Readings and Cases in International Human Resource Management

This new edition of *Readings and Cases in International Human Resource Management* is a classic edited textbook, taking account of recent developments in the international human resources management (IHRM) field, such as the pandemic, the role of diversity, equity, and inclusion, as well as climate change. It includes a range of key readings that are essential for understanding the field and contextualizes each one with a selection of real-life case studies that demonstrate their meaning and impact in practice.

The book aims to sensitize the reader to the complex human resource issues that exist in the global business environment. To that end, it strives to publish "tried and true" readings and cases that provide stimulating and intellectually challenging material and are written in ways that engage both the student and the instructor.

Key features include:

- New readings and case studies that account for recent changes in the field, positioned alongside "tried and true" material
- Integration of contemporary themes such as remote working, digitization, sustainability, and social issues throughout the book
- An expanded introductory chapter, new discussion questions, and consistent pedagogy throughout
- Supplemental tutor support material, additional cases, and teaching notes to enhance instructors' abilities to use the readings and cases with their students
- Bringing together well-known contributors and field experts into one encompassing text, this textbook is ideal for any class in international human resource management, international organizational behaviour, or international business.

This seventh edition is thoroughly updated to enable students to understand the complexity of human resource issues in the post-pandemic era of global, remote, and technology-mediated working.

B. Sebastian Reiche is a Professor of Managing People in Organizations at IESE Business School, Spain.

Günter K. Stahl is Professor of International Management, Chair of the Institute for Responsibility and Sustainability in Global Business, and Co-Director of the Center for Sustainability Transformation and Responsibility at WU Vienna, Austria.

Mark E. Mendenhall is the J. Burton Frierson Chair of Excellence in Business Leadership in the Gary W. Rollins College of Business at the University of Tennessee, Chattanooga, USA.

Gary R. Oddou is Professor Emeritus of International Management and former Director of the Global Business Management program at California State University, San Marcos, USA.

Readings and Cases in International Human Resource Management

Seventh Edition

Edited by

B. Sebastian Reiche,
Günter K. Stahl,
Mark E. Mendenhall, and
Gary R. Oddou

 Routledge
Taylor & Francis Group

NEW YORK AND LONDON

Designed cover image: © Getty Images

Seventh edition published 2024
by Routledge
605 Third Avenue, New York, NY 10158

and by Routledge
4 Park Square, Milton Park, Abingdon, Oxon, OX14 4RN

Routledge is an imprint of the Taylor & Francis Group, an informa business

First edition published by Routledge 1991

Sixth edition published by Routledge 2016

ISBN: 978-1-032-13664-6 (hbk)
ISBN: 978-1-032-16151-8 (pbk)
ISBN: 978-1-003-24727-2 (ebk)

DOI: 10.4324/9781003247272

Typeset in Bell Gothic
by Deanta Global Publishing Services, Chennai, India

Access the Support Material: www.routledge.com/9781032161518

Contents

PART IV
People Issues in Global Teams, Alliances, Mergers, and Acquisitions   287

Illustrations

EXHIBITS

TABLES

CHARTS

Preface

WELCOME TO THE SEVENTH EDITION of *Readings and Cases in International Human Resource Management*. If you are a long-time user of this text, we would like to thank you for continuing to use the book in your teaching or consulting endeavors. We originally put this book together because we couldn't find one ourselves, and we wanted such a book to use in our classes. Since then, with your help, the book has evolved and become a standby for teachers of international management, international human resource management (HRM), and international organizational behavior (OB).

As digitalization is making rapid inroads into our daily personal and professional lives and mega events like the pandemic, #BlackLivesMatter, or climate change are sweeping across the globe, virtually all organizations and the people working in them experience increasing—and novel—forms of global dependencies and interconnectedness. Within this context, many business decisions become critical. While some of those decisions pertain to a firm's financial or physical resources, the most neglected and perhaps most important decisions to be made concern the management of the firm's international human resources. Indeed, one of the greatest problems is the continued lack of a global perspective on the part of a firm's managerial cadre. As a member of one cultural and institutional context, the manager tends to see physical and virtual situations or encounters from that perspective, to judge events from that perspective, and to make decisions based on that perspective. In an increasingly interconnected global business environment, such a perspective breeds failure.

Our principal objective for this book is to sensitize the reader to the complex human resource issues that exist in the global business environment. With this primary objective in mind, we have attempted to represent many regions of the world, balanced by the quality of information and discussion potential of the reading or case.

Most publishing companies are turning to online creation of packets of readings and cases. Although a good idea in theory, it requires a great deal of research in case repositories and online journal systems to design a supplemental text of one's own. Most instructors are too busy with other obligations to spend the time necessary to design and create supplemental texts online, particularly if there is a good alternative, and we believe a book such as this one is just that alternative. We believe there is a continued need for books to publish "tried and true" readings and cases that provide stimulating and intellectually challenging material and are written in ways that engage both the student and the instructor. If you are a new adopter of the book, we are grateful to you, and we look forward to your comments concerning your experience in using the book. Feel free to contact us with your feedback.

In this new edition of our book, we have kept the best readings and cases from the previous editions, thoroughly updating the materials whenever copyright agreements permitted this. However, we also added a range of new readings and cases that have the same type of "feel" as the old, "tried and true" ones. Although the format of the book and the conceptual groupings of each major section have not changed significantly compared to the most recent previous edition, some of the subthemes have been adapted to reflect critical current concerns and lines of thought in international HRM. We have also added an introductory chapter that provides a more integrative overview of the main themes and pillars of international HRM that the book—and typical courses on international HRM— cover. A few of the readings and cases included in this book, however, seemed to us to be classics. In other words, the issues they address seem to transcend time (and copyright date)! We chose to keep these in the book, since we like to teach from them, and we know that most of you do as well.

This book can be used in a variety of ways in HRM, management, and OB courses. It can stand alone if the instructor's preference is to teach predominately a case course. It can be used in tandem with other textbooks that have an international HRM, management, or OB focus, or as a supplement to them. Or the book can be used as a main text in HRM or other related courses, supplemented with other readings and texts with which the instructor is comfortable.

The instructor's manual is available on this book's website at Routledge. Contained in the instructor's manual are teaching notes for the cases as well as class discussion notes and guidelines for some of the readings. It also contains a few additional cases from previous editions that have been replaced by newer material in the book, but that some of you may want to continue to use in your courses. Our goal is to support you as an instructor in all your needs.

As stated earlier, our main objective for the book is simply this: to sensitize the reader to the complex human resource issues that exist in a globally interconnected business environment. With this objective in mind, we have attempted to represent many regions of the world in terms of the locations in which the readings and cases are based: Bulgaria, Canada, China, Czech Republic, Finland, France, Germany, India, Italy, Japan, Nigeria, Senegal, Spain, Sweden, Switzerland, the UK, and the US.

Additionally, our readings and cases involve cross-cultural interaction between people and cultures and human resource systems in the following combinations: US–India, US–Japan, Senegal–France, China–India, Germany–US, Austria–Bulgaria, Finland–Bulgaria, Nigeria–UK, Nigeria–US, Canada–France, Sweden–China, and China–US.

However, in providing for this diversity of location and interaction, we chose not to "force fit" something into the book for the sake of regional or geographic representation. We included what we and our editors felt were quality readings and cases in the field of international human resource management. We do not view this book as a North American HR text nor a European HR text. Our goal was to create a book of readings and cases that would focus on the points of confluence between cultures, human resource systems, and people in an era of post-pandemic globalization.

Acknowledgments

WE WOULD LIKE TO THANK all those who have contributed to this book. Many of the authors willingly sent us cases, articles, manuscripts in progress, and bibliographies that they had developed over the years. We regret that we could not include all the sources offered to us.

We would like to express our gratitude to three people, for without their assistance and support, this new edition of the book would not have occurred: our editor at Routledge, Alexandra McGregor, for her determined support and belief in this edition of the book and for her patience and flexibility in working with our needs; Alexandra's editorial assistant, Ella McFarlane, who was instrumental in navigating us through the project; and Fiona Shoro, who liaised with several publishers to allow us to include key published materials on International Human Resource Management in our new edition.

A special thanks goes to Megan, Dorit, Janet, and Jane, and our families for their unwavering support of us over the years as we have pursued our fascination with "things international"—they make all we accomplish possible and our gratitude to them is eternal.

B. SEBASTIAN REICHE
Barcelona, Spain

GÜNTER K. STAHL
Vienna, Austria

MARK E. MENDENHALL
Signal Mountain, Tennessee

GARY R. ODDOU
Oceanside, California

Contributors

Joanne Barnes
Division of Leadership & Followership
  Studies
DeVoe School of Business, Technology,
  and Leadership
IWU-National & Global
DEI&B Consultant and Coach
Indiana Wesleyan University
1900 W. 50th Street
Marion, Indiana 46953-9393
United States
Joanne.Barnes@indwes.edu

Ingmar Björkman
Rector
Hanken School of Economics
Arkadiankatu 22
00100 Helsinki
Finland
ingmar.bjorkman@hanken.fi

J. Stewart Black, PhD
Global Chief Leadership and Strategy
  Officer
Squire Patton Boggs
1500 W 3rd Street, Suite 450
Cleveland, OH 44113
United States

Jaime Bonache
Full Professor of Management
Universidad Carlos III de Madrid
Business Department
Calle Madrid, 123
Getafe, Madrid
Spain
Jaime.bonache@uc3m.es

David Bowen
Robert & Katherine Herberger Chair in
  Global Management
Thunderbird School of Global
  Management
Arizona State University
1 Global Place
Glendale, AZ 85306–6000
United States
david.bowen@thunderbird.edu

Maggie Boyraz
Department of Management
Jack H. Brown School of Business and
  Public Administration
California State University, San
  Bernardino
5500 University
  Parkway JB-424
San Bernardino, CA 92407
United States
Maggie.Boyraz@csusb.edu

Paula Caligiuri
Northeastern University
312C Hayden Hall
360 Huntington Avenue
Boston, MA 02115-5000
United States
p.caligiuri@northeastern.edu

Celia Chui
Assistant Professor of Management
HEC Montréal
3000, Chemin de la
    Côte-Sainte-Catherine
Montréal, Québec
H3T 2A7
Canada
celia.chui@hec.ca

David G. Collings
Professor of Sustainable Business
Trinity Business School
Trinity College Dublin
Dublin 2
Ireland
david.collings@gmail.com

Barbara Coudenhove-Kalergi
Federation of Austrian Industries
Policy Advisor Education & Society
Schwarzenbergplatz 4
1030 Vienna
Austria
Barbara.Coudenhove-kalergi@iv.at

C. Brooklyn Derr
Emeritus Professor
The Marriott School of Management
Brigham Young University
Provo, UT
United States
brooke_derr@byu.edu

Mihaela Dimitrova
Vienna University of Economics and
    Business (WU Vienna)
Department of Global Business and
    Trade
Welthandelsplatz 1
Vienna 1020
Austria
mihaela.dimitrova@wu.ac.at

Robin J. Ely
Diane Doerge Wilson Professor of
    Business Administration
Harvard Business School
Soldiers Field
Boston, MA 02163
United States

Paul Evans
INSEAD
Boulevard de Constance
77305 Fontainebleau
France
paul.evans@insead.edu

Stacey R. Fitzsimmons
University of Victoria
Peter B. Gustavson School of Business
PO Box 1700 STN CSC
Victoria BC, V8W 2Y2
Canada
sfitzsim@uvic.ca

Alexander Fleischmann
Research Affiliate
IMD International Institute for
    Management Development
Ch. de Bellerive 23
1001 Lausanne
Switzerland
alexander.fleischmann@affiliate.imd.org

Pankaj Ghemawat
Anselmo Rubiralta Chair of Strategy and
    Globalization
Emeritus Professor of Strategic
    Management
IESE Business School
Ave. Pearson 21
08034 Barcelona
Spain
and
Global Professor of Management and
    Strategy
Director of the Center for the
    Globalization of Education and
    Management
New York University
Leonard N. Stern School of Business
Kaufman Management Center
44 West Fourth Street, 8-93
New York, NY 10012
United States
PGhemawat@iese.edu

Nana Yaa A. Gyamfi
OBHRM Department
China Europe International Business
     School (CEIBS)
699 Hongfeng Road
Shanghai, 201206
P.R. of China
gnana@ceibs.edu

Roger Hallowell
HEC Paris
96 Sears Rd.
Brookline MA 02445
United States
rogerhallowell@comcast.net

Carin-Isabel Knoop
Case Research & Writing Group
Harvard Business School
Boston, MA 02163
Unites States
Cknoop@hbs.edu

Henry W. Lane
Northeastern University
316 Hayden Hall
360 Huntington Ave
Boston, MA 02115-5000
United States
ha.lane@northeastern.edu

Yih-teen Lee
IESE Business School
People Management Department
Ave. Pearson 21
08034 Barcelona
Spain
ylee@iese.edu

Yuan (Echo) Liao
Discipline of International Business
University of Sydney Business
     School
The University of Sydney
Rm 4136, Abercrombie
     Building H70
New South Wales 2006
Australia
yuan.liao@sydney.edu.au

Martha Maznevski
Professor of Organizational Behaviour
Ivey Business School, Western University
1255 Western Road
London, Ontario
N6G 0N1
Canada
mmaznevski@ivey.ca

Amy McCarter
National University of Ireland, Galway
University Road
Galway
Ireland

Anthony McDonnell
Professor of Management
Cork University Business School
University College Cork
Ireland
anthony.mcdonnell@ucc.ie

Mark E. Mendenhall
J. Burton Frierson Chair of Excellence in
     Business Leadership
Gary W. Rollins College of Business
University of Tennessee, Chattanooga
422 Fletcher Hall
615 McCallie Avenue
Dept 6056
Chattanooga, TN 37403
United States
mark-mendenhall@utc.edu

Philip H. Mirvis
Senior Fellow in Social Innovation
Babson Social Innovation Lab
Babson College
231 Forest Street
Babson Park, MA 02457
United States

Christof Miska
Vienna University of Economics and
     Business (WU Vienna)
Welthandelsplatz 1, 1020
Vienna
Austria
christof.miska@wu.ac.at

Evalde Mutabazi
EM Lyon Business School
23, av. Guy de Collongue
BP 174
69132 Ecully Cedex
France
contact@mutabazi.com

Emma Nordbäck
Department of Management and
  Organisation
Hanken School of Economics
Arkadiankatu 22
00100 Helsinki
Finland
emma.nordback@hanken.fi

Laura J. Noval
Department of Management and
  Organization
Rennes School of Business
2 rue Robert d'Arbrissel
CS 76522 35065
Rennes
France
and
Affiliate Professor
Imperial College Business School
Imperial College of London
South Kensington Campus
London SW7 2AZ
UK
laura.noval@rennes-sb.com

Gary R. Oddou
Emeritus Professor
California State University San Marcos
333 S. Twin Oaks Valley Rd.
San Marcos, CA 92096–0001
United States
goddou@csusm.edu

Nicola M. Pless
Chair and Professor of Management
UniSA Business
University of South Australia
47-55 North Terrace
Adelaide, South Australia 5000
Australia
Nicola.Pless@unisa.edu.au

Vladimir Pucik
Visiting Professor Emeritus
International Business Group
Aalto University
Helsinki
Finland
vladimir.pucik@aalto.fi

Markus Pudelko
Department of International Business,
  Director
School of Business and Economics
University of Tübingen
Melanchthonstr. 30
72074 Tübingen
Germany
markus.pudelko@uni-tuebingen.de

B. Sebastian Reiche
IESE Business School
People Management Department
Ave. Pearson 21
08034 Barcelona
Spain
sreiche@iese.edu

Mike Rosenberg
Professor of the Practice of Management
IESE Business School
Ave. Pearson 21
08034 Barcelona
Spain
mrosenberg@iese.edu

Carlos Sánchez-Runde
IESE Business School
Ave. Pearson 21
08034 Barcelona
Spain
CSanchez-Runde@iese.edu

Álvaro San Martín
IESE Business School
People Management Department
Camino del Cerro del Águila 3
28023 Madrid
Spain
ASanmartin@iese.edu

Christian Seelos
Distinguished Fellow
Director, Global Innovation for Impact
    Lab
Stanford University
Stanford CA
United States
cseelos@stanford.edu

Atri Sengupta
Indian Institute of Management
    Sambalpur
Jyoti Vihar, Burla, Sambalpur
768019, Odisha
India
atrisengupta@iimsambalpur.ac.in

Günter K. Stahl
Professor of International Management
Chair, Institute for Responsibility and
    Sustainability in Global Business
    (RSGBI)
Co-Director, Center for Sustainability
    Transformation and Responsibility
    (STaR)
Vienna University of Economics and
    Business (WU Vienna)
Welthandelsplatz 1, Gebäude D1
1020 Vienna
Austria
E-mail: güenter.stahl@wu.ac.at

Luigi Stirpe
Associate Professor of Management
Universidad Carlos III de Madrid
Business Department
Calle Madrid, 123
Getafe, Madrid
Spain
lstirpe@emp.uc3m.es

Mary Sully de Luque
Associate Dean of Graduate Programs
    and Research
Professor of Global Management
Academic Director, Women Entrepreneur
    Programs in Rising Economies
Arizona State University
Thunderbird School of Global
    Management
401 North 1st Street
Phoenix, AZ 85004
United States
Mary.Sullydeluque@thunderbird.asu.edu

Satu Teerikangas
School of Economics
University of Turku
Rehtorinpelllonkatu 3
20500 Turku
Finland
satu.teerikangas@utu.fi

David A. Thomas
President
Morehouse College
Morehouse School of Medicine
720 Westview Drive
Atlanta, GA 30310
United States

Vlad Vaiman
School of Management
California Lutheran University
60 W. Olsen Rd., #3550
Thousand Oaks, CA 91360
United States
vvaiman@callutheran.edu

Josefine van Zanten
Senior Advisor Equity, Inclusion &
  Diversity
IMD International Institute for
  Management Development
Ch. de Bellerive 23
1001 Lausanne
Switzerland
josefine.vanzanten@imd.org

Celia Zárraga-Oberty
Associate Professor of Management
Universidad Carlos III de Madrid
Business Department
Calle Madrid, 123
Getafe, Madrid
Spain
Czarraga@emp.uc3m.es

B. Sebastian Reiche, Günter K. Stahl, Mark E. Mendenhall, and Gary R. Oddou

INTRODUCTION: CHRISTINE TSENG'S JOURNEY THROUGH DIFFICULT INTERNATIONAL HUMAN RESOURCE MANAGEMENT TERRAIN

W E THINK THE BEST WAY to introduce the textbook is with an introductory reading and case. It sets the tone of the book, helps integrate the various subsections, and, if you like, also makes an excellent reading assignment to begin class with.

The tectonic shifts that we have been experiencing over the recent past—such as grappling with a global pandemic and the disruptions it has brought to our ways of working, the increasingly forceful calls for creating inclusive work environments and societies following #BlackLivesMatter, the ever more visible impact climate change has on our livelihoods, as well as the resurgent geopolitical tensions and uncertainties over future international relations as the Ukraine crisis has vividly demonstrated—all have a fundamental human element. As a result, the effective and purposeful alignment, configuration, and engagement of people in organizations, for which human resource (HR) managers carry responsibility, should play a critical part in guiding individual and organizational decision-making in navigating and helping address such complexity.

And yet executives, HR managers, and scholars alike have been lamenting the lack of impact that human resource management (HRM) has in organizations and wider society. Consider the following words from a prominent figure in the HR field:

> [As HR managers] we feel we aren't valued in our own organizations, that we can't get the resources we need. We complain that management won't

buy our proposals and wonder why our advice is so often ignored until the crisis stage. But the human resources manager seldom stands back to look at the total business and ask: Why am I at the bottom looking up? The answer is painfully apparent. We don't act like business managers—like entrepreneurs whose business happens to be people.[1]

The statement illustrates one of the key dilemmas that HR managers face in many organizations: how to move from an operational and administrative focus to more value-adding strategic activities, especially when it comes to navigating the complexities and uncertainties of the global context in the 21st century. In fact, when business leaders themselves are asked about the desired role of HR, a majority emphasize that the international HR function needs to become more strategically aligned with an organization's business needs.[2]

This in itself is good news—after all, who wouldn't want to have her own function elevated to a more strategic status? However, the call to move to more strategic waters comes with an important caveat: how do you demonstrate the strategic value you are tasked to contribute? That this is not an easy challenge is, perhaps, reflected in the time that has elapsed from when the opening statement was made: It was over four decades ago when Jac Fitz-enz most candidly outlined the common struggles of the HR function.[3] How much has changed thus far is a matter of perspective, but the HR function has worked to raise its profile ever since.

In many ways, the prevalence of Big Data and the additional analytical tools and metrics that HR has at its disposal have facilitated this endeavor. Yet you don't demonstrate strategic value by justifying the existence of the HR function per se, but rather by directly assisting to execute business strategy through taking core people management decisions. We believe it is critical for HR managers to develop a sound understanding of the landscape in which international HR decisions need to be taken, and be able to prioritize the most essential international HR decisions in order to serve and contribute to the business. The book is organized to outline these key areas of decision-making and activities for international HR managers.

To summarize and illustrate the many HR decisions and activities that the book will discuss in much greater depth—as organized across five principal parts—let us take you on a journey to accompany Christine Tseng as she navigates the difficult terrain of international HRM. Christine is a Cantonese HR director working in a British company in London. However, she could just as easily be a manager in any medium-sized North or Latin American, Asian, Australian or New Zealand, or African company. The issue is not her gender, her nationality, or the nationality of her firm, but rather the challenges she faces due to globalization.

CHRISTINE TSENG'S CHALLENGES

Christine Tseng is Director of Human Resources for TechPub, a technology firm that develops software and data analytical tools for the publishing industry.

TechPub has been very successful over the past ten years. Sales have increased at an annual rate of 10 percent and profits have correspondingly surged. TechPub has had an international sales team for several years already to build relationships with large national newspapers and publishers. Recently, TechPub's top management has been mulling over the possibility of setting up offices abroad to be able to better serve its growing number of international clients through after-sales service, software maintenance, and on-demand support in the same time zone. This would involve a physical footprint in South America and Asia—and possibly even in other regions. Doing so would also allow TechPub to take advantage of cheaper labor rates for its increasing pool of software developers in some of these countries and move toward being a truly global firm.

Christine was asked by the firm's CEO to prepare an analysis (due on his desk in two weeks) of the human resource impact such moves would have on the firm. As Christine sat down at her desk, she began to jot down ideas. She found herself somewhat baffled by this global angle of HRM, as she had little experience or training in managing human resources internationally. The following are some of her thoughts as she attempted to create an outline for her report.

I. The Context of International HRM Decisions

Her first thoughts wandered to the broader social, political and economic context in which the decisions would be made. The COVID-19 pandemic and the Ukraine conflict had posed important risks to continued globalization, forcing organizations to rethink global supply chains, the sourcing of energy and raw materials and how to circumvent drastic travel restrictions. *How much global footprint was really necessary for her firm to reach its future growth potential?* These were of course all strategic questions, and Christine started to ponder whether TechPub indeed had a clearly focused business strategy for becoming a multinational firm. She made a mental note to call Carlos Fernandez, the VP of Finance, to see how far the thinking of the top management team had progressed on that front. *How will the development of TechPub's staff fit into such a plan? I wonder why I am not on that planning team?* Christine thought about how she could insert herself into that process without being suspected of having ulterior motives.

There were also important implications for TechPub's senior leaders and talent pipeline. *What kind of perspective and experience should future top management have if they will be leading a true multinational firm? How will that experience be best obtained—through international assignments or the use of consultants? Am I going to be responsible for educating management regarding international issues? If so, it's the blind leading the blind*, she thought, *for she would not even be sure how to evaluate the validity of an external consultant's proposals.* Christine figured that she could always hire experts to evaluate the bid proposals of consulting firms, but that would run into serious budget squeezes for her department. *Who should we send—our high potentials that are destined to lead the company in the next ten years or our non-designated personnel? How important will it be to have a global perspective at the top versus having one throughout the levels of the company? And who are the most critical positions for which we need to develop successors internally?* She realized that this would be considerably more complex to determine once the firm straddled different international offices.

Christine shifted her thinking to the HR policies and practices that she had developed over the past years as TechPub had grown into a more mature company and had to formalize its systems. She was proud of the various initiatives she had advanced but now she started to have second thoughts. *How would these policies and practices translate to foreign offices? Should I promote the same practices in areas such as hiring, development, and performance appraisal across the entire firm, or would we need to adapt them to different local preferences?* Christine realized that she would need to weigh up the benefits of a simpler, standardized approach with the varying talent needs in each locale. *The cost of hiring new workers—not to mention well-qualified managers—is not going to be loose change. I hope they aren't ignoring the cost of hiring well-qualified managers and retaining them in their financial analyses*, Christine thought. *How will we retain the best and the brightest? What do South Americans want? What about Eastern Europeans? Is a good salary enough or are other factors involved?*

Christine realized that she needed to consider other institutional conditions of potential target countries for TechPub's international expansion. *Which countries have educational systems that would best support the knowledge base that our talent will need? Which countries have social systems that favor unions more than management? Which countries have governments that are stable and are not likely to change and upset the equilibrium of our workers' and managers' work schedules?*

This prompted yet deeper questions. *What about the possibility of terrorism? Will I have to devise a terrorism-prevention training program? Which countries are friendly to us, not just business-wise but in their perceptions of the West and their right to manage the local residents? I wonder how much kidnap insurance costs?* Christine's mind began to wander. She envisioned herself in a small, box-like hole covered with rusty iron bars. *When would her kidnappers give her water?* Her reverie was broken by a string of other concerns that flashed across her mind.

II. Cross-cultural and Diversity Management-related Decisions

Christine reminded herself that she needed to keep the big picture in mind before getting too involved in solving details, and there were still broader questions to address. *Where exactly should TechPub's international offices be located?* She remembered reading a newspaper article that mentioned that one of the factors important to Japanese firms locating in the US was finding compatible regional cultural norms. The Japanese liked the Southern US culture because of its regard for interpersonal relations in business settings, tradition, and respect for elders and persons in positions of authority. *Which cultures within these regions are most favorable to British expatriates and their families? Most importantly, which cultures promote a strong work ethic?* Christine now contemplated TechPub's overarching management system. *Would the system be in harmony with the work culture of the foreign countries? Probably. Okay, so, how do we train local staff to understand how we do things at TechPub? Will I have to design those training programs too?*

Christine also wondered whether TechPub's managers will have to develop unique incentive systems to get their subordinates to work. *No, probably not ... well, then again, maybe. After all, the people under me have different buttons that make them work harder—those buttons are not the same for everyone here in the UK. Is it possible,* Christine thought, *for some cultures to have work norms that are antithetical to promotion and pay inducements? I think those would be universal motivators! Maybe this won't be a major problem. Maybe it will be more of a fine-tuning issue in terms of adapting our job design, incentive systems, and motivational techniques to the country where we decide to set up shop.*

Christine started to think about the composition and make-up of TechPub's future workforce. *Will local managers—if we use local managers—desire to be promoted to the British headquarters? Will top management desire that? Fifteen years from now, what will, and what should, TechPub's top management look like: an Asian managing a South American office and a mixture of South Americans, Asians, Europeans, and Americans at headquarters?* Christine thought about her own multicultural experience that had brought her from her native Hong Kong to study in Australia and ultimately accept a job in London. She was certain of the many advantages her experience had to offer. *How could TechPub benefit from multiculturals to better connect with and serve our international clients? And how can we ensure that multiculturals work effectively side-by-side their monocultural colleagues?*

As she pondered these questions, she reminded herself that TechPub's current workforce was fairly homogenous, so they still had a long way to go. *Perhaps the international expansion might give the necessary push to diversify our workforce, especially the software developers? But how could we create a safe and inclusive environment that would be attractive for diverse talent?* Christine started to think that she might as well revisit TechPub's corporate culture and ensure it was sufficiently accommodating for its global and more diverse workforce. As she paused to charge her Apple Pencil, with which she had taken notes on her tablet, her thoughts shifted to the more urgent challenge of how to staff the foreign offices.

III. Decisions Regarding Global Staffing and the Management of Global Mobility

Christine wondered whether TechPub should send its own staff overseas or instead hire talent locally. *Which countries in Asia, South America, or possibly even Eastern Europe, have the most qualified personnel to staff sales and key account, software development and technology support positions? Do some countries have laws that require hiring a certain percentage of local workers?*

Christine remembered meeting a man once at a professional convention who had worked for a services company in Qatar. He reported having had to hire local workers for most positions below middle management level, with the promise to phase out all foreign expatriates within ten years.

Can or should the subsidiary management come from TechPub's head-quarters? If not, where would we find local managers to hire? The universities? Christine recalled reading once that, in France, the norm was to hire managers from the "Grandes Écoles" and not from the universities. *If we send our own talent, who should go? How long should their assignments be? How expensive will it be to house a British family at their accustomed standard of living in the new country? How should we select whom to send? Should we base our decisions on experience in the company, adaptability potential, or desire to relocate? What if nobody wants to go?* Christine's thoughts wandered to dual-career couple issues. *Just how hard will it be to attract our best people to go to a foreign country if their spouse has a good career here,* she wondered. She had heard about some firms that have formed a consortium in the foreign country to help provide employment for expatriates' spouses. Working together, they had more flexibility than if they were trying to go it alone. *But with virtual work interactions having become more prevalent due to COVID-19, perhaps TechPub leaders could, at least partly, manage the foreign subsidiaries remotely?*

Provided Christine would be able to identify a sufficient pool of internal candidates, she wondered how much training they would need before they relocate. *How in depth will it need to be? Do they need language training or is English good enough?* Christine thought that most business people around the world speak English, so maybe this was not really an issue. *Will the firm budget my department the resources necessary to do quality training, or will I be left with a budget that will allow nothing more than bringing in a few local professors for a couple of hours each to do area briefings? Who can I call on to do the training?*

Christine felt somewhat relieved when she remembered reading about a few cross-cultural training providers in the ad section of an HRM newsletter she subscribed to. But her confidence ebbed when the following thought occurred to her: *How will I know if the training these external consultants provide is valid and helpful or just a dog and pony show? Can I, with my staff, develop my own training program? What kind of time and money will such an endeavor require?* As Christine began mentally planning a strategy to develop training programs with her staff, her mind switched to yet another problem.

Clearly, training and development were only part of the challenge. *What would be the career implications of these foreign assignments? Should the assignments be developmental, or should slots simply be filled as they open up, regardless of whether or not the move will develop the employee?* Christine was vaguely aware that companies such as IBM, Adidas, and Ciba-Geigy viewed international assignments as an integral part of their management development for senior posts. *If the assignment is developmental, what will we do when the employee returns?* Christine wondered if TechPub would give her authority to dictate what position returning managers should receive ... She doubted they would give her that authority. *But what would happen to these experienced internationalists if they didn't have a clear career path for them when they returned? How will we reintegrate these employees into TechPub's home operations? We'll lose them,* Christine thought to herself, *if we can't offer them a good position when they return. How will the HR department keep informed of the needs, concerns, performance, and evaluation of all overseas employees? By email? Videoconferencing? Site visits?* Christine wondered whether she could justify trips to the Far East as site visits. *They may be necessary, but might be viewed by others as a new perk for the HRM department.*

The re-entry part kept bothering Christine. Not only was there the position transition issue to plan for, but she wondered how they might best capture their learning about the foreign operations. *This could be really valuable,* she thought. *It could help us coordinate our efforts better and understand the challenges of our foreign operations.* She would somehow need to work out how to encourage the transfer of learning more explicitly. Then the thought occurred to her that she would also need to think through how to motivate and evaluate the expatriates while they are overseas.

Can we just use the same forms, procedures, and criteria, or is there something unique about a foreign assignment that requires unique performance evaluation systems? When should we evaluate people? Christine remembered reading in a professional newsletter that expatriate employees require at least six months to settle into their overseas assignments. *Would it be fair to evaluate employees before six months? When would it be valid? After eight, ten, or twelve months? This is getting very messy,* Christine sighed. *Should the criteria by which to judge performance in South America and other places be relative to the country in question, or should we use the same evaluation criteria everywhere?* The last thing Christine felt like doing was overseeing the development of a new performance evaluation system! *We can get by with our current one,* she mentally noted. *Who should do the evaluating? Headquarters, the regional subsidiary superiors, peers, or a mixture of superiors and subordinates? Should the criteria revolve around bottom-line figures or staff objectives? If financial-type performance criteria are emphasized, what happens if the pound depreciates significantly against the local currency and wipes out the expatriate manager's cost savings and profits? How can the expatriate manager be evaluated, motivated, and rewarded under such conditions?*

Christine also contemplated whether nationality differences mattered in performance evaluation. *If a British manager is being evaluated by a Peruvian subsidiary manager, will the evaluation be fair or is there potential for some sort of cultural bias? What if the British manager is a woman? Will we be able to put together an attractive, but not too costly, compensation package for our expatriates? I wonder what such a package would look like. We need to offer something good to entice the employee to go, especially if the employee might lose the spouse's income, yet if there's too great a difference in the package between the expatriate and local staff, that will create "us vs. them" problems.*

IV. Decisions Regarding People Issues in Global Collaborations

As the list of issues regarding TechPub's necessary pool of international staff that Christine had populated over the last 30 minutes grew, her thoughts wandered to more general questions of how TechPub could ensure effective collaborations among its workforce across the globe. *How would TechPub's international expansion affect its future ability to connect staff and tasks across the various offices? And to what extent would that be necessary?* Christine knew that staff had become more accustomed to interacting regularly through virtual means over the past few years, but opening offices in Asia and South America meant that colleagues would be distributed in global virtual teams across vastly different locales and time zones. *How could HR help bridge the distance and the barriers that would inevitably exist? How could she avoid new siloes emerging when she had worked so hard to tear them down between TechPub's developers and sales representatives?*

Her mind raced anew to more specific questions. *Should she script specific rules and procedures to help the global virtual teams communicate more effectively? Or should she leave this to the team leaders? But how could we ensure common practices across the organization? And what about the meeting times?* Christine recalled talking to a colleague in a large multinational who was leading a globally dispersed team. He had recently started to rotate meeting times so the Australian team members wouldn't always have to connect to the virtual team meetings exceptionally early. *Heck, these are all additional aspects I will need to incorporate as we revamp our leadership training,* she moaned.

Christine was also acutely aware that given TechPub's recent growth trajectory, the firm would likely increase its size further. *Once they had opened international offices, could they continue to grow organically, or would they need to look for partners to diversify their software and service offering further? But how could they identify a suitable alliance partner?* She realized that she needed to form part of this decision making to avoid the business storming ahead without people issues in mind. Perhaps she could start a common interest group with other HR directors of similar firms to help her prepare for such possible scenarios.

This made her wonder whether top management would be interested in partnerships given the past focus on maintaining full ownership through organic growth. *Perhaps a foreign acquisition was a more likely possibility,* Christine thought. It started to dawn on her that this would open a whole new set of HR issues she would need to grapple with. *How could she be proactive in assessing possible acquisition targets together with top management? And how do you integrate an acquired company without overwriting the unique capabilities it had to offer?* Christine had heard that HR played a crucial role in the post-acquisition integration process to help form a unified culture and craft common work processes and practices. But moving from hearsay to getting her hands dirty would be no small feat, she knew. For a moment, she allowed herself a comforting thought because she knew that she wouldn't be alone in this ... senior managers would similarly need to up their game and learn to shepherd TechPub through its future growth. But reality brought her quickly back to earth: *Isn't it also my responsibility to help our senior leaders do so, and do so in a sustainable and responsible manner?*

V. Decisions on How to Nurture Responsible Global Leadership

At this point, Christine was glad that she had had the foresight to cancel her remaining meetings for the afternoon. Her list was getting longer and longer and yet she felt she hadn't yet thought through all critical issues. She realized that she not only had to determine the most relevant decisions for herself but also support the leaders—well, ultimately all employees—in her organization to take the right decisions themselves. As she pondered TechPub's planned international expansion, she sensed that this might become increasingly more complex. She wondered whether taken-for-granted practices in the UK would necessarily work in another country that might have different standards of ethical conduct. *How could she ensure that the ethical standards she believed in prevailed as TechPub ventured abroad? How could she help her company's managers resolve situations in which codes of conduct might clash?*

Christine's thoughts were now racing between problems. *I remember reading somewhere,* she mused, *that in order to shut down an operation in France (or was it Germany or Sweden?), management had to give the workers a full year's notice, retrain them, and then find them new jobs!* While the technology sector was generally much less regulated, she knew that her firm's top management would find such a contingency troubling at best. *Well, maybe this was less problematic in the Asian or South American labor markets.* Then Christine recalled meeting a public relations spokeswoman for a US services provider at a party, and the nightmare she had described. It seemed that the US management of her company had pressured the local teams in Colombia to increase their workload dramatically to fulfill a large and time-sensitive service contract for a major client. The press had gotten hold of cases where junior female workers were working 16-hour days with no breaks; if the employees complained, they were terminated on the spot. What was more, some of the female workers were subjected to sexual harassment from their male managers. It was a public relations nightmare. *Maybe dealing with complex and extensive labor laws wouldn't be all bad … maybe employment regulation would protect us from questionable ethical nightmares,* Christine thought. But then she thought of codetermination laws in countries such as Germany and worker's representatives sitting on the local boards of directors—that would not be easy for British managers to stomach.

Suddenly, another set of doubts took hold of her. She recalled a recent discussion with the board that had highlighted concerns over TechPub's sustainability commitments as top management considered a possible move into blockchain technology. *You would want to carefully evaluate the environmental impact this would generate, especially in the eyes of the big publishers among your clients,* Christine heard one board member say. She was under no illusion that TechPub would be under closer scrutiny as the company expanded internationally. *Plus without a credible promise on how TechPub can contribute to a more sustainable society, we will likely lose a good chunk of our current and prospective talent in the future anyway,* she thought. *But where should sustainability ideally sit in the organizational structure? Is it the responsibility of the top management team? Or should it feature as a key HR responsibility?* This might have far-reaching consequences for the scope of HR and the capabilities she would need to develop within her team. She also pondered how she could get her senior leaders to role model sustainable behavior themselves?

As Christine put down her pen, the obvious complexity of the report loomed before her. She had just scratched the surface of the basic human resources issues associated with globalizing their business and there seemed to be no end to the potential permutations around each problem. *This will be no easy task,* she concluded. As she left her office and made her way to the parking garage, she wondered, *Where can I go for help?*

TechPub is a fictive company, yet its situation closely parallels the initial path which virtually all companies must tread as they choose to expand internationally, grapple with the issues, challenges, and opportunities associated with the globalization of business, and work to configure their management and work systems across their global operations. For HR managers to effectively support a company on this path and have a strategic impact on the company's global business, it is essential to understand the complex terrain in which international HR decisions occur, and then initiate coherent and sustainable HR activities that help align the firm's purpose, people, and products. We hope this book will enable the reader to do so.

NOTES

1.   Fitz-enz, J. (1980). Quantifying the human resources function. *Personnel*, 57, 41–52.
2.   Santa Fe Relocation (2021). *Global Mobility Survey 2020/21: Challenging Change.* London: Santa Fe Relocation.
3.   Fitz-enz (1980), p. 41.

PART I

The Context of IHRM: Challenges, Strategies, and External Forces

DOI: 10.4324/9781003247272-1

Paul Evans, Vladimir Pucik, Ingmar Björkman, and B. Sebastian Reiche

PUTTING THE CHALLENGES OF INTERNATIONAL HUMAN RESOURCE MANAGEMENT INTO HISTORICAL PERSPECTIVE[1]

L IKE MANY OTHER COMPANIES, THE Swedish-Swiss corporation ABB that was born out of a merger in 1988 wanted to be a fast-growing firm with a wide international presence. Percy Barnevik, its Swedish CEO, is notable for recognizing the dilemmas that this involved, adopting the now well-known corporate mantra of "acting local but thinking global." His vision was to create an international company that was able to deal effectively with three internal contradictions: being global and local, big and small, and radically decentralized with centralized reporting and control.[2] The key principle was local entrepreneurship, so most of the decision-making was to be done at the lowest possible level, in the 5,000 independent profit centers, the business units that became the foundation of the ABB organization.

Influential country managers controlled operations in countries, within a matrix structure of regions and business segments. ABB also established business steering committees and functional councils to coordinate the different units, exploit synergies and help transfer knowledge and best practices across the network of local units. The firm developed a management information system called ABACUS that contained data on the performance of the profit centers. Barnevik and his team of top managers traveled extensively to ensure communication and knowledge-sharing across units, while international assignments

DOI: 10.4324/9781003247272-2

helped instill all units with the corporate ethos that Barnevik was pursuing: initiative, action, and risk-taking.

However, after becoming one of the most admired companies in the world during its first ten years, ABB encountered significant problems in its second decade. Hit by the economic downturn in Europe, limitations in the firm's management started to emerge. While flexible and responsive to local contexts, ABB had failed to achieve sufficient global synergies and efficiency. Conflicts between business areas and national units meant that many managers felt that decision-making was unclear. The local profit centers continued to operate their own human resources management (HRM) systems, which were at best aligned at national levels, but not at regional or global levels.

Barnevik's successors between 1997 and 2005 tried to impose more clarity and discipline by eliminating the country managers and regions, giving more power to global businesses, also introducing centralized corporate processes to improve global control, coordination, and efficiency. However, these top-down initiatives further increased the complexity of the firm, and without country managers in place to coordinate local operations, the company verged on paralysis. Country managers were reintroduced; the structure was simplified by selling all businesses except for two (power and automation), and a new global ABB People Strategy was launched, aimed at linking HRM with the business. By 2005, ABB was profitable once again, but had shrunk from 213,000 employees (in 1997) to 102,000. A new CEO, Fred Kindle, found a firm with a high degree of local entrepreneurship and innovation, but with limited coordination and still unsatisfactory global efficiency. Barnevik's contradictions were still on the table.

In this reading, we examine the challenges facing ABB from the historic perspective of internationalization of the firm and the concomitant evolution of HRM. The dilemmas faced by ABB have always existed. What has changed is the nature and speed of communication between a company's headquarters and its subsidiaries around the world. But the essential problems of being flexible and responsive to local market needs while promoting global efficiency, avoiding duplication, and coordinating and controlling diverse units and people remain.

As we will discuss, some modern firms have adopted a *multidomestic* strategy, with autonomous local operations that can respond readily to local needs, while others pursue a centralized, *meganational* strategy to prevent duplication and make global operations more efficient. Their approach to human resource management is radically different.

However, both strategies have limitations, leading to the idea that contemporary global corporations face many contradictions, as ABB recognized. They have to be simultaneously local and global in scope, centralized and decentralized, capable of delivering short-term results while developing future assets, managing multiple alliances without full control, and responding to market pressures to do things better *and* cheaper *and* faster. In the light of this, we examine the concept of the *transnational organization*, at the heart of which is the notion of contradiction,[3] and we explore the implications for people management.

EARLY INTERNATIONALIZATION

International business is not a recent phenomenon; nor is international HRM a product of the 20th or 21st centuries. The Assyrians, Phoenicians, Greeks, and Romans all engaged in extensive cross-border trade. Roman organizations spanning Asia, Africa, and Europe are often heralded as the first global companies, in that they covered the whole of the known world.

The pioneers of international business were the 16th- and 17th-century trading companies—the English and Dutch East India companies, the Muscovy Company, the Hudson's Bay Company, and the Royal African Company.[4] They exchanged merchandise and services across continents and had a geographical spread to rival today's multinational firms. They signed on crews and chartered ships and engaged the services of experts with skills in trade negotiations and foreign languages, capable of assessing the quality of goods and determining how they should be handled and loaded. These companies were obliged to delegate considerable responsibility to local representatives running their operations in far-away countries, which created a new challenge: how could local managers be encouraged to use their discretionary powers to the best advantage of the company? The trading companies had to develop control structures and systems to monitor the behavior of their scattered agents.

Formal rules and procedures were one way of exercising control, but this did not eliminate the temptations of opportunistic behavior for those far from the center. Other control measures were therefore developed, such as employment contracts stipulating that managers would work hard and in the interests of the company. Failure to do so could lead to reprimand or dismissal. Setting performance measures was the next step. These included the ratio of capital to tonnage, the amount of outstanding credit on advance contracts, whether ships sailed on time, and the care taken in loading mixed cargoes. There were also generous financial incentives, such as remuneration packages comprising a fixed cash component and a sizeable bonus. Such a mix of control approaches was not far off contemporary methods used to evaluate and reward managerial performance in large multinationals.

The Impact of Industrialization

The Industrial Revolution originated in Britain in the late 18th century. The emergence of the factory system in Europe and the US had a dramatic impact both on international business and on the management of people. The spread of industrialization in Europe and the US provided growing markets for minerals and foodstuffs and prompted a global search for sources of supply.

Cross-border manufacturing began to emerge by the mid-19th century. But it was difficult to exercise real control over distant operations. The rare manufacturing firms that ventured abroad often used family members to manage their international operations. For example, when Siemens set up its St Petersburg factory in 1855, a brother of the founder was put in charge. In 1863, another brother established a factory to produce sea cables in Britain. Keeping it in the family was the best guarantee that those in distant subsidiaries could be trusted not to act opportunistically.

The international spread of rail networks and the advent of steamships in the 1850s and 1860s brought new speed and reliability to international travel, while the invention of the telegraph uncoupled long-distance communication from transportation. It became possible for firms to manufacture in large batches and to seek volume distribution in mass markets. The rapid growth in firm size provided a domestic platform from which to expand abroad, paving the way for a surge in international business activity in the last decades of the 19th century.[5]

The late 19th and early 20th centuries saw several developments in international business and in people management practices. In parallel with developments in transport and communication, industrialization was having a significant impact on the organization of firms. They were being reshaped by new manufacturing techniques, by the increased specialization and division of labor, and by a change in the composition of the workforce from skilled tradesmen to unskilled workers, previously agrarian, who were unaccustomed to industry requirements like punctuality, regular attendance, supervision, and the mechanical pacing of work effort—similar to the situation in labor-intensive industries in China over the past 40 years. Early personnel management practices were shaped in factories experiencing discipline and motivation problems, where entrepreneurs like Robert Owen in Scotland (often referred to as the father of modern personnel management) began to pay more attention to employees' working conditions and welfare.

The growth in international manufacturing sustained a flourishing service sector, which provided the global infrastructure—finance, insurance, transport— to permit the international flow of goods. All this led to a degree of internationalization that the world would not see again until it had fully recovered from the damage to the global economy created by two world wars. It was a golden age for multinationals, with foreign direct investment (FDI) accounting for around 9 percent of world output.[6]

War and Economic Depression

The outbreak of World War I, followed by a period of economic depression and then World War II, transformed management practices and multinational activity in very different ways, stimulating the development of people management practices but suppressing international trade.

The sudden influx of inexperienced workers (many of them women) into factories in 1915 to service war needs increased the pressure on managers to find ways to improve productivity rapidly. Tasks had to be simplified and redesigned for novices. To contain labor unrest, more attention had to be paid to working conditions and employee demands, which also meant training first line supervisors. These initiatives centralized many of the aspects of employment relations previously discharged by individual line managers. In some progressive firms, employees began to be viewed as resources and the alignment of interest between the firm and workers was emphasized. The 1920s also saw the development of teaching and research, journals, and consulting firms in personnel management.[7]

However, the Great Depression was the start of a bifurcation in employment practices in the US and Japan, the latter having gone through a period of rapid industrialization and economic growth. Leading firms in both the US and Japan were experimenting with corporate welfarism in the 1920s.[8] However, the depth of the Depression in the US in the 1930s meant that many firms had no option except to make lay-offs and repudiate the welfare arrangements that had been established in many non-unionized firms. They turned instead to a path of explicit and instrumental contracts between employee and employer, with wages and employment conditions often determined through collective bargaining.[9] Because of the militarization of the Japanese economy, the impact of the Depression was much less severe on that side of the Pacific. Under legislation fostering "social peace" in the name of national unity, large firms maintained these welfare experiments, leading step-by-step to an HRM orientation built around implicit contracts (lifetime employment, corporate responsibility for the development of staff, and low emphasis on formalized performance evaluation). Endorsed by the strong labor unions that emerged in post-war Japan, these practices became institutionalized, reinforcing and reinforced by Japanese societal values.

In the West, World War II intensified interest in the systematic recruitment, testing, and assigning of new employees to leverage their full potential. Psychological testing used by the military spilled over into private industry.[10] In addition, the desire to avoid wartime strikes led the US government to support collective bargaining, strengthening the role of the personnel function as a result.

If these external shocks had some salutary consequences for the development of personnel practices, they had quite the opposite effect on multinational activities. The adverse conditions during the interwar years encouraged firms to enter cross-border cartels rather than risk foreign investments. By the late 1920s, a considerable proportion of world manufacturing was controlled by these cartels—the most notorious being the "seven sisters" controlling the oil industry.[11]

World War II dealt a crushing blow to these cartels, and after the war, the US brought in aggressive antitrust legislation to dismantle those that remained. While US firms emerged from the war in excellent shape, European competition was devastated, and Japanese corporations (known as *zaibatsu*) had been dismembered. The war had stimulated technological innovation, and American corporations had no desire to confine their activities to the home market. A new era of international business had begun.

THE MODERN MULTINATIONAL

Although Europe had a long tradition in international commerce, it was the global drive of US firms after World War II that gave birth to the multinationals as we know them today. American firms that had hardly ventured beyond their home markets before the war now began to flex their muscles abroad, and by the early 1960s, US companies had built an unprecedented lead in the world economy.

American firms also found faster ways of entering new markets. Many moved abroad through acquisitions, followed by investment in the acquired subsidiaries to benefit more fully from economies of scale and scope.[12] This was the approach taken by Procter & Gamble (P&G), which established a presence in Continental Europe by acquiring an ailing French detergent plant in 1954. An alternative strategy was to join forces with a local partner, as in the case of Xerox, which entered global markets through two joint ventures, with the English motion picture firm, the Rank Organisation, in 1956, and with Fuji Photo Film in Japan in 1962.

In professional services, McKinsey and Arthur Andersen scrambled to open their own offices in foreign countries through the 1950s and 1960s. Others, such as Price Waterhouse and Coopers & Lybrand, built their international presence through mergers with established national practices in other countries. For most others, the route was via informal federations or networks of otherwise independent firms.

Advances in transport and communications—the introduction of commercial jet travel, the first transatlantic telephone link in 1956, then the development of the telex—facilitated this rapid internationalization. More significant still was the emergence of computers. By the mid-1970s, computers had become key elements in the control and information systems of industrial concerns, paving the way for later complex integration strategies. Taken together, the jet plane, the new telecommunications technology and the computer contributed to a "spectacular shrinkage of space."[13]

Alongside these technological drivers of internationalization, powerful economic and political forces were at work. Barriers to trade and investment were progressively dismantled with successive General Agreement on Tariffs and Trades (GATT) treaties. Exchange rates were stabilized following the Bretton Woods Agreement (July 1944), and banks started to play an international role as facilitators of international business. The 1957 Treaty of Rome established the European Community. US firms, many of which already perceived Europe as a single entity, were the first to exploit the regional integration. European companies were spurred by "the American challenge" (the title of a bestselling call-to-arms book by the French journalist and politician Jean-Jacques Servan-Schreiber in 1967), encouraging them to expand beyond their own borders.

Staffing for International Growth

In the decades following World War II, virtually all medium- and large-sized firms had personnel departments, typically with responsibility for industrial (union) relations and for the operational aspects of employment, including staffing subsidiaries abroad.[14] The newly created international personnel units focused on expatriation, sending home country managers to foreign locations.

The largest 180 US multinationals opened an average of six foreign subsidiaries each year during the 1960s.[15] This rapid international expansion opened up new job possibilities, including foreign postings. While US firms in the immediate postwar period had been "flush with veterans who had recently returned from the four corners of the globe [and who] provided a pool of eager expatriates,"[16] more managers were now urgently needed. People had to be persuaded to move abroad, both those with much needed technical skills and managers to exercise control over these expanding foreign subsidiaries. In most companies at the time, this meant paying people generously as an incentive to move abroad.

In the late 1970s, horror stories of expatriate failure gained wide circulation—the technically capable executive sent out to run a foreign subsidiary being brought back prematurely as a borderline alcoholic, with a ruined marriage, and having run the affiliate into the ground. Academic studies seemed to confirm this problem,[17] which for some companies became a major handicap to international growth. It was no longer just a question of persuading people to move abroad, it was a question of "How can we help them to be successful?" While the reluctance to move abroad was increasing, often for family reasons but also because of the mismanagement of reentry to the home country, concern over the rising costs of expatriation was growing.

International business also became a subject of academic study during this period. In the early 1980s, the challenges of expatriation started to attract the attention of researchers, reinforced by the new-found legitimacy of HR, and the concern of senior managers anxious about growth prospects abroad. While it was too early to talk of an international HRM field, international growth was leading to new challenges beyond expatriation that were to shape this emerging domain.

Organizing for International Growth

Rapid international growth brought with it the problems of controlling and coordinating increasingly complex global organizations—where **control** refers to visible and hierarchical processes and structures while **coordination** signifies tools that facilitate alignment through lateral interactions such as cross-boundary project teams and informal social networks. The awareness that international HRM is crucial not just for international staffing but also for building corporate cohesion and inter-unit collaboration grew and matured between the 1960s and 1990s. It was becoming increasingly apparent that the traditional structures were not sufficient to cope with the growing complexities of managing international business.

Many firms selling a wide range of products abroad opted for a structure of worldwide product divisions, whereas those with few products but operating in many countries would typically organize themselves around geographic area divisions, as did IBM.[18] The tricky question was how to organize when the firm had many different products sold in many different geographic markets. It was not at all clear how companies should deal with this zone of maximum complexity.

In practice, two responses emerged. Some firms implemented matrix organizations involving both product and geographic reporting lines, others increased the number of headquarters staff in coordinating roles. Both routes were ultimately to show their limitations, but the two paths gave rise to a growing understanding of the potential role of HRM in dealing with the fundamental problems of cross-border coordination and control.

The Matrix Structure Route

By the early 1970s, several US and British companies (Citibank, Corning, Dow, Exxon, and Shell, among others) had adopted the idea of matrix as a guiding principle for their worldwide organization. Right from the start, some management scholars urged caution, pointing out that matrix is much more complex than reporting lines and structural coordination.[19] Matrix had to be built into leadership development, control and performance appraisal systems, teamwork, conflict resolution mechanisms, relationships, and attitudes, anticipating the later insight that matrix has more to do with HRM than it has to do with structure.[20] Few of the companies that opted for the matrix solution had such supporting elements in place.

A focus on *reporting lines*, the first dimension of coordination, was not sufficient. Attention also had to be paid to the second dimension of coordination, *social architecture*—the conscious design of a social environment that encourages a pattern of thinking and behavior supporting organizational goals. This includes interpersonal relationships and inter-unit networks, the values, beliefs, and norms shared by members of the organization, and the mindsets that people hold. ABB's Percy Barnevik was conscious of the importance of the social elements of the international firm, and thus the need for extensive communication, travel, and relocation of people across units.

Common management processes are a third element of coordination, including processes for managing talent (including recruitment, selection, development, and retention of key personnel), performance and compensation management, and knowledge management and innovation. As ABB's problems compounded, it became increasingly obvious to executives that they had to develop and implement global management processes, although it was less clear how to do this.

Many companies found matrix structures difficult. They led to power struggles, ambiguity over resource allocation, buck-passing, and abdication of responsibility. In theory, a manager reported to two bosses, and conflicts between them would be reconciled at the apex one level higher up. However, it was not unusual to find companies where managers were reporting to four or five bosses, so that reconciliation or arbitration could only happen at a very senior level. While matrix might ensure the consultation necessary for sound decision-making, it was painfully slow. By the time the firm had decided, say, to build a new chemical plant in Asia, nimbler competitors were already up and running. By the early 1980s, many firms reverted to structures where accountability lay clearly with the product divisions, although some (such as ABB) retained a structure with many matrix features.[21]

But if matrix structures were gradually going out of fashion, the matrix problem of organization was more alive than ever. Practitioners and researchers argued that the traditional hierarchic tools of control (rules, standard operating procedures, hierarchical referral, and planning) could not manage the growing complexity of information processing.[22] Organizations required strong capabilities in two areas: first in information processing and second in coordination and teamwork. There was an explosion of interest in how to improve coordination while keeping the reporting relationships as clear and simple as possible.[23]

Gradually, it became clear that the matrix challenges of coordination in complex multinational firms were essentially issues of people and information technology management. Matrix, as two leading strategy scholars were later to say, is a "frame of mind" nurtured more than anything else by careful human resource management.[24]

The Headquarters Coordination Route

Most organizations took the well-trodden path of keeping control of international activities with central staff. This was particularly true for German and Japanese companies, but was also the dominant organizing pattern in Anglo-Saxon firms. As with matrix, this approach was initially successful but eventually led to inefficiencies and paralysis. Again, speed was shown to be the Achilles heel.

It took a long time to work through decisions in German *Zentralbereiche* (central staff departments), and particularly in Japanese *nemawashi*[25] (negotiation) processes of middle-up consultative decision-making. However, multinationals from both of these countries were largely export-oriented with sales subsidiaries abroad, and the disadvantages were initially outweighed by the quality of decision-making and commitment to implementation that accompanied the consensus-oriented decision-making. The complex consultative processes worked reasonably well as long as everyone involved was German or Japanese.[26]

The strains of staff bureaucracy began to show in the US in the early 1980s as companies started to localize, acquiring or building integrated subsidiaries abroad. By localizing the management of foreign units, the coordination of decision-making by central staff became more difficult, slowing down the process at a time when speed was becoming more important. Local managers in lead countries argued for more autonomy and clearer accountability, while the costly overhead of the heavy staff structures associated with central coordination contributed to the erosion of competitiveness.

Faced with the second oil-shock and recession in the late 1970s, American firms were the first to begin the process of downsizing and de-layering staff bureaucracies, followed by Europeans in Nordic and Anglo-Saxon countries. The Japanese and Germans followed more slowly. After decades of postwar international growth, attention in HRM shifted to the painful new challenges of dealing with organizational streamlining and job redesign, layoffs, and managing change under crisis.

Firms that had pursued the headquarters-coordination route came to the same conclusion as firms that had invested in a matrix structure: they had to develop non-bureaucratic coordination and control mechanisms by building lateral relationships facilitated by human resource management. The control and coordination problem became another important strand in the development of international HRM.

HRM Goes International

During the 1980s, the idea that HRM might be of strategic importance gained ground. The insight that strategy is implemented through structure had taken hold—and it was then logical to argue that strategy is also implemented through changes in selection criteria, reward systems, and other HR policies and practices. In turn, this challenged the notion that there might be a "best" approach to HRM—the approach would depend on the strategy.

Perhaps appropriate HRM practices also depend on cultural context? This question was prompted by the difficulties that expatriates had experienced in transplanting management practices abroad, and was supported by growing research on cultural differences, pioneered by Geert Hofstede's study based on the global IBM opinion survey. This showed significant differences in the understanding of management and organization.[27]

The emergence of "the Japanese challenge" in the 1980s as both threat and icon further highlighted the issue of cultural differences, as well as the strategic importance of soft issues, such as HRM. Numerous studies attempted to explain how the Japanese, whose country was destroyed and occupied after World War II, had managed to rebound with such vigor, successfully taking away America's market share in industries such as automobiles and consumer electronics. How had they managed to pull this off with no natural resources apart from people? A large part of the answer seemed to lie in distinctive HRM practices that helped to provide high levels of skill, motivation, and collective entrepreneurship, as well as collaboration between organizational units.[28] This was a shock for Western managers, who suddenly realized that other approaches to management could be equally or even more successful.

New international human resource challenges also emerged. Many governments began to apply pressure on foreign firms to hire and develop local employees. Given the cost of expatriation, this persuaded some multinational firms to start aggressively recruiting local executives to run their foreign subsidiaries. This often required extensive training and development, but as one observer pointed out, "The cost must be weighed against the cost of sending an American family to the area."[29] At Unilever, for example, the proportion of expatriates in foreign management positions dropped from 50 percent to 10 percent between 1950 and 1970.[30]

However, there was a Catch-22 in localizing key positions in foreign units: the greater the talent of local people, the more likely they were to be poached by other firms seeking local skills. Consequently, localization was a priority for only a minority of multinational firms until well into the 1990s, except for operations in highly developed regions such as North America, Europe, and Japan.[31]

Some firms used expatriate assignments for developmental reasons rather than just to solve an immediate job need. In these corporations, high-potential executives would be transferred abroad to expose them to international responsibilities. The assumption was that with growing internationalization, *all* senior executives needed international experience, even those in domestic positions. For example, the vice-president of P&G had already pointed out in 1963 that the company would never appoint anyone simply because of his or her nationality: "A Canadian runs our French company, a Dutch person runs the Belgian company, and a Briton runs our Italian company. In West Germany, an American is in charge; in Mexico, a Canadian."[32] This meant that P&G was able to attract the very best local talent, quickly developing an outstanding reputation around the globe for the quality of its management. For local firms in France, Singapore, Australia, and Brazil, P&G was the management benchmark, and not only in the fast-moving consumer goods sector. Other firms started to adopt the P&G approach, although this created new challenges for international HRM. How does one manage the identification, development, transfer, and repatriation of talent spread out across the globe?

The link between international management development and the problems of coordination and control was established by the landmark research of Edström and Galbraith. They studied the expatriation policies of four multinationals of comparable size and geographic coverage in the mid-1970s, including Shell.[33] The research showed that these companies had quite different levels and patterns of international personnel transfer.[34] There were three motives for transferring managers abroad. The first and most common was to meet an immediate need for particular skills in a foreign subsidiary. The second was to develop managers through challenging international experience. However, the study of Shell revealed a third motive for international transfers—as a mechanism for control and coordination. The managers sent abroad were steeped in the policies and style of the organization, so they could be relied on to act appropriately in diverse situations. Moreover, frequent assignments abroad developed a network of personal relationships that facilitated coordination.

It appeared that Shell was able to maintain a high degree of control and coordination while at the same time having a more decentralized organization than other firms. This suggested that appropriate HRM practices could allow a firm to be globally coordinated and relatively decentralized at the same time, avoiding the matrix and corporate staff traps. Global control and coordination, it appeared, could be provided through socialization, minimizing the necessity for centralized headquarters control or bureaucratic procedures.

These findings drew attention to expatriation, mobility, and management development as a vital part of the answer to the matrix/bureaucracy problem of coordination. In truth, the concept was not entirely new—the Romans had adopted a similar approach to the decentralization dilemma two millennia before, staffing far-flung regions with trusted governors socialized to safeguard the interests of the Empire.

By the mid-1990s, with globalization deepening, surveys consistently showed that global leadership development was one of the top three HRM priorities in major US corporations.[35] In some companies in Europe and the US, international management development was seen to be so critical that this department was separated from the corporate HR function and reported directly to the CEO.

ENTER GLOBALIZATION

By the end of the 1980s, the traditional distinction between domestic and multinational companies had started to become blurred. International competition was no longer the preserve of industrial giants; it was affecting everybody's business. Statistics from the 1960s show that only 6 percent of the US economy was exposed to international competition. By the late 1980s, the corresponding figure was over 70 percent and climbing fast.[36]

Globalization surfaced as the new buzzword at the beginning of the 1990s, though it has different meanings for different people, sometimes with strong negative overtones. Viewed as interdependence and interconnectedness, many of the ingredients of globalization had actually been around for several decades. The steady dismantling of trade barriers in Western Europe and in North and South America, the increasing availability of global capital, advances in computing and communications technology, the progressive convergence of consumer tastes and, in particular, the universal demand for industrial products had all been underway for some time. What made a difference was that these trends now reached a threshold where they became mutually reinforcing.

Widespread deregulation and privatization opened new opportunities for international business in both developing and developed countries. The multinational domain, long associated with the industrial company, was shifting to the service sector, which by the mid-1990s represented over half of total world foreign direct investment. Problems of distance and time zones were further smoothed away as communication by fax gave way to e-mail and fixed phone networks gave way to wireless mobile technology. Globalization was further stimulated by the fall of communism in Russia and Eastern Europe. Together with China's adoption of market-oriented policies, huge new opportunities were opened to international business as most of the world was drawn into the integrated global economy.

Multinationals increasingly located different elements of their value-adding activities in different parts of the world. Formerly hierarchical companies with clean-cut boundaries were giving way to complex arrangements and configurations, often fluctuating over time. The new buzzword from GE was "the boundaryless organization."[37] With increasing cross-border project work and mobility, the image of an organization as a network was rapidly becoming as accurate as that of hierarchy. For example, a European pharmaceutical corporation could have international R&D partnerships with competitors in the US and manufacturing joint ventures with local partners in China, where it also outsourced local sales of generic products to a firm strong in distribution.

Traditionally, the only resources that multinationals sought abroad were raw materials or cheap labor. Everything else was at home: sources of leading-edge technology and finance, world-class suppliers, pressure-cooker competition, the most sophisticated customers, and the best intelligence on future trends.[38] Global competition was now dispersing some of these capabilities around the world. India, for example, developed its software industry using a low-cost strategy as a means of entry, but then quickly climbed the value chain, just as Japan had done previously in the automobile industry. The implication of such developments was that multinational firms could no longer assume that all the capabilities deemed strategic were available close to home.

With the erosion of traditional sources of competitive advantage, multinationals needed to change their perspective. To compete successfully, they had to do more than exploit scale economies or arbitrage imperfections in the world's markets for goods, labor, and capital. Toward the end of the 1980s, a new way of thinking about the multinational enterprise came out of studies of how organizations were responding to these challenges. The concept of the transnational organization was born.

The Roadmap for Managing Globalization

If there is a single perspective that has shaped the context for our understanding of the multinational enterprise and its HRM implications, it is Bartlett and Ghoshal's research on the transnational organization.[39] To this we can add Hedlund's related concept of heterarchy and Doz and Prahalad's studies on the multi-focal organization, all of which have origins in Perlmutter's geocentric organization.[40] These strategy and management researchers grew to believe that people management is perhaps the single most critical domain for the multinational firm. None of them had any interest in HRM by virtue of their training, but all were drawn to the HRM field by findings from their research.

Doz and Prahalad began to link the fields of multinational strategy and HRM when researching the patterns of strategic control in multinational companies.[41] As they saw it, multinational firms faced a central problem: responding to a variety of national demands while maintaining a clear and consistent global business strategy. This tension between strong opposing forces, dubbed local responsiveness and global integration, served as a platform for much subsequent research on multinational enterprises, and it was captured by Sony's "think global, act local," aphorism, also adopted by ABB as its guiding motto.

Bartlett and Ghoshal developed these concepts further in their study of nine firms in three industries (consumer electronics, branded packaged goods, and telephone switching) and three regions (North America, Europe, and Japan).[42] They discovered that these companies seemed to have followed one of three internationalization paths, which they called "administrative heritage":

- One path emphasized responsiveness to local conditions, leading to what they called a "multinational enterprise" and which we prefer to call **multi-domestic**. This led to a decentralized federation of local firms led by entrepreneurs who enjoyed a high degree of strategic freedom and organizational autonomy. The strength of the multidomestic approach was local responsiveness to customers and infrastructure. Some European firms, such as Unilever and Philips, and ITT in the US, embodied this approach.
- A second path to internationalization was that of the "global" firm, typified by US corporations such as Ford and Japanese enterprises such as Matsushita and NEC. Since the term *global* is today applied like the term multinational to any large firm operating on a worldwide basis, we prefer to call such a firm the **meganational** firm. Here, worldwide facilities are typically centralized in the parent country, products are standardized, and overseas operations are considered as delivery pipelines to access international markets. The global hub maintains tight control over strategic decisions, resources, and information. The competitive strength of the meganational firm comes from efficiencies of scale and cost.
- Some companies appeared to have taken a third route, a variant on the meganational path. Like the meganational, their facilities were located at the centre. But the competitive strength of these "**international**" firms was their ability to transfer expertise to less advanced overseas environments, while allowing local units more discretion in adapting products and services. They were also capable of capturing learning from such local initiatives and then transferring it back to the central R&D and marketing departments. The "international" enterprise was thus a tightly coordinated federation of local firms. Some American and European firms, such as Ericsson, fitted this pattern, heralding the growing concern with global knowledge management.

It was apparent to Bartlett and Ghoshal that specific firms were doing well because their internationalization paths matched the requirements of their industry. Consumer products required local responsiveness, so Unilever had been thriving with its multidomestic approach, while Kao in Japan—centralized and meganational in heritage—had hardly been able to move outside its Japanese borders. The situation was different in consumer electronics, where the centralized meganational heritage of Matsushita (Panasonic and other brands) seemed to fit better than the more localized approaches of Philips' and GE's consumer electronics business. And in telecommunications switching, the international learning and transfer ability of Ericsson led its "international" strategy to dominate the multidomestic and meganational strategies of its competitors.

Perhaps the most significant of Bartlett and Ghoshal's observations was that accelerating global competition was changing the stakes. In all three industries, it was clear that the leading firms had to become more **transnational** in their orientation—more locally responsive *and* more globally integrated *and* better at sharing learning between headquarters and subsidiaries. What had been driving this change? Increasing competition was shifting the competitive positioning of these firms from *either/or* to *and*. The challenge for Unilever (like ABB in the opening story) was to maintain its local responsiveness, but at the same time to increase its global efficiency by eliminating duplication and integrating manufacturing. Conversely, the challenge for Matsushita was to keep the economies of centralized product development and manufacturing, but to become more local and responsive to differentiated niches in markets around the world.

The Transnational Solution

The defining characteristic of the transnational enterprise is its capacity to steer between the contradictions that it confronts. As Ghoshal and Bartlett put it:

> Managers in most worldwide companies recognize the need for simultaneously achieving global efficiency, national responsiveness, and the ability to develop and exploit knowledge on a worldwide basis. Some, however, regard the goal as inherently unattainable. Perceiving irreconcilable contradictions among the three objectives, they opt to focus on one of them, at least temporarily. The transnational company is one that overcomes these contradictions.[43]

However, it is not clear that all multinational firms are destined to move in a transnational direction. While all companies are forced to contend with the dimensions of responsiveness, efficiency, and learning, and intensified competition heightens the contradictory pressures, these features are not equally salient in all industries. Moreover, the pressures do not apply equally to all parts of a firm. One subsidiary may be more local in orientation, whereas another may be tightly integrated. Even within a particular function, such as marketing, pricing may be a local matter whereas distribution may be controlled from the center. In HR, performance management systems may be more globally standardized, whereas reward systems for workers may be left to local discretion. Indeed, this differentiation is another aspect of the complexity of the transnational—one size does not fit all.

In many ways, the transnational concept drew its inspiration from the concept of matrix. But transnational is neither a particular organizational form, nor a specific strategic posture. Rather it is an "organizational model," a "management mentality," and a "philosophy."[44] The transnational challenge is therefore to create balanced perspectives[45] or a "matrix in the mind of managers."[46] The challenge for senior management is to build a common sense of purpose that will guide local strategic initiatives, to coordinate through a portfolio of processes rather than via hierarchic structure, and to shape people's attitudes across the globe.[47]

This has led international HRM researchers to examine the local–global tension in multinationals.[48] On the one hand, there are pressures for HRM policies and practices to be adapted to fit local institutional rules, regulations, and norms, as well as the cultural context. Yet if the multinational decentralizes the responsibility for HRM to local units, this can result in duplication, excessive cost, and lack of regional or global scale advantages within the HR function. Even more importantly this may handicap inter-unit learning within the corporation while handicapping coordination. For example, a failure to address issues related to corporate social responsibility in a globally consistent manner can cost the company dearly. Siemens experienced this when a corruption scandal erupted in 2007, as did Nike, severely criticized for not having tightly supervised labor practices across its global network of suppliers.

Given the persistent challenges to address the local–global tension, multinationals have also started to complement their primarily structural solutions with people-related approaches. One such approach consists of staffing with multicultural individuals, who by virtue of their upbringing and experience have gained familiarity with norms and behaviors of multiple country contexts and can flexibly switch among them. Fast-moving consumer goods multinational L'Oréal is a case in point, staffing its product development teams by one third with multiculturals.[49]

Capabilities and Knowledge as Sources of Competitiveness

Today, management, strategy, and international business scholars are increasingly focused on capabilities and knowledge as drivers of competitive advantage. A core organizational capability is a firm-specific bundling of technical systems, people skills, and cultural values.[50] To the extent that they are firm-specific, such organizational capabilities are difficult to imitate because of the complex configuration of the various elements. The capabilities can therefore be a major source of competitive advantage (although their very success can also create dangerous rigidities).

The distinguishing feature of a capability is the integration of skills, technologies, systems, managerial behaviors, and work values. For example, FedEx has a core competence in package routing and delivery. This rests on the integration of barcode technology, mobile communications, systems using linear programming, network management, and other skills.[51] The capability of INSEAD or IMD in executive education depends on faculty know-how integrated with program design skills, marketing, relationships with clients, the competence and attitude of support staff, reward systems, and a host of other interwoven factors that have evolved over the years.

Another crucial source of competitive advantage comes from the firm's ability to create, transfer, and integrate knowledge.[52] At the heart of the surge of academic and corporate interest in management of knowledge lies the distinction between explicit and tacit knowledge. The former is knowledge that you know that you have, and in organizations explicit knowledge is often codified in texts and manuals. The latter is personal, built on intuition acquired through years of experience and hard to formalize and communicate to others. One of the main approaches to knowledge management is to build collections of explicit knowledge (customer contacts, presentation overheads, etc.) using software systems, and to make that knowledge available via an intranet. Another approach is to focus on building connections or contacts between people in the organization that can be used to transfer tacit knowledge.[53] Many professional firms have gone down this route, for instance by creating yellow page directories that allow consultants to find individuals who have relevant experience and encouraging the development of informal relationships among people interested in a certain topic area. In a world where the retention of people is more difficult, it is particularly important to retain and transfer their knowledge.

These ideas about the source of competitive advantage are related to the *resource-based perspective* of the firm, which views it as a bundle of tangible and intangible resources. If such resources are valuable to the customer, rare, difficult to purchase or imitate, and effectively exploited, then they can provide a basis for superior economic performance that may be sustained over time. This view quickly attracted the attention of HRM scholars because its broad definition of resources could be applied to HRM-related capabilities, such as training and development, teamwork and culture. Resource-based theory helped to reinforce the interrelationship between HRM and strategy. It provided a direct conceptual link between an organization's more behavioral and social attributes and its ability to gain a competitive advantage. This influential view, based largely on research on multinational enterprises, has continued to play an important role in current strategy and HRM thinking.

THE EVOLUTION OF INTERNATIONAL HRM

As we have seen, the challenges of foreign assignments, adapting people management practices to foreign situations, and coordinating and controlling distant operations have existed since antiquity. It is only during the last 50 years that specialized personnel managers have begun to assume a responsibility for these tasks. With the acceleration of globalization, these and other international HRM issues have developed into a central competitive challenge for corporations. As Floris Maljers, former co-chairman of Unilever, put it: "Limited human resources—not unreliable or inadequate sources of capital—has become the biggest constraint in most globalization efforts."[54] Many scholars studying the multinational firm would agree.

The centrality of these HRM issues has increased over time. For example, as the bottom-line consequences became more visible, concern over expatriation broadened to include the understanding that it was not just about sending managers abroad but also about helping expatriates to be successful in their roles and future careers. The scope of expatriation has changed—today expatriates come not only from the multinational's home country but also from other, third countries—and they come in increasingly varied forms and shapes that include international business travelers, global domestics, and self-initiated assignees, to name but a few.[55] Localization of staff in foreign units became a new imperative, leading to the complex task of tracking and developing a global talent pool. As globalization started to have an impact on local operations, for example, in China, it also became clear that even local executives need to have international experience. Globalization has raised awareness of the pivotal role played by managerial talent in implementing global strategies, and multinationals from different parts of the world are increasingly competing for talent from the same global talent pools.

Over the past two decades, multinationals from high-growth emerging markets have become major global investors. Large international acquisitions by firms like Tata Steel from India and CEMEX from Mexico, the world's largest building material company, have transformed industries that were traditionally dominated by firms from developed countries. The shift away from countries such as the US and Japan dominating lists of the world's largest companies is clear. Out of the world's 500 largest corporations, the US lost no less than 56 of its 177 spots between 1999 and 2019, and Japan lost 29 of its 81. The winners were emerging countries, foremost China with a whopping increase (from 10 to 119), but also South Korea (12 → 16), India (1 → 7), Taiwan (1 → 9), Mexico (2 → 4), and Brazil (3 → 8).[56] Even Western scholars increasingly look to these emerging markets for new lessons in human resource management and building capabilities.[57]

As the ABB story illustrated, the failure of structural solutions to address the problems of coordination and control led to an increased focus on how HR practices might assist in providing cohesion to the multinational firm. HRM and strategy came together in the transnational concept that helped to dissolve many of the traditional boundaries in organizational thinking. Today, the strategic importance of international HRM is widely recognized. Recent crises like the COVID-19 pandemic and the Ukraine conflict have raised additional challenges for international HRM but have also pointed to the HR function as uniquely positioned for navigating global companies through a "new normal."[58] For example, the travel bans and the shift to full remote work due to pandemic-induced lockdowns have led to lasting changes in the way work is designed and performed while also reshaping the global mobility landscape and triggering a broader discussion about what sustainable performance and meaningful work may look like. Similarly, the global supply chain disruptions caused by the Ukraine conflict—together with a more emphatic focus on sustainability considerations—have led multinationals to rethink their global footprint, which has important implications for how and where global talent could and should be sourced.

The increasing centrality of international HRM issues has blurred the boundaries between this domain of academic study and others. Once no more than an appendix to the field of personnel/HR management, international HRM has become a lens for the study of the multinational enterprise, the form of organization that continues to dominate the world economy. Understanding the complex challenges facing today's global organizations calls for interdisciplinary work with scholars of strategy, institutional economics, organization, cross-cultural management, leadership, change management, organizational culture, and others.

NOTES

1. Many of the observations in this reading are drawn from Evans, Pucik, and Björkman (2011). This is a further revision by the authors of their article that appeared in the previous edition of this book.
2. Barham and Heimer (1998).
3. Bartlett and Ghoshal (1989).
4. Carlos and Nicholas (1988). On the other side of the world, southern Chinese clans spread their hold across Southeast Asia in the 14th and 15th centuries.
5. Wilkins (1970).
6. Even by the early 1990s, foreign direct investment had only rallied to around 8.5 percent of world output (Jones, 1996). Recent data show the stock of FDI to be 30 percent of global GDP in 2019 (World Investment Report 2021, UNCTAD—available at https://unctad.org/webflyer/world-investment-report-2021).
7. Kaufman (2007).
8. Moriguchi (2000).
9. Kaufman (2007).
10. Jacoby (1985).
11. Sampson (1975); Vernon, Wells, and Rangan (1997). Similarly in pharmaceuticals, electric light bulbs, steel, and engineering industries, elaborate arrangements were established among national champions allowing them to focus on their home markets and to suppress international competition.
12. Chandler (1990).
13. Vernon (1977).
14. Kaufman (2007).
15. Vaupel and Curhan (1973).
16. Hays (1974).
17. Tung (1982), although see Harzing (1995), for a detailed analysis.
18. Stopford and Wells (1972).
19. Argyris (1967).
20. Davis and Lawrence (1977).
21. It would be misleading to say that matrix structure is dead. Some organizations introduced matrix organizations in the late 1980s and 1990s. The matrix structure that ABB employed until 1998 is perhaps the most well-known example. Research suggests that matrix structure can be appropriate as a transition organization, facilitating the development of a "matrix culture," leading to different forms of multi-dimensional organization, facilitated by coordination mechanisms that the matrix introduced (Egelhoff and Wolf, 2017; Galbraith, 2008).
22. Egelhoff and Wolf (2017); Galbraith (1977).
23. Martinez and Jarillo (1989).
24. Bartlett and Ghoshal (1990).
25. The *nemawashi* process in Japanese firms is an informal process of consultation, typically undertaken by a high-potential individual, involving talking with people and gathering support for an important decision or project.

26. Many German international firms had an unusual structure abroad, where the sales subsidiary was run jointly by a local general manager with a German commercial manager on a *primus inter pares* basis, facilitating this consensual approach.
27. Hofstede (1980).
28. See Pucik and Hatvany (1981), and Pucik (1984). The success of Japan threw the spotlight on HR ingredients such as long-term employment, intensive socialization, team-based appraisal and rewards, slow promotion, and job rotation. Distinctive features of Japanese management that received attention in the West included continuous improvement, commitment to learning, quality management practices, customer-focused production systems, and consultative decision-making.
29. Oxley (1961).
30. Kuin (1972).
31. Even today, localization (how to develop the talent of local staff) remains one of the most neglected areas of international human resource management.
32. "Multinational companies: Special report" (1963, p. 76).
33. Edström and Galbraith (1977).
34. "Three times the number of managers were transferred in Europe at (one company rather than the other), despite their being of the same size, in the same industry, and having nearly identical organization charts" (Edström and Galbraith, 1977, p. 255). For recent research examining why multinationals transfer headquarters managers to staff foreign subsidiaries see Lee, Yoshikawa, and Harzing (2022).
35. See the SOTA (State of the Art) surveys, run annually since 1995 by the Human Resource Planning Society, reported each year in the journal *Human Resource Planning*; see also a survey undertaken in Fortune 500 firms by Gregersen, Morrison, and Black (1998).
36. Prescott, Rothwell, and Taylor (1999).
37. Ashkenas, Ulrich, Jick, and Kerr (1995).
38. Such clusters of critical factors helped particular nations to develop a competitive advantage in certain fields—such as German firms in chemicals or luxury cars, Swiss firms in pharmaceuticals, and US firms in personal computers, software, and movies.
39. Bartlett and Ghoshal (1989).
40. See Hedlund (1986); Prahalad and Doz (1987); and Perlmutter (1969).
41. Doz, Bartlett, and Prahalad (1981); Doz and Prahalad (1984, 1986).
42. Bartlett and Ghoshal (1989).
43. Ghoshal and Bartlett (1998, p. 65).
44. Bartlett and Ghoshal (1989).
45. Doz and Prahalad (1986).
46. Bartlett and Ghoshal (1989).
47. Ghoshal and Bartlett (1997).
48. Rosenzweig and Nohria (1994); Björkman and Lu (2001); Reiche and Minbaeva (2019).
49. Hong and Doz (2013).
50. Hamel and Prahalad (1994); Wilden, Devinney, and Dowling (2016).
51. This example is taken from Hamel and Prahalad (1994), who provide a more complete definition, emphasizing that core competences should be gateways to the future.
52. Kogut and Zander (1992); Kim, Reiche and Harzing (2022).
53. Polanyi (1966); Nonaka and Takeuchi (1995).
54. Cited by Bartlett and Ghoshal (1992).
55. McNulty and Brewster (2017).
56. See https://fortune.com/global500/.
57. For example, Cappelli, Singh, Singh and Useem (2010) examine the lessons of business leaders in India. See also Mellahi, Frynas, and Collings (2016).
58. Caligiuri, De Cieri, Minbaeva, Verbeke, and Zimmermann (2020); Collings, Nyberg, Wright, and McMackin (2021).

REFERENCES

Argyris, C. (1967). "Today's problems with tomorrow's organizations." *Journal of Management Studies* 4(1): 31–55.

Ashkenas, R.N., D. Ulrich, T. Jick, and S. Kerr (1995). *The boundaryless organization: Breaking the chains of organizational structure.* San Francisco, CA: Jossey-Bass.

Barham, K., and C. Heimer (1998). *ABB: The dancing giant.* London: Financial Times/ Pitman.

Bartlett, C.A., and S. Ghoshal (1989). *Managing across borders: The transnational solution.* Cambridge, MA: Harvard Business School Press.

Bartlett, C.A., and S. Ghoshal (1990). "Matrix management: Not a structure, a frame of mind." *Harvard Business Review* 68(4): 138–145.

Bartlett, C.A., and S. Ghoshal (1992). "What is a global manager?" *Harvard Business Review* 70(5): 124–132.

Björkman, I., and Y. Lu (2001). "Institutionalization and bargaining power explanations of HRM practices in international joint ventures: The case of Chinese–Western joint ventures." *Organization Studies* 22(3): 491–512.

Caligiuri, P., H. De Cieri, D. Minbaeva, A. Verbeke, and A. Zimmermann (2020). "International HRM insights for navigating the COVID-19 pandemic: Implications for future research and practice." *Journal of International Business Studies* 51(5): 697–713.

Cappelli, P., H. Singh, J. Singh, and M. Useem (2010). *The India way: How India's top business leaders are revolutionizing management.* Boston, MA: Harvard Business School Publishing.

Carlos, A.M., and S. Nicholas (1988). "Giants of an earlier capitalism: The chartered trading companies as modern multinationals." *Business History Review* 62(Autumn): 398–419.

Chandler, A.D. (1990). *Scale and scope: The dynamics of industrial capitalism.* Cambridge, MA: Harvard University Press.

Collings, D.G., A.J. Nyberg, P.M. Wright, and J. McMackin (2021). "Leading through paradox in a COVID-19 world: Human resources comes of age." *Human Resource Management Journal* 31(4): 819–833.

Davis, S.M., and P.R. Lawrence (1977). *Matrix.* Reading, MA: Addison-Wesley.

Doz, Y., and C.K. Prahalad (1984). "Patterns of strategic control within multinational corporations." *Journal of International Business Studies* 15(2): 55–72.

Doz, Y., and C.K. Prahalad (1986). "Controlled variety: A challenge for human resource management in the MNC." *Human Resource Management* 25(1): 55–71.

Doz, Y., C.A. Bartlett, and C.K. Prahalad (1981). "Global competitive pressures and host country demands: Managing tensions in MNCs." *California Management Review* 23(3): 63–74.

Edström, A., and J.R. Galbraith (1977). "Transfer of managers as a coordination and control strategy in multinational organizations." *Administrative Science Quarterly* 22(2): 248–263.

Egelhoff, W.G., and J. Wolf (2017). *Understanding matrix structures and their alternatives: The key to designing and managing large, complex organizations.* London: Palgrave Macmillan.

Evans, P., V. Pucik, and I. Björkman (2011). *The global challenge: International human resource management.* Boston, MA: McGraw-Hill.

Galbraith, J.R. (1977). *Organization design.* Reading, MA: Addison-Wesley.

Galbraith, J. (2008). *Designing matrix organizations that actually work: How IBM, Proctor & Gamble, and others design for success.* Jossey-Bass.

Ghoshal, S., and C.A. Bartlett (1997). *The individualized corporation.* New York: Harper-Business.

Ghoshal, S., and C.A. Bartlett (1998). *Managing across borders: The transnational solution* (2nd ed.). London: Random House.

Gregersen, H.B., A.J. Morrison, and S. Black (1998). "Developing leaders for the global frontier." *MIT Sloan Management Review* 40(1): 2–32.

Hamel, G., and C.K. Prahalad (1994). *Competing for the future*. Boston, MA: Harvard Business School Press.

Harzing, A.W.K. (1995). "The persistent myth of high expatriate failure rates." *International Journal of Human Resource Management* 6(2): 457–475.

Hays, R.D. (1974). "Expatriate selection: Insuring success and avoiding failure." *Journal of International Business Studies* 5(1): 25–37.

Hedlund, G. (1986). "The hypermodern MNC: A heterarchy?" *Human Resource Management* 25(1): 9–35.

Hofstede, G. (1980). *Culture's consequences: Comparing values, behaviors, institutions, and organizations across nations*. Beverly Hills, CA and London: Sage.

Hong, H.-J., and Y. Doz (2013). "L'Oréal masters multiculturalism." *Harvard Business Review* 91(6): 114–119.

Jacoby, S.M. (1985). *Employing bureaucracy: Managers, unions and the transformation of work in American industry, 1900–1945*. New York: Columbia University Press.

Jones, G. (1996). *The evolution of international business*. London: Routledge.

Kaufman, B. (2007). "The development of HRM in historical and international perspective." In P. Boxall, J. Purcell, and P. Wright (Eds.), *The Oxford handbook of human resource management* (pp. 19–47). New York: Oxford University Press.

Kim, H., B.S. Reiche, and A.-W. Harzing (2022). "How does successive inpatriation contribute to subsidiary capability building and subsidiary evolution? A longitudinal perspective on inpatriates' knowledge transfer." *Journal of International Business Studies* 53(7): 1394–1419.

Kogut, B., and U. Zander (1992). "Knowledge of the firm, combinative capabilities, and the replication of technology." *Organization Science* 3(3): 383–397.

Kuin, P. (1972). "The magic of multinational management." *Harvard Business Review* 50(6)(November–December): 89–97.

Lee, H.-J., K. Yoshikawa, and A.-W. Harzing (2022). "Cultures and institutions: Dispositional and contextual explanations for country-of-origin effects in MNC 'ethnocentric' staffing practices." *Organization Studies* 43(4): 497–519.

Martinez, J.I., and J.C. Jarillo (1989). "The evolution of research on coordination mechanisms in multinational corporations." *Journal of International Business Studies* 20(3): 489–514.

McNulty, Y., and C. Brewster (2017). "Theorising the meaning(s) of 'expatriate': Establishing boundary conditions for business expatriates." *The International Journal of Human Resource Management* 28(1): 27–61.

Mellahi, K., J.G. Frynas, and D.G. Collings (2016). "Performance management practices within emerging market multinational enterprises: The case of Brazilian multinationals." *The International Journal of Human Resource Management* 27(8): 876–905.

Moriguchi, C. (2000). "Implicit contracts, the great depression, and institutional change: The evolution of employment relations in US and Japanese manufacturing firms, 1910–1940." Working Paper. Boston, MA: Harvard Business School.

Nonaka, I., and H. Takeuchi (1995). *The knowledge-creating company: How Japanese companies create the dynamics of innovation*. New York: Oxford University Press.

Oxley, G.M. (1961). "The personnel manager for international operations." *Personnel* 38(6): 52–58.

Perlmutter, H.V. (1969). "The tortuous evolution of the multinational corporation." *Columbia Journal of World Business* 4: 9–18.

Polanyi, M. (1966). *The tacit dimension*. London: Routledge and Kegan Paul.

Prahalad, C.K., and Y. Doz (1987). *The multinational mission: Balancing local demands and global vision*. New York: Free Press.

Prescott, R.K., W.J. Rothwell, and M. Taylor (1999). "Global HR: Transforming HR into a global powerhouse." *HR Focus* 76(3): 7–8.

Pucik, V. (1984). "White-collar human resource management in large Japanese manufacturing firms." *Human Resource Management* 23(3): 257–276.

Pucik, V., and N. Hatvany (1981). "An integrated management system: Lessons from the Japanese experience." *Academy of Management Review* 6(3): 469–480.

Reiche, B.S., and D. Minbaeva (2019). "HRM in multinational companies." In A. Wilkinson, N. Bacon, S. Snell, and D. Lepak (Eds.), *SAGE handbook of human resource management* (2nd ed., pp. 541–556). London: Sage.

Rosenzweig, P.M., and N. Nohria (1994). "Influences on human resource management practices in multinational corporations." *Journal of International Business Studies* 25(2): 229–251.

Sampson, A. (1975). *The seven sisters: The great oil companies and the world they made*. London: Hodder and Stoughton.

Stopford, J.M., and L.T. Wells (1972). *Managing the multinational enterprise*. London: Longman.

Tung, R.L. (1982). "Selection and training procedures of US, European, and Japanese multinationals." *California Management Review* 25(1): 57–71.

Vaupel, J.W., and J.P. Curhan (1973). *The world's largest multinational enterprises*. Cambridge, MA: Harvard University Press.

Vernon, R. (1977). *Storm over the multinationals: The real issues*. Cambridge, MA: Harvard University Press.

Vernon, R., L.T. Wells, and S. Rangan (1997). *The manager in the international economy*. Englewood Cliffs, NJ: Prentice Hall.

Wilden, R., T.M. Devinney, and G.R. Dowling (2016). "The architecture of dynamic capability research identifying the building blocks of a configurational approach." *Academy of Management Annals* 10(1): 997–1076.

Wilkins, M. (1970). *The emergence of multinational enterprise*. Cambridge, MA: Harvard University Press.

Vlad Vaiman and David G. Collings

GLOBAL TALENT MANAGEMENT
Past, Present, and Future[*]

INTRODUCTION

ONE OF THE MOST IMPORTANT developments in international human resource management (HRM) over the past quarter century has been the increased focus on the effective management of those individuals with high levels of human capital who are central to organizational success, both at home and abroad (Vaiman & Collings, 2015). Ever since the second half of the 1990s, talent management (TM) has become a key area of focus for both practitioners and academics. Even though at first some scholars were somewhat doubtful of the academic value of TM, its rapid development, especially over the last decade, has proven them wrong. TM now is a growing area with an increasing consensus on definitions, theoretical frameworks, and levels of analysis.

Five major TM conceptualizations have emerged in the academic community during the past 15 years. Lewis and Heckman (2006) have identified the first three of them. The first was to simply rebrand HRM as TM, which did not sit well with academics who saw it as a relabeling of the same old thing, as mentioned above. The second idea helped to refocus the succession planning conversation from an organizational chart-centric perspective to one that is more dynamic and focused on anticipating staffing requirements and establishing talent pools to fulfill those needs (Cappelli & Keller, 2014). Managers should pay special attention to those employees who regularly outperform their peers, known as "A-players," rather than those who fall into the "B" or "C" performance categories. The main goal of managers, according to the third conceptualization, was to focus on A-players and ultimately manage out the C-players. Although

[*] This reading is an updated version of an earlier chapter published in D.G. Collings, G.T. Wood & P.M. Caligiuri (2015). *The Routledge Companion to International Human Resource Management.* London: Routledge.

DOI: 10.4324/9781003247272-3

there were advocates for this strategy (chief among them Jack Welch of GE), the principle of forced distribution on which it was founded is increasingly viewed as outdated owing to the damage it might do to individuals, groups, organizations, and society as a whole (Collings et al., 2022). In 2009, Collings and Mellahi identified a fourth topic, which centers on the distinction of crucial (or critical, pivotal) employment positions in businesses. These positions are defined by the potential for significant variation in the quality or quantity of output when the quality or quantity of employees increase, and their alignment with the organization's strategic intent (i.e., mission, vision, strategy, etc.). According to Collings (2017), this line of research contributed to a major conceptual shift in TM by changing the locus of differentiation in TM from employee inputs to outputs. The use of big data and people analytics to help businesses make better personnel investment decisions was a fifth, more recent topic that transpired during TM's development (see Vaiman & Khoreva, 2021; Minbaeva & Vardi, 2019; Vaiman et al., 2012).

In conjunction with the theoretical conceptualizations mentioned earlier, the scholarly literature pertaining to TM's conceptual foundations has mostly developed along two different approaches. The first and, without a doubt, most prevalent approach focuses on *exclusive* TM, which emphasizes the disproportionate contribution of high-performing and high-potential employees frequently engaged in crucial areas. In line with this approach, Collings and Mellahi's (2009) definition of talent management states that it entails:

> activities and processes that involve the systematic identification of key positions which differentially contribute to the organisation's sustainable competitive advantage, the development of a talent pool of high potential and high performing incumbents to fill these roles, and the development of a differentiated human resource architecture to facilitate filling these positions with competent incumbents and to ensure their continued commitment to the organisation.
>
> (p. 305)

Even though this definition of TM is not the only one that is considered valid, it is by far the most common used in TM literature.

The second approach concentrates on a more *inclusive* TM, which emphasizes the strengths (in terms of knowledge, skills, ability, expertise, etc.) that individual employees bring to the workplace and how organizations can build upon those strengths (Swailes, 2013, 2020). The term "inclusive TM" refers to the understanding and acceptance that all employees in an organization should be viewed as talent, that everyone is capable of contributing something important to their organization, and that each and every employee should be provided with the opportunity to develop and be deployed in positions in which they may benefit their organization the most. This focus, in contrast to the exclusive approach, does not place an excessive emphasis on an individual's performance, which may be advantageous to collaboration and the contributions made by teams. Although this strategy has a number of clear advantages and advocates among TM researchers, applying it in organizations is arguably more idealistic and aspirational.

We argue, however, that this exclusive/inclusive divide should not be seen as an either/or proposition, but rather as a continuum, with some companies using an "exclusive extreme" characterized by a disproportionate investment in highly talented individuals, with a greater focus on talent attraction and acquisition, and others using an "inclusive extreme" characterized by equal resource allocation and investment in low performers to balance the books. However, most businesses fall somewhere in the middle, doing their best to invest in employees' growth at all stages of their careers (Morris et al., 2016). Therefore, this chapter treats TM as a multifaceted phenomenon.

There is little doubt that TM as an area of research is just as important and relevant now as it was when it first surfaced from the world of management consulting in the early 2000s (see Michaels et al., 2001). Even though there are some critical issues, some of which have already been discussed, talent shortages continue to be a pivotal issue for organizations all over the world, and global leaders continue to cite talent challenges as the most important issue that impacts their ability to deliver on both short-term and long-term organizational objectives (Collings et al., 2022).

This chapter has four main aims. First, it seeks to review several important contemporary issues pertaining to TM. Second, it examines the global context of talent management by analyzing the five key developments and challenges affecting global talent management (GTM) and looking into their potential impact on TM policies and strategies. Third, it reviews various issues related to TM in multinational enterprises (MNEs) and the role of the HR function in managing talent. Finally, the chapter seeks to identify some research areas which may serve as a foundation for future studies in talent management.

CONTEMPORARY ISSUES IN TM

As noted previously, in the past 15 years, there have been several academic and practical advancements in the field of talent management. Following, the 2007–2009 global recession, many of the initial challenges which motivated the initial interest in talent management either persisted or reemerged, including tight labor markets; more complex talent demands in terms of incumbents' knowledge, skills, and abilities; more complex technology and organizational structures; and increasing job mobility (Vaiman et al., 2021). Recent years have also resulted in an increasing emphasis on talent management in times of crisis. This is largely due to the COVID-19 pandemic, which has not only resulted in tremendous human suffering on a worldwide scale, but also produced huge disruptions that led to profound changes in how individuals and organizations live, work, and operate (Collings et al., 2021). From a talent perspective, there may be a silver lining, as this challenge created multiple opportunities for more flexible working arrangements, which are initially associated with increased employee satisfaction, productivity, and retention (Wang & Heyes, 2020; Baeza et al., 2018), as well as the opportunity to access more geographically diverse talent pools. The jury is still out on the longer-term implications of these flexible working arrangements, though.

Indeed, the pandemic has shown that in some circumstances remote and/or hybrid working can be relatively successful alternative to full-time attendance at a workplace. As a result, companies are allowing some of their traditionally office-based workers to perform at least some their duties remotely or in a hybrid setting (i.e., letting them work sometimes from home and the rest on-site). This is occurring throughout the world: for instance, McKinsey (2021) predicted that up to 25% of the workforce in industrialized nations and roughly 10% in poorer countries will continue working from home even after the pandemic. As we write this chapter in mid-2022, many businesses are now preparing to welcome workers back to the office as vaccines and other interventions have eased the public health challenges around the pandemic in many developed countries. Most commentators recognize, however, that things cannot go back to "business as usual," and that the "new normal" will be hybrid calling for more adaptability in terms of remote work. A key challenge for businesses is figuring out how to adapt to and benefit from these changes. The trend toward remote and hybrid work necessitates a rethinking of traditional TM practices, such as the formation of decentralized rather than centralized talent pools, the redistribution of top performers to the most important positions, the elimination of annual performance reviews, and the development of the most positive working environment possible.

Other contemporary TM-related issues are related to the post-pandemic recovery, with employers predicting strong demand for talent across key sectors (Manpower Group, 2022), although this demand may be tempered by the ongoing war in Ukraine and wider economic challenges as we look towards the latter part of 2022. This demand will influence the shape of the labor landscape, which in turn will impact on TM strategies employed by organizations worldwide. Among major trends shaping the labor landscape are increases in employee power, continuing scarcity of talent, rapid technological advances, and profound organizational transformations. Speaking of the increasing power of employees, they expect their employers to go above and beyond the basics of providing a comfortable workplace, a fair wage, and opportunities for professional growth, in addition to a sense of meaning and fulfillment in their job. Many people also anticipate a firmer position on socioeconomic concerns, including matters of social justice and inclusion, given the importance of holding consistent beliefs. According to Manpower Group's "What Makes Workers Thrive" survey, 64% of employees want their work to help better society (Manpower Group, 2022).

The second trend deals with talent shortages which are a result of changing demographics, including falling birth rates, decreased cross-border movement, and an increase in early retirement. Innovative strategies for acquiring new skills, enhancing old ones, and keeping valuable talent with an organization are needed now more than ever. For instance, 69% of employers currently cannot find skills they require (Manpower Group, 2022). The generational shift to those 35 years of age and below (by 2030 they will represent 75% of the overall workforce) will exacerbate the proverbial war for talent among organizations looking for talent.

Due to the COVID-19 pandemic, investments in digitalization have increased, and both consumers and workers anticipate that this will improve their daily lives and productivity. This trend emphasizes a pressing need for businesses to train their staff to analyze data, draw conclusions based on that analysis, and mix the best of human and machine learning to create new value. For instance, one in three organizations plans to invest more in AI technology, including machine learning, over the next year (Manpower Group, 2022).

The last trend concerns organizational transformation. As a result of increased competition, unpredictability, and transparency, businesses are aiming to be more intelligent, evolving, and looking for more agile operating models, robust supply chains, greener solutions, and consolidated partners. To illustrate this, 83% of organizations surveyed by Manpower Group (2022) responded that they need greater speed and agility to cope with change. Responsible, empathetic leaders, along with talented employees, are key to implementing this transformation. These trends challenge many taken-for-granted assumptions in talent management research and require researchers and practitioners to reflect carefully on their assumptions about what works and why when it comes to talent management (see Lazarova et al., 2023).

Even though the area of TM has seemingly reached maturity, which is evidenced by the emergence of greater consensuses regarding the delineation of TM and its intellectual boundaries, we should not overlook evident differences in the ways talent management is defined and conducted around the world. These differences, attributed to variations in national contexts, should help to effectively balance an excessively Western conceptualization of talent management, which is not necessarily reflective of practice in many national contexts (Vaiman & Vance, 2023; Collings et al., 2019; Sparrow et al., 2015; Holden & Vaiman, 2013; Mellahi & Collings, 2010). However, from an academic perspective, at a minimum it is important that scholars define how they conceptualize and operationalize talent management in the context of individual research studies. We now turn to considering the global context of talent management.

THE GLOBAL CONTEXT OF TALENT MANAGEMENT

As indicated earlier, much of the theoretical and empirical base that talent management is premised upon has evolved from a North American paradigm and research tradition. Indeed, the seminal work of the McKinsey consultants (Michaels et al., 2001) who coined the term "the war for talent" was based on the issues that US organizations confronted regarding both the aging workforce and shrinking labor markets in the American context. This work has undoubtedly initiated the debate on talent management and provided some important insights into the understanding of the concept. However, as the research base was maturing, it became increasingly important that perspectives from different national contexts enter the debate and influence the definitions and boundaries of talent management as we know it (Vaiman et al., 2012). For example, one of the most important discussions in global talent management from the very beginning was on the question of convergence versus divergence of TM practices across cultures, regions, and countries

(Tarique & Schuler, 2012; 2010). Earlier debates showed limited consensus, but more recently, researchers have identified evidence of convergence at least in some areas of TM (e.g., Froese et al., 2020; Stahl et al., 2012). Stahl et al. (2012), for instance, identified a few reasons that compel organizations to move toward convergence. Perhaps the most relevant is: firms compete for the same pool of talented employees and want to standardize the way in which they select and develop their talent (Stahl et al., 2012). At the same time, the authors note that while striving for consistency in their TM efforts, organizations continue to adapt to local contexts and standards, given national differences. Scholars must be cautious in unpacking and exploring these differences to understand their origin and influence. As Vaiman and Brewster (2014) noted, researchers need to be mindful of the assumptions that they make about explanations for national differences (or similarities) in HRM practices and how they influence organizations operating internationally. These authors contend that it would be erroneous to look only at cultural differences among nations; rather, a balanced view should be adopted to analyze the HRM environment. We argue that these insights are equally relevant for considerations of talent management.

Insights from the wider HRM literature are instructive in this regard. There has been a burst of activity in the mid-2000s, where scholars recorded the importance of institutional factors and proved that they matter more in such HRM activities as recruitment and selection (Collings & Isichei, 2018; Wood et al., 2014), training (Goergen et al., 2012), flexible working practices (Richbell et al., 2011), turnover (Croucher et al., 2012), and downsizing (Wood et al., 2013). It is also noteworthy that differences in how these practices are implemented across nations are quite stable and may last for decades (Mayrhofer et al., 2011). The connection between these practices and societal cultural differences is not that clear. However, in areas where the institutional factors are not that pronounced, cultural differences may be more significant (Vaiman & Brewster, 2014). Some examples of HRM processes where cultural differences play perhaps a decisive role include the use of appraisal systems (Hempel, 2001; Bailey et al., 1997), communication (Papalexandris & Chalikias, 2002), performance management systems (Woods, 2003), personnel selection (Huo et al., 2002), and development (Holden & Vaiman, 2013), among many others. So, once again, a more balanced approach to explaining the cross-national differences in TM activities is needed.

In the early literature, with some notable exceptions (Collings & Mellahi, 2009; Dries, 2013; Mäkelä et al., 2010; McDonnell et al., 2010; Farndale et al., 2010; Vance & Vaiman, 2008; Holden & Vaiman, 2013), more international perspectives on talent management remained in the minority. Later, however, there have been a good number of papers and special issues dedicated specifically to talent management in different national contexts and world regions (see Preece et al., 2013; McDonnell et al., 2012; Collings et al., 2011). While building on early North American scholarship, more recent contributions (Ahlvik & Björkman, 2015; Dries, 2013; Van den Brink et al., 2013) clearly move beyond the US context by providing both academic and practical insights from different nations and regions and broadening our understanding of talent management in the global context. Talent management is bound to remain a major issue for organizations in all the major economies around the world, with the latest research indicating that talent management challenges may even be more pronounced in emerging markets (Froese, 2020; Muyia et al., 2018; Skuza et al., 2016). The unprecedented growth in these markets has offered valuable insights and provided important implications for talent management strategies. Recent studies demonstrate that even after the much-discussed global financial crisis of 2008–2009, talent challenges remain a top priority for many organizations in China and India (Patel et al., 2019; Teagarden et al., 2008; Stumpf et al., 2010; Iles et al., 2010; Doh et al., 2011; Shi & Handfield, 2012). Equally, despite the general lack of research on talent management in Central and Eastern Europe, most recent works in this area highlighted the significance of the TM issues for both private and public organizations there. Moreover, the complex history and cultural peculiarities in post-communist countries provide an additional context for talent management efforts, which in turn makes it more difficult to understand and practice (Skuza et al., 2013; Vaiman & Holden, 2011; Holden & Vaiman, 2013).

Some talent management researchers have recently shifted their focus to the external environment in which firms operate. Businesses, especially those with a global presence, operate within one or more very complex and generally volatile external contexts, each of which represents a unique, context-based macro talent management (MTM) system. A variety of political, legal, economic, technical, and socio-cultural elements create any MTM system, which in turn affects the organizations that function inside those systems and their internal operations (King & Vaiman, 2019). As GTM increasingly takes place in a macro (or extra-organizational) context, understanding the MTM system is becoming crucial. The term MTM refers to "the activities that are systematically developed by government and nongovernmental organizations expressly for the purpose of enhancing the quality and quantity of talent within and across countries and regions to facilitate innovation and competitiveness of their citizens and corporations" (Khilji et al., 2015, p. 237). Considering this, it is expected that MTM will have a significant impact on GTM and its efficacy, despite the fact that empirical research on the processes behind this impact has been scant thus far.

To encompass all these different international, national, and regional perspectives, include the ever-present influence of globalizing business world, and underscore the importance of talent management in the global context, several definitions of GTM have been offered over the years. However, after more than 20 years of practitioner rhetoric and academic discussion on the definition of global talent management, there is still no firm consensus on what it entails. Historically, GTM centered on a small core group of personnel – those who matter most in terms of a company's ability to create value and maintain a competitive edge. For instance, Stahl et al. (2012) defined GTM as recruiting, selecting, training, and keeping key personnel throughout the world. Another line of research, spearheaded by Collings and Mellahi (2009), argues that any TM system should begin with the value of the jobs filled by these exceptional workers. For Vaiman, Scullion, and Collings (2012), GTM refers to all organizational operations with the intention of recruiting, selecting, developing, and keeping the pivotal talent in the most strategic jobs worldwide. Drawing from Mellahi and Collings' (2010) work, Collings, Mellahi, and Cascio (2019) refine their definition of GTM as follows: (a) the systematic identification of pivotal positions that differentially contribute to an organization's sustainable competitive advantage on a global scale; (b) the development of a talent pool of high-potential and high-performing incumbents who reflect the global scope of the MNE; and (c) the development of a differentiated HR architecture to fill these roles with the most qualified candidates. This is the definition we are going to use for the purposes of this chapter.

This definition is universal enough to emphasize the fact that organizations face increasing competition for talent on a global scale and encounter major problems in attracting, developing, and retaining their key employees. To better understand the main challenges of GTM, it is necessary to look at some of the main external developments that impact every organization's TM efforts (Collings et al., 2019; Morris et al., 2016; Tarique & Schuler, 2012; Schuler et al., 2011). Along with long-standing problems like an aging population (especially in developed economies), tight labor markets, decreasing availability of talent, ever-widening skill gaps, and shifting patterns of labor mobility, there are several recent developments that will undoubtedly alter the dynamics of GTM, now and in the future.

First, as mentioned earlier, there are crisis-driven challenging conditions prompted by severe environmental disruptions (Farndale & Vaiman, 2022; Vaiman et al., 2021). The COVID-19 pandemic is not the first of its kind, but it is certainly among the most notable and consequential disruptions for individuals, organizations, and societies alike. In addition, there are changes in weather patterns, extreme temperatures, political unrest, and large-scale technological failures, all of which would have far-reaching effects on people's daily routines and the ways in which businesses operate. Therefore, one of the major challenges modern organizations have to confront is talent management during times of crisis.

Second, there is a clear trend of so-called "de-globalization" (Witt, 2019), a term that has emerged from a string of protectionist policies enacted by governments of major economies over the past five years. A series of trade wars waged by the United States against Canada, China, and the European Union in 2018 resulted in the introduction of tariffs and other protectionist measures that significantly slowed the flow of commodities across borders (Farndale & Vaiman, 2022). The Brexit referendum vote of 2016 in which the United Kingdom voted to leave the European Union after nearly half a century of membership was perhaps the most visible relic of the de-globalization era. All of these resulted in much more stringent immigration restrictions, reduced talent flows across national boundaries, and a slowdown in globalization. The COVID-19 pandemic has undoubtedly exacerbated this trend when health-related travel prohibitions were implemented globally. So, despite becoming accustomed to relying on international talent, many organizations have found themselves with shrinking global talent pools and a resulting need to rely more heavily on scarce local talent (Farndale & Vaiman, 2022).

Third, both de-globalization and the COVID-19 epidemic have increased the importance of remote and hybrid work arrangements to organizations. Organizations were already investigating increased usage of virtual work in response to the diminishing global talent pool before the epidemic hit. With the pandemic, the realization that hybrid work is here to stay is slowly sinking in with organizational leaders. As mentioned earlier in this chapter, talent management strategies must evolve in tandem with the rise of remote and hybrid work by, among other things, shifting the focus from centralizing to decentralizing talent pools, eliminating the old performance management system, and providing the greatest possible employee experience that includes such important features as flexibility, asynchrony, trust, professional development opportunities, and a holistic focus on well-being, among others (LinkedIn, 2022).

The hybrid working arrangement has another side, though, of which managers should be aware. As it turns out, many remote and hybrid workers are experiencing burnout, which they blame in part on management's inability to communicate openly and, at times, unambiguously. Employees who are anxious or burned out are more likely to leave their jobs voluntarily, which can have a direct impact on the company's talent pool and its GTM strategy. Organizational leadership should establish transparent rules on a wide range of topics, including but not limited to communication tools, working hours, expectations for cooperation, available assistance, and so on, in order to successfully handle these critical problems. Human resources professionals should assist managers in facilitating and reinforcing the consistent and clear dissemination of these standards, methodologies, and expectations. There is more to be done in this area, since it appears that most companies are just now beginning to build the nuts and bolts of hybrid work models. As indicated earlier, the post-pandemic trend toward greater remote work flexibility has led to a rising recognition of the need to shift emphasis away from managing employees' physical presence and toward managing employees' intellectual assets (Vaiman & Vance, 2023).

The fourth development is the establishment and growth of the contingent – or fluid – workforce (Boudreau, 2021). When it is more efficient to bring in outside talent for a specific project or task than to train employees in-house, organizations turn to a fluid workforce to fill the gap as quickly as possible (Lau, 2020). This strategy also helps businesses save money by cutting down on overhead expenses like health insurance, retirement plans, and office space, while also improving output quality and boosting productivity (and can help provide expertise in certain new markets, without exposing the organization to the risks associated with international expansion). It's worth noting that as the COVID-19 epidemic got underway, more and more companies started tapping into the skills of the contingent labor force in addition to their regular staff. Cap Gemini found that approximately 80% of companies throughout the globe had adopted a fluid workforce in the year prior to the emergence of COVID in 2019 (Paolini et al., 2020). Although the role of GTM experts in this development is not yet obvious, the rise of fluid labor and the allure of this sort of (beyond) employment for both businesses and people are transforming the way organizations manage their workforce.

Dealing with these challenges requires a rethinking of global talent strategies. Indeed, the findings of the Microsoft's 2021 World Trend Index report propose the following possible solutions (Microsoft, 2021), although these represent important areas where academic research could facilitate a more informed discussion:

- *Create a plan to empower people for extreme flexibility.* A human-centered strategy that considers policy, physical space, and technology is essential for every company. It all begins with addressing fundamental concerns such as, for example, "How many people will have access to remote work?", "Who will need to concentrate, and where can they do it?", "Where can people do collaborative work?", etc. Given that constant upheaval and crises are now the norm worldwide, the ability to adapt quickly to unexpected events is essential for leaders.
- *Invest in space and technology to bridge the physical and digital worlds.* Most businesses will need a variety of spaces for focused individual working, collaborating in small groups, or holding large events, as well as open areas for informal discussions, get-togethers, and group activities. Investment in technology that allows for full participation from home, the office, the road, etc., should be just as important as investing in physical space.
- *Combat digital exhaustion from the top.* Managers should consider where they can bolster the existing team with more people or tools to better assist them in dealing with the pressures of day-to-day operations. It is also important to embrace a balance of synchronous and asynchronous collaboration.
- *Prioritize rebuilding social capital and culture.* Evidence suggests that restoring social capital and culture is more than a nice-to-have for companies. Meeting new people and expanding our professional networks is time-consuming in any workplace, but it's considerably more time-consuming when employees are constantly switching between meetings. Restoring social capital, however, is crucial since it is connected to major results like productivity and innovation.
- *Rethink employee experience to compete for the best and most diverse talent.* With 40% of employees actively looking for other opportunities, a company's willingness to be extremely flexible is essential if it wants to keep and attract the best employees. Moreover, as the pandemic subsides, flexible work is an excellent chance for executives to develop a more diverse workforce, since Generation Z-ers (who are most at risk of leaving) and many other employees are more likely to select distant work roles.

We now turn our attention to the remaining two forces that drive talent management efforts in organizations – namely, changes in the attitudes of employees toward work and national differences.

Evidence shows that the attitudes toward work are changing in many parts of the world (Tarique & Schuler, 2012). The traditional psychological contract, which implicitly stipulates mutual loyalty and commitment between an employee and their organization, seems to be fading away fast. Nowadays, employees expect to change jobs frequently, use their employability (that comprises a winning combination of technical and social skills) to look for better opportunities elsewhere, and use global mobility as a self-development tool to increase their attractiveness to other potential employers. This suggests that top talent will be willing and able to work for multiple employers, have excellent social and professional connections, and move from one job to another, despite geographic distances (Vaiman & Collings, 2015). To deal with these changing attitudes, organizations must put extra effort into their talent management activities, and particularly into attracting/identifying and retaining top talent.

Along with the changing attitudes, national cultures and institutional differences also continue to play a significant role in the ways people are managed in organizations (Tarique & Schuler, 2012). More specifically, culture has both a direct and indirect impact on how HR policies, procedures, and techniques are designed and implemented, and how employees' behaviors are influenced. For example, in some Scandinavian cultures, many managers are uncomfortable and/or unwilling to acknowledge performance differences among employees – an important step that is required to improve performance, etc. – due to the prevalence of egalitarianism in these cultures. In high-power-distance and rather hierarchical Russia, the developmental efforts are severely restricted by a limited tradition of empowerment in Russian organizations (Outila et al., 2018; Holden & Vaiman, 2013). These and similar culture-bound factors present major challenges for global talent management, especially for those multinational companies that are trying to converge their TM practices. Equally, institutional factors such as legislative context and national infrastructural support for business have significant potential to impact the nature of talent management practices in different regions.

To summarize, all the aforementioned challenges and developments – environmental disruptions, de-globalization trends, proliferation of remote and hybrid work, growth of the fluid workforce, changing attitudes toward work, and national differences – do strongly impact global organizational efforts to attract, develop, mobilize, and retain key employees. This impact first and foremost affects how global TM procedures, policies, and strategies are designed, configured, used, and evaluated (Collings et al., 2019; Tarique & Schuler, 2012).

MANAGING TALENT GLOBALLY: THE ROLE OF THE HR FUNCTION

As noted earlier, a key area of focus in research on global talent management has been on the HR practices that support effective GTM. However, how these practices and global talent flows more generally are managed and coordinated at a global level has received far less attention (cf. Farndale et al., 2010; Scullion

& Starkey, 2000; Sparrow, 2012). We argue that this is a key limitation, as the organizational structures that support and organize GTM will have a significant impact on global talent flows within the MNE and ultimately potentially correlate with organizational performance. In this regard, a key antecedent to the global orientation that many MNEs strive for is the effective management of staffing flows throughout the MNE network. As Taylor, Beechler, and Napier (1996) argue, "in order to provide value to the business, the (strategic international) HRM system of global firms should be constructed around specific organizational competences that are critical for securing competitive advantage in a global environment" (1996, p. 960). In this regard, Gong (2003) explicitly calls for a heterogeneous staffing composition (i.e., an appropriate mix of parent-country nationals, host-country nationals, and third-country nationals) to facilitate innovation and organizational learning in the MNE. Focusing on the subsidiary level, he argues that a heterogeneous staffing composition facilitates access to and recognition of diverse sources of innovation and organizational learning, and improves performance regarding both the interpretation of information and integrative learning. More generally, the effective positioning of the corporate HR or global talent function is central in terms of managing the tensions between global integration and local responsiveness of key talent issues and the management of the MNE more generally (Scullion & Starkey, 2000).

However, managing global talent is challenging, and there is evidence that ethnocentric tendencies prevail (if only subconsciously) in many MNEs, with parent-country nationals dominating key leadership positions in the headquarters operation (Carpenter et al., 2001; Mäkelä et al., 2010; Mellahi & Collings, 2010). However, Scullion and Starkey's (2000) study pointed to an optimistic emerging agenda for corporate HR in international companies with a focus on senior management development, succession planning, and the development of a cadre of internationally capable managers. We argue that the development of an effective talent management function, or responsibility for such within the corporate HR function, is central to maximizing the contribution of the MNE's global talent pool and tapping into local talent markets that reflect the MNE's global footprint. For example, Collings, McDonnell, Gunnigle, and Lavelle's (2010) empirical study of foreign-owned subsidiaries in Ireland, points to the significance of corporate structures and systems in facilitating staffing flows from subsidiary operations to the corporate headquarters as inpatriate employees. Sparrow, Scullion, and Farndale (2011) note that in addition to this top-down (management-controlled) approach to managing talent flows, a bottom-up (self-initiated, culture-driven) approach also impacts on the corporate HR role. This highlights the potential for tapping into local talent pools or self-initiated expatriates in the local market to fill key talent gaps in the MNE.

Farndale, Paauwe, and colleagues (2010) identify four important corporate HR (CHR) roles which significantly impact on corporate efforts in managing talent globally. CHR's role as "Champion of Process" is premised upon the requirement for improved horizontal coordination of processes and practices of talent management internally. This is achieved through effective management of what Farndale and colleagues term "global expertise networks," and a designated "Champion of Process" role aimed at monitoring the global implementation of the GTM strategy and related objectives. Second, as "Guardian of Culture," CHR is focused upon the implementation of global values and culture and the management of the employer brand globally. Third, CHR can play a key role in "Network Leadership and Intelligence." This involves a developed awareness of leading trends and developments in the MNE's internal and external labor markets, the capacity to deploy human capital appropriately, and a sensitivity to the contexts in which the MNE operates. The role of networking (both by the HR function itself and the facilitation of same more generally in the organization) emerges as key. Finally, as "Managers of Internal Receptivity" CHR's role in the management of the careers of international employees is emphasized. Clearly, this role is targeted at senior management and high potential development and career management. These four roles are not mutually exclusive, and Farndale et al.'s (2010) research points to overlaps between them, which lead to additional value generation owing to the associated complementarities.

The key role of the corporate HR function in terms of managing talent flows, both top-down and bottom-up, to utilize Sparrow and colleagues' (2015, 2011) terminology, represents an important element of global talent management which, with the notable exceptions identified above, remains largely underdeveloped. This argument aligns with Boxall's (1996) distinction between human capital advantage and organization process advantage. While the former relates to the knowledge, skills, and abilities of the organization's employees, the latter refers to the systems and processes that facilitate their effective deployment and management. However, worryingly, there is little evidence that strategic oversight of global talent is widely evident in many corporate HR or global mobility functions, with a transactional and compliance focus far more common (Collings et al., 2019; Collings, 2014). Thus, a key focus of research moving forward should be on assisting MNEs to better understand the importance of the corporate HR role in effectively managing talent flows and coordinating talent on a global scale.

One example of the global talent function's role in practice relates to facilitating knowledge creation and knowledge sharing in the MNE. Knowledge is increasingly seen as a critical source of competitive advantage in the MNE (see Doz et al., 2001; Kogut & Zander, 1993). Thus, a key question for the global HR function is how to maximize the contributions of those individuals who span geographic and cultural boundaries and who are high-value-added contributors to both the coordination process and to the knowledge creation and sharing process. This group can be classified as high-value boundary spanners (HVBSs) (see Kostova & Roth, 2003; Taylor, 2007). These individuals can be located anywhere in the multinational network, and the challenge is to identify them and ensure their effective deployment in the multinational network. However, it is important to recognize that knowledge transfer does not occur without several conditions being met, and there are significant latent barriers to knowledge sharing (Michailova & Husted, 2003). First, in terms of the HVBSs, the importance of their motivation and ability to share knowledge emerges as important. This has been termed disseminative capacity (Minbaeva, 2005). For the receiver, the ability and motivation of subsidiary employees (absorptive capacity) also emerge as important (Minbaeva et al., 2003). Of particular importance to the consideration of talent practices that can facilitate this critical organizational routing (knowledge sharing) are the underlying HR practices that maximize knowledge sharing.

Broader perspectives from the HR literature provide insights on how HR practices can assist in knowledge sharing and more broadly the role of HR in knowledge creation and dissemination. Much of this research is theoretically positioned in the social capital literature. While a thorough discussion of the construct is beyond the scope of the current chapter, social capital is broadly defined as:

> the sum of the actual and potential resources embedded within, available through and derived from the network of relationships possessed by an individual or social unit. Social capital comprises the network and the assets that may be mobilized though that network.
>
> (Nahapiet & Ghoshal, 1998, p. 243)

Nahapiet and Ghoshal (1998) further elucidate three types of social capital. Structural social capital focuses on the patterns of interactions between individuals in a network. In the multinational context, it contributes to the flow of knowledge and coordination by spanning sub-units or networks in the MNE's global operations (Kostova & Roth, 2003). Relational social capital focuses on the nature of personal relationships developed over time and brings trust to the fore. Finally, cognitive social capital focuses on the shared goals, norms, and values that are built though relationships over time (Inkpen & Tsang, 2005). Theoretical and empirical insights point to some important perspectives on how HR practices can facilitate knowledge sharing, and these provide important insights for the global talent management function (see Raab et al., 2014; Cabrera & Cabrera, 2005; Foss et al., 2009; Minbaeva et al., 2012). For example, relational social capital points to the importance of norms and identifications within the group, while cognitive social capital points to the importance of shared goals, norms, and values. Considering their role in knowledge creation and sharing, this brings forward the importance of identifying prospective employees who have a higher probability of sharing the same norms and identifying with each other, pointing to the importance of shared values (Cabrera & Cabrera, 2005). This is in line with posited best practice in talent management, which points to the importance of a focus on values in recruitment and selection (Stahl et al., 2012). Theoretically, person–organization fit is a useful lens to further unpack this relationship.

Work design has also been identified as significant in facilitating knowledge creation and sharing. Cabrera and Cabrera (2005) argue that work design is strongly tied to structural social capital by establishing interdependencies, more frequent interactions, and information flow among employees. While stable jobs with concrete tasks might constrain knowledge flows, more fluid work arrangements where work is organized as sequence of assignments with employees working with diverse employees on a project basis might facilitate knowledge flows (Cabrera & Cabrera, 2005). Empirically, Foss et al. (2009) found that job characteristics such as autonomy, task identity, and feedback determine individuals' motivations to share knowledge, which in turn predicts employees' knowledge sharing behavior. However, the recent shift to hybrid and virtual workplaces has raised important questions for how work design can continue to facilitate such knowledge collaboration and sharing in this context (Lazarova et al., 2023).

Organizational culture also emerges as key. It can play a role in developing social norms around knowledge sharing (De Long & Fahey, 2000) and in terms of creating a climate of trust which is central to the emergence of relational social capital (Cabrera & Cabrera, 2005). Indeed, Minbaeva et al. (2012) empirically demonstrated that employees' perception of the organization's commitment to knowledge sharing combined with extrinsic motivation directly influence the extent to which employees engage in firm-internal knowledge exchange. Additionally, individuals' intrinsic motivation combined with engagement in social interaction mediated the relationship. Given Minbaeva and colleagues' conclusion that HR can influence these conditions through the signaling effect of HR practices combined with the practices themselves, this reinforces the key role of the global HR function in driving knowledge creation and sharing in the MNE. Again, this is an area which requires further research in the context of evolving work structures. How can culture be shared and maintained in the absence of a shared workplace?

Clearly, the above examples are illustrative, and there are several other important HR practices that can facilitate knowledge creation and sharing. They are presented as illustrative of how careful alignment of HR practices can support a strategic talent objective (in this example, knowledge creation and sharing). In line with recent advancements in the HR literature and models of talent management (see Collings et al, 2019; Morris et al., 2016; Lepak & Snell, 1999), we advocate a differentiated HR architecture, where such HR practices are directly targeted at the employee group for whom they are developed.

CONCLUSIONS AND FUTURE RESEARCH OPPORTUNITIES

This chapter set out to provide a relatively broad-brush overview of the maturing field of global talent management. There is little doubt that global talent management has gained significant traction as a key global strategic HR process to leverage the competitive advantage of the MNE. However, the extant literature suggests that organizations continue to struggle with the challenges of managing global talent, and indeed a key challenge for the academic community is the continued development of a body of research to better inform managerial practice in this regard.

Our review touches upon both the macro and organizational contexts of GTM. Our understanding of the macro context is one that has been seriously underdeveloped in previous work (cf. Schuler et al., 2011; Tarique & Schuler, 2012; section 3 of Scullion & Collings, 2011), but is now gradually getting due attention from scholars (cf. King & Vaiman, 2019; Vaiman et al., 2018a, 2018b). We contend that more work in this direction is needed, since a better understanding of the macro context of (G)TM will provide a base for a comparative understanding of the nature of talent management on a global basis. We define comparative talent management in this sense as variations in talent management practice between different nations or regions that can largely be traced to differences in the macro institutional, legislative, and cultural context in which business unfolds in the nation state. In a similar fashion to which comparative HR has established itself as a key field of study, building a comparative understanding of talent management in different nation states that reflects the particular macro context in which talent management unfolds will provide a useful stream of research in the global TM space. Understanding the differences in how talent is managed in different nation states and regions will be valuable in understanding the global–local tension which MNEs must balance in developing and implementing effective global TM systems.

Additionally, research needs to continue to develop our understanding of the role of effective GTM in organizational performance. In a similar vein to the importance of the work of Mark Huselid and others in illustrating the linkage between investments in human resources and organizational performance, well-designed empirical studies that could explore the relationship between effective GTM and organizational performance would significantly advance the standing of the field of study. However, the effective design of such studies is not without challenges. Indeed, such studies would benefit from imaginative outcome variables, more sophisticated methods, more attention to context, and tighter conceptual clarity (see Arnold & Cohen, 2008, for a similar call in the context of careers research). Research in this vein will provide an evidence-based logic for discussions around best-practice GTM. While this terminology is utilized presently, as yet we have no research to identify what is best practice and how such practices translate into organizational outcomes such as sustainable performance.

A further avenue which merits empirical consideration is deepening our understanding of the interaction between employee mobility and global talent management. There are two key elements to this debate. First, we require a better understanding of how organizations can tap into global talent in local labor markets. For example, research on self-initiated expatriation brings a focus on individuals who relocate internationally of their own accord without organizational support (Haslberger & Vaiman, 2013; Al Ariss & Crowley-Henry, 2013; Cohen et al., 2011). This research indicated that these individuals are often under-employed in host economies and that organizations are failing to capture the potential value of these employees (Al Ariss et al., 2013; Fang et al., 2013). Understanding the potential value of these talent pools and how best to realize it in the context of global talent management represents an important stream of research. Second, although global employee mobility is often considered central to global talent management, the reality is that it often sits in different functions in practice, and we have little theoretical and empirical guidance for global mobility professionals in developing effective practice in this regard (Collings, 2014). Better understanding how global mobility and global talent interact and work together to ensure that employees with high levels of human capital globally are aligned with talent needs across the multinational network remains under researched. All these important questions have now to be taken in a slightly different light though, given the aforementioned COVID-19 pandemic, de-globalization trends, and rapid developments in information technology, all of which are making global mobility a much more complicated issue (Lazarova et al., 2023).

Finally, it would be useful to better understand the institutional and cultural factors which emerge as significant in managing the balance between global standardization versus local adaptation of GTM policies and practices in the MNE. This would move the debate on best practices in GTM forward in a significant way by providing an understanding of the types of practices which are more globally acceptable and effective versus those which require a greater degree of adaptation to local cultural and institutional norms. More broadly, it would provide a better understanding of differences in talent practices between different national contexts.

In conclusion, we find ourselves at an exciting juncture in the evolution of the field of GTM. While there clearly is some work remaining to firmly establish the boundaries of the field, we do not feel that a single agreed definition of GTM is necessarily required. However, at a minimum, there is a requirement for scholars and practitioners alike to be precise in defining how they utilize the terminology in their own work. What is clear is that there is a significant appetite for academic research to inform practice and better understand the nature of talent and its deployment in the contemporary MNE.

REFERENCES

Ahlvik, C., & Björkman, I. (2015). Towards explaining subsidiary implementation, integration, and internalization of MNC headquarters HRM practices. *International Business Review*, 24(3): 497–505.

Al Ariss, A., & Crowley-Henry, M. (2013). Self-initiated expatriation and migration in the management literature: Present theorizations and future research directions. *Career Development International*, 18(1): 78–96.

Al Ariss, A., Vassilopoulou, J., Ozbilgin, M., & Game, A. (2013). Understanding career experiences of skilled minority ethnic workers in France and Germany. *The International Journal of Human Resource Management*, 24(6): 1236–1256.

Arnold, J., & Cohen, L. (2008). The psychology of careers in industrial and organizational settings: A critical but appreciative analysis. *International Review of Industrial and Organizational Psychology*, 23: 1–44.

Baeza, M. A., Gonzalez, J. A., & Wang, Y. (2018). Job flexibility and job satisfaction among Mexican professionals: A socio-cultural explanation. *Employee Relations*, 40(5): 921–942.

Bailey, J., Chen, C., & Dou, S. (1997). Conceptions of self and performance-related feedback in the US, Japan and China. *Journal of International Business Studies*, 28(3): 605–625.

Boudreau, J. W. (2021). *Economic Recovery after COVID-19: The Future of Work*, VCEDA Virtual Conference, January 15.

Boxall, P. (1996). The strategic HRM debate and the resource-based view of the firm. *Human Resource Management Journal*, 6(3): 59–75.

Cabrera, E. F., & Cabrera, A. (2005). Fostering knowledge sharing through people management practices. *International Journal of Human Resource Management*, 16(5): 720–735.

Cappelli, P., & Keller, J. R. (2014). Talent management: Conceptual approaches and practical challenges. *Annual Review Organizational Psychology and Organizational Behavior*, 1(1): 305–331.

Carpenter, M. A., Sanders, W. G., & Gregersen, H. B. (2001). Bundling human capital with organizational context: The impact of international assignment experience on multinational firm performance and CEO pay. *Academy of Management Journal*, 44(3): 493–511.

Cohen, L., Arnold, J., & O'Neill, M. (2011). Migration: Vocational perspectives on a complex and diverse transition. *Journal of Vocational Behavior*, 78(3): 321–324.

Collings, D. G. (2014). Integrating global mobility and global talent management: Exploring the challenges and strategic opportunities. *Journal of World Business*, 45(2): 161–168.

Collings, D. G. (2017). Workforce differentiation. In D. G. Collings, K. Mellahi, & W. F. Cascio (Eds.), *The Oxford Handbook of Talent Management*. Oxford: Oxford University Press.

Collings, D. G., & Isichei, M. (2018). The shifting boundaries of global staffing: Integrating global talent management, alternative forms of international assignments and non-employees into the discussion. *International Journal of Human Resource Management*, 9(1): 165–187.

Collings, D. G., McDonnell, A., Gunnigle, P., & Lavelle, J. (2010). Swimming against the tide: Outward staffing flows from multinational subsidiaries. *Human Resource Management*, 49(4): 575–598.

Collings, D. G., & Mellahi, K. (2009). Strategic talent management: A review and research agenda. *Human Resource Management Review*, 19(4): 304–313.

Collings, D. G., Mellahi, K., & Cascio, W. F. (2019). Global talent management and performance in multinational enterprises: A multilevel perspective. *Journal of Management*, 45(2): 540–566.

Collings, D. G., Nyberg, A. J., Wright, P. M., & McMackin, J. (2021). Leading through paradox in a COVID-19 world: Human resources comes of age. *Human Resource Management Journal*, 31(4): 819–833.

Collings, D. G., & Scullion, H. (2009). Global staffing. *International Journal of Human Resource Management*, 20(6): 1249–1272.

Collings, D. G., Scullion, H., & Vaiman, V. (2011). European perspectives on talent management. *European Journal of International Management*, 5(5): 453–462.

Collings, D. G., Scullion, H., & Vaiman, V. (2022). *Talent Management: A Decade of Developments*. Bingley, Emerald Publishing.

Croucher, R., Wood, G., Brewster, C., & Brookes, M. (2012). Employee turnover, HRM and institutional contexts. *Economic and Industrial Democracy*, 33(4): 605–620.

De Long, D. W., & Fahey, L. (2000). Diagnosing cultural barriers to knowledge management. *Academy of Management Perspectives*, 14(4): 113–127.

Doh, J., Smith, R., Stumpf, S., & Tymon, W. (2011). Pride and professionals: Retaining talent in emerging economies. *Journal of Business Strategy*, 32(5): 35–42.

Doz, Y., Santos, J., & Williamson, P. J. (2001). *From Global to Metanational: How Companies Win in the Knowledge Economy*. Harvard, MA: Harvard Business Press.

Dries, N. (2013). Talent management, from phenomenon to theory: Introduction to the special issue. *Human Resource Management Review*. http://doi.org/10.1016/j.hrmr.2013.08.006 (accessed June 22, 2014).

Fang, T., Samnani, A.-K., Novicevic, M. M., & Bing, M. N. (2013). Liability-of-foreignness effects on job success of immigrant job seekers. *Journal of World Business*, 48(1): 98–109.

Farndale, E., & Vaiman, V. (2022). HR professionals and talent management: Navigating the dynamic macro context. In D. G. Collings, V. Vaiman, & H. Scullion (Eds.), *Talent Management: A Decade of Development*. London: Emerald Publishing, pp. 107–126.

Farndale, E., Paauwe, J., Morris, S. S., Stahl, G. K., Stiles, P., Trevor, J., & Wright, P. M. (2010). Context-bound configurations of corporate HR functions in multinational corporations. *Human Resource Management*, 49(1): 45–66.

Farndale, E., Scullion, H., & Sparrow, P. (2010). The role of the corporate human resource function in global talent management. *Journal of World Business*, 45(2): 161–168.

Foss, N. J., Minbaeva, D. B., Pedersen, T., & Reinholt, M. (2009). Encouraging knowledge sharing among employees: How job design matters. *Human Resource Management*, 48(6): 871–893.

Froese, F. (2020). Ready for global success? Strengths and weaknesses of Korean HRM. *Asian Business and Management*, 19: 179–183.

Goergen, M., Brewster, C., Wood, G. T., & Wilkinson, A. (2012). Varieties of capitalism and investments in human capital. *Industrial Relations: A Journal of Economy and Society*, 51(2): 501–527.

Gong, Y. (2003). Toward a dynamic process model of staffing composition and subsidiary outcomes in multinational enterprises. *Journal of Management*, 29(2): 259–280.

Haslberger, A., & Vaiman, V. (2013). Managing talent of self-initiated expatriates: A neglected source of the global talent flow. In V. Vaiman & A. Haslberger (Eds.), *Managing Talent of Self-Initiated Expatriates: A Neglected Source of the Global Talent Flow*. London: Palgrave Macmillan, pp. 1–18.

Hempel, S. P. (2001). Differences between Chinese and Western managerial views of performance appraisal. *Personal Review*, 30(2): 203–226.

Holden, N., & Vaiman, V. (2013). Talent management in Russia: Not so much war for talent as wariness of talent. *Critical Perspectives on International Business*, 9(1/2): 129–146.

Huo, Y. P., Huang, H., & Napier, N. K. (2002). Divergence or convergence: A cross-cultural comparison of personnel selection practices. *Human Resource Management*, 41(1): 31–44.

Iles, P., Chuai, X., & Preece, D. (2010). Talent management and HRM in multinational companies in Beijing: Definitions, differences and drivers. *Journal of World Business*, 45(2): 179–189.

Inkpen, A., & Tsang, E. (2005). Social capital, networks, and knowledge transfer. *Academy of Management Review*, 30(1): 1146–1165.

Khilji, S. E., Tarique, I., & Schuler, R. S. (2015). Incorporating the macro-view in global talent management. *Human Resource Management Review*, 25(3): 236–248.

King, K. A., & Vaiman, V. (2019). Enabling effective talent management through a macro-contingent approach: A framework for research and practice. *BRQ Business Research Quarterly*, 22(3): 194–206.

Kogut, B., & Zander, U. (1993). Knowledge of the firm and the evolutionary theory of the multinational corporation. *Journal of International Business Studies*, 24(4): 625–645.

Kostova, T., & Roth, K. (2003). Social capital in multinational corporations and a micro-macro model of its formation. *Academy of Management Review*, 28(2): 297–317.

Lau, Y. (2020). How (and why) companies should engage the liquid workforce. *Forbes*, January 6.

Lazarova, M., Caligiuri, P., Collings, D. G., & De Cieri, H. (2023). Global work in a rapidly changing world: Implications for MNEs and individuals. *Journal of World Business*, 58(1): 101365.

Lepak, D. P., & Snell, S. A. (1999). The human resource architecture: Toward a theory of human capital allocation and development. *Academy of Management Review*, 24(1): 31–48.

Lewis, R. E., & Heckman, R. J. (2006). Talent management: A critical review. *Human Resource Management Review*, 16(2): 139–154.

LinkedIn. (2022). The Reinvention of Company Culture, 2022 Global Talent Trends report.

Mäkelä, K., Bjorkman, I., & Ehrnrooth, M. (2010). How do MNCs establish their talent pools? Influences on individuals' likelihood of being labelled as talent. *Journal of World Business*, 45(2): 134–142.

Manpower Group. (2022). *The Great Realization: Accelerated Trends, Renewed Energy*. Milwaukee, WI: Manpower Group.

Mayrhofer, W., Brewster, C., Morley, M., & Ledolter, J. (2011). Hearing a different drummer? Evidence of convergence in European HRM. *Human Resource Management Review*, 21(1): 50–67.

McDonnell, A., Lamare, R., Gunnigle, P., & Lavelle, J. (2010). Developing tomorrow's leaders – Evidence of global talent management in multinational enterprises. *Journal of World Business*, 45(2): 150–160.

McDonnell, A., Collings, D. G., & Burgess, J. (2012). Asia Pacific perspectives on talent management. *Asia Pacific Journal of Human Resources*, 50(4): 391–398.

McKinsey & Company. (2021). Grabbing hold of the new future of work. *Organizational Practice*, May 2021.

Mellahi, K., & Collings, D. G. (2010). The barriers to effective global talent management: The example of corporate élites in MNEs. *Journal of World Business*, 45(2): 143–149.

Michaels, E., Handfield-Jones, H., & Axelrod, B. (2001). *The War for Talent*. Boston, MA: Harvard Business School Press.

Michailova, S., & Husted, K. (2003). Knowledge-sharing hostility in Russian firms. *California Management Review*, 45(3): 59–77.

Microsoft. (2021). *2021 Work Trend Index: Annual Report*. Microsoft Corporation.

Minbaeva, D., Mäkelä, K., & Rabbiosi, L. (2012). Linking HRM and knowledge transfer via individual-level mechanisms. *Human Resource Management*, 51(3): 387–405.

Minbaeva, D., Pedersen, T., Bjorkman, I., Fey, C., & Park, H. (2003). MNC knowledge transfer, subsidiary absorptive capacity and knowledge transfer. *Journal of International Business Studies*, 34(6): 586–599.

Minbaeva, D., & Vardi, S. (2019). Global talent analytics. In D. G. Collings, H. Scullion, & P. Caligiuri (Eds.), *Global Talent Management* (2nd ed.). New York: Routledge.

Minbaeva, D. B. (2005). HRM practices and MNC knowledge transfer. *Personnel Review*, 34(1): 125–144.

Morris, S., Snell, S., & Björkman, I. (2016). An architectural framework for global talent management. *Journal of International Business Studies*, 47(6): 723–747.

Muyia, M. H., Wekullo, C. S., & Nafukho, F. M. (2018). Talent development in emerging economies through learning and development capacity building. *Advances in Developing Human Resources*, 20(4): 498–516.

Nahapiet, J., & Ghoshal, S. (1998). Social capital, intellectual capital, and the organizational advantage. *Academy of Management Review*, 23(2): 242–266.

Outila, V., Vaiman, V., & Holden, N. (2018). Marco talent management in Russia: Addressing entangled challenges in managing talent on the country level. In V.

Vaiman, R. Schuler, P. Sparrow, & D. Collings (Eds.), *Macro Talent Management in Emerging and Emergent Markets: A Global Perspective*. New York and London: Routledge, pp. 25–45.

Paolini, S., Buvat, J., Abirami, B., Crummenerl, C., Schastok, I., & Manchanda, N. (2020). *The Fluid Workforce Revolution*. Paris: Capgemini Research Institute.

Papalexandris, N., & Chalikias, J. (2002). Changes in training, performance management and communication issues among Greek firms in the 1990s: Inter-country and intra-country comparisons. *Journal of European Industrial Training*, 26(7): 342–352.

Patel, P., Boyle, B., Bray, M., Sinha, P., & Bhanugopan, R. (2019). Global staffing and control in emerging multinational corporations and their subsidiaries in developed countries: Indian IT EMNCs in Australia. *Personnel Review*, 48(4): 1022–1044.

Preece, D., Iles, P., & Jones, R. (2013). MNE regional head offices and their affiliates: Talent management practices and challenges in the Asia Pacific. *The International Journal of Human Resource Management*, 24(18): 3457–3477.

Raab, K. J., Ambos, B., & Tallman, S. (2014). Strong or invisible hands? Managerial involvement in the knowledge sharing process of globally dispersed knowledge groups. *Journal of World Business*, 49(1): 32–41.

Richbell, S., Brookes, M., Brewster, C., & Wood, G. (2011). Non-standard working time: An international and comparative analysis. *International Journal of Human Resource Management*, 22(4): 945–962.

Schuler, R., Jackson, S., & Tarique, I. (2011). Framework for global talent management: HR actions for dealing with global talent challenges. In H. Scullion & D. Collings (Eds.), *Global Talent Management*. London: Routledge, pp. 17–36.

Scullion, H., & Collings, D. G. (Eds.). (2011). *Global Talent Management*. New York: Routledge.

Scullion, H., & Starkey, K. (2000). In search of the changing role of the corporate human resource function in the international firm. *International Journal of Human Resource Management*, 11(6): 1061–1081.

Shi, Y., & Handfield, R. (2012). Talent management issues for multinational logistics companies in China: Observations from the field. *International Journal of Logistics Research and Applications*, 15(3): 163–179.

Skuza, A., Scullion, H., & Collings, D. G. (2016). Talent management in Europe. In M. Dickmann, C. Brewster, & P. Sparrow (Eds.), *International Human Resource Management: Contemporary HR Issues in Europe*. New York: Routledge, pp. 329–353.

Skuza, A., Scullion, H., & McDonnell, A. (2013). An analysis of the talent management challenges in a post-communist country: The case of Poland. *International Journal of Human Resource Management*, 24(3): 453–470.

Sparrow, P. (2012). Globalising the international mobility function: The role of emerging markets, flexibility and strategic delivery models. *The International Journal of Human Resource Management*, 23(12): 2404–2427.

Sparrow, P., Hird, M., & Cooper, C. L. (2015). Strategic talent management. In P. Sparrow & C. Cooper (Eds), *Do We Need HR?* London: Palgrave Macmillan, pp. 177–212.

Sparrow, P., Scullion, H., & Farndale, E. (2011). Global talent management: New roles for the corporate HR function? In H. Scullion & D. G. Collings (Eds.), *Global Talent Management*. New York: Routledge, pp. 39–55.

Stahl, G., Björkman, I., Farndale, E., Morris, S., Paauwe, J., & Stiles, P. (2012). Six principles of effective global talent management. *MIT Sloan Management Review*, 53(2): 25–32.

Stumpf, S. A., Doh, J. P., & Tymon, W. (2010). Capitalising on human resource management in India: The link between HR practices and employee performance. *Human Resource Management*, 49(3): 351–373.

Swailes, S. (2013). The ethics of talent management. *Business Ethics: A European Review,* 22(1): 32–46.

Swailes, S. (Ed.). (2020). *Managing Talent: A Critical Appreciation.* Bingley: Emerald Publishing.

Tarique, I., & Schuler, R. (2012). Global talent management literature review: A special report for SHRM foundation. Alexandria, VA, SHRM Foundation.

Tarique, I., & Schuler, R. S. (2010). Global talent management: Literature review, integrative framework, and suggestions for future research. *Journal of World Business,* 45(2): 122–133.

Taylor, S. (2007). Creating social capital in MNCs: The international human resource management challenge. *Human Resource Management Journal,* 17(4): 336–354.

Taylor, S., Beechler, S., & Napier, N. (1996). Toward an integrative model of strategic international human resource management. *Academy of Management Review,* 21(4): 959–985.

Teagarden, M. B., Meyer, J., & Jones, D. (2008). Knowledge sharing among high-tech MNCs in China and India: Invisible barriers, best practices and next steps. *Organizational Dynamics,* 37(2): 190–202.

Vaiman, V., & Brewster, C. (2014). How far do cultural differences explain the differences between nations? Implications for HRM. *International Journal of Human Resource Management.* http://doi.org/10.1080/09585192.2014.937969.

Vaiman, V., & Collings, D. G. (2015). Global talent management. In D. G. Collings, G. T. Wood, & P. M. Caligiuri (Eds.), *The Routledge Companion to International Human Resource Management* (pp. 210–225). London: Routledge.

Vaiman, V., Collings, D., Cascio, W., & Swider, B. W. (2021). The shifting boundaries of talent management. *Human Resource Management,* 60(2): 253–257.

Vaiman, V., Collings, D., & Scullion, H. (2012). Global talent management: Trends, challenges, and opportunities. *Management Decision,* 50(5): 925–941.

Vaiman, V., & Holden, N. J. (2011). Talent management in Central and Eastern Europe. In H. Scullion & D. Collings (Eds.), *Global Talent Management.* London: Routledge, pp. 178–193.

Vaiman, V., & Khoreva, V. (2021). Talent management: Decision making in the global context. In I. Tarique (Ed.), *Routledge Companion to Talent Management.* London: Routledge, pp. 81-93.

Vaiman, V., Schuler, R., Sparrow, P., & Collings, D. (Eds.). (2018a). *Macro Talent Management: A Global Perspective on Managing Talent in Developed Markets.* New York and London: Routledge.

Vaiman, V., Schuler, R., Sparrow, P., & Collings, D. (Eds.). (2018b). *Macro Talent Management in Emerging and Emergent Markets: A Global Perspective.* New York and London: Routledge.

Vaiman, V., & Vance, C. M. (Eds.). (2023). *Smart Talent Management* (2nd ed.). Northampton, MA: Edward Elgar Publishing, forthcoming.

Vance, C. M., & Vaiman, V. (2008). Smart talent management: On the powerful amalgamation of talent management and knowledge management. In V. Vaiman & C. Vance (Eds.), *Smart Talent Management: Building Knowledge Assets for Competitive Advantage.* Northampton, MA: Edward Elgar, pp. 1–15.

Van den Brink, M., Fruytier, B., & Thunnissen, M. (2013). Talent management in academia: Performance systems and HRM policies. *Human Resource Management Journal,* 23(2): 180–195.

Wang, W., & Heyes, J. (2020). Flexibility, labour retention and productivity in the EU. *The International Journal of Human Resource Management,* 31(3): 335–355.

Witt, M. A. (2019). De-globalization: Theories, predictions, and opportunities for international business research. *Journal of International Business Studies,* 50(7): 1053–1077.

Wood, G. T., Brewster, C., Demirbag, M., & Brookes, M. (2014). Understanding contextual differences in recruitment and selection. In G. Wood, C. Brewster, & M. Brookes (Eds.), *Varieties of HRM: A Comparative Study of the Relationship between Context and Firm*. London: Routledge, pp. 25–38.

Wood, G. T., Goergen, M., & Brewster, C. (2013). The effects of the national setting on employment practice: The case of downsizing. *International Business Review*, 22(6): 1051–1067.

Woods, P. (2003). Performance management of Australian and Singaporean expatriates. *International Journal of Manpower*, 24(5): 517–534.

Markus Pudelko

GLOBAL INTEGRATION VERSUS
LOCAL RESPONSIVENESS

STRATEGIC CHOICE OF MULTINATIONAL CORPORATIONS:
GLOBAL INTEGRATION VERSUS LOCAL RESPONSIVENESS

THE TENSION BETWEEN GLOBAL INTEGRATION versus local responsiveness may be regarded as one of the most crucial issues multinational corporations (MNCs) face. As such, the study of these two conflicting requirements constitutes one of the primary research agendas in global strategic management and in international human resource management (HRM) of the last four decades.

The starting point of our discussion is the MNC, a cornerstone of today's globalized economies and therefore central to the studies of international business (IB). An MNC can be defined as an integrated network of collective entities, formed by a corporate headquarters (HQ) and numerous subsidiaries across various countries. Such a network demands that MNCs develop cross-border control and coordination mechanisms among their dispersed entities. In this context, control refers to vertical, top-down HQ–subsidiary relations, while coordination addresses horizontal relations among subsidiaries.

Early research focused on the definition of the "one best way" MNCs should adopt in their management practices, irrespective of any contextual consideration. However, subsequent literature called the generalizability of normative management theory into question and followed more the so-called "contingency theory", a term attributed to the seminal scholars Paul Lawrence and Jay Lorsch (e.g., Lawrence & Lorsch, 1967, 1969). According to this framework, different business environments impact organizations in a variety of ways. Consequently, companies are required to align their strategies and structures with the respective business environment they operate in, to assure maximum performance.

The contingency framework was further adapted to the MNC context by seminal scholars such as C.K. Prahalad and Yves Doz (e.g., Prahalad & Doz, 1987) as well as Chris Bartlett and Sumantra Ghoshal (e.g., Bartlett & Ghoshal,

DOI: 10.4324/9781003247272-4

1988). These authors specified the need of MNCs to adapt to the various business environments they operate in by proposing two dimensions of pressures: integration versus differentiation. These dimensions are instrumental for establishing a corporate strategy under the contingency paradigm. Even after 35 years, the writings of these authors continue to be the main reference points when discussing what became known as the "(global) integration versus (local) responsiveness framework" (IR-framework). According to this conceptualization, the key challenge MNCs face is the necessity to exploit their comparative advantages through standardized corporate processes, which are generally developed at HQs across countries (global integration or standardization), while also having to adapt to the particularities of each business environment they operate in (local responsiveness or localization).

Global integration and local responsiveness can therefore be understood as two opposing pressures all MNCs experience. Consequently, their challenging task is to resolve this specific trade-off between synergies and autonomy by deciding which dimension to choose over the other. Eventually, the ability of MNCs to manage the competing forces of global integration and local responsiveness is essential for their survival and prosperity.

Since its development as a paradigm for modeling international corporate strategies and practices, the IR-framework has been empirically frequently validated and has proven its outstanding conceptual relevance. It is commonly employed to analyze the advantages and disadvantages of global integration or local responsiveness in terms of the corporate strategy, a particular business function (such as HRM), a particular management practice (such as pay for performance), or the products and services a company offers to its customers. According to Luo (2002, p. 189), "global strategies are most frequently analyzed using the global integration–local responsiveness (I-R) paradigm".

In this context, global integration has been defined as "the centralized management of geographically dispersed activities on an ongoing basis" (Prahalad & Doz, 1987, p. 14). It is driven by economies of scale and scope, and focuses on cost reduction through globally standardizing products and processes. In addition, efficiency seeking and integrated learning through knowledge sharing by HQ are further central building blocks of global integration.

In contrast, local responsiveness can be classified as the ability of MNCs to successfully cope with relevant institutional differences such as legal and regulatory stipulations imposed by governments and agencies, variations of local market conditions regarding consumer tastes and demands as well as differences regarding expectations of local employees. Instead of adopting standardized procedures handed down from HQ, subsidiaries are expected to adapt their operations to the unique circumstances of the respective local business environment. Local responsiveness further implies that foreign subsidiaries closely interact with local actors to become locally embedded, establishing local legitimacy, and thus overcoming their liability of foreignness. This "liability of foreignness" (LOF) is a common notation in IB research, which refers to the risk MNCs have in foreign markets of being identified as foreign and being discriminated against on these grounds. Contrary to the concept of global integration, due to this risk MNCs frequently choose to act like a local company, thus going against the concept of global integration.

Adherents of the IR-framework generally stress external environmental aspects, such as industrial forces, as drivers for either integration or responsiveness. Industrial forces pushing for global integration include worldwide business resource sourcing and deployment; by contrast, industrial forces pressing for local responsiveness are those requiring local context-sensitive management and quick responses to each local market.

In addition to such external environmental forces, internal organizational factors are of relevance for the IR-framework. In this context, we refer to studies integrating the IR-framework with the so-called "resource-based theory". This "grand theory" within management studies stipulates that company resources which are valuable, rare, difficult to imitate and non-substitutable are pivotal for the company's long-term success. Firms should therefore examine their organization to distinguish their sources of competitive advantage. Human resources are usually perceived as a key resource on which a competitive advantage can be built. According to the research direction, which integrates the resource-based theory into the IR-framework, the organizations' respective strategic capabilities (such as foreign experience and resource distinctiveness) and the organizational infrastructure (such as coordination systems and resource and information flows) play essential roles in pushing for either the integration or the responsiveness argument, depending on each individual MNC's resource set-up.

Early IB literature regarded corporate HQ as the main source of innovation and management know-how. It was therefore the task of HQ to pass down this knowledge to its subsidiaries abroad. However, later research acknowledged the possibility for subsidiaries to develop localized approaches that are either particularly suited for their respective business environment or function as best practice for the entire corporation. In the latter case, local responsiveness can lead to new learning and the introduction of innovation capabilities for the entire corporate network.

Global integration and local responsiveness are usually perceived as largely incompatible, implying that MNCs must either standardize or localize their corporate network, various business functions, and single management practices. However, a series of researchers claim that MNCs are required to find integrated solutions, by negotiating between standardization and localization. As such, Bartlett and Ghoshal suggested that "retaining local flexibility while achieving global integration" is the key requirement for successful MNCs.

While the IR-framework has mostly been applied to global strategic management, it was also widely tested for specific business functions, in particular international HRM and international marketing. Both business disciplines are concerned with the people of the countries MNCs operate in. Thereby, international HRM is concerned with local employees working for foreign subsidiaries, and international marketing is concerned with local customers from various countries. Consequently, to determine to which degree subsidiaries should rely on standardized practices defined by HQ as well as to establish the degree to which subsidiaries should adapt to the local employee or customer context is a particularly difficult dilemma to resolve. As such, much of the international HRM literature is informed by the IR-framework, investigating the following more specific research questions: first, to which degree should MNCs globally integrate their HRM policies to control and coordinate the HRM practices of their foreign subsidiaries; and secondly, to which degree should they adjust their HRM policies to the respective cultural and institutional context of their host countries, thereby adopting policies which are practiced by local firms? This dilemma becomes especially acute when operating in country contexts that strongly differ from the MNCs' home country context. The conflicting relationship between global integration and local responsiveness has been specifically studied in the area of HRM (see, e.g., Schuler, Dowling, & De Cieri, 1993). Chen and Wilson (2003) argue that HRM also lends itself to the study of the dialectic between both dimensions. First, HRM has particularly distinctive national characteristics across countries; and second, HRM has been defined as central to the success of MNCs' internationalization efforts.

GLOBAL INTEGRATION

Global integration and local responsiveness can be understood as inversely related. Nevertheless, their underlying determinants are not necessarily on the same scale and so they should not be understood as extreme and mutually excluding positions on a continuum.

Global integration is a key element for companies which seek to acquire a global advantage from a competitive advantage originally developed in the home country. Coordination and control are central in assuring consistency of standardized processes across all corporate entities. The downside of this strategy, however, is evident: by insisting on the implementation of overly ethnocentric approaches, HQ might be blind to instances where those approaches might prove ineffective in the respective host companies. At the extreme, such approaches might even conflict with local laws or regulations. Therefore, it is the responsibility of the local employees of foreign subsidiaries to intervene in order to avoid scandals or outright conflicts with authorities. Nevertheless, in less drastic situations, approaches dictated by HQ might alienate local employees and final products might not find the approval of local customers. As such, MNCs might be exposed to the previously mentioned risk of "liability of foreignness".

According to the aforementioned resource-based theory, global integration is concerned with leveraging corporate resources and competencies from the home country to the international environment. However, these resources and competencies are often tacit in nature, i.e., not codified in written manuals. As such, they are embedded in the human resources, who might even be unaware of possessing these uncodified competencies. Consequently, these competencies cannot be easily transferred given the time this takes, and can only be acquired through observation and experience. While this makes it difficult for competitors to adopt such competencies, even entities of the own corporations, such as foreign subsidiaries, will have difficulties to acquire these competencies. Therefore, international assignments such as expatriation, inpatriation, or even (in case of learning from other subsidiaries) from third-country nationals are of fundamental importance.

Using international assignees, particularly expatriates, may be the best way to ensure effective integration of management practices. As they are familiar with the corporate culture and specific management practices as developed by HQ in the home country context, they can serve as ambassadors of HQ, promoters of the "way to do things" as defined by HQ, and as teachers of explicit and, arguably even more important, of tacit knowledge. Developing a cohort of globally competent managers is an important objective of MNCs pursuing an integration strategy, as they are relevant for the encouragement of local employees around the world to follow the paths set out by HQ.

In addition, global integration will assist companies to reap economies of scale and scope for cost reduction purposes. Empirical research (Birkenshaw, Hulland, & Morrison, 1995; Yip, 1995) has shown a strong relationship between economies of scale and global integration. Ruth and Morrison (1990) list the following aspects from the external business environment that should push an MNC towards applying global integration: (1) high degree of standardization of customer needs worldwide; (2) high degree of standardization of purchasing practices worldwide; (3) existence of the same competitors in key markets worldwide; (4) high intensity of competition worldwide; (5) high concentration of distribution channels worldwide; (6) high susceptibility of economies of scale worldwide; (7) high degree of product awareness worldwide; (8) high degree of standardization of product technology worldwide; and (9) high degree of standardized products sold by competitors worldwide. While an adaptation to local conditions might increase market share, the costs associated with an adaption to each and every market might increase costs to such an extent that standardized products and production processes might be a more profitable strategy. Standardization based on global integration will also ensure the same product quality and reduce the risk that the brand image might suffer from differing product qualities.

Global integration also ensures that subsidiaries are not pursuing practices which might be accepted in the local context but would alienate customers on a worldwide basis. Looking at "the bigger picture", particularly regarding ethical issues, could save the entire MNC from embarrassment and loss of brand value.

According to the aforementioned resource-based theory, global integration is generally about leveraging corporate resources to the international environment. In this instance, it is assumed that the sources of competitive advantage lie within the home country, more specifically within HQ. Given that MNCs are embedded in the institutional and cultural context of their home country, they must continue to gain approval by their "referent audiences" (Greenwood, Raynard,

Kodeih, Micelotta, & Lounsbury, 2011) such as owners in their original national environment as companies internationalize. The pressure to conform to local standards when expanding internationally is referred to as "country of origin effect" (Ferner, 1997). This leads to distinct patterns of management coordination and control among MNCs of different nationalities (Edwards, Sánchez-Mangas, Jalette, Lavelle, & Minbaeva, 2016). However, MNCs might equally decide to emulate what they perceive to be the "best practices" of other management models across their corporate network. For example, a comparative study of HRM practices by Pudelko and Harzing (2007) revealed that subsidiaries of Japanese firms in Germany were neither following the Japanese model (home country) nor the German model (host country), and vice versa for subsidiaries of German companies in Japan. In both instances, they rather adopted HRM practices that were more similar to US practices. Consequently, the authors of this study did not observe global integration around HQ practices (country of origin effect) nor local responsiveness, but global integration around what they call "perceived best practices" stemming from the "dominant model" in management, the US model. Smith and Meiskins (1995) labeled this the "dominance effect", which is stronger the more actors of other countries are interested in adopting it. Apparently, companies also follow "logics of appropriateness" in their management (DiMaggio & Powell, 1983). Such logics reflect isomorphic pressures to conform to dominant models and practices, in order not to be perceived as outsiders or as less qualified by peers (such as other managers) or key audiences (such as investors). A comprehensive adoption of a dominant management model in the pursuit of "best practices" would have major implications, as it would ultimately result in a global convergence of management practices, a position Pudelko (2006, 2020) labeled "(context-free) universalism approach". Hence, we can deduce that we should always specify what the focus point of global integration is: HQ (respectively, home country) practices or perceived best practices (deriving from a "dominant" model). Representatives of the dominant model (e.g., US MNCs) have a significant incentive to also apply domestic management practices abroad (by combining the country of origin effect with the dominance effect). Accordingly, empirical studies also seem to suggest that in particular US MNCs adopt standardized approaches around domestic practices (Edwards & Ferner, 2002; Ferner, Belanger, Tregaskis, Morley, & Quintanilla, 2013; Edwards et al., 2016).

While the focus of research has mainly been on the integration of corporate strategy, less attention has been directed towards the global integration of single business functions, such as HRM. This might be surprising, given the calls for the integration of the HRM function in particular, to create the necessary cohesion across policies and practices to achieve a transnational configuration (Bartlett & Ghoshal, 1989) of MNCs.

According to Chen and Wilson (2003), HRM global integration can be perceived as a rational management initiative by HQ to transfer its HRM practices to the companies' foreign subsidiaries, executed with the belief that such integrated policies and practices will lead to the adoption of best practices around the world. At least in principle, the adoption of HQ practices through corporate subunits, such as foreign subsidiaries, should be executed without resistance as HQ are the owners and can insist on full compliance. Especially, expatriates are very important in the implementation of the global integration strategy, as they play a key role in assuring that each foreign subsidiary also executes its responsibilities according to the directives of HQ. Given the strategic relevance of expatriates for the MNC, the HRM function needs to put a strong focus on the professional management of the MNC's expatriates, including aspects such as recruitment, training, evaluation, remuneration, and promotion, in order to ensure that expatriates execute their important but also challenging tasks to the full satisfaction of the MNC.

A series of studies have empirically demonstrated that HQ is frequently the main source from which HRM practices are standardized, as comparative studies between HQ and subsidiaries indicate (see, e.g., Bartlett & Goshal, 1989; Björkman, 2006; Rosenzweig, 2006). This is explained by the attitude of HQ, which commonly takes it for granted that its respective way of managing human resources is also the best way and that this "administrative heritage" (Taylor, Beechler, & Napier, 1996) will also be equally effective abroad. While this logic possesses a lot of face value, one should not underestimate the attraction force of perceived best practices stemming from dominant management models, as the studies by Pudelko and Harzing (2007) have shown. In addition to the global integration of HRM practices (around HQ or dominant practices), MNCs can of course also decide to employ hybrid approaches, combining globally integrated and localized elements (Brewster, Sparrow, & Harris, 2005).

LOCAL RESPONSIVENESS

MNCs implement local responsiveness strategies, i.e., the adaptation of foreign subsidiary practices to the local business environment, to address the complexity and dynamism of the local context in the various host countries. Local responsiveness leads to better compatibility of management practices with local conditions in terms of regulations, implicit norms, values, and expectations of relevant actors, such as governments agencies, customers, or employees. This, in return, results in a greater legitimacy of the foreign entity and a reduced liability of foreignness in the various host countries. A higher degree of congruence between own management practices and the local business environment can thus lead to improved performance of local subsidiaries. By contrast, if foreign subsidiaries were, knowingly or unknowingly, to ignore national laws, norms, and values, they could be penalized, lose customers, employees, and ultimately, profits.

Furthermore, as the local responsiveness approach generally implies a delegation of authority towards local managers, it can be inferred that those who are in the best position to determine what is best for the subsidiary are also in an adequate position to make the relevant decisions on the ground. In addition, if those locals are relatively free to decide what is best for subsidiary performance, they can follow their own evaluations without being constrained by HQ directives or by HQ representatives, i.e., expatriates who may not necessarily have the interest of local profit maximization at heart.

In addition, adherents of global integration should keep in mind that cost reduction measures based on economies of scale and scope could eventually lead to opposite results. As global integration requires significant efforts of global coordination and control, MNCs usually operate with a strong expatriate presence, to ensure the effective implementation of standardized practices determined by HQ. As expatriates tend to be very costly, increased costs of coordination and control due to expatriation might ultimately outweigh the savings global integration is intended to generate.

Furthermore, subsidiary performance can be significantly determined by situational and dynamic conditions. External players' actions, such as those by local regulatory agencies, competitors, suppliers, and customers, need to constantly be monitored, and reactions and countermeasures have to be developed and implemented without delay. To determine the adequate degree of local responsiveness is therefore not an easy task, as the appropriate level might vary across time, countries, business functions, or products.

In addition to pursuing local interests, foreign subsidiaries might also generate in a bottom-up fashion new knowledge, insights, ideas, and innovations that could become of relevance for the entire corporate network if properly distributed. However, to develop such knowledge, subsidiaries must have a sufficient degree of autonomy, as guaranteed by local responsiveness approaches.

All the more, the uninterrupted relevance of cross-country cultural and institutional differences results in the continued differentiation of management models across nations. Hall and Soskice (2001) labeled these differences between country systems "varieties of capitalism". To build on global integration strategies on the premise of management models, consumer tastes and employee preferences being in the process of converging might therefore have been precipitated. MNCs will continue to operate in culturally and institutionally diverse business environments, and therefore need to assure that their local entities have enough leeway to locally embed themselves and to establish local legitimacy.

Furthermore, while globalization trends over various decades might have pushed MNCs towards the implementation of more and more globally integrated management approaches, for more than a decade, we have witnessed counter-trends, frequently labeled de-globalization. As such, we observe a reduction of foreign direct investment streams, increasing political tensions among major trading blocks, efforts to become less dependent on products previously provided by real or potential adversaries, a resurgence of nationalistic sentiments and, last but not least, disturbances of the flow of goods, services, and people due to the COVID pandemic. Consequently, such aspects of de-globalization on the macro level appear to push the pendulum between integration and localization on the micro level to swing more towards localization. Defining the right balance between integration and localization can therefore never be determined in an abstract fashion, but is always subject to the context on the macro and the micro level, and is therefore always subject to changes over time.

HRM has previously been described as being of major relevance for the implementation of global integration strategies, and it is of equal importance in the application of local responsiveness policies. While HRM under the global integration paradigm focuses on expatriates, local responsiveness can most convincingly be implemented by local employees. This indicates the necessity for HRM to ensure that excellent local talent is recruited against the competition of established local employers that might be more attractive for potential recruits. Moreover, of equal importance is thorough training, as local employees who are meant to have a high degree of autonomy need to be at least familiarized with the overall objectives of the MNC and its products. Furthermore, their regular performance evaluation will be of great importance to ensure that the right local decision makers are also adhering to the responsibilities they are entrusted with. Finally, to motivate high-performing local employees to continue working for the subsidiary, they will need to be well remunerated and have at least the chance to become promoted to the top without expatriates blocking these positions. While HRM is vital for the implementation of the principles of local responsiveness in general, HRM practices themselves also need to adhere to these principles and follow local practices in order not to alienate (potential) local employees.

CONSEQUENCES OF GLOBAL INTEGRATION AND LOCAL RESPONSIVENESS FOR INTERNATIONAL STRATEGIES

From the abovementioned, it appears that global integration and local responsiveness are opposite ends of the same continuum, only allowing for a trade-off between both positions. Indeed, earlier studies from the 1980s and 1990s regarded both dimensions as opposite poles of the same scale (Roth & Morrison, 1990). However, this perspective was subsequently challenged (Prahalad & Doz, 1987), arguing that both concepts are not mutually exclusive, but should be perceived as a duality which can be pursued simultaneously, provided that MNCs embrace a collaborative corporate culture, develop certain organizational capabilities and implement a matrix structure. As such, it has been frequently recommended that companies should find a strategic balance between both concepts. On this basis, the IR-framework allows international corporate strategies to be conceptualized by three single strategies.

The most classic differentiation is that by Perlmutter (1969), who differentiated between "ethnocentrism", "polycentrism" and "geocentrism" (with "regiocentrism" as an additional strategy, as a compromise between polycentrism and geocentrism). According to this classification, an MNC following the global integration paradigm by standardizing its foreign subsidiary policies around HQ (i.e., home country) practices, would implement an "ethnocentric strategy": Whatever management practices are employed in the domestic environment should be implemented everywhere else in the world, irrespective of local contextual conditions. In terms of consequences for HRM, the "ethnocentric strategy" implies that the foreign subsidiary employees regard themselves as merely executing HQ's directives and that key subsidiary employees are expatriates sent by HQ to assure the correct completion of its instructions.

By contrast, an MNC following the local responsiveness paradigm would implement the "polycentric strategy": Every foreign subsidiary forms its own independent decision-making center around which own strategies and practices are formulated in accordance with the local contextual conditions. For HRM, the "polycentric strategy" entails that foreign subsidiary employees regard themselves as fully embedded in their local country, and not as part of a foreign entity. They also hold all key positions, with expatriates being the absolute exception.

Finally, an MNC following a combined global integration–local responsiveness paradigm would implement the geocentric international strategy: Whatever appear to the top management of HQ to be best management practices, no matter where these practices originated from, either from HQ or from one of the foreign subsidiaries, should be implemented everywhere in the world, wherever and whenever possible. Only when certain local contextual conditions prevent this standardization around best practices should local solutions be adopted. The implications for HRM are, in comparison, more complex: Foreign subsidiary employees perceive themselves as belonging to a global company in which they still represent local interests. In addition, there is a high number of international assignees to ensure an intense exchange of views. International assignments can, however, occur in all directions: expatriates, inpatriates, and third country nationals, with the latter also ensuring lateral exchanges. Figure 1 summarizes the relationship between the strategic choice of global integration versus local responsiveness on one side, and the three models of ethnocentrism, polycentrism, and geocentrism on the other.

With certain modifications, a series of scholars developed other sets of three generic international strategies, yet always with the same principle: two opposite strategies plus an integrated one. As such, Prahalad and Doz (1987) developed the "multi-focal" strategy, which is at the same time globally integrated

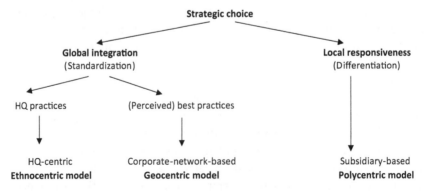

Figure 1 Global integration versus localization

and locally responsive. Similarly, Jarillo and Martinez (1990) identified on the basis of the degree of integration and localization for foreign subsidiaries three roles: the "receptive," the "active," and the "autonomous." The conceptualization by Prahalad and Doz was further developed into the highly influential systematization by Bartlett and Goshal (1989), who developed a 2 by 2 matrix of international strategies based on the dimensions of global integration and local responsiveness. As a result, they identified the "global strategy" (based on global integration at the expense of local responsiveness), the "multi-domestic strategy" (based on local responsiveness at the expense of global integration), and the "transnational strategy" (integrating both strategies) (to complete the 2 by 2 matrix, they defined a fourth, the "international strategy," which is low on both dimensions and therefore regarded as inferior). This typology, and in particular, the conceptualization of the "transnational company," fully integrating global integration and local responsiveness, has become a benchmark for subsequent research and the basic knowledge explained in every international strategy textbook. The transnational strategy, which is regarded as the superior but also most complex one, is based on high levels of intra-MNC exchanges of goods, services, personal and in particular vertical, but also lateral knowledge.

The overarching conceptualization is that MNCs using the geocentric/multi-focal/transnational strategy with foreign subsidiaries taking on an autonomous role can achieve both global integration and local responsiveness by internally breaking management down into various activities. Thereby, some of these activities will be globally integrated, and others will remain differentiated according to national context. This way, an MNC can highly integrate some activities while being highly locally responsive with others. Overall, i.e., in aggregation, MNCs can thus achieve aspects of both global integration and local responsiveness at the same time. Other authors, such as Doz and Prahalad (1986) and Bartlett and Ghoshal (1989), insist that achieving both global integration and local responsiveness is less a question of breaking management down into single activities and finding for each one a particular degree of integration relative to localization. In contrast, a truly transnational strategy implies the definition of a strategic, dynamic, and simultaneous balance between both approaches on a higher level, based on organizational learning due to intensive knowledge flows in all directions, integrating and exploiting geographically dispersed expertise. As such, foreign subsidiaries are not just recipients of knowledge from HQ (as with the global strategy based on global integration) or independent actors (as with the multi-domestic strategy based on local responsiveness), but important sources of knowledge to be transferred as best practices throughout the corporate network. The following quote by Bartlett and Ghoshal (1998, p. 65) illustrates this approach:

> Managers in most worldwide companies recognize the need for simultaneously achieving global efficiency, national responsiveness, and the ability to develop and exploit knowledge on a worldwide basis. Some, however, regard the goal as inherently unattainable. Perceiving irreconcilable

contradictions among the three objectives, they opt to focus on one of them, at least temporarily. The transnational company is one that overcomes these contradictions.

The new paradigm is not about a pendulum swinging back and forth between global integration and local responsiveness, but about meeting simultaneously paradoxes, opposites, dualities, and contradictory strategic demands, and keeping a dynamic balance between them.

Authors such as Bartlett and Ghoshal were fully aware of the complexity of the transnational strategy they were propagating, particularly with regard to coordination and control. To address this issue, they directed the attention away from "hard" strategy and structural aspects and more towards "soft" factors of a shared collaborative corporate culture and central values of the organization. More specifically, they replaced the traditional focus on vertical HQ–subsidiary relationships with the coordination of complex webs of mainly horizontal relationships. To establish such a cooperative culture and relationship-oriented values, a key focus was put on the management of human resources. A central idea was that under highly complex conditions, self-control appears more efficient to establish cohesion across activities if the transnational configuration is to be achieved rather than boss-control, and that self-control is essentially implemented via HRM.

Evans et al. (2002) thus remarked that while some of the most significant strategy scholars had a (micro) economics background, they subsequently redirected their attention to HRM. They did so as they came to recognize the human factor to be the central resource of organizations, which needs to be properly managed. As examples, Evans and colleagues mentioned Howard Perlmutter ("geocentric organization"), Yves Doz and C.K. Prahalad ("multi-focal organization"), Gunnar Hedlund ("heterarchy"), and Sumatra Ghoshal and Chris Bartlett ("transnational company"). Firms should therefore look inside their organization to define resources that could be the sources of their competitive advantage. As mentioned before, human resources are usually perceived as a key resource on which a competitive advantage can be built. The emergence of the "resource-based theory" has already been described. An outflow from this shift of attention towards (internal) resources, competencies and capabilities of organizations as sources of competitive advantage and away from the positioning of the company in the (external) market was that HRM also grew in relevance within the area of strategy research since the 1990s (in particular in comparison to marketing, which in the 1980s, under the strong influence of Michael Porter, was more the center of attention in strategy research). As such, Evans et al. (2002) argued that in a global era, the most relevant insights into management processes will come from studying human resource management in an international context. Before this shift in perception in the 1990s, HRM was regarded more as a task of helping strategy to be executed. However, the concept of the transnational company was highly instrumental in integrating strategy and HRM. As a consequence, HRM came to be seen as an integral part of the MNC, spurred by the failure of structural solutions to problems of coordination and control, by inflexible systems, and by the fact that strategic innovations increasingly come from local units rather than HQ. As a result, the boundaries between the HR function and line management also became fuzzier.

While various authors have suggested that global integration and local responsiveness are qualitatively different constructs, they also suggested that the integrated international strategy, which combines elements of both integration and localization, is a superior choice and should therefore be pursued. Nevertheless, reality has depicted a somewhat different picture: in strategy and international HRM research and practice, the constructs of global integration and local responsiveness continue to be at least implicitly considered as opposite poles of a single continuum. Moreover, the propagation of the integrated approach of integration and localization under the umbrella of the transnational strategy turned out to be somewhat overly idealistic and non-pragmatic, given its inherent complexity in terms of internal coordination and control as well as knowledge flows.

This becomes particularly evident when the actual practices are studies by which the IR-framework is meant to be implemented. With this focus, the question of global integration and local responsiveness quickly becomes an either-or choice again (Evans, Pucik, & Barsoux, 2002; Chung, 2015). Even those MNCs which Bartlett and Ghoshal described as role models for their transnational strategy have since abandoned this approach due to its being overly complex, frequently adopting the less demanding "global" approach. More recent textbooks, such as those by Peng (2021) and Verbeke (2013), therefore characterize the transnational strategy as a possibly overly demanding and over-ambitious exercise, stressing more clear-cut either-or choices between integration and localization. As a result, the balance appears to swing back to the contingency approaches described earlier, assessing the advantages and disadvantages of alternative (instead of integrated) strategies.

HRM IMPLICATIONS

When investigating the implications of the IR-framework, research has attached significantly less attention to single business functions compared to overall corporate strategy. This also applies to HRM, even though this business function is particularly susceptible to IR aspects. Every organization has a set of implicit but in most cases explicitly formulated HRM policies. They are highly relevant for the implementation of the chosen international strategy and ultimately for the overall performance of an MNC. After all, HRM policies are essential in forming the key resource of any organization: the human resources.

We have already discussed how essential HRM is for implementing the combined configuration of global integration and local responsibility for which the transnational company stands exemplary. We also mentioned that recent research again focused on either-or choices regarding both dimensions. Therefore, we have to state: no matter whether an MNC focuses more on global integration or on local responsiveness, HRM is highly relevant in implementing either configuration. To globally integrate operations, coordination and control mechanisms are of central importance. Research has established that the use of expatriates in MNCs is a central control mechanism. Hence, it is the role of HRM to choose, prepare, evaluate, and incentivize expatriates for this important role. On the other side, to implement local responsiveness, local knowledge and expertise is of relevance, which can only be provided by local managers. Yet again, HRM is also central in the provision of local talent and expertise.

To evaluate the degree of global integration versus local responsiveness within the function of HRM, Rosenzweig and Nohria (1994) suggested breaking HRM down into different practices, as the degree of global integration versus local responsiveness in HRM can vary between those practices. For instance, recruitment and training activities are regarded as rather similar across countries as they are based on technical expertise that is less prone to local differentiation. Hence, companies might consider using relatively more global integration than local responsiveness approaches for these two HRM functions. This might differ for performance evaluation and incentive aspects such as remuneration and promotion, which are more susceptible to cultural differences and where aspects of local responsiveness might therefore be more relevant.

Recruitment decisions for foreign subsidiaries are a crucial mechanism to ensure either global integration or local responsiveness. If MNCs are more interested in ensuring global responsiveness, they should focus on expatriates. As expatriates have been trained by HQ, socialized into the HQ culture, and have internalized the corporate values, they have an in-depth explicit and tacit knowledge of relevant aspects they can transmit to subsidiaries. Especially for transmitting tacit knowledge, their personal interactions with local employees may be vital. Consequently, they possess a high degree of social capital with the organization, and have a greater ability to transfer knowledge from HQ, integrate activities across entities, transmit a shared vision and control execution. In addition, they are considered to be more committed to the overall organization than local managers, who might show more loyalty to the particular interest of their subsidiary or the business environment they have been socialized in.

Expatriates are also in a better position to evaluate whether the local subsidiary adheres to the ethical standards of HQ, the HQ country, and the global customer base, and not just those of the local country. This will be of particular relevance where local ethical norms deviate strongly from global standards. Moreover, this could lead to serious consequences if the global customer base becomes outraged, for example in cases of insufficient worker rights, the neglect of safety issues or the discrimination of minorities. Furthermore, to relay the interests of the local subsidiary back to HQ, it might be practical to have expatriates communicating with HQ, as their voices might be heard and accepted more than those of local managers. However, while expatriates can better ensure the execution of standardized management practices, MNCs should also consider a variety of factors: local employees might resent them for not being sufficiently committed to the local subsidiary, for ignoring local values and customs, or for their highly paid jobs, which they might consider should be filled by local employees.

If embeddedness into the local business environment is of great relevance, local managers with a high degree of local expertise and external social capital within their country are in most cases a better choice. As they have a deep personal knowledge of the local business environment, share the same culture and language with local stakeholders such as local suppliers, customers, regulatory agencies, and local employees, they are therefore able to communicate more effectively with them than expatriates. Expatriates would not only differ from the local environment in terms of culture and language, but if coming from a more developed country, might also show a certain arrogance and condescendence towards the local population.

In addition to these communication aspects, local managers are likely to deal with local idiosyncrasies, recontextualize general corporate approaches towards the particular local context, develop locally adapted strategies, and preempt or react to actions of local competitors in more effective ways and therefore help the MNC to gain local legitimacy. Local managers also tend to be committed more long-term to the local subsidiary than expatriates who already know when they will return to HQ. In addition, to foster their own career, expatriates are well aware that they have to pursue the interests of HQ and not those of the local subsidiary. MNCs should also consider that the failure rate of expatriates (usually defined as a premature return home due to private or professional problems related to expatriation) is exceptionally high. Furthermore, the fact that local managers can make it to the top of a subsidiary and won't have to always report to expatriates who come and go will motivate more local talent to seek positions in these subsidiaries. And even if MNCs were to prefer employing more expatriates in their subsidiaries abroad, often local governments limit this approach by enforcing the recruitment of local employees.

If subsidiaries are newly introduced in a foreign country, it is quite normal to commence with expatriates in key positions, irrespective of strategic preferences, as only they are acquainted with the functioning of certain core processes. More telling is who will succeed the expatriates of the first generation: in case of global integration strategies, this will most likely again be expatriates; however, in terms of local responsiveness, a switch to local managers will most likely occur. Finally, in regard to their recruitment practices, MNCs also have to pay attention to avoid employing selection methods and criteria that local applicants might consider inappropriate and contradicting their cultural values. The questions of whether interviews and tests are appropriate, to what degree applicants should stress their capabilities or remain modest, how necessary capabilities are to be defined, whether such capabilities matter more than connections, and how differences in gender, social background, sexual orientation, etc., should be considered need to be carefully evaluated.

The global integration versus local responsiveness divide also has an implication for *training* measures. As global integration implies the use of expatriates in foreign subsidiaries, training refers first of all to general training measures for HQ employees, of whom some will, after various years of employment, be chosen for an expatriate assignment. An abundance of studies have shown that a specific preparation program (e.g., cross-cultural training and language studies) of those having been selected for such an expatriation assignment is also highly useful.

Where the MNC follows a local responsiveness strategy, the training of local employees of foreign subsidiaries becomes much more relevant, as the company will have to fully rely on them as key decision makers. From this follows that the MNC must invest time and money in intensive training. In this case, training is also not simply an issue of transferring technical and managerial skills, but also about passing on the corporate philosophy, values, and principles. For this purpose, mentoring and coaching activities are also of relevance. In addition, an MNC might even consider inpatriation, i.e., the assignment of local talent to HQ for a few years, as an excellent way not only to learn technical aspects, but also to adopt the corporate philosophy, values, and principles.

While local responsiveness would ideally imply that local employees hold all key positions, this might be very difficult in some countries if the local educational system does not provide locals with the necessary basic skill sets. In this case, it will be the MNC's responsibility to train the local workforce of their subsidiaries more comprehensively, so that those who benefit from such programs can take over wider decision-making authority in the future. As such, MNCs will have to take a much longer-term perspective, as training will become much more a question of fostering the future potential of local talent, and not simply a question of passing on technical competence under a global integration regime where expatriates are able to control the activity of locals.

Also regarding *performance evaluation*, practices will differ depending on which strategy an MNC is pursuing. Under the global integration perspective, the evaluation of expatriates will be of major relevance, also in the context of future top management positions back at HQ. Regarding locals, job positions are likely to be defined in a more fixed and narrow way. Consequently, the performance evaluation will be carried out on a short-term and restricted basis, focusing on current productivity and performance. By contrast, with a local responsiveness perspective, positions for locals are likely to be more flexible and developmental. This will also be reflected in the performance evaluation, which will include more developmental aspects, such as the willingness to take on decision-making responsibilities in managerial positions.

Finally, regarding incentive instruments such as *remuneration* and *promotion* practices, the IR-framework will also be of relevance. MNCs pursuing the global integration strategy will have to take into account that expatriate compensation packages (including translocation and accommodation costs, school fees for children, hardship allowances, etc.) are typically significantly more expensive than the salaries for local managers. Nevertheless, as they will have to rely on expatriates, they will need to bear these additional costs. Furthermore, companies will have to offer expatriates attractive positions once they rotate back to HQ, as they may otherwise be demotivated and leave the corporation. An abundance of studies has shown how critical the repatriation phase is and how many (by then former) expatriates leave the company at this stage. Furthermore, as local employees under a global integration regime have only limited promotion prospects, MNCs that still want to attract high-performing local employees will need to pay them well to compensate for the lack of future career possibilities.

If an MNC pursues the local responsiveness approach, the motivation of locals is easier as they are aware that they may potentially be promoted to the top of their subsidiary and thus obtain salaries in accordance with their position. Consequently, local employees might also view their career at the foreign subsidiary from a longer-term perspective, while locals working for an MNC with a global integration strategy might leave their employer as soon as a competitor is offering a more attractive salary.

CONTEXTUAL DIFFERENTIATION

Having introduced and discussed the two dimensions of global integration and local responsiveness and their implications, specifically for the business function of HRM, it is relevant to understand under which configurations and contexts which strategy should be chosen. The following relevant criteria will be described: entry mode, industry, business function, home country, and host country.

Regarding *entry mode*, an MNC striving for global integration is likely to establish a wholly owned subsidiary (instead of engaging in a joint venture with a local partner) as it will allow the MNC to exert full control over its subsidiary. As a result, it can standardize management practices around HQ (or perceived best) practices without having to negotiate arrangements with a local partner which might be eager to establish its own management practices. In addition, an MNC seeking global integration would be well advised to establish its subsidiary as a greenfield entity (instead of acquiring an already established local company). This way, it can recruit employees according to its own selection criteria and imprint its own corporate values and principles in the newly established subsidiary through expatriates sent over from HQ. HRM as a business function will be key in ensuring the transfer of the corporate culture to each foreign subsidiary via training and mentoring. As a result, local employees of a greenfield entity are much more likely to follow and implement standardized management practices established at HQ compared to employees of an acquired company who might attempt to keep management as it was under the previous local ownership, resisting any change.

By contrast, an MNC seeking local responsiveness should have fewer problems entering a new market via a joint venture with a local partner, as from the start, the latter would be able to ensure local embeddedness in the new entity, establish local legitimacy, and avoid the liability of foreignness. Should an MNC striving for local responsiveness enter a new market via a wholly owned subsidiary, it might consider acquiring an established local company which could retain its own corporate values and philosophy, thus again assuring the continuity of local legitimacy.

Independent of the MNC's choice between global integration and local responsiveness, some *business functions* have been found to be more conducive towards global integration than others. For example, research and development, manufacturing and managerial accounting are more likely to gain from standardization across countries and units. In contrast, HRM and marketing (including sales and customer service) are business functions in which MNCs are likely to seek adaptation to the local context, given the greater influence of culture and cultural differences in these areas. This is also reflected in the number of expatriates in foreign subsidiaries, which have been found in an empirical study to be three times as high in research and development than in HRM (Harzing, Pudelko, & Reiche, 2016). Furthermore, even within business functions, certain differences might exist. As previously described in the context of HRM, recruitment and training tend to be more globally integrated compared to incentive aspects such as remuneration and promotion. Despite these differences between (and even within) business functions regarding global integration and local responsiveness, the chosen international strategy will still push those functions in one or the other direction. As such, a globally integrated MNC will, for example, in marketing, seek a more standardized product policy for the sake of economies of scale, while a locally responsive MNC is likely to offer products with local specifications to best cater for the differing tastes of customers from different countries.

In addition, whether an MNC is leaning more towards global integration or towards local responsiveness is often not only a question of the individual corporate strategy, but also influenced by the *industry* in which the company is offering its products and services. If the MNC operates in a more globalized industry, an industry that is characterized by standardized products, or a business-to-business industry, it will more likely lean towards a global integration strategy. If the MNC produces for the end consumer, the question will be whether consumer tastes for these products tend to be more homogeneous (e.g., consumer electronics, automotive industry), whether the industry is more technology- and (global) advertisement-intensive, whether the industry allows for possibilities of economies of scale, and whether the industry is characterized by a high intensity of global competition and a low intensity of local competition. In all those cases, it is again highly likely that the MNC will pursue a global integration strategy. By contrast, industries with a high degree of demand heterogeneity (e.g., the food industry), fierce local competition and location-bound competitive advantages will require substantial autonomy of local subsidiaries, and are therefore likely to favor a local responsiveness strategy.

Another important aspect regarding the IR-framework is the *home country* of the MNC, as HQ practices emerge within the particular cultural and institutional environment of the respective home country. Depending on how this environment influences the HQ practices, standardization efforts around HQ practices under a global integration strategy may differ substantially (an effect called isomorphic pressure of the home country). Particularly, companies from Japan and the US are known for implementing the global integration approach.

Japan has frequently been described as having a highly particularistic, insular, and ethnocentric culture. As a result, Japanese MNCs traditionally go to great lengths to ensure that their management practices are also implemented in their foreign subsidiaries. As discussed earlier, one important way to coordinate and control foreign subsidiaries is via expatriates. And indeed, as a study by Harzing, Pudelko, and Reiche (2016) established, foreign subsidiaries of Japanese companies tend to have a very high number of expatriates. They usually make all the important decisions by keeping in very close contact with HQ, while local managers are usually excluded from high-level decision-making processes. To obtain qualified local managers despite this, Japanese companies typically offer very attractive salaries.

Albeit for a different reason, the United States is also a home country of MNCs which frequently employ a global integration approach. In probably no other country is the above-mentioned dominance effect based on perceived best practices so relevant. The competitiveness, profitability, and general appeal of US companies (e.g., Apple) and entire industries (e.g., high tech), the strength of the US economy (number one in the world), the relevance of the currency (global lead currency), the dominance of US management teaching and research (MBA schools), the attractiveness as an immigration country (the country with the highest number of foreign-born residents), and soft factors such as the pervasiveness of its pop culture (e.g., Hollywood movies) are all factors rendering the US model highly attractive for outsiders and worth emulating (an effect called mimetic isomorphism). This and a widespread conviction to represent the "best country in the world" triggers the attitude among US managers that the own management model should also be employed abroad. This particularly applies to HRM practices such as individualistic incentive systems.

Very different is the situation in successful but small countries (e.g., Scandinavian countries, the Netherlands, Switzerland). Given their small size, their practices tend to be not known enough for the dominance effect to play a major role. In addition, and given their small size, they are often willing to adapt to larger and more powerful neighbors and business partners. Consequently, their MNCs are often leaning towards the local responsiveness strategy. The same applies, though for a different reason, to MNCs from emerging economies. In this instance, their foreign subsidiaries are often struggling with their liability of origin. In order not to be overly identified with their country of origin (and its perceived backward status), MNCs often adapt a local responsiveness approach, thus increasing their local legitimacy. Chinese MNCs have been known for this and their resulting reaction of pursuing a local responsiveness strategy.

Finally, not only the home country, but also the *host country* matters for defining an MNC's positioning regarding the IR-framework. In developing countries, the general education and specialized training levels of the local workforce are frequently insufficient, so that local employees are often not regarded as qualified enough to take on certain key positions in a foreign subsidiary. As a result, expatriates have to take on these positions, pursuing a more globally integrated approach. In addition, given that MNCs often come from rich and developed countries, they often enjoy a high status in less-developed countries (an advantage of foreignness rather than a liability of foreignness). Consequently, their management practices are met with acceptance and respect (dominance effect). Furthermore, given the economic muscle of MNCs, local government authorities often lack the power to resist the requests of their foreign guests. A striking exception has been China, where government authorities have been highly successful in restricting certain market entry forms (wholly owned subsidiaries), pushing towards joint ventures with local partners. This has greatly assisted Chinese companies to profit from the resulting technology transfer (an effect labeled coercive isomorphism).

By contrast, local responsiveness strategies are particularly relevant in host countries with a distinct local business environment, which impedes the smooth transfer of standardized management practices from HQ. Furthermore, environmental complexity such as diversity of consumer tastes or local sourcing imperatives, segmented markets according to regions and different regulations or incongruence of regulations by different local regulatory bodies all result in a high degree of uncertainty that local managers are best equipped to deal with. An example of intra-country institutional heterogeneity is the US, where foreign automotive companies have set up manufacturing sites specifically in states with low labor representation. The resulting freedom from labor interference allowed them to standardize their management practices, specifically in HRM, around HQ country practices. Furthermore, public policy might also restrict globally integrated approaches, forcing MNCs to adopt more local responsiveness strategies (e.g., by allowing only a limited number of expatriates into the country or by exerting informal pressure to adapt to local practices). Finally, local employees are likely to be more motivated working for a subsidiary that has adopted local management practices and is run by their compatriots. By contrast, expatriates are more inclined to apply HQ home country practices to which they are more accustomed and which they take for granted, but this may alienate local employees.

All these differences among home and host countries suggest that MNCs need to find highly differentiated approaches regarding their strategic choices between global integration and local responsiveness. Finally, it is important to consider the home and host context not only separately, but also in conjunction. Where there are only limited cultural and institutional differences between home and host country (e.g., among Anglophone countries), barriers to transferring management practices will be low, which would facilitate global integration. By contrast, substantial cultural and institutional differences between home and host country (e.g., between highly individualistic Western and highly collectivistic African, Asian, or South American countries) create barriers for standardized management practices, which would be an argument for local responsiveness.

CONCLUSION

After all these considerations regarding the tension between global integration versus local responsiveness, what is ultimately the bottom line? Various studies have attempted to empirically determine which strategy works best and towards which strategy MNCs should gravitate, yet they have obtained contradictory results. Some studies see local responsiveness as prevailing (e.g., Brock & Siscovick, 2007; Luo, 2002), while others (e.g., Edwards et al., 2016; Pudelko & Harzing, 2007) perceive a stronger trend towards global integration. From this we can conclude that there is no single pathway, as either global integration or local responsiveness can, under certain conditions, prove to be the more advantageous strategy. Hence, what matters is to define what these conditions are and how they impact the choice of global integration versus local responsiveness. These conditions might refer to the corporate context, the home, or the host country context, demonstrating the complexity of the circumstances in which MNCs operate. In addition, MNCs not only have to decide which strategy to choose, but also to what degree. To further add to the complexity, the degree of global integration in terms of local responsiveness might even differ between (and within) business functions. HRM in particular has been described as a business function requiring more local responsiveness approaches. Moreover, as the discussion around the transnational corporation has indicated, MNCs might under certain conditions strive for both global integration and local responsiveness. Consequently, it is evident that there is no "one-size-fits-all solution" and that MNCs need to carefully establish which path to pursue not only in their overall strategies, but also in their HRM practices, while always being prepared to revise their original strategy should changes in the contextual factors require it.

REFERENCES

Bartlett, C.A. and Ghoshal, S. (1988) 'Organizing for Worldwide Effectiveness: The Transnational Solution', *California Management Review*, 31(1): 54–74.

Bartlett, C.A. and Ghoshal, S. (1989) *The Transnational Solution*, Harvard Business School, Boston, MA.

Birkenshaw, J., Hulland, J.S. and Morrison, A. (1995) 'Structural and Competitive Determinants of a Global Integration Strategy', *Strategic Management Journal*, 16(8): 637–655.

Björkman, I. (2006) 'International Human Resource Management Research and Institutional Theory', in *Handbook of Research in International Human Resource Management*, eds. G.K. Stahl and I. Björkman, Edward Elgar, Cheltenham and Northampton, 463–447.

Brewster, C., Sparrow, P.R. and Harris, H. (2005) 'Towards a New Model of Globalizing HRM', *International Journal of Human Resource Management*, 16(6): 949–970.

Brock, D.M. and Siscovick, I.G. (2007) 'Global Integration and Local Responsiveness in Multinational Subsidiaries: Some Strategy, Structure, and Human Resource Contingencies', *Asia Pacific Journal of Human Resources*, 45(3): 353–373.

Chen, S. and Wilson, M. (2003) 'Standardization and Localization of Human Resource Management in Sino-Foreign Joint Ventures', *Asia Pacific Journal of Management*, 20(3): 397–408.

Chung, C. (2015) 'The Conceptualization of Global Integration and Local Responsiveness in International HRM Research: A Review and Directions for Future Research', *Discussion Paper JHD-2015-02*.

DiMaggio, P.J. and Powell, W.W. (1983) 'The Iron Cage Revisited: Institutional Isomorphism and Collective Rationality in Organizational Fields', *American Sociological Review*, 48(2): 147–160.

Doz, Y. and Prahalad, C.K. (1986) 'Controlled Variety: A Challenge for Human Resource Management in the MNC', *Human Resource Management*, 25(1): 55–71.

Edwards, T. and Ferner, A. (2002) 'The Renewed "American Challenge": A Review of Employment Practice in US Multinationals', *Industrial Relations Journal*, 33(2): 94–111.

Edwards, T., Sanchez-Mangas, R., Jalette, P., Lavelle, J. and Minbaeva, D. (2016) 'Global Standardization or National Differentiation of HRM Practices in Multinational Companies? A Comparison of Multinationals in Five Countries', *Journal of International Business Studies*, 47(8): 997–1021.

Evans, P., Pucik, V. and Barsoux, J.-L. (2002) *The Global Challenge: Framework for International Human Resource Management*, McGraw-Hill Irwin, New York.

Ferner, A. (1997) 'Country of Origin Effects and HRM in Multinational Companies', *Human Resource Management Journal*, 7(1): 19–37.

Ferner, A., Bélanger, J., Tregaskis, O., Morley, M. and Quintanilla, J. (2013) 'US Multinationals and the Control of Subsidiary Employment Policies', *ILR Review*, 66(3): 645–669.

Greenwood, R., Raynard, M., Kodeih, F., Micelotta, E.R. and Lounsbury, M. (2011) 'Institutional Complexity and Organizational Responses', *Academy of Management Annals*, 5(1): 317–371.

Ghoshal, S., and Bartlett, C.A. (1998). *Managing across borders: The transnational solution* (2nd ed.). Random House, London.

Hall, P.A. and Soskice, D. (2001) *An Introduction to Varieties of Capitalism*, Oxford University Press, Oxford.

Harzing, A.-W., Pudelko, M. and Reiche, S. (2016) 'The Bridging Role of Expatriates and Inpatriates in Knowledge Transfer in Multinational Corporations', *Human Resource Management*, 55(4): 679–695.

Jarillo, J.C. and Martinez, J.I. (1990) 'Different Roles for Subsidiaries: The Case of Multinational Corporations in Spain', *Strategic Management Journal*, 11(7): 501–512.

Lawrence, P. and Lorsch, J. (1967) *Organization and Environment: Managing Differentiation and Integration*, Division of Research, Graduate School of Business Administration, Harvard University, Boston, MA.

Lawrence, P. and Lorsch, J. (1969). *Developing Organizations: Diagnosis and Action*, Addison-Wesley, Boston.

Luo, X. (2002) 'Organizational Dynamics and Global Integration: A Perspective from Subsidiary Managers', *Journal of International Management*, 8(2): 189–215.

Peng, M.W. (2021) *Global Strategy*, Cengage Learning, Boston, MA.

Perlmutter, H.V. (1969) 'The Tortuous Evolution of the Multinational Corporation', *Columbia Journal of World Business*, 4(1): 9–18.

Prahalad, C.K. and Doz, L.Y. (1987) *The Multinational Mission: Balancing Local Demand and Global Vision*, Simon and Schuster, New York.

Pudelko, M. (2006) 'Universalities, Particularities and Singularities in Cross-National Management Research', *International Studies of Management & Organization*, 36(4): 9–37.

Pudelko, M. (2020) 'Bringing Context Back into International Business Studies: Own Research Experiences, Reflections and Suggestions for Future Research', *International Studies of Management & Organization*, 50(4): 317–333.

Pudelko, M. and Harzing, A.W. (2007) 'Country-of-Origin, Localization, or Dominance Effect? An Empirical Investigation of HRM Practices in Foreign Subsidiaries', *Human Resource Management*, 46(4): 535–559.

Rosenzweig, P.M. (2006) 'The Dual Logics behind International Human Resource Management: Pressures for Global Integration and Local Responsiveness', In G.K. Stahl and I. Björkman (Eds.), *Handbook of Research in International Human Resource Management*, 36–48. Edward Elgar, Cheltenham.

Rosenzweig, P.M. and Nohria, N. (1994) 'Influences on Human Resource Management Practices in Multinational Corporations', *Journal of International Business Studies*, 25(2): 229–251.

Roth, K. and Morrison, A.J. (1990) 'An Empirical Analysis of the Integration-Responsiveness Framework in Global Industries', *Journal of International Business Studies*, 21(4): 541–564.

Schuler, R., Dowling, P. and De Cieri, H. (1993) 'An Integrative Framework of Strategic International Human Resource Management', *Journal of Management*, 19(2): 419–459.

Smith, C. and Meiksins, P. (1995) 'System, Society and Dominance Effects in Cross-National Organizational Analysis', *Work, Employment & Society*, 9(2): 241–267.

Taylor, S., Beechler, S. and Napier, N. (1996) 'Toward an Integrative Model of Strategic International Human Resource Management', *Academy of Management Review*, 21(4): 959–985.

Verbeke, A. (2013) *International Business Strategy*, Cambridge University Press, Cambridge.

Yip, G.S. (1995) *Total Global Strategy: Managing for Worldwide Competitive Advantage*, Prentice Hall, Englewood Cliffs, NJ.

Ingmar Björkman

PAULA JOHNSON: BUILDING A WORLD-CLASS PRODUCT DEVELOPMENT CENTER IN CHINA[1]

INTRODUCTION

PAULA JOHNSON, THE HEAD OF the Product Development Center (PDC) of Advanced Technologies Systems in Shanghai, had been in China for five months. She was the first person in the Product Development Center when she arrived in Shanghai in April 2018. Thinking back over the period she had spent in China so far, she felt that things had gone quite well. The PDC was now up and running, and today, on September 12, 2018, Paula welcomed its 16th employee.

Nonetheless, Paula still had a number of concerns. The PDC was still rather small, and it was possible for her to interact with and influence all employees. As the PDC would grow significantly over the next year, she wanted to make sure to create a healthy and positive atmosphere and orientation towards work. Her vision was to create a world-class PDC in Shanghai, but how to do that in a country that traditionally had been a recipient of technological know-how from abroad, and what measures should be taken to convince other parts of Advanced Technologies Systems to engage in joint development projects with the PDC? And even if she managed to develop the capabilities needed to build a world-class PDC through careful recruitment and selection as well as good investments in training and development, how were they to retain the employees in a market where job hopping was common, money apparently an important reason why people switched jobs, and well-educated people had ample opportunities in other companies? Basically, her question was: Would lessons on how to manage people obtained in North America and Europe also apply in the People's Republic of China?

PRODUCT DEVELOPMENT IN HI TECH SYSTEMS

Advanced Technologies Systems was established in Stockholm, Sweden, in 1986. Already by the late 1990s, Advanced Technologies Systems had become known

DOI: 10.4324/9781003247272-5

as one of Europe's most innovative firms in its industry. The growth continued in the new century, with firm profitability remaining healthy. The company is currently one of the three largest firms in its industry. Advanced Technologies Systems' global manufacturing comprises six production facilitates in five different countries on three different continents. Approximately 45 percent of sales come from Europe, but the United States and Japan and, increasingly, China have become important markets.

Product development is seen as key to the success of Advanced Technologies Systems. Almost 20 percent of Advanced Technologies Systems' employees are working in research and development. Advanced Technologies Systems has PDCs in Sweden, the United Kingdom, the United States, Japan, Hong Kong (China), and, most recently, Mainland China. There is a global PDC management group headed by Johan Lind that consists of all the PDC heads and which convenes once a month. Johan Lind reports to the head of global product development in Advanced Technologies Systems, Anders Jonsson.

The responsibility for product development programs resides with the global business lines and the so-called "platforms" (such as the Japanese user interface). Research programs within the business lines that lead to actual products also draw on the work being done within the platforms. In each PDC, people work on projects related to both Advanced Technologies Systems' business lines and platforms.

A full-grown PDC has some 4–500 employees, a variety of competencies, and is expected to have the capabilities needed to develop an entire new product. There are several reasons why the company has established a whole portfolio of PDCs. First, different areas vary in terms of technologies and standards relevant for the business. Therefore, it makes sense to locate research and development activities in locations where the technologies reside. Second, by dispersing PDCs to different parts of the world, the company can move product creation activities in response to environmental and market changes. Third, it enables Advanced Technologies Systems to draw on human resources not available in one location. Advanced Technologies Systems has traditionally done most of its product creation in Sweden, but as a result of the growth of Advanced Technologies Systems, there are not enough engineering students in the whole country to satisfy its needs. Fourth, products need to be locally adapted, and this is easier to carry out locally than in a distant PDC.

In a typical research program, most of the work on the key components of a new product is done within one single "core" PDC. Within each project, there is a fairly clear distribution of responsibilities across the PDCs involved. Other "peripheral" PDCs are typically involved in developing locally adapted variants of the product. Most of the work has typically already been done in the core PDC before the other PDCs get involved (although in order to ensure that the necessary local adaptations of the final product can be made at a later stage, people from each of the geographical regions are involved in steering groups during the conceptualization stage). The knowledge transfer mostly takes place through people from the PDCs who visit the core PDC for one to three months to work with the product development people before they return to their own units. At the point when the project has been established in the peripheral PDCs, the focal project leader reports to the global head of the focal product development project and to the head of their own PDC. Heavy emphasis is put on establishing and following up project milestones.

ADVANCED TECHNOLOGIES SYSTEMS IN CHINA

The People's Republic of China started opening up to the outside world in 1979. In 1995, the Advanced Technologies Systems group established a representative office in Shanghai, and in 2006 its first subsidiary was established. By the beginning of 2018, Advanced Technologies Systems already had four subsidiaries in China. Advanced Technologies Systems had become a significant player in the rapidly growing Chinese market, where it was competing with Western, Japanese, and also increasingly strong local competitors. China had become one of Advanced Technologies Systems' most important markets. Most of the products sold in China were produced in the firm's local factories.

However, Advanced Technologies Systems so far had no Product Development Center in China. After 2016, there was a growing consensus that this neglect had to be rectified. A decision to establish a PDC in Shanghai was made by Advanced Technologies Systems' management board in January 2018. Paula Johnson was chosen to head the PDC.

PAULA JOHNSON

Paula Johnson was born in California in 1979. After graduating from college with a major in management her first job was with a major US industrial firm. As a part of this job, in 2007, she spent six months in Hong Kong. During her assignment in Hong Kong, she "fell in love with Asia and China. Since that moment she knew that she was going to return to Asia." Paula also met her future partner, who moved with her to the United States. In 2012 Paula did an MBA and then started to work in a small start-up company. In 2014 Paula was persuaded by one of her previous colleagues to join Advanced Technologies Systems. When joining Advanced Technologies Systems, Paula was appointed operations manager. After some months, she was asked to head the Engineering unit of the new Product Development Centers that was built in Philadelphia. Paula accepted the job, which meant that she would be responsible for the largest unit of the PDC. Paula and her new boss, Curtis O'Neill, soon became very close, with Paula acting as the second in charge of the PDC. Paula recalls:

> I learnt a lot from Curtis. He was very people-oriented. He would make sure that you get an opportunity to get into an environment where you either learn or you don't. He gave people lots of challenges, lots of learning opportunities, where they could prove themselves. He would also quite

directly point to areas of improvement. He also underlined the importance of networking, how to build networks of people that you can draw on."

One of the things that Paula learnt soon after joining Advanced Technologies Systems was the importance of having good personal contacts within the company. Advanced Technologies Systems' global product development worked to a significant extent through informal contacts across units, and it was crucial to be well connected. Her choice of the five product line managers in the department reflected this view. While people in the Philadelphia-unit expected and pressured her to choose local people for the positions, she selected three expatriates and only two local employees:

> People thought I was taking promotions away from Philadelphia. I had my own views in mind – we needed to be connected to the other centers. If you're well connected people trust you to do a good job within a research program, and it is also easier to get technical help if needed. I then used lots of interviews with the candidates to convince people about their capabilities and to get some buy-in from the other managers. I also made sure to tell people that the objective was to fill the positions with local people in two to three years. In fact, the line managers had as an explicit objective to develop a local replacement for themselves.

During the next 18 months, Paula visited Sweden several times. She often took part in the global PDC group meetings as O'Neill's stand-in. The global PDC management also knew that she was interested in returning to Asia, something Paula had mentioned from the outset in her performance management discussions.

ESTABLISHING THE PRODUCT DEVELOPMENT CENTER

During the summer of 2017, the global PDC management group decided that a feasibility study on the possible creation of a PDC in the People's Republic of China should be carried out. In October, Paula was asked to become involved in the project. Her task was to examine the data and write a report on whether or not a PDC should be established, and, if so, where in China it should be located. By that time Paula also knew that she would be the preferred candidate as head of the PDC (if approved). In January 2018, Advanced Technologies Systems' global management board approved the establishment of a PDC in Shanghai. One of the advantages of Shanghai was that the PDC would be able to use the existing Advanced Technologies Systems organization in the city. It would be easier to learn from the experiences of Advanced Technologies Systems' largest Chinese production site and its China headquarters, both of which were located in Shanghai. In February, Paula went to China on a pre-visit mainly to meet with people in the Advanced Technologies Systems-organization.

When it became clear that the PDC would be established, Paula started to look for staff. There was no established policy for people management within the global product creation organization, but Paula was told to draw on the HR department at the Advanced Technologies Systems group in China for support. She thought that she would initially need approximately ten positions for expatriates, and it would be of crucial importance to find suitable people for the key positions.

> It was networking all the way – the social networks were very important! There were many people who knew that I would do it and some of them contacted me. I contacted and spoke to lots of people in all parts of the Advanced Technologies Systems organization. I wanted the candidates to have experience in launching Advanced Technologies Systems products in China. They should know the Chinese environment and culture. This meant that there were only a very small number of people who fulfilled my criteria. And they had to commit to staying at least two or even three years, which is not usual in Advanced Technologies Systems. Towards the end of the period they start hunting for another job anyhow.

Paula finally identified four persons she wanted: one Swede, and three persons from the People's Republic of China who had studied and worked for several years abroad (two in the United States, one in Sweden). One of them she already knew in advance, the others she had identified through her networking activities. All the Chinese candidates had a strong education background, with degrees from top Chinese universities before leaving the country for overseas graduate studies. Everybody had at least some experience in leading own teams:

> I talked a lot to them. Have they thought about living in China? Were they (the Chinese) conscious about the challenges involved in going back to China? For instance, people may be jealous of them making much more money, traveling abroad and having much higher positions than they themselves had? Have they realized that it's going to be a start-up operation, and that it may be difficult to get things started and people on board?

To persuade the persons she wanted to accept relocating to China, Paula tried to create a positive and challenging vision for the PDC. To date, Advanced Technologies Systems had probably not done enough to meet the needs of the Chinese-speaking countries. Did it want to become a part of the process of creating a world-class PDC in China? The PDC would become responsible for the Chinese user interface platform – did it want to participate in the challenge of its development? Being restricted by the company's expatriate compensation policy, which was built on a standardized job grading system, she was able to offer competitive but not exceptional salaries. She finally managed to persuade her four top candidates to accept a job in the PDC. They all knew each other from their previous jobs. During the late Spring of 2018, she found some additional people in the global Advanced Technologies Systems organization who also agreed to take up jobs in Shanghai:

A part of my strategy was to get people from different Product Development Centers. By having these people in my organization we are able to easily reach into the other PDCs which is particularly important in the beginning as we are dependent on doing parts of larger projects in collaboration with other centers. If we have good people who have credibility from each of the other PDCs, we will be recognized and seen as trustworthy.

But Paula did not see technical competence as the only important criterion. In her view:

> 80 percent is attitude. It doesn't matter what you can if you lack drive. With drive you can always fill in the gaps … Perhaps it has something to do with my own background. I have had to manage without an engineering education in an organization and industry that are extremely technology-intensive.

The PDC was to report to the Global PDC management and to Advanced Technologies Systems' China country management. As agreed upon with the Global PDC management group, PDC Shanghai would be responsible for product creation in the Chinese language area, including Mainland China, Hong Kong, Singapore, and Taiwan. In the beginning, it would mostly work on limited parts of larger products in collaboration with other global PDCs, for example, on software and on Chinese-specific applications. The long-term vision was eventually to have the capabilities to build new products in China.

THE START OF THE PRODUCT DEVELOPMENT CENTER

Paula and her family finally arrived in Shanghai on April 12, 2018. The next employee arrived from overseas in May, and by September, the unit already had 16 employees, half of whom had been recruited from abroad. Paula's estimate was that long-term, 10–15 percent of the employees would be from overseas, but that it would take three to four years to decrease the proportion of expatriates to that level:

> When you build a home, first you build the foundations. You need to make sure that the foundations are in place – the recruitment process, human resources management, finance. Then you need key managers to build the organization around it.

In the recruitment of local employees, the PDC was collaborating closely with Advanced Technologies Systems' human resources department. After job descriptions and job grade levels had been determined by the PDC, the HR department would announce the position using both advertisements and the home page of the corporation, receive CVs, carry out initial screening of the candidates, and arrange for interviews and assessment of the applicants.

The interviews were conducted by a minimum of two PDC managers, who also acted as observers in the assessment centers organized by the HR department. For the assessment of applicants in China, Advanced Technologies Systems used "The Space Shuttle," a game where the applicants worked together in a group with the objective of reaching an agreement on how to build a space shuttle. By observing the applicants involved in a problem-solving situation where they also interacted with each other, the observers could draw their own conclusions about the applicants. Recruitment and selection of local employees largely resembled practices used elsewhere in the global Advanced Technologies Systems organization.

Some other Western firms had apparently made larger adjustments in their selection practices in China. For instance, Paula had heard that Shell already many years ago had changed its selection practices based on an in-depth study of its existing Chinese managers and entry-level management trainees. Traditionally, Shell focused on analytical and problem-solving abilities. However, when, for example, applicants were asked to identify the strengths and weaknesses of the Chinese educational system and then say what they would do to remedy deficiencies if they were the Minister of Education, if there were any responses at all, they tended to be uniformly bland. It was also found that the kind of "Who would you throw out of the airplane?" question commonly used in the West tended to engender a "learned helplessness effect" on the part of Chinese university graduates, who had excelled at clearly defined tasks in a familiar environment and who had "learnt" to respond to the unfamiliar by simply freezing. Shell's system identified the Chinese education system as the chief culprit. The educational system is hierarchical, extremely competitive, and largely based on examination of rote learning. Problem-oriented interaction among strangers is unnatural and problematic for most Chinese people. Therefore, evaluating the decision-making skills, communication skills, analytical problem-solving abilities, and leadership capabilities of applicants based on hypothetical cases solved in assessment situations may be very difficult. As a result, Shell's study recommended the use of real case studies rather than hypothetical questions.[2]

Competence development would probably be key to the success of the PDC, both in terms of localizing its operations and in producing good results. By mid-September, the new employees had mostly worked on small projects, like setting up the IT system. A couple of people had also been sent to other units to work in the field with experienced engineers for three weeks. Formal training would be important, and the PDC would need to collaborate with Advanced Technologies Systems' HR department on the course program offered to the PDC employees. To what extent should the Chinese employees receive the same content and delivery as Advanced Technologies Systems employees elsewhere? In China, the Confucianist and Communist-influenced Chinese educational system, in which the learner is a mostly passive receiver who is obedient to the instructor, tends to create linear rather than lateral thinking and precedent-based problem-solving where the focus in on getting the "right" answer.

Nonetheless, hands-on on-the-job coaching would be even more important for the development of the new employees. Most of the responsibility for coaching would obviously fall on the experienced Advanced Technologies Systems employees, but it would also be important to bring in people from other PDCs for visits in Shanghai. Coaching of the expatriates would be extremely important, Paula thought. She had already been discussing it at length with the managers she had hired, but she was not sure whether that was enough, especially when the unit would grow over the next couple of years. She certainly would not be able to coach all the expatriates by herself.

In Advanced Technologies Systems' globally standardized performance management system, all employees should hold performance management discussions with their superiors. Within this system, individual objectives are established and followed up. According to company policy, the individual's objectives must be specific and if possible measurable, key activities for how to reach the objectives must be specified, criteria for how to evaluate the performance agreed upon, and finally, development plans decided upon. Paula's aim was that every new employee would take part in their first performance management discussion within a month after they joined the organization. All Advanced Technologies Systems superiors in China were trained in how to use the system, but there was still a question of how the "Western" system would be implemented in the Chinese culture characterized by respect for hierarchy, "face," and harmonious personal relationships.

Paula had also given the question of the relationship between employee competence development and career progress quite a lot of thought. In Advanced Technologies Systems worldwide, people achieved high status by having excellent technological knowledge and skills rather than having made a successful career as managers. However:

> In China especially the young people expect to get a new title every year; otherwise they had better start looking for another company. The speed of expected career progression clearly differs from the West. To develop the level of competence required for the next career step will be a challenge. Can they achieve it once a year? I think very few will.

The compensation of employees would follow Advanced Technologies Systems' policies. Managers and team leaders were compensated based on both business and individual performance. High-level executives and senior managers had a large business performance component in their bonus system, while the compensation of lower-level employees was mostly based on their individual performance. In the Shanghai PDC, individual performance would be evaluated based on four to five objectives. Paula required that the objectives had to be measurable on a ten-point scale. For instance, a manager's performance could be evaluated based on the manager's ability to fill positions in their group, employee satisfaction (as measured by company-wide surveys), employee turnover, the team's ability to stay within budget, and some measure of quality (to be determined in discussions between the manager and Paula). Each person's performance was evaluated every six months, and bonuses paid accordingly. The target bonus was 10 percent of the person's base salary, with 20 percent as maximum. People working on a specific development project were not evaluated every six months, the evaluation followed the milestones of the project instead. The bonus element was also somewhat larger for people working on projects than for other PDC members.

Paula believed that the compensation system would work well in China. Having clear objectives and rewards linked with their fulfillment would help send a clear message to the employees: your performance equals what you deliver – not the personal connections, or *guanxi*, that you have! Nonetheless, at least in the start-up phase of the PDC, it might be somewhat difficult to establish feasible objectives for the employees. Additionally, there had been reports from other foreign firms that there was a tendency among local employees to set objectives that would be easily accomplished by the subordinates.

LOOKING TOWARDS THE FUTURE

Analyzing the start-up phase of the PDC, Paula found that many things had gone quite smoothly. For instance, the two Chinese "returnees" who had joined the PDC so far (the third was still in Sweden, but would relocate next month) appeared to be doing well. Although China had changed a lot since they left the country some ten years earlier, their interaction with the local employees seemed to go smoothly.

Managing the growth would certainly be a challenge in the next couple of years, Paula thought. For instance, local employees would have to be taught to manage themselves and to take responsibility – behaviors not automatically understood and accepted in the Chinese environment. While Advanced Technologies Systems' culture was non-hierarchical and meritocratic, the Chinese culture is hierarchical, and the "face" of superiors could be at stake if subordinates took their own initiatives rather than waiting for orders from their superiors. Furthermore, during the Communist regime since 1949 Chinese people had been discouraged from engaging in competitive and entrepreneurial behavior. The Chinese proverb "the early bird gets shot" aptly illustrates the reluctance on the part of Chinese employees to engage in the kind of innovative behavior that Paula wanted to see in the PDC. On the other hand, Paula had seen several Chinese employees changing their behavior significantly abroad. What should they do to promote this behavior in the Shanghai PDC?

Paula was also looking for somebody to work closely with Advanced Technologies Systems' HR function. This person would work closely with her and the line managers to define future competence needs and how they could be met. "So far, I guess I have fulfilled this role, but I'm afraid that neither I nor line managers will have time enough to pay sufficient attention to this issue in the future."

Finally, Paula was concerned about retention: "I have also been told by [a human resources expert] that a small salary difference may make a person switch job." Paula believed that money would not be key to retaining employees, though. Creating a positive, family-like atmosphere might help. Paula had started a tradition of everyone in her unit meeting for a snack on Monday mornings. She also made a conscious effort to spend time talking to people in the department. Furthermore, she had invited people out for lunch and dinner. To maintain a positive relationship between the foreign and local employees, she tried to coach the expatriates to do the same. All this had apparently contributed to their starting to circulate rumors that "things are done a bit differently in the PDC." She was now thinking about whether to involve the employees' families in some way. Formal team building exercises should probably also be undertaken.

There were so many things to do ... Paula looked out of her window in one of the many fashionable buildings in the Pudong area of Shanghai – where should she start?

PLEASE ANSWER THE FOLLOWING QUESTIONS

1. Evaluate the staffing of key positions (i.e., who has been chosen for different positions, and how) in the Product Development Center. What has Paula Johnson done well/poorly? Why?
2. Please evaluate the people management practices for (i) expatriates and (ii) local employees in the Product Development Center. What has Paula Johnson done well/poorly? Why?
3. What should Paula Johnson now do in terms of people management? Why?

NOTES

1. While the names, dates, and some other information have been changed in order not to reveal the identities of the company and individuals, this chapter is based on real events.
2. Economist Intelligence Unit (1998): *China on the Couch*. September 28, 3–4.

Evalde Mutabazi and C. Brooklyn Derr

SOCOMETAL
Rewarding African Workers

I T WAS A MOST UNUSUAL meeting at a local cafe in Dakar. Diop, a young Senegalese engineer who was educated at one of France's elite engineering *grandes écoles* in Lyon, was meeting with N'Diaye, a model factory worker to whom other workers from his tribe often turned when there were personal or professional difficulties. N'Diaye was a chief's son, but he didn't belong to the union and he was not an official representative of any group within the factory.

Socometal is a metal container and can company. While multinational, this particular plant is a joint venture wherein 52 percent is owned by the French parent company and 48 percent is Senegalese. Over the last 20 years, Socometal has grown in size from 150 to 800 employees, and it has returns of about 400 million FCFA (African francs) or $144 million. The firm is often held up as a model in terms of its Africanization of management policies, whereby most managers are now West African, with only eight to ten top managers coming from France.

During the meeting, N'Diaye asked Diop if he would accept an agreement to pay each worker for two extra hours in exchange for a 30 percent increase in daily production levels. If so, N'Diaye would be the guarantor for this target production level that would enable the company to meet the order in the shortest time period. N'Diaye said with a smile:

> If you accept my offer, we could even produce more. We are at 12,000 [units] a day, but we've never been confronted with this situation. I would never have made this proposal to Mr. Bernard but, if you agree today, I will see that the 20,000 [unit] level is reached as of tomorrow evening. I'll ask each worker to find ways of going faster, to communicate this to the others and to help each other if they have problems.

DOI: 10.4324/9781003247272-6

Mr. Olivier Bernard, a graduate of Ecole Centrale in Paris (one of France's more prestigious engineering schools), was the French production manager, and Diop was the assistant production manager. Mr. Bernard was about 40, and had not succeeded at climbing the hierarchal ladder in the parent company. Some reported that this was due to his tendency to be arrogant, uncommunicative, and negative. His family lived in a very nice neighborhood in Marseille, and it was his practice to come to Dakar, precisely organize the work using various flowcharts, tell Diop exactly what was expected by a certain date, and then return to France for periods of two to six weeks. This time, he maintained that he had contracted a virus and needed to return for medical treatment.

Shortly before Mr. Bernard fell ill, Socometal agreed to a contract requiring it to reach, in a short time, a volume of production never before achieved. Mr. Bernard, after having done a quick calculation, declared: "We'll never get that from our workers – *c'est impossible!*" After organizing as best he could, he left for Marseille.

Diop pondered what N'Diaye had proposed, and then he sought the opinions of influential people in different departments. Some of the French and Italian expatriates told him they were sure that the workers would not do overtime, but most agreed it was worth a try. Two days after his meeting with N'Diaye, Diop felt confident enough to take the risk. The next morning, N'Diaye and Diop met in front of the factory and Diop gave his agreement on the condition that the 30 percent rise in daily production levels be reached that evening. He and the management would take a final decision on a wage increase only after assessing the results and on evaluating the ability of the workers to maintain this level of production in the long run.

The reasons given by the French and Italian expatriates for why the Senegalese would not perform overtime or speed up their productivity are interesting. One older French logistics manager said: "Africans aren't lazy but they work to live, and once they have enough they refuse to do more. It won't make any sense to them to work harder or longer for more pay." And the Italian human resource manager exclaimed:

> We already tried two years ago to get them to work faster. We threatened to fire anyone caught going too slow or missing more than one day's work per month, and we told them they would all get bonuses if they reached the production target. We had the sense that they were laughing behind our backs and doing just enough to keep their jobs while maintaining the same production levels.

Four days after their first negotiation, the contract between Diop and N'Diaye went into action. Throughout the day, N'Diaye gave his job on the line to two of his colleagues in order to have enough time and energy to mobilize all the workers. The workers found the agreement an excellent initiative. "This will be a chance to earn a bit more money, but especially to show them [the French management] that we're more capable than they think," declared one of the Senegalese foremen. From its first day of application, the formula worked wonders. Working only one extra hour per day, every work unit produced 8 percent more than was forecast by Diop and N'Diaye. Over the next two months, the daily production level varied between 18,000 and 22,000 units per day – between 38 and 43 percent more than the previous daily production. It was at this production level, never experienced during the history of the company, that Mr. Bernard found things when he returned from his illness.

Diop said:

> I was very happy to see the workers so proud of their results, so satisfied with their pay raise, and finally really involved in their work ... In view of some expatriates' attitudes, it was a veritable miracle ... But, instead of rejoicing, Mr. Bernard reproached me for giving two hours' pay to the workers, who were only really doing one hour more than usual. "By making this absurd decision," he said, "you have put the management in danger of losing its authority over the workers. You have acted against house rules ... You have created a precedent too costly for our business. Now, we must stop this ridiculous operation as quickly as possible. We must apply work regulations." And he slammed the door in my face before I had the time to say anything. After all, he has more power than me in this company, which is financed 52 percent by French people. Nevertheless, I thought I would go to see the managing director and explain myself and present my arguments. I owed this action to N'Diaye and his workers, who had trusted me, and I didn't care if it made Bernard any angrier.

In the mean time, the workers decided to maintain the new production level in order to honor their word to N'Diaye and Diop. A foreman and friend of N'Diaye stated, "At least he knows how to listen and speak to us like men."

The foreman indicated, however, that they might return to the former production level if Bernard dealt with them as he did before.

CASE DISCUSSION QUESTIONS

1. What are the underlying cultural assumptions for Mr. Bernard, and how are these different from the basic assumptions of N'Diaye and Diop?
2. What would you do if you were Bernard's boss, the managing director?
3. In what ways is a reward system a cultural phenomenon? How might you design an effective reward system for Senegal?

Roger Hallowell, David Bowen, and Carin-Isabel Knoop

FOUR SEASONS GOES TO PARIS*

Europe is different from North America, and Paris is very different. I did not say difficult. I said different.

— A senior Four Seasons manager

THE LINKAGE BETWEEN SERVICE CULTURE AND COMPETITIVE ADVANTAGE

THE ENDURING SUCCESS OF SERVICE organizations such as Southwest Airlines, the Walt Disney Company, Wal-Mart, and USAA (among others) is frequently attributed in no small degree to their corporate cultures. These companies have built and maintained organizational cultures in which everyone is focused on delivering high customer value, including service, and individuals behave accordingly. The culture influences how employees behave, which, in turn, shapes the value that customers receive, in part through the thousands of daily encounters between employees and customers.

Corporate culture has been linked to competitive advantage in companies, for better or worse,[1] and in service companies, in particular.[2] Culture is so important in service companies because of its effect on multiple factors affecting customer value, factors as critical as employee behavior and as mundane (but important) as facility cleanliness. These aspects are especially visible to customers, who often co-produce a service with employees. In many services, employee and customer interactions take place continually, in many parts of the organization, so that no realistic amount of supervision can ever exercise sufficient control over employee behavior. Under these circumstances, culture becomes

* Originally published in The Academy of Management Executive.

DOI: 10.4324/9781003247272-7

one of management's most effective, if unobtrusive, tools to influence employee thoughts, feelings, and, most importantly, behavior.

UNDERSTANDING CORPORATE CULTURE

Our model of corporate culture, which uses Schein[3] as a point of departure, consists of the following four components: underlying assumptions, values, employee perceptions of management practices, and cultural artifacts.

Underlying Assumptions

These are basic assumptions regarding the workplace, such as the assumption that subordinates should fulfill their job requirements as a condition of employment.

Values

These are those things that are viewed as most important in an organizational setting, such as cost control, customer satisfaction, and teamwork.

Values exist in two forms in organizations. The first is what can be termed "espoused values," which are what senior managers or company publications say the values are.

The second form is "enacted values," which are what employees infer the values to be. Although enacted values, per se, are invisible, employees infer what they are by examining the evidence found in the next two components of culture: management practices and cultural artifacts. These two components are more readily observed than assumptions and values.

Employee Perceptions of Management Practices (Particularly Relating to Human Resources): Policies and Behaviors

Employees' views of practices such as selection, training, performance appraisal, job design, reward systems, supervisory practices, and so on shape their perceptions of what values are actually being enacted in a setting. For example, although customer service may be an espoused value, if job applicants are not carefully screened on service attitude, or if employees who provide great service are not recognized and rewarded, then employees will not believe that management truly values service. In short: culture is what employees perceive that management believes.

Cultural Artifacts

These include heroes, rituals, stories, jargon, and tangibles such as the appearance of employees and facilities. Again, given the espoused value of customer service, if jargon used to characterize customers is usually derogatory, then a strong service culture is unlikely to emerge.

In contrast, if espoused values are enacted — and thus reflected in policies, management behaviors, and cultural artifacts — then a culture may emerge in which senior management and employees share similar service-relevant thoughts, feelings, and patterns of behavior. This behavior has the potential to enhance customer value and contribute to competitive advantage.

EXPORTING CORPORATE CULTURE: CAN CULTURE TRAVEL ACROSS BORDERS?

If a company succeeds in creating a corporate culture that contributes to competitive advantage in its home country, can it successfully "export" that corporate culture to another country — particularly if that country's national culture is strongly distinct, as is the case in France?

The Issue of Flexibility versus Consistency

Will an organization's *corporate* culture "clash" or "fit" with a different *national* culture? The key consideration here is what components of corporate culture link most tightly to competitive advantage and, as a consequence, must be managed *consistently* across country borders — even if they seem to clash with the culture of the new country. Alternatively, are there components of culture that are not critical to the linkage? If so, *flexibility* may enhance the competitiveness of the corporate culture given the different national culture.[4]

One way to frame this analysis is around whether the potential clash between corporate and national culture is over the corporate values themselves, i.e., *what* they are, or over the manner of their implementation, i.e., *how* they are enacted (specifically, management practices and cultural forms). Is there a clash between core corporate values and core country values? If so, and if those core values are critical to competitive advantage, then perhaps the company cannot be successful in that setting. If the clash is over how values are enacted, then some management practices or cultural forms can be modified in the new setting. However, this requires managers to ask which practices or forms can be modified, enhancing the competitive advantage of the corporate culture, and which practices, if modified, will undermine corporate culture.

In short, all of the elements of corporate culture can be thought of as the threads in a sweater: when a thread sticks out of a sweater, sometimes it is wisely removed, enhancing the overall appearance. However, sometimes removing a thread will unravel the entire sweater. Managers must determine which aspects of their corporate cultures will "stick out" in a new national environment and whether modifying or eliminating them will enhance the organization or weaken it.

FOUR SEASONS HOTELS AND RESORTS: OVERVIEW

In 2002, Four Seasons Hotels and Resorts was arguably the world's leading operator of luxury hotels, managing 53 properties in 24 countries. Being able to replicate "consistently exceptional service" around the world and across cultures was at the heart of the chain's international success and sustained advantage.

For Four Seasons, "consistently exceptional service" meant providing high-quality, truly personalized service to enable guests to *maximize the value of their time*, however guests defined doing so. Corporate culture contributed to the firm's success in two ways. First was through the values that the organization espoused. For Four Seasons, these were personified in the Golden Rule: "Treat others as you wish they would treat you." Second was the set of behaviors that employees and managers displayed, in effect the enactment of the firm's values. The organizational capability of translating core values into enacted behaviors created competitive advantage at Four Seasons. Doing so required managers to address a central question as they expanded into new countries: what do we need to keep consistent, and what should be flexible, i.e., what should we adapt to the local market?

Performance

Four Seasons generally operated (as opposed to owned) mid-sized luxury hotels and resorts. From 1996 through 2000 (inclusive), Four Seasons increased revenues from $121 million to $347.5 million and earnings from $55.7 million to $125.8 million, a 22.6 percent compounded annual growth rate (CAGR). Operating margins increased from 58.8 percent to 67.9 percent during the same period. Four Seasons' 2001 revenue per room (RevPAR), an important hospitality industry measure, was 32 percent above that of its primary US competitors and 27 percent higher than that of its European competitors. Growth plans were to open five to seven new luxury properties per year, predominantly outside of North America.

Four Seasons entered the French market by renovating and operating the Hotel George V, a historic Parisian landmark. The hotel was renamed the Four Seasons Hotel George V Paris (F. S. George V).

International Structure

Each Four Seasons property was managed by a general manager responsible for supervising the day-to-day operations of a single property. Compensation was, in part, based on the property's performance. Hotel general managers had a target bonus of 30 percent of base compensation; 25 percent of the bonus was based on people measures (employee attitudes), 25 percent on product (service quality), and 50 percent on profit.

Four Seasons' management believed that the firm's regional management structure was a key component of its ability to deliver and maintain the highest and most consistent service standards at each property in a cost-effective manner. General managers reported directly to one of the 13 regional vice presidents or directly to one of the two senior vice presidents, operations. A regional marketing director, an area director of finance, and a regional human resources director completed each support team. The majority of these individuals were full-time employees of a Four Seasons-managed property, with a portion of their time devoted to regional matters, including both routine management and deciding how to customize Four Seasons' operating practice to the region.

Management

Four Seasons' top management team was noted for its longevity, many having been at the firm for over 25 years. Characteristics that executives attributed to their peers included an international flair, a respect for modesty and compassion, and a "no excuses" mentality.

Italian in Italy, French in France

The firm's top managers were very comfortable in a variety of international settings. Antoine Corinthios, president, Europe, Middle East, and Africa, for example, was said to be "Italian in Italy, French in France." Born and educated in Cairo, Corinthios then spent 20 years in Chicago but described himself as a world citizen. He was as much of a cultural chameleon as he wanted Four Seasons hotels to be. "When I speak the language of the environment I am in, I start to think in the language I am in and adapt to that culture. If you are going global, you cannot be one way," he explained.

No Bragging, No Excuses

Modesty, compassion, and discipline were also important. A manager who stayed with Four Seasons from the prior management of the George V described the Four Seasons due diligence team that came to the property as "very professional and not pretentious; detail-oriented; and interested in people. They did not come telling me that all I did was wrong," he remembered, "and showed a lot of compassion. The people are good, but still modest — many people in the industry can be very full of themselves." Importantly, excuses were not tolerated at Four Seasons. "Oh, but we have just been open a year" or "The people here do not understand" were not acceptable statements.

Strong Allegiance to the Firm

Both corporate and field managers often referred to the firm as a "family," complete with rules, traditions, and tough love. There was a strong "one-firm sentiment" on the part of managers in the field; they worked for the firm, not for the individual property to which they were assigned. For example, a general manager explained, "We are happy to let stars go to other properties to help them."

Service Orientation

Customer service extended to all levels in the organization. Managers sometimes assisted in clearing restaurant tables in passing. "If I see that something needs to get done," a manager explained, "I do it."

FOUR SEASONS' APPROACH TO INTERNATIONAL GROWTH

> Today, we have opened enough properties overseas that we can go into any city or town and pull people together to fulfill our mission.
>
> Isadore Sharp, Founder and CEO

Diversity and Singularity

One of the things Four Seasons managers were wary about was being perceived as an "American" company. They found it useful in Europe to position Four Seasons as the Canadian company it was. One noted:

> The daughter of a property owner once told us, "I do not want you to be the way Americans are." She assumed that Americans say, "Do it my way or take the highway." Canadians are seen as more internationally minded and respectful of other value systems.

According to Corinthios, "Our strength is our diversity and our singularity. While the essence of the local culture may vary, the process for opening and operating a hotel is the same everywhere." He continued:

> My goal is to provide an international hotel to the business or luxury leisure traveler looking for comfort and service. The trick is to take it a couple of notches up, or sideways, to adapt to the market you are in. Our standards are universal, e.g., getting your message on time, clean room, good break-fast; being cared for by an engaging, anticipating and responding staff; being able to treat yourself to an exciting and innovative meal – these are global. This is the fundamental value. What changes is that people do it with their own style, grace, and personality; in some cultures you add the strong local temperament. For example, an Italian concierge has his own style and flair. In Turkey or Egypt you experience different hospitality.

As a result, "Each hotel is tailor made" and adapted to its national environment, noted David Crowl, vice president sales and marketing, Europe, Middle East, and Africa:

> Issy Sharp once told me that one of our key strengths is diversity. McDonald's is the same all over. We do not want to be that way. We are not a cookie cutter company. We try to make each property represent its location. In the rooms, we have 40 to 50 square meters to create a cul-tural destination without being offensive. When you wake up in our hotel in Istanbul, you know that you are in Turkey. People know that they will get 24-hour room service, a custom-made mattress, and a marble bathroom, but they also know that they are going to be part of a local community.

According to David Richey, president of Richey International, a firm Four Seasons and other hotel chains hired to audit service quality:

> Four Seasons has done an exceptional job of adapting to local markets. From a design perspective, they are much more clever than other companies. When you sit in the Four Seasons in Bali, you feel that you are in Bali. It does not scream Four Seasons at you.

A manager explained Four Seasons' ability to be somewhat of a cultural chameleon with an analogy to Disney:

> Unlike Disney, whose brand name is so strongly associated with the United States, Four Seasons' brand doesn't rigidly define what the product is. The Four Seasons brand is associated with intangibles. Our guests are not looking to stay in a Canadian hotel. Our product has to be 100 percent Four Seasons, but in a style that is appropriate for the country.

According to Crowl, Four Seasons learned from each country and property:

> Because we are an international hotel company, we take our learning across borders. In Egypt, we are going to try to incorporate indigenous elements to the spa, but we will still be influenced by the best practices we have identified at our two spas in Bali.

Globally Uniform Standards

The seven Four Seasons "service culture standards" expected of all staff all over the world at all times are:

1. SMILE: Employees will actively greet guests, smile, and speak clearly in a friendly manner.
2. EYE: Employees will make eye contact, even in passing, with an acknowledgment.
3. RECOGNITION: All staff will create a sense of recognition by using the guest's name, when known, in a natural and discreet manner.
4. VOICE: Staff will speak to guests in an attentive, natural, and courteous manner, avoiding pretension, and in a clear voice.
5. INFORMED: All guest contact staff will be well informed about their hotel, their product, will take ownership of simple requests, and will not refer guests elsewhere.
6. CLEAN: Staff will always appear clean, crisp, well-groomed, and well-fitted.
7. EVERYONE: Everyone, everywhere, all the time, shows their care for our guests.

In addition to its service culture standards, Four Seasons had 270 core worldwide operating standards (see Appendix 1 for sample standards). Arriving at these standards had not been easy; until 1998, there were 800. With the firm's international growth, this resulted in an overly complex set of rules and exceptions. The standards were set by the firm's senior vice presidents and Wolf Hengst, president, worldwide hotel operations, who explained:

> We had a rule about the number of different types of bread rolls to be served at dinner and number of bottles of wine to be opened at lounges. But in countries where no bread is eaten at dinner and no wine is consumed, that's pretty stupid.

"While 270 standards might seem extensive," Richey noted, "if there are only 270, there are thousands of things that are not covered over which the general manager and local management team have a lot of control."

In addition, exceptions to the standards were permitted if they made local sense. For example, one standard stated that the coffee pot should be left on the table at breakfast so that guests could choose to refill their cups. This was perceived as a lack of service in France, so it was amended there. Standards were often written to allow local flexibility. While the standards require an employee's uniform to be immaculate, they do not state what it should look like. In Bali, uniforms were completely different from uniforms in Chicago. Managers underlined the fact that standards set *minimum expectations*. "If you can do something for a client that goes beyond a standard," they told staff, "do it." As a result, stories about a concierge taking a client to the hospital and staying with that person overnight were part of Four Seasons lore, contributing to cultural artifacts.

To evaluate each property's performance against the standards, Four Seasons used both external and internal auditors in its measurement programs. "Our standards are the foundation for all our properties," a senior manager noted. "It is the base on which we build." "When you talk to a Four Seasons person," Richey concluded, "they are so familiar with each of the standards, it is astonishing. With many managers at other firms this is not the case."

"We have been obsessed by the service standards," Hengst concluded. "People who come from the outside are surprised that we take them and the role they play in our culture so seriously. But they are essential. Talk to me about standards and you talk to me about religion." Another manager added, "Over time, the standards help to shape relationships between people, and those relationships contribute to building our culture."

Delivering Intelligent, Anticipatory, and Enthusiastic Service Worldwide

A manager stated:

> We decided many years ago that our distinguishing edge would be exceptional, personal service – that's where the value is. In all our research around the world, we have never seen anything that led us to believe that

"just for you" customized service was not the most important element of our success.

Another manager added:

> Service like this, what I think of as "intelligent service," can't be scripted. As a result, we need employees who are as distinguished as our guests – if employees are going to adapt, to be empathetic and anticipate guests' needs, the "distance" between the employee and the guest has to be small.

There were also tangible elements to Four Seasons' service quality. The product was always comfortable – so much so that at guests' requests, the company made its pillows, bedspreads, and mattresses available for sale. Guests could also count on a spacious bathroom, which was appreciated by the world traveler, especially in Europe where bathrooms tended to be small. "However, there are differences in the perception and definition of luxury," explained Barbara Talbott, executive vice president of marketing:

> In the US, our properties have public spaces with a luxurious, but intimate, feeling. In the Far East, our properties have large lobbies enabling guests to see and be seen. People around the world also have different ways of using a hotel – restaurants, for example, are more important in hotels in Asia, so we build space for more restaurants in each property there.

Human Resources and the Golden Rule

Four Seasons' managers believed that human resource management was key to the firm's success. According to one senior manager, "People make the strength of this company. Procedures are not very varied or special. What we do is fairly basic." Human resource management started and ended with "the Golden Rule," which stipulated that one should treat others as one would wish to be treated. Managers saw it as the foundation of the firm's values and thus its culture. "The Golden Rule is the key to the success of the firm, and it's appreciated in every village, town, and city around the world. Basic human needs are the same everywhere," Sharp emphasized. Appendix 2 summarizes the firm's goals, beliefs, and principles.

Kathleen Taylor, president, worldwide business operations, provided an example of how Four Seasons went about enacting the Golden Rule as a core value:

> We give employees several uniforms so they can change when they become dirty. That goes to their dignity, but it is uncommon in the hospitality industry. People around the world want to be treated with dignity and respect, and in most organizational cultures that doesn't happen.

Managers acknowledged that many service organizations made similar statements on paper. What differentiated Four Seasons was how the chain operationalized those statements. Crowl noted, "A service culture is about putting what we all believe in into practice. We learn it, we nurture it, and most importantly, we do it."

In 2002, for the fifth year in a row, Four Seasons was among *Fortune* magazine's list of the top 100 best companies to work for in North America. While turnover in the hospitality industry averaged 55 percent, Four Seasons' turnover was half that amount.

GOING TO PARIS

However it developed its approach and philosophy, Four Seasons management knew that entering France would be a challenge.

The George V Opportunity

The six hotels in Paris classified as "Palaces" were grand, historic, and luxurious. Standard room prices at the F. S. George V, for example, ranged from $400 to $700. Most palaces featured award-winning restaurants, private gardens, and expansive common areas. For example, the Hotel de Crillon, a competitor to the F. S. George V, was an eighteenth-century palace commissioned by King Louis XV. The nine-story George V was designed in the 1920s by two famous French art deco architects. The property was located in one of Paris' most fashionable districts. For comparative data on Parisian palaces, please refer to Appendix 3.

Observers of the Paris hotel scene noted that by the 1980s and 1990s, the George V, like some of its peers, was coasting on its reputation. In December 1996, HRH Prince Al Waleed Bin Talal Bin Abdulaziz al Saud purchased the hotel for $170 million. In November 1997, Four Seasons signed a long-term agreement to manage the hotel. "We needed to be in Paris," John Young, executive vice president, human resources, explained:

> We had looked at a new development, but gaining planning permission for a new building in Paris is very hard. Since we look for the highest possible quality assets in the best locations, the George V was perfect. It established us very powerfully in the French capital.

In order to transform the George V into a Four Seasons, however, an extensive amount of effort had to be placed into both the tangible and experiential service that the property and its people could deliver.

Physical Renovations

Four Seasons' challenge was to preserve the soul of the legendary, almost mythical, George V Hotel while rebuilding it for contemporary travelers. Four Seasons closed the hotel for what ended up being a two-year, $125 million total renovation. Because the building was a landmark, the facade had to be maintained. The interior of the hotel, however, was gutted. The 300 rooms and suites were reduced to 245 rooms of larger size (including 61 suites). Skilled craftsmen restored the facade's art deco windows and balconies, the extensive wood paneling on the first floor, and the artwork and seventeenth-century Flanders tapestries that had long adorned the hotel's public and private spaces.

The interior designer hired by Four Seasons, Pierre Rochon, noted:

> My main objective was to marry functionality with guest comfort, to merge twenty-first-century technology with the hotel's "French classique" heritage. I would like guests rediscovering the hotel to think that I had not changed a thing – and, at the same time, to notice how much better they feel within its walls.[5]

The fact that the designer was French, Talbott pointed out, "signaled to the French that we understood what they meant by luxury."

While Four Seasons decided to build to American life-safety standards, it also had to adhere to local laws, which affected design and work patterns. For example, a hygiene law in France stipulates that food and garbage cannot travel the same routes: food and trash have to he carried down different corridors and up/down different elevators. Another law involved "right to light," stipulating that employees had the right to work near a window for a certain number of hours each day. As a result, employees in the basement spa also worked upstairs in a shop with a window for several hours a day, and as many windows as possible had to be programmed into the design.

The new Four Seasons Hotel George V opened on December 18, 1999, at 100 percent effective occupancy (occupancy of rooms ready for use). Managers credited extensive publicity, the millennium celebration, and the profile of the property for that success. The opening was particularly challenging because Four Seasons only took formal control of operations on December 1, in part due to French regulations. "The French are very particular about, for example, fire regulations, but the fire department would not come in and inspect until everything else was complete," a manager said.

BECOMING A FRENCH EMPLOYER

Entering the French hospitality market meant becoming a French employer, which implied understanding French labor laws, business culture, and national idiosyncrasies.

Rules

France's leaders remained committed to a capitalism that maintained social equity with laws, tax policies, and social spending that reduced income disparity and the impact of free markets on public health and welfare.[6] France's tax burden, 45 percent of GDP in 1998, was three percentage points higher than the European average – and eight points higher than the OECD average. A further burden on employers was the 1999 reduction of the work week to 35 hours. Unemployment and retirement benefits were generous. Importantly, Four Seasons' management was not unfamiliar with labor-oriented government policy. "Canada has many attributes of a welfare state, so our Canadian roots made it easier to deal with such a context," Young explained.

The country was known for its strong unions.[7] "In France, one still finds a certain dose of antagonism between employees and management," a French manager underlined. The political party of the Force Ouvrière, the union that was strongest at the F. S. George V, garnered nearly 10 percent of the votes in the first round of the 2002 French presidential election with the rallying cry, "Employees fight the bosses!"

"If you look at the challenges of operating in France," noted Corinthios, "they have labor laws that are restrictive, but not prohibitive. The laws are not the same as, for example, in Chicago. You just need to be more informed about them." The law did give employers some flexibility, allowing them to work someone a little more during peak business periods and less during a lull. A housekeeper, for example, might work 40-hour weeks in the summer in exchange for a few 30-hour weeks in the late fall. Furthermore, French employers could hire 10–15 percent of staff on a "temporary," seasonal basis.

A particularly tricky area of labor management in France involved terminations. A Four Seasons manager explained:

> Wherever we operate in the world, we do not fire at will. There is due process. There is no surprise. There is counseling. So Paris isn't that different, except to have the termination stick is more challenging because you really need a very, very good cause and to document *everything* carefully. If you have one gap in the documentation, you will have to rehire the terminated employee.

National and Organizational Culture

Geert Hofstede's seminal work, *Culture's Consequences*,[8] indicates a great disparity between North American (US and Canadian) national culture and that of France. While Hofstede's work has been criticized for the construction of the dimensions along which cultures differ,[9] there is general agreement with the principle that cultures do differ. Further, Hofstede's work and that of other scholars indicate that the differences between North American and French organizational culture are large. Corinthios identified attitudes surrounding performance evaluation as one difference:

> European and Middle Eastern managers have a hard time sitting across from people they supervise and talking about their weaknesses. The culture

is not confrontational. It is more congenial and positive. It is very important to save face and preserve the dignity of the person being reviewed.
Some Four Seasons managers using standard forms might even delete certain sections or questions or reprogram them in different languages.

For Didier Le Calvez, general manager of the F. S. George V and recently
appointed regional vice president, another significant difference was the degree
to which middle and front-line managers felt accountable. "The greatest challenge in France is to get managers to take accountability for decisions and policies," he said. "In the French hierarchical system there is a strong tendency to
refer things to the boss."

Le Calvez was also surprised by managers' poor understanding of human
resource issues. In France, when a manager has a problem with an employee, the
issue generally gets referred to the human resources department. "We, at Four
Seasons, on the other hand, require that operating managers be present, deal
with the issue, and lead the discussion."

"Seeing Is Believing"

When reflecting on their experiences with employees in France, several Four
Seasons managers mentioned Saint Thomas ("doubting Thomas"). "They must
see it to believe it," Le Calvez explained. "They do not take things at face value.
They also tend to wait on the sidelines once they see that something works, they
come out of their shells and follow the movement." A Four Seasons manager
continued:

> Most of the workforce in France did not know what Four Seasons was all
> about. For example, they did not think we were serious about the Golden
> Rule. They thought it was way too American. Initially, there were some
> eyebrows raised. Because of this skepticism, when we entered France, we
> came on our tiptoes, without wanting to give anyone a lecture. I think *how*
> we came in was almost as important as *what* we did.

More Differences

For several Four Seasons managers, working in France required a "bigger cultural adjustment" than had been necessary in other countries. "In France, I
always knew that I would be a foreigner," a manager explained. "It took me a
while to adjust to the French way." "There is simply an incredible pride in being
French," added another. "The French have a very emotional way to do things,"
an F. S. George V manager explained. "This can be good and bad. The good side
is that they can be very joyous and engaging. On the bad side, sometimes the
French temper lashes out."

According to Four Seasons managers, what was referred to in the cultural
research literature as the French "logic of honor"[10] was strong. While it would

be degrading to be "in the service of" (*au service de*) anybody, especially the boss, it was honorable to "give service" (*rendre service*), with magnanimity, if asked to do so with due ceremony. In this context, management required a great deal of tact and judgment.

Managing differing perceptions of time could also be a challenge for North Americans in France. North Americans have been characterized as having a "monochronic" culture based on a high degree of scheduling and an elaborate code of behavior built around promptness in meeting obligations and appointments.[11] In contrast, the French were "polychronic," valuing human relationships and interactions over arbitrary schedules and appointments. These differences created predictable patterns, summarized in Appendix 4.

Specific areas where Four Seasons and French national culture differed often related to either (French) guest expectations of a palace hotel, including its physical structure and tangible amenities, or manager–employee relationships. For example, in France, hotel guests expected a palace hotel to have a world-class gastronomic restaurant. They also expected exquisite floral arrangements and to be wowed by the decor. In contrast, Four Seasons hotels generally have excellent, although not necessarily world-class, restaurants and are known for their understated, subtly elegant look. An example of differences in employee–manager relationships can be found in the French managerial practice of being extremely cautious in providing employee feedback to the degree that, according to Four Seasons' managers, the practice is unusual. In contrast, Four Seasons' management practice involved a great deal of communication, including feedback on an individual employee's performance, which managers believed critical to solving problems and delivering superior service.

Cultural Renovation at the F. S. George V

Awareness and management of French cultural patterns were especially important to Four Seasons managers in Paris because a significant portion of the former operator's management and staff remained. Young explained:

> When we explored options for refashioning the George V into a Four Seasons hotel, we realized that without being able to start from scratch, the task would be Herculean. The existing culture was inconsistent with ours. In a North American environment you can decide whom to keep after an acquisition at a cost you can determine in advance on the basis of case law. In France, the only certainty is that you cannot replace the employees. You are acquiring the entity as a going concern. Unless you do certain things, you simply inherit the employees, including their legal rights based on prior service.

To be able to reduce headcount, by law an enterprise had to plan to be closed for over 18 months. Because the F. S. George V owner wanted the renovation to be complete in 12 months, staff were guaranteed a position with Four Seasons unless they chose to leave.[12] "Many of the best employees easily found other jobs, while the most disruptive were still there when the hotel reopened," Young said. "The number of people we really did not want was somewhere in the region of 40 out of 300 coming back on reopening."

Managers uniformly noted that the cultural renovation necessary to enable Four Seasons to be able to deliver its world-class service was on par with the extent of the physical renovation. Young provided an example:

> During the due diligence process, the former general manager went to lunch with one of our senior staff. Even though guests were waiting, the maître d' immediately tried to escort the general manager and his party to the general manager's customary table. At Four Seasons this is seen as an abuse of privilege. For us, "the guest always comes first."

Fortunately, in taking over The Pierre in New York, Four Seasons had been through a somewhat similar process. The scale of change necessary in each situation was enormous, as illustrated by this quotation from a senior Four Seasons manager:

> Shortly after we bought The Pierre in 1981, a bell captain lamented that the times of the big steamer trunks were over. The staff had not adjusted to jet travel, despite its prevalence for two decades. This is the same kind of recalibration we had to do at the George V.

Apples and Oranges

Young described the firm's approach to cultural transformation in acquired properties with existing staffing:

> If we can achieve a critical mass of individuals among the workforce who are committed to doing things differently, to meeting our standards, that critical mass overcomes the resistance of what becomes a diminishing old guard. Progressively, that old guard loses some of its power. If one rotten apple can ruin the barrel, then you have to seed the organization with oranges that cannot be spoiled by the apples. As a result, a departing old-guard employee is very carefully replaced. Concurrently, individuals with the right culture and attitude are promoted. That creates a new culture, bit by bit by bit. At the F. S. George V, we also appealed to the national pride of our staff to help us restore a French landmark – to restore the pride of France.

"UN BOSS FRANCO-FRANÇAIS"

To effect this cultural change, Four Seasons picked Le Calvez to be general manager. Le Calvez was described as both demanding and "Franco-Français,"[13] an expression used in France to describe someone or something "unequivocably French." At the same time, Le Calvez brought extensive Four Seasons and North American experience. Prior to opening the Regent Hotel in Singapore, he spent 25 years outside France, including 11 years at The Pierre. "He is very international, yet also very French, very attached to his country and its culture," an executive explained. "He knows everyone and has an unbelievable memory for names and events (what happened to so-and-so's mother-in-law, etc.). He is very visible and accessible to the staff, eating in the staff cafeteria."

An F. S. George V manager noted, "The hotel's culture is embodied in the general manager – he shows a lot of love and respect for others and promotes social and cultural and ethnic integration." In a country where people typically referred to each other as Monsieur and Madame with their last name, Le Calvez encouraged the use of the first name. "It is more direct, relaxed, and straight-forward. It represents the kind of relationship I want to have with my staff," he stated.

Young commented on the choice of Le Calvez:

> The choice of senior leadership is absolutely critical. Adherence to our values and operational goals has to be extremely strong. Hotel openings require a lot of patience and tolerance because results are likely to be less positive as you manage through periods of major change.

The Task Force – "Culture Carriers"

To help Le Calvez and his team "Four Seasonize" the F. S. George V staff and ensure a smooth opening, Four Seasons assigned a 35-person task force, as it did to every new property. A manager noted:

> The task force helps establish norms. We help people understand how Four Seasons does things. Members listen for problems and innuendoes and communicate the right information to all, and squash rumors, especially when there are cultural sensitivities. The task force also helps physically getting the property up and running. Finally, being part of the task force exposes managers who may one day become general managers to the process of opening a hotel.

The task force, composed of experienced Four Seasons managers and staff, reflected the operating needs of each property. For example, if an experienced room service manager had already transferred to the opening property, those skills would not be brought in via the task force.

> The approach supports allegiance to the firm and not just one property – because members of the task force are not associated with one hotel. We

are excited to participate, even if it means working long hours for weeks away from home.

Most task force members, who typically stayed three weeks for an opening, stayed seven to eight weeks at the F. S. George V.

Strong Tides

After working for 25 years abroad, Le Calvez admitted that he was hesitant to return to work in France in light of the general tension he sensed between labor and management. However, he was encouraged by what he had seen at The Pierre, where Four Seasons managers noted that they had fostered a dialogue with the New York hospitality industry union. Le Calvez felt he could do the same in Paris:

> When I arrived I told the unions that I did not think that we would need them, but since the law said we had to have them, I said "Let's work together." I do not want social tensions. Of course, this is not unique to me; it is Four Seasons' approach. We have to be pragmatic. So we signaled our commitment to a good environment.

Le Calvez communicated this commitment by openly discussing the 35-hour work week, the Four Seasons retirement plan, and the time and attendance system, designed to make sure that staff would not work more than required.

At the outset of negotiations, in preparation for the reopening, Le Calvez took the representatives of the various unions to lunch. As work progressed, he organized tours of the site so that union representatives could see what was being done and "become excited" about the hotel. He noted that, "Touring the property in hard hats and having to duck under electric wires builds bonds. Witnessing the birth of a hotel is exciting." Managers stated that the unions were not used to such an inclusive approach in France.

Young felt that dealing with unions in France was easier than in New York: "In France, you are dealing with an institution backed by stringent, but predictable, laws. In the United States, you are dealing with individuals in leadership who can be much more volatile and egocentric."

Four Seasons' experience with The Pierre proved invaluable. According to Young:

> In New York, we redesigned working spaces, and trained, and trained, and trained staff. But we also burned out a couple of managers. The old culture either wears you down or you wear it down. In an environment with strong labor laws, management sometimes gives up the right to manage. At some point, managers stop swimming against the tide. If that continues long enough, the ability to manage effectively is lost. The precedents in a hotel

are those that the prior managers have permitted. If the right to manage has been given up, standards are depressed, productivity decreases, margins decrease, and eventually you have a bad business. Regulars are treated well, but many guests are not. Reversing this process requires enormous management energy. It is very wearing to swim against a strong tide. You are making decisions that you believe reasonable and facing reactions that you believe unreasonable.

The 35-hour Work Week

Managers believed that Four Seasons' decision to implement the 35-hour work week at the F. S. George V to meet the letter and spirit of French law was a major signal to the unions and workforce about the way the company approached human resource issues. "When we hire staff from other hotels, they are always surprised that we obey the law," an F. S. George V manager noted. "They were working longer hours elsewhere."

A 35-hour work week yielded 1,820 annual workable hours per full-time staff equivalent. But since the French had more holidays and vacation than American employees, French employees provided 1,500 to 1,600 workable hours. This compared to about 2,050 hours in the US for a full-time equivalent. The manager added:

> We did not really understand the impact of the 35-hour work week. Each of our 80 managers has to have two consecutive days off a week, and each of the staff can work 214 days a year. Not 215. Not 213. But 214.

In 2002, 620 staff covered 250 rooms, or 2.5 staff per room. On average, Four Seasons hotels had 1.6 employees per room. Depending on food and banquet operations, that average could rise or fall significantly. Table 1 shows employees-to-room ratios at selected Four Seasons properties.

Young felt that labor laws explained about 15 percent of the need for increased staff ratios in Paris; vacations and holidays, 10 percent; with the rest

Table 1 Employees-to-room ratios at selected Four Seasons properties

Property	Employees-to-Rooms Ratio
Four Seasons worldwide average	1.6
The Pierre New York	2.3
Four Seasons Hotel New York	1.6
Four Seasons Hotel George V Paris	2.5
Four Seasons Hotel Berlin	0.9
Four Seasons Hotel London	1.2
Four Seasons Hotel Canary Wharf, London	1.4
Four Seasons Hotel Milano	2.2

Source: Four Seasons.

explained by other factors including some logistics of the operation, e.g., a historic building, all compared to US norms. Corinthios elaborated:

> In Paris, you have six palaces competing for the same clients. It is a more formal operation. Guest expectations are very high, as is the level of leisure business (which requires higher staffing). People stay four to six days and use the concierge extensively. The concierge staffing at the F. S. George V is as big as anything we have in the chain. Then there is more emphasis on food and beverage. We have a fabulous chef and more staff in the kitchen for both the restaurant and room service — expectations of service in the gastronomic restaurant are very high.

RUNNING THE F. S. GEORGE V

Recruitment and Selection

Four Seasons wanted to be recognized as the best employer in each of its locations. In Paris, F. S. George V's wages were among the top three for hotels. Salaries were advertised in help wanted ads, a first in the industry in Paris according to F. S. George V managers, who believed doing so would help them attract high-quality staff.

At the F. S. George V, as across the firm, every potential employee was interviewed four times, the last interview with the general manager. According to one executive, "In the selection process, we try to look deep inside the applicant. I learned about the importance of service from my parents — did this potential employee learn it from hers?" "What matters is attitude, attitude, attitude," Corinthios explained. "All around the world it is the same. Without the right attitude, they cannot adapt." Another manager added, "What we need is people who can adapt, either to guests from all over the world, or to operating in a variety of countries." One of his colleagues elaborated on the importance of hiring for attitude, and its challenges:

> You would think that you would have a lot of people with great experience because there are so many palace hotels in Paris. But because we hire for attitude, we rarely hire from the other palaces. We hire individuals who are still "open" and tend to be much younger than usual for palace hotels. Then we bet on training. Of course, it takes much longer to train for skills when people do not have them. We look for people persons, who are welcoming and put others at ease, who want to please, are professional and sincerely friendly, flexible, smiley, and positive. At the F. S. George V, people apply for jobs because they have friends who work here.

To spread the culture and "de-demonize" the US, the new F. S. George V management recruited staff with prior Four Seasons and/or US experience to serve as ambassadors. A manager noted, "Staff with US experience share with other staff what the United States is about and that it is not the terrible place some French people make it out to be." Several managers had international experience. About 40 individuals had prior US experience.

"Anglo-Saxon" Recognition, Measurement, and Benefits

Le Calvez and his team launched an employee-of-the-month and employee-of-the year program. "This had been controversial at Disney. People said it could not be done in France, but we managed to do it quite successfully. It all depends how it is presented," Le Calvez noted. "We explained that the program would recognize those who perform. Colleagues can tell who is good at their job."

Le Calvez used the same spirit to introduce annual evaluations, uncommon in France:

> People said evaluations would be unpopular, but the system seems to work. We told the staff that it would be an opportunity for open and constructive dialogue so that employees can know at all times where they stand. This allows them to adapt when need be. We wanted to make clear that there would be no favoritism, but rather that this would be a meritocracy. Here your work speaks for itself. The idea that your work is what matters could be construed as very Anglo-Saxon!

In another "Anglo-Saxon" action, a "Plan d'Epargne d'Entreprise" was set up for George V employees. This was a combination of a tax-deferred savings account and 401(k)-type retirement plan. "This is totally new in France," Le Calvez claimed. Employees could contribute up to 4 percent of their salary, and the hotel would match it with 2 percent, to be raised based on profitability. The unions signed the agreement, although they were opposed to the principle of a non-government-sponsored retirement plan.

IMPLEMENTING THE GOLDEN RULE

The Golden Rule was at work at the F. S. George V, as its human resource director illustrated:

> Cooks, before joining Four Seasons, used to have very long days starting in the morning to prepare for lunch, having a break during the afternoon, and coming back to prepare dinner. Today they work on either the morning or afternoon shift, enabling a better organization of their personal lives.

"All these gestures take time to work," Le Calvez summarized. "At first employees do not think we mean it. Some new hires think it's artificial or fake, but after a few months they let their guard down when they realize we mean what we say."

Managers believed that the effect of Four Seasons' human resource practices was reflected in customer satisfaction. Indeed, Le Calvez proudly reported that guest cards often included comments on how friendly and attentive the staff were. "All the other palace hotels in Paris are beautiful, but we believe that we have a special focus on friendly and personable service." He continued, "We offer friendly, very personal service. We have a very young and dynamic brigade with an average age of 26, spanning 46 different nationalities."

Communication

To promote communication and problem-solving, the F. S. George V management implemented a "direct line." Once a month, the general manager met with employees, supervisors, and managers in groups of 30. The groups met for three consecutive months so that issues raised could be addressed, with results reported to the group. Managers believed that the F. S. George V was the only palace hotel in France with such a communication process. It was important to note that the groups met separately – that is, employees met separately from supervisors – because subordinates in France did not feel comfortable speaking up in front of superiors.

French law mandated that a *comité d'entreprise* (staff committee) be established in organizations with more than 50 employees. It represented employees to management on decisions that affected employees (e.g., salaries, work hours). At the F. S. George V, Le Calvez chaired the committee's monthly meeting, which included union representatives. "We would do these things anyway, so it is easy to adjust to these laws," Corinthios said. "We do it in France because it is required by law. But we do the same around the world; it just has a different name."

Every morning, the top management team gathered to go over glitches – things that may have gone wrong the day before and the steps that had been, or were being, taken to address the problem. "Admitting what went wrong is not in the French culture," a French Four Seasons manager explained. "But the meetings are usually very constructive."

Finally, about three times a year, Le Calvez and his team hosted an open-door event, inviting employees and their families to spend some time at the hotel. "This is to break down barriers," he explained:

> We take people around the hotel, into the back corridors. Try to remind people of a notion that is unfortunately being lost – that of the "*plaisir du travail*" – or enjoying one's work. Furthermore, we celebrate achievement.

Good property rankings, for example, are recognized with special team celebrations.

The property also cultivated external communication with the press in a way that was culturally sensitive. Le Calvez and his team felt that they had been very open and responsive to the press (which they stated was unusual in France), and that as a result, "Not a single negative article had been written about Four Seasons Hotel George V since its opening". A colleague added, "The press appreciated that they were dealing with locals. It was not like Disney where everyone was American."

CULINARY *COUP D'ÉTAT*

In a significant diversion from typical Four Seasons practice, a non-Four Seasons executive chef was hired. "In France, having a serious chef and serious food is important," the F. S. George V food and beverage director noted. "You cannot be a palace hotel without that." "We knew that what mattered in Paris was food and decor," Talbott added. Although only 7 percent of room guests were French, most restaurant patrons were French.

Chef Philippe Legendre from the world-famous Parisian restaurant Taillevent was recruited. "Didier came to me through a common friend," Legendre explained. Legendre accepted Four Seasons' offer because "there was something exciting about being part of opening a hotel." He also liked their language, which he described as "optimistic" and "about creating possibilities."

Legendre felt that Four Seasons' real strength was around relationship management (with clients and among staff), which:

> is not something that we are that good at in France, or place particular emphasis on. We have a lot to learn in the social domain. Everything at Four Seasons is geared towards the needs of the guest. At first it was hard, especially the training. Perhaps because in France we think we know everything.

He continued, "After three years I might not talk the Four Seasons talk, I might not use the same words, but I have the same view and adhere to the same system."

Despite Legendre's success (earning two Michelin stars), a colleague added that, "bringing in such an executive chef was problematic. The challenge is that with this chef you have someone with extraordinary talent, but who must still adjust to the way service is delivered at Four Seasons." Coexistence was not always easy. Legendre described a situation illustrating miscommunication and cultural differences that required tremendous patience on the part of the restaurant, guests, and management:

> Recently a man ordered an omelet and his wife ordered scrambled eggs. The man returned the omelet because he decided he wanted scrambled eggs. We made them. Then he sent them back because they did not meet his expectations. Of course, we realize that our oeufs brouillés are different from scrambled eggs, which don't contain cream. Because we are Four Seasons we cooked the eggs as he wanted them, like American scrambled eggs, and didn't charge for them. But cooking is about emotion – if you want to please someone, you have to do it with your heart. *We live differently in France.*

RESULTS

A Cultural Cocktail

The F. S. George V was, in effect, a cultural cocktail. Le Calvez explained:

> The F. S. George V is not *only* a French hotel – it is French, but it is also very international. We want to be different from the other palaces that are oh so very French. We want to project the image of a modern France, one that does not have to be dusty. We want to be a symbol of a France that is in movement, a European France, a France that stands for integration and equality.

The cultural cocktail also contained a number of elements unusual in France. At the time of the opening, journalists asked about the "American" smiling culture, which was referred to in France as "la culture Mickey Mouse." Le Calvez replied, "If you tell me that being American is being friendly and pleasant, that is fine by me. People tell me everyone smiles at the Four Seasons George V."

The spectacular flowers in the lobby of the F. S. George V (a single urn once contained 1,000 roses) were both very French and extremely international. "Paris is a city of fashion and culture, artistic and innovative," Le Calvez explained. "That is why, for example, we have the flowers we do. We can do that here." However, the flowers were designed by a young American. Another departure from French standard was the decision to hire women as concierges and men in housekeeping. These were viewed by managers as revolutionary steps in Paris.

Service Quality

Richey summarized the results of the first F. S. George V service quality audit in October 2000, identifying some differences between French and North American business culture:

> Keep in mind that this occurred less than one year after opening, and it takes at least a year to get things worked out. There were three things we talked to Four Seasons' executives about, mostly related to employee attitude. First, the staff had an inability to apologize or empathize. I think that could be construed as typically European, and especially French. Second, the team had a very tough time doing anything that could be described as selling. This is also typically European. For example: say your glass is empty at the bar. In Paris, they may not ask you if you want another drink. Third, the staff were rules and policy oriented. If something went wrong, they would refer to the manual instead of focusing on satisfying the guest.

Things had changed considerably by Richey's second audit in August 2001, when "they beat the competitive market set." The scores showed a significant improvement, raising the property to the Four Seasons' system average.

More good news came in July 2002 with the results of an Employee Opinion Survey, in which 95 percent of employees participated. The survey yielded an overall rating of 4.02 out of 5. The questions that ranked the highest were: "I am proud to work for Four Seasons Hotels and Resorts" (4.65) and "I would want to work here again" (4.61).

The property also received several industry awards, including Andrew Harper's Hideaway Report 2001 and 2002, World's Best Hotels and Resorts, Travel & Leisure Readers' Choice Awards 2001, #2 Best Hotel in Europe, and #5 World's Best Hotel Spa.

CONCLUSION: CULTURE, CONSISTENCY, AND FLEXIBILITY

The Four Seasons Hotel George V case illustrates how a service firm with a strong, successful organizational culture expanded internationally into a country with a distinct, intense national culture. When Four Seasons entered France, some elements of organizational culture were held constant, while others were treated flexibly. Managers never considered altering their *organizational values*, whether related to the service provided to guests, which had to be engaging, anticipating, and responding; the property, which had to be beautiful, luxurious, and functional; or how managers would treat employees, insisting that employees be treated as managers would like to be treated if they performed those jobs. While these values remained constant despite considerable differences in operating environments, the ways those values were enacted did sometimes change. This required changes in policies, management practices, and the use of cultural artifacts.

The tangible elements of service provide clear evidence of flexibility. Like all Four Seasons properties, the F. S. George V is luxurious. However, in France, the first floor of the hotel is adorned with gilt and seventeenth-century tapestries. No other Four Seasons property is decorated this way. The hotel elected to have a two-Michelin-star restaurant, despite the challenges of working with a famous chef in a country where there may be no more distinguished form of celebrity. More subtly non-tangible elements of service quality changed, requiring changes in policies. For example, a coffee pot is never left on the table for guests to help themselves. This change enables the hotel to meet the standard for service set by a Four Seasons' organizational value ("anticipatory") as interpreted in France, where one should not have to pour coffee oneself.

Management practices also changed. In order to have an engaging, anticipating, and responding staff, managers relied upon employee selection even more heavily than at other properties. In this way, management practice was intensified in response to a new national culture. However, the goal of those intensified selection efforts was to hire a less experienced staff than typical for other palace hotels and the chain. This was because of underlying, inflexible assumptions that many more experienced workers in France have about employment and how they should treat guests. Less experienced individuals are less set in attitudes and cultural stereotypes contrary to delivering the service for which Four Seasons is renowned. Management therefore focused more sharply on hiring based on attitudes rather than prior work experience. Thus, this management practice changed in France to enable Four Seasons to remain true to its organizational values.

The use of cultural artifacts also changed. While a typical Four Seasons property opening would be accompanied by information to the press on the world-renowned service for which the chain is famous, including legendary service stories, in France, this was an afterthought to the glory of the property and the appropriateness of the renovations for a *French* architectural landmark.

Many management practices did not change upon arrival in France. Employee-of-the-month and employee-of-the-year recognition programs, feedback practices, and meetings to discuss problems were implemented despite a general belief that they would be found incompatible with the French environment. Yet they were successful because of *how* they were implemented – using the words of one manager, "on tiptoes." Their more awkward (from a French perspective) elements were amended, and their purpose was communicated gently, but repeatedly. The individuals carefully selected into the Four Seasons' environment did not object to their use because they understood the intent of the practices, as well as their effect. The practices ultimately contributed to achieving the changes in organizational culture that Four Seasons managers believed were necessary, helping to ensure that the "oranges" (new employees) carefully selected into the property became the dominant culture carriers, overwhelming the leftover "apples" who refused to change, creating an environment in which those apples no longer fit comfortably.

Perhaps the most important element of management practice contributing to Four Seasons' success in France was management discipline. This took two forms, both of which can be viewed as contributing to the enactment of organizational values. First, discipline can be seen in the way Four Seasons managers lived the values they espoused; allowing guests to be seated first in the dining room; treating employees with dignity; and adhering to local labor laws and internal policies designed to protect employees. Second, Four Seasons managers had the discipline to insist that employees deliver outstanding service to guests. This occurred through adherence to the core service culture standards and 270 operating standards (as occasionally amended). Meeting these standards has resulted in customer loyalty. Thus, discipline acts as a glue, ensuring that organizational values actually *drive* a culture, which in turn *contributes* to competitive advantage.

Managers in widely diverse service industries can benefit from Four Seasons' approach to global management when entering countries with distinct, intense national cultures. To do so, they must understand their own organizational culture: what are their (1) underlying assumptions, (2) values, (3) employee perceptions of management practices (policies and behaviors), and (4) cultural artifacts? Managers must then ask what elements of their culture are essential to competitive advantage in existing environments, and how the new environment will change that linkage. When there is a change, does the element of culture itself need to change (coffee pot no longer left on the table), or does the way the element is implemented, the way a value is enacted, need to change, such as the implementation "on tiptoes" of an employee-of-the-month recognition program. In general, *values core to the organization's "value proposition" (what customers receive from the firm relative to what they pay for it) will not change, but elements of how they are enacted may.*

While organizations eventually come to understand how to operate in a new national environment, successful organizations cannot afford the type of negative publicity and poor financial performance that accompany blundering into a new national culture, as Disney discovered after opening Euro Disney in France. The Four Seasons case study is a single case, based on a single organization. As such, we do not claim that its findings are necessarily applicable to other firms. However, it illustrates an approach to global management that managers of other services may find useful, but which they must customize to their own organizational and cultural needs.

APPENDIX 1: SAMPLE CORE STANDARDS

Reservations

Mission: To provide crisp, knowledgeable, and friendly service, sensitive to the guest's time, and dedication to finding the most suitable accommodation.

- Phone service will be highly efficient, including: answered before the fourth ring; no hold longer than 15 seconds; or, in case of longer holds, call-backs offered, then provided in less than three minutes.
- After establishing the reason for the guest visit, reservationist automatically describes the guest room colorfully, attempting to have the guests picture themselves in the room.

Hotel Arrival

Mission: To make all guests feel welcome as they approach, and assured that details are well tended; to provide a speedy, discreet, and hassle-free arrival for business travelers; to provide a comforting and luxurious arrival for leisure travelers.

- The doorman (or first contact employee) will actively greet guests, smile, make eye contact, and speak clearly in a friendly manner.
- The staff will be aware of arriving vehicles and will move toward them, opening doors within 30 seconds.

- Guests will be welcomed at the curbside with the words "welcome" and "Four Seasons" (or hotel name), and given directions to the reception desk.
- No guest will wait longer than 60 seconds in line at the reception desk.

Hotel Departure

Mission: To provide a quick and discreet departure, while conveying appreciation and hope for return.

- No guest will wait longer than five minutes for baggage assistance once the bellman is called (eight minutes in resorts).
- No guest will wait longer than 60 seconds in line at the cashier desk.
- Staff will create a sense of recognition by using the guest's name, when known, in a natural and discreet manner.

Messages and Paging

Mission: To make guests feel that their calls are important, urgent, and require complete accuracy.

- Phone service will be highly efficient, including: answered before the fourth ring; no longer than 15 seconds.
- Callers requesting guest room extensions between 1 a.m. and 6 a.m. will be advised of the local time and offered the option of leaving a message or putting the call through.
- Unanswered guest room phones will be picked up within five rings, or 20 seconds.
- Guests will be offered the option of voice mail: they will not automatically be routed to voice mail OR they will have a clear option to return to the operator.

Incoming Faxes and Packages

Mission: To make guests feel that their communications are important, urgent, and require complete accuracy.

- Faxes and packages will be delivered to the guest room within 30 minutes of receipt.

Wake-up Calls

Mission: To make certain that guests are awakened exactly on time in a manner that gently reassures them.

- When wake-up calls are requested, the operator will offer a second reminder call.
- Wake-up calls will occur within two minutes of the requested time.

Guest Room Evening Service

Mission: To create a sense of maximum comfort and relaxation. When meeting guests, to provide a sense of respect and discretion.

- Guest clothing that is on the bed or floor will be neatly folded and placed on the bed or chair – guest clothing left on other furniture will be neatly folded and left in place; shoes will be paired.
- Newspapers and periodicals will be neatly stacked and left on a table or table shelf in plain view; guest personal papers will not be disturbed in any way.
- Guest toiletries will be neatly arranged on a clean, flat cloth.

Laundry and Valet

Mission: To provide excellent workmanship and make guests feel completely assured of the timing and quality of our service.

- Laundry service will include same-day service; express four-hour service; and overnight service (seven days per week).
- Dry cleaning service will include same-day service; express four-hour service (seven days per week).
- Pressing service will be available at any time, and returned within one hour; and can be processed on the normal laundry schedule.

Room Service

Mission: To provide a calm, competent, and thorough dining experience, with accurate time estimates and quick delivery.

- Phone service will be highly efficient, including: answered before the fourth ring; no hold longer than 15 seconds; or, in the case of longer holds, call-backs offered, then provided in less than three minutes.
- Service will be prompt and convenient; an estimated delivery time (an hour and minute, such as "nine-fifteen p.m.") will be specifically mentioned; and the order will be serviced within five minutes (earlier or later) than that time.
- Continental breakfast will be delivered within 20 minutes, other meals within 30 minutes, and drinks-only within 15 minutes.
- Table/tray removal instructions will be provided by a printed card, and tables will be collected within 12 minutes of guest call.

APPENDIX 2: FOUR SEASONS GOALS, BELIEFS, AND PRINCIPLES

Who We Are: We have chosen to specialize within the hospitality industry, by offering only experiences of exceptional quality. Our objective is to be recognized as the company that manages the finest hotels, resorts, residence clubs, and other residential projects wherever we locate. We create properties of enduring value using superior design and finishes, and support them with a deeply instilled ethic of personal service. Doing so allows Four Seasons to satisfy the needs and tastes of our discriminating customers, to maintain our position as the world's premier luxury hospitality company.

What We Believe: Our greatest asset, and the key to our success, is our people. We believe that each of us needs a sense of dignity, pride, and satisfaction in what we do. Because satisfying our guests depends on the united efforts of many, we are most effective when we work together cooperatively, respecting each other's contribution and importance.

How We Behave: We demonstrate our beliefs most meaningfully in the way we treat each other and by the example we set for one another. In all our interactions with our guests, business associates, and colleagues, we seek to deal with others as we would have them deal with us.

How We Succeed: We succeed when every decision is based on a clear understanding of and belief in what we do and when we couple this conviction with sound financial planning. We expect to achieve a fair and reasonable profit to ensure the prosperity of the company, and to offer long-term benefits to our hotel owners, our shareholders, our customers, and our employees.

APPENDIX 3: COMPARATIVE DATA ON PARISIAN PALACES

Property	Construction/Style	Capacity (Rooms and Suites)	Amenities	Price (Dollar/ Single Room)	Owner	Lessee/Operator
Bristol	Built in 1829/Louis XV–XVI style	180	1 restaurant: Le Bristol 1 interior garden 1 swimming pool 1 fitness center 1 beauty salon	480–600	Société Oetker[cc] (1978)	Independent
Crillon	Built in the 18th century/Louis XV–XVI style	152	2 restaurants: L'Ambassadeur and L'Obélix 1 fitness center Guerlain Beauty Institute	460–550	Groupe Hôtels Concorde[aa] (1907)	Groupe Hôtels Concorde[aa] (1907)
Four Seasons Hotel George V Paris	Built in 1928/Art Deco style	245	1 restaurant: Le Cinq 1 swimming pool 1 fitness center 1 beauty salon	670	Prince Al Waleed Bin Talal[dd] (1996)	Four Seasons Hotels and Resorts (2000)
Meurice	Built in the 18th century/Louis XV–XVI style	161	1 restaurant: Le Meurice 1 fitness center Caudalie Beauty Institute	470–550	The Sultan of Brunei (1997)	The Dorchester Group[bb] (2001)
Plaza Athenée	Built in 1889/Belle Epoque style	144	2 restaurants: Le Relais Plaza	490–508	The Sultan of Brunei (1997)	The Dorchester Group[bb] (2001)
Ritz	Built in 1898/Louis XV–XVI style	139	1 restaurant: L'Espadon Escoffier-Ritz cooking school 1 fitness center 1 beauty salon 1 swimming pool	From 580	Mohammed Al Fayed (1979)	Independent

Notes: [a] Groupe Hôtels Concorde was created in 1973 to regroup the luxury hotels such as the Crillon, the Lutetia, and the Hôtel Concorde Saint-Lazare (all in Paris) owned by La Société du Louvre. [b] The Dorchester Group, a subsidiary of the Brunei Investment Agency, was established in 1996 as an independent United Kingdom-registered company to manage luxury hotels, including The Dorchester in London, The Beverly Hills Hotel California, and the Hotel Meurice in Paris. [c] The Oetker Group is a German agribusiness group which owns four luxury hotels in addition to the Bristol: the Cap Eden Roc in Antibes, France; the Park Hotel in Vitznau, Switzerland; the Brenner's Park Hotel in Baden-Baden, Germany; and the Château du Domaine Saint-Martin in Vence, France. [d] Al Waleed Bin Talal owns 21.9 percent of Four Seasons' stocks. Investments by Prince Al Waleed in Four Seasons' properties include F. S. George V and Riyadh (100 percent); London (majority); Cairo, Amman, Alexandria, Sharm El Sheikh and Beirut (unspecified); and Aviara (minority).

Sources: "Four Seasons Hotels and Resorts," Brian D. Egger et al., Crédit Suisse First Boston, April 5, 2002, p. 21. http://meuricehotel.com, www.ritz.com, www.hotel-bristol.com, www.four-seasons.com/paris/vacations/index.html, www.plaza-athenee-paris.com, www.crillon.com. All accessed June 2002.

APPENDIX 4: PREDICTABLE PATTERNS OF MONOCHRONIC AND POLYCHRONIC CULTURES

Monochronic People (Americans)	Polychronic People (French)
Do one thing at a time	Do many things at once
Concentrate on the job	Can be easily distracted and manage interruptions well
Take time commitments (deadlines, schedules) seriously	Consider an objective to be achieved, if possible
Are low-context and need information	Are high-context and already have information
Are committed to the job	Are committed to people and human relationships
Adhere religiously to plans	Change plans often and easily
Are concerned about not disturbing others; follow rules of privacy and consideration	Are more concerned with those who are closely related (family, friends, close business associates) than with privacy
Show great respect for private property; seldom borrow or lend	Borrow and lend things often and easily
Emphasize promptness	Base promptness on the relationship
Are accustomed to short-term relationships	Have strong tendency to build lifetime relationships

Source: Adapted from Edward T. Hall, *Understanding cultural differences, German, French, and Americans*. Yarmouth, ME: Intercultural Press, 1990.

NOTES

1. Kotter, J. P. and Heskett, J. L. 1990. *Corporate culture and performance*. New York: The Free Press.
2. Heskett, J. L., Schlesinger, L. A. and Sasser, W. E., Jr. 1997. *The service profit chain*. New York: The Free Press; Schneider, B. and Bowen, D. E. 1995. *Winning the service game*. Boston, MA: Harvard Business School Press; and Berry, L. L. 1995. *On great service*. New York: The Free Press.
3. Schein, E. H. 1990. Organizational culture. *American Psychologist*, 45(2): 109–19.
4. The theory behind this discussion finds its roots in the contingency work of scholars such as Lawrence and Lorch; see Lawrence, P. and Lorsch, J. 1967. *Organization and environment*. Boston, MA: Harvard Business School Press. Other scholars, including James Heskett, have used the contingency perspective as a starting point for theories of internationalization of services; see Loveman, G. 1993. *The internationalization of services*. Harvard Business School Module Note No. 9–693–103, Boston, MA: Harvard Business School Publishing. Heskett's views have influenced ours considerably. We are indebted to Professor Caren Siehl, Thunderbird, for much of the framework on managing the potential clash between organizational culture and country culture, which she developed for her organizational behavior MBA classes. In turn, Caren always acknowledges an intellectual debt to Professor Joanne Martin, Stanford University.
5. *Interior Design*, March 2000, p. S24.
6. For example, maternity leave for a salaried employee's first child was six weeks of prenatal leave and ten weeks of paid leave after birth; for a third child, it was eight weeks off before and 18 weeks after birth.

7. Communist-controlled labor union (Confédération Générale du Travail) or CGT, nearly 2.4 million members (claimed); independent labor union or Force Ouvrière, 1 million members (estimated); independent white-collar union or Confédération Générale des Cadres, 340,000 members (claimed); Socialist-leaning labor union (Confédération Française Démocratique du Travail) or CFDT, about 800,000 members (estimated). Source: www.cia.gov/cia/publications/factbook/goes/fr.html, accessed June 10, 2002.
8. Hofstede's work was based on a survey conducted by questionnaire with IBM employees in 50 different countries; see Hofstede, G. 1982. *Culture's consequences: international differences in work-related values*. Thousand Oaks, CA: SAGE.
9. Hofstede's approach has not been without its critics, but, as Hickson comments, Hofstede had "frail data, but robust concepts"; see Hickson, D. 1996. The ASQ years then and now through the eyes of a Euro-Brit. *Administrative Science Quarterly*, 41(2): 217–28.
10. See d'Iribarne, P. 1996/97. The usefulness of an ethnographic approach to the international comparison of organization. *International Studies of Management and Organisation*, 18(4): 32.
11. Van der Horst, B. Edward T. Hall – a great-grandfather of NLP, www.cs.ucr.edu/gnick/bvdh/print_edward_t_hall_great_htm, accessed April 20, 2002. The article reviews Hall, E. 1959. *The silent language*. New York: Doubleday.
12. One alternative was to give the staff a significant enough severance package to encourage them to go. However, as Young explained, "The government deplores that approach."
13. Usually used to describe a meal – say a first course of fromage de tête (pig's head set in jelly) or bouillabaisse (fish soup), followed by a main course of blanquette de veau (veal stew with white sauce), and rounded off with a plateau de fromage (cheese platter) or tarte aux pommes (apple tart).

PART II

Cross-cultural and Diversity Management

DOI: 10.4324/9781003247272-8

Robin J. Ely and David A. Thomas

GETTING SERIOUS ABOUT DIVERSITY

Enough Already with the Business Case[*]

T HE BUSINESS CASE HAS BEEN made to demonstrate the value a
diverse board brings to the company and its constituents.

The case for establishing a truly diverse workforce, at all organizational
levels, grows more compelling each year. ... The financial impact—as
proven by multiple studies—makes this a no-brainer.

The business case is clear: When women are at the table, the discussion
is richer, the decision-making process is better, and the organization is
stronger.

These rallying cries for more diversity in companies, from recent statements
by CEOs, are representative of what we hear from business leaders around the
world. They have three things in common: All articulate a business case for hiring
more women or people of color; all demonstrate good intentions; and none of the
claims is actually supported by robust research findings.

We say this as scholars who were among the first to demonstrate the potential benefits of more race and gender heterogeneity in organizations. In 1996, we
published a *Harvard Business Review* article, in which we argued that companies
adopting a radically new way of understanding and leveraging diversity could
reap the real and full benefits of a diverse workforce. This new way entailed
not only recruiting and retaining more people from underrepresented "identity
groups," but also tapping their identity-related knowledge and experiences as
resources for learning how the organization could perform its core work better.
Our research showed that when companies take this approach, their teams are
more effective than either homogeneous teams or diverse teams that don't learn

* Originally published by Harvard Business Publishing.

DOI: 10.4324/9781003247272-9

from their members' differences. Such companies send a message that varied points of view are valued and don't need to be suppressed for the sake of group cohesion. This attitude encourages employees to rethink how work gets done and how best to achieve their goals.

We called this approach the learning-and-effectiveness paradigm. We argued that cultivating a learning orientation toward diversity—one in which people draw on their experiences as members of particular identity groups to reconceive tasks, products, business processes, and organizational norms— enables companies to increase their effectiveness. We stand by the research on which that article was based, and we continue to advocate its conclusions.

> *Increasing diversity does not, by itself, increase effectiveness; what matters is how an organization harnesses diversity, and whether it's willing to reshape its power structure.*

The problem is that nearly 25 years later, organizations have largely failed to adopt a learning orientation toward diversity and are no closer to reaping its benefits. Instead, business leaders and diversity advocates alike are advancing a simplistic and empirically unsubstantiated version of the business case. They misconstrue or ignore what abundant research has now made clear: Increasing the numbers of traditionally underrepresented people in your workforce does not automatically produce benefits. Taking an "add diversity and stir" approach, while business continues as usual, will not spur leaps in your firm's effectiveness or financial performance.

And despite all the rhetoric about the value of diversity, white women and people of color remain seriously underrepresented in many industries and in most companies' senior ranks. That lack of progress suggests that top executives don't actually find the business case terribly compelling.

On that point, we have to agree: The simplistic business case isn't persuasive. A credible and powerful case can be made, however, with three critical modifications. First, platitudes must give way to sound, empirically based conclusions. Second, business leaders must reject the notion that maximizing shareholder returns is paramount; instead, they must embrace a broader vision of success that encompasses learning, innovation, creativity, flexibility, equity, and human dignity. Finally, leaders must acknowledge that increasing demographic diversity does not, by itself, increase effectiveness; what matters is how an organization harnesses diversity, and whether it's willing to reshape its power structure.

In this reading, we expose the flaws in the current diversity rhetoric and then outline what a 21st-century learning-and-effectiveness paradigm could look like—and how leaders can foster it.

A CRITIQUE OF THE BUSINESS CASE FOR DIVERSITY

Let's start with the claim that putting more women on corporate boards leads to economic gains. That's a fallacy, probably fueled by studies that went viral a decade ago reporting that the more women directors a company has, the better its financial performance. But those studies show correlations, not causality. In all likelihood, some other factor—such as industry or firm size—is responsible for both increases in the number of women directors and improvement in a firm's performance.

In any case, the research touting the link was conducted by consulting firms and financial institutions, and fails to pass muster when subjected to scholarly scrutiny. Meta-analyses of rigorous, peer-reviewed studies found no significant relationships—causal or otherwise—between board gender diversity and firm performance. That could be because women directors may not differ from their male counterparts in the characteristics presumed to affect board decisions, and even if they do differ, their voices may be marginalized. What is more pertinent, however, is that board decisions are typically too far removed from firms' bottom-line performance to exert a direct or unconditional effect.

As for studies citing the positive impact of racial diversity on corporate financial performance, they do not stand up to scrutiny either. Indeed, we know of no evidence to suggest that replacing, say, two or three white male directors with people from underrepresented groups is likely to enhance the profits of a Fortune 500 company.

The economic argument for diversity is no more valid when it's applied to changing the makeup of the overall workforce. A 2015 survey of Harvard Business School alumni revealed that 76% of those in senior executive positions believed that "a more diverse workforce improves the organization's financial performance." But scholarly researchers have rarely found that increased diversity leads to improved financial outcomes. They have found that it leads to higher-quality work, better decision-making, greater team satisfaction, and more equality—under certain circumstances. Although those outcomes could conceivably make some aspects of the business more profitable, they would need to be extraordinarily consequential to affect a firm's bottom line.

Moreover, advocates who justify diversity initiatives on the basis of financial benefits may be shooting themselves in the foot. Research suggests that when company diversity statements emphasize the economic payoffs, people from underrepresented groups start questioning whether the organization is a place where they really belong, which reduces their interest in joining it. In addition, when diversity initiatives promise financial gains but fail to deliver, people are likely to withdraw their support for them.

Still another flaw in the familiar business case for diversity is the notion that a diverse team will have richer discussions and a better decision-making process simply because it is diverse. Having people from various identity groups "at the table" is no guarantee that anything will get better; in fact, research shows that things often get worse, because increasing diversity can increase tensions and conflict. Under the right organizational conditions, though, employees can turn cultural differences into assets for achieving team goals.

Studies have shown, for example, that diverse teams realize performance benefits in certain circumstances: when team members are able to reflect on and discuss team functioning; when status differences among ethnic groups are minimized; when people from both high- and low-status identity groups believe the team supports learning; and—as we reported in our earlier article—when teams orient members to learn from their differences rather than marginalize or deny them. But absent conditions that foster inquiry, egalitarianism, and learning, diversity either is unrelated to or undermines team effectiveness.

> *When diversity initiatives promise financial gains but fail to deliver, people are likely to withdraw their support for them.*

Many progressive companies today recognize the conditional nature of the diversity–performance link and have moved beyond "diversity," the catchword of the 1990s, to "diversity and inclusion." They understand that just increasing the number of people from underrepresented groups is not meaningful if those employees do not feel valued and respected. We applaud the emphasis on inclusion, but it is insufficient because it doesn't fundamentally reconfigure power relations.

Being genuinely valued and respected involves more than just feeling included. It involves having the power to help set the agenda, influence what—and how—work is done, have one's needs and interests taken into account, and have one's contributions recognized and rewarded with further opportunities to contribute and advance. Undertaking this shift in power is what the learning-and-effectiveness companies we wrote about in 1996 were doing, and it's what enabled them to tap diversity's true benefits.

THE LEARNING-AND-EFFECTIVENESS PARADIGM, REDUX

What we've learned since we wrote our original article is that embracing a learning orientation toward diversity turns out to be quite difficult. To make real progress, people—and the organizational cultures they inhabit—must change. But instead of doing the hard work involved, companies have generally stuck with easier, more limited approaches that don't alter the status quo.

We previously identified four actions that were helping business leaders and managers shift to a learning-and-effectiveness approach. We still consider those actions fundamental, but we present them anew here to underscore the message in light of today's challenges and opportunities.

Build Trust

The first task for those in charge is to build trust by creating a workplace where people feel safe expressing themselves freely. That requires setting a tone of honest discourse and getting comfortable with vulnerability—one's own and others'. At no time has this need been greater in the United States than during the current unrest spurred by outrage over police brutality against Black men and women—a legacy of centuries of racism. Two weeks into the nationwide protests that began in May, white leaders in companies across the country struggled with how to respond. Publicly expressing support for the Black Lives Matter movement was one thing; knowing what to say to Black employees, who might already have been feeling marginalized or undervalued at work, was quite another. Leaders who were used to wielding authority grounded in their subject-matter expertise had no comparable expertise to handle the deep grief, rage, and despair felt by many of their employees—especially their Black employees.

And Black leaders, many with firsthand experience of police mistreatment and other forms of racial oppression, faced the challenge of managing their own strong emotions and speaking their truth without appearing biased against whites.

Yet troubling times provide opportunities for leaders to begin conversations that foster learning. In response to public acts of racial injustice, for example, white leaders can reach out from a place of vulnerability, as a way of creating connection and psychological safety, rather than staying silent from a place of privilege and self-protection. This was the choice made by a white senior partner in a global professional services firm when he decided to convene a special virtual meeting with his teams across the country. He knew that if he said nothing about the recent racist incidents, his silence would speak for him, with a message not of neutrality but of complicity. Just weeks before, he'd been eloquent in addressing the distress wrought by the COVID-19 pandemic, but when it came to race, he felt at a complete loss. What he astutely realized, though, was that people needed him simply to begin a dialogue, acknowledge his pain and theirs, and give them the space to talk about their experiences inside and outside the firm, if they wished. He had no solutions, but that moment required none—just a willingness to speak from the heart and listen compassionately to whatever his colleagues might share. Perhaps most important, he was willing to risk not getting his own words or actions exactly right, and he was ready to receive feedback with openness and equanimity.

Actively Work against Discrimination and Subordination

Creating psychological safety and building employees' trust can be an excellent starting point for the second action: taking concrete measures to combat forms of discrimination and subordination that inhibit employees' ability to thrive. This action calls for both individual and collective learning aimed at producing systemic change.

Over the years we've seen the emergence of a multibillion-dollar industry dedicated to advancing such goals. Companies have adopted a slew of initiatives as a result: affinity groups, mentoring programs, work–family accommodation policies, and unconscious bias training, to name a few. But the sad truth is that these efforts largely fail to produce meaningful, sustained change—and sometimes even backfire.

Leaders are the stewards of an organization's culture; their behaviors and mindsets reverberate throughout the organization. Hence, to dismantle systems of discrimination and subordination, leaders must undergo the same shifts of heart, mind, and behavior that they want for the organization as a whole and then translate those personal shifts into real, lasting change in their companies.

To that end, a first step for leaders is to learn about how systems of privilege and oppression—racism, sexism, ethnocentrism, classism, heterosexism—operate in the wider culture. Numerous excellent books and articles can help with this work; they have the added benefit of relieving those on the receiving end of oppressive systems from the burden of educating their majority-group counterparts. And the impact can be surprising. For example, major news organizations picked up the story of a Black flight attendant who noticed a white male passenger reading a book about white people's reluctance to confront racism. She struck up a conversation with the man and had a moving exchange with him, eventually learning that he was the CEO of a major airline. The encounter filled her with hope: Here was a powerful executive—someone in a position to effect change—making a genuine effort to understand systemic racism.

> Learning from cultural differences is more likely once leaders have created trust, begun to dismantle systems of discrimination and subordination, and embraced a range of styles.

Educating oneself is important, but it will be meaningless unless leaders take the next step: investigating how their organization's culture has reproduced systems of oppression, undercutting some groups' opportunities to thrive and succeed, while giving others a boost. As part of that investigation, leaders must examine what stereotypes and assumptions they hold about employees' competencies and suitability for jobs, acknowledge that they have blind spots, and come to see how their personal defenses can shut down learning—their own and their organization's. Working with hundreds of leaders over the years, we have seen how this individual learning journey can be a transformational experience that often leads to individual behavioral change.

But that's not enough. The critical final step in rooting out systems of discrimination and subordination is for leaders to use their personal experience to spur collective learning and systemic change. It is here that even the most progressive leaders' efforts tend to stall. Such efforts require a well-articulated, widely shared organizational mission to motivate and guide change, together with a collective process of continuous reflection and consciousness-raising, experimentation, and action—followed by sustained attention, monitoring each change for impact, and making adjustments accordingly.

An example of this process comes from a midsize consulting firm whose partners—almost all white men—had begun to fear that high turnover among the white women and people of color they employed meant they were losing talent, potentially undermining the firm's competitiveness. Taking a hard look at their culture, they identified a flawed approach to project assignment that was inadvertently contributing to systematic inequities. Plum projects were going disproportionately to white men; it was the old story of people having an easier time identifying talent when it comes in a package that looks like them. When a particularly challenging project for an important client came up—the kind that can stretch and give exposure to a promising young consultant—the white male partners staffed it with their go-to people: other white men. Meanwhile, white women and people of color, despite having been recruited from the same highly competitive MBA programs as their white male counterparts, regularly were assigned the more mundane projects. They got stuck doing tasks they had long ago mastered, which led many to leave the firm. Come promotion time, the few who remained were either counseled out or told they still weren't ready for partnership; women waited two years longer than men, on average, to make partner.

But were the go-to people actually better? Did they really have more "raw horsepower," as the partners believed? When those leaders examined their developmental practices, they were chagrined to see clear patterns in who received coaching, whose mistakes were forgiven, and who got second and even third chances to prove themselves: the white men. So after an uncomfortable reckoning with their biases, the partners decided to experiment with making comparable investments in people they'd previously overlooked—people they might have automatically, if not quite consciously, written off simply as hires to meet diversity goals. When they started treating white women and people of color more like the white men they'd favored, they were surprised to find a bigger, more diverse pool of talent than they'd expected.

Embrace a Wide Range of Styles and Voices

The third necessary action for leaders and managers involves actively trying to understand how organizational norms might implicitly discourage certain behavioral styles or silence certain voices. For example, in companies where the prototypical leader is a white man who earns respect by speaking assertively, women and Black men, who are often penalized for being assertive, may find themselves in a double bind: They can conform to the organization's norms and deviate from cultural prescriptions for their group, or they can do the opposite. But either way, they violate one set of expectations, risking marginalization and diminished chances for advancement.

Managers may believe they're giving helpful feedback when they tell a large Black man to smile more so that his white colleagues won't fear him, when they ask a Latina who advocates passionately for a project to dial it down, when they encourage a no-nonsense white woman to be "nicer," or when they urge a soft-spoken woman of East Asian descent to speak more forcefully. But all such messages communicate that these employees must be ever-mindful of how others see them in relation to stereotyped images of their group, making it harder for them to bring their talents and perspectives to the table. Companies need performance management systems that tie feedback and evaluation criteria to bona fide task requirements rather than group stereotypes.

Make Cultural Differences a Resource for Learning

For companies shifting to a learning-and-effectiveness paradigm, the fourth action is to encourage—and draw lessons from—open discussions about how identity groups shape employees' experiences inside and outside the organization. Leaders should frame those experiences as a valid source of ideas for enhancing the organization's work and culture. Even if employees champion ideas that are at odds with the company's profit goals, those ideas may still be worth pursuing if they help the organization achieve its mission or uphold its values.

Over the years, we have seen that learning from cultural differences is more likely to occur once the previous three actions are under way: Leaders have created trust, begun to dismantle systems of discrimination and subordination, and embraced a broad range of styles. Without such efforts, talking about differences happens (if it happens at all) only in reaction to diversity-related crises—when discussions tend to be fraught and people's capacity to learn is diminished.

An example of learning from gender diversity comes from Boris Groysberg's study of top-ranked research analysts on Wall Street. In exploring whether they take their star status with them when they switch firms, he found a fascinating sex difference: Unlike their male counterparts, whose performance worsened upon changing firms, women who made a move experienced no such performance drop. The reason, Groysberg concluded, was that women analysts faced sex discrimination, and so they had to do the job differently from men. Women had a more difficult time building support networks inside their firm, had fewer mentors, and were neglected by high-status groups such as the firm's institutional sales force—an important source of industry information. And so, unlike men, women built their franchises on portable, external relationships with clients, companies, and the media. In addition, they forged unconventional in-house relationships with their firm's retail sales force—also an important source of industry information, but a low-status group that male analysts typically ignored. Not only were women stars able to maintain their performance upon switching firms but, generally speaking, they outperformed their male peers over the nine-year period of the study. In short, women were not only different; they were better.

In a follow-up set of case studies, coauthored with Ashish Nanda and Laura Morgan Roberts, respectively, Groysberg showed how a Wall Street firm's research director leveraged women's "difference" to everyone's advantage. He aggressively recruited talented women for the analyst role and then set out to create the conditions that would enable them to thrive, emphasizing team culture, allowing flexible work arrangements, and instituting systems that gave analysts regular, unbiased feedback to help them set personal improvement goals. Additionally, he encouraged people to develop their own style and voice. As one woman star in the firm noted, "We have always been given the freedom to be ourselves." Another said, "I never felt I had to pretend to be male to fit in here." Within three years this firm had the highest percentage of top-ranked women analysts of any firm on Wall Street and the lowest rate of female turnover. Furthermore, the research department moved in the rankings from 15th to first, and the unique approach that women had developed for building their franchises became the basis for training all the firm's analysts. What the research director figured out was that gender had given women analysts a unique set of experiences, and those, together with their resilience and ingenuity, led to new insights into how to do the job better.

We have also seen how the mere act of learning across employees' differences can have a positive impact, even when the content of the learning is unrelated to people's identities. The benefits are particularly strong when the differences have been historically fraught with tension. In a study of more than 400 retail bank branches in the northeastern United States, we, together with Irene Padavic of Florida State University, found that the more racially diverse the branch, the better its performance—but only for branches in which all employees, across all racial groups, experienced the environment as conducive to learning. Some of that learning definitely came from sharing cultural knowledge—for example, a white branch manager described how his Chinese coworker's explanations of norms in the Chinese community helped him better serve that segment of customers. But many of the branches' tasks were technical and unrelated to people's cultural backgrounds. In those cases, the benefit from diversity seemed to stem mainly from the process of learning—a process that involves taking risks and being unafraid to say "I don't know," "I made a mistake," or "I need help." Showing such vulnerability across divisive lines of difference, such as race, and being met with acceptance rather than judgment or rejection, strengthens relationships. Stronger relationships in turn increase resilience in the face of conflict and other stressors. In short, for culturally diverse teams, the experience of learning across racial differences can, in and of itself, improve performance.

Inequality is bad for both business and society. Organizations limit their capacity for innovation and continuous improvement unless all employees are full participants in the enterprise: fully seen, heard, developed, engaged—and rewarded accordingly. Moreover, such treatment can unleash enormous reserves of leadership potential too long suppressed by systems that perpetuate inequality.

When the only legitimate conversation about diversity is one that links it to economic gains, we tend to discount the problem of inequality. In fact, studies have shown that making the economic case diminishes people's sense that equality is itself important, limits socially conscious investors' ability to promote it, and may even increase bias. Furthermore, focusing on financial benefits sends a message to traditionally underrepresented employees that they are worth hiring and investing in only because having "their kind" in the mix increases the firm's profitability.

Companies will not reap benefits from diversity unless they build a culture that insists on equality. Treating differences as a source of knowledge and connection lays the groundwork for such a culture. But as part of that process, firms may have to make financial investments that they won't recoup, at least in the short run, and more will be required of top leaders, managers, and rank-and-file employees alike. Everyone will have to learn how to actively listen to others' perspectives, have difficult conversations, refrain from blame and judgment, and solicit feedback about how their behaviors and company practices might be impeding the push for a culture that supports learning, equality, and mutual respect. Developing those capacities is no small feat in any context; it is even more challenging for people working across cultural identity differences. But teams that truly embrace the learning-and-effectiveness paradigm will come to understand that homogeneity isn't better; it's just easier. They'll realize, too, that the benefits of diversity arise as much from the collective work of developing those key capacities as from the collective learning they enable.

Finally, while there is a business case for diversity—one that rests on sound evidence, an expansive definition of what makes a business successful, and the presence of facilitating conditions—we are disturbed by the implication that there must be economic grounds to justify investing in people from underrepresented groups. Why should anyone need an economic rationale for affirming the agency and dignity of any group of human beings? We should make the necessary investment because doing so honors our own and others' humanity and gives our lives meaning. If company profits come at the price of our humanity, they are costing us too much. And if diversity initiatives fail to reckon with that trade-off, they will amount to little more than rearranging the deck chairs on a sinking ship.

Josefine van Zanten and Alexander Fleischmann

INCLUSION IN ORGANIZATIONS

Taking Stock and Going Forward in Turbulent Times

INTRODUCTION

THE TECTONIC CHANGES WE HAVE witnessed so far in the early 2020s have brought equity, inclusion, and diversity (EI&D) to the top of CEOs' priority lists. Today's societies are changing, at a faster pace than ever before, and so should global organizations to stay in tune with the markets they operate in. First and foremost, this means adapting corporate cultures, and hence behaviors.

We now know that the business case for EI&D is well proven (see, e.g., van Knippenberg, Nishii, & Dwertmann, 2020; Creary, McDonnell, Ghai, & Scruggs, 2019; Gompers & Kovvali, 2018), and leading companies have been working for decades towards establishing a diverse workforce and inclusive cultures, measuring their progress along the way. Indeed, EI&D has by now become an imperative for global organizations (Romansky, Garrod, Brown, & Deo, 2021) to adapt to an ever faster-changing socioeconomic and political context that shapes brand identities and consumer behavior and is needed to attract bright talents from all walks of life. Global social movements like #MeToo and Black Lives Matter (BLM) have reached the last corners of global societies, and call for organizations to advance equity and increase visibility of underrepresented groups. With Millennials growing into management positions and Gen Zs entering the workforce, ever more global employees see diversity no longer as just a "nice thing to have," but as a standard, and organizational cultures characterized by equity and inclusion as issues organizations must actively strive for. As if the above changes weren't enough, COVID-19 disrupted work lives globally, and highlighted and exacerbated socioeconomic inequalities. This added inclusive hybrid work settings and the socioeconomic background to the list of issues organizations must deal with. In addition, the war in Ukraine and the uprising in Iran are the latest examples of the turbulent 2020s.

DOI: 10.4324/9781003247272-10

How can organizations act proactively in such a complex environment today to increase inclusiveness? And how can organizations validate their progress and measure inclusion reliably?

To work towards answering these questions and to guide organizations in their EI&D efforts, the International Institute for Management Development (IMD) ran a rigorous academic research project called *Inclusive Future*, sponsored by a Fortune 500 organization, on which this reading is based.[1]

INCLUSION AS KEY TO PROMOTING EI&D

Equity, inclusion, and diversity have been on the agenda of business to attract and retain talents from all walks of life, to serve and represent a broad group of customers and stakeholders, and to build an open and safe culture where *everyone* can thrive. Still, not enough progress has been made when it comes to the diversification of senior leadership positions (Nkomo, Bell, Roberts, Joshi, & Thatcher, 2019) as the management of corporations, and especially their C-suites, do not mirror the communities they serve.

Research shows that diversity can have positive and negative effects on team performance as it may lead not only to increased creativity and satisfaction, but also to lower social integration and increased conflict (Stahl, Maznevski, Voigt, & Jonsen, 2010). It is inclusion and inclusive leadership that "unlock" the positive potential of a diverse workforce (Hewlett, Marshall, Sherbin, & Gonsalves, 2013).

Indeed, diversity (the representation of people from underrepresented groups) can exist without inclusion, as an organization may have a diverse workforce, but only a privileged group is in key decision-making positions – and inclusion can also exist without diversity in cases of a homogenous workforce being able to participate in organizational decision making (Mor Barak, 2017: 492). While diversity management aims to ensure that individuals from underrepresented groups are part of the organization, it can only be "the initial step toward workplace inclusion" (Mor Barak, 2017: 363), and requires psychological and physical safety to deliver the many EI&D promises (Edmondson, 2019; Prime & Salib, 2015) – see also Box 1.

BOX 1: Diversity and inclusion

It is worth pointing out that while diversity can be present in an organization without inclusion, it is diversity that tests the strength of inclusion. Indeed, only when diversity is present we can talk about real inclusion – without the presence of diversity, it is a group of like-minded people from similar backgrounds who happily agree they feel included. When there is visible diversity in an organization, it becomes important to foster inclusive behaviors through daily interactions.

Hence, instead of focusing solely on representing the diversity of its environment within an organization, inclusion aims to create organizational structures, team environments, behaviors, and leadership potentials that foster an environment where everyone feels part of the organization (see, e.g., Nkomo, 2014; Shore, Cleveland, & Sanchez, 2018) – ways to achieve this are discussed in Box 2. Unlocking the potential of diversity through inclusion today implies also taking intersectionality into account, which means that individuals are different and similar along various – intersecting – lines. For instance, in terms of race/ethnicity, sexual orientation: for example, a Black leader might also be female and part of the LGBTQ+ community.

BOX 2: Fostering EI&D – review talent pipeline, fast-tracking, and inclusive leadership

Organizations can act on power imbalances by reviewing their talent pipeline, fast-tracking members of underrepresented groups, and reviewing their external hiring policies. Whilst many organizations are already working on these steps, few have mastered the fine nuances and **behavioral influences** that impact the end result. Most still require a thorough review of these steps to identify key decisive moments to improve the selection and promotion of *all* talents. Inclusive leadership, i.e., **leaders acting as visible allies and vocal advocates**, plays a pivotal role in progressing towards further equity in organizations. It would mean leaders visibly speak about talents from different backgrounds in formal and in informal settings; they openly sponsor their work; regularly highlight their achievements; vocally and convincingly recommend them for the next promotion, among others.

In light of the many changes in society in recent years and based on an analysis that demonstrated just how much expectations about inclusion changed as a result, we developed a comprehensive and future-proof inclusion model (see Figure 1). It contains all the core components of inclusion as they stand today, and will allow organizations to foster a comprehensive and truly inclusive culture.

Whilst we have known for some time that psychological safety is the core to inclusion, other components were added in practice over time, such as belonging, as well as participation and fairness, the latter pointing to equity in EI&D. Newer areas that percolated to the surface as a result of recent societal shifts include authenticity and uniqueness. Today's core inclusion components span as follows:

- **belongingness, authenticity, and uniqueness** as aspects that account for the personal level,
- **participation and fairness** as organizational components pointing to equity,
- **psychological safety** being at the center, as it establishes an environment that allows individuals to speak up freely without fear of retribution,
- and **diversity** to ensure that individuals from *all* walks of life are included.

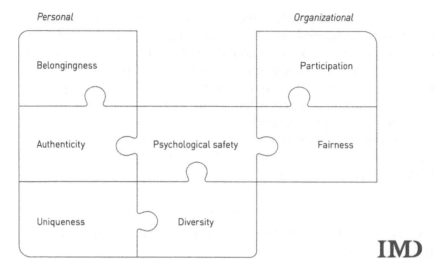

Personal   *Organizational*

Belongingness   Participation

Authenticity   Psychological safety   Fairness

Uniqueness   Diversity

IMD

Figure 1 Components of inclusion.
Source: IMD.

Indeed, it is equally documented that to foster inclusion, inclusive leadership is a key driver: Leaders must manage the balance of two seemingly contradictory needs of both employees and leaders themselves: the needs to feel part of the whole ("belongingness") while remaining true to one's own identities ("unique-ness") at the same time – as conceptualized in optimal distinctiveness theory (Brewer, 1991). Leaders who show inclusive leadership behaviors are not only able to create an inclusive environment; by showcasing inclusive traits – such as cognizance, courage, curiosity, commitment, cultural intelligence, and collabora-tion (Dillon & Bourke, 2016) – they also act as visible role models and advocates.

CHANGING GLOBAL SOCIETIES: IMPACT ON INCLUSION AND INCLUSIVE LEADERSHIP

Corporations that are committed in word and action to EI&D foster inclusion and inclusive cultures with all the opportunities and hurdles this brings along – as discussed in Box 3. The tremendous changes we've witnessed in the early 2020s call for a renewed focus on inclusion to prevail in fast-changing business environ-ments and to continue to engage a new profile of employees.

BOX 3: Leadership strategies and talent competency frameworks

The socioeconomic and political turbulences of early 2022 raised many pressing questions and development opportunities for organizations as well as leaders and pointed to a refreshed focus on leadership strategies and tal-ent competency frameworks to include explicit inclusive behaviors and inclu-sive leadership. More specifically, it highlighted the importance of different styles in daily interactions and behaviors to reflect the ability to foster inclusion in broad ways, encompassing newer inclusion components, for all talents to progress.

Global social movements like #MeToo are having a long-term impact as they have popularized talking about concepts like patriarchy and toxic masculinity to point towards systemic inequalities pervasive in societies around the globe (see, e.g., Lee & Murdie, 2021). The latter impose and normalize a toxic and patriarchal male culture from which both women and men suffer, though not equally so. Behavior that has long been unwelcome but often seen as "normal" became "denormalized." For example, men interrupt women 30–40% more than men (Hancock & Rubin, 2015), affecting women's ability to contribute equally and elaborate on their ideas and know-how, impacting their creditability and confidence, and ultimately negatively affecting their image as leaders. Organizations must address toxic masculinity and patriarchy, both sensitive but crucial topics, in order to go to the root causes of inequalities on gender as well as other areas of diversity. See Box 4 for practical implications.

BOX 4: Stepping up, role modeling – and discussing patriarchy as well as toxic masculinity

In such prevalent situations, leaders from all backgrounds, aware of this dynamic, can firmly yet constructively counter multiple interruptions. For example, open statements such as "Tereza wasn't quite finished with her idea, let's give her an opportunity to share it in full" or "I know you want to contribute, John, and I think we ought to give Jing the opportunity to finish her comments first" are easy to adopt and implement. By displaying these simple behaviors, the habit of interrupting people from underrepresented groups will fade as leaders ensure new behaviors are adopted. In addition, men should become active allies and advocates in debating patriarchy and toxic masculinity.

Another social evolution – or even revolution – in the form of BLM has had and is still having a large impact on inclusion. BLM started in 2013, and became a global social movement in 2020 (see, e.g., Anderson, Barthel, Perrin, & Vogels, 2021). It raised our attention to systemic racism and another complex topic: white privilege. In tune with the world in which they operate, many companies supported BLM vocally, yet questions were raised about the visibility and lives of underprivileged groups working in the manual roles within their organizations. Both #MeToo and BLM sparked waves of advocacy and allyship – avidly picked up by Gen Zs – but also waves of resistance. As explored in Box 5, organizations in the 2020s must proactively navigate this space to represent their clients, partners and stakeholders, as well as keep close contact with *all* their employees and changing expectations around inclusion.

BOX 5: Intersectionality – bringing visibility to members of underrepresented groups

Leaders need to be aware of the power dynamics that are at play at work and in society. Black people and People of Color remain less visible in Europe as well as in North America. Black and Asian women especially are too often not heard nor seen, yet key social movements were started by them (BLM and #MeToo). Hence, intersectionality is key. With this knowledge, leaders ought to focus on getting to know talents from this pool and spend time with them. They may be the source of ground-breaking ideas that are dismissed or get ridiculed. It is helpful to understand their ambitions and their daily realities, which are often filled with hurdles and discrimination their leaders may not be aware of. Inclusive leaders ought to be open to learn with humility, reflect on their (white) privilege, and use their position to support and sponsor them. Becoming a member of a People of Color employee resource group (ERG) is a good first step, providing leaders step in with an open mindset to listen and learn.

In addition to the social movements discussed earlier, the 2000s have seen rising socioeconomic inequalities (Piketty, 2014, 2020) – with organizations inadvertently perpetuating socioeconomic inequalities (Amis, Mair, & Munir, 2020). This means, at the same time, that organizations are and must be part of the solution. Indeed, with socioeconomic inequality being seen as "one of the most pernicious threats to our society" (Amis et al., 2020: 431), a threat to democracy (Wolf, 2017) and the IMF seeing economic growth threatened by unequal opportunities (Aiyar & Ebeke, 2019), addressing socioeconomic inequalities must become a priority of organizations – as discussed in Box 6.

BOX 6: Addressing socioeconomic inequalities

Socioeconomic background should be added as a new diversity dimension, and leaders are well advised to add socioeconomic diversity to their teams, thereby ensuring a more realistic representation of the world the organization operates in. This requires sourcing for a larger university pool, accepting different clothing, language, and writing styles, as well as discouraging "code switching," and supporting uniqueness instead, whilst bridging similar values and beliefs. In addition, the scope of inclusion should be broadened beyond a focus on talent and high potential.

In addition to the global social movements listed earlier, it was COVID-19 that unexpectedly disrupted our lives globally, at the workplace and beyond. COVID-19 made already existing socioeconomic inequalities glaringly apparent – and exacerbated them for many underprivileged groups. The list of impacts is almost endless, ranging from the unequal distribution of child and elder care work among women and men that made working from home more stressful for female employees to more women resigning (Adams-Prassl, Boneva, Golin, & Rauh, 2020); it continues with Black people, younger employees, and manual and precarious workers being dismissed in disproportional numbers: these groups were hit hardest in the labor market (Joyce & Xu, 2020; OECD, 2021), and in the case of women, were set back several decades (United Nations, 2020).

Whilst COVID-19 disrupted the work life of nearly all white-collar workers globally, it set in motion a gigantic investment in remote work. This resulted in working from home becoming a new norm, albeit in different formats, for most organizations; many have now adopted a hybrid form of work (Lund et al., 2021). Organizations must take this opportunity to make hybrid work settings inclusive, as explored in Box 7.

BOX 7: Hybrid work – inclusion is not guaranteed, but must be strived for

Whilst hybrid work means the organization can reap the benefits of including employees from around the world, the hybrid workplace is not a guarantee for inclusion: Proactive enactment of inclusive leadership is needed to make all work settings inclusive and reap the full extent of their opportunities.

During hybrid meetings, leaders need to ensure accessibility for those online and oversee how airtime is shared; they need to manage side conversations in the room, and ensure those online stay in the conversation. It is wise to co-create a clear hybrid meeting protocol with the team, and ensure it is implemented and sustained successfully over time through ongoing enhancements.

These tremendous shifts are being accelerated by the ever-faster pace of technological transformation and, last but not least, by newer generations in the workplace. Millennials – those born between 1981 and 1996 – are currently stepping into management positions; this is the first digital native generation whose members strive to express themselves at work. These employees are driven by purpose and meaning, and aim to make a difference in the world *as well as* within their organizations. Work–life balance is high on their list of priorities, contrary to Baby Boomers (Whitney Gibson, Greenwood, & Murphy, 2009). Coupled with the next generation – Gen Zs – entering the workforce, these trends are being further highlighted and accelerated. In addition to purpose and work–life balance, Gen Zs demand frequent feedback, have a high need for social connection (Gabrielova &

Buchko, 2021), are outspoken supporters of the Black Lives Matter and #MeToo movements (Business Insider, 2020), and together with Millennials, they push hard for climate change action (Pew Research Center, 2021) and see equity, inclusion, and diversity as far more relevant than previous generations (Schroth, 2019). Organizations must reflect this, as explored in Box 8.

BOX 8: Including younger generations to advance sustainability and EI&D

Leaders are wise to tap into these sources of energy from Gen Z and Millennials to help drive sustainability topics in their organization, including EI&D. Encouraging and rewarding ERG participation, giving them space and a platform to share their views and mindsets on a regular basis, as well as giving them a voice to contribute to creating inclusion at all levels of the organization may unleash a tsunami of engagement and enhanced loyalty. Often, fostering inclusion is decided in the nuanced behaviors, the informal conversations and coaching, where reverse coaching and mentoring may equally prove to be insightful for inclusive leaders and *all* talents.

The model in Figure 2 summarizes the many changes witnessed recently, and how they impact EI&D. Organizations are well advised to both understand and take into account these shifts and their impact when setting EI&D ambitions and developing inclusive leaders.

For organizations, the macro trends documented earlier in this reading call for a new and increased focus on inclusion and inclusive leadership: On the individual level, social movements and socioeconomic inequalities call for focusing on listening with humility and crediting input from underrepresented groups. Acting as their visible allies and vocal advocates, employees at all levels should educate themselves on the issues raised. At the team level, inclusive leadership should be understood as a collective process where everyone is able to speak up to establish an inclusive culture. As organizations are increasingly scrutinized, fact-checked, and held accountable, inclusive leadership at the organizational level means to take a stand – also in potentially heated debates – and back this up with broad and sustainable systems and processes to help organizations becoming themselves visible allies.

TRACKING PROGRESS: MEASURING INCLUSION

To track their progress, organizations are well advised to measure inclusion. The common approach to measuring taken by leading companies is to ask their employees about their individual perception of inclusion in a recurring survey (referred to as an inclusion index, and usually embedded in an annual or bi-annual employee survey). Whilst an inclusion survey is better than none, we know that these surveys are not comparable for many reasons, and that today, the full components of inclusion are not addressed. As a result, there is no "golden standard" for measuring inclusion. While many organizations have been relying

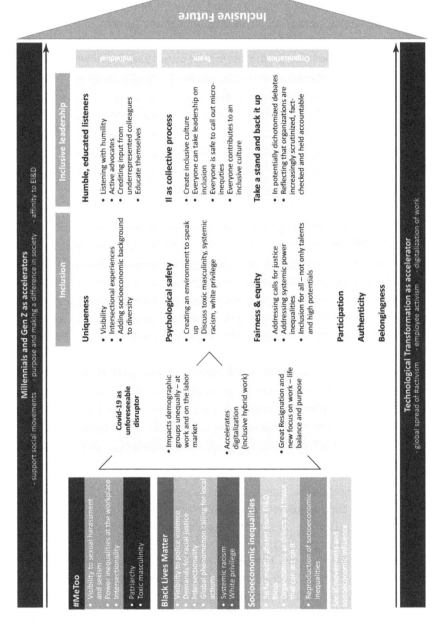

Figure 2 Impact of changing socioeconomic framework on inclusion and inclusive leadership.

Source: IMD.

on inclusion indices for decades, academic scales provide validated scores based on a multitude of questions that in their entirety are often not applicable in a corporate environment with over-surveyed employees.

Hence, key to measuring inclusion in organizations is to balance practicality, thoroughness, and reliability. Measuring inclusion is key in developing an organizational culture where everyone can thrive, equity and fairness are taken into account, and psychological safety allows everyone to take risks and address sensitive topics. Key to measuring inclusion in recent and future disruptive times is to maintain a core of key elements that can be tracked over time to allow assessing progress while being at the same time open to new challenges as they occur. Accordingly, all actions should aim at creating an environment that cherishes differences, rather than eliminates them.

Based on the recent and ongoing influences on inclusion, yearly inclusion indexes are no longer sufficient to understand how included employees feel in the moment. We recommend a comprehensive approach to measuring inclusion that mixes quantitative and qualitative approaches, coupling short-term and long-term input, to gain in-depth and reliable insights related to inclusion that can be acted upon when needed. It is composed of the following steps.

Quantitative Steps

1. **Update your existing inclusion index, or start an inclusion index that covers questions related to** *all* **six components of inclusion**

   Organizations that already actively measure inclusion might start by asking themselves if they have updated their questions to reflect *all* the six components of inclusion, to create a comprehensive inclusion index in tune with today's expectations of inclusion.

2. **Consider adding an Inclusion Net Promoter Score (iNPS) and Inclusion Nudges**

   Both tools are simple and easy to implement, they take little time, and yet the iNPS can give you a pulse on whether employees would recommend your organization to members of underrepresented groups, and nudges can spur employees to adjust their behaviors and foster more inclusion.

3. **Allow for self-identification – in a secure, safe, and legal way**

   Leading organizations have started to encourage their employees to self-identify in their employee surveys whether they belong to an underrepresented group. Utmost care must be taken to comply with local data protection laws and to set up a system where self-identification is secure and safe for employees globally. The benefit of investing in such a program is in-depth knowledge of the experiences of employees with specific intersectional characteristics, e.g., women with disabilities.

4. **Analyze your inclusion index and iNPS results to "hear" all voices, especially underrepresented ones**

   Ensure your provider has the experience and know-how to analyze the results by using several sub-groups to raise the voices of underrepresented groups, lest their input is drowned in the majority group's input. More often than not, the experience of inclusion is different based on different diversity aspects coupled with seniority, business, location, and more. Without this in-depth analysis, the most valuable insights to focus on targeted actions will be lost.

5. **Consider, if feasible, running an in-depth dedicated survey focused exclusively on inclusion**

    Several organizations have decided to spend time and effort to address inclusion in more depth and breadth than the inclusion index allows. These surveys are usually based on questions tested for their reliability and meaningfulness and are rolled out every two or three years. The same analysis requirements as stated in point 4 apply.

Qualitative Steps

6. **Add qualitative insights to the quantitative inclusion measures and give both visibility**

    Qualitative insights – such as quarterly lunch and learns, blogs, digital boards, and leader-led speaking sessions – offer a sense of what is happening right now and may raise topics unaddressed in yearly quantitative surveys. This is useful to avoid employees picketing online against decisions or other activities that feel exclusive and/or not in line with their values, an activity Millennials and Gen Z have started to adopt. In addition, they offer opportunities to open dialogues on difficult conversations such as white privilege and patriarchy.

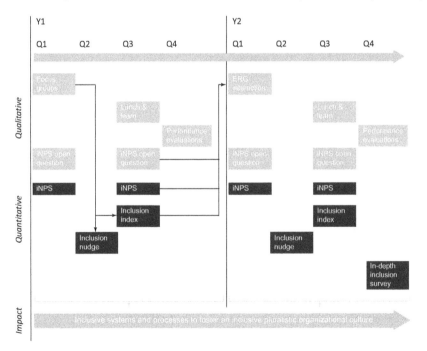

• illustrative arrows depict how the results of focus groups can be used to launch targeted inclusion nudges and adapt the inclusion index results later discussed with ERGs

Figure 3 Comprehensive approach to measuring inclusion.

Source: IMD.

CONCLUSION: PRACTICAL RECOMMENDATIONS FOR CREATING PLURALISTIC INCLUSIVE CULTURES

There are many ways formal and informal systems and processes foster inclusion. Since organizations were designed mostly by white men and for white men, it is no surprise that they still include invisible hurdles for people from underrepresented groups. It is, however, worth noting that more and more attention is given to systems and processes, and that as a result, progress is made to make them equitable. Pay equity and parental leave are two examples that demonstrate hurdles are slowly being recognized and eliminated. Figure 4 summarizes the practical recommendations we bring forward to create pluralistic inclusive cultures, as explored in more detail below.

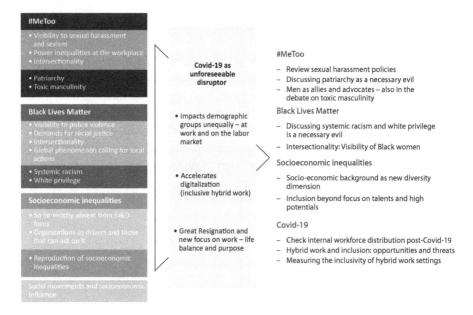

Figure 4 Creating pluralistic inclusive cultures.

Source: IMD.

Leaders can foster inclusion daily through formal and informal interactions. **It is therefore highly recommended that leadership development and talent frameworks list inclusive leadership as a core leadership and talent requirement, and that leaders are held accountable to deliver.** Leaders must actively educate themselves on issues raised by social movements and their calls for social justice. As a result, the culmination of their interactions contributes largely to living and breathing the corporate culture. Hence, we offer a non-exhaustive list of inclusive behaviors taking new aspects of inclusion into account for consideration, reflection, and/or adoption:

1. **Organizations must review and refresh their sexual harassment policies,** as recent years have demonstrated that sexual harassment is still prevalent – and that it is systematic. Indeed, less than 10% of sexual harassment accusations turn out to be "fake" (Orchowski, Bogen, & Berkowitz, 2020). Hence, leaders can make a difference by role modeling zero tolerance towards bullying and harassment, including sexual harassment. The key is to be aware of the fact that a homogeneous workforce is a risk factor for sexual harassment – and to consider this when composing teams.

2. Similarly, **discussing systemic racism and white privilege is a "necessary evil" if organizations want to address EI&D seriously.** This includes understanding that some individuals are more visible than others, which means that some voices and talent go unheard (McKinsey & Lean In, 2020). Asian and Black women remain in the background, which means that their know-how, knowledge, and insights remain untapped. Lesbian women from these two underrepresented groups are even more absent from the mindset. It is worth noting that two of the most recent social movements were initiated by lesbian Black women: #MeToo and BLM. What are these women saying in organizations that is not being heard today? Managers should educate themselves on intersectionality and proactively reach out to women from these underrepresented groups and both sponsor and mentor them, giving them a more equal shot at advancement and contribution. What message does the leader give to ensure (white) privilege is understood and accepted? How can they encourage people to use their (white) privilege to support others?

3. **With COVID-19 highlighting and exacerbating already existing socioeconomic inequalities, organizations must embrace their role in combating them.** Accordingly, the socioeconomic background must be taken up as an additional diversity dimension – and inclusion must go beyond a pure focus on talent and high potential.

4. To benefit from the promise of hybrid work settings to include various voices from all over the world, **leaders and all employees must take active efforts to make hybrid work inclusive by using the latest technology to ensure equity and accessibility for those online,** and oversee how airtime is shared. Also, conversations on-site must be managed actively to ensure that those online stay in touch. A clear hybrid meeting protocol must be implemented and enhanced frequently.

To summarize, leaders' ability to listen, versus jumping to a "fixing" mode right away, contributes to a psychologically safe environment. In addition, the complex societal shifts we are witnessing in the 2020s call for leadership to be a collective process where everyone can speak up. For example, all employees should feel safe to come forward to discuss sexual harassment or everyday sexism, racism, or homo- and transphobia without feeling judged, dismissed, or ridiculed. It is highly recommended that managers listen to and support employees of all genders and backgrounds when uncomfortable conversations are placed on the table. Creating a pluralistic inclusive organizational culture means, accordingly, that various voices are heard and acted upon, and that participation and fairness prevail.

While a well-known metaphor to distinguish inclusion from diversity is to see diversity as being invited to the party and inclusion as being invited to dance, a pluralistic culture is one where everyone can contribute to choosing the music that is played at every party.

ACKNOWLEDGMENTS

This reading is based on the *Inclusive Future* project, an independent academic research project conducted with full editorial control by IMD, funded by Philip Morris International. See https://www.imd.org/inclusivefuture.

REFERENCES

Adams-Prassl, A., Boneva, T., Golin, M., & Rauh, C. 2020. Inequality in the Impact of the Coronavirus Shock: Evidence from Real Time Surveys. *Journal of Public Economics*, 189: Article 104245.

Aiyar, S., & Ebeke, C. 2019. *Inequality of opportunity, inequality of income and economic growth* (vol. WP/19, 34). Washington, DC: International Monetary Fund.

Amis, J., Mair, J., & Munir, K. A. 2020. The Organizational Reproduction of Inequality. *Academy of Management Annals*, 14(1): 195–230.

Anderson, M., Barthel, M., Perrin, A., & Vogels, E. A. 2021. *#BlackLivesMatter surges on Twitter after George Floyd's death*. Washington, DC: Pew Research Center.

Brewer, M. B. 1991. The Social Self: On Being the Same and Different at the Same Time. *Personality and Social Psychology Bulletin*, 17(5): 475–482.

Business Insider. 2020. How Gen Z Really Feels about Race, Equality, and its Role in the Historic George Floyd Protests, Based on a Survey of 39,000 Young Americans. *Business Insider*, June 10. https://www.businessinsider.com/how-gen-z-feels-about -george-floyd-protests-2020-6.

Creary, S. J., McDonnell, M.-H., Ghai, S., & Scruggs, J. 2019. When and Why Diversity Improves Your Board's Performance. *Harvard Business Review*, March 26: 1–6.

Dillon, B., & Bourke, J. 2016. *The six signature traits of inclusive leadership*. Deloitte. https://www2.deloitte.com/content/dam/Deloitte/au/Documents/human-capital/ deloitte-au-hc-six-signature-traits-inclusive-leadership-020516.pdf.

Edmondson, A. 2019. The Role of Psychological Safety: Maximizing Employee Input and Commitment. *Leader to Leader*, 2019(92): 13–19.

Gabrielova, K., & Buchko, A. A. 2021. Here Comes Generation Z: Millennials as Managers. *Business Horizons*, 64(4): 489–499.

Gompers, P., & Kovvali, S. 2018. The Other Diversity Dividend. *Harvard Business Review*, 96(4): 72–77.

Hancock, A. B., & Rubin, B. A. 2015. Influence of Communication Partner's Gender on Language. *Journal of Language and Social Psychology*, 34(1): 46–64.

Hewlett, S. A., Marshall, M., Sherbin, L., & Gonsalves, T. 2013. *Innovation, Diversity and Market Growth*. New York: Center for Talent Innovation.

Joyce, R., & Xu, X. 2020. *Sector shutdowns during the coronavirus crisis: Which workers are most exposed?* London: The Institute for Fiscal Studies.

Lee, M., & Murdie, A. 2021. The Global Diffusion of the #MeToo Movement. *Politics and Gender*, 17(4): 827–855.

Lund, S., Madgavkar, A., Manyika, J., Smit, S., Ellingrud, K., et al. 2021. *The future of work after COVID-19*. Washington D.C.

McKinsey & Lean In. 2020. *Women in the workplace*. McKinsey & Lean In.

Mor Barak, M. E. 2017. *Managing diversity: Toward a globally inclusive workplace* (4th ed.). Thousand Oaks, CA: Sage.

Nkomo, S. 2014. Inclusion: Old Wine in New Bottles? In B. M. Ferdman & B. R. Deane (Eds.), *Diversity at work: The practice of inclusion*, 580–592. San Francisco, CA: Jossey-Bass.

Nkomo, S. M., Bell, M. P., Roberts, L. M., Joshi, A., & Thatcher, S. M. B. 2019. Diversity at a Critical Juncture: New Theories for a Complex Phenomenon. *Academy of Management Review*, 44(3): 498–517.

OECD. 2021. *OECD Employment Outlook 2021*. OECD. https://doi.org/10.1787/19991266.

Orchowski, L., Bogen, K. W., & Berkowitz, A. 2020. False Reporting of Sexual Victimization: Prevalence, Definitions, and Public Perceptions. In R. Geffner, J. W. White, L. K. Hamberger, A. Rosenbaum, V. Vaughan-Eden, et al. (Eds.), *Handbook of interpersonal violence and abuse across the lifespan*, 1–23. Cham: Springer International Publishing.

Pew Research Center. 2021. *Gen Z, Millennials stand out for climate change activism, social media engagement with issue*. Washington, DC: Pew Research Center.

Piketty, T. 2014. *Capital in the twenty-first century*. Cambridge, MA: Belknap Press of Harvard University Press.

Piketty, T. 2020. *Capital and ideology*. Cambridge, MA and London: Belknap Press of Harvard University Press.

Prime, J., & Salib, E. R. 2015. *The secret to inclusion in Australian workplaces: Psychological safety*. New York: Catalyst.

Romansky, L., Garrod, M., Brown, K., & Deo, K. 2021. How to Measure Inclusion in the Workplace. *Harvard Business Review*, May 27, 2001. https://hbr.org/2021/05/how-to-measure-inclusion-in-the-workplace.

Schroth, H. 2019. Are You Ready for Gen Z in the Workplace? *California Management Review*, 61(3): 5–18.

Shore, L. M., Cleveland, J. N., & Sanchez, D. 2018. Inclusive Workplaces: A Review and Model. *Human Resource Management Review*, 28(2): 176–189.

Stahl, G. K., Maznevski, M. L., Voigt, A., & Jonsen, K. 2010. Unraveling the Effects of Cultural Diversity in Teams: A Meta-analysis of Research on Multicultural Work Groups. *Journal of International Business Studies*, 41(4): 690–709.

United Nations. 2020. *Policy brief: The impact of COVID-19 on women*. United Nations. https://www.unwomen.org/en/digital-library/publications/2020/04/policy-brief-the-impact-of-covid-19-on-women.

van Knippenberg, D., Nishii, L. H., & Dwertmann, D. J. G. 2020. Synergy from Diversity: Managing Team Diversity to Enhance Performance. *Behavioral Science and Policy*, 6(1): 75–92.

Whitney Gibson, J., Greenwood, R. A., & Murphy, Jr., E. F. 2009. Generational Differences in the Workplace: Personal Values, Behaviors, and Popular Beliefs. *Journal of Diversity Management (JDM)*, 4(3): 1–8.

Wolf, M. 2017. Inequality Is a Threat to Our Democracies. *Financial Times*, 12(20): 9. December 19.

Pankaj Ghemawat and B. Sebastian Reiche

NATIONAL CULTURAL DIFFERENCES AND GLOBAL BUSINESS*

THE EMINENT DUTCH PSYCHOLOGIST AND culture expert Geert Hofstede interviewed unsuccessfully for an engineering job with a US company early in his career. Later, he wrote of the cross-cultural misunderstandings that crop up when US managers interview Dutch recruits and vice versa:

> American applicants, to Dutch eyes, oversell themselves. Their CVs are worded in superlatives … during the interview they try to behave asser-tively, promising things they are very unlikely to realize … Dutch applicants in American eyes undersell themselves. They write modest and usually short CVs, counting on the interviewer to find out by asking how good they really are … To an uninitiated American interviewer an uninitiated Dutch applicant comes across as a sucker. To an uninitiated Dutch interviewer an uninitiated American applicant comes across as a braggart.[1]

Cultural differences can be important even in life-and-death situations. Consider Korean Air's high incidence of plane crashes between 1970 and 2000. Analysis of conversations recorded in the black boxes of downed planes showed that even when a crash was likely, Korean Air co-pilots and flight engineers rarely sug-gested actions that would contradict the judgments of their captains. Challenging one's superior in Korea was considered culturally inadequate behavior.[2]

The Korean Air example is particularly noteworthy for two reasons. First, if national culture can have significant—not to say existential—consequences among people of the same cultural origin, we need to be very cautious in dealing with

* Originally published by IESE Publishing.

DOI: 10.4324/9781003247272-11

national cultural *differences* in cross-border interactions. Second, the cultural pre-dispositions of Korean Air co-pilots and flight engineers persisted in a very highly regulated environment, suggesting that national culture's influence on behavior reaches beyond administrative attributes such as governmental policies, laws and institutions. This reading focuses on different ways of thinking about culture and how cultural differences affect the operation of firms around the globe.

For the purpose of this reading, *culture shall be defined as a set of shared values, assumptions, beliefs, morals, customs, and other habits that are learnt through membership in a group, and that influence the attitudes and behaviors of group members.* Note three implications of this definition. First, culture is defined as a group-level phenomenon. From this perspective, cultures exist at many different levels, including organizational functions or business units, organizations, industries, regions, and nations.[3] This reading focuses in particular on national culture and the role of cultural differences across countries rather than other cultural groups because this level of culture is particularly relevant for global businesses. Second, the definition implies that culture is acquired through a process of socialization rather than being innate. Shared values, assumptions, and beliefs are learned through interactions with family, teachers, officials, experiences, and society at large. In this respect, Geert Hofstede speaks of culture as a process of "collective programming of the mind."[4] Third, it is this collective programming that determines what is considered acceptable or attractive behavior. In other words, cultural values provide preferences or priorities for one behavior over another.

Also implicit in that group-level definition of culture is that such attempts to characterize behavior are necessarily approximate since they abstract away from individual-level factors that also matter. As a result, it is important not to treat cultural characterizations as fully explaining or determining behavior. Rather, the operational criterion for assessing the usefulness of cultural characterizations is whether they offer more insight into behavior than would be obtained if one were to ignore them.

With those caveats, evidence from sources such as the World Values Survey, a study of 65 countries reflecting 75% of the world's population, *does* suggest that national cultural traits have, at a deep level, remained fairly stable over time despite superficial evidence of some convergence in cultural habits, artifacts, and symbols (e.g., the spread of American consumer culture across the globe).[5] And cultural differences remain prominent in a host of different contexts. Consider the following high-stakes example. You are riding in a car with a close friend, who hits a pedestrian:

> You know that he was going at least 35 miles per hour in an area of the city where the maximum allowed speed is 20 miles per hour but there are no other witnesses. His lawyer says that if you testify under oath that he was only driving at 20 miles per hour, it may save him from serious consequences.

More than 90% of managers in Canada, the United States, Switzerland, Australia, Sweden, Norway, and Western Germany reported that they would *not* testify falsely under oath to help their close friend, while fewer than half of managers in South Korea (26%), Venezuela (34%), Russia (42%), Indonesia (47%), and China (48%) said they would refuse to testify falsely in this hypothetical situation.[6] This exemplified the point that some cultures put more emphasis on *universal* commitments (like honesty), while others put more weight on loyalty to *particular* people and relationships.

Societies' responses to the COVID-19 pandemic similarly displayed material cultural differences. For example, in Taiwan, a sense of collective prudence shaped by the country's recent history and deep-seated community-oriented values allowed the government to implement far-reaching measures such as strict border control with community-backed quarantine and a comprehensive tracking system integrating travel and health data of all citizens. This allowed the country to keep infections low. Contrast this with Spain, where a culture of strong familial ties and high physical proximity in social interactions enabled the virus to spread rapidly in the first months of the pandemic. The government responded with a near-total lockdown to cut social contact, yet its subsequent loosening resulted in a rapid return to pre-COVID cultural habits and a renewed rise in infections.[7] Clearly, crisis situations like the pandemic give rise to deep-seated—and often unconscious—cultural preferences that determine decision-making and action.

The persistence of cultural value differences is particularly relevant for large global companies that are exposed to *multiple* national cultures in their daily operations. This adds to complexity because it forces companies to adapt their practices and approaches to every culturally distinct context they operate in. So although the concepts discussed in this reading apply more broadly, the primary focus here is on global firms.

Sections 1 and 2 of this reading focus, respectively, on frameworks of national cultural value differences and observable indicators of national culture and some of their documented implications for international business. Section 3 provides a broader discussion of how global companies can manage to adapt to cultural (and other) differences.

1. FRAMEWORKS OF NATIONAL CULTURAL VALUE DIFFERENCES

Cultural differences at the level of behavior form the basis for much of the casual comparison that takes place in diverse settings like business schools, for both serious and humorous purposes. Citizens in the United States maintain a culture around owning guns that most Europeans can't fathom. The Czechs drink far more beer than people in Saudi Arabia, and even more than the Irish, who come in second. India and China are so close geographically that they still haven't resolved their territorial disputes, but couldn't display more distinct food cultures, particularly around which animals and parts of animals should or shouldn't be eaten. Argentines see psychotherapists more often than other nationalities. Brazilians spend a higher proportion of their income on beauty products than the citizens of any other major economy. Japanese exchange business cards very intensively, and in a highly ritualized way. And so on.

Unless one is focused on a particular country or, at most, a handful, it quickly becomes overwhelming to try to look at the world in terms of countries where business cards are received in particular ways or the local cuisine has particular ingredients. As a result, most frameworks for understanding culture have sought to identify a limited number of cultural value dimensions that underlie behavior and that provide a basis for classifying countries. Thus, the Japanese consider it rude not to study a business card carefully because it reflects a person's professional identity, title, and social status. So the ritual of exchanging business cards (a behavior) can only be fully understood by taking into account the underlying importance of respect for seniority and status in that culture (basic values). More broadly, dealing with national cultural differences therefore requires not only knowledge about adequate behaviors, but also understanding deeper values and assumptions that explain why certain behaviors are more appropriate than others.

Hofstede's Cultural Dimensions

The most widely used framework for categorizing national cultures is the one developed by Geert Hofstede, a Dutch social psychologist.[8] Based on surveys of more than 100,000 IBM employees in more than 50 countries between 1967 and 1973, Hofstede argued that national cultures differed systematically across four dimensions: *power distance, individualism/collectivism, uncertainty avoidance,* and *masculinity/femininity*.

Power distance is probably the most important cultural dimension identified by Hofstede: it concerns the degree to which a culture accepts and reinforces the fact that power is distributed unevenly in society. Members of high *power distance* cultures such as Malaysia accept status differences and are expected to show proper respect to their superiors. Status differences may reflect organizational hierarchy, but they may also be based on age, social class, or family role. Low *power distance* cultures such as Denmark are less comfortable with differences in organizational rank or social class and are characterized by more participation in decision-making and a frequent disregard of hierarchical level. The concept of *power distance* helps to explain the importance of deference that Korean Air's co-pilots showed towards their captains.

A second dimension Hofstede identified is *individualism/collectivism*. Individualist cultures tend to emphasize the individual over the group. Members of *individualist* cultures such as the UK maintain loose social structures marked by independence, the importance of individuals' rights, and the recognition of personal initiative and achievement. In contrast, *collectivist* cultures such as Venezuela place more emphasis on the overall good of and loyalty to the group. Members of *collectivist* societies distinguish more clearly between in-groups and out-groups and are expected to subordinate their individual interests to those of their in-groups (e.g., family, organization). Hofstede's research also suggested a strong correlation with *power distance*: *individualist* cultures tend to exhibit lower *power distance*, although there are exceptions (e.g., France).

Uncertainty avoidance concerns the degree to which cultural members are willing to accept and deal with ambiguous situations. Cultures with high levels of *uncertainty avoidance* such as Greece prefer structure and predictability, which results in explicit rules of behavior and strict laws. Members of such cultures tend to be relatively averse to changing employers, embracing new approaches, or engaging in entrepreneurship. In societies with low *uncertainty avoidance*, such as Singapore, there is more acceptance of unstructured situations and ambiguity, favoring risk taking, innovation, and the acceptance of different views.

The fourth dimension Hofstede identified is *masculinity/femininity*. *Masculine* cultures such as Japan are thought to reflect a dominance of "tough" values such as achievement, assertiveness, competition, and material success, which are stereotypically associated with male roles. In contrast, *feminine* cultures focus on "tender" values such as personal relationships, care for others, and quality of life. In addition, *feminine* cultures such as Sweden are also characterized by less distinct gender roles. Firms in feminine cultures place a stronger emphasis on overall employee well-being than on bottom-line performance.

Hofstede's research has been replicated by himself and other scholars and extended to over 80 countries.[9] Exhibit 1 lists the scores along each dimension for 30 of them. Using these scores, Hofstede developed national cultural profiles to compare cultures and highlight cultural differences (see Exhibit 2). Applying such a comparative lens to the Ukraine–Russia conflict reveals that the two neighbors are culturally—and indeed also linguistically—very similar along the four dimensions: power distance (Russia 93 vs. Ukraine 92), individualism (Russia 39 vs. Ukraine 25), uncertainty avoidance (Russia 95 vs. Ukraine 95), and masculinity (Russia 36 vs. Ukraine 27). This has led scholars to characterize the conflict as a "clash of brothers, not cultures."[10] Such profiling is supposed to highlight similarities and differences to be expected in interactions with cultures other than one's own. It is important to note that a culture's position along a certain cultural dimension (e.g., the higher level of power distance in Korea) is not an evaluation of whether members of that culture approach situations better or worse than in other cultures. Instead, the cultural dimensions simply demonstrate different preferences or priorities for how issues should be approached. Note also that such cultural preferences do not always capture people's broad political views. In fact, despite their cultural value similarities, Russians and Ukrainians show marked differences in their aspirations towards and satisfaction with democratic political institutions, as data from the European Values Study reveal.[11]

Some Applications

The most obvious application of Hofstede's framework is based on the idea that improving the alignment between management practices and cultural contexts yields tangible business benefits. Consider some examples:[12]

Exhibit 1 Hofstede's cultural value scores for 30 countries

Country	Power Distance	Individualism/ Collectivism	Uncertainty Avoidance	Masculinity/ Femininity
Argentina	49	46	86	56
Australia	38	90	51	61
Brazil	69	38	76	49
Canada	39	80	48	52
Chile	63	23	86	28
China	80	20	30	66
Colombia	67	13	80	64
Denmark	18	74	23	16
France	68	71	86	43
Germany	35	67	65	66
Greece	60	35	112	57
India	77	48	40	56
Indonesia	78	14	48	46
Iran	58	41	59	43
Israel	13	54	81	47
Italy	50	76	75	70
Japan	54	46	92	95
Korea (South)	60	18	85	39
Malaysia	104	26	36	50
Mexico	81	30	82	69
Netherlands	38	80	53	14
Philippines	94	32	44	64
Poland	68	60	93	64
Portugal	63	27	104	31
Russia	93	39	95	36
Singapore	74	20	8	48
Spain	57	51	86	42
Sweden	31	71	29	5
United Kingdom	35	89	35	66
United States	40	91	46	62

Source: Compiled and adapted from Geert Hofstede, Gert Jan Hofstede, and Michael Minkov (2010). *Cultures and Organizations: Software of the Mind* (3rd ed.), New York: McGraw-Hill.

- Participative management can improve profitability in low *power distance* cultures, but worsen it in high *power distance* cultures.
- Quick fixes can improve profitability in more *short-term-oriented* cultures, but worsen it in more *long-term-oriented* cultures.
- Merit-based pay and promotion policies can improve profitability in more *masculine* cultures, and reduce it in more *feminine* cultures.
- During performance appraisal, feedback quality and relational quality between supervisor and subordinate tend to be higher when the cultural preference of the performer (*individualistic* vs. *collectivistic*) is matched with the performance perspective (focus on the individual performer vs. the collective performing unit).
- Emphasizing individual contributions can improve profitability in more *individualistic* cultures, and worsen it in more *collectivistic* cultures.

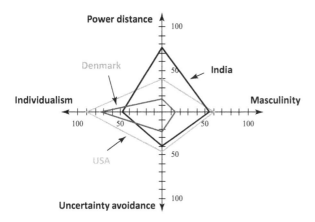

Exhibit 2 Cultural profiles based on Hofstede's cultural dimensions

To provide a more systematic treatment, this subsection begins by considering the implications of Hofstede's cultural dimensions, particularly power distance, for a range of business functions or activities. It goes on to discuss some of the ways in which they have also been used to understand cross-border interactions.

Let's begin with marketing. One example of how marketing communications are affected by Hofstede's cultural dimensions is provided by the finding that the use of humor in advertising is more prevalent in countries with lower *power distance* as well as low *uncertainty avoidance*.[13] And according to another study, 63% of humorous television advertisements in Thailand and Korea (countries with high *power distance*) contain characters of unequal status, versus only 29% in the US and Germany (countries with low *power distance*).[14] High *power distance* is also related to a tendency for consumers to make purchase decisions based on emotion rather than information. In addition, in countries with high *power distance* and *collectivism*, public relations focus more on building and maintaining relationships, whereas in low *power distance* and *individualistic* cultures, it entails more explicit dissemination of information. Further, consider online marketing where the larger gap between marketers and consumers in high *power distance* cultures entails less consumer–marketer interactivity. There also tend to be higher service expectations in high *power distance* cultures, and even the organization of products in retail stores has been shown to vary with this dimension of culture.[15]

The link between marketing and innovation/new product development seems to work better when managed in a centralized way in cultures with high *power distance*.[16] And looking at innovation more broadly, studies indicate that countries with low *power distance* tend to have stronger innovation capabilities, which might affect a company's decisions about where to locate its innovative activities. Low *uncertainty avoidance* and high *individualism* also correlate with innovation capability.[17] In cultures with high *power distance*, consumers are more likely to want products that help them demonstrate their status.

National culture has also been shown to have an impact on manufacturing and supply chain practices, which can be useful to consider in a variety of contexts: analyzing manufacturing footprints, managing multi-plant operations, assessing competitors and suppliers and different countries, and so on. Consider the adoption of quality management practices. One European study indicates that in cultures with low *power distance* and low *uncertainty avoidance*, implementation of formal quality management systems may require external market pressure.[18]

Entire books have been written on cross-cultural negotiations. A typical prescription is that in higher *power distance* cultures, the seniority of the negotiator (and size of the negotiating team) send important signals. Companies from low *power distance* cultures can run into trouble by sending a junior negotiator (who might be better versed in the content) or by trying to save money by limiting the size of the negotiating team. There are also indications that negotiators from high *power distance* cultures may be less attuned to joint gains, as they may be more accustomed to power differences simply determining outcomes.

There are also important organizational or human resources implications of national culture. In countries with high (versus low) *power distance*, employee selection tends to give more emphasis to social class (over education), training tends to emphasize conformity (versus autonomy), evaluations focus on compliance or trustworthiness (over performance), wage differences between managers and workers are larger, leadership is more authoritarian (instead of participative), motivation is based on the assumption that subordinates dislike work and hence is more coercive (instead of reward-based), and organizations are more hierarchical (versus flat).[19] Achieving significant change in high *power distance* cultures requires putting senior staff front and center in communication efforts, using legitimate authority, and "tell[ing] subordinates what to do." In lower *power distance* cultures, it is more important to explain the reasons for change, "allow for questions and challenges," and involve employees in figuring out how to implement the desired change.[20]

The implications of *power distance* for human resources also reach beyond individual firms to affect the design of institutions and governance structures. For example, high *power distance* is related to more stringent employment protection legislation.[21] The protections afforded to labor in such cultures are also associated with less external equity financing and a greater degree of family ownership. Hofstede further asserted a link between *power distance* and accounting:

> In large *power distance* countries, the accounting system will be used more frequently to justify the decisions of the top power holder(s); in fact it usually is their tool to present the desired image, and figures will be twisted to this end.[22]

Subsequent research has cast doubt on the impact of *power distance* on accounting disclosure, but does indicate that high levels of *uncertainty avoidance* fit with low disclosure and conservatism in accounting.[23]

In addition to these country-level characterizations of the effects of cultural dimensions, Hofstede's framework has also been used to study cross-border phenomena such as the choice of entry mode, and international diversification. A survey article reports that "firms from countries with large *power distance* prefer subsidiary and equity JV entry modes whereas firms from countries high in *uncertainty avoidance* prefer contract agreements and export entry modes."[24] The same summary article also cites various studies analyzing the effects of overall cultural distance—typically calculated as the sum of the squared differences between countries along Hofstede's value dimensions[25]—on entry modes:

> As the cultural distance between countries increased, the tendency to choose a joint venture (JV) over an acquisition increased. Also, as cultural distance increased, Japanese firms were more likely to choose green-fields or wholly owned subsidiaries over shared ownership; the tendency to choose licensing over JVs or wholly owned subsidiaries increased; the tendency to choose a greenfield over an acquisition increased; wholly owned subsidiaries were less preferred than either shared-equity ventures or technology licensing; [and] the tendency to choose management-service contracts over franchising increased ....[26]

It has also been shown that cultural distance is a significant deterrent to foreign portfolio investment.[27]

Limitations and Alternative Frameworks

Although Hofstede's framework remains the most widely used approach to classify and compare national cultures, it has several limitations. The data are relatively old and, despite attempts at replication, may not fully capture recent changes in the political environment (e.g., the end of the Cold War and the decline of communism) or the workplace (a stronger focus on cooperation, knowledge-sharing, and empowerment). Second, the reliance on data from employees of a single organization, IBM, offers a narrow—and arguably biased—basis for generalizing about national cultural characteristics.[28] Third, the dimension of *uncertainty avoidance* did not emerge as a distinct cultural dimension in a later study that Hofstede conducted using a Chinese equivalent of his original survey developed by Chinese social scientists.[29] Based on data from 23 countries, including 20 from Hofstede's original study, the scholars identified a different fourth dimension representing Chinese values, originally termed Confucian Work Dynamism and later re-labeled *long-term/short-term orientation*. Fourth, the content of the *masculinity/femininity* dimension has also been challenged. It is also less clear what exactly this dimension involves. For example, the high masculinity score for Japan appears to contradict the high levels of concern and care that Japanese organizations usually show towards their employees, which would seem to be more indicative of a *feminine* culture as defined by Hofstede.

Criticisms have also been leveled against the frequent use of Hofstede's framework to compute aggregate cultural distances between countries. For one thing, such an approach suggests that distances are symmetric. In other words, a Swedish firm investing in China is supposed to face exactly the same cultural distance as a Chinese firm investing in Sweden, which seems unlikely.[30] In addition, the assumption of homogeneity within each nation underlying Hofstede's data raises even more questions when the data are used to compute distance scores between countries in ways that ignore both intranational variation and noncultural dimensions of distance (e.g., physical). For example, we would expect the cultural differences encountered by a Spanish firm investing in France to depend on whether the home and host units are located in Barcelona and Perpignan (very close by) or in Seville and Le Havre (much farther away). This point is particularly relevant for large and diverse countries like the BRICS (Brazil, Russia, India, China, and South Africa), but it also applies to smaller countries. Thus, the computed cultural distance between the Czech Republic and Slovakia, which shared the same national flag for a long time, is higher than for most other cultural pairs! This not only highlights the role of intra-cultural variation, but also the limits of using countries to define cultural regions.

Finally, the subjectivity of Hofstede's framework also makes for some arbitrariness in terms of the value dimensions highlighted: other researchers have used survey responses to categorize national cultures differently. Box 1 provides very brief overviews of some other frameworks of this sort. One worth mentioning here is a framework developed recently by Michele Gelfand and coauthors that provides insight into variations within as well as across 33 countries by classifying them in terms of their "tightness."[31] *Tight cultures* such as India or Korea have many strong behavioral norms across everyday situations (e.g., in classrooms, libraries, public parks) and low tolerance for deviations from them, whereas *loose cultures* such as Ukraine or the Netherlands have weaker social norms and higher tolerance of deviant behavior. Individuals in tight cultures are supposed to focus on avoiding mistakes and behaving properly, and to have higher self-regulatory strength (higher impulse control) and a greater need for structure. The tightness–looseness distinction is related to, yet somewhat distinct from, the value dimensions that have already been discussed. For example, tightness is positively but only partially correlated with collectivism and power distance. It also has some other interesting correlates. Thus, tight cultures tend to have less open media and a higher incidence of religious observance by their members. Members of tight cultures also seem more likely to perceive their own culture to be superior than members of loose cultures. Recent research also found that tight cultures experienced fewer cases and deaths per million during the early stages of the COVID-19 pandemic compared with loose cultures. The results demonstrate that tight groups cooperate much faster under threat and have higher survival rates than loose groups, which suggests that tightening social norms might confer an evolutionary advantage in times of collective threat.[32]

BOX 1: Some alternative cultural frameworks

In addition to the cultural dimensions identified by Hofstede, a range of other cultural frameworks aim to classify national cultures along various value dimensions. While some dimensions match or overlap with the ones proposed by Hofstede, the following well-known frameworks also include other dimensions:

- Fons Trompenaars, another Dutch researcher, collected more recent data in over 40 countries. Out of the seven dimensions identified in his study, five focus on relationships between people (e.g., the relative importance of applying universal and standardized rules as reflected in the earlier example of whether or not to testify against a friend, or the extent to which people are free to express their emotions in public), whereas the remaining two dimensions concern time management and a culture's relationship with nature.[33]

- Shalom Schwartz, an Israeli psychologist, provided yet another approach to describe and classify national cultures. Schwartz argues that cultural values reflect three basic issues societies are confronted with: the nature of the relation between the individual and the group, how to guarantee responsible behavior, and how to regulate the relation of people to the natural and social world. Using data from schoolteachers and university students in over 60 countries, Schwartz derived three dimensions that represent solutions to the above issues.[34]

- Robert House, along with an international team of researchers, engaged in an ambitious effort to characterize cultures that was mainly focused on cultural differences in leadership. Termed the GLOBE (Global Leadership and Organizational Behavior Effectiveness) study, this research derived nine cultural dimensions that addressed both previously identified value dimensions (e.g., power distance and individualism/collectivism) and new ones (e.g., gender egalitarianism and performance orientation). For each dimension, the research team differentiated between societal practices (as things are) and societal values (as things should be). While this distinction perhaps better reflects the richness of a society's cultural fabric, it also makes cross-cultural comparisons more complex.[35]

---

2. OBSERVABLE CULTURAL INDICATORS

The proliferation of cultural frameworks for analyzing culture has led some researchers, particularly economists, to focus on more observable indicators of cultural differences, particularly religion and language. The impact of religion on certain aspects of behavior is particularly easy to discern. The difference in Czech and Saudi Arabian levels of beer consumption, for instance, can be related to the fact that the largest religion in the Czech Republic is Christianity (in which wine is consumed as part of ritual practice) while the official religion of Saudi Arabia is Islam, which prohibits the consumption of alcohol. Similarly, we can understand dietary differences between Indians and Chinese in large part based on religious distinctions

Most research using religion as a marker of differences in national culture has focused on whether or not countries share a common religion. According to the *World Christian Encyclopedia*, "there are 19 major world religions, which are subdivided into 270 large religious groups, and many smaller ones," with Christianity (33% of the world population in 2000), Islam (21%), and Hindu (14%) being the largest high-level groupings.[36] Based on a sample of 163 countries, 51% of country pairs have at least 30% or more of both populations practicing the same major religion. But that analysis does not account for differences between denominations within religions: the world's 2.1 billion Christians, for instance, are subdivided into some 34,000 separate groupings![37] More nuanced characterizations treat commonalities at the level of denomination or sect as closest (e.g., Methodist), then consider matches at broader levels of aggregation within a single religion (e.g., Protestant), then at the level of a religion (e.g., Christianity), and then most broadly combine groups of religions with a similar origin and some common beliefs (e.g., "monotheistic religions of a common Middle-Eastern origin," the category that encompasses Judaism, Christianity, and Islam).[38]

Language is another observable aspect of culture that, according to some researchers, offers a window into deeper beliefs and thought processes.[39] Work on the implications of linguistic differences for thought patterns across cultures dates back at least to early work by Edward Sapir (1921)[40] and Benjamin Whorf (1940).[41] One scholar provided the following description of the language's deeper impact: "Language carries with it patterns of seeing, knowing, talking, and acting ... patterns that mark the easier trails for thought and perception and action."[42] Later, scholars such as Noam Chomsky moved away from this view to focus on universal patterns across languages, but more recent research has again shown an "appreciation of how interpretive differences can be rooted as much in systematic uses of language as in its structure."[43]

One way to summarize the extent of linguistic differences is to note that among the sample of 163 countries referenced above, in only 10% of the country pairs do 20% or more of the populations of both countries speak a common language.[44] The genealogical classification of languages permits more nuanced characterizations of linguistic distance based on whether or not two languages have common ancestors. Exhibit 3 presents a table of linguistic distance from the United States according to such analysis. More sophisticated statistical tests have also validated linguistic distance as a marker of cultural distance.

Exhibit 3 Linguistic distance from the United States, 25 largest economies

Linguistic Distance from United States	Countries
1 (same language)	Australia, Canada, India, Nigeria, United Kingdom
2 (same sub-branch at the 1st level but different at the 2nd level)	Belgium, Germany, Netherlands, Switzerland
3 (same branch but different at the 1st sub-branch level)	Sweden
4 (same family but different branches)	Argentina, Brazil, France, Italy, Mexico, Poland, Russia, Spain
5 (different families)	China, Indonesia, Japan, Korea, Saudi Arabia, Taiwan, Turkey

Note: This table is compiled based on the distance between the two closest major languages for each pair of countries.
Source: "L1" variable from Douglas Dow and Amal Karunaratna (2006). Developing a multidimensional instrument to measure psychic distance stimuli, *Journal of International Business Studies*, 37(5), pp. 578–602.

What is particularly interesting about the use of linguistic distance as an observable indicator of cultural differences is that it has been shown to correlate with cultural distinctions such as those described in the previous section. Two examples will be presented here, based on distinctions between English and Spanish that will be familiar to many readers. First, consider Hofstede's dimension of *individualism/collectivism*. English-speaking cultures are considered more *individualistic* (they score 84 on this dimension), whereas Spanish-speaking cultures are deemed more *collectivistic* (22). Linguistically, the requirement in Spanish, but not English, to specify a person's gender when describing his or her occupation reflects the collectivist pattern of rooting description in social context. English, by casting aside the need to communicate such contextual information, "tends to elevate individuals vis-à-vis their groups."[45] Hofstede's dimension of *power distance* is also related to linguistic differences between Spanish and English. Spanish-speaking countries score much higher on this dimension (69) than English-speaking countries (32). And in Spanish, we note the distinct formal (*usted*) and informal (*tu*) forms of the English "you." This hierarchical emphasis is also seen in speech patterns such as the tendency in Mexico to introduce an engineer as *ingeniero* or a lawyer as *licenciado*, whereas both would just be called "mister" in English.[46]

In addition to serving as observable markers of cultural differences at deeper levels than behavior, religion and language are also useful bases for grouping countries. It can be helpful to think in terms of countries where English is the main language or where most of the population are Catholic, although—as always—one has to be careful to avoid oversimplification. More sophisticated efforts at classifying countries into cultural clusters have often relied on geography, language, and religion as primary factors, while others have also used cultural frameworks such as Hofstede's as well as levels of economic development.[47]

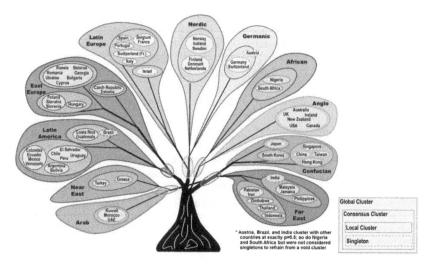

Exhibit 4 Clusters of national culture.

Source: Figure 2, p. 881 in Simcha Ronen and Oded Shenkar (2013). Mapping world cultures: Cluster formation, sources and implications, *Journal of International Business Studies,* 44(9): pp. 867–897.

The clusters resulting from a synthesis across ten such studies are shown in Exhibit 4.

Some Applications

The comparative, country-by-country implications for business have been studied in less detail for observable cultural indicators than for the cultural value dimensions discussed in the previous section. The cross-country implications of observable cultural indicators have attracted more attention, and yield some striking conclusions about how cultural distance, measured thus, tends to reduce cross-border interactions. In contrast, research of this sort that relies on Hofstede's original four dimensions (and their aggregation into a single measure of cultural distance) has produced results that don't fit as well with theory and intuition. Thus, some research suggests that Hofstedian cultural distance actually increases bilateral trade![48] This seems to suggest that distance is not always a barrier per se. For example, distance has been shown to lead decision-makers to prepare and plan more extensively for foreign activities or to actively anticipate differences and potential misunderstandings.[49]

To provide a more systematic treatment, this subsection will focus on reviewing the effects of observable cultural indicators, particularly language, on four types of cross-border flows: flows of products and services, of capital, of people, and of information.[50]

Let's start with trade, which has been studied more intensively than other types of cross-border flows. A common language has been shown to increase the bilateral merchandise trade between a pair of countries significantly—by

42%, according to one study.[51] There is less research on services trade, but one study indicates that a common language increases services trade by even more, which seems intuitively plausible.[52] Digging deeper into the effects of linguistic differences, while communication via a translator can indeed facilitate trade, one analysis indicates that direct communication appears to be about three times more effective than indirect communication in promoting trade. The same study also suggests that linguistic diversity within a country as well as higher levels of literacy promote foreign trade relative to domestic activity.[53]

Analogously, countries that share a common religion have been shown to trade more than countries that don't, with one study indicating that a common religion increases trade by 22%.[54] Not all religions are created equal in this respect: some religious communities turn out to be more conducive to the development of international trade networks than others.[55]

A common language has also been shown to have a significant positive effect on certain types of capital flows. Thus, according to one study that looked across a range of capital flows, "when both countries speak the same language FDI stocks in host countries are 54% higher and portfolio equity investment 38% larger, whereas portfolio debt investment and loans are not statistically significantly different."[56]

Turning to long-run flows of people, 60% of migrants move to a country with the same major religion, and 40% go to a country with the same major language.[57] Research on diasporas and international business networks has also shown migration to have an important effect on all the other types of cross-border flows considered in this section, reminding us of the complementarities across them.

Information flows tend to be more elusive, but one way of quantifying the impact of language barriers on information flows is to look at the intensity of international telephone calls on a population-weighted basis. The intensity of minutes of phone calls between countries where at least 20% of the populations share a common language is ten times greater than between countries that lack that commonality.[58] The impact of language barriers is also evident in studies that use patent citations as proxies for knowledge flows. According to a study conducted in Europe, "having the same language increases the amount of knowledge flows between two regions by up to 28 percent."[59] Of course, one can easily think of other, more subtle ways in which cultural differences impede information flows, ranging from misinterpretation to unwillingness to share information across cultural boundaries.

That last point calls attention to an important underlying factor: trust. One broad indicator of the effects of cultural differences on trust is provided by patterns of trust within versus between countries. The best available data, from Eurobarometer surveys, indicate that Western Europeans trust their fellow citizens more than twice as much as citizens of other Western European countries and nearly four times as much as citizens of countries outside of Western Europe.[60] Disaggregated analysis of these data suggests that trust falls as the populations of any two countries grow more different in terms of their languages, religions, genes, body types, geographic distance, and incomes, and if they have a history of being at war with each other.[61] Lack of trust, of course, complicates cross-border interactions of all types.

3. MANAGING ADAPTATION TO CULTURAL DIFFERENCES

We have seen that operating in ways that fit with diverse cultural contexts can improve business performance. In thinking through how far to push efforts to adapt to local cultural conditions, it is important to account for industry characteristics that increase or decrease sensitivity to cultural differences. Businesses that sell directly to consumers (rather than to other businesses) are more sensitive to cultural differences, as is the service sector compared to businesses that sell physical products. For example, while they sell to other businesses, most kinds of IT services are highly sensitive to language differences. In contrast, industrial machinery (sold to other companies for use in their factories) tends to be relatively insensitive to cultural distance. This is one factor that helps explain the global success of Germany's *Mittelstand* (small and medium-sized) firms in many such sectors even though they have fewer resources for cultural adaptation than larger firms.

That said, companies with broad footprints generally do need to adapt their operating practices to cultural (and other) differences across countries. As companies push farther with such variation, complementary moves such as decentralizing decision-making, indigenizing in-country management teams, and *in*patriating foreign subsidiary staff to the company's home country to tap their cultural and local market knowledge can help.[62] But the extreme solution of varying practices everywhere to maximize local fit usually isn't a good idea either because it creates enormous complexity and involves sacrificing all international economies of scale, implying performance no better (and perhaps even worse) than standalone local firms. So managing adaptation entails finding ways to limit the need for or cost of variation.[63]

Focus is one way to reduce the need for variation. The simplest way to do this is by focusing operations on countries with similar cultures. Focusing on serving—or hiring from—the diaspora from a company's home country can ease entry into new markets by reducing the cultural distance that has to be crossed to reach local customers and manage people. Other options for focus involve concentration on products, segments, or vertical stages that require relatively little variation from country to country.

Externalization, e.g., via joint ventures or franchising, is another way that companies can reduce the cost of local adaptation. Partnering with a local firm can provide access to local cultural understanding, business networks, and so on that would be costly and time-consuming for a foreign company to develop on its own. As long as the partners can set up an effective interface to address cultural (and other) differences in managing the partnership, better local fit can be achieved. Of course, companies can also acquire foreign firms to gain access to local knowledge and networks while maintaining control, but that requires the acquiring firms to have sufficient cross-cultural capability to manage and, in most cases, integrate the acquired firms.

Designing business systems to separate clearly elements that can be varied across countries from elements that are "integral" and therefore not to be tampered with on a piecemeal basis can also ease adaptation. A particularly interesting expedient is to promote a strong corporate culture while allowing variation on operational or tactical elements. However, it's important not to place too much confidence in corporate culture entirely overpowering national cultural differences. Recall that Hofstede's original research took place within a single company with a strong corporate culture—IBM—and still revealed large national cultural differences. In fact, some research suggests that bringing employees from different cultures together in the same company might strengthen rather than mitigate national cultural differences among them.[64]

More broadly, an organization can also improve its internal capabilities for bridging cultural differences. Hiring for adaptability and investing in cross-cultural training can improve workforce capabilities and flexibility. Exposure to and deeper experience with foreign locations and cultures via participation in international teams, travel, expatriation, and inpatriation can inform and grow these kinds of capabilities. For many companies with high growth targets in foreign markets, increasing the diversity of their management teams should also be a priority—especially given how monocultural most such teams still tend to be. Of the 2013 *Fortune* Global 500 companies, only 13% had a nonnative CEO. The share of nonnative executives in the entire top management team of 2013 *Fortune* Global 500 companies faired only marginally better, and stood at 15%.[65] Most firms from emerging markets have even less internationalized leadership teams. Another way for organizations to bridge cultural differences is to hire—and then continue to develop and promote—bicultural or multicultural individuals who, through their upbringing and experience, have internalized the norms and behavioral sets that are appropriate in different cultural, ethnic, and linguistic environments and can easily shift between them.[66]

Finally, an organization's efforts to manage differences can only be as effective as the individuals within it that deal with these differences on a regular basis. Effectiveness in this regard requires learning about and awareness of cultural heterogeneity. Often, such learning is developed through personal experiences in foreign cultures which, in addition to developing knowledge about other cultures, also foster more reflection about one's own culture and in which ways it differs from others. Cultural learning can also occur through cultural assimilation exercises in which participants are confronted with various critical incidents of crosscultural encounters, need to select among alternative behaviors to deal with the encounter, and then receive feedback from a cultural expert. Tools such as the Global Attitude Protocol survey or the Cultural Agility self-assessment can help you test your own cultural awareness.[67]

NOTES

1. Geert Hofstede (1991). *Cultures and Organizations: Software of the Mind, Intellectual Cooperation and Its Importance for Survival*, New York: HarperCollins, p. 79.
2. The cultural analysis of Korean Air's plane crashes is described in Malcolm Gladwell (2008). *Outliers: The Story of Success*, New York: Little, Brown. For a more detailed discussion of the role of national cultural differences in commercial aviation, see Robert L. Helmreich (2000). Anatomy of a system accident: The crash of Avianca Flight 052, *International Journal of Aviation Psychology*, 4(3), pp. 265–284.
3. Kwok Leung, Rabi S. Bhagat, Nancy R. Buchan, Miriam Erez, and Christina B. Gibson (2005). Culture and international business: Recent advances and their implications for future research, *Journal of International Business Studies*, 36(4), pp. 357–378.
4. Geert Hofstede (1980). *Culture's Consequences: International Differences in Work-Related Values*, Beverly Hills, CA: SAGE, p. 25.
5. Ronald Inglehart and Wayne E. Baker (2000). Modernization, cultural change, and the persistence of traditional values, *American Sociological Review*, 65(1), pp. 19–51. Shalom Schwartz found similar levels of stability over time in his own research; see Shalom H. Schwartz (2008). *Cultural Value Orientations: Nature and Implications of National Differences*, Moscow, Russia: Publishing House of SU HSE.
6. Alfons Trompenaars and Charles Hampden-Turner (1998). *Riding the Waves of Culture: Understanding Cultural Diversity in Global Business* (2nd ed.), New York: McGraw-Hill, pp. 33–35.
7. The following article traces national responses to the pandemic in a range of different countries across the globe: Nancy Adler and Sonja Sackmann (2022). The grand challenge none of us chose: Succeeding (and failing) against the global pandemic. In J. S. Osland, B. S. Reiche, B. Szkudlarek, and M. E. Mendenhall (Eds.), *Advances in Global Leadership*, Bingley, UK: Emerald, vol. 14, pp. 3–85.
8. Hofstede (1980).
9. See, e.g., Geert Hofstede, Gert Jan Hofstede, and Michael Minkov (2010). *Cultures and Organizations: Software of the Mind* (3rd ed.), New York: McGraw-Hill.
10. Akos Lada (2014). Russia vs. Ukraine: A clash of brothers, not cultures, *The Washington Post*, March 4, 2014. https://www.washingtonpost.com/news/monkey-cage/wp/2014/03/04/russia-vs-ukraine-a-clash-of-brothers-not-cultures/, accessed March 24, 2022.
11. Tim Reeskens (2022). Are Ukrainian values closer to Russia or to Europe? *London School of Economics Blog*, March 4, 2022. https://blogs.lse.ac.uk/europpblog/2022/03/04/are-ukrainian-values-closer-to-russia-or-to-europe/, accessed March 24, 2022.
12. The following bullet points are drawn from Karen L. Newman and Stanley D. Nollen (1996). Culture and congruence: The fit between management practices and national culture, *Journal of International Business Studies*, 27(4), pp. 753–779; Evert Van De Vliert, Kan Shi, Karin Sanders, Yongli Wang, and Xu Huang (2004). Chinese and Dutch interpretations of supervisory feedback, *Journal of Cross-Cultural Psychology*, 35(4): pp. 417–435.
13. Marieke de Mooij (2021). *Global Marketing and Advertising: Understanding Cultural Paradoxes* (6th ed.), Thousand Oaks, CA: SAGE.
14. Dana L. Alden, Wayne D. Hoyer, and Chol Lee (1993). Identifying global and culture-specific dimensions of humor in advertising: A multinational analysis, *Journal of Marketing*, 57(2), pp. 64–75.
15. This paragraph is based on material in Chapter 7 of Marieke de Mooij (2021). *Global Marketing and Advertising: Understanding Cultural Paradoxes* (6th ed.), Thousand Oaks, CA: SAGE.

16. Tony C. Garret, David H. Buisson, and Chee Meng Yap (2006). National culture and the use of R&D and marketing integration mechanisms: A cross cultural study between Singapore and New Zealand, *Industrial Marketing Management*, 35(3), pp. 293–307.

17. Hongyi Sun (2009). A meta-analysis on the influence of national culture on innovation capability, *International Journal of Entrepreneurship and Innovation Management*, 10(3–4), pp. 353–360.

18. Brian P. Matthews, Akiko Ueno, Tauno Kekale, Mikko Repka, Zulema Lopes Pereira, and Graca Silva (2001). European quality management practices: The impact of national culture, *International Journal of Quality & Reliability Management*, 18(7), pp. 692–707. (Note: this study is based on research conducted only in the UK, Finland, and Portugal).

19. This paragraph is based on material in Chapter 2 of John B. Cullen and K. Praveen Parboteeah (2013). *Multinational Management: A Strategic Approach* (6th ed.), Mason, OH: South-Western CENGAGE Learning.

20. John W. Bing (2004). Hofstede's consequences: The impact of his work on consulting and business practices, *Academy of Management Perspectives*, 18(1): pp. 80–87, at p. 85.

21. Pankaj Ghemawat and Thomas M. Hout (2011). *Differences in Business Ownership and Governance around the World*, Globalization Note Series.

22. Geert Hofstede (1987). The cultural context of accounting, in *Accounting and Culture: Plenary Session Papers and Discussants' Comments*, Annual Meeting of the American Accounting Association, p. 8.

23. Nigel Finch (2009). Towards an understanding of cultural influence on the international practice of accounting, *Journal of International Business and Cultural Studies*, 2(1), pp. 1–6.

24. Bradley L. Kirkman, Kevin B. Lowe, and Cristina B. Gibson (2006). A quarter century of *Culture's Consequences*: A review of empirical research incorporating Hofstede's cultural values framework, *Journal of International Business Studies*, 37(3), pp. 285–320, at p. 301.

25. Bruce Kogut and Harbir Singh (1988). The effect of national culture on the choice of entry mode, *Journal of International Business Studies*, 19(3), pp. 411–432.

26. Bradley L. Kirkman, Kevin B. Lowe, and Cristina B. Gibson (2006). A quarter century of *Culture's Consequences*: A review of empirical research incorporating Hofstede's cultural values framework, *Journal of International Business Studies*, 37(3), pp. 285–320, at p. 299.

27. Raj Aggarwal, Colm Kearney, and Brian Lucey (2009). Is gravity a cultural artefact? Culture and distance in foreign portfolio investment, FMA Annual Meeting. www.efmaefm.org/0EFMAMEETINGS/EFMA%20ANNUAL%20MEETINGS/2009-Milan/papers/EFMA2009_0455_fullpaper.pdf.

28. Brendan McSweeney (2002). Hofstede's model of national cultural differences and their consequences: A triumph of faith—a failure of analysis, *Human Relations*, 55(1), pp. 89–118.

29. Geert Hofstede and Michael H. Bond (1988). The Confucian connection: From cultural roots to economic growth, *Organizational Dynamics*, 16(1), pp. 4–21.

30. Oded Shenkar (2012). Cultural distance revisited: Towards a more rigorous conceptualization and measurement of cultural differences, *Journal of International Business Studies*, 43(1), pp. 1–11. See also Anne-Wil Harzing (2004). The role of culture in entry-mode studies: From neglect to myopia? In Joseph L. C. Cheng and Michael A. Hitt (Eds.), *Advances in International Management*, Oxford, UK: Elsevier, vol. 15, pp. 75–127 .

31. Michele J. Gelfand et al. (2011). Differences between tight and loose cultures: A 33-nation study, *Science*, 332, pp. 1100–1104.

32. Michele J. Gelfand, Joshua C. Jackson, Xinyue Pan, Dana Nau, Dylan Pieper, Emmy Denison, Munqith Dagher, Paul A. M. Van Lange, Chi-Yue Chiu, and Mo Wang (2021). The relationship between cultural tightness–looseness and COVID-19 cases and deaths: A global analysis, *The Lancet Planetary Health*, 5(3), e135–e144.

33. Fons Trompenaars and Charles Hampden-Turner (1997). *Riding the Waves of Culture: Understanding Cultural Diversity in Business* (2nd ed.), London: Nicholas Brealey.

34. Shalom H. Schwartz (2008). *Cultural Value Orientations: Nature and Implications of National Differences*, Moscow: Publishing House of SU HSE.

35. Robert J. House, Paul J. Hanges, Mansour Javidan, Peter W. Dorfman, and Vipin Gupta (Eds.) (2004). *Culture, Leadership, and Organizations: The Globe Study of 62 Societies*, Thousand Oaks, CA: SAGE.

36. Quoted in B. A. Robinson (2011). Religions of the world: Numbers of adherents of major religions, their geographical distribution, date founded, and sacred texts. Last modified December 2, 2015. www.religioustolerance.org/worldrel.htm.

37. See www.adherents.com/Religions_By_Adherents.html and www.religioustolerance.org/worldrel.htm.

38. Douglas Dow and Amal Karunaratna (2006). Developing a multidimensional instrument to measure psychic distance stimuli, *Journal of International Business Studies*, 37(5), pp. 578–602.

39. The material on language covered in this section draws from Joel West and John L. Graham (2004). A linguistic-based measure of cultural distance and its relationship to managerial values, *Management International Review*, 44(3), pp. 239–260.

40. Edward Sapir (1921). *Language*, New York: Harcourt, Brace, and World.

41. Benjamin L. Whorf (1940). Science and linguistics, *Technology Review*, 42(6), pp. 229–248.

42. Michael Agar (1994). *Language Shock: Understanding the Culture of Conversation*, New York: Quill, p. 71.

43. John J. Gumperz and Stephen C Levinson (1996). Introduction: Linguistic relativity re-examined. In John J. Gumperz and Stephen C. Levinson (Eds.), *Rethinking Linguistic Relativity*, Cambridge, UK: Cambridge University Press, pp. 1-18, at pp. 2–3.

44. Calculation based on a subset of 163 countries from www.cepii.fr/anglaisgraph/bdd/distances.htm.

45. Joel West and John L. Graham (2004). A linguistic-based measure of cultural distance and its relationship to managerial values, *Management International Review*, 44(3), pp. 239–260, at p. 244.

46. Ibid., p. 246.

47. Simcha Ronen and Oded Shenkar (2013). Mapping world cultures: Cluster formation, sources and implications, *Journal of International Business Studies*, 44(9): pp. 867–897.

48. Gert-Jan M. Linders, Arjen Slangen, Henri L. F. de Groot, and Sjoerd Beugelsdijk (2005). Cultural and institutional determinants of bilateral trade flows, Tinbergen Institute Discussion Paper, No. 05-074/3, Amsterdam and Rotterdam, the Netherlands: Tinbergen Institute.

49. Jody Evans and Felix T. Mavondo (2002). Psychic distance and organizational performance: An empirical examination of international retailing operations, *Journal of International Business Studies*, 33(3), pp. 515–532.

50. Pankaj Ghemawat (2010). *The Globalization of Markets*, Globalization Note Series.

51. Pankaj Ghemawat and Rajiv Mallick (2003). The industry-level structure of international trade networks: A gravity-based approach. Working paper, Boston, MA: Harvard Business School.

52. Fukunari Kimura and Hyun-Hoon Lee (2006). The gravity equation in international trade in services, *Review of World Economics*, 142(1), 92–121.

53. Jaques Melitz (2008). Language and foreign trade, *European Economic Review*, 52(4), pp. 667–699.

54. Linders et al. (2005).

55. Joshua J. Lewer and Hendrik Van den Berg (2007). Religion and international trade: Does the sharing of a religious culture facilitate the formation of trade networks? *American Journal of Economics and Sociology*, 66(4), pp. 765–794.

56. Christian Daude and Marcel Fratzscher (2008). The pecking order of cross-border investment, *Journal of International Economics*, 74(1), pp. 94–119, at p. 104.

57. Jeni Klugman (2009). *Human Development Report 2009, Overcoming Barriers: Human Mobility and Development.* UNDP-HDRO Human Development Reports.

58. This analysis is based on a sample of 63 countries with data from 1995–1999. Domestic calling minutes are from the International Telecommunications Union World Telecommunication/ICT Indicators 2009 database. International calling minutes are from International Telecommunications Union (1999). "Direction of Traffic, 1999: Trading Telecom Minutes.". Population data from World Development Indicators and data on proportion of national populations speaking particular languages from the Centre d'Études Prospectives et d'Informations Internationales.

59. Per Botolf Maurseth and Bart Verspagen (2002). Knowledge spillovers in Europe: A patent citations analysis, *Scandinavian Journal of Economics*, 104(4), pp. 531–545, at p. 541.

60. Survey respondents were actually asked to rate the citizens of other countries as well as their own on a spectrum ranging from "no trust at all" to "a lot of trust." An academic article based on this survey summarizes data about the percentage of citizens of each West European country surveyed who report trusting others "a lot": see Luigi Guiso, Paola Sapienza, and Luigi Zingales (2009). Cultural biases in economic exchange? *Quarterly Journal of Economics*, 124(3), 1095–1131.

61. Ibid.

62. Heejin Kim, B. Sebastian Reiche, and Anne-Wil Harzing (2022). How does successive inpatriation contribute to subsidiary capability building and subsidiary evolution? A longitudinal perspective on inpatriates' knowledge transfer, *Journal of International Business Studies*. doi.org/10.1057/s41267-021-00494-3.

63. For an extended discussion of adaptation that includes but goes beyond the levers discussed in this note, see Chapter 4 of Pankaj Ghemawat (2007). *Redefining Global Strategy*, Brighton, MA: Harvard Business School Press.

64. Nancy J. Adler and Allison Gundersen (2008). *International Dimensions of Organizational Behavior* (5th ed.), Mason, OH: South-Western CENGAGE Learning.

65. Pankaj Ghemawat and Herman Vantrappen (2015). How global is your C-suite? *MIT Sloan Management Review*, 56(4): pp. 73–82.

66. Davina Vora, Lee Martin, Stacey R. Fitzsimmons, Andre A. Pekerti, C. Lakshman, and Salma Raheem (2019). Multiculturalism within individuals: A review, critique, and agenda for future research, *Journal of International Business Studies*, 50(4), pp. 499–524.

67. To take the Global Attitude Protocol (GAP) survey, see https://ghemawat.com/surveys/gap-survey; the Cultural Agility self-assessment can be found at www.myGiide.com.

Reading 2.4

Nana Yaa A. Gyamfi, Stacey R. Fitzsimmons, Christof Miska, and Günter K. Stahl

MULTICULTURAL INDIVIDUALS
What Can They Bring to Global Organizations?

GLOBAL BUSINESSES ARE FAST-MOVING PLACES with technologies that enable people to be more mobile than ever. Not only do individuals travel more frequently and connect with people from societal cultures that are different from their own, but as globalization dissolves geographical barriers, more individuals find themselves identifying with not only one culture, but with two or even more. Statistics indicate that this demographic is both large and growing. By 2021, more than 40 million people in OECD countries were foreign-born (OECD, 2022), and multicultural individuals have become so important that UNESCO has discussed their impact in reports since 2009 (UNESCO, 2009).

Multiculturalism varies along three dimensions: knowledge of, internalization of, and identification with more than one culture (Vora, Martin, Fitzsimmons, Pekerti, Lakshman, & Raheem, 2019). Knowledge refers to individuals' understanding of cultural content such as norms, values, beliefs, etc. Internalization refers to the cognitive aspect, encompassing the degree to which societal cultural values, assumptions, beliefs, and practices are reflected in an individual's own values. Finally, identification represents an emotional component whereby individuals see themselves as group members and value group membership. Indra Nooyi and Carlos Ghosn could both be poster children for multiculturalism, though they illustrate both its upside and potential dark sides. Indra Nooyi, former CEO and Chair of PepsiCo, who was ranked the #1 most powerful woman in business on the *Fortune 50* list from 2006 to 2009 (CNN Money, 2009), drew on her multicultural identity to shape PepsiCo as a global company. Nooyi moved

DOI: 10.4324/9781003247272-12

to the United States to complete her Master's degree at Yale, after degrees at the Indian Institute of Management and Madras Christian College. Under her watch, PepsiCo ramped up its international sales, and she turned PepsiCo into a corporation that truly appreciates and derives benefit from its diverse employees. She also spoke out – sometimes controversially – in favor of working globally:

> Although I'm a daughter of India, I'm an American businesswoman. ... Graduates, as you aggressively compete on the international business stage, understand that the five major continents and their peoples – the five fingers of your hand – each have their own strengths and their own contributions to make. Just as each of your fingers must coexist to create a critically important tool, each of the five major continents must also coexist to create a world in balance. You, as an American businessperson, will either contribute to or take away from, this balance.
>
> (Nooyi, 2005)

Carlos Ghosn, another well-known multicultural, was President and CEO of both Renault and Nissan. He speaks five languages, was born in Brazil, spent time in Lebanon as a child, graduated with engineering degrees from Paris, and is a French citizen. When he successfully merged Renault with Nissan, he drew on his Brazilian–Lebanese–French background in order to succeed in Japan, a country that was foreign to him at the time. However, later he became better known as a wanted fugitive who had escaped from Japanese house arrest in a cargo box (Jordan & Jack, 2021). As we discuss later, his multiculturalism might have been a factor in taking an overly relativistic approach to ethics.

A decade ago, we published the first version of this reading that held up both Nooyi and Ghosn as exemplars of multiculturalism (Fitzsimons, Miska, & Stahl, 2011). At that time, we only considered the potential benefits of multiculturalism. Now, we take a more critical eye to considering the potential double-edged sword nature of multiculturalism. Furthermore, although multiculturals' knowledge and abilities can be valuable in the world of international business and global organizations, few global organizations leverage their multicultural employees' potential, whether due to lack of awareness or missing processes required to leverage the distinct skills of multiculturals. Examples include selection or placement processes to put them in positions where they can realize their full potential (Hong & Minbaeva, 2022).

HOW CAN MULTICULTURAL EMPLOYEES CONTRIBUTE TO GLOBAL BUSINESS?

In order to understand how organizations can best use their multicultural employees' skills, we will explore multiculturals' impact on key international business activities – international teams, intercultural connection and negotiations, global mobility and talent development, and global leadership and ethics.

Multiculturals' Impact on Teams

Professional football (soccer) player Zlatan Ibrahimović was born and raised in Sweden to immigrant parents from Bosnia and Croatia. His multicultural background helped him connect others within his teams:

> He found a divided dressing room at Inter [Italy] and told President Massimo Moratti that winning under such conditions would be impossible. ... And just like that, Ibrahimović ... changed the soul of the club, becoming the leader of a Scudetto-winning machine.
>
> (Adams, 2020)

Ibrahimović's tenure at Inter Milan, from 2006 to 2009, saw three consecutive wins of the Serie A. Similarly, Ibrahimović is credited with fostering cohesiveness within AC Milan and inspiring teammates to improve their level of play, thus enabling them to win the Serie A titles when he played on loan in 2011 and again on his return in 2021 (Burns, 2022). Ibrahimović's example illustrates how multicultural individuals might influence team effectiveness: they might act as bridges across cultural faultlines, and strategically steer teams towards international or cross-cultural opportunities. Since global teams are usually multicultural, divisions within groups often develop along cultural lines, promoting disharmony, dissatisfaction, and poor performance (Lau & Murnighan, 2005; Polzer, Crisp, Jarvenpaa, & Kim, 2006). These faultlines develop when the group's composition emphasizes cultural divisions, such as with teams composed of members representing only two cultures. In order to avoid this tendency of culturally diverse teams to divide into factions based on cultural background, managers can include multicultural individuals on the team to make subgroup divisions less obvious (Gibson & Vermeulen, 2003). When team members straddle the cultural divide and belong in both groups, they become bridges across the faultline, reducing its detrimental effect (Lau & Murnighan, 2005).

An experiment found that multicultural individuals bridge across cultural faultlines differently, depending on whether their cultures overlap with those of their teammates (Jang, 2017). *Cultural insiders* – who shared at least one culture with their teammates, such as an Indian–Australian person on an Indian–American team – tended to integrate knowledge across cultures, such as suggesting ways to combine aspects from both cultures. In contrast, *cultural outsiders* – people who did not share cultures with their teammates, such as a Brazilian–British person on that same Indian–American team – tended to elicit knowledge from other cultures, such as asking questions about cultural norms. Another study found that multicultural employees had more culturally diverse social networks than monocultural employees, even beyond their own cultural groups (Fitzsimmons, Liao, & Thomas, 2017). Together, these findings suggest that multicultural individuals can reduce the likelihood that diverse teams develop cultural faultlines and increase the likelihood they integrate or elicit cultural knowledge.

The strategic benefit of multicultural individuals on teams is that multicultural individuals may shift team activities towards capturing innovative international or cross-cultural opportunities. Cross-cultural creativity or innovation gains are common reasons to strategically build multicultural teams. Yet multicultural teams also incur process losses, such as taking longer to coordinate or resolve misunderstandings (Schippers, Den Hartog, Koopman, & Wienk, 2003). As a result, research on cultural diversity in teams is lately shifting away from exploring the main effects of cultural diversity on team performance towards understanding how the strategic management of team cultural diversity affects performance and other outcomes (Minbaeva, Fitzsimmons, & Brewster, 2021).

For example, both longitudinal and cross-sectional data support the claim that when football (soccer) teams compete internationally, teams with multicultural managers outperform teams with monocultural managers, due to the multicultural managers' ability to build their teams' international competitive advantage (Szymanski, Fitzsimmons, & Danis, 2019). Similar dynamics may have helped support Ibrahimović's success as described in our opening quotes. Further, findings from 574 R&D participants across 82 teams in a Chinese branch of a large German global organization supported the claim that multicultural team leaders leveraged their teams' cultural diversity to improve team innovation through enhanced communication inclusion (Lisak, Erez, Sui, & Lee, 2016). Therefore, multicultural employees can contribute to international team performance by facilitating team innovation and internationally oriented strategic activities.

Overall, multicultural individuals on diverse teams can weaken faultlines, improve intercultural connections, facilitate innovation, and shift strategic activities to improve performance of internationally oriented tasks. These effects may be most pronounced in diverse teams that are expected to perform complex, internationally focused tasks.

Multiculturals' Impact on Intercultural Connection and Negotiations

Related to the faultline bridging role explained in the previous section, multiculturals often have the ability to connect easily with people from different cultures. This capacity is due to their heightened abilities to process content from different cultures (also known as integrative complexity; Tadmor, Galinsky, & Maddux, 2012), sensitivity to hot button issues across cultures (Varela, 2019), and adaptive skills developed while internalizing multiple cultures. Take the example of Bozoma Saint John, marketing professional who has worked for global brands such as Pepsi, Apple Music, Uber, and Netflix. Saint John was born in Connecticut, USA, to Ghanaian parents, moved to Ghana as an infant, and relocated to the United States as a teen. In an interview with Forbes, Saint John attributed her unique ability as a marketing executive to connect with minds and hearts across cultures, belief systems, and other faultlines, to her experience of adapting to American culture as a teenager:

Part of it was also the need to fit in, and so trying to find the points of connection ... it doesn't really matter if somebody doesn't hold the same belief
systems as you or doesn't come from the same place that you do. There is
going to be some connection. You just have to find it.

(Bozoma Saint John, quoted by McCormick, 2020)

The ability to connect across cultures enables multiculturals to communicate
effectively with essential stakeholders and thereby achieve ends that others
may not be able to. Dr. Uğur Şahin of German vaccine manufacturer BioNTech
has said in interviews that he bonded with Albert Bourla, Chief Executive of
Pfizer, over their shared backgrounds as immigrants. The flourishing partnership
between BioNTech and Pfizer yielded a vaccine that was more than 90% effective in preventing COVID-19. Dr. Şahin shared:

We realized that he is from Greece and that I'm from Turkey ... it was very
personal from the beginning.

(Dr. Uğur Şahin, quoted by Gelles, 2020)

With their innate ability to pick up on cultural nuances and connect with others, multiculturals are well-positioned to negotiate across cultures. Good negotiators find a balance between maximizing individual objectives and common
goals simultaneously. It is therefore important that negotiators understand their
counterparts' goals, expectations, and negotiation strategies, which in a cross-
cultural setting frequently turns out to be an obstacle. When negotiators share
a culture, they usually share common expectations about acceptable negotiation
strategies, behavior, and the sequence of the bargaining process. However, when
negotiators from different cultures meet, they are often used to different cultural norms and standards (Cohen, 1997). For example, people from Argentina,
France, and India are often used to top-down approaches, from general to specific principles, whereas people from Mexico, Japan, and Brazil are often used
to building agreement from the bottom up (Salacuse, 2005). Because of these
differing expectations, same-culture negotiations, like US–US or Japanese–
Japanese, tend to have better outcomes than cross-cultural bargaining (Brett &
Okumura, 1998). We propose two ways multiculturals may be able to mitigate
some of these intercultural negotiation challenges.

First, rather than seeing dissimilarities as obstacles, multicultural negotiators might be more appreciative of differences in perspectives and negotiation
strategies than monoculturals. Multiculturals may develop this skill because they
are constantly confronted with diverse or even contradicting realities, so they
learn how to deal with such situations and how to make the best of them (Tadmor,
Tetlock, & Peng, 2009). If negotiations are complex and require creative solutions, multicultural experience may be even more of an advantage. Second,
multicultural negotiators may be able to positively influence their negotiation
partners' communication experience. Research shows that although cross-
cultural negotiations are often fraught with tensions and misunderstandings,

international negotiations can produce higher joint gains than same-cultural negotiations when the communication experience is pleasant for both parties (e.g., when both parties feel comfortable and make efforts reciprocating and adapting to the other party's norms and expectations; Liu, Chua, & Stahl, 2010). To minimize cross-cultural tensions and misunderstanding, multiculturals may leverage homophily, the human inclination to interact with people who are similar to themselves (McPherson, Smith-Lovin, & Cook, 2001), generated by their ability to signal similarity or familiarity across cultures, to enhance their negotiation partners' communication experience.

Multiculturals' Impact on Global Mobility and Talent Deployment

Despite growing anti-globalization sentiments and immigration barriers in many parts of the world, global mobility – the ability of a workforce to be deployed seamlessly from one country to another – is more important than ever in supporting the globalization efforts of multinational companies (Pucik, Björkman, Evans, & Stahl, 2023; Reiche, Lee, & Allen, 2019; Shaffer, Kraimer, Chen, & Bolino, 2012). However, firms struggle to support the movement of talent globally and to prepare their managers and high-potential employees for global leadership roles. Not everybody is well equipped for a "boundaryless career", and research has consistently shown that most companies lack a systematic approach to developing global leadership capabilities and leveraging the competences of managers and professionals who have gained international experience through past work or education abroad (Lazarova & Cerdin, 2007; Reiche, Kraimer, & Harzing, 2011). Given expected demands for globally competent managers and professionals, organizations need to become more effective in leveraging the competences of internationally experienced managers or finding those who already possess these competencies (Caligiuri & Bonache, 2016).

Recruiting multicultural individuals is one way to expand the global talent pool and fill key positions involving international responsibilities. Multiculturals have already gained an in-depth understanding of multiple cultures, can switch among them, and tend to show stronger integrative complexity, creativity, and boundary-spanning skills (Hong & Minbaeva, 2022; Vora et al., 2019). For example, L'Oréal Paris has about 40 product development teams, most of them headed by multicultural managers recruited from the company's international subsidiaries or other global companies (Pucik et al., 2023). L'Oréal found that teams comprising multiculturals were effective in new-product development because of multicultural members' sensitivity to both their own and other cultures, cultural empathy, and multilingual skills which allowed them to overcome communication barriers, respond to the needs of a diverse set of stakeholders, and spot new product opportunities in global markets (Hong & Doz, 2013; Ramarajan, Dessain, & Moloney, 2020).

In most countries, immigrants or the children of immigrants are the largest pool of multicultural individuals. They also represent one of the most under-tapped talent pools in the world as well as an unparalleled track record of entrepreneurship (Hajro, Caprar, Zikic, & Stahl, 2021). The BioNTech founders we alluded to earlier, who developed a potent vaccine against COVID-19, have foreign roots. Uğur Şahin and Özlem Türeci, the co-founders of BioNTech SE, are both German citizens born to Turkish immigrants. A profile on *Bloomberg* (Kluth, 2020) reveals that Şahin was four years old when he moved with his mother to join his father, one of the "guest workers" who came to work in a car factory during Germany's postwar economic boom. Türeci was born in Germany to a Turkish father who was working as a doctor in a small hospital. Katalin Karikó, BioNTech's head of R&D, and considered a strong contender for the Nobel prize for her groundbreaking work on mRNA, left Hungary for the US to continue her post-doctoral work, then later moved to Germany to join BioNTech.

Migrants exhibit a higher level of entrepreneurial activity than non-immigrants, due to a combination of self-selection, where individuals who pack up and move countries are more likely to be highly motivated and capable, and lack of opportunity in more traditional labor markets due to discrimination and exclusion (Dabić, Vlačić, Paul, Dana, Sahasranamam, & Glinka, 2020; Levie, 2007; Vandor & Franke, 2016a). One explanation for immigrants' entrepreneurial successes is that cross-cultural experiences make people more open-minded and creative (Maddux, Lu, Affinito, & Galinsky, 2021). Recent research suggests that the constant switching of perspectives that comes with having a multicultural background helps in identifying promising entrepreneurial opportunities (Vandor & Franke, 2016b).

The foregoing may partly explain why multicultural individuals tend to be more effective in foreign or cross-cultural contexts, such as cross-border project work or international postings. Edman's (2016) work has explored the paradox of foreignness, demonstrating how being a foreigner may result in disorientation, vulnerability, and outsider status, yet may also offer an opportunity to grow, explore, and reinvent. In the context of international assignments, there is evidence that the skills, abilities, and perspectives that multiculturals posses help them adapt to foreign and culturally diverse environments (Hong & Minbaeva, 2022; Vora et al., 2019). For example, Brannen, Garcia, and Thomas (2009) found that multicultural individuals have higher cultural metacognition than monoculturals, a key aspect of cultural intelligence that facilitates cross-cultural adjustment and cultural learning (Thomas et al., 2008).

However, multiculturalism's impact on international assignment success is not straightforward, for several reasons. Global mobility today covers a broad array of international assignment types and ways of global working, not just traditional expatriate assignments, including inpatriation, short-term assignments, "flexpatriation" and international commuting, the use of self-initiated expatriates, global virtual teams, and the COVID-19-induced need for organizations to offer remote-work options (Collings, Scullion, & Morley, 2007; Lazarova, Caligiuri, Collings, & De Cieri, 2023). The global mobility types differ in the demographic composition of international assignees, required company support, and attendant work experiences. They can be classified in terms of three dimensions (Shaffer et al., 2012):

- *Physical mobility* is the degree to which the work role requires that employees travel, or relocate, internationally;
- *Cognitive complexity* is the degree to which the global work requires employees to adjust their thought patterns, scripts, and behaviors to effectively interact with people and adapt to situational demands across cultures; and
- *Nonwork disruption* is the degree to which the work role requirements interfere with employees' activities and routines outside of work (e.g., lead to family separation).

By classifying the global mobility types along these three dimensions, it is possible to identify a matrix of global work experiences that differ in terms of physical mobility, cognitive flexibility, and nonwork disruption, as illustrated by Figure 1.

We propose that multiculturals have an advantage over monoculturals primarily in assignment contexts that require high levels of cognitive flexibility and cultural adaptability, such as expatriation. Both corporate and self-initiated expatriates are required to relocate to a foreign country to live and work; therefore, these types of assignments are high on physical mobility and need for cognitive flexibility and cultural adaptability. By contrast, short-term assignees are required to physically travel to a foreign country for months at a time, but due to the short-term and often project-specific nature of the work, they typically require less adaptability. Therefore, demands for cognitive flexibility and adaptability are comparatively low (Shaffer et al., 2012).

Multiculturals' Impact on Global Leadership and Ethics

Leading in the global environment implies the need to span boundaries across organizations, diverse constituencies, and countries (Lane, Maznevski, Mendenhall, & McNett, 2004). This global context is increasingly labeled VUCA – volatile, uncertain, complex, and ambiguous (Miska, Economou, & Stahl, 2020). Research indicates that global leaders in particular must manage contexts that range widely in terms of both relationship and task complexity (Reiche, Bird, Mendenhall, & Osland, 2017). Several types of multiculturals are likely

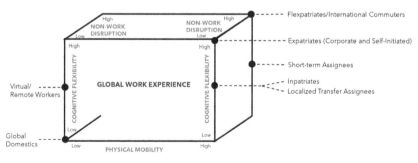

Adapted from Shaffer et al., 2012

Figure 1 Taxonomy of global mobility types and attendant work experiences.
Source: Adapted from Shaffer et al. (2012).

to naturally possess the skill sets facilitating global leadership. For example, Fitzsimmons, Lee, and Brannen (2013) emphasized the global leadership potential among multiculturals who did not feel like they belonged in any of their cultures. Their dual status as both insiders with deep cultural understanding and outsiders able to assume unconstrained cultural perspectives may help them analyze complex issues associated with global leadership from different viewpoints.

A key challenge that differentiates global from domestic leadership relates to how leaders safeguard ethical conduct across their countries of operation and how they contribute to sustainable development. Therefore, leaders operating in cultures that are not their own must decide whether to use their own ethical principles, or to adopt local ethical principles. For example, when working in countries where bribery is common, some managers refuse to take part because bribery is universally wrong and illegal in most legal systems, while others nonetheless accept some level of bribery – such as "facilitation payments" – as normal in that context. These two perspectives are called universalist and relativist ethical perspectives, respectively, and they represent two broad categories of ethical argumentation across cultures (Windsor, 2004). Ethical universalism assumes that the situation does not influence what is ethical; only universal rules do. In contrast, ethical relativism assumes that each culture has the right to determine its own set of rules about right and wrong.

Multiculturals' ability to switch between cultures and their greater cultural adaptability and culture-based creativity (Hong & Minbaeva, 2022; Vora et al., 2019) may help them to be effective in cross-cultural contexts, but they may also facilitate espousing a culturally and ethically relativistic attitude, thereby increasing their propensity to engage in unethical behavior. As illustrated by Carlos Ghosn's downfall, we see potential downsides to having multiple ethical frames of reference. Carlos Ghosn's high level of multiculturalism might have made it easier for him to take an overly relativistic approach to ethics, thus contributing to his alleged financial misconduct. Among other things, Ghosn is accused of under-reporting his earnings in filings to the Tokyo Stock Exchange to hide 5.2 billion yen ($48 million) over five years from 2010, having illegally misappropriated $5 million from Nissan between July 2017 and July 2018, using company funds for personal purposes, and misrepresenting the company's investments (Reuters, 2020). Ghosn was simultaneously operating Nissan and Renault across France and Japan, while also drawing on his Brazilian–Lebanese–French background, giving him a wide range of ethical norms to draw upon when evaluating his own ethical behavior.

Further, multiculturals are classified as marginal, separated, integrated, or cosmopolitan, depending on their levels of identification with and interrelationships between their cultural identities (see Table 1); and these classifications may have implications for their ethical decision-making.

Multicultural individuals who separate their cultural identities have been found to be more inclined towards ethical relativism, and this effect is even stronger than that of identifying with cultures where ethical relativism is normative (Hrenyk, Szymanski, Kar, & Fitzsimmons, 2016). Similarly, marginals

Table 1 Multicultural types, by identification with cultures

Multicultural Type	Description	Example
Marginals	Marginals have more than one culture, but feel disassociated with both or all of them	April Raintree, Métis character in a Native Canadian novel: "It would be better to be a full-blooded Indian or full-blooded Caucasian. But being a half-breed, well, there's just nothing there." (Mosionier, 1999, p. 142)
Separated	Separated multiculturals keep their cultural identities apart and identify with one or the other depending on the context	Andrea Jung, former CEO of Avon, and Chinese–American: "I've definitely become more assertive. ... It really was critical to have that Western versus Eastern aspect, and still feel like I never had to change who I am." (Jung, 2009)
Integrated	Integrated multiculturals merge their cultures together, resulting in a new, hybrid culture	Eric Liu, former speechwriter for President Clinton, and Chinese–American: "I could never claim to be Chinese at the core. Yet neither would I claim, as if by default, to be merely 'white inside.' I do not want to be white. I only want to be integrated." (Liu, 1998)
Cosmopolitans	Cosmopolitans identify with many cultures, are usually frequent travelers, and have lived in several different countries	Carlos Ghosn, former President and CEO of Renault and Nissan, and French–Brazilian–Lebanese: "He is the quintessential global executive." "When you are an outsider and you cannot be categorized into one culture, it makes people feel that you are unlikely to be biased." (Najjar, 2008)

may be more likely to lean towards ethical relativism than cosmopolitans, who primarily associate with other globally mobile individuals.

Despite the potential pitfalls of an overreliance on ethical relativism, we speculate that some multicultural employees may be able to reconcile relativistic with universalist ethics. This balance strikes the appropriate balance between global consistency and local sensitivity – what ethics scholars Donaldson and Dunfee have described as "a need to retain local identity with the acknowledgement of values that transcend individual communities" (1999, p. 50). It invites managers to assess behaviors against fundamental norms that are commonly sourced from international agreements such as the UN's Universal Declaration of Human Rights, such that they can be used to evaluate and critique specific norms generated by local communities (Donaldson, 2016).

In direct contrast to our earlier warnings that multicultural individuals may be more inclined towards ethical relativism, monocultural individuals may be overly inclined towards ethical universalism due to their reliance on one singular set of culture-based ethical norms. This risks adopting colonial attitudes towards the ethical norms in countries where global leaders operate. Multicultural identity is especially likely to help global leaders succeed when engaged in sustainable development projects, which tend to be complex, multi-party, and multi-country tasks. In these contexts, global leaders aiming to achieve the UN's Sustainable Development Goals need to be proficient in managing VUCA contexts while transcending cultural differences and boundaries.

THE DOWNSIDES OF MULTICULTURALISM AND ORGANIZATIONAL INTERVENTIONS

In the fifth edition's version of this reading, we exclusively examined potential benefits of multicultural individuals (Fitzsimons, Miska, & Stahl, 2011). Yet this does not necessarily align with many peoples' experiences of multiculturalism. While the benefits of multiculturalism are still significant and hopefully more influential for most people than the downsides, we want to be clear that multiculturalism is not a universally positive experience. Beyond the cautions we discussed earlier in relation to relativist ethics, we also introduce reasons why people often find it difficult to be multicultural, and how other people's expectations are instrumental to explaining potential penalties experienced by multicultural individuals. Further, starting from the premise that multiculturals' benefits to organizations may be latent rather than assured, we explain what organizations can do to avoid the downsides we identify, and unlock the potential of multicultural employees.

Multicultural individuals spend more time introspecting about where they belong and how they identify themselves than monoculturals, because the former have more options for belonging and identity than the latter. These can be uncomfortable and difficult experiences. Findings from 1196 participants across three separate samples of employed students, hotel employees, and health care employees all supported expectations that multiculturals who separate their cultural identities tend to experience lower levels of personal well-being (as measured by higher identity uncertainty and feeling overburdened with cultural translation work) than those who integrate their cultural identities (Fitzsimmons, Liao, & Thomas, 2017). Therefore, despite all the potential advantages of multiculturalism, it also comes at a cost of personal well-being for some.

Although the experience of being multicultural is intensely personal, it is also experienced in the context of other people's reactions. Olympic snowboarder Eileen Gu, American-born and raised by her Chinese immigrant mother, switched from her original Olympic team USA to team China in 2019, before becoming the youngest gold medalist ever in freestyle skiing. Her switch from team USA to team China received abundant media coverage in both countries, with strangers loudly questioning her allegiance to either country (Larmer, 2022). Although most people do not receive this level of scrutiny for their cultural identities, people often experience more muted versions of pushback from others. This can result in a person feeling torn between cultures, or feeling caught between societal expectations imposed by each culture. Research on ethnic identity confirmation among expatriates (Fan, Cregan, Harzing, & Köhler, 2018; Fan & Harzing, 2017) shows that multicultural expatriates cannot control how others see them. For example, they found that local Chinese employees sometimes viewed Chinese–British expatriates as Chinese, and therefore expected them to behave according to Chinese norms, even when that was not how the expatriates saw themselves.

The foregoing indicates that simply hiring multicultural employees is not enough; it is also essential to set up the conditions that allow their skills to emerge. Although we have identified many potential benefits to firms in employing multicultural employees, their accrual depends on how multiculturals are managed (Hong & Minbaeva, 2022). Multicultural employees have the potential to add value in the four key areas described above (teams, intercultural connection and negotiation, global mobility and talent deployment, and leadership and ethics), but only when organizations implement the procedures necessary to use their skills (for example, selection processes and career development practices to place them in positions where they can be most useful). Given that multinational organizations often fail to take advantage of the knowledge, skills, and experiences of their global employees, organizations with the right processes in place have an opportunity to enhance their competitive advantage.

Organizations should first develop an organizational culture that encourages diversity of thought and perspectives. Organizations that value multiple cultures are more likely to benefit from cultural diversity (Jackson, Joshi, & Erhardt, 2003), because when they don't, they risk suppressing employees' multicultural identities and the skills that emerge from being multicultural (Ely & Thomas, 2001). Organizations with especially strong organizational cultures often train employees to think, behave, and react similarly to one another, resulting in a cohesive workforce. Yet these strong and cohesive cultures may miss out on the unique benefits of its multicultural employees (Jackson et al., 2003). Therefore, organizations should create visible signs that the company values employees with a multicultural background, and that international experience or orientation will improve one's career advancement within the organization. For example, leaders could create multicultural role models by promoting multiculturals to top management positions, or by instituting international experiential programs, explained later.

Next, organizations can hire people with multicultural backgrounds and place them strategically into positions where they can be most useful. Otherwise, their unique skills could be wasted. According to our analysis, multiculturals are most likely to contribute to the success of diverse teams when they are working on complex tasks requiring creativity, especially within an international or cross-cultural context (Hong & Minbaeva, 2022; Godart, Maddux, Shipilov, & Galinsky, 2015). Therefore, organizations should identify tasks and teams with these characteristics, and try to place multicultural employees on those teams. For example, multicultural employees are more likely to benefit an international coordination team, rather than a team focused on coordinating with a stable local supplier. Since it is not practical to measure how much individuals identify with their cultures for recruitment purposes, we recommend hiring people with a wide variety of multicultural backgrounds and placing them strategically once more is known about their particular skill sets. This approach will also help shift the organizational culture in the right direction in terms of valuing diversity.

Finally, organizations should train and develop multicultural employees to further enhance their skills with respect to the organization's requirements. We recommend using corporate training and development programs to achieve two goals: supporting multiculturals to become more conscious of their skills and abilities, and developing similar skill sets among monocultural employees. Mentorship and coaching are best suited to achieving the first goal, while global experiential programs could achieve both. Monocultural employees may particularly benefit from multicultural experiences afforded them by employing organizations. Although monoculturals are not likely to develop these skills to the same degree as multiculturals, multicultural experiences such as short-term international assignments may bring them a step towards closing the gap by shifting employees' interpersonal attitudes and behaviors towards a more global orientation (Maddux et al., 2021).

For example, Pless, Maak, and Stahl (2011) studied a global experiential program at PricewaterhouseCoopers, where high-potential employees worked with local partners in developing countries for eight weeks. The program helped managers acquire skills similar to those of multiculturals. Experiencing the heightened ambiguity, competing tensions, and challenging ethical dilemmas associated with working in a foreign culture can trigger a transformational experience and produce new mental models in managers. Evidence shows that this program helped participants broaden their horizons, reduce stereotypes and prejudices, learn how to perceive the world through the eyes of people who are different, and work effectively with a diverse range of stakeholders. These qualities are similar to those of multicultural employees, and are essential for leading responsibly in a global and interconnected world. If a program like this one is not feasible because of cost or time constraints, then organizations could use short-term field experiences to expose employees to sub-cultures within their own countries (for example, by looking after homeless people, working with juvenile delinquents, or living with immigrants seeking asylum) to provide significant cultural immersion experiences and perspective-taking skills (Mendenhall & Stahl, 2000).

Organizations can compensate for downsides related to higher levels of ethical relativism and individuals' difficulty deciding where they belong by designing organizational practices that strategically leverage multiculturals' unique skills, and build similar skills among monocultural employees. However, the benefits and downsides of multiculturalism also depend on other organizational members' perceptions of a multicultural's legitimacy, explained next.

LEGITIMACY CONSIDERATIONS

This chapter has so far focused on potential skills and abilities of multicultural employees, as well as the downsides of multiculturalism. Another way in which multiculturalism may be a double-edged sword relates to perceptions held by other organizational members about multiculturals' legitimacy. Returning to the definition of who a multicultural is, Vora et al.'s (2019) dimensions of knowledge, internalization, and identification may be necessary but not sufficient conditions for an uncontested claim to multiculturalism. This is because the three dimensions focus on an individual's own perspective of self: cultures known, internalized, and identified with; however, as described in the prior section on downsides, identity is both personal and social in nature, such that audiences may accept or reject claims an individual makes to an identity (DeRue & Ashford, 2010). Legitimacy refers to the quality of being considered, by oneself *and* by relevant audiences, to be a member of a specific cultural group through natural, immersive, legal, or other broadly accepted means (Lee & Gyamfi, 2023). A professional may consider himself or herself to be multicultural, but may fail to reap the benefits of multiculturalism if he or she lacks legitimacy before the relevant audience.

Expanding the example from prior sections, while the Chinese populace accepted Eileen Gu's claim of identification with China, they rejected that of Zhu Yi, another American-born athlete of Chinese descent who also opted to compete for China at the 2022 Beijing Winter Olympics. Chinese media articles considered Yi to not be "Chinese enough", despite her Chinese—American heritage, citing her lack of fluency in Mandarin and comparing her with Gu, who not only speaks fluent Mandarin but also appears to have more fully embraced Chinese culture (CNN, 2022). An example such as the foregoing illustrates that businesses who hope to employ or deploy multiculturals to certain positions should be cautious about assuming that ethnic heritage is enough for others to accept multiculturals as belonging to their cultural groups. Similar to the examples we offered earlier about Chinese—British expatriates sent on assignment to China, it is possible for audiences to brand multiculturals as "fake" or illegitimate if they don't also speak the relevant languages and behave in ways associated with cultural norms (Fan, Cregan, Harzing, & Köhler, 2018; Fan & Harzing, 2017). For example, a multicultural manager whose job in a multinational enterprise involves persuading or negotiating with local authorities may be more effective if in addition of having local heritage, she speaks the local language, demonstrates familiarity with the local cultural context and norms, or otherwise signals the same (e.g., having grown up or completed school in the local context). Here also, the onus is placed on employers to be circumspect in their hiring and training of multiculturals, by selecting and training them according to the skills and characteristics that would most enhance their legitimacy among relevant stakeholders.

CONCLUSION

Multicultural individuals may contribute valuable skills to teams, negotiations, global mobility, ethics, and leadership. Although this discussion has focused primarily on multiculturals' overall contributions, their experiences are not universal, and organizations are at risk of alienating their multicultural employees unless they consider the different ways to be multicultural. Furthermore, organizations have an important role to play in ensuring the success of multicultural employees, by aligning selection, training, and organizational culture to harness the potential in their multicultural employees.

REFERENCES

Adams, T. (2020). The Zlatan effect: How Ibrahimovic changed Europe forever. *Eurosport*. Retrieved from https://www.eurosport.com/football/the-zlatan-effect-how -ibrahimovic-changed-europe-for-ever_sto6715841/story.shtml.

Brannen, M. Y., Garcia, D., & Thomas, D. C. (2009). *Biculturals as natural bridges for intercultural communication and collaboration*. Paper presented at the International Workshop on Intercultural Collaboration, Palo Alto, CA.

Brett, J., & Okumura, T. (1998). Inter- and intracultural negotiation: U.S. and Japanese negotiatiors. *Academy of Management Journal*, 41(5), 495–510.

Burns, E. (2022). Ex-Inter coach: "Milan able to afford to build, Ibrahimovic changed everything". *Sempremilan*. Retrieved from https://sempremilan.com/inter-milan -ibrahimovic-changed-everything.

Caligiuri, P., & Bonache, J. (2016). Evolving and enduring challenges in global mobility. *Journal of World Business*, 51(1), 127–141.

CNN. (2022). Fame and fury: China's wildly different reactions to US-born Olympians. *CNN*, February 12, 2022. Retrieved from: https://edition.cnn.com/2022/02/11/ china/eileen-gu-zhu-yi-nathan-chen-comparison-intl-hnk-dst/index.html.

CNN Money. (2009). 50 most powerful women in business: Fortune's annual ranking of America's leading business women. Retrieved January 22, 2010, from https://money .cnn.com/magazines/fortune/mostpowerfulwomen/2009/full_list/.

Cohen, R. (1997). *Negotiating Across Cultures*. Washington, DC: United States Institute of Peace.

Collings, D. G., Scullion, H., & Morley, M. J. (2007). Changing patterns of global staffing in the multinational enterprise: Challenges to the conventional expatriate assignment and emerging alternatives. *Journal of World Business*, 42(2), 198–213.

Dabić, M., Vlačić, B., Paul, J., Dana, L. P., Sahasranamam, S., & Glinka, B. (2020). Immigrant entrepreneurship: A review and research agenda. *Journal of Business Research*, 113, 25–38.

DeRue, D. S., & Ashford, S. J. (2010). Who will lead and who will follow? A social process of leadership identity construction in organizations. *Academy of Management Review*, 35(4), 627–647.

Donaldson, T. (2016). Values in tension: Ethics away from home. In B. S. Reiche, G. K. Stahl, M. E. Mendenhall, & G. R. Oddou (Eds.), *Readings and Cases in International Human Resource Management* (6th ed.). New York: Routledge, pp. 403–415.

Donaldson, T., & Dunfee, T. W. (1999). When ethics travel: The promise and peril of global business ethics. *California Management Review*, 41(4), 45–63.

Edman, J. (2016). Reconciling the advantages and liabilities of foreignness: Towards an identity-based framework. *Journal of International Business Studies*, 47(6), 674–694.

Ely, R. J., & Thomas, D. A. (2001). Cultural diversity at work: The effects of diversity perspectives on work group processes and outcomes. *Administrative Science Quarterly*, 46(2), 229–273.

Fan, S. X., & Harzing, A. W. (2017). Host country employees' ethnic identity confirmation: Evidence from interactions with ethnically similar expatriates. *Journal of World Business*, 52(5), 640–652.

Fan, S. X., Cregan, C., Harzing, A. W., & Köhler, T. (2018). The benefits of being understood: The role of ethnic identity confirmation in knowledge acquisition by expatriates. *Human Resource Management*, 57(1), 327–339.

Fitzsimmons, S. R., Lee, Y. T., & Brannen, M. Y. (2013). Demystifying the myth about marginals: Implications for global leadership. *European Journal of International Management*, 7(5), 587–603.

Fitzsimmons, S. R., Liao, E., & Thomas, D. C. (2017). From crossing cultures to straddling them: An empirical examination of outcomes for multicultural employees. *Journal of International Business Studies*, 48(1), 63–89.

Fitzsimmons, S. R., Miska, C., & Stahl, G. K. (2011). What bicultural individuals bring to global organizations. In G. K. Stahl, M. E. Mendenhall, & G. Oddou (Eds.), *Readings and Cases in International Human Resource Management and Organizational Behavior* (5th ed.). New York: Routledge, pp. 155–171.

Gelles, D. (2020). The husband-and-wife team behind the leading vaccine to solve Covid-19. *The New York Times*. Retrieved from https://www.nytimes.com/2020/11/10/business/biontech-covid-vaccine.html.

Gibson, C. B., & Vermeulen, F. (2003). A healthy divide: Subgroups as a stimulus for team learning behavior. *Administrative Science Quarterly*, 48(2), 202–239.

Godart, F. C., Maddux, W. M., Shipilov, A. V., & Galinsky, A. (2015). Fashion with a foreign flair: Professional experiences abroad facilitate the creative innovations of organizations. *Academy of Management Journal*, 58(1), 195–220.

Hajro, A., Caprar, D. V., Zikic, J., & Stahl, G. K. (2021). Global migrants: Understanding the implications for international business and management. *Journal of World Business*, 56(2), 101192.

Hong, H. J., & Doz, Y. (2013). L'Oreal masters multiculturalism. *Harvard Business Review*, 91(6), 114–118.

Hong, H. J., & Minbaeva, D. (2022). Multiculturals as strategic human capital resources in multinational enterprises. *Journal of International Business Studies*, 53(1), 95–125.

Hrenyk, J., Szymanski, M., Kar, A., & Fitzsimmons, S. R. (2016). Understanding multicultural individuals as ethical global leaders. In J. S. Osland, M. Li, & M. E. Mendenhall (Eds.), *Advances in Global Leadership*, Vol. 9, pp. 57–78. Bingley: Emerald.

Jackson, S. E., Joshi, A., & Erhardt, N. L. (2003). Recent research on team and organizational diversity: SWOT Analysis and implications. *Journal of Management*, 29(6), 801–830.

Jang, S. (2017). Cultural brokerage and creative performance in multicultural teams. *Organization Science*, 28(6), 993–1009.

Jordan, D., & Jack, S. (2021). Ex-Nissan boss Carlos Ghosn: How I escaped Japan in a box. *BBC News*. Retrieved from https://www.bbc.com/news/business-57760993

Jung, A. (2009). The premier beauty products seller: Andrea Jung. *Talks at Google*. Retrieved from: https://www.youtube.com/watch?v=D7Rc62PWBRA

Kluth, A. (2020). Here's to the immigrant heroes behind the BioNTech vaccine. *Bloomberg*. November 13, 2020. Retrieved from https://www.bloomberg.com/opinion/articles/2020-11-13/here-s-to-the-immigrant-heroes-behind-the-biontech-pfizer-vaccine?leadSource=uverify%20wall.

Lane, H. W., Maznevski, M. L., Mendenhall, M. E., & McNett, J. (Eds.). (2004). *The Blackwell Handbook of Global Management: A Guide to Managing Complexity*. London: Blackwell.

Larmer, B. (2022). Cold warrior: Why Eileen Gu ditched Team USA to ski for China at the Beijing Olympics: The superpower rivalry will be played out on the slopes. *The Economist*, February 3, 2022 (updated February 16, 2022). Retrieved from https://www.economist.com/1843/2022/02/03/cold-warrior-why-eileen-gu-ditched-team-usa-to-ski-for-china.

Lau, D. C., & Murnighan, J. K. (2005). Interactions within groups and subgroups: The effects of demographic faultlines. *Academy of Management Journal*, 48(4), 645–659.

Lazarova, M., Caligiuri, P., Collings, D. G., & De Cieri, H. (2023). Global work in a rapidly changing world: Implications for MNEs and individuals. *Journal of World Business*, 58(1), 101365.

Lazarova, M. B., & Cerdin, J. L. (2007). Revisiting repatriation concerns: Organizational support versus career and contextual influences. *Journal of International Business Studies*, 38(3), 404–429.

Lee, Y. T., & Gyamfi, N. Y. A. (2023). Multicultural identities at work. In *Oxford Research Encyclopaedia of Business and Management*. doi: https://doi.org/10.1093/acrefore/9780190224851.013.351.

Levie, J. (2007). Immigration, in-migration, ethnicity and entrepreneurship in the United Kingdom. *Small Business Economics*, 28(2), 143–169.

Lisak, A., Erez, M., Sui, Y., & Lee, C. (2016). The positive role of global leaders in enhancing multicultural team innovation. *Journal of International Business Studies*, 47(6), 655–673.

Liu, E. (1998). *The Accidental Asian*. Toronto: Random House.

Liu, L. A., Chua, C. H., & Stahl, G. K. (2010). Quality of communication experience: Definition, measurement, and implications for intercultural negotiations. *Journal of Applied Psychology*, 95(3), 469–487.

Maddux, W. W., Lu, J. G., Affinito, S. J., & Galinsky, A. D. (2021). Multicultural experiences: A systematic review and new theoretical framework. *Academy of Management Annals*, 15(2), 345–376.

McCormick, M. (2020). Netflix appoints Bozoma Saint John as chief marketing officer. *Forbes*. Retrieved from https://www.forbes.com/sites/meghanmccormick/2020/07/01/netflix-appoints-bozoma-saint-john-as-chief-marketing-officer/?sh=43557c4a1a61.

McPherson, M., Smith-Lovin, L., & Cook, J. M. (2001). Birds of a feather: Homophily in social networks. *Annual Review of Sociology*, 27(1), 415–444.

Mendenhall, M., & Stahl, G. (2000). Expatriate training and development: Where do we go from here? *Human Resource Management*, 39(2–3), 251–265.

Minbaeva, D., Fitzsimmons, S., & Brewster, C. (2021). Beyond the double-edged sword of cultural diversity in teams: Progress, critique, and next steps. *Journal of International Business Studies*, 52(1), 45–55.

Miska, C., Economou, V., & Stahl, G. K. (2020). Responsible leadership in a VUCA world. In M. E. Mendenhall, M. Žilinskaitė, G. K. Stahl, R. Clapp-Smith (Eds.) *Responsible Global Leadership*. New York: Routledge, pp. 11–28.

Mosionier, B. C. (1999). *In Search of April Raintree*. Winnipeg: Portage & Main Press.

Najjar, G. (2008, August). *Carlos Ghosn Tells Students to Embrace Diversity*. Retrieved July, 2010, from http://www.aub.edu.lb/news/archive/preview.php?id=74360.

Nooyi, I. (2005). Indra Nooyi's graduation remarks. *Bloomberg*. Retrieved from https://www.bloomberg.com/news/articles/2005-05-19/indra-nooyis-graduation-remarks.

OECD. (2022). *International Migration Outlook 2021*. Paris: OECD. Retrieved from https://data.oecd.org/migration/stocks-of-foreign-born-population-in-oecd-countries.htm.

Pless, N. M., Maak, T., & Stahl, G. K. (2011). Developing responsible global leaders through international service-learning programs: The Ulysses experience. *Academy of Management Learning & Education*, 10(2), 237–260.

Polzer, J. T., Crisp, C. B., Jarvenpaa, S. L., & Kim, J. W. (2006). Extending the faultline model to geographically dispersed teams: How colocated subgroups can impair group functioning. *Academy of Management Journal*, 49(4), 679–692.

Pucik, V., Björkman, I., Evans, P., & Stahl, G. K. (2023). *The Global Challenge: Managing People Across Borders*. Cheltenham: Edward Elgar Publishing.

Ramarajan, L., Dessain, V., & Moloney, E. (2020). Leading change in talent at L'Oréal. *Harvard Business School Case*, 420–106.

Reiche, B. S., Bird, A., Mendenhall, M. E., & Osland, J. S. (2017). Contextualizing leadership: A typology of global leadership roles. *Journal of International Business Studies*, 48(5), 552–572.

Reiche, B. S., Kraimer, M. L., & Harzing, A. W. (2011). Why do international assignees stay? An organizational embeddedness perspective. *Journal of International Business Studies*, 42(4), 521–544.

Reiche, B. S., Lee, Y. T., & Allen, D. G. (2019). Actors, structure, and processes: A review and conceptualization of global work integrating IB and HRM research. *Journal of Management*, 45(2), 359–383.

Reuters. (2020). Factbox: Financial wrongdoing allegations against Carlos Ghosn. *Reuters*, January 8, 2020. Retrieved from https://www.reuters.com/article/us-nissan-ghosn -allegations-factbox-idUSKBN1Z71QI.

Salacuse, J. W. (2005). *Leading Leaders: How to Manage Smart, Talented, Rich and Powerful People*. New York: AMACOM.

Schippers, M. C., Den Hartog, D. N., Koopman, P. L., & Wienk, J. A. (2003). Diversity and team outcomes: The moderating effects of outcome interdependence and group longetivity and the mediating effect of reflexivity. *Journal of Organizational Behavior*, 24(6), 779–802.

Shaffer, M. A., Kraimer, M. L., Chen, Y. P., & Bolino, M. C. (2012). Choices, challenges, and career consequences of global work experiences: A review and future agenda. *Journal of Management*, 38(4), 1282–1327.

Szymanski, M., Fitzsimmons, S. R., & Danis, W. M. (2019). Multicultural managers and competitive advantage: Evidence from elite football teams. *International Business Review*, 28(2), 305–315.

Tadmor, C. T., Galinsky, A. D., & Maddux, W. W. (2012). Getting the most out of living abroad: Biculturalism and integrative complexity as key drivers of creative and professional success. *Journal of Personality & Social Psychology*, 103(3), 520.

Tadmor, C. T., Tetlock, P. E., & Peng, K. (2009). Acculturation strategies and integrative complexity: The cognitive implications of biculturalism. *Journal of Cross-Cultural Psychology*, 40(1), 105–139.

Thomas, D. C., Stahl, G., Ravlin, E. C., Poelmans, S., Pekerti, A., Maznevski, M., et al. (2008). Cultural intelligence: Domain and assessment. *International Journal of Cross Cultural Management*, 8(2), 123–143.

UNESCO. (2009). *Investing in Cultural Diversity and Intercultural Dialogue*. UNESCO (United Nations Educational, Scientific and Cultural Organization).

Vandor, P., & Franke, N. (2016a). See Paris and… found a business? The impact of cross-cultural experience on opportunity recognition capabilities. *Journal of Business Venturing*, 31(4), 388–407.

Vandor, P., & Franke, N. (2016b). Why are immigrants more entrepreneurial? *Harvard Business Review* . Retrieved from: https://hbr.org/2016/10/why-are-immigrants -more-entrepreneurial

Varela, O. E. (2019). Multicultural competence: An empirical comparison of intercultural sensitivity and cultural intelligence. *European Journal of International Management*, 13(2), 177–197.

Vora, D., Martin, L., Fitzsimmons, S. R., Pekerti, A. A., Lakshman, C., & Raheem, S. (2019). Multiculturalism within individuals: A review, critique, and agenda for future research. *Journal of International Business Studies*, 50(4), 499–524.

Windsor, D. (2004). The development of international business norms. *Business Ethics Quarterly*, 14(4), 729–754.

Joanne Barnes

WTC

The Challenge to Create a Culture of
Equity, Inclusion, and Belonging

THE IMPORTANCE OF DIVERSITY IN organizations really started in
the 1960s, but gained more recent attention in the 1990s. The movement
became synonymous with the position of Chief Diversity Officer (CDO)—despite
the fact that having a CDO was more often symbolic than substantive. As organizations gained an awareness that the role and scope of CDOs was limiting and
didn't really respond to the need for all individuals to feel represented, the focus
changed to include equity, inclusion, and belonging. Organizations found the need
to focus on more than diversity of numbers or quotas related to race, ethnicity,
and gender. The emerging question shifted to employees and their feelings of
equitable treatment, inclusive behaviors, and sense of belonging.

WHY INCLUSION IN THE TELECOMMUNICATIONS INDUSTRY
IS MORE IMPORTANT THAN EVER

Telecommunication companies, especially those that work in the wireless communication arena, serve a very diverse clientele. At a time when meeting customer
needs is increasingly important, every level of the organization must understand
the importance of diversity, equity, inclusion, and belonging (DEIB), but also
act upon creating a culture of inclusion and belonging. The job satisfaction rate
for Black, Indigenous, and People of Color (BIPOC) has decreased in wireless
communication industries because they do feel excluded from the mainstream
organizational culture. Leaders in the wireless communications industry recognized that voices were not being heard, BIPOC individuals were not a part of the
leadership teams, and the customer service for BIPOC individuals was declining
due to the lack of knowledge of differences. In WTC, the executive leadership

DOI: 10.4324/9781003247272-13

team found they did not have a good understanding of diversity, equity, inclusion, and belonging and wanted to do something about it.

THE CELLULAR ORGANIZATION

WTC was founded in the early 1990s and is a major telecommunications competitor in the United States. The organization has over 800 locations in more than 30 states and employs more than 2,000 individuals.

The employees of WTC hold positions ranging from sales associates, sales consultants, and information technologists to an executive leadership team. At face value, WTC has a mission that appears to be inclusive, with a focus on positive and sustainable impact for all stakeholders. The values presented by WTC promote care, connection, authenticity, inspiration, and business acumen. However, values must be acted upon. The executive leadership team (ELT) recognized this and realized that DEIB had not been a priority.

The organization's ELT is centrally located and consists of the owner, president, chief financial officer, chief legal officer, and regional team officers. The regional team officers have responsibilities to lead middle-level managers who are either co-located or distal-located in the various regions where WTC has offices.

THE DRIVE TO BE MORE INCLUSIVE

One of the major problems within WTC was that the membership of the ELT did not represent its employees or customer base. The 14-member team was comprised of 86 percent white males and 14 percent white females. There was no BIPOC representation on the team. The leader assigned to change and educate the ELT on inclusive competencies was not a member of the team, had no direct voice on the team, and was always only an invited guest to ELT meetings. In other words, DEIB was an agenda item to the ELT. The company still realized that to retain diverse talent, something needed to be done. Although the plan for DEIB training and development was clouded with obstacles, the director of inclusion (we'll refer to her as Alyssa) was given permission to contact and contract with a consultant to help them get started. The consultant suggested that a good starting point would be to have the ELT members take an assessment to determine how likely they themselves were to be inclusive. Since the ELT members were not aware that there are specific competencies that enable inclusiveness and that they can be measured, the idea of an assessment was met with some hesitancy. Alyssa recognized the importance of benchmarking competencies to be able to measure progress over time, and that if the program to be more inclusive as a company was going to work, it had to start at the top. The ELT needed to understand their personal strengths and weaknesses in order to be inclusive. In addition, the BIPOC employees needed a voice. How could Alyssa be the voice for employees, she wondered, when she did not have a seat at the table?

RESISTANCE

Not only was the ELT hesitant to give any credence to an assessment, but the sentiment from the ELT was, "Yes, we want to be inclusive, and we think we already are, so what can you tell us that we do not already know?" The leadership of WTC wondered if there would be measurable benefit to the organization to undergo training in such things as inclusiveness, unconscious bias, micro-aggressions, micro-inequities, and more that the consultant talked about. The first point of resistance in this line of thinking was cost—not so much the cost of training and development, but the time taken from already busy executives' schedules to learn and incorporate inclusiveness into their leadership paradigm—and for what seemed like an intangible benefit! And even though the ELT finally gave its nod of approval, the practical issue of actually finding time in these exec-utives' schedules was a real problem. As Alyssa tried to coordinate setting up a series of training/development sessions as well as a time to complete the Inclusive Competency Inventory (ICI; see www.kozaigroup.com/inclusion-competencies/), most of the ELT did not want to commit more than one or two hours for the sessions. The proposal was to have the training take place during ELT meetings, but those meetings already had full agendas. Although the ELT had empowered Alyssa to act on behalf of the ELT and hire a consultant, the leadership of WTC once again delayed the progress by wanting to have multiple conversations with the proposed consultant to determine if it was really worth it. Finally, though perhaps not thoroughly, convinced, a schedule was created, and all ELT members agreed to dedicate two-and-a-half hours a month to training and development in the area of inclusiveness, along with completing a one-on-one coaching session with the consultant after receiving their ICI results. However, whether overtly resistant or not, many of the leaders were pre-occupied or had other commit-ments that deterred them from being available and having a real motivation to learn more about the topic and their relationship to it. Scheduling their training and coaching sessions required patience and perseverance.

ACTION

Now it was time to implement the plan. Beginning with the basics, the consultant provided an overview of the assessment they had taken, the Inclusion Competency Inventory (see Appendices A and B). The members of the ELT had completed the assessment but did not fully grasp what was being measured and its importance to changing the culture at WTC. The discussion in the room was challenging. Each ELT member moved into a comparative, competitive mode by sharing who had the highest score in each of the three domains. Most of the conversation centered around the dimension of *Bridging Differences*, which includes *Valuing Different Perspectives (VP)* and *Power Sensitivity (PS)* (see Appendix C). As top executives in the organization, of course, they wanted to appear open to all ideas and people. Yet during part of the subsequent training, when asked to do a simple exercise by leaving the conference room and having a conversation with their employees, it was challenging. It was clear that a divide existed between us (Alyssa and the consultant) and them (the ELT) about what needed to be done and what the ELT members were ready and willing to do.

REASONING

WTC struggled with understanding the difference between inclusion and inclusive values, and whether there was a connection to their personal *and* company values. Inclusion, especially for the ELT, meant having language that appeared to be inclusive, pictures on walls that represented various cultures, racial and ethnic representation in the company, and an individual leading DEIB efforts. The ELT believed their values demonstrated the inclusive nature of the company but failed to recognize that inclusion is more than words and requires a change in behaviors, actions, and often the organizational culture. WTC's values included *promoting care, fostering connection, leading with authenticity, being inspirational,* and *having business acumen.* Since the ELT perceived that their company values naturally led to a culture of inclusion, they believed their collective group ICI score (see Figure 1) would validate, as a collective, that they were creating the culture they aspired to in their organization's documentation. The group report revealed that there were two ELT members who did not even participate in the assessment. (Alyssa was included in the group report, which accounted for a total of 13 participants.) Second, the ELT did not demonstrate a high level of inclusion competencies. However, if sufficiently motivated, this could lead to an opportunity for the ELT to develop a plan to improve their inclusion competencies. There was also an opportunity for leaders to move forward by leveraging the competencies where they were already strong. Both Alyssa and the consultant were hopeful that the collective scores of the ELT would be a catalyst for change; however, that was not the case. The owner of the company did not believe the leadership team had room for development, and most of the members felt they

Groups Averages & Distributions

	Low		Moderate			High	
	1	2	3	4	5	6	7
Knowing Yourself		2	1	6	4		
Openness to Change		1	4	2	4	2	
Adaptability		2	4	2	3	1	1
Knowing Others		1	1	8	1		2
Connecting with Others	1		4	7		1	
Reading Others		1		7	2	1	2
Bridging Differences	3	1	5	3			1
Valuing Different Perspectives		2	5	3		2	1
Power Sensitivity	5	1	3	2	1		1
ICI Total Score		2	5	3	2		1

N=13

Figure 1 Group averages and distributions.

Source: Used with permission, Kozai Group © 2022.

did not have time. As the ELT openly discussed the group scores, there was some defensiveness related to the domain of *Bridging Differences*. As leaders, they felt there was an openness to the different perspectives of organizational members; however, each member was far removed from their employees, and the only channel to hear other opinions was through Alyssa, who did not have a seat at the table. While the group scores surrounding *Knowing Yourself* were mostly in the moderate range, there was pushback on how their own self-awareness could be an influencer for inclusion. After spending considerable time breaking down the group results and how each one would facilitate growth among the leadership team and have a positive impact on the organization, Alyssa, along with the consultant pursued actions to move the group forward.

DEVELOPMENTAL STEPS

After multiple training and development sessions with the ELT, the consultant provided individual coaching sessions with each leader so they could create a personal development plan (PDP). The focus was that change needed to begin with the ELT. If the leadership of an organization are not willing to change themselves and their behaviors, the organizational culture will not and cannot change and become more inclusive. Each ELT member who had completed the assessment met with the consultant for a minimum of one hour to review their PDP and determine whether the plan of action would facilitate personal change. The two members who did not complete the ICI were offered several opportunities to complete it and to have a one-on-one meeting with the consultant. Both members decided not to participate in the one-on-one sessions; however, the entire ELT team did participate in the trainings. Since Alyssa had also taken the ICI, the consultant included her in the PDP process. The fact that Alyssa was not a member of the ELT seriously hindered WTC from truly developing a more inclusive environment, which is why Alyssa developed a PDP specifically focused on getting a seat at the table and being the voice she knew she needed to be to represent WTC's employees (see Appendix D). In other words, Alyssa needed to use her inclusive competencies to be more included. WTC's executive leadership team, in an effort to promote the ideals of diversity, equity, inclusion, and belonging in the organization, created a multi-disciplinary team that represented middle-level managers within the organization, called the Connection Team. Creating the Connection Team provided Alyssa with the avenues needed to be a liaison between the employees and the ELT. One member of the ELT was also added to the team, and the addition of George (name changed) demonstrated to middle-level managers that the leadership was behind the DEIB initiative. The Connection Team met once or twice a month to discuss WTC's diversity and inclusion efforts. Alyssa was appointed the leader for the Connection Team and believed the team members could be a catalyst for change. As an advocate for DEIB, Alyssa noticed that George, a member of the ELT as the executive leader of a region, and a member of her Connection Team, also believed that their culture needed to change, and that meant that individuals in leadership positions needed to change. Alyssa asked George if he would be willing to introduce the ICI to his regional team members. Both Alyssa and George had their respective teams take the ICI assessment and engage in one-on-one coaching with the consultant.

RESULTS

The ELT, George, and Alyssa felt they could go no further. Without the full support of the ELT, the actions from the PDP for some of the ELT, Connection Team, and regional team members had come to an end. The consultant worked with the owner and president of WTC to help them understand that DEIB initiatives would not be effective and the work Alyssa was doing would be hindered if she was not a member of the ELT. Moreover, one of the actions on Alyssa's PDP was to work on being "visible and heard" to facilitate positive change. Alyssa was able to use the steps she had outlined in her PDP to demonstrate the importance of her becoming a member of the ELT. Alyssa now has a seat at the table and her voice is heard. She is a regular part of the ELT meetings, and though it was not an easy process and she was only given 15 minutes to speak, this has evolved. Alyssa was persistent. She was not demanding, but used the ideas of inclusion being a value-added process that would eventually impact the bottom line. She is recognized as an asset to the team and continues to make progress. A few team members continue to follow through with the action items on their plan, but support from the ELT is minimal. The organization still experiences turnover and dissatisfaction as it relates to BIPOC voices being heard and understood. However, Alyssa believes that now that she has a regularly scheduled seat at the table, she can recreate the momentum that has been lost in the day-to-day business of profit and loss.

Alyssa continues to use the actions she outlined in her PDP. However, as she reflected on the progress she had made, Alyssa wondered what she could to do to further embed DEIB into the organization and how she could find more allies on the ELT to help in this endeavor. Alyssa knew that for the organizational culture to change, DEIB had to be a lived value, not just words. How could WTC's employees live out these values in their daily work? And how could the leaders, at all levels of the organization, contribute to an inclusive culture and reflect the inclusive values?

DISCUSSION QUESTIONS

a. Who is the protagonist in the case, and does that matter?
b. What went right, and what went wrong?
c. What would you do differently?
d. Where should WTC go from here?
e. Does the ELT need to restructure its team? Why or why not?
f. Can an organization where leaders and followers are not co-located be successful in implementing DEIB initiatives? Why or why not?
g. How and why will an inclusive culture at WTC assist in its future growth?

APPENDIX A: INCLUSIVE COMPETENCY INVENTORY

We live, work, and play within diverse contexts. The forms of diversity we encounter reflect a wide range of types: race, ethnic group, gender, age, religion, political views, ability, and a host of others. Each type often carries with it a set of values, beliefs, and customs that vary from one individual or group to another. When diverse people come into contact, the outcome can be confusion, conflict, or apathy. Other potential outcomes include heightened interest in diversity, intriguing questions, learning, innovation, and synergies.

Other than significant historical and organizational reasons, what explains which of these potential outcomes will occur? This is determined at the individual level by personal competencies—predispositions, cognitive orientations, attitudes, knowledge, and behaviors—that are linked to superior performance in diverse settings. In other words, the difference between positive versus negative outcomes in response to diversity is: (a) our attentiveness to the differences involved, (b) our understanding of why they exist, and (c) our ability to navigate them effectively.

To assess these competencies, the ICI measures these three key factors, explained in greater detail in the following sections.

1) **Knowing Yourself:** Your awareness of "who you are" and how open you are to changing, as well as your likelihood to adapt to challenging contexts.
2) **Knowing Others:** Your interest in and actions to develop relationships with people who differ from you and your ability to understand them.
3) **Bridging Differences:** Your interest in multiple perspectives and your ability to see and value them and to be sensitive to the inequities present in many contexts.

Used with permission, Kozai Group © 2022

APPENDIX B: ICI AND DEI

The ICI Relative to the DEI Space
Building Individual Competencies

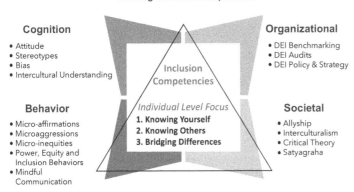

Cognition
- Attitude
- Stereotypes
- Bias
- Intercultural Understanding

Organizational
- DEI Benchmarking
- DEI Audits
- DEI Policy & Strategy

Inclusion Competencies

Individual Level Focus
1. **Knowing Yourself**
2. **Knowing Others**
3. **Bridging Differences**

Behavior
- Micro-affirmations
- Microaggressions
- Micro-inequities
- Power, Equity and Inclusion Behaviors
- Mindful Communication

Societal
- Allyship
- Interculturalism
- Critical Theory
- Satyagraha

Social Action and Social Justice

Used with permission, Kozai Group © 2022

APPENDIX C: BRIDGING DIFFERENCES

Kozai Group © 2022

Bridging Differences comprises two ICI dimensions: valuing different perspectives and Empowering Others. Before we can take thoughtful action to remedy inequity, we need two types of perception: the ability to see and understand power differentials and inequities, and to see situations from others' point of view.

Valuing Different Perspectives (VP)

This dimension measures your openness to diverse perspectives and the effort you devote to appreciating and understanding them. It assesses your ability to look beyond your personal opinions to respect and comprehend the logic of perspectives held by people who are different from you.

Why is VP important to inclusion? Many of us live in settings characterized by diversity, which provides a valuable opportunity to share opinions and learn about our differences—if we take advantage of it. Hearing and respecting others' voices, especially marginalized voices, is essential for inclusion. The ability to understand different perspectives leads to greater understanding, empathy, and compassion for others' behavior and goals, which can set the stage for better situation diagnosis and for collaboration that could lead to more equitable solutions.

Power Sensitivity (PS)

This dimension measures your degree of awareness of power dynamics in both organizational structures and individual relationships. It assesses your awareness of the impact of power and privilege on inclusion and equity.

Why is PS important to inclusion? In every social system, be it a social group, a workplace, or government, there is a power structure. To address inequity in laws, policies and practices, we must recognize where power is located and how it might need to shift.

APPENDIX D: ALYSSA'S PERSONAL DEVELOPMENT PLAN

Personal & Confidential

Create Your Own Personal Development Plan

ELEMENT	YOUR PLAN
Assessment: What is your weakest dimension that, if developed, would have the greatest positive impact, would be the easiest to change, and is the most urgent?	Power sensitivity Adaptability (emotional resilience)
General Plans: List a few broad objectives to help you focus your efforts. Set a deadline by which you will accomplish these plans.	1. Ability to speak up and have presence. 2. Observe behaviors that exclude you at TCC 3. Meet with individuals who are representative of a marginalized group.

Tactics: These are the concrete "how-to's" that help you achieve your general plan. Tactics need to be Specific, Measurable, Achievable, Relevant to the larger objective, and with a clear Time frame for achievement (that is, they should be SMART goals). How will you know if you've been successful?	1. You will be placed on the Executive Leadership Team meeting calendar at least once per month to share concerns related to DEI at TCC.
	2. Journal any occurrences where you feel excluded and document your feelings.
	  a. Include how you reacted to others.
	  b. Include how others reacted to you (verbal/non-verbal)
	3. After 24–48 hours, you will journal what you believe should have been your action/reaction based on what was observed.
	4. Listening – listen to understand what behaviours or feelings are being displayed by members of the ELT
	  a. Reflect on what you have learned.

Reporting Results: Results are better when we tell others about our plans. Without this accountability, it is too easy to fail to follow through. Find someone who will hold you accountable in a positive way, and decide when and how you will report to them.	Select your accountability partner. Meet with him/her at least every two weeks. Reflect on the process (lessons learned).

Used with permission, Kozai Group © 2022

Álvaro San Martín

HIRING A CHEF – DECISION MAKING SIMULATION*

YOU AND SEVERAL OTHER PARTNERS are looking for a lucrative investment where the return on your money is attractive. After a lot of research, you have narrowed the investment choice down to the restaurant industry. The niche you are going to focus on is the 3-star restaurant category. From your experience and research, you know that the most critical component of a successful restaurant at this level ultimately is hiring the right chef.

Broadly speaking, the success of a luxury restaurant depends on its value proposition in four key dimensions: the choice and quality of the food and drink, the type of service the customers experience, and the overall atmosphere of the restaurant. The role of the executive chef is the most critical in making the choices that create this unique dining experience. Some of the specific responsibilities of the executive chef include the menu design, recipe development, procurement and cost control, kitchen team training, and coordination with the dining room. As the saying goes, "Behind a great restaurant, there is a great chef." Therefore, it is crucial for the investment partners to choose the right executive chef for this luxury restaurant.

In casting the net as wide as possible for the initial phase of recruitment, chefs from three continents were considered. After further consideration, including interviews of the owners and head chefs where the chefs previously worked, discussions with the chefs' present associates and actual in-dining experiences to see first-hand the food and drink quality and choice, the service and overall atmosphere, the search was narrowed to three outstanding candidates, referred to here as Chef A, Chef B, and Chef C. All have suitable résumés and appear equally qualified, though different in some ways. Your partners may have also done their own research on the candidates.

* Originally published by IESE Publishing.

DOI: 10.4324/9781003247272-14

TO THE STUDENT

You will be formed into groups. In preparation for making a collective decision on the three candidates, information about each candidate will be provided to all of you. Individually, you will then be asked to rate each chef based on several relevant criteria. You will be asked to maintain the confidentiality of your personal decision. Once all of you have made your personal decisions, you will discuss your ratings as a group and come to a team decision.

B. Sebastian Reiche and Yih-Teen Lee

UWA ODE

Embracing Life and Career across Cultures*

THE INSTRUMENT HAD BEEN THERE all this time, but I never quite understood how to play it. During my travels I learned all that I needed to bring MY music alive.

Uwa Ode

Uwa Ode was standing on the terrace of a Barcelona-based business school moments after graduating from a 17-month-long Global Executive MBA program. It was a quiet moment before rejoining the family and fellow graduates for the graduation dinner, following the rush of accomplishment. A number of life events had taken Uwa from a childhood in Nigeria, then to England, Northern Ireland, Texas, and finally, Louisiana.

With the MBA program ending, a decision had to be made: continue a career in an oilfield services company headquartered in the United States or make a professional pivot?

Uwa's current company would most likely require a relocation every two to three years from one country to the next, or alternatively, relocations within the same country. However, another option would be to make a career change and move to a place that would feel like home, and where there would be an opportunity to finally start building a more permanent life. Yet another path would be to start a company in Africa to contribute to the business landscape there and move back to the continent after being away for 17 years. Uwa felt a responsibility to Nigeria and strived to preserve its cultural heritage, after learning from many other cultures and countries. This was clearly more than just a sentimental wish, seeing that Africa offered a myriad of business opportunities and a lot of room for economic development. It

* Originally published by IESE Publishing.

DOI: 10.4324/9781003247272-15

would be exciting to return home and contribute to the country's development. At the same time, cultural dilemmas might arise, since Uwa was not a typical Nigerian.

A number of personal and professional decisions were looming large on the horizon. The decision was much more complex than simply weighing up the financial benefits or the opportunities to travel and see the world. This decision would be pivotal for life and the future.

A MULTI-CULTURAL CHILDHOOD

Uwa's parents were both from Edo State in Nigeria (see Exhibit 1 for a geo-political map of Nigeria). They both spoke English as their first language, but because they were from the same ethnic culture, they also shared a local language, which they spoke with each other. However, they left Edo State when they were teenagers and moved to Lagos State, also in Nigeria. As for their university educations, Uwa's father studied in England and Uwa's mother in France. After several years, they returned to Nigeria, where the father started his career with a multinational company that relocated him every three years. That gave the family the opportunity to work and live in the Netherlands twice, in England, in the United States, in Singapore and in several different states in Nigeria. In the parents' view, some of those moves began to cause too much instability for their children, so the father began to relocate to some of the countries by himself while the rest of the family remained in Nigeria and visited him during vacations.

Uwa's father began his career in Rivers State, which had a different culture from their culture of origin. The children often wondered why, as a family, they did not eat the same food or speak the same Nigerian language as their local friends who were from Rivers State. The Ode family had one culture at home, and spoke the parents' language, but the children played, went to school and interacted with classmates in a different cultural context. Very early on, Uwa started to feel displaced, not only because the family had relocated from one state to another, but also because the parents themselves felt and acted displaced. This had a lasting impact on how cultural heritage was viewed. Today, the three siblings defined themselves differently from their parents, in spite of understanding their parents' culture and language. While they would say they were from Port Harcourt city (Rivers State), the parents would cite Benin City as their cultural origin. Aside from the relocations themselves, Uwa's father's work context also affected the way the family lived. As Uwa recalled:

> During the first 16 years of my life in Nigeria, in between the relocations, we lived in a purpose-built international, multi-racial, inter-racial and cross-cultural environment. All my friends who lived in the camp with me were also displaced from their parents' cultures. We had friends who were non-Nigerians growing up and going to school with us. Going to school, we "camp kids" were always "odd" compared to the other kids who did not live in our 20-square-mile camp. The camp was artificially designed to remind everyone from different nationalities of their homes: there were

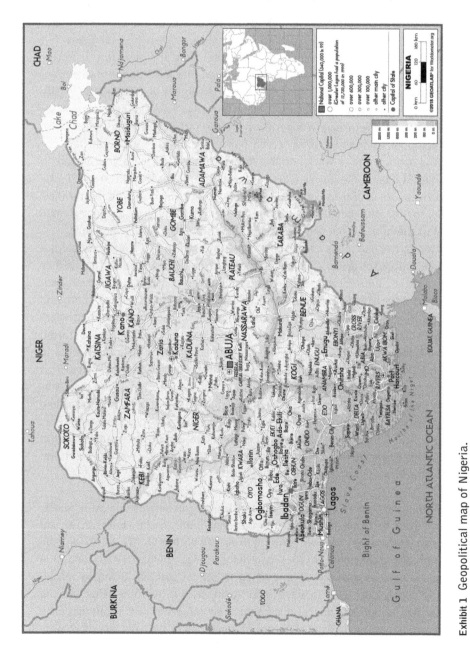

Exhibit 1 Geopolitical map of Nigeria.

Source: Nations Online Project (www.nationsonline.org).

swimming pools, tennis clubs, golf courses, a grocery store, recreational centers, a salon – you get the idea. Once you drove into the camp, it was really like we did not live in Nigeria. So even though we were Nigerian, we were living in our own bubble, separated from our country.

After high school, a month after turning 16 years old, Uwa relocated to London to join an older sister, who had left two years earlier, and start A-levels. Uwa would go on to finish tertiary education in London as well. The process of adjusting to a new life in London began on the first day, as Uwa recalled:

> I realized that I didn't understand the jokes or subtle witty comments, and I sounded very different and dressed differently from the people around me. Back in Nigeria, I had graduated as head student of my school. I was very popular, I had the best grades at my high school, my mum was a known entrepreneur in town ... Everyone knew me: the other kids, the teachers, the parents. And now, for the first time in my life the people around me wanted me to explain who I was. They didn't know my personality, my jokes, who my family was, how many siblings I had. In 16 years, I had never been unknown, undefined – and there I was. Worst of all, everyone would ask what country I was from, and this immediately separated me in teenage social circles. The Nigerian teenagers were the funniest – the ones who were either born in London or who had moved there many years before me. They would identify with me, but their first question was always: "When did you move to London?" The longer you had been in London, the more accepted you were because you sounded like them, understood the culture and could navigate your way around. So I would lie awake wishing for time to go by so I could say that I had been in London for three years, instead of three months.

The adjustment process involved many different steps that all happened at the same time. In the first year in London, Uwa never referred to the time spent in London in terms of months. Instead, this period was always characterized as "almost a year." This offered a pass to be accepted and hang out with potential friends. Changes in clothes and accent were also required during this time:

> The first weekend in London I went shopping with my mum and my older sister and her Nigerian boyfriend, who had been going to school in London for the previous two years. That weekend I allowed the two to choose all the clothes my mum bought for me – after all, I was about to start the same school they were going to and I didn't want to look different. I also realized my sister's accent had changed. That weekend I spent hours going through teenage magazines looking at how teenagers my age dressed and I watched television for countless hours trying to fine-tune my ears. I would practice the words and repeat my new-found accent over and over again. After a while, when I said that I was from Nigeria people would remark: "Wow, I never would have guessed except for your name!"

ENTERING THE PROFESSIONAL WORLD

After earning a degree in engineering, Uwa took a job at a local engineering company in London, choosing to work in the oil industry like the father. However, the fear that London would become permanent turf soon began to take hold:

> I worried that I would stop absorbing other cultures and experiences that the world has to offer. Besides, there were still days when London did not feel like "home" and I was not going to return to Nigeria – I was too different now. In a way, I was searching for what I had been used to growing up: the promise of the move.

After eight years in London, an international company offered a great opportunity. Uwa was relocated to Belfast, Northern Ireland for three years. This time in Belfast coincided with strong feelings of being uprooted and led to a pivotal decision: Uwa purchased a house in order to be able to own and go back home to something. Up to now, nothing had ever felt permanent. However, it turned out that a long-term home in Belfast was not possible, so a move to the United States with the same company came next. With this move came another dance of adaptation and assimilation.

After almost five years in Texas and one year in Louisiana, Louisiana was supposed to be the last non-permanent move. Yet no friends lived nearby. Unmarried and without children, Uwa hadn't yet put down any roots. This was the opposite of the life Uwa had aspired to have. While studying in London and with parents living in Amsterdam, Uwa remembered begging them to go home. The parents replied: "But where do you want to go back to? We are in Amsterdam now and there is nobody in Nigeria." After relocating to Louisiana, Uwa was tired of exploring so many new places that were ultimately only temporary. Weary of building roots, making friends and establishing traditions in a place, only to leave again, Uwa had accepted life would revolve around work, an apartment, and the gym.

Up to now, Uwa's moves had been linked to promotions as opposed to places where a life could be built. In those places, most people were expatriates like Uwa, all coming and going with multiple cultural experiences. Now, it was time to find out where long-term friendships could be made and a more permanent life, a home and a family could be created. In fact, an important reason for embarking on the Global Executive MBA was that the program would mean coming back to Europe. It would offer sufficient new experiences and time to explore the world, in addition to providing academic fluidity. Uwa hoped to identify where to live and find the opportunity to relocate to a place that could be called home.

Uwa realized how important this was after being offered a job back in London, an opportunity that was rejected straight away. Uwa's boss couldn't understand the refusal, because it would mean returning to a very familiar city. As tempting as it was to return to Europe, London just didn't seem like the right place. With so many cultural experiences that stretched far beyond London, it was difficult to walk away from the last six years in the United States. What's more, Uwa's British accent had given way to American English that stood out in the United Kingdom and from family members who had lived there much longer. More time was needed before choosing a final home.

THE MULTICULTURAL DIVIDEND

In contemplating future personal and professional steps, Uwa reflected on the advantages of living a multicultural life. Each culture had been like a beautifully different and unique song, and the process of living through each was the art of mastering a new dance. These experiences were treasures in a truly enriching life:

> I feel like I have many personas living inside me. It is almost an exciting feeling. I know that I can change accents, the tone of my conversation, my way of thinking, my body language, my emotional intelligence, the interpretation of my surroundings, my point of view and even my jokes if I come across anyone who shares a cultural commonality with any of the places I have lived in. It means I am never afraid of change and I am never without friends. These are some of the many beautiful aspects of moving and experiencing the world the way I have.

These experiences were also beneficial from a career perspective, as they had been instrumental in leading multicultural teams successfully and bringing out the best in others. In fact, Uwa had often been selected for job promotions because of this very experience and skill. By and large, Uwa had a good understanding of how to make decisions across many cultures to create a win–win result for everyone and was often involved in client negotiations. Most of the company's clients were international, so Uwa would be selected to be part of the contract negotiations as a way of developing relationships and understanding with clients. As yet another sign that the company valued these skills, Uwa had worked with the executive board on several occasions to redefine company policy, and a few times had also been selected as part of a team of 20 – out of a workforce of over 150,000 – to be the voice of the employees and help the company define effective policies across its global organization.

Further, when engaging with people who did not share the experiences of several cultures, Uwa had learned to quickly bring a new point of view into the discussion, and was always able to understand several points of view at a time. Uwa also felt privileged to have few prejudices and a high sense of tolerance and empathy. Even when not understanding another person or a cultural practice, Uwa would ask for clarification rather than making a quick judgment, because it constituted a key learning moment. Uwa also tried to instill this cultural understanding in the team:

> In the United States, when an employee is expecting a baby it is common for coworkers to plan a party called a "baby shower." I had one non-US

employee, though, who did not tell anyone that his wife was pregnant. One day he happily announced that he had just become a father. His coworkers took this badly; they felt deceived and couldn't understand how they could have worked with him for nine months without him mentioning it once. Some went as far as questioning whether they could still trust him if he would keep such a secret. When I heard about this issue, I assembled my team to explain that in some cultures there are superstitions about celebrating, naming a baby or buying gifts before the baby's safe arrival. They were all shocked because they had not heard of this before. But with the help of Google, everyone came to understand. I then called the employee and asked him to explain his motivations to his teammates. Needless to say, a party was planned after the baby arrived.

THE MULTICULTURAL BAGGAGE

Yet there was a flipside to a multicultural life. Because Uwa had had to say goodbye several times, there was a permanent fear of loss – whether it was being separated from friends and loved ones or the initial rejection people may face in a new society while they are still different from the people around them. On the positive side, this meant that Uwa was very cautious about never causing other people any kind of pain or feelings of rejection. Afraid to lose another set of friends and move again, Uwa's biggest question was about belonging:

> Where is home? Where am I from? Which culture should I identify with? Is home where I work – even though it is not permanent? Or is home where my parents' house is? Because with all this moving I have not put down any roots anywhere, yet. What is the correct response to the first time someone asks: "Where are you from?" Should I reply that I am Nigerian? But when I say so, the immediate connotations are not true and the last 17 years of my life go missing unless I respond with further detail. Should I say I am English because of my second citizenship? But you can tell that I obviously have African heritage! Saying I am English also leaves out the first 16 years of my life. Worse yet, I have adopted an American-sounding accent and have lost my British accent. Is that even a plausible response? After all, I have a UK passport to back up my claim, which isn't the case if I say that I am American just because I might sound it slightly, because I don't have US citizenship or a green card. In fact, I'm in the United States on a visa, with the looming reality that it will expire and I will have to move again.

There was also the question of national identity and loyalty. Was it right to pick a political party in the United States or join a cause? What about voting in the English elections and contributing to charities that might benefit from Uwa's time and skills? Or was it better to focus on national loyalty to Nigeria and the African continent, which was in dire need of foreign-trained Africans? In addition, so many experiences abroad had changed Uwa's personality. It was laughable when people remarked Uwa was quiet. How could someone think this about such a sociable and approachable person? Even the family didn't seem to recognize all of Uwa's personality anymore. While living in the United States, one sister once mentioned:

> Each time I see you it is as if another part of your personality has gone. Where is the loud laughter [people thought it was too gregarious at that time, so Uwa decided to suppress it], where are the jokes [no one seemed to understand the English jokes, so Uwa stopped telling them], and where is the fire and the passion in your soul [people seemed to think it was aggressive, so Uwa suppressed that too]?

It took a few days for the sisters to adjust. As one of them exclaimed: "It's like you are able to be multiple people depending on the situation." What had also changed was Uwa's relationship with the base culture. Experiences over the course of many moves showed that the skills Uwa's parents had taught did not always apply in every new cultural situation. This meant a whole new set of skills had to be learned in order to excel. In fact, along the way several better modes of conduct had been picked up. While Uwa's parents were hesitant to accept this deviation from some of their own cultural traditions, they also acknowledged the positive perspectives that this brought to the family's habits and activities.

THE DECISION

All this made the decision to move exceedingly difficult. Maybe a move to a new country, coupled with the experiences from the Global Executive MBA, would provide a fresh inspiration even if the choice was made to stay with the current employer. After all, excitement always comes with moving to a new place. Maybe a nomadic life, the thrill of discovering new cultures and the challenge of reinventing oneself in new cultures remained enticing. While feeling rootless, there was still a fair share of restlessness, a fixation on moving and avoiding anything permanent that might take away the freedom of packing the bags and starting all over again. On the other hand, maybe the next move would turn out to be the ideal place. Uwa also still felt strangely attached to Africa, and Nigeria in particular. Uwa's parents had decided to retire in Nigeria, so there was some family there now. Yet one sister who had also moved back to Nigeria earlier was unhappy because she felt people did not really understand her and she did not share the views of Nigerian society. And there were not too many friends back in Nigeria.

One thing was clear. The Global Executive MBA had been undertaken in order to make a drastic career change, one that could help identify someplace to call home. Uwa had also wanted to be around likeminded people who had colorful cultural backgrounds themselves and who were citizens of the world: people who would understand what it was like to be a citizen of many countries and to possess many different cultural experiences. Given the transience of past relationships, Uwa wanted lifelong friends who could be part of a permanent future.

PART III

Global Staffing and Management of Global Mobility

DOI: 10.4324/9781003247272-16

David G. Collings, Anthony McDonnell, and Amy McCarter

TYPES OF INTERNATIONAL ASSIGNEES[*]

INTRODUCTION

INTERNATIONAL ASSIGNMENTS HAVE LONG REPRESENTED a critical mechanism by which organisations that operate on a global scale can effectively manage and develop their global operations. Such assignments serve multiple purposes, including management development, co-ordination and control, information exchange, and succession planning (Black et al., 1999; Cheong et al., 2019; Edstrom & Galbraith, 1977; Harzing, 2001). For employees, it is claimed that international assignments are "the single most influential force for the development of managers" (Stroh et al., 2004) and can contribution significantly to the development of one's career in the global organization. Historically, much of the research surrounding international assignments has centred around "traditional" international assignments (Andersen, 2021) – purpose-driven transfers to a foreign location with a duration of 12–36 months (Dowling et al., 2008) or up to 60 months. This is unsurprising as such assignments traditionally represented the most dominant form of global staffing arrangement (Collings et al., 2007), and recent indications suggest that assignments of this duration remain prevalent among organisations (Collings & Isichi, 2018; Finaccord, 2018; McDonnell et al., 2011).

However, the landscape of global mobility has altered significantly over the past decades, and the topography of global staffing is far more heterogeneous in the contemporary multinational enterprise (MNE) than has been the case in the past (Jooss et al., 2021). Additionally, the COVID-19 pandemic represented one of the most significant challenges ever to the movement of people globally (Caligiuri et al., 2020; Collings & Sheeran, 2020). This forced many MNEs to recall international assignees and halt mobility programmes, at least temporarily

[*] This reading is an updated version of an earlier chapter published in D.G. Collings, G.T. Wood & P.M. Caligiuri (2015). *The Routledge Companion to International Human Resource Management.* London: Routledge.

DOI: 10.4324/9781003247272-17

(Lazarova et al., 2023). The pandemic also shifted many assumptions around the nature of global work which may have lasting impacts on how MNEs deploy international assignees (Jooss et al., 2022a, 2022b). This has important implications for the study and practice of international human resource management (IHRM). First, it creates a question as to the utility of academic theories and models based on samples of traditional longer-term assignments. Do the findings and recommendations hold true in different modes of international staffing? Second, for IHRM practitioners, it demands a wider range of policies and practices to reflect the differing requirements of different staffing types (Jooss et al., 2021, 2022b). Also, it is important to consider the extent to which these differing global staffing options meet the strategic objectives of the sending organisation and the individual employees. Finally, how does our understanding around the use and effectiveness of international mobility evolve in the context of our understanding of the post-pandemic world of work and assumptions around where and how work is done and by whom (Jooss et al., 2022b; Lazarova et al., 2023)?

This reading begins by considering the role of international assignees in the MNE. The challenges to traditional models of global mobility which relied on longer-term assignments are then outlined. Emerging alternatives to global mobility are then introduced, followed by a consideration of the HR challenges, and issues emerging from a portfolio approach to global mobility. We conclude with some directions for further study.

EXPATRIATE DEPLOYMENT AND THE MNE

Organizations have physically relocated managers to foreign locations where business operations are based since approximately 1900 BC. Indeed, even at this stage, locals were viewed as inferior and restricted to lower-level jobs while parent country nationals (PCNs – individuals from the headquarters country) were afforded superior conditions, similar to modern-day expatriates (Moore & Lewis, 1999: 66–67).

Edstrom and Galbraith (1977) were amongst the first to theorise on the differing objectives of International assignments. Broadly following their conceptualisation, literature on international management and IHRM has consistently focused on three core purposes for using international assignments. First, in position filling: where particular knowledge, skills, and abilities are not available in the host country, organisations may fill the existing gap with expatriates sourced from other geographic areas. Second, they serve as vehicles for the training and development of current and future international managers. Finally, international assignments may act as a means of organisational development, through knowledge transfer and information sharing among subsidiaries as well as the co-ordination and control of subsidiary units. Others such as Salt and Millar (2006) identify the key drivers of international working as building new international markets, providing temporary and short-term access to talent to execute overseas projects, and to perform boundary spanning roles and facilitate the exchange of knowledge within the firm.

Pucik (1992) further elaborated on the definition of international assignments, categorising them by *demand*-driven or *learning*-driven purposes. Those which are demand-driven are identified as serving skill requirements to solve specific problems which arise in the host location. In contrast, learning-driven assignments are characterised as providing a means of developing managerial talent at the individual level as well as for organisational learning. While evidently organisations may use international assignments for an array of motives, it should be noted that these are not mutually exclusive, and indeed international assignments may serve multiple functions at any one time. Nonetheless, these broad objectives provide a basis for understanding the objectives of global mobility.

The objectives of global mobility have important implications in judging the success or otherwise of international assignments. For example, assignments premised on management development have been shown to result in personal change and role innovation, as acclimatizing to the new environment results in the assignee adapting their frame of reference. Indeed, successfully completing an international assignment has long been a springboard for career progression for high-potential managers. Given recent calls for managers to develop higher levels of cross-cultural competence, such as being more resilient and tolerant of greater levels of ambiguity, this is an important objective of global mobility (Hitt et al., 2021). However, these assumptions have been challenged during the COVID-19 pandemic, when MNEs were forced to develop new ways of achieving such personal change in the absence of opportunities for international relocation (Lazarova et al., 2023). Positively, research supports the idea that even short-term international experiences can lead to the development of cross-cultural competencies such as a tolerance for ambiguity, and humility (Caligiuri & Tarique, 2016).

Alternatively, in control-driven assignments, the emphasis is on locals absorbing the new demands of the expatriate manager, and success is considered as locals changing their frames of reference (Shay & Baack, 2004). The relationship between differing objectives of global mobility and the nature of HR support required by assignees also emerges as an important consideration (see Collings, 2014).

However, the relationship between international assignments and MNEs has been somewhat tortuous, with some suggesting that there remains a significant underestimation of the complexities which surround them (Dowling et al., 2017). Indeed, there are a number of emerging challenges which constrain the potential value that organisations reap from expatriate deployment. While, on one hand, they have served well for achieving organisational objectives, on the other hand, they are fraught with challenges which affect many of the stakeholders involved in the international assignment. This has prompted some debate surrounding the viability of international assignments for organisations. We will now briefly consider some of these challenges before moving on to consider the various alternatives to the traditional international assignment which are commonplace in the contemporary MNE.

CHALLENGES TO LONG-TERM ASSIGNMENTS

The first key challenge relating to the traditional international assignment emerges in terms of recruitment and selection. Organisations face an increasingly difficult task in attracting employees willing to take on international assignments. A multiplicity of reasons cited for such difficulties include the rise of dual-career couples, increase in difficult assignment locations, family influence, less generous expatriate compensation packages, and career concerns (e.g., Collings et al., 2007; Shortland, 2016; Tang et al., 2022).

With the widening participation of women in the labour market during the last half-century, relationships increasingly involve dual careers. Individuals engaged in dual-career relationships may be less willing to accept international assignments, and therefore exclude themselves from the selection phase because of the impact the international phase may have on their partner and their career or the disruption it may cause to personal and family situations (Collings et al., 2007; Doherty et al., 2011; Forster, 2000; Shortland, 2016). Women tend to be less represented in international assignments, and research indicates that the organisational rationale behind the use of expatriate assignments differs to that of female expats. Specifically, women appear more likely to decide on taking on an assignment based on how it can contribute to family life, their career and financial potential (Shortland, 2016). Additionally, political and cultural constraints of host countries have been argued to deter employees from accepting international assignments. This issue became particularly evident during the Trump government's term in the US and in the ongoing Brexit process in the UK. In both of these countries, the governments created significant barriers to the entry and employment of even skilled employees. This was evidenced in the reduction in H1B visas in the US, for example. The challenges created have resulted in some MNEs establishing units in more favourable locations to facilitate talent flows (Horak et al., 2019). Also, host countries involved in war, civil unrest, and political instability may be conceived as dangerous to relocate to (Ipek & Paulus, 2021). Increasingly, international assignees are likely to factor criteria such as the health care system into their decision making around potential locations, an issue which was highlighted as countries responded to the COVID-19 pandemic (Lazarova et al., 2023). Locations which are culturally distant from the home country and may prove challenging for assignees may also be more unattractive when compared to locations which are culturally and perhaps geographically close to the home country.

An additional challenge emerges when those considering undertaking international assignments reflect on the experiences of previous expatriates through direct communication or through observation. This may influence the decision to accept or decline an international assignment (Tung, 1988). Witnessing the challenges which other expatriates faced on repatriation may result in potential international assignees concluding that an international assignment will hinder rather than benefit their own career should they accept (Gregersen, 1992; Lazarova & Cerdin, 2007). Relatedly, the shift to remote and virtual working during the pandemic has undoubtably caused many employees to reflect on career and other priorities ,and in some commentators' words, has led to a "great resignation". While globally the evidence on the scale of this great resignation is mixed, there is little doubt that employees are indeed reflecting on their career priorities (Akkermans et al., 2021; Lazarova et al., 2023), and this may result in a decreased willingness to locate personally and with their families. If this becomes a trend, it may significantly impact the supply of international assignees.

Further challenges for organisations relate to costs, and expatriate "failure". While the true cost of an international assignment is difficult to measure, typically traditional international assignments incur huge financial as well as other costs. Traditional estimates indicate that the average cost of maintaining expatriates abroad was between three and five times the cost of employing them at their home location (Forster, 2000). Indeed, there has been a consistent drive to reduce the costs of global mobility over the past decades. Balance sheet compensation packages are regularly being replaced with local-plus packages or tiered compensation packages which reward based on the strategic function of the individual assignment (see Tornikoski et al., 2014).

Expatriate failure has been a significant and indeed controversial issue within the literature. Expatriate failure is commonly defined as a premature return from an international assignment. Although high expatriate failure rates of 20–30% have been frequently highlighted in the literature (Black et al., 1999; Tung, 1981, 1982), such high rates have been challenged by others suggesting that the indicated failure rates are exaggerated and are not supported by empirical investigation (Harzing, 1995, 2002). However, there have been calls to conceptualise the issue of expatriate failure more broadly (Scullion & Collings, 2006). Such an approach recognises the potential costs it can lead to – both directly in terms of salaries, relocation expenses, legal issues, etc., and indirectly through the possibility of market share loss and strained relationships (Collings et al., 2007).

More broadly, the issue of the wellbeing of international assignees has become an increasing consideration in recent years. While such wellbeing concerns surfaced in earlier discussions (Collings et al., 2007), it is only in recent times that this has gained any significant traction in academic research. There is little doubt that the COVID-19 pandemic was one key driver of this increasing focus (Collings & Sheeran, 2020). Indeed, the differing public health measures introduced by governments across the globe, placed significant pressure on international HR professionals in terms of implementing organizational health and safety measures and ensuring their approaches to global mobility are designed to deliver on their duty of care to keep their employees healthy and safe (Lazarova et al., 2023). However, there is also broader recognition of the unique demands and pressures that international assignees can be exposed to and the risks that make them more vulnerable to hazards in comparison to colleagues who are located in a set workplace (De Cieri & Lazarova, 2021). Indeed, De Cieri and Lazarova (2021) provide an excellent review of how international HR practitioners can learn from parallel fields in understanding how to manage the health and safety of international cohorts.

Finally, issues around retention of expatriate employees after repatriation have emerged as a challenge to the traditional assignment. Arguably, repatriation presents the most problematic phase of the international assignment cycle, and was identified as the biggest single problem by UK companies over 20 years ago (Forster, 2000). Although the expectation may be that repatriation should be relatively straightforward as the expatriate is "coming home" (Stroh et al., 2000), research suggests this phase is often the most problematic for employees and the sending organisation. Despite acknowledgement of the fact that retention is a serious problem, there is little evidence to suggest that organisations are developing effective re-entry programmes for expatriates returning from international experience. Previous reports suggest that often 10–25% of repatriated employees leave their organisation within the first year of return (Black et al., 1999; Bonache et al., 2001; Collings, 2014). This is a critical concern for the organisation, particularly when the primary purpose of the assignment is learning-driven, where it is crucial that organisations proactively plan to reintegrate employees into their organisation on return in order to profit from the investment made (Reiche & Harzing, 2022). Causes for high rates of turnover have been connected with frustration felt by the employee. For the returning expatriate, coming home is often a difficult transition due to the development of the organisation since their departure. However, perhaps it is concerns around career development where repatriated employees feel most of their frustration. Although the academic literature and practitioner reports emphasise the benefits of international assignments for one's career in terms of advancement, empirical evidence to support these claims, at least within the sending organisation, is rather scant (Welch, 2003).

Furthermore, many empirical accounts report that those who undertook international assignments often experienced negative career implications in terms of missed opportunities while they were abroad or broken promises of promotion when they returned from their assignments, and difficulties in finding a suitable position upon return (Stahl & Chua, 2006). In reality, many employees find themselves in "holding patterns" upon their return, as organisations who fail to effectively plan for their return struggle to find suitable positions which merit the newly acquired competencies by the employee (Feldman & Thomas, 1992; Bonache et al., 2001). Furthermore, concerns are raised by repatriates over the underutilisation of their newly acquired skills. Many perceive their positions upon re-entry as lacking in authority (Lazarova & Cerdin, 2007). Former expatriates perceive that organisations do not value the knowledge and experience they have acquired while on assignment (Selmer, 1995). Consequently, employees are overcome with feelings of underemployment and disillusion, and leave the organisation through frustration with the treatment they have received.

However, Kraimer et al. (2009) found that those who undertook developmental assignments were more likely to progress within the organisation upon return than those who accepted assignments which related to problem solving etc. Notwithstanding this, developmental-driven international assignees are more likely to leave their organisation upon return (Dickmann & Doherty, 2010). While international assignments evidently pose complex problems for organisations, they also present a complex challenge for employees. International assignments provide excellent opportunities for skill and knowledge development, general management skill acquisition, as well as unique intercultural awareness and global leadership development (Black et al., 1999; Collings & Mellahi, 2018; Mendenhall, 2001). However, from a more negative perspective, international assignments are often reported to have detrimental career effects. Despite the concerns over the particularly negative implications of international assignments for expatiates and repatriates, some researchers have started to consider why employees continue to accept such postings (Lazarova & Cerdin, 2007; Stahl et al., 2002). However, the question remains open as to understanding how individuals weigh up the posited negative implications of international assignments with decisions to undertake international relocations.

CHANGING FORMS OF GLOBAL MOBILITY

The challenges identified above mean that both organisations and individuals alike are re-evaluating their attitudes towards global mobility, and indeed the international staffing options available to meet organisational operational objectives and individual career objectives (Jooss et al., 2021). Briscoe and Schuler (2004: 223) concluded almost two decades ago that the definition of the international employee within the organisation has expanded, and that the "tradition of referring to all international employees as expatriates ... falls short of the need for international HR practitioners to understand the options available ... and fit them to evolving international business strategies". Although there is a growing literature which focuses on the experiences of self-initiated expatriates, or those employees who relocate to another country without organisational support and gain employment in the host country (see Doherty, 2013; Kubovcikova & van Bakel, 2022; Singh et al., 2021; Vaiman & Haslberger, 2013), for this reading, we will focus on corporate expatriates – "employees who are temporarily relocated by their organization to another country ... to complete a specific task or accomplish an organizational goal" (Shaffer et al., 2012: 1287).[1]

A key point of differentiation between the traditional international assignment and emerging alternatives is temporal. While international assignments typically involved sojourns abroad of between one and five years, there is far more variety in modern forms of international mobility. Pucik et al. (2023) argue that the traditional long-term orientation of international assignments derived from rather ethnocentric objectives of the traditional assignment. Such assignees predominantly acted as corporate agents in establishing control mechanisms in newly established subsidiaries or by transferring knowledge. Additionally, developmental objectives may have been conceived in more traditional terms as building cross-national organisational coordination capabilities (see also Collings &

Scullion, 2012). However, more recently, problem-solving objectives which are defined by their singular purpose mean that such long-term sojourns are less necessary. Additionally, it is increasingly recognised that shorter periods abroad can have beneficial effects on individuals' careers. For example, many international graduate programmes now incorporate one or two short international assignments. Such assignments are considered attractive to younger employees entering the workforce, who consider global experience as a key desire in their early careers.

The first alternative form of global mobility which we will consider is the *international business traveller* (IBT). The IBT or frequent flyer is defined as "one for whom business travel is an essential component of their work" (Welch & Worm, 2006: 284). For such employees, business travel can account for 25–75% of their working time (Jooss et al., 2022a). Employees who take up these international assignments travel and communicate regularly between the host location and home office, but they will not relocate as their roots remain in their home country. While not a new phenomenon, the IBT is increasingly being considered as an alternative to international relocation, and hence merits discussion. IBTs provide the advantage of face-to-face interaction in conducting business transactions without the requirement of physical relocation. The IBT has also been identified as key in developing cross-unit social ties and sustaining social networks in MNEs. Bozkurt and Mohr (2011: 150) argue, based on their empirical study, that business travel "offer[s] continuity to social ties established via all the different forms of social mobility, but among all the different forms it emerged as the one that allowed the greatest discretion".

By definition, international business travel generally involves relative short stays in specific locations, the durations of which are dictated by the objective of the visit. IBTs tend to be utilised for specialised tasks which occur rather irregularly, such as budgeting or production scheduling. Tracking the utilisation of the IBT as an alternative to conventional assignments, survey reports have presented the increasingly active position IBTs hold for MNEs. This trend appears to be consistent with recent survey reports suggesting that international business travel is an increasingly viable alternative option. Given the extensive number of people involved in business travel, it is a significant challenge for MNEs to establish an accurate account of the number of IBTs in their organisations (Welch et al., 2007; Welch & Worm, 2006). Clearly, the implications of failure to track such assignments from a tax perspective are significant, and organisations are increasingly putting extended travel policies in place to accurately track their populations of IBTs (Brookfield, 2013). This challenge was particularly evident during the COVID-19 pandemic, when lockdowns meant that offices were closed and individuals could choose to work from anywhere, which was particularly challenging for organisations to track and account for. For individual IBTs, the potential for stress and poor lifestyle is significant, and managing the health and safety of IBTs should be a key priority for MNEs (De Cieri & Lazarova, 2021; Jooss et al., 2022a).

A second alternative form of global mobility is the *commuter assignment*. A longer-term arrangement, commuter assignments generally involve an assignee commuting from their home base to a post in another country, generally on a weekly or bi-weekly basis. Similar to IBTs, commuter assignments involve heavy travel, but these assignments are likely to be of a more structured, defined pattern (Stahl et al., 2007). While it is difficult to quantify the extent of usage of such assignments, Mayrhofer and Scullion (2002) cite the example of German quality engineers with managerial and technical responsibilities in the clothing industry who travelled frequently in several countries in Eastern Europe, returning regularly for briefings and to spend weekends with their families. Indeed, Mayrhofer and Brewster (1997) argue that the geographic situation in Europe means that Euro-commuting and frequent visiting is a viable alternative to expatriate transfers. The shift to virtual working has the potential to drive increasing levels of commuter assignments which may become more viable as individuals are required to spend less time on site, making such options more practical. However, such assignments have profound effects on the lives of the individuals concerned and are frequently incompatible with family life and familiar daily routines, and often do not sustain adequate work–life balance. Additionally, individual burnout, fatigue, and tax management are important concerns (Meyskens et al., 2009; Mayrhofer et al., 2008). Such arrangements can be used in a wide range of circumstances where an individual may not wish to relocate their family when taking on a role in a new location.

Thirdly, *rotational assignments* involve an individual working for a set period of time in a foreign location followed by a break in the home country. This type of assignment is most common in the oil and gas industries, where drilling locations are often incompatible with family life. Again, such assignments tend to be longer-term arrangements and are often a function of the industries concerned. Commuter and rotational assignments are two types of assignments where the empirical evidence is particularly limited (Collings & Isichei, 2018) and there is considerable potential for further research around both types of assignment.

The most common alternative to the traditional assignment is the *short-term assignment*. These assignments are generally viewed as being of a longer duration than a business trip and usually do not last longer than one year (Collings & Isichei, 2018). Similar to previous alternative forms discussed, they generally do not involve relocation of the assignee's spouse or family (Star & Currie, 2009). Such assignments are suited to organisational, or to a lesser degree individual, development objectives which could be achieved at a fraction of the costs associated with expatriate assignments (Scullion & Collings, 2006). Empirical data on the use of short-term assignments are limited but indicative of the increasing usage of short-term assignments: 86% of firms in the Brookfield GMAC (2013) survey had short-term assignment policies in place. The key advantages of short-term assignments include increased flexibility, simplicity and cost-effectiveness (Tahvananinen et al., 2005: 667–668). Common disadvantages include: (1) taxation issues, particularly for assignments over six months' duration; (2)

potential for side-effects such as alcoholism and marital problems; (3) failure to build effective relationships with local colleagues and customers; and (4) the need for work visas and permits (Tahvanainen et al., 2005; Dickmann & Debner, 2011). Short-term assignments have a wide range of applications, from leadership development through problem solving to project-type roles. Short-term assignments represent another important area of global staffing that would benefit from increased empirical investigation, including how they may need to be supported (Conroy et al., 2018).

The final alternative to the traditional assignment where temporality emerges as a key concern is the *permanent transfer*, where the individual is permanently transferred to local payroll and local terms and conditions in the host country. Such arrangements have been increasing in popularity over the past decade, and are seen as a cost-effective means of transferring staff globally, with some two-thirds of firms reporting an increase in the numbers of permanent transfers (ECA International, 2018). This type of mobility has largely been neglected by the academic literature despite its increasing utilisation in practice. Collings et al.'s (2008) study unearthed some evidence of permanent transfers as a staffing option, which they traced to operating in low-margin industries where the cost constraints of global mobility were particularly significant. However, findings from Tait, De Cieri, and McNulty's (2014) exploratory study questioned the cost savings of permanent transfers, arguing that the assignment type may be at odds with the MNE's longer-term goals regarding talent and knowledge management. However, the area of permanent transfers is largely unresearched, and the extent of their usage, the implications on employee outcomes and organisation performance all merit further consideration. Permanent transfers have wide applications, although empirical research is required to understand individual employees' motivations to accept such assignments. In terms of utilisation levels, 61% of organisations indicated that they expect to see a continued increase in the use of permanent transfers as a form of international assignment (ECA International, 2018).

We will now turn to spatial issues around alternative forms of global mobility, with a particular focus on where the assignee and their family are located during the assignment episode. Indeed, a key characteristic of the traditional expatriate assignment was that assignees and their family generally relocated to the host location for the duration of the assignment. The emergence of these alternative forms of global mobility shift the boundaries of location for the assignees and their families alike. For example, in the case of IBTs and short-term assignees, their base is generally retained in their home country. This means the assignee's family often remain in the home country, while salary, pension, and social security benefits are also handled there (Tahvanainen et al., 2005). However, where a short-term assignment lasts beyond six months, this can create tax and social security issues, and it may not be possible for the assignee to retain tax status in their home country. For similar reasons, commuter and rotational assignees are often classified as residents in their host countries for tax and social security purposes, particularly when they spend in excess of six months of the year in the location. However, their family will remain in the home country. Permanent transfers will by definition be located for tax and social security purposes in the host country.

Inpatriation also emerges as a further categorisation of alternative international assignee when the location issue is considered. Harvey, Novecevic, and Speier (2000) define inpatriates as employees from multinational subsidiaries transferred to the HQ on a permanent or semi-permanent basis. Thus, a key difference between inpatriates and traditional assignees is that inpatriates are located at the HQ or in the home country of the MNE. As part of a global network, such assignees can act as "linking pins" between foreign subsidiaries and HQ. Indeed this boundary-spanning role can aid the global competitiveness of the MNE (Harvey et al., 1999). Inpatriation also facilitates the embedding of employees from outside the MNE's country of origin into the organisation, while potentially providing subsidiary talent with defined career paths, and facilitating the learning of organizational cultures, values and decision making processes (Duvivier et al., 2019; Harvey et al., 2001). Similarly, the return of inpatriates to their home country on completion of their assignment can aid the localization process. Indeed, one recent study highlighted the key role which inpatriates' knowledge transfer plays in subsidiary capability-building and subsidiary evolution over time, and the authors argue that successive inpatriation plays a key role in enhancing subsidiary performance (Kim et al., 2022). Although there is limited empirical evidence on the extent of usage of inpatriate assignments, Collings et al. (2010) concluded that although the absolute number of inpatriate assignees within individual organisations was small, they were used in a wide range of MNEs in the sample of multinational subsidiaries in Ireland.

HR'S ROLE AND CHALLENGES

The expansion in the variety of assignment types available and utilised by organisations presents particular implications for the HR function. As a starting point for HR, the expansion in the portfolio of assignments available inevitably enlarges the scale of workload for HR as each alternative form of assignment is likely to present its own set of issues similar to, but distinct from, those of traditional assignments. At a basic level, this implies an increased administrative burden, but there are also high-value connotations in terms of organisations adopting a more strategic approach to global staffing, which will mean new policy development and implementation. A key issue across many of the alternative forms of assignment is that they are viewed as outside the remit of the global mobility function owing to many being viewed as non-expatriates, typically seen as more the responsibility of line management (Jooss et al., 2022a; Welch & Worm, 2006). We will now turn to considering some of the main HR challenges and implications of alternative types of assignments in the context of the traditional expatriate cycle, consisting of recruitment and selection of assignees, pre-departure preparation, support during the assignment, repatriation, and career management.

With respect to recruitment and selection, it appears that formal processes for alternative assignments are especially uncommon, which is not selection given that informal methods appear to be dominant for long-term expatriates (Brewster, 1991). Tahvanainen et al. (2005) found formal selection in the case of short-term assignments to be an extreme rarity. We suggest that formal selection regarding many of the other forms of alternative assignment is likely to be similarly unusual. Scholarship has shown selection criteria for international assignments to be strongly based on technical skills and a person's track record in their domestic role (Sparrow et al., 2004). While the skills and characteristics that should be incorporated into selection decisions for traditional assignments have been debated and critically discussed, little is known about whether there are specific criteria for alternative forms of assignment. We suggest that job descriptions and selection decisions should address such issues in the case of roles that will incorporate forms of global mobility (e.g., frequent international business travel). As a result, there needs to be due consideration of the skills and capabilities that, if possessed, will increase the likelihood of a successful assignment.

With respect to preparation, Mayerhofer et al.'s (2004) research on flexpatriate assignments (defined as individuals who travel away from their home base and across borders for brief assignments) found that the predominant role of the HR function was providing general information on travel, health, and safety regulations in the countries people were travelling to, taking care of travel insurance, visas, and so forth. They noted that preparation for the assignment/travel and ongoing support was of secondary importance compared to ensuring the correct travel arrangements had been put in place (typically done by an external travel agency). Of some note was that despite the lack of organisational support, each interviewee emphasised the importance of informal relationships and networks in assisting them with preparing for an assignment – a point reinforced more recently by Conroy et al. (2018). There was acknowledgement from the organisation of the potential importance of cross-cultural skills for flexpatriates, but the HR function had not established specific training initiatives for these individuals due to doubts as to whether they would be effective and necessary. Finally, no consideration was given to preparing flexpatriates for dealing with any stresses that might occur on the different assignments undertaken. The lack of preparation and consideration of the different situations faced by individuals in the different types of assignments undertaken is likely to be a negative for both organisational and individual outcomes. We see this as a major issue. Issues may include simplistic things like working out the most appropriate accommodation – for example, hotel versus serviced apartment, which may impact health and wellbeing – and the provision of pre-departure training specific to the assignment being undertaken.

Unsurprisingly, there is little evidence in the research literature that families of individuals undertaking non-traditional expatriate assignments are considered at any point in the assignment cycle. In other words, they are not considered at the assignee selection stage nor are they involved in any forms of preparation or ongoing support. We feel that this is an area HR departments need to consider in a comprehensive manner given the emerging research which shows that individuals undertaking various alternative types of international work suffer negative quality of work–life outcomes and struggle to keep a balance between their work and private/family lives (e.g., De Cieri & Lazarova, 2021; De Frank et al., 2000). A multitude of research has called for MNEs to be more strategic and proactive in their use of expatriate assignments to allow for more effective recruitment, selection, preparation, and management. However, the reactive use of alternative assignments such as IBTs and short-term assignments is especially vivid. Mayerhofer et al. (2004) pointed to the case of an HR department holding a second passport for its international staff due to the need for individuals to travel on very short notice. One interviewee recommended having a travel bag ready at all times, both at home and in the office, such was their experience of needing to undertake international travel at short notice. While it is important to acknowledge that much of this may be unavoidable, there needs to be greater appreciation of the impact this may have on the individual and their spouse/family. Recent research by Jooss et al. (2022a) highlights the substantial pressures placed on IBTs and how these demands are intensified due to an inadequate support infrastructure.

Expatriate scholarship has long noted the importance of the provision of support during an assignment (Stroh et al., 2004; Tung, 1981; 1988;), but it appears from the limited research undertaken in this area and our own discussions with professionals charged with managing global mobility that no support is provided in the case of most alternative forms. The case organisation in Mayerhofer et al.'s (2004) research was very strong in terms of support to expatriates and their families, but no recognition was provided to those on shorter/alternative types of global mobility work (see also Conroy et al., 2018). We feel that there is a need for consideration of whether HR can involve itself more in the case of different forms of global mobility to ensure that support is available when required. When we consider the earlier point about the short notice often afforded to those having to undertake international travel, the provision of support may have a positive impact. Indeed, the act of considering whether an individual and family can be provided with some useful support by the organisation may act as a positive effect in its own right.

A key reasoning behind the emergence and utilisation of IBTs, short-term assignments, and so forth is that the assignee's family and spouse tend to remain in the home country, meaning that there is a cost-saving benefit for the organisation. We have seen a significant increase in interest in how to better determine the success and effectiveness of international assignments (see, e.g., McNulty et al., 2009). While it appears that alternative global mobility forms have, in part, emerged due to being less costly than traditional expatriates, they have not been immune to a further drive to lower costs. For example, research from Australia found that reduced international travel was the most common impact of the global financial crisis on MNEs (see Boyle & McDonnell, 2013). Similarly, Salt and Wood (2012) found that business travel was an area where savings were especially sought when the downturn at that time. An interviewee (from an IT consultancy) made the point that "like most companies, we're now much more careful about who goes on business trips for cost reasons" (Salt & Wood, 2012: 437). How the COVID-19 pandemic will translate into longer-term trends in international business travel is an open question (Collings & Sheeran, 2020), but early indications suggest some change may be likely (Jooss et al., 2022b). However, a key challenge for organisations and the HR function is measuring and tracking the level of international travel taking place, as well as other forms of alternative assignments. Anecdotal evidence points to great difficulty in tracking the extent to which alternative international assignments are being used. Consequently, when tracking the numbers is proving difficult, it logically points towards there being a very limited appreciation of whether these assignments are effective or successful, and of the bottom-line cost/benefit to the organisation. From both an organisational and individual perspective, there is very little understanding of the returns garnered from the different forms of global mobility. It also points to the additional challenges of measuring the return on investment of alternative forms of global mobility. Moreover, this points to the lack of an appropriate organisational infrastructure in tracking, managing, and supporting these key global workers (Jooss et al., 2022a).

The nature of careers in organisations and career management has also evolved substantially over the last half-century. We note that while careers traditionally have been demonstrated to develop within a single organisation, careers developed more recently are most appropriately viewed as complex and unstructured. The way in which individuals think about their career has changed. Traditional careers saw secure lifetime employment with single organisations and largely vertical career progression which was controlled by the organisation. Gradual changes in the employment relationship due to the environmental forces at play have generally seen shorter terms of employment, increases in inter-firm mobility and career development managed to a greater degree by the employee (Arthur & Rousseau, 1996). With the emergence of more contemporary theoretical underpinnings, alternative schools of thought have come to the fore offering insights into why employees continue to accept international assignments despite the potential negative implications that may be experienced. Lazarova and Cerdin (2007) propose the notion of the "proactive repatriate". The proactive repatriate is one who is actively engaged with their own personal and professional career development. For such individuals, the degree of organisational support they receive during and at the end of their experience is of secondary importance, and instead they use international experience as a tradable asset to advance their careers in the direction which best matches their personal needs and values. In this regard, Lazarova and Cerdin (2007) suggest that while the issue of increased turnover upon repatriation may be considered as a consequence of poor organisational support, it may also be stimulated by individuals who proactively look to advance their careers by seeking opportunities external to the organisation which appropriately fit their personal and professional career objectives. These individuals may in fact have had little intention of remaining with the sending organisation. Research of this kind has focused on long-term expatriate assignments, meaning that we do not know if individuals feel similarly in respect to undertaking other types of international assignments. The high turnover of repatriates has been noted for some time, but whether such an issue exists in the case of shorter assignment methods is unknown. What we can suggest is that there is likely to be little or no consideration of the repatriation process by organisations for assignments of short duration.

MANAGERIAL IMPLICATIONS AND FUTURE RESEARCH

The global mobility landscape is far from homogenous, which has consequences for both practitioners and scholars in the area. HR practitioners need to establish systems of tracking and managing the different mobility portfolios, which we argue will demand a considerable range of policies and practices that are aligned to the different challenges and requirements of different mobility forms. Failing to consider the characteristics and circumstances of different types of international work is likely to fuel negative outcomes, on both an individual and organisational level. For example, at an individual level, organisations cannot continue to turn a blind eye to the issue of workload and travelling time for those undertaking regular international travel (Jooss et al., 2022a, 2022b). In particular, there is a need for organisations to consider the impact such travel may have on the individual (e.g., jet lag, dietary changes), as well as on their family life (e.g., the individual may be provided with time off as a result of the personal/family time taken for travel). For example, Jooss et al. (2022a) pointed to IBTs regularly taking medication to keep going, and note that this had become normalised behaviour. There is also a strong case that job descriptions, person specifications, and employment contracts account for the different forms of global mobility that may be encompassed in the role and the additional characteristics or issues that may be involved (Demel & Mayrhofer, 2010). Issues around pay and performance management also emerge as significant. For example, the structure of pay for an individual undertaking a short-term assignment is likely to differ to that for a long-term assignee. With respect to performance management, the question of how a person's performance on assignment is evaluated emerges. Can an organisation adopt the same system to evaluate a person on a long-term assignment, a short-term assignment, or international business travel?

The area of global mobility is ripe for theoretical advancement and empirical investigation, with numerous research questions of importance worthy of consideration (see Collings & Isichei, 2018; Jooss et al., 2021; Shaffer et al., 2012). A simplistically worded yet inherently difficult question to answer due to measurement challenges is: what is the actual extent and use of different global mobility types? Brewster et al. (2001), in a UK-based study of international assignment types, found that approximately one-third of organisations had no idea how many staff were frequent flyers, though they had detailed data on all long-term assignees. Leading on from this, there is a key need to understand which types of assignments are most cost-effective, and in what cases (e.g., business purpose/situation) particular types of assignments are chosen, and why. There has been discussion about the need for expatriate assignments to be used more strategically and for closer linkages between global mobility and global talent (Cerdin & Brewster, 2014; Collings, 2014), but there is limited understanding of how various types of global mobility are influenced by international organisation strategies.

On more HR-related points, there is a need for research that examines the HR practices and systems used to support the different forms of global mobility. In other words, how do selection, training, rewards and support vary with the type of assignment, and how do differing HR practices relate to key performance outcomes? While the indications suggest there tend not to be formal processes and support for flexpatriates (e.g., Mayrhofer et al., 2004), there has been little empirical investigation in this area. Undertaking this type of research is important because even if there is little being done by the majority of organisations, it may help in identifying best practices that are being used by some pioneering firms with respect to how they manage global mobility. Overall, there is scope for considerable research into the role of both corporate and subsidiary HR functions in the management of alternative international assignments.

For instance, in the case of selection, flexpatriate assignments are by nature briefer than traditional expatriate assignments, which means that there is a more limited time period to adjust to the different culture and working with people from that country. An interesting question that logically follows concerns the selection criteria for different types of global mobility. Does having cross-cultural competence become more important in shorter assignments due to not having the time to develop such skills, or is the opposite true, that cross-cultural agility is less important because the duration is short? Are all measures of cross-culturally suitability useful and valid for each type of international working? Considerable attention has been paid to shortages of global talent, leading to discussion around the development of international managers, but what this actually means and how international assignments assist has not received much attention (Selmer, 1998). Relatedly, we know very little about how different types of international assignments fit in with approaches to career development within MNEs, a shortcoming that should be addressed.

On an individual level, we call on researchers to investigate the individual motivations underscoring people undertaking international assignments and whether there are differences in these according to the different mobility forms. There is an acute need to better appreciate the non-work issues and challenges faced by different international workers. For example, the high potential of international frequent flyers to suffer from burn-out is a key consideration (Collings et al., 2007; Jooss et al., 2022a). There is consequently a need for studies that investigate the strains and pressures on individuals and their partners/families involved in different mobility forms and how organisations can help ease these.

Table 1 Summary of alternative global mobility types

Assignment	Assignment Definition	Potential Uses	Temporal Issues	Challenges	HR Issues
International Business Travel	Regular travel and communication between home and host location of an undefined duration	Specialised irregular tasks, e.g. production scheduling, budgeting, individual development, managerial control, development of networks	Delineation of work and life roles, travel on personal time	Burnout, stress, cost management, work–life balance	Policy formation and implementation, recruitment, selection, training, rewards, health and safety
International Commuter	Periodic travel between home and host location, frequently on a weekly, bi-weekly, or monthly basis	Project based tasks, network building, individual development, short-term skills gap	Tax Issues, social security issues, compensation issues	Costs, burnout, stress, cost management, work–life balance	Work permit issues, policy formation and development, recruitment, selection, training, rewards, health and safety
Rotational Assignment	Assignment of a prescribed period of time in host location followed by a break in home location before further relocation	Managerial development, organisational functionality	Tax and social security issues	Work–life balance, strain on relationships	Training and retention
Short-term Assignment	Assignment of a duration longer than a business trip and shorter than one year	Technical roles, organisational and individual development objectives; specific skill transfers	Tax and social security issues	Strain on personal relationships, health issues, work–life balance, failure to build effective relationships	Work permit issues, policy, recruitment, training, rewards, health and safety
Permanent Transfer	One-way transfer in which assignee works and resides in host location indefinitely	Low-margin industries, less strategic transfers	Permanent break with home base	Return on investment, identity, support	Attracting individuals to undertake transfers given relatively lower financial benefits

Mayerhofer et al. (2004) found evidence of flexpatriates being active in gathering information from the internet and colleagues and friends to improve their experience and chances of succeeding on the assignment. Consequently, it would be useful to better understand how individuals manage the demands that are placed on their work and non-work life. The impact of undertaking an international assignment on one's career has started to gain a lot of attention (e.g., Suutari, 2003; Cappellen & Janssens, 2005). Much has been made of the learning experience garnered from an expatriate assignment leading to the development of three types of career capital (e.g., Jokinen et al., 2008): know-how (the ability to see how things work differently in various situations), know-whom (the development of relationships), and know-why (appreciating what is important to them). Research that investigates the career outcomes from different global mobility forms would make a very useful addition to existing understanding of the impact of international experience on one's career.

CONCLUSION

In this reading, we have highlighted the changing topography of global mobility approaches in international organisations (see Table 1 for a summary). In particular, we have highlighted that while the traditional corporate expatriate remains a mainstay in MNEs globally, there are a significant range of other types of global staffing assignments occurring which have received comparatively less attention by scholars. Practitioners also appear to have paid less attention to these global mobility forms, which might be based on the premise that they avoid many of the issues that are associated with long-term international assignments (Brewster et al., 2001). While this may be the case, it is not a truly accurate picture because it appears that alternative forms of global mobility bring new issues and challenges, as we have highlighted. An overarching issue in this is that there appears to be a lack of HR involvement in non-long-term assignments, where in forms such as international business travel it is line management that appears to bear the main responsibility. As a result, a key challenge is enacting a set of consistent and appropriate policies and practices for the different global mobility types.

NOTE

1.   Shaffer et al. (2012) prioritise assignments lasting several years in their definition. Given the incorporation of short-term assignments in the present discussion, we recognise the importance of such shorter-duration assignments.

REFERENCES

Andersen, N. (2021). Mapping the expatriate literature: A bibliometric review of the field from 1998 to 2017 and identification of current research fronts. *The International Journal of Human Resource Management*, 32(22): 4687–4724.

Akkermans, J., Collings, D. G., da Motta Veiga, S. P., Post, C., & Seibert, S. (2021). Toward a broader understanding of career shocks: Exploring interdisciplinary connections with research on job search, human resource management, entrepreneurship, and diversity. *Journal of Vocational Behavior*, 126: 103563.

Arthur, M. B., & Rousseau, D. M. (1996). *The boundaryless career: A new employment principle for a new organizational era*. Boston, MA, Cambridge University Press.

Black, J. S., Gregersen, H. B., Mendenhall, M. E., & Stroh, L. K. (1999). *Globalizing people through international assignments*. New York, Addison-Wesley.

Brewster, C. (1991). *The management of expatriates*. London, Kogan Page.

Bonache, J., Brewster, C., & Suutari, V. (2001). Expatriation: A developing research agenda. *Thunderbird International Business Review*, 43(1): 3–20.

Boyle, B., & McDonnell, A. (2013). Exploring the impact of institutional and organisational factors on the reaction of multinational companies to the global financial crisis. *Asia Pacific Business Review*, 19(2): 247–265.

Bozkurt, Ö., & Mohr, A. T. (2011). Forms of cross-border mobility and social capital in multinational enterprises. *Human Resource Management Journal*, 21(2): 138–155.

Brewster, C., Harris, H., & Petrovic, J. (2001). Globally mobile employees: Managing the mix. *Journal of Professional Human Resource Management*, 25: 11–15.

Briscoe, D. R., & Schuler, R. S. (2004). *International human resource management*, 2nd edition. New York, Routledge.

Brookfield GMAC. (2013). *Global relocation trends: 2013 survey report*. Brookfield, IL, Bun Ridge.

Caligiuri, P., De Cieri, H., Minbaeva, D., Verbeke, A., & Zimmermann, A. (2020). International HRM insights for navigating the COVID-19 pandemic: Implications for future research and practice. *Journal of International Business Studies*, 51(5): 697–713.

Caligiuri, P., & Tarique, I. (2016). Cultural agility and international assignees' effectiveness in cross-cultural interactions. *International Journal of Training and Development*, 20(4): 280–289.

Cappellen, T., & Janssens, M. (2005). Career paths of global managers: Towards future research. *Journal of World Business*, 40(4): 348–360.

Cerdin, J. L., & Brewster, C. (2014). Talent management and expatriation: Bridging two streams of research and practice. *Journal of World Business*, 49(2): 245–252.

Cheong, A., Sandhu, M. S., Edwards, R., & Ching Poon, W. (2019). Subsidiary knowledge flow strategies and purpose of expatriate assignments. *International Business Review*, 28(3): 450–462.

Collings, D. G. (2014). Integrating global mobility and global talent management: Exploring the challenges and strategic opportunities. *Journal of World Business*, 49(2): 253–261.

Collings, D. G., McDonnell, A., Gunnigle, A., & Lavelle, J. (2010). Swimming against the tide: Outward staffing flows from multinational subsidiaries. *Human Resource Management*, 49(4): 575–598.

Collings, D. G., Morley, M. J., & Gunnigle, P. (2008). Composing the top management team in the international subsidiary: Qualitative evidence on international staffing in US MNCs in the Republic of Ireland. *Journal of world business*, 43(2): 197–212.

Collings, D. G., & Scullion, H. (2012). Global staffing. In G. K. Stahl & I. Bjorkman (Eds.), *Handbook of research in international human resource management*, pp. 142–161, second edition. Edward Elgar Publishing.

Collings, D. G., Scullion, H., & Morley, M. J. (2007). Changing patterns of global staffing in the multinational enterprise: Challenges to the conventional expatriate assignment and emerging alternatives. *Journal of World Business*, 42(2): 198–213.

Collings, D. G., & Isichei, M. (2018). The shifting boundaries of global staffing: Integrating global talent management, alternative forms of international assignments and non-employees into the discussion. *The International Journal of Human Resource Management*, 29(1): 165–187.

Collings, D. G., & Sheeran, R. (2020). Research insights: Global mobility in a post-Covid world 1. *The Irish Journal of Management*, 39(2): 77–84.

Conroy, K. M., McDonnell, A., & Holzleitner, K. (2018). A race against time: Training and support for short-term international assignments. *Journal of Global Mobility: The Home of Expatriate Management Research*, 6(3/4): 299–315.

De Cieri, H., & Lazarova, M. (2021). "Your health and safety is of utmost importance to us": A review of research on the occupational health and safety of international employees. *Human Resource Management Review*, 31(4): 100790.

DeFrank, R. S., Konopaske, R., & Ivancevich, J. M. (2000). Executive travel stress: Perils of the road warrior. *Academy of Management Perspectives*, 14(2): 58–71.

Demel, B., & Mayrhofer, W. (2010). Frequent business travelers across Europe: Career aspirations and implications. *Thunderbird International Business Review*, 52(4): 301–311.

Dickmann, M., & Debner, C. (2011). International mobility at work: Companies' structural remuneration, social security and risk considerations. In M. Dickmann & Y. Baruch (Eds.), *Global careers*, pp. 268–293. London, Routledge.

Dickmann, M., & Doherty, N. (2010). Exploring organizational and individual career goals, interactions, and outcomes of developmental international assignments. *Thunderbird International Business Review*, 52(4): 313–324.

Doherty, N. (2013). Understanding the self-initiated expatriate: A review and directions for future research. *International Journal of Management Reviews*, 15: 447–469.

Doherty, N., Dickmann, M., & Mills, T. (2011). Exploring the motives of company-backed and self-initiated expatriates. *The International Journal of Human Resource Management*, 22(3): 595–561.

Dowling, P. J., Festing, M., & Engle, A. D. (2008). *International human resource management*, 5th edition. London, Cengage Learning.

Dowling, P. J., Festing, M., & Engle, A. E. (2017). *International human resource management*, 7th edition. Boston, MA, Cengage.

Duvivier, F., Peeters, C., & Harzing, A. W. (2019). Not all international assignments are created equal: HQ-subsidiary knowledge transfer patterns across types of assignments and types of knowledge. *Journal of World Business*, 54(3): 181–190.

ECA International. (2018). Permanent transfers—a growing trend. Retrieved from https://www.eca-international.com/insights/blog/november-2018/permanent-transfers [accessed November 1st 2022].

Edstrom, A., & Galbraith, J. R. (1977). Transfer of managers as a coordination and control strategy in multinational organizations. *Administrative Science Quarterly*, 22(2): 248–263.

Feldman, D. C., & Thomas, D. C. (1992). Career management issues facing expatriates. *Journal of International Business Studies*, 23: 271–293.

Finaccord. (2018). *Global expatriates: Size, segmentation and forecasts for the worldwide market*. Singapore, Finnacord.

Forster, N. (2000). The myth of the "international manager". *International Journal of Human Resource Management*, 11(1): 126–142.

Gregersen, H. (1992). Commitments to a parent company and a local work unit during repatriation. *Personnel Psychology*, 45(1): 29–54.

Harvey, M., Speier, C., & Novicevic, M. M. (1999). The role of inpatriation in global staffing. *International Journal of Human Resource Management*, 10(3): 459–476.

Harvey, M., Speier, C., & Novecevic, M. M. (2001). A theory-based framework for strategic global human resource staffing policies and practices. *International Journal of Human Resource Management*, 12(6): 898–915.

Harvey, M. G., Speier, C., & Novicevic, M. M. (2000). Strategic global human resource management: The role of inpatriate managers. *Human Resource Management Review*, 10(2): 153–175.

Harzing, A. W. (2001). Of bears, bees and spiders: The role of expatriates in controlling foreign subsidiaries. *Journal of World Business*, 26: 366–379.

Harzing, A. W. (2002). Acquisitions versus greenfield investments: International strategy and management of entry modes. *Strategic Management Journal*, 23(3): 211–227.

Harzing, A. W. K. (1995). The persistent myth of high expatriate failure rates. *International Journal of Human Resource Management*, 6(2): 457–474.

Hitt, M. A., Holmes Jr, R. M., & Arregle, J. L. (2021). The (COVID-19) pandemic and the new world (dis)order. *Journal of World Business*, 56(4): 101210.

Horak, S., Farndale, E., Brannen, M. Y., & Collings, D. G. (2019). International human resource management in an era of political nationalism. *Thunderbird International Business Review*, 61(3): 471–480.

Ipek, E., & Paulus, P. (2021). The influence of personality on individuals' expatriation willingness in the context of safe and dangerous environments. *Journal of Global Mobility: The Home of Expatriate Management Research*, 9(2): 264–288.

Jokinen, T., Brewster, C., & Suutari, V. (2008). Career capital during international work experiences: Contrasting self-initiated expatriate experiences and assigned expatriation. *The International Journal of Human Resource Management*, 19(6): 981–1000.

Jooss, S., Conroy, K. M., & McDonnell, A. (2022a). Discretion as a double-edged sword in global work: The perils of international business travel. *Human Resource Management Journal*, 32(3): 664–682.

Jooss, S., Conroy, K., & McDonnell, A. (2022b). From travel to virtual work: The transitional experiences of global workers during Covid-19. *International Business Review*, 31(6): 102052.

Jooss, S., McDonnell, A., & Conroy, K. (2021). Flexible global working arrangements: An integrative review and future research agenda. *Human Resource Management Review*, 31(4): 100780.

Kim, H., Reiche, B. S., & Harzing, A. W. (2022). How does successive inpatriation contribute to subsidiary capability building and subsidiary evolution? An organizational knowledge creation perspective. *Journal of International Business Studies*, 53(7): 1394–1419.

Kraimer, M. L., Shaffer, M. A., & Bolino, M. C. (2009). The influence of expatriate and repatriate experiences on career advancement and repatriate retention. *Human Resource Management*, 48(1): 27–47.

Kubovcikova, A., & van Bakel, M. (2022). Social support abroad: How do self-initiated expatriates gain support through their social networks? *International Business Review*, 31(1): 101894.

Lazarova, M., Caligiuri, P., Collings, D. G., & De Cieri, H. (2023). Global work in a rapidly changing world: Implications for MNEs and individuals. *Journal of World Business*, 58(1): 101365.

Lazarova, M. B., & Cerdin, J. L. (2007). Revisiting repatriation concerns: Organizational support versus career and contextual influences. *Journal of International Business Studies*, 38(3): 404–429.

Mayerhofer, H., Hartmann, L. C., Michelitsch-Riedl, G., & Kollinger, I. (2004). Flexpatriate assignments: A neglected issue in global staffing. *International Journal of Human Resource Management*, 15(8): 1371–1389.

Mayrhofer, W. & Brewster, C. (1997) Ethnocentric staffing policies in European multinationals. *International Executive*, 38: 749–778.

Mayrhofer, W., & Scullion, H. (2002). Female expatriates in international business: Empirical evidence from the German clothing industry. *International Journal of Human Resource Management*, 13(5): 815–836.

Mayrhofer, W., Sparrow, P., & Zimmerman, A. (2008). Modern forms of international working. In M. Dickmann, C. Brewster, & P. Sparrow (Eds.), *International human resource management: A European perspective*, pp. 219–239. London, Routledge.

McDonnell, A., Russell, H., Sablok, G., Burgess, J., Stanton, P., Bartram, T., Boyle, B., & Manning, K. (2011). *Report: A profile of human resource management in multinational enterprises operating in Australia.* Adelaide, University of South Australia.

McNulty, Y., De Cieri, H., & Hutchings, K. (2009). Do global firms measure expatriate return on investment? An empirical examination of measures, barriers and variables influencing global staffing practices. *The International Journal of Human Resource Management,* 20(6): 1309–1326.

Mendenhall, M. E. (2001). New perspectives on expatriate adjustment and its relationship to global leadership development. In M. E. Mendenhall, T. M. Kühlmann and G. K. Stah *Developing global business leaders: Policies, processes, and innovations,* London, Quorum Books. pp. 1–18.

Meyskens, M., Von Glinow, M. A., Werther, W. B. Jr, & Clarke, L. (2009). The paradox of international talent: Alternative forms of international assignments. *The International Journal of Human Resource Management,* 20(6): 1439–1450.

Moore, K., & Lewis, D. (1999). *Birth of the multinational.* Copenhagen, Copenhagen Business Press.

Pucik, V. (1992). Globalization and human resource management. *Globalizing Management: Creating and Leading the Competitive Organization,* 61: 84.

Pucik, V., Björkman, I., Evans, P., & Stahl, G. K. (2023). *The global challenge: Managing people across borders,* 4th edition. Cheltenham, Edward Elgar.

Reiche, B. S., & Harzing, A.-W. (2022). International assignments. In B. S. Reiche, H. Tenzer, & A.-W. Harzing (Eds.), *International human resource management,* 6th edition, pp. 153–189. London, Sage.

Salt, J., & Millar, J. (2006). International migration in interesting times: The case of the UK. *People and Place,* 14(2): 14–25.

Salt, J., & Wood, P. (2012). Recession and international corporate mobility. *Global Networks,* 12(4): 425–445.

Scullion, H. & Collings, D. G. (Eds.). (2006). *Global staffing,* London, Routledge.

Selmer, J. (1995). *Expatriate management: New ideas for international business.* Westport, CT: Greenwood Publishing Group.

Selmer, J. (1998). Expatriation: Corporate policy, personal intentions and international adjustment. *The International Journal of Human Resource Management,* 9(6): 996–1007.

Shaffer, M. A., Kraimer, M. L., Chen, Y. P., & Bolino, M. C. (2012). Choices, challenges, and career consequences of global work experiences: A review and future agenda. *Journal of Management,* 38(4): 1282–1327.

Shay, J. P., & Baack, S. A. (2004). Expatriate assignment, adjustment and effectiveness: An empirical examination of the big picture. *Journal of International Business Studies,* 35: 216–232.

Shortland, S. (2016). The purpose of expatriation: Why women undertake international assignments. *Human Resource Management,* 55(4): 655–678.

Singh, S. K., Vrontis, D., & Christofi, M. (2021). What makes mindful self-initiated expatriates bounce back, improvise and perform: Empirical evidence from the emerging markets. *European Management Review.* DOI: 10.1111/emre.12456.

Sparrow, P., Brewster, C., & Harris, H. (2004). *Globalizing human resource management.* London, Routledge.

Stahl, G. K., Miller, E. L., & Tung, R. L. (2002). Toward the boundaryless career: A closer look at the expatriate career concept and the perceived implications of an international assignment. *Journal of World Business,* 37(3): 216–227.

Stahl, G. K., Björkman, I., Farndale, E., Morris, S. S., Paauwe, J., Stiles, P., ... Wright, P. M. (2007). *Global talent management: How leading multinationals build and sustain their talent pipeline MIT Sloan Management Review* 53(2):25–32.

Stahl, G. K., & Chua, C. H. (2006). Global assignments and boundaryless careers: What drives and frustrates international assignments? In M. J. Morley, N. Heraty, & D. G. Collings (Eds.), *International human resource management and international assignments*, pp. 135–152. Basingstoke, Palgrave Macmillan.

Starr, T. L., & Currie, G. (2009). "Out of sight but still in the picture": Short-term international assignments and the influential role of family. *The International Journal of Human Resource Management*, 20(6): 1421–1438.

Stroh, L. K., Black, J. S., Mendenhall, M. E., & Gregersen, H. B. (2004). *International assignments: An integration of strategy, research, and practice*. Boca Raton, FL, CRC Press.

Stroh, L. K., Gregersen, H. B., & Black, J. S. (2000). Triumphs and tragedies: Expectations and commitments upon repatriation. *International Journal of Human Resource Management*, 11(4): 681–697.

Suutari, V. (2003). Global managers: Career orientation, career tracks, life-style implications and career commitment. *Journal of Managerial Psychology*, 18(3): 185–207.

Tahvanainen, M., Welch, D., & Worm, V. (2005). Implications of short-term international assignments. *European Management Journal*, 23(6): 663–673.

Tait, E., De Cieri, H., & McNulty, Y. (2014). The opportunity cost of saving money: An exploratory study of permanent transfers and localization of expatriates in Singapore. *International Studies of Management and Organization*, 44(3): 80–95.

Tang, Q. T., Rammal, H., & Michailova, S. (2022). Expatriates' families: A systematic literature review and research agenda. *Human Resource Management Review*, 32(4): 100877.

Tornikoski, C., Suutari, V., & Festing, M. (2014). Compensation package of international assignees. In D. G. Collings, G. T. Wood, & P. M. Caligiuri (Eds.), *The Routledge companion to international human resource management*, pp. 315–333. London, Routledge.

Tung, R. (1982). Selection and training procedures of US, European and Japanese multinationals. *California Management Review*, 25(1): 57–71.

Tung, R. L. (1981). Selection and training of personnel for overseas assignments. *Columbia Journal of World Business*, 16(1): 68–78.

Tung, R. L. (1988). Career issues in international assignments. *Academy of Management Perspectives*, 2(3): 241–244.

Vaiman, V., & Haslberger, A. (Eds.). (2013). *Talent management of self-initiated expatriates: A neglected source of global talent*. Basingstoke, Palgrave Macmillan.

Welch, D. E. (2003). Globalisation of staff movements: Beyond cultural adjustment. *MIR: Management International Review*: 43(2), 149–169.

Welch, D. E., Welch, L. S., & Worm, V. (2007). The international business traveller: A neglected but strategic human resource. *The International Journal of Human Resource Management*, 18(2): 173–183.

Welch, D. E., & Worm, V. (2006). International business travellers: A challenge for IHRM. In G. Stahl & I. Bjorkman (Eds.), *Handbook of research in international research management*, pp. 283–301. Cheltenham, Edward Elgar.

Mark E. Mendenhall, Gary R. Oddou, and B. Sebastian Reiche

THE EXPATRIATE PERFORMANCE APPRAISAL CONUNDRUM*

HUMAN RESOURCE PERFORMANCE MANAGEMENT (PM) systems in large companies are commonly made up of the following functions: performance appraisal, goal setting, training and development, continuous feedback, and performance-based pay (Bader et al., 2021). Ideally, they are designed to be a "cyclical process that allows both the organization and the employee an opportunity to align employee performance with both job-specific and organizational goals" (Varma, Wang, & Coleman, 2022: 47). Implementing PM systems in organizations, while conceptually rational, turns out to be very difficult to do (DeNisi, Murphy, Varma, & Budhwar, 2021; Murphy, 2020). In a study conducted by the consulting firm Mercer, only 2% of companies believed that their PM systems deliver exceptional value, and 70% stated "they need to improve the link between performance management and other talent decisions," such as development, promotions, and succession planning (Mercer, 2019: 1).

One of the difficulties in creating an effective PM system is *accurately* measuring an employee's performance when sometimes a myriad of variables can affect the performance outcomes. Another challenge is knowing *how* to measure the employee's performance. Quantifiable data related to someone's performance can overlook many of the qualitative achievements of the employee (e.g., a more cohesive team, increased motivation, better team member communication, etc.). A third difficulty is knowing who has the information best used to measure the employee's performance. Sometimes it's not the boss. The challenge, then, in developing a sound PM system is to minimize the error-proneness of such systems and ensure a broad perspective when looking at an individual's influence on the

---

* This is a revision by the authors of their article that appeared in the previous edition of this book.

DOI: 10.4324/9781003247272-18

unit's overall performance. The problems prevalent in PM systems are especially exacerbated as the context for measuring performance becomes increasingly complex. In a global company with expatriate workers, managers, and executives, careful thought must be given to addressing the challenges.

THE CHALLENGE OF MEASURING PERFORMANCE OF EXPATRIATES

Unlike most employees, expatriates serve highly strategic control, knowledge transfer, and global leadership roles for their firms (Bebenroth & Froese, 2020; Harzing, Pudelko, & Reiche, 2016; Kobrin, 1988). Additionally, they are often "high potentials" who have been purposely sent on overseas assignments to develop global business skills and a global mindset in preparation for higher-level leadership responsibilities (Cerdin & Brewster, 2014; Vaiman, McNulty, & Haslberger, 2021). And they must perform their roles, unlike their domestically based counterparts, in new, unfamiliar cultures where relationship building, diplomacy, interpersonal influence, stakeholder relations, and ethical nuance are manifested quite differently from their native business cultures. This latter aspect of job performance that deals with human competency is called "contextual performance," and it involves being able to navigate within the social contexts of a business situation in such a way as to produce successful outcomes (Motowidlo & Van Scotter, 1994). It requires dealing with "broader organizational and societal goals," and "can be thought of as related to aspects of helping and cooperating, which are essential to individual and organizational success" (Caligiuri & Day, 2000: 156).

To engage in effective contextual performance, expatriate managers require timely, accurate, and valid evaluations of "how they are doing on the job, and whether they need to change course" in their interpersonal actions (Varma, Wang, & Budhwar, 2020: 80). Why? Because failures on their part can have significant bottom-line effects on their companies. In global PM systems, the most common way of ensuring that expatriate managers receive timely, accurate, and valuable feedback about their contextual performance is through the use of performance appraisals (PAs). And as has already been explained, creating an effective and valid expatriate performance appraisal is easier said than done.

APPRAISING EXPATRIATE PERFORMANCE

Several problems are inherent in appraising an expatriate's contextual and task performance. First, let's consider those who evaluate an expatriate's job performance – host national managers and executives and home office managers and executives.

Host National Management's Perceptions of Actual Job Performance

For expatriates on long-term overseas assignments and who have managerial roles overseas, the most common source of their performance appraisals is their superior in the host country (Bader et al., 2021; Suutari & Tahvanainen, 2002). That local management evaluates the expatriate is probably necessary; however, such a process sometimes is problematic. Local managers often evaluate expatriates' performance from their own cultural frame of reference or needs (Pucik, Evans, Björkman, and Morris (2017). For example, one American expatriate manager we talked to used participative decision-making in India, but was viewed by his local rater as being incompetent because of the cultural expectation that managers in India, partly owing to their social class level, are seen as experts who should not have to ask subordinates for ideas and input. Being seen as incompetent negatively affected local management's review of this expatriate's performance, and he was denied a promotion on return to headquarters. Similarly, in one major multinational, local staff members were politely praiseworthy of even overtly incompetent expatriates. They knew that if they said anything negative, they would be saddled with the individual for a longer period of time (Pucik et al., 2017: 279)!

From these two brief case examples, several important issues can be drawn that apply broadly to the challenge of expatriate performance appraisal. For instance, were expatriates given helpful feedback over a reasonable time period about the need to adjust their managerial behavior before the PAs were conducted? And if so, were sufficient training or consulting resources available to them to assist them in making the difficult transition from their managerial styles that had been successful for them in their home country but were now less effective in different cultures? Was there a hyper-focus on their contextual performance vs. task performance, thus rendering an imbalanced overall evaluation of their total performance? To what degree should local management be responsible for developing expatriates' abilities to be successful in their contextual performance, or should the onus be upon expatriates to develop themselves? Should local raters consider the degree and amount of cross-cultural training that expatriates receive before and during their overseas assignments when evaluating their contextual performance? That is, should there be a higher "degree of difficulty" component considered by local raters when an expatriate received no or little training? Should local raters lower their expectations for high performance from expatriates until such training could be conducted?

Each of these issues holds important implications for how HR systems should approach the PM of expatriates, and we will address possible solutions later in this reading. However, local management's appraisal is not the only potential challenge associated with conducting valid expatriate PAs.

Home Office Management's Perceptions of Actual Job Performance

Because home office management is geographically, culturally, and often philosophically distanced from the milieu that expatriates live and work within, home office raters often are not fully aware of the complete picture of what is happening overseas. As a result, home office management will often use different variables than local management when evaluating expatriates' contextual and task performance (Pucik et al., 2017). It is common for the home office to use task-related performance criteria to measure expatriate success, such as rate of return on investment, market share, profits, and the hitting of other company-specific targeted outcomes. The danger lies in only using these types of criteria for expatriate PAs while ignoring other variables that can drastically affect the company's performance. Local events such as strikes, devaluation of the currency, political instability, and runaway inflation are examples of phenomena that are beyond the control of the expatriate (Pucik et al., 2017). Consider the situation of the following expatriate we interviewed and ask yourself, "Was he a high performer or a low performer?"

He was assigned to work in a country where, at the time, labor–management relations were problematic. During his tenure there, he almost singlehandedly stopped a strike that would have completely shut down his firm's manufacturing facility for months. In a country where strikes were commonplace, such an accomplishment was quite a coup, especially for a Westerner. The numerous meetings and talks with labor representatives, government officials, and local management required an acute understanding of their culture and a sensitivity beyond the ability of most expatriate managers. However, because of exchange rate fluctuations with primary trading partners in the region, the demand for the product the facility produced temporarily decreased by 30 percent during his tenure. Rather than applauding the efforts of this expatriate executive to avert a strike and recognizing the superb negotiation skills he demonstrated, the home office viewed the expatriate as being only somewhat better than a mediocre performer. In other words, because for home office management the most visible criterion of his performance was rather negative (sales figures), they assumed that he had not performed adequately. And though the home office knew that a strike had been averted, the bottom-line concern for sales dollars overshadowed for them any other significant accomplishments on the part of the expatriate.

In this case, though home office management may have agreed with an argument put forward to them by an objective observer that this expatriate's contextual performance was high, task-related criteria for them trumped contextual performance criteria. Whether or not this expatriate was a high performer is simply in the eye of the beholder – the criteria lenses one looks through. Thus, expatriates must walk a tightrope. They must learn to navigate a new culture, determine how to work with a foreign boss, and essentially learn an entirely new cultural business system. Simultaneously with that effort, they must also be attuned to the home office's expectations during their overseas assignments. It is difficult, and sometimes impossible, to please both parties. Attempting to satisfy both parties can result in a temporary or permanently railroaded career. So it was with an individual we interviewed, who was considered a "high potential" in a semiconductor firm. She was sent to an overseas subsidiary without pre-departure or post-arrival cross-cultural training about the country's marketing system. Due to this lack of preparation, she barely kept her head above water because of the difficulties of cracking what, in her mind, was a nearly impossible market to comprehend. On returning to the US, she was physically and mentally exhausted from the battle, so she sought a much less challenging position, and got it because top management believed they had overestimated her potential. In fact, top management never did understand what the expatriate had been up against in the foreign market.

From others' and our own experiences in working with expatriates, it is clear that home office management often does not understand the value of an international assignment or strategically utilize expatriates' gained experience when they return to the home office (Akkan, Lazarova, & Reiche, 2018). There are various issues involved with this tendency (see Akkan et al., 2018), but we will focus on one that we believe is at the forefront of the problem: cultural ethnocentricity.

Two of the most significant aspects of home office management's inability to understand expatriates' experience and thereby more accurately measure their performance are (1) the communication gap between the expatriate and the home office while they are abroad, and (2) the lack of home office managers' global and cultural acumen.

Being physically separated by thousands of miles and in different time zones in today's world does not pose distinct problems for communication like it did 20 or 30 years ago. Despite not having difficulty talking directly with their home office managers, expatriates (and their home office managers) have plenty of other responsibilities to attend to. Fixing day-to-day problems tends to take precedence over other concerns, such as maintaining contact with one's boss (or subordinate) so they can be kept up to date on the expatriate's status. Thus, an "out of sight, out of mind" relationship can often evolve despite modern technology that allows for constant contact. Without high motivation on the part of both parties to mutually and consistently stay in touch with one another to keep each other informed, when it comes time to conduct PAs, the home office manager may operate from a non-nuanced, relatively simplistic understanding of the expatriate's work reality. Added to this conundrum is the following issue: how can one understand what another person's overseas managerial experience is like – its inherent difficulties, challenges, stresses – without having lived and worked overseas oneself? If home office managers have not lived or worked overseas, and if the expatriate and the home office manager are not communicating regularly about the assignment, this adds to the low probability of the home office manager being able to evaluate the expatriate's performance accurately.

Up to now, we have discussed challenges associated with the local and home office managers' perceptions of expatriate performance. Let's now turn our attention to what usually composes expatriates' actual performance to understand better why evaluating it can be problematic.

ACTUAL JOB PERFORMANCE

The primary factors relating to expatriates' actual job performance include their technical job expertise that relates to task performance, personal adjustment to the culture that relates to contextual performance, and various other environmental factors.

Technical Job Expertise (Task Performance)

As with all jobs, one's success abroad partly depends on one's expertise in the technical area of the job. One study indicates that approximately 95 percent of expatriates believe that technical competency is crucial to successful job performance (Oddou & Mendenhall, 1991). Although common sense supports this notion, research shows that technical competence is necessary but not sufficient for successful expatriate job performance (Varma et al., 2022). For example, an engineer who is an expert in her field and who tends to ignore cultural variables that are important to job performance will likely be ineffective. She might be less flexible with local personnel, policies, and practices because she relies on technical know-how or because of differences in cultural views. As a result, the local employees might become alienated by her managerial and working style and become quite resistant to her objectives and strategies. We have run across numerous examples where this has been the case. One expatriate we interviewed worked for a large construction firm and was sent to a worksite in India. The expatriate was an expert in their field and operated in the same fashion as they did in their home country. They unintentionally ignored local work customs and became an object of hatred and distrust. The project was delayed for more than six months because of the expatriate's behavior.

A less experienced engineer with less technical competence but who is highly culturally sensitive might be more willing to defer to the host country's employees and their procedures and customs (Neeley & Reiche, 2022). A shade of humility is always more likely to breed flexibility. In the long run, the less experienced engineer might develop the trust of the local employees and might well be more effective than the experienced engineer.

Adjustment to a New Culture (Contextual Performance)

Expatriates' ability to adapt to the host culture environment enables them to work with the people within it effectively. Nearly every research study ever conducted on expatriates has found that understanding the host culture, having the ability to communicate with the host nationals, and being able to manage stress were essential to successful job performance (Han, Sears, Darr, & Wang, 2022; Shaffer, Harrison, & Gilley, 1999). Regardless of how much expatriates know about the technical aspects of their work role, if they cannot communicate well with and understand the perspectives of the host nationals, the work will not get done.

An expatriate's adjustment overseas is also related to the support the expatriate receives from the accompanying spouse and other family members (Dang, Rammal, & Michailova, 2022). The stress on the expatriate's spouse from the overseas assignment can negatively affect the expatriate's adjustment and job performance (Dang et al., 2022). Company variables affecting cultural and work adjustment also come into play. The thoroughness of the company's expatriate selection method and the type and degree of pre-departure and post-arrival cross-cultural training will affect expatriate adjustment and performance (Chenyang, 2022; Gai, Brough, & Gardiner, 2021). In other words, if the firm is not selective about the personality of the expatriate or does not adequately prepare the employee and their dependents with cross-cultural training, the firm may be building in failure before the manager ever departs for their overseas assignment.

All these factors influence an expatriate's learning curve in a foreign business environment. More time is thus required to learn the ins and outs of the job than for the expatriate's domestic counterparts who might have just taken a comparable position in their home country. Hence, performance evaluations at the company's normal time interval may be too early to accurately and fairly reflect the expatriate's performance.

In summary, expatriates' overall performance is based on overseas adjustment (contextual performance), technical expertise (task performance), and various relevant environmental factors. PAs, however, are based on raters' perceptions of ratee' performance, which is based on a set of fairly complex variables that can affect the raters' evaluations. Much of the perceived performance flows from perceptions of expatriates and their situations, and can be skewed or biased. The performance appraisal will be more or less valid depending on whether the manager assessing the expatriate's performance has had personal overseas experience or is otherwise sensitive to problems associated with overseas work. The bottom line for the expatriate is that the performance appraisal will influence their promotion potential and the type of position the expatriate receives on returning to headquarters. Because expatriates generally return from their experience with valuable managerial skills, especially for firms pursuing an international or global market path, it behooves organizations to carefully review their process of appraising expatriates and their evaluation criteria.

GUIDELINES ON HOW TO APPRAISE AN EXPATRIATE'S PERFORMANCE

Human Resources Department: Give Guidelines for Performance Evaluation

Human resources departments can do a couple of things to help guide evaluators' perspectives when assessing expatriate performance. First, a basic breakdown of the difficulty level of expatriate assignments should be produced to evaluate performance. For example, working in Japan is generally considered more difficult than working in England or English-speaking Canada for American expatriates. The learning curve in Japan will take longer for them because of the very different ways business is conducted, the language barrier, and the isolation many

Americans can feel within the Japanese culture. Significant variables such as the following should be considered when determining the difficulty level of the assignment:

- The operational language used in the firm.
- "Cultural distance" between the expatriate's home country and the country of the assignment.
- Stability of external factors that will affect the expatriate's performance (for example, labor force, exchange rate, political stability, etc.).

English has become the lingua franca for day-to-day business operations in some global firms. However, while many local workers in global companies speak English, their proficiency varies, and often there are many who do not speak it effectively or comfortably, so they rely on their native language whenever possible. In addition, they usually do not speak English among themselves while at work. In Spain, for example, American expatriates' reliance on English may allow them to perform at an adequate level, but if they do not speak Spanish, this will limit their effectiveness. Secretaries, for example, often have minimal English-speaking skills, and it is common for Spanish employees to rarely speak English together. When this happens, they unknowingly exclude expatriates from casual and sometimes work-related conversations. Also, many Spaniards outside the company either do not speak English or do not speak it well. Thus, outside of work, expatriates have to spend up to three to four times the amount of time to accomplish the same things if they cannot speak Spanish well.

Although sharing the same language facilitates effective communication, it is only the first level of communication. More deep-rooted, cultural-based phenomena can more seriously affect an expatriate's performance. Countries or regions where a company sends its expatriates can be reasonably divided into categories such as these: (1) minor level of cultural difficulty for adjustment, (2) culturally difficult for adjustment, and (3) a significant level of cultural difficulty for adjustment. Plenty of information is available to help evaluate the difficulty level of assignments from academic research (see, for example, Ronen & Shenkar, 2017). In addition, feedback from a firm's expatriate cadre can help build a picture of the varying difficulty level of specific international assignments.

Rather than having home office managers try to subjectively design the difficulty level of the assignment into their performance appraisal, HR departments could have a built-in, numerical difficulty factor that is multiplied times the quantity obtained by the regular evaluation process (for example, somewhat more difficult = × 1.2; more difficult = × 1.6; much more difficult = × 1.8).

Evaluator: Try to Objectify the Evaluation

Several things can be done to try to make the evaluator's estimation more objective:

1. It makes sense to focus carefully on the on-site manager's appraisal of the employee's performance since this is the individual who has been working with the expatriate and has more day-to-day information to use in their evaluation. Also, if the on-site manager who evaluates the expatriate is of the same nationality as the expatriate, this can be useful given the similar cultural background of both the rater and the ratee, though personality differences can still influence such evaluations (Caligiuri & Day, 2000). Increasingly, integrated evaluation teams are used by multinational corporations to triangulate perceptions of performance to try to develop more nuanced evaluations that can be of higher-level benefit to expatriate managers (Kossek et al., 2017). We argue that integrating the home office manager and the on-site manager in a "co-performance appraisal team" where they combine their scoring, discuss discrepancies, and then come to a holistic evaluation that synthesizes both of their perceptions is the most beneficial way, at present, to generate helpful assessments to both the firm and the expatriate.

2. In cases where a home-site manager creates the written performance evaluation, we argue that the home-site manager should be a former expatriate from the same location. If it is impossible to match locations, the home-site manager should at least have had some expatriate work experience, preferably in the same region as the current expatriate. This is important because when the home-site manager is trying to evaluate the expatriate against criteria with which the home-site manager is unfamiliar relative to the overseas site, inaccurate evaluations can easily occur. For example, in regions of Africa, the dynamics of the workplace can be considerably different from those of, say, Denmark. Whereas stability characterizes Denmark, instability often characterizes some regions of Africa. Labor unrest, political upheavals, different labor laws, and other elements all modify the actual effects a supervisor can have on the labor force's productivity in a company located in these regions of Africa. A manager who has not personally experienced these frustrations will not be able to evaluate an expatriate's productivily accurately. If production is down under the Danish expatriate's watch, their Danish boss may tend to believe it is because the supervisor was not effective.

3. On the other hand, when a local on-site manager is making the written, formal evaluation, the home-site manager should be consulted before the on-site manager completes a formal terminal evaluation. This makes sense because consulting the home-site manager can balance possible hostile evaluations caused by intercultural misunderstandings. An American expatriate we interviewed related the following experience. In France, women are legally allowed to take several months off to have a baby. They are paid during that time, but are not supposed to do any work related to their job. This expatriate had two of the three secretaries take maternity leave simultaneously. Because they would eventually return to work, they were

not replaced with temporary help. The same amount of work, however, still existed. The American expatriate asked them to do some work at home, not really understanding the legalities of such a request as the French women could be fired from their jobs for working at home. One of the women agreed to do it because she felt sorry for him. When the American's French boss found out one of these two secretaries was helping, he became angry and intolerant of the American's actions. The French manager assumed the American should have been aware of French laws governing maternity leave. As a result, the American felt he was given a lower performance evaluation than he deserved. After the American asked his former boss at the home office to intercede and help his French boss understand his reasoning, and after speaking with the home office manager, the French manager decided to modify the performance evaluation to account for the American's learning curve associated with French business law and culture.

Performance Criteria

Here again, special consideration needs to be given to the expatriate's experience. Expatriates are not only performing a specific function, as they would in their domestic operation, but they are also broadening their understanding of their firm's global operations and the inherent interdependencies thereof. As a result, two recommendations are suggested.

MODIFY THE NORMAL PERFORMANCE CRITERIA FOR THE PARTICULAR POSITION TO FIT THE OVERSEAS POSITION AND SITE CHARACTERISTICS

We will use the following example to illustrate this recommendation. Maintaining positive management–labor relations is not a primary performance evaluation criterion in most American firms. Stabilizing the workforce is not highly valued because the workforce is already usually a stable entity. Instead, productivity in terms of the number of units produced or services provided is a highly valued outcome. As such, motivating the workforce to work faster and harder is viewed as being important. In many parts of the world, however, the workforce is not as stable as in the USA. Stability is related to constant production – not necessarily to increasing production – and a steady production amount can be crucial to maintaining market share. In this case, if an expatriate can maintain positive management–labor relations such that the workforce goes on strike only twice instead of 25 times, the expatriate should be rewarded commensurately. In other words, while the expatriate's US counterpart might be rated primarily on production increases, the American expatriate in another country that is less stable in terms of the workforce should be rated on the constancy of production.

How can such modifications in the standard performance criteria be determined? Ideally, returned expatriates who worked at the same site or in the same country should be involved in developing the appropriate measures or ranking of the performance criteria. Only they have first-hand experience of what the possibilities and constraints are like at that site. This developmental cycle should occur approximately every two years, depending on the stability of the site – its culture, personnel, and business cycles. Re-evaluating the criteria and their prioritization periodically will make sure the performance evaluation criteria remain current with the reality of the overseas situation. If expatriate availability is a problem, outside consultants specializing in international human resource management issues can be hired to help create country-specific performance evaluation forms and criteria.

INCLUDE AN EXPATRIATE'S INSIGHTS AS PART OF THE EVALUATION

"Soft" criteria are difficult to measure and therefore legally challenging to support. Nevertheless, every attempt should be made to give the expatriate credit for relevant insights into the interdependencies of domestic and global operations. For example, if an Australian expatriate learns that the reason the firm's plant in Vietnam needs supplies by certain dates is to accommodate cultural norms – or even local laws – such information can be invaluable. Previously, no one at the domestic site understood why the plant in Vietnam always seemed to have such odd or erratic demands about delivery dates. And no one in Vietnam bothered to think that their Australian supplier didn't operate the same way. If delivering supplies on specific dates asked for by their Vietnamese colleagues ensures smoother production or increased sales and profits for the Vietnamese operation, and if the Australian expatriate is a critical link in the communication gap between the Australian and Vietnamese management teams, the expatriate should be given credit for such insights. This should be reflected in the expatriate's performance review.

To obtain this kind of information, either human resources or operational personnel should hold a debriefing session with the expatriate on their return. It should be in an informal interview format so that specific and open-ended questions can be asked. Questions specific to the technical nature of the expatriate's work that relate to the firm's interdependencies should be asked. General questions concerning observations about the relationship between the two operations should also be included.

There is another, even more effective way this aspect of performance review can be handled. At regular intervals – say, every three to six months – the expatriate could be questioned by human resources or operational personnel in the domestic site about how the two operations might better work together. Doing it this way helps maximize the possibility of noting all relevant insights.

CONCLUSION

In the global marketplace, firms that carefully select and manage their internationally assigned personnel will reap the benefits. Today, we continue to see high turnover rates for expatriates when they return (Cave, Roberts, & Muralidharan, 2022). This is primarily due to firms not managing their expatriates' careers well. Firms are not prepared to appropriately reassign expatriates on their re-entry. This indicates that firms do not value the expatriate's experience. This further carries over into the lack of emphasis on adequately evaluating an expatriate's performance. Appropriately evaluating an expatriate's performance is an issue of both fairness to the expatriate and competitive advantage to the firm. With the valuable experience and insights that expatriates gain, retaining them and effectively positioning them in a firm will mean the firm's business strategy will be increasingly guided by those who understand the companies' worldwide operations and markets.

REFERENCES

Akkan, E., Lazarova, M., & Reiche, B.S. (2018). The role of repatriation in and for global careers. In Dickmann, M., Suutari, V., & Wurtz, O. (Eds.), *The management of global careers*. Cham, Switzerland: Palgrave Macmillan, 223–256.

Bader, A.K., Bader, B., Froese, F.J., & Sekiguchi, T. (2021). One way or another? An international comparison of expatriate performance management in multinational companies. *Human Resource Management*, 60(5): 737–752. https://doi.org/10.1002/hrm.22065.

Bebenroth, R., & Froese, F.J. (2020). Consequences of expatriate top manager replacement on foreign subsidiary performance. *Journal of International Management*, 26(2). https://doi.org/10.1016/j.intman.2019.100730.

Caligiuri, P., & Day, D.V. (2000). Effects of self-monitoring on technical, contextual, and assignment-specific performance: A study of cross-national work performance ratings. *Group and Organization Management*, 25(2): 154–174.

Cave, A.H., Roberts, M.J.D., & Muralidharan, E. (2022). Examining antecedents of repatriates' job engagement and its influence on turnover intention. *The International Journal of Human Resource Management*. https://doi.org/10.1080/09585192.2022.2145911.

Cerdin, J.-L., & Brewster, C. (2014). Talent management and expatriation: Bridging two streams of research and practice. *Journal of World Business*, 49(2): 245–252.

Chenyang, L. (2022). Meta-analysis of the impact of cross-cultural training on adjustment, cultural intelligence, and job performance. *Career Development International*, 27(2): 185–200.

Dang, Q.T., Rammal, H.G., & Michailova, S. (2022). Expatriates' families: A systematic literature review and research agenda. *Human Resource Management Review*, 32(4):100877

DeNisi, A., Murphy, K., Varma, A., & Budhwar, P. (2021). Performance management systems and multinational enterprises: Where we are and where we should go? *Human Resource Management*, 60(5): 701–713.

Gai, S., Brough, P., & Gardiner, E. (2021). Psychological adjustment and post-arrival cross-cultural training for better expatriation: A systematic review. In Brough, P., Gardiner, E., & Daniels, K. (Eds.), *Handbook on management and employment practices*, Handbook Series in Occupational Health Sciences. Cham, Switzerland: Springer, 1–28.

Han, Y., Sears, G.J., Darr, W.A., & Wang, Y. (2022). Facilitating cross-cultural adaptation: A meta-analytic review of dispositional predictors of expatriate adjustment. *Journal of Cross-Cultural Psychology*, 53(9): 1054–1096.

Harzing, A., Pudelko, M., & Reiche, B.S. (2016). The bridging role of expatriates and inpatriates in knowledge transfer in multinational corporations. *Human Resource Management,* 55(4): 679–695.

Kobrin, S.J. (1988). Expatriate reduction and strategic control in American multinational corporations. *Human Resource Management,* 27(1): 63–75.

Kossek, E.E., Huang, J.L., Piszczek, M.M., Fleenor, J.W., & Ruderman, M. (2017). Rating expatriate leader effectiveness in multisource feedback systems: Cultural distance and hierarchical effects. *Human Resource Management,* 56(1): 151–172.

Mercer. (2019). *Global performance management study insights: Performance transformation in the future of work.* Last accessed on 5 April 2022 at https://www .mercer.us/our-thinking/career/global-performance-management-study-2019.html.

Motowidlo, S., & Van Scotter, J. (1994). Evidence that task performance should be distinguished from contextual performance. *Journal of Applied Psychology,* 79(4): 475–480.

Murphy, K.R. (2020). Performance evaluation will not die, but it should. *Human Resource Management Journal,* 30(1): 13–31.

Neeley, T.B., & Reiche, B.S. (2022). How global leaders gain power through downward deference and reduction of social distance. *Academy of Management Journal,* 65(1): 11–34.

Oddou, G., & Mendenhall, M. (1991). Succession planning in the 21st century: How well are we grooming our future business leaders? *Business Horizons,* 34(1): 26–34.

Pucik, V., Evans, P., Björkman, I., & Morris, S. (2017). *The global challenge: International human resource management* (3rd ed.). Chicago, IL: Chicago Business Press.

Ronen, S., & Shenkar, O. (2017). *Navigating global business: A cultural compass.* Cambridge: Cambridge University Press.

Shaffer, M., Harrison, D., & Gilley, K. (1999). Dimensions, determinants, and differences in the expatriate adjustment process. *Journal of International Business Studies,* 30(3): 557–581.

Suutari, V., & Tahvanainen, M. (2002). The antecedents of performance management among Finnish expatriates. *The International Journal of Human Resource Management,* 13: 55–75.

Vaiman, V., McNulty, Y., & Haslberger, A. (2021). Herding cats: Expatriate talent acquisition and development. In Tarique, I. (Ed.), *The Routledge companion to talent management.* New York: Routledge, 359–371.

Varma, A., Wang, C., & Budhwar, P. (2020). Performance management for expatriates. In Bonache, J., Brewster, C., & Froese, F. (Eds.), *Global mobility and the management of expatriates,* Cambridge Companions to Management. Cambridge: Cambridge University Press, 80–99.

Varma, A., Wang, C., & Coleman, T. (2022). Performance management for expatriates. In Toh, S.M., & DeNisi, A. (Eds.), *Expatriates and managing global mobility,* New York: Routledge, 45–57.

Jaime Bonache, Celia Zárraga-Oberty, and Luigi Stirpe

THE COMPENSATION OF CORPORATE EXPATRIATES

INTRODUCTION

THE DIVIDE BETWEEN THE PROFESSIONAL and academic world, analysed at length in the general management literature, finds an illustrative example in the field of international compensation. While the academic literature has paid this subject very little attention, it is a very important factor in the professional world. Human resource professionals working in multinational corporations (MNCs) report that the problems associated with the design and management of expatriates' pay packages take up most of their time and energy (Bonache, Sánchez, & Zárraga-Oberty, 2009; Caligiuri & Bonache, 2016; Festing & Perkins, 2008). This is logical due to the complexity of the matter, the impact this remuneration has on corporate expenditure, and, above all, its influence on the firm's ability to attract, retain, and galvanize the talent it requires to successfully undertake its international operations. This topic is not adequately addressed in the academic literature, although it is relatively easy to find studies that analyse topics such as (1) the goals and approaches for the design and implementation of global mobility, (2) the typical challenges and difficulties to be addressed in this area, (3) the trends that may be observed in this policy, and (4) the issues and key contingency factors deserving more attention from the literature. This reading reviews the relatively scarce literature on these four issues and provides a summary of the current landscape of international compensation.

APPROACHES TO COMPENSATING GLOBAL MOBILITY

When we talk about compensating international mobility in a multinational company, we have to clarify which employees we are talking about. Firstly, there are

DOI: 10.4324/9781003247272-19

the so-called flexpatriates, employees who travel for brief assignments across cultural and national borders, leaving their families at home (Shortland, 2018). Included in this category, for example, are commuters (employees travelling usually weekly from home to their assignment locations), rotational assignees (employees travelling abroad to work shifts for regular, set periods followed by rest periods off-shift at home), and international business travellers (employees who take multiple short business trips to various locations). The sending company is responsible for the flexpatriates' compensation, there are no tax implications, and it will depend on the company's travel policy.

Another type of corporate expatriate is the short-term assignee. Their assignments typically last between three and 12 months, are usually unaccompanied, and assignment lengths may reflect taxation implications (Shortland, 2018). When employees are assigned a short-term posting, firms may use the information provided by consultancies (e.g., regarding the amounts usually paid in a series of expense categories, such as food, hotels, transportation, etc.) to set each employee's corresponding allowances. As with the flexpatriates, the sending unit will be responsible for the specific method of compensation for short-term assignees, which will depend on the company's travel policy. As mentioned earlier, taxation may be an issue – depending on duration – and it is therefore very normal for companies to rely on an external consultant. Indeed, according to KPMG's (2018) Global Assignment Policies and Practices Survey, outsourcing tax preparation not only for short-term assignees, but also (particularly) for long-term assignees is a practice used by over 90% of companies.

Long-term assignees are corporate expatriates who are sent abroad on a temporary basis to complete a time-based task or accomplish an organizational goal. They are typically sent abroad for more than one year and up to a maximum of three or four years, and their immediate family (if they have them) usually accompany them. The process of designing the compensation package for long-term assignees is especially complex (Bonache, 2006; Harvey, 1993a, 1993b; Suutari & Tornikoski, 2000, 2001; Shortland, 2018). Within this ambit, a whole series of factors or critical elements need to be taken into careful consideration, which nonetheless tend to be omitted when the aim is to set the salary for domestic employees or host-country nationals (HCNs). We are referring here to elements such as the employee's home country, their family circumstances (e.g., number and ages of children and their partner's employment status), the quality and size of their home, floating exchange rates, differences in living costs, taxes and inflation rates, the need to reconcile home- and host-country compensation laws and regulations, and the geographically imposed problems of communication and control. These issues increase both the complexity of the situation and the information needed with regard to individuals and their postings (Suutari & Tornikoski, 2001; Bonache, 2006). We will be focusing on the compensation of long-term assignments in this reading.

Compensation and benefits arrangements for long-term assignees typically follow one of two main approaches: the balance sheet system and the local-plus system. The balance sheet is the most popular expatriate reward approach

(Shortland, 2018). According to Mercer (2020), two-thirds of participating companies in a survey use a home-based balance sheet as the typical remuneration approach for long-term assignees. The idea of this approach is that expatriates maintain their home-country standard of living and retain equity with home peers. By keeping expatriates in line with conditions at home, they can seamlessly slot back into their lives after their overseas posting.

The system was designed by a group of economists in the 1950s and 60s, with one of the leading lights being G. F. Dickover, who is considered to be its foremost champion (Dickover, 1957). His work was probably naïve on a theoretical level, but original and full of potential on a practical level. The system's point of departure involves the five goals to which an international remuneration system should aspire (Bonache, 2006): (1) to ease the transfer of international employees in the most cost-effective manner, (2) to be consistent and fair in the treatment of all its employees, (3) to attract (and satisfy) personnel in the areas where the MNC has its greatest needs and opportunities, (4) to facilitate the retention of international assignees in the home country at the end of the foreign assignment, and (5) to foster the expatriate behaviours required for implementing effective global strategies.

With these goals in mind, the balance sheet approach begins with the employee's reference salary. This is the pay employees receive either in their home country (as mentioned earlier, the most frequent option), in their receiving or host country, or according to an international salary scheme as per their job duties. This reference salary is then divided into four items or categories of expenditure: goods and services, housing, taxes, and savings. The amount allocated to each one of these items will depend largely on the level of income and the size of the household. It is fair to say that the more we earn and the larger our household, the more we spend, for example, on goods and services (i.e., transport, food, clothing, and entertainment). Therein lies the need for tables that specify what people with different income levels and personal circumstances spend on each one of the four blocks of expenditure.

Once the reference salary has been divided into these four elements, the system makes a series of calculations and adjustments to specify the host-country salary. These include differentials or allowances conceived as *equalizers* (i.e., cost of living differential, housing allowance, and tax differential), designed to guarantee expatriates' purchasing power by making sure that employees are no better and no worse off than if they had not taken the assignment, or as *motivators*, designed to incentivize employees to take the international assignment by compensating them for the "inconveniences" of living abroad (Philips & Fox, 2003). These motivators have different technical terms, such as "overseas premiums" (Reynolds, 1997), which are a percentage of the reference salary paid monthly during expatriation, or "mobility premiums", which are lump-sum payments made at the beginning and end of an assignment (Philips & Fox, 2003).

In addition to the reference salary, the equalizers, and the motivators, one should add performance bonuses as well as a number of other services and benefits, conceived as *enablers* (i.e., services and benefits provided to help the employee relocate and focus on their role). This category may include medical insurance, flights home, support for the accompanying partner, and schooling for the accompanying children.

With the local-plus system (see Figure 1), an expatriate receives a salary that is consistent with the pay scales in the host or receiving country, but it is increased by a series of allowances, such as those for transport, housing, and children's schooling (McNulty, 2015). The package of allowances is not the same for all expatriates. The decision is made by the firm, being determined largely by the assignment's location (i.e., the location's degree of hardship), among other factors. This approach is attractive for employees when the levels of pay for a given position are significantly higher in the host country (O'Really, 1996). It is also used for the early stages of permanent moves abroad. The employee is helped to relocate, to be later treated as a local employee.

The local-plus compensation system is different to the localization system, which is a much less generous compensation method for international work. In this system, the employee simply receives a salary that is consistent with the salary levels in their receiving country, and the "expatriate" status is removed from their package (McNulty, 2015). Localization used to be a rare approach as it was difficult to find expatriates receiving only local terms and conditions (Shortland, 2018). However, according to Mercer (2020), a majority of companies have localized assignees during the last two years, and localization is now part of the long-term assignment policy for 43% of the respondents. The countries in which a majority of respondents have localized assignees are the US (53%), UK (15%), Singapore (14%), China (11%), Germany (10%), and Australia (8%).

The local-plus and localization compensation systems are an alternative to the balance sheet approach. Their advocates contend that they are better suited

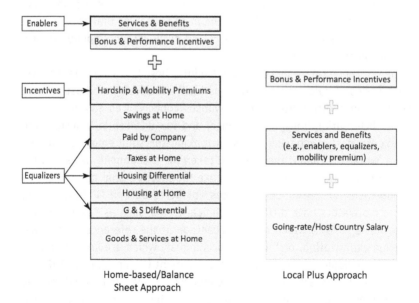

Figure 1 Approaches to compensating long-term assigned expatriates.

to the new global mobility scenario in the highly globalized 21st century. As mentioned at the beginning of this section, we now have a huge variety of profiles and situations that fall within the category of international mobility. We can no longer simply assume, as the balance sheet approach does, that expatriates will return to their country of origin after a relatively short period of time (one to four years), that interest in the assignment lies above all with the company (consider, for example, employees who, for personal or family reasons, wish to work abroad; Shortland, 2016), that repatriation will always take place or be planned, and that equity with employees in the home country is the essential type of equity to be kept (Phillips & Fox, 2003). We require greater variety in the nature of compensation to accommodate the different types of global mobility, and the local-plus compensation system can often be the most suitable.

A number of consultants (e.g., Mercer, KPMG, etc.) provide companies with data on the allowances and benefits most commonly provided for long-term assignees. Some of them may go unnoticed by the expatriates, who will come to consider them as part of their destination salary (e.g., the cost of living differential), but others may be very important for them. In this respect, there are studies that examine, from the employees' point of view, how important the different elements of compensation are when deciding to accept or reject an assignment. For example, Warneke and Schneider (2011) conducted an empirical study in which they analysed 21 benefits, each with two or three levels, that were being offered by a German company to Spanish and German expatriates. When the respondents were asked to select the five most important characteristics out of these 21 attributes, the elements most frequently mentioned were the salary (71%), support for the accompanying partner (60%), the reintegration guarantee (58%), schooling for the accompanying children (41%), and the location bonus (32%). Clearly, the specific importance of these attributes for the expatriates depended on their individual profile. For example, single, young expatriates may not care as much about schooling and partner support as middle-aged employees with children and an accompanying partner. It is interesting to see how some of these preferences were subject to certain societal effects. For example, for a hypothetical assignment in the USA, the attribute "look-and-see trip" was important for 33% of the German respondents, but for only 9% of the Spanish respondents. These preferences within the company cannot be understood unless the larger institutions of a society are analysed. This opens the way for studying international compensation from a cross-cultural perspective, an approach that is under-used.

CHALLENGES AND DIFFICULTIES TO BE ADDRESSED IN THE DESIGN OF EXPATRIATION PACKAGES

The balance sheet approach and the local-plus approach are excellent arrangements for avoiding a strictly individual negotiation. This explains their popularity when it comes to setting the salary of many employees posted abroad. Nevertheless, they are not without difficulties. Let us focus on some of the key challenges and issues in this area.

The Issue of Costs

This is the most common challenge, and also the most obvious one. The expatriate package identifies and includes a whole series of salary items (i.e., bonuses, allowances, and benefits) that make international assignments a very expensive option (Bonache et al., 2009; Tornikoski, Suutari, & Festing, 2014). It has been calculated that the cost of international staff is now 2.4 times higher than that of their equivalent HCNs of the same level and category (Mercer, 2020). In addition to direct costs, there are also indirect ones, such as administrative costs, which although lower, are not insignificant (Nowak & Linder, 2016). Expatriation packages require at least regular attention and updating, but this may sometimes need to be continuous. Let us take, for example, the cost of living allowance, which offsets the difference in the shopping basket (for the same range and quantity of products that include transport, food, clothing, household items, and entertainment) in the host country compared to the home country. Depending on the host country's stability, this allowance is reviewed on a yearly, half-yearly, or even monthly basis by a specialized outside firm with which regular contact needs to be maintained. All this requires staff time and effort (Nowak & Linder, 2016). The increasingly more common practice of subcontracting the collection and calculation (including cost estimates) of assignment compensation, which now extends to 45% of organizations (KPMG, 2018), is a good reflection of the indirect costs associated with this activity.

One element that affects the high cost of assignments is the "foreign service premium". Why is there a need to include a "foreign service premium"? Traditionally, before the onset of globalization in the 1990s, the need to incentivize mobility through assignment premiums seemed obvious (Caligiuri & Bonache, 2016). In the 1960s, Dickover, the system's pioneer, mentioned earlier, provided us with a very clear explanation:

> A construction worker, nomadic by background, may be enticed by high wages to undertake a two-year stint in Iceland or Patagonia, but career employment in Cuba or Venezuela holds little attraction for this year's graduating chemical engineer – or his wife or sweetheart – or even less for the married man with three or five or 12 years of domestic service with the company.
>
> (Dickover, 1957: cited by Reynolds, 1997)

If we overlook the text's sexist tone, it is this type of reasoning that is still used today to justify premium incentives. In addition to family and personal issues (such as the growing importance of quality of life considerations; Shaffer, Harrison, & Gilley, 1999), and the continued uncertainty regarding international terrorism and the political and social unrest in certain destinations (Welch, Welch, & Tahvanainen, 2008), it is frequently mentioned that the career implications of international assignments are often frustrating (Warneke & Schneider, 2011). A lack of respect for acquired skills, loss of status, and reverse culture shock upon return are recurring problems in many companies (Stahl, Miller, & Tung, 2002). For these reasons, or barriers to international mobility, many individuals will not agree to move unless they are offered a generous compensation system (Shortland, 2018). In other cases, however, the trade-off between pay, living conditions (e.g., housing, schooling, partner assistance, etc.), and career aspects can lead to a different result. For example, the salary during the assignment may be lower if the employee receives a credible promise of a subsequent promotion (Warneke & Schneider, 2011). It has also been shown that, contrary to the opinion of their HR managers, while monetary compensation is appreciated by female expatriates, if they reject a location on the grounds of living conditions (e.g. spouse employment, education being unsuitable for their families), additional incentive payments do not serve to change their minds (Shortland, 2016).

The Issue of Fairness

In order to be motivating, the rewards need to be perceived as fair. According to equity theory (Festinger, 1954; Adams, 1965), this perception arises in a social medium as the result of comparing the ratio of our contributions and rewards with that same ratio among other individuals, who thereby act as referents for comparison purposes. Dissimilar ratios lead to perceptions of inequity. This proposition implies that the same organizational circumstance may be perceived as fair or unfair depending on which individual or group of individuals the worker chooses for the comparison. Accordingly, a major concern when analysing people's satisfaction with their compensation system involves identifying the referent used in the individual's comparisons.

The problem faced by expatriate employees is that there are multiple potential referents (Bonache, 2006). They may compare themselves not only to other expatriates within the same company and host country, but also to expatriates within the same company and other host countries, expatriates from other companies within their host country, HCNs, and so forth. The home-country balance sheet approach, for example, insists on the need to refer to a person's peers in the home country (Philips & Fox, 2003). The assumption is that as expatriates will be repatriated after a relatively short period of time (three to five years), it is more appropriate to compare them to employees in their home country (Phillips & Fox, 2003).

Unfortunately, prioritizing a sense of fairness has the drawback in salary terms of discriminating against HCNs, as they are very likely to consider this situation to be unfair. This is regrettable because HCNs are valuable socializing agents, sources of social support, assistance, and friendship for expatriates (Toh & DeNisi, 2003). The disparity in pay may induce HCNs to become uncooperative or antagonistic, which could even compromise the expatriate's performance.

The issues of unfairness with regard to HCNs are so important that many studies have sought to identify the factors that may offset or attenuate the negative influence a pay differential has on the inequity perceived among HCNs (e.g., Chen, Choi, & Chi, 2002; Bonache et al., 2009; Leung, Zhu, & Ge, 2009; Paik,

Parboteeah, & Shim, 2007). Thanks to these studies, we know that this perception is especially marked, for instance, when an HCN does not perceive a salary advantage over locals in other companies, when they do not see logical reasons for high expatriate compensation, and when expatriates do not have the appropriate interpersonal skills.

Expatriation Packages and Cross-cultural Development

The generous compensation packages traditionally offered to expatriates typically favour or foster a type of experience in which expatriates live in cultural bubbles or relatively isolated and well-"sheltered" communities, with globally neutral shops, language, schools, and activities. Needless to say, this is not the best way of encouraging enculturation or an understanding of what it is like to live and work in another country. Instead, what it does is stop the expatriate from facing a new situation and adjusting to local salary conditions and standards. Engaging in work challenges in cultures that differ from the predominant societal values of expatriates' home culture are the hallmark of what makes these global mobility experiences truly developmental (Caligiuri & Bonache, 2016), and compensation should not be an exception.

Furthermore, it is not simply that the traditional expatriation packages do not favour development, but that they might often negate it. For example, the differential of goods and services in the home-country balance sheet approach assumes that expatriates and their families wish to maintain the same lifestyle. They are not expected to change their shopping habits, yet this assumption is highly debatable. People change as a result of their international experience, and part of the intercultural learning process actually involves assimilating habits and products from beyond one's own frontiers.

The Tension between Attraction and Retention

Although people may accept an international assignment for a variety of reasons (e.g., career development, a more satisfactory position in the host country or upon repatriation, a spirit of adventure, the enjoyment of a cosmopolitan lifestyle, or the opportunity for children to become proficient in another language), money is one of the more tangible assets and is easier to quantify, which explains why organizations, in full awareness of the significant role money plays in the decision to accept an international assignment, have made generous salary packages the simplest and most widely used strategy for attracting talent to foreign postings (Bonache, 2006).

It is arguable whether this emphasis on the monetary component is equally effective when the aim is to retain talent once the person is working in the host country. The turnover of expatriates in host countries is not a topic that has been widely studied, although there is circumstantial evidence that it might be significant. Existing evidence shows that when analysing the factors that induce people to stay with the organization, money does not play a key role (Reiche, Kraimer,

& Harzing, 2011). The decisive factors are career openings or perspectives, recognition, support from and relationships with supervisors, or emotional ties with the organization's management or members. If an expatriate lacks these elements, and only has financial reasons for staying with the company, other companies will not find it difficult to attract them through an equal salary offer. Likewise, competitors will find it very difficult to recruit expatriates if they are content and satisfied (Yan, Zhu, & Hall, 2002).

The problem, nevertheless, is not that generous salary packages may help to attract but not retain staff during the assignment period, but that they may even be the trigger for turnover once the posting has ended. Research has consistently reported high turnover rates among repatriates, which some studies place at 20–50% (Reiche et al., 2011). Although there are numerous reasons for this high turnover (e.g., greater opportunities elsewhere, new contacts, and lack of recognition), compensation has its role to play. The incentives and allowances designed to encourage employees to take up a foreign assignment are not sustained when the expatriate returns home, leading to a substantial loss of income. In fact, such a loss of income is cited as one of the main difficulties upon return (Bonache, 2006).

The possible downside of generous salary packages on the retention of repatriates is not so paradoxical when we analyse it in the light of more recent research into job turnover (Chen, Ployhart, Thomas, Anderson, & Bliese, 2011). This has highlighted how the essential trigger for job turnover is the nature of the change in satisfaction, rather than overall levels of satisfaction. Let us take as an example the situation depicted in Figure 1. It shows two individuals, α and β, who at the time of repatriation have identical levels of job satisfaction. According to the standard literature on job turnover, and all other things being equal (openings in other companies, recognition of their experience within the company, etc.), they will be equally likely to accept a job in another company. Nevertheless, as Figure 2 shows, α has held a foreign posting, a situation that was very satisfactory because of the generous incentives received. By contrast, β was subject to local employment conditions, which were not nearly as favourable; α sees this opportunity as a change for the worse, while β considers it an improvement. Let us assume that by taking a job in another company, α loses out by 10% and β gains by that same 10%. By applying the logic of Prospect Theory (Kahneman & Tversky, 1984) formulated by Daniel Kahneman, a Nobel Prize winner, the more likely scenario is that the loss of that percentage by α will generate more dissatisfaction than the satisfaction gained by β from that same figure (10%). As posited within the framework of this theory, the problem is that we hate losing more than we love winning. This will make α more inclined than β to accept exactly the same job offer. While the former will be risk-seeking, the latter will be more risk-averse. If this is indeed the case, an attractive pay package abroad may drive global mobility, but reduce a company's ability to retain employees upon their return.

The problem of retaining employees is also an issue in the localization system. Throughout the entire posting, the firm has to deal with local competition.

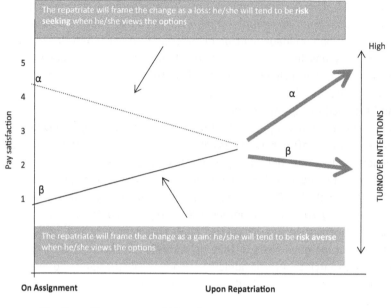

α Employee with a generous expatriate package

β Employee with an average local contract

Figure 2 Pay satisfaction change and turnover intentions.

Source: Bonache & Zárraga-Oberty (2017)

Localization systems mean that employees' opportunity cost is greatly reduced, and they will therefore be more willing to swap their allegiance more readily than if they were subject to the traditional balance sheet system. This therefore clearly increases the firm's risk of losing employees (McNulty, 2014). For international staff, the opportunity cost of leaving the firm is very low, both in terms of salary (they do not receive the traditionally high pay packages) and emotionally (psychological contract) as they do not create an employment relationship whereby they are obliged to give more because they receive more.

TRENDS IN INTERNATIONAL COMPENSATION

Following an analysis of the possible ways of compensating international postings and the challenges and issues companies need to address in this area, we will now highlight what firms are actually doing. There are three core tendencies: reducing costs, increasing the internal differentiation of compensation packages, and focusing more on the value of assignments.

More Cost Control

According to a recent survey (KPMG, 2018), 40% of companies consider that expatriates are overpaid. However, there is nothing new about this view of expatriation as being very costly. Quite the opposite, it is an opinion that has been regularly reflected in all the surveys conducted over the past 20 years. Indeed, a survey by Brookfield Global Relocation Services (2015) indicates that 23% of companies report that the cost of these postings is the main challenge they face within the field of global mobility.

The increasing use of the localization approach can be interpreted as a way of reducing expatriation costs. Another initiative has been to increase the number of short-term postings and commuter assignments involved in working abroad (Bonache, 2006). These two solutions are more economical, as they do not involve – or they do so to a lesser extent – many of the costly items included in the compensation package of many long-term assignments (e.g., education or partner allowance).

A third way of reducing costs has involved examining traditional items of expenditure and looking for ways of applying cuts to each of them. When we compare the data on the conditions of expatriation, there is a noticeable increase in the number of companies that, for example, reduce costs by: (1) merging all the incentives and allowances into a single item (with a lower allocation than the sum of their separate amounts); (2) paying allowances as lump sums, paying part upfront and the rest when the assignment has been successfully completed (with the ensuing cost saving in the event of non-completion); (3) using tax equalization (the employee pays neither more nor less tax than they would have paid in the home country) as opposed to a tax protection policy (the employee pays no more than they would have paid in the home country, but may pay less in certain situations); or (4) making alternative downward adjustments in other differentials such as cost of living or housing. All-in-all, over a period of 20 years, those companies that remunerate their expatriates using the balance sheet approach have reduced the gap between the average costs of expatriates and those of equivalent local managers significantly, going from a ratio of 3.5 in 1997 (Reynolds, 1997) to one of 2.4 (Mercer, 2020).

Salary Differentiation among Expatriates (and Its Legitimization)

Despite the advantages of one or other international compensation system, we have stressed that no arrangement is without its difficulties, which are due to the numerous goals that the system seeks to achieve. Some understand or restrict the purpose of the system to simply being an instrument for attracting and motivating employees to accept an international posting in order to enable the firm to compete globally. But this general objective must be accompanied by more specific ones, such as cost control, facilitating repatriation, or upholding equity across groups of employees (Bonache, 2006; Bonache & Zárraga-Oberty, 2020). This is an extremely challenging issue because it is almost impossible to achieve all these objectives at the same time. For example, the objective of attracting staff can be readily achieved by offering a generous pay package, although, as we have seen, such a policy may have a number of negative consequences: it incurs high costs for the firm in terms of both gross and management expenses, it leads to inequity perceptions among HCNs, and it may make repatriation more difficult.

The tension between conflicting objectives results in internal differentiation between groups of expatriates (AIR Inc, 2010, 2011; Bitten, 2001; Bonache & Zárraga-Oberty, 2020), in which, depending on the group involved, some objectives will be prioritized over others. For executive postings, the balance sheet approach with high premiums and benefits is normally used (Phillips & Fox, 2003). This system makes assignments financially very attractive for employees, albeit at the cost of impeding the achievement of other objectives, such as costs, equity, and cultural integration. These other objectives, however, can be pursued through alternative systems, such as local-plus or localization (McNulty, 2015), and can be applied to other expatriates (e.g., women whose assignment is driven by the expatriation of their partners employed by the same firm; see Shortland, 2016), who in some cases will be compensated according to the salary conditions in the host country (localization), or in others, also according to the host country, but increased by a series of allowances. In short, it is common today to encounter a broad range of formal arrangements (Yan et al., 2002), with the same company applying both contractual relationships (those based on long-term service and loyalty) and transactional ones (project-based), as well as very attractive compensation packages for some expatriates, and more modest ones for others.

How can this internal differentiation in salary conditions between expatriates be justified? It is obvious that it cannot be explained in terms of needs, as these should be the same, for example, for both a key executive and a veteran employee with children who are relocated abroad. The way the compensation literature justifies an unequal allocation of rewards is by referring to the respective contributions of the different employees. This requires calling upon the merit-based equity norm, whereby rewards should be proportional to contributions. It is the reference norm, and also the most representative one within the sphere of MNCs (Toh & DeNisi, 2003). The person assigned to an executive position is valued as crucial, requiring the company to offer an attractive salary and the substantial benefits traditionally associated with expatriate positions. This preference has a moral sense: it is understood to be the most legitimate way of distributing rewards, particularly in Western thinking, where it is considered unfair to compensate individuals on an equal basis when their inputs or contributions are unequal.

This way of legitimizing differences both promotes and justifies a series of relative comparisons in which each individual will be comparing their respective inputs and outputs. It is highly likely that this process will create problems of inequity (e.g., between expatriate groups subject to very different conditions), although it is often assumed to be the price that has to be paid if the organization is to compete globally in a cost-effective manner (Toh & DeNisi, 2003).

More Focus on the Value of Assignments

As we have seen, companies have paid a great deal of attention to costs. This explains the steady fall in the number of management expatriates, and their replacement with other options that are more economical and satisfactory not only for the parent company, but also for the subsidiary. If an assignment's value added is not readily apparent, it is highly unlikely to take place (Farndale, Scullion, & Sparrow, 2010; McNulty, De Cieri, & Hutchings, 2009). In any case, as argued in the next section, although companies are paying increasing attention to the value of assignments, more research is needed on the actual impact of international assignments on both the company and the employee.

A FUTURE RESEARCH AGENDA

So far, we have focused on the challenges and difficulties of different approaches to compensate global mobility. Though discussion of these systems will continue to attract the attention of practitioners, there are a number of more strategic topics which should also attract academics' interest and guide future research in this area. We will classify these topics into three main areas: (1) the determinants of expatriate compensation, (2) the effects of different expatriate compensation systems, and (3) the way to study global compensation. The following is a brief analysis of these topics as well as the theories that support their investigation.

The Determinants of Expatriate Compensation

VIRTUAL MOBILITY AND INCREASED FLEXIBILITY

The context must be considered as an essential contingency factor in the design and implementation of expatriates' compensation packages. One essential context change is growing virtual mobility. In the Brookfield Global Relocation Services (2021) Talent Mobility Survey, which explored the views of 123 mobility professionals on what lies ahead for mobility beyond 2020, respondents said that employee mobility was at a turning point as physical mobility remains resilient, while virtual mobility was emerging; 82% of respondents believed that more flexibility would have a direct impact on the mobile employee experience. We need research focused on the impact of those trends and changes on expatriate packages and on how the mobile employee experience is affected by the ability of firms to administer flexible benefits programmes.

THE TYPE OF ORGANIZATION

In contrast to the early assumption from the literature that the type of organization is irrelevant to compensation decisions (Edström & Galbraith, 1977), a recent qualitative interpretive study (Bonache & Zárraga-Oberty, 2020) on the challenge of designing expatriation pay in a workers' cooperative has highlighted the impact of the organizational context on the way that compensation is understood and managed. As opposed to the conventional view analysed in this reading, which involves supporting the business by meeting multiple and conflicting objectives (e.g., satisfying expatriates' needs and expectations, controlling costs, ensuring equity with local employees, facilitating repatriation, etc.), the challenge is understood in the cooperative as redesigning the policy so that its organizational identity is respected and upheld. The debates that are normally the focus of attention in the literature (e.g., How can we attract staff to an expatriate assignment without it becoming too costly? How can we avoid a situation of inequity with local staff? How can we ensure the return is not seen as a pay cut?) are not the ones discussed by cooperative members, nor do they even feature on their agendas. Instead, they are predominated by discussions on how to achieve a remuneration policy that while being competitive, is still consistent with the cooperative's social mission and (democratic) decision-making process. The tension between financial and social performance, which characterizes a large part of the literature on social enterprises, also appears in relation to this specific HR policy. Once the challenge is thus understood, the way of managing it and the compensation decisions adopted are also very different to the conventional approach (see Bonache & Zárraga-Oberty, 2020). Clearly, we need more qualitative interpretive research on how the type of organization, including non-governmental organizations, political organizations, armed forces, charities, not-for-profit corporations, etc., may follow a very different logic from the one that we have represented in the rest of this reading for conventional MNCs.

CONTROL AND MONITORING NEEDS

Agency theory (Gómez-Mejía, Berrone, & Franco-Santos, 2014) offers a useful perspective on analysing how the need to control executive decisions impacts compensation packages. This theory is relevant to situations that have a principal–agent structure. The HQ–expatriate relationship corresponds to a principal–agent structure: HQ (the principal) delegates work and responsibilities to expatriates (the agents). In this type of relationship, there is a risk that the "agency problem" may arise. This refers to the possibility that agents will pursue their own interests, which may diverge from the interests of the principal. This is a real possibility in the multinational arena. For example, in a subsidiary located in a culturally different environment, it is possible for an expatriate to enjoy excellent work conditions while making very little effort. Their resulting poor performance can then be excused by attributing it to the lack of fit of the company's procedures to the local culture. Incentive alignment is a traditional device used to address the agency problem. This is defined as the extent to which the reward structure is designed to induce managers to make decisions that are in the best interests of the principal (Gómez-Mejía et al., 2014). Properly designed, the reward structure promotes self-monitoring as it provides performance incentives that encourage agents to minimize opportunism and promote their alignment with the principal's interests. Through these performance incentives, expatriates pursuing their own goals will also be pursuing the goal of the HQ. From an agency perspective, future research could analyse how different configurations of the expatriate incentives (i.e., the proportion of bonuses and long-term incentives versus salary and benefits, the short and long time horizons of incentives, the quantitative and qualitative criteria used to trigger rewards), respond to the intentions of the MNC to solve the agency problem, and procure an appropriate alignment of interests between the company and expatriates.

STRATEGIC POSITION OF THE EXPATRIATE

While in the literature it is usual to refer to long-term corporate expatriates as a homogenous group of employees, a closer look at the strategic position they can occupy abroad allows us to make some distinctions that have important implications for international compensation strategies. Just as in other categories of employees, long-term corporate expatriates can perform different sorts of jobs. Specifically, we can discern between "star" and "guardian" positions (Baron & Kreps, 1999; Bonache & Noethen, 2014). This distinction is based on the possible effects on total company performance of the individual outcomes of the employees who occupy these positions. Star jobs are those in which bad performance is not particularly critical, but good performance is very beneficial for the company. A long-term corporate expatriate performing a star job would be a manager who runs a subsidiary that has very little dependence on HQ (e.g., in terms of its products, brand image, or procedures) and where what is essential is developing new projects highly tailored to the local market. Guardian jobs are those in which exemplary performance will be of little consequence for the company's accomplishments, but bad performance will cause a disaster. A guardian job for a long-term corporate expatriate would be that of representing the firm to important external constituencies of the host country, the reputation of the firm being a valuable asset. Subsidiary managers in the financial industry typically fall within this category.

Effects of Compensation Packages

EXAMINING THE EFFECTS OF ALTERNATIVE COMPENSATION APPROACHES

As mentioned earlier, organizations can use different approaches for compensating their expatriates (e.g., balanced scorecard, local-plus). However, little is known about the relative performance outcomes of these approaches, and research aimed at filling these actual knowledge gaps is therefore desirable. The outcomes to be explored may involve different analytical levels (e.g., expatriates, HCNs, organization). Furthermore, these outcomes can be examined considering individual and organizational contingencies. Research endeavours should also be dedicated to the effects of compensation schemes based on so-called idiosyncratic deals (i-deals) – that is, customized reward packages negotiated individually by expatriates with the organization. Like other HR i-deals, compensation i-deals are driven by individual-level factors, such as personal goals and needs (see Rousseau, Ho, & Greenberg, 2006). Previous research suggests that HR i-deals affect a wide range of employee attitudes and behaviours, with i-dealers showing higher levels of performance and organizational attachment (Liao,

Wayne, & Rousseau, 2016). Social exchange theory is used as the explanatory mechanism of these positive effects. One would therefore expect that compensation i-deals also boost expatriates' productive contributions, while improving their overall experience abroad. Yet, despite such personalized reward systems gaining increased popularity (Fulmer & Li, 2022), organizations seem to consider them only marginally when it comes to expatriate compensation. Indeed, more than three-quarters of the organizations surveyed by Mercer (2020) had a standard policy applied globally, with only 5% handling assignments on a case-by-case basis. On the other hand, Mercer's (2020) survey also highlighted that the expatriate profile was becoming more multifaceted in terms of gender, sexual orientation, generation, and family status. This diversity calls for reward systems that are more meaningful from an individual perspective. Importantly, however, while they may be highly valuable from expatriates' perspectives, compensation i-deals may exacerbate perceptions of unfairness among HCNs and also trigger similar perceptions among expatriates (see Rousseau et al., 2006), thus generating increasing implementation costs. These potential tensions may further inform future research projects.

CROSS-CULTURAL RESEARCH ON EXPATRIATES' SATISFACTION WITH THEIR COMPENSATION

As mentioned earlier, MNCs commonly design different compensation systems for different types of expatriates. It would be reasonable to expect that this would lead to different levels of satisfaction among expatriates regarding their compensation. The evidence on this point is, however, non-existent. The influence of nationality on expatriates' attitudes toward their salaries is another important, and complementary, topic to examine. As mentioned earlier, some studies have analysed the existence of societal effects on employees' preferences for certain components of the expatriation package (Warneke & Schneider, 2011). Other studies have also analysed the cross-cultural and motivational utility of various compensation strategies on managers and the workforce at large (e.g., Lowe, Milliman, De Cieri, & Dowling, 2002). Their goal was to compare pay practices or preferences for pay practices across cultures. For example, when compared to individualist cultures, collectivist countries have been found to place more value on seniority. They see compensation according to needs as being fairer. Drawing on these types of studies, it would be illustrative to conduct in-depth academic cross-cultural research analysing the motivational utility of various compensation strategies on expatriates from different nationalities. Such research would aim at providing some clues for companies as to which expatriate compensation strategy is most likely to be a good match for the values of a particular culture.

THE ISSUE OF TRANSACTION COSTS

It is very common to say that expatriates are very expensive. Some studies (Bonache & Pla-Barber, 2005) based on transaction cost theory have nonetheless questioned the general validity of this affirmation. In particular, they consider a series of costs which, although omitted in the traditional literature on expatriation, should be taken into account when making decisions to recruit expatriates or local managers in an MNC's subsidiaries, such as the costs incurred by the recruitment, training, and assessment of the subsidiary's technical and management staff. For example, whenever the foreign subsidiary is a new venture or located in environments that are culturally very different, these costs may be very high, with the result that the overall cost of using HCNs may be higher than the salary costs incurred through deploying expatriates. This explains the apparent contradiction whereby firms in a business context defined by the need to reduce expenditure may continue to make intensive use of such an apparently costly solution as expatriation. If expats really do add value to the organization, they may be a more efficient option and offset the high costs incurred by their deployment. In any case, measuring the return on investment from global assignments remains an onerous challenge for organizations. Without a doubt, determining when the transaction costs of using expatriates are lower than those of using local managers is of interest and deserves more attention in the literature.

JUSTICE PERCEPTIONS AND OTHER THEORETICAL VIEWS

As mentioned earlier, a number of empirical studies on the determinants and effects of salary inequity among local employees and expatriates have been recently published. It would be interesting to extend this type of research to comparisons among expatriates belonging to different categories. In this sense, while equity theory is the traditional reference used to analyse organizational justice, other approaches regarding justice are also possible. One possible and complementary alternative is Rawls' theory of justice (see Bonache, 2004, for an analysis of this theory as applied to HR management). According to this theory, different work arrangements for expatriates and local employees will be fair in cases where (a) the groups have the same basic labour rights and opportunities, (b) greater rewards correspond to greater merits, and (c) the greater rewards of the expatriates group (the most favoured group) improve those of the less-favoured group of local employees. Theoretical and empirical research on the topic using this (or other) theoretical frameworks may be very instructive.

PAY ATTRIBUTIONS AND THEIR EFFECTS ON EXPATRIATES' ATTITUDES AND BEHAVIOURS

A topic worth analysis is expatriates' evaluation of their pay, and specifically their pay attributions. Nishii, Lepak, and Schneider (2008) highlighted that employees make causal attributions about why management adopts HR initiatives. They identified two different HR attributions: the "workforce control" attribution (HR initiatives are believed to be intended to control costs) and the "workforce welfare" attribution (HR initiatives are believed to be intended to enhance employee well-being). While control attributions are negatively related to employee contributions, welfare attributions elicit productive attitudes and behaviours, and in turn, organizational performance. HR attribution research may be extended to expatriate compensation to improve our understanding of its relationship with expatriate attraction, motivation, and retention. Arguably, if expatriates perceive their pay package as being intended to reduce mobility costs rather than supporting their well-being, they may experience the international assignment less positively, thus delivering suboptimal performance. This may occur, for example, when the organization chooses the (less costly) local-plus or localization systems instead of the balance sheet approach. Notably, individual attributions may deviate from the actual intentions of the organization. Thus, while the organization may use local-plus or localization compensation systems with the constructive intent to foster cultural development in the host country, expatriates may perceive these systems as being intended to reduce overheads. This implies that how the organization "sells" the pay package may be pivotal vis-à-vis expatriate attributions of their pay (see Guest, Sanders, Rodrigues, & Oliveira, 2021), a topic that future research could also elaborate on. Importantly, HR attributions are not the only kind of evaluation employees make of the HR initiatives they encounter. Other constructs, such as "HR salience" (the degree to which HR initiatives are appraised as meaningful by employees) (Garg, Jiang, & Lepak, 2021) and "HR satisfaction" (the degree to which HR initiatives are viewed by employees as fulfilling their work-related needs) (Stirpe, Profili, & Sammarra, 2022) have been recently introduced. Bringing these constructs into expatriate compensation research may shed additional light on the complexities of expatriate compensation and its related effects.

IMPACT ON COMPETITIVE ADVANTAGE

More research is also needed on the effects of expatriate compensation systems on firms' competitive advantages. In this regard, and contrary to the basic assumption underlying much of the research on traditional compensation literature, competitive advantage cannot be attained if companies simply implant a "state of the art" compensation package. As is well explained by the resource-based view of the firm, a competitive advantage must come from a resource that is valuable, rare, and difficult to imitate (Barney, 2001). Accordingly, instead of focusing on standard compensation packages, competitive advantage will come from crafting compensation and reward systems to create employment relationships that extract the value of firm-specific resources. We have no information about the way in which expatriate packages can be designed to create a shared mindset, extract tacit knowledge among expatriates and repatriates, encourage innovation, creativity, and responsiveness, and stimulate the development of productive relationships among people. Investigation along this line would undoubtedly be of great academic and professional interest.

Other Ways of Seeing Compensation Issues

The studies we have reviewed in this reading are based, with one exception (Bonache & Zárraga-Oberty, 2020), on the positivist paradigm. Perhaps now is a good time to encourage studies from other epistemological perspectives. Interpretivist or critical studies can help us not only to analyse the subject from other perspectives, but also to challenge many of the assumptions that have dominated the compensation literature in recent decades and to discover other approaches, challenges, and solutions encountered by companies in relation to this policy. It could also lead to the construction of theories that may be more interesting and better reflect the way in which these issues are experienced in the business community, both from the company and employee point of view. It is a question of analysing many of the issues that have occupied us in this reading, but doing so from other perspectives and assuming a different way of producing knowledge in the area (See Bonache, 2021).

CONCLUSIONS

The compensation of corporate expatriates is one of the issues taking up most of the time and energy of HR professionals working in multinational companies. For over half a century now, the balance sheet approach has been used as the basis for calculating the most suitable compensation for both the individual and the company. Nevertheless, when judged according to the goals it aspires to accomplish, this system has a series of shortcomings that are becoming increasingly apparent, and which need to be resolved by HR departments. Local-plus and localization are alternative approaches for compensating expatriates, which, despite providing certain advantages, are not without their own problems and difficulties. Given the lack of an "ideal system", companies have been distinguishing between types of assignments, with different conditions and approaches for each of them. This is not the only feature defining the current landscape of international compensation. Other trends include implementing different initiatives to reduce expatriation costs, and analysing the expatriation's value added for a company. Examining how the organizational context and other variables affect the way in which the challenge of designing an expatriation package is understood and addressed and analysing the impact of expatriate compensation on a number of individual and organizational outcomes are research areas deserving of attention in the specialized literature. If, furthermore, this is undertaken from different epistemological paradigms, the area will move forward in a direction that is not only relevant for business practice, but also for those wishing to understand and explain one of the most important policies of international human resource management. We hope that this reading encourages at least one reader to move in this direction.

REFERENCES

Adams, J. S. (1965). Inequity in social exchange. In L. Berkowitz (Ed.), *Advances in experimental social psychology* (Vol. 2, pp. 267–299). New York: Academic Press.

AIR Inc. (2010). *Diverse expatriate populations – Alternative remuneration packages*. New York: AIRINC.

AIR Inc. (2011). *Local-plus: Tips, tools and trends.* New York: AIR Inc.

Barney, J. B. (2001). Resource-based theories of competitive advantage: A ten-year retrospective on the resource-based view. *Journal of Management,* 27(6), 643–650.

Baron, J. N., & Kreps, D. M. (1999). HRM in emerging companies. In J. N. Baron & D. M. Kreps (Eds.), *Strategic Human Resources.* New York: Wiley.

Bitten, J. (2001). Compensation strategies for international assignments: Alternatives to the balance sheet. *HR Professional,* 18(2), 29–31.

Bonache, J. (2004). Towards a re-examination of work arrangements: An analysis from Rawls' theory of justice. *Human Resource Management Review,* 14(4), 395–408.

Bonache, J. (2006). The compensation of expatriates: A review and a future research agenda. In G. Stahl & I. Bjorkman (Eds.), *Handbook of research in international human resource management* (pp. 158–175). Cheltenham: Edward Elgar Publishing.

Bonache, J. (2021). The challenge of using a "non-positivist" paradigm and getting through the peer-review process. *Human Resource Management Journal,* 31(1), 37–48.

Bonache, J., & Noethen, D. (2014). The impact of individual performance on organizational success and its implications for the management of expatriates. *The International Journal of Human Resource Management,* 25(14), 1960–1977.

Bonache, J., & Pla-Barber, J. (2005). When are international managers a cost effective solution? The rationale of transaction cost economics applied to staffing decisions in MNCs. *Journal of Business Research,* 58(10), 1320–1329.

Bonache, J., Sanchez, J. I., & Zárraga-Oberty, C. (2009). The interaction of expatriate pay differential and expatriate inputs on host country nationals' pay unfairness. *The International Journal of Human Resource Management,* 20(10), 2135–2149.

Bonache, J., & Zárraga-Oberty, C. (2017). The traditional approach to compensating global mobility: Criticisms and alternatives. *The International Journal of Human Resource Management,* 28(1), 149–169.

Bonache, J., & Zárraga-Oberty, C. (2020). Compensating global mobility in a workers' cooperative: An interpretive study. *Journal of World Business,* 55(5), 59–68.

Brookfield Global Relocation Services. (2015). *Global relocation trends survey report.* Woodridge, IL: Brookfield Global Relocation Services.

Brookfield Global Relocation Services. (2021). *Talent mobility trends survey.* Woodridge, IL: Brookfield Global Relocation Services.

Caligiuri, P., & Bonache, J. (2016). Evolving and enduring challenges in global mobility. *Journal of World Business,* 51(1), 127–141.

Chen, C. C., Choi, J., & Chi, S. C. (2002). Making justice sense of local–expatriate compensation disparity: Mitigation by local referents, ideological explanations, and interpersonal sensitivity in China-foreign joint ventures. *Academy of Management Journal,* 45(4), 807–826.

Chen, G., Ployhart, R. E., Thomas, H. C., Anderson, N., & Bliese, P. D. (2011). The power of momentum: A new model of dynamic relationships between job satisfaction change and turnover intentions. *Academy of Management Journal,* 54(1), 159–181.

Dickover, G. F. (1957). Employee relations in foreign operations. In International Management Association (Ed.), *Case studies in foreign operations* (pp. 118–133). New York: Author.

Edström, A., & Galbraith, J. R. (1977). Transfer of managers as a coordination and control strategy in multinational organizations. *Administrative Science Quarterly,* 22(2), 248–263.

Farndale, E., Scullion, H., & Sparrow, P. (2010). The role of the corporate HR function in global talent management. *Journal of World Business,* 45(2), 161–168.

Festing, M., & Perkins, S. (2008). Rewards for internationally mobile employees. In M. Dickmann, C. Brewster, & P. Sparrow (Eds.), *International human resource management: A European perspective* (pp. 150–173). Oxon: Routledge.

Festinger, L. (1954). A theory of social comparison processes. *Human Relations*, 7(2), 117–140.

Fulmer, I. S., & Li, J. (2022). Compensation, benefits, and total rewards: A bird's-eye (re)view. *Annual Review of Organizational Psychology and Organizational Behavior*, 9(1), 147–169.

Garg, S., Jiang, K., & Lepak, D. P. (2021). HR practice salience: Explaining variance in employee reactions to HR practices. *The International Journal of Human Resource Management*, 32(2), 512–542.

Gómez-Mejía, L. R., Berrone, P., & Franco-Santos, M. (2014). *Compensation and organizational performance: Theory, research, and practice*. New York: Routledge.

Guest, D. E., Sanders, K., Rodrigues, R., & Oliveira, T. (2021). Signalling theory as a framework for analysing human resource management processes and integrating human resource attribution theories: A conceptual analysis and empirical exploration. *Human Resource Management Journal*, 31(3), 796–818.

Harvey, M. G. (1993a). Designing a global compensation system: The logic and a model. *Colombia Journal of World Business*, 28(4), 56–72.

Harvey, M. G. (1993b). Empirical evidence of recurring international compensation problems. *Journal of International Business Studies*, 24(4), 785–799.

Kahneman, D., & Tversky, A. (1984). Choices, values and frames. *American Psychologist*, 39(4), 341–350.

KPMG. (2018). *Global assignment policies and practices*. London: KPMG.

Leung, K., Zhu, Y., & Ge, C. (2009). Compensation disparity between locals and expatriates: Moderating the effects of perceived injustice in foreign multinationals in China. *Journal of World Business*, 44(1), 85–93.

Liao, C., Wayne, S. J., & Rousseau, D. M. (2016). Idiosyncratic deals in contemporary organizations: A qualitative and meta-analytical review. *Journal of Organizational Behavior*, 37, S9–S29.

Lowe, K. B., Milliman, J., De Cieri, H., & Dowling, P. J. (2002). International compensation practices: A ten-country comparative analysis. *Human Resource Management*, 41(1), 45–66.

McNulty, Y. (2014). The opportunity costs of local-plus and localization approaches to expatriate compensation. In L. Berger & D. Berger (Eds.), *The compensation handbook* (6th ed., pp. 1–21). Columbus, OH: McGraw-Hill Education.

McNulty, Y. (2015). Employing novel compensation approaches to compete for expatriate talent. In L. Berger & D. Berger (Eds.), *The compensation handbook: A state-of-the-art guide to compensation strategy and design* (6th ed., pp. 503–518). Columbus, OH: McGraw-Hill Education. ISBN-13: 978-0071836999. Reprinted in: Mendenhall, M., Oddou, G., Stahl, G., & Reiche, R. S. (Eds.). (2016). *Readings and cases in international HRM and OB* (5th ed.). In press.

McNulty, Y., De Cieri, H., & Hutchings, K. (2009). Do global firms measure expatriate return on investment? An empirical examination of measures, barriers and variables influencing global staffing practices. *International Journal of Human Resource Management*, 20(6), 1309–1326.

Mercer. (2020). *Worldwide survey of international assignment policies and practices*. Geneva: Mercer.

Nishii, L. H., Lepak, D. P., & Schneider, B. (2008). Employee attributions of the "why" of HR practices: Their effects on employee attitudes and behaviors, and customer satisfaction. *Personnel Psychology*, 61(3), 503–545.

Nowak, C., & Linder, C. (2016). Do you know how much your expatriate costs? An activity-based cost analysis of expatriation. *Journal of Global Mobility*, 4(1), 88–107.

O'Really, M. (1996). Expatriate pay: The state of the art. *Compensation and Benefits Review*, 12(1), 54–60.

Paik, Y., Parboteeah, K. P., & Shim, W. (2007). The relationship between perceived compensation, organizational commitment and job satisfaction: The case of Mexican workers in the Korean Maquiladoras. *International Journal of Human Resource Management*, 18(10), 1768–1781.

Phillips, L., & Fox, M. A. (2003). Compensation strategy in transnational corporations. *Management Decision*, 41(5), 465–476.

Reiche, B. S., Kraimer, M. L., & Harzing, A. W. (2011). Why do international assignees stay? An organizational embeddedness perspective. *Journal of International Business Studies*, 42(4), 521–544.

Reynolds, C. (1997). Expatriate compensation in historical perspective. *Journal of World Business*, 32(2), 118–132.

Rousseau, D. M., Ho, V. T., & Greenberg, J. (2006). I-deals: Idiosyncratic terms in employment relationships. *Academy of Management Review*, 31(4), 977–994.

Shaffer, M. A., Harrison, D., & Gilley, M. (1999). Dimensions, determinants, and differences in the expatriate adjustment process. *Journal of International Business Studies*, 30(3), 557–581.

Shortland, S. (2016). The purpose of expatriation: Why women undertake international assignments. *Human Resource Management*, 55(4), 655–678.

Shortland, S. (2018). What seals the deal? How compensation and benefits affect women's decisions to accept expatriation in the oil and gas industry. *Personnel Review*, 47(3), 765–783.

Stahl, G. K., Miller, E., & Tung, R. (2002). Toward the boundaryless career: A closer look at the expatriate career concept and the perceived implications of an international assignment. *Journal of World Business*, 37(3), 216–227.

Stirpe, L., Profili, S., & Sammarra, A. (2022). Satisfaction with HR practices and employee performance: A moderated mediation model of engagement and health. *European Management Journal*, 40(2), 295–305.

Suutari, V., & Tornikoski, C. (2000). Determinants of expatriate compensation – Findings among expatriate members of SEFE. *Finnish Journal of Business Economics*, 49(4), 517–539.

Suutari, V., & Tornikoski, C. (2001). The challenge of expatriate compensation: The sources of satisfaction and dissatisfaction among expatriates. *The International Journal of Human Resource Management*, 12(3), 389–404.

Toh, S. M., & DeNisi, A. (2003). Host country national reactions to expatriate pay policies: A model and implications. *Academy of Management Review*, 28(4), 606–621.

Tornikoski, C., Suutari, V., & Festing, M. (2014). Compensation package of international assignees. In D. G. Collings, G. T. Wood, & P. M. Caligiuri (Eds.), *The Routledge Companion to International Human Resource Management*, (pp. 289–307). New York: Routledge.

Warneke, D., & Schneider, M. (2011). Expatriate compensation packages: What do employees prefer? *Cross Cultural Management: An International Journal*, 18(2), 236–256.

Welch, C. L., Welch, D. E., & Tahvanainen, M. (2008). Managing the HR dimension of international project operations. *The International Journal of Human Resource Management*, 19(2), 205–222.

Yan, A., Zhu, G., & Hall, D. T. (2002). International assignments for career building: A model of agency relationships and psychological contracts. *Academy of Management Review*, 27(3), 373–391.

J. Stewart Black

FRED BAILEY

An Innocent Abroad[1]

FRED GAZED OUT THE WINDOW of his office at the tranquil beauty of the
Imperial Palace amidst the traffic jam 24 floors below. It had only been six
months ago that Fred had arrived with his wife and two children for this three-
year assignment as the managing director (MD) of Kline & Associates' Tokyo
office. Kline & Associates was a multinational consulting firm with seven offices
in the US and in nine other countries worldwide. Fred was now trying to decide
if he should simply pack up and tell the home office that he was coming home or
whether he should try to somehow convince his wife and himself that they should
stay and try to finish the assignment. Given how excited Fred thought they all were
about the assignment to begin with, it was a mystery to him as to how things had
gotten to this point. As he watched the swans glide across the water in the moat
that surrounds the Imperial Palace, Fred reflected back on the past seven months.

Seven months ago, the Global Managing Director (GMD), Dave Steiner,
based in the firm's home office in Boston, asked Fred to lunch to discuss "business." To Fred's surprise, the "business" was not the major project that he and
his team had just successfully finished, but was instead a very big promotion and
career move. Fred was offered the MD position of the firm's relatively new Tokyo
office. The office had five partners, two were non-Japanese—one from the US
and one from the UK. There were 15 associate consultants, of whom five were
not Japanese, and ten research associates, of whom four were not Japanese.
The non-Japanese staff hailed from various countries, including Singapore, the
US, France, Brazil, and India. Fred would be in charge of the whole office and
would report to a senior partner (located in Singapore) who was overseeing the
Asian region. It was implied to Fred that if this assignment went as well as his
past assignments had, it would be the last step before becoming a senior partner
in the firm. Making senior partner mattered to Fred for a couple of reasons.

DOI: 10.4324/9781003247272-20

First, making senior partner would effectively double his compensation. Kline was one of the few consulting firms that still based the majority of fixed compensation on seniority and "rank" rather than billable hours and still allocated the highest percentage of profits to senior partners as well. It did this in an effort to encourage collegiality and collaboration across offices and across practice areas. Second, making senior partner was an essential step in Fred's ambition of becoming the Global Managing Director of the firm down the road.

However, if Fred returned home early, it would hurt, not help, his career ambitions and perhaps be his kiss of death at Kline. But Jenny was not in a mood to discuss things. As far as she was concerned, there was nothing to discuss. She was fed up with the assignment and Japan. She felt the company and Fred had oversold the country and how "well they would be looked after." Fred worked 80+ hours a week because of all the after-hours socializing he had to do with clients. That level of hours was part of the package when Fred was trying to make partner, but having made partner three years ago, his being gone this much was not the deal Jenny had signed up for. Because Fred was never home, he "had no idea what life was really like in Japan," so she had given him an ultimatum: Either they packed up together, or she went home alone. That things had escalated this far just didn't seem possible to Fred. What was he supposed to do? Sacrifice everything he had worked for over the years? His partner status and Harvard MBA would no doubt get him another job, but his ultimate ambitions were just within reach if he could do well in this assignment. But if he walked away, his chance of making senior partner and eventually GMD were potentially doomed. On the other hand, he loved his wife and children and did not want to be unhappy. What had gone wrong?

FRED AND JENNY

Fred and Jenny met during their last year in college in a senior seminar class on business ethics. Fred was instantly attracted to Jenny's warm smile and flair for fashion. Jenny recognized in Fred high ambition, but also a kind heart. The two started dating only a week after the class started.

Jenny came from a well-to-do family in Connecticut. Her father was a senior executive with a major firm headquartered in New York. She had majored in fashion merchandising as a way of combining her interest and talent for fashion and her father's advice to study something practical.

Fred was the oldest of six children and the first to go to college. His father was a construction worker and his mother a beautician. Fred had worked hard in high school and graduated second in his class. Even with a partial scholarship, tuition help from his parents put a real financial burden on them. Fred was determined to take advantage of every opportunity and make his parents proud.

Before and after getting married, Fred and Jenny talked at length about careers and family. Out of college, he had landed a great job with American Express and hoped that with three years of experience in New York, his stellar college grades, and good Graduate Management Admission Test scores, he could get into a top MBA program. Jenny wanted to be a buyer for a major store like Saks Fifth Avenue and later have her own shop. They both wanted children, but thought they would wait until Fred finished his MBA before starting a family. At that point, Jenny would take a few years off and then start her own small clothing store once the kids were in school. They both thought that owning her own shop would give Jenny the flexibility and time to spend with their children that she wanted.

After three years with American Express, Fred was thrilled when he was accepted to Harvard's MBA program. Upon graduating, he joined Kline & Associates. Kline was largely a business strategy and innovation consulting firm. Given its long-time focus on innovation and its recent focus on digital transformation, its three main US hubs were Boston, San Francisco, and Austin, with Boston as the home office.

Fred had a couple of other offers coming out of Harvard, but including expected performance bonuses, the job at Kline paid 20% more. After accepting, Fred was assigned to the San Francisco office and put on the team of the hardest-charging associate at Kline—Rick Savage.

Rick was bright and had an MBA from Stanford. He was one year away from the magical "up or out" decision concerning partner. This decision usually happened about the seventh year of employment for typical MBA hires, though only about 10–15% made partner. In this final year, Rick was going to do anything and everything needed to make partner. Whereas he had put in 80+ hour weeks since starting, in the year before his potential promotion to partner, he worked many 100-hour weeks and expected members of his team to do the same.

To no one's surprise, Rick made partner. To the surprise of some, he poured praise on his team, particularly Fred for the past year's success. With this solid start and Rick's model in front of him, Fred thought he had a very good shot at making partner in another six years.

Fred worked hard, learned from Kline's best, took on extra projects, and spent endless hours understanding clients and impressing them with his insights. To no one's surprise, in his seventh year at Kline, Fred made partner; he was both thrilled and relieved.

A year after making partner, Fred was asked to transfer to Austin because several key clients had moved their headquarters from California to Texas. Knowing that Texas was not high on Fred or Jenny's places to live and work, Fred was told that if he wanted, the move could be considered temporary. Work in Austin went great. Fred brought in nearly double the business of any other new partner in the office—most of it in the IT space. However, Fred's undergraduate training and real loves were biology and chemistry, so when the chance to move to Boston came up, he jumped on it. Boston had a thriving ecosystem of bio-tech and pharmaceutical companies and start-ups. Jenny was delighted to move back east and be closer to her family.

The move to Boston couldn't have gone better. While still maintaining some of his clients in Texas, Fred built up new ones in Boston's bio-innovation hub. The kids settled into school quickly. As planned, Jenny opened her clothing shop. A year after its opening, it was doing well.

Everything was going according to plan until the offer to go to Japan.

THE OFFER

Fred was stunned by the Tokyo offer. The Tokyo office was opened in part to serve major US and European clients' operations in Japan, which was a hub for robotics and automation. From this same base, Kline would begin to develop relationships with Japanese firms, which were starting to get very serious about digital transformation. Kline strategized that not only could it do business in Japan with new Japanese clients, it could leverage its offices in key innovation centers around the world (Tel Aviv, Singapore, Paris, London, Sydney, Berlin, Seoul, Amsterdam, and Dubai) as well as those in the US with new Japanese clients. The two-way strategic significance of the office and of his assignment were not lost on Fred.

Fred's predecessor in Japan, George Woodward, had opened the office 18 months ago. George was a senior partner with a mixed reputation. He had friends at the very top of Kline, but he could be a bit of a "prickly fellow," so he had his detractors as well. Fred wasn't sure why George had been suddenly transferred back to London. Because the transfer back was taking place "right away," Dave told Fred that he and his family had about three weeks to get prepared.

When Fred told his wife about the unbelievable opportunity, he was shocked at her less than enthusiastic response. Jenny thought that it would be rather difficult to have the children live and go to school in a foreign country for three years. Besides, Jenny had opened her clothing shop just a year ago. What was she supposed to do? Sell it? Close it? Run it from Japan?

Fred explained that the career opportunity was just too good to pass up and that the company's overseas package would make living in Japan terrific. The company would pay all the expenses to move whatever the Baileys wanted to take with them. The company had a very nice house in a nice district of Tokyo that would be provided rent-free. Additionally, the company would rent their house in Boston during their absence. The firm would provide education expenses for the children to attend an international school, and a cost-of-living adjustment to neutralize the higher cost of living in Japan. After two days of consideration and discussion, Fred told Mr. Steiner he would accept the assignment.

PREPARING FOR THE MOVE

Between getting things at the office transferred to Bob Newcome, who was taking over from Fred, and the logistic hassles of arranging for furniture and the like to be moved, neither Fred nor his family had much time to really find out much about Japan other than what they read on Wikipedia.

Kline handled many of the logistical and relocation details internally. Unfortunately, a number of things went wrong. For example, when the packers came, they were totally unprepared for the fact that not all of the Baileys' belongings were being shipped to Japan; some were going into storage. This determination had come about because on their "look-see visit" a week after Fred had accepted the assignment, Jenny saw that their house in Japan would not accommodate all their belongings. In fact, some family antiques Jenny had recently received from her folks would not even fit through the door.

For Jenny and her shop, the timing was not convenient. Jenny's shop was in a great location in Boston and still had four years left on its five-year lease. She probably could have sold the shop or found someone to take over the lease, but she didn't want to. In the end, she felt that the shop was doing well and the staff were experienced enough that she could run it over Zoom from Japan, with a few trips back each year.

FRED'S EARLY EXPERIENCES

When the Baileys arrived in Japan, they were greeted at the airport by one of the young associate consultants and one of the Japanese partners. Fred and his family were exhausted from the long trip, and the 90-minute ride back to Tokyo was a rather quiet one. After a few days of just settling in, Fred spent his first full day at the office.

Fred's first order of business was to have an all-hands meeting with the partners and employees of associate rank and higher. Although Fred didn't really notice it at the time, all the Japanese staff sat on one side of the room and all the non-Japanese sat on the other. After Fred introduced himself and his general ideas about the potential and future directions of the Tokyo office, he opened it up to questions and comments.

The first to speak up was Paulo Nakamura, an associate consultant who hailed from Brazil and was a recent graduate from INSEAD. Next was a research associate from India. Several others spoke up, but none of the partners and none of the Japanese associates offered up any thoughts. Fred sensed they had opinions, but he just wasn't sure why they weren't coming out. Rather than drag things out, Fred thanked everyone for coming and said he looked forward to their all working together to make the Tokyo office the fastest-growing office in the company.

Less than a month after arriving, Fred had a "pitch meeting" with a large Japanese multinational. Accompanying him from Kline was Ralph Webster, a partner who was married to a Japanese. Ralph had moved from San Francisco to the Tokyo office as soon as it was opened. Also on the Kline team was Kenichi Kurokawa, a new Japanese research associate who had recently graduated from Sophia University. The Japanese client team consisted of four members—the VP of administration, the Chief Digital Officer, and two staff specialists. After shaking hands and a few awkward bows, the Japanese offered to exchange business cards. Fred's staff had prepared his cards in advance with Japanese on one side and English on the other. Fred handed his cards to each Japanese with the English side up.

After the card exchange, Fred said that he knew the Japanese gentlemen were busy and he didn't want to waste their time, so he would get right to the point. Fred then had Ralph Webster lay out Kline's proposal for the project and what the project would cost. After the presentation, Fred asked the Japanese for their reaction to the proposal. The Japanese did not respond immediately, so Fred launched into his summary version of the proposal, thinking that the translation might have been insufficient. But again, at the end, the Japanese had only the vaguest of responses to his direct questions.

The recollections of the frustration of that meeting were enough to shake Fred back to reality. The reality was that in the four weeks that followed that first meeting, Kline made little progress with the client. Fred remembered saying to himself in frustration at the time, "I can never seem to get a direct response from these guys."

About six weeks after the first meeting, Fred had decided that the reason not much progress was being made was because Fred and his group just didn't know enough about the client to adequately customize their proposal. Consequently, Fred had suggested to Ralph that Kurokawa develop a report on the client so the proposal could be re-evaluated and changed where necessary.

To impress upon Kurokawa the importance of this task and the great potential they saw in him, Fred decided to have the young Japanese associate meet with both Fred and Ralph. In the meeting, Ralph laid out the nature and importance of the task. At the end, Fred leaned forward in his chair and said:

> You can see that this is an important assignment and that we are placing a lot of confidence in you by giving you this assignment. We need the report this time next week so that we can revise and re-present our proposal. What do you think?

After a somewhat pregnant pause, Kurokawa responded somewhat hesitantly, "I don't know what to say." At that point Fred smiled, got up from his chair, and walked over to the young Japanese associate, extended his hand, and said, "Hey, there's no need to thank us. We're just giving you the opportunity you deserve."

The day before the report was due, Fred asked Ralph how the report was coming. Ralph said that since he had heard nothing from Kurokawa, he assumed everything was under control, but he would double-check. Ralph later ran into Paulo Nakamura. Paulo, like the more than 1.5 million ethnic Japanese in Brazil, traced his Japanese ancestry in Brazil back to a major immigration of Japanese to the country between 1907 and 1917. Over the generations, Paulo's family had not only maintained cultural ties to Japan, but had preserved the Japanese language in the family as well. Ralph knew that Paulo was hired because of his language ability and that, unlike many of the other non-Japanese associates, Paulo often went out after work with some of the Japanese research associates, including Kurokawa. So Ralph asked Paulo if he knew how Kurokawa was doing on the report. Paulo then recounted that last night at the office, Kurokawa had asked if Americans sometimes fired employees for being late with reports. Paulo had sensed that this was more than a hypothetical question, and asked Kurokawa why he wanted to know. Kurokawa did not respond immediately, and since it was 7:30 in the evening, Paulo suggested they go out for a drink. At first Kurokawa resisted, but then Paulo assured him that they would grab a drink at a nearby bar and come right back.

At the bar, Paulo got Kurokawa to open up. Kurokawa explained the nature of the report that he had been requested to produce. He continued to explain that even though he had worked long into the night every night to complete the report, it was just impossible, and that he had doubted from the beginning whether he could complete the report in a week.

At this point, Ralph asked Paulo, "Why the hell didn't Kurokawa say something in the first place?" Ralph didn't wait to hear whether Paulo had an answer to his question or not. He headed straight to Kurokawa's desk.

The incident just got worse from that point. Ralph chewed Kurokawa out, and then went to Fred explaining that the report would not be ready and that Kurokawa didn't think it could be from the start. "Then why didn't he say something?" Fred asked. No one had any answers, and the whole thing just left everyone more skeptical of and uncomfortable with each other than ever.

There were other incidents, big and small, over the last six months that had driven Fred nuts, but at this point he was too tired to remember them all. To Fred, it seemed that working with Japanese both inside and outside the firm was like working with people from another planet. He felt he just couldn't communicate with them, and he could never figure out what they were thinking. But in fairness, the cross-cultural challenges were not with the Japanese. For example, the two Indian research associates seemed to constantly have problems with the senior research associate, Bolin Chang, who was from Singapore. However, when the two Indian research associates were having conflicts with Bolin, they were fighting with each other. Someone in the office had mentioned that it had to do with one hailing from Kashmir and the other from Goa, but the difference was lost on Fred.

JENNY'S EARLY EXPERIENCES

Jenny's life in Japan was equally frustrating. Jenny was determined at first to make an adventure out of living in Japan. During the first week, she went down to the local grocery store to buy some food and basic household supplies. However, not being able to read the labels, she had mistakenly bought a bottle of bluish-colored liquid that was in a bottle of the same shape as "Scope" mouthwash back home. She discovered that it was actually bathroom cleaning liquid after swishing and gargling and nearly choking to death on the stuff.

After about a month, Jenny tried to take the Tokyo subway from her house to the famous Meiji Shrine. What was supposed to be a 15-minute ride turned into a two-hour ordeal. Jenny missed her stop, but didn't discover it for several more. Then, when she did, she got off the train, only to discover she had no idea how to get to the other side of the tracks and head back the opposite way. She exited the station and tried to ask how to get to the other side. Finally, someone in English pointed out some stairs that led to a tunnel that went under the tracks to the other side. However, arriving there, she found, that she had no idea how much a ticket would cost to the stop she wanted, and even though the map had had the stops in both English and Japanese, there were so many subway lines and stops that it was just overwhelming.

At this point, she was frustrated nearly to the point of tears. The tears came when she saw a small group of young grade-school kids buy tickets and go through the turnstile without a second thought. Though she didn't want to, she called Fred on her mobile. She reached his assistant, who said he was in a meeting. "I understand, but I need to speak with him," Jenny said firmly. When Fred came to the phone, Jenny was clearly upset. Fred tried to be understanding, but his irritation at being called out of a meeting because she was lost on the subway seeped through. This only amplified Jenny's frustration.

After a brief discussion, Fred and Jenny reasoned that she should take the escalator up out of the subway and hail a taxi. Fortunately, the Japanese taxi driver understood "Meiji Shrine," and Jenny was able to tour the shrine, but not with the same attitude she had started with that morning.

After about five months in Japan, Jenny was finding life quite frustrating. Both kids were doing OK in school, but their commute by subway was longer than anticipated. Consequently, between the commute and actual school time, they were gone a good part of the day. Having them gone all day and not being at the shop turned out to produce a bigger "blank" than Jenny expected.

Managing the shop by Zoom was working fine enough, but the 12-hour time difference was a non-trivial challenge. Also, information that Jenny knew simply by being in the shop, like daily traffic and revenue, now had to be sent over to her. At times, she got the impression that the staff felt micro-managed by those information requests, even though the information requested was the same as she had when she managed the shop in person.

On top of all this, Jenny had not really met or become friends with anyone. The Baileys lived in a nice neighborhood in Ebisu. Jenny knew there were Japanese families in many of the houses on their block, but she rarely saw them. Even if she did, she didn't know if they spoke English. She had seen some other foreigners at the local grocery store and shops and had exchanged greetings and some small pleasantries, but she really hadn't made any friends yet. Back in Boston, she was only three hours away from her folks and her younger sister. She missed them. Fred's being gone 10–16 hours a day did not help any. A few days ago, Jenny was explaining some of this to Fred, but unfortunately, Fred was a bit preoccupied, thinking about his upcoming meeting between his firm and a significant prospective client—a top 100 Japanese multinational company.

THE BOMBSHELL

For Jenny, these incidents were only the tip of the iceberg. Recently, their oldest daughter had complained about not fitting in at school. She said she missed her friends back home. Jenny had wanted Japan to be an adventure, but it just seemed like incident after incident chipped away at her sense of competence. Of the few foreigners she had met who were new to Japan, many had lots of complaints about the country and how life back in France, or Switzerland, or Singapore was so much better. For herself, one of the things she missed most was driving. Back in Boston, Jenny could drive to visit friends, family, or to take a trip to New York to check on some potential new clothing lines she might bring into her shop. She had not gotten the nerve up to drive in Japan. Tokyo was crowded, bumper-to-bumper traffic, and sometimes the signs had only Japanese characters. To top it all off, in Japan they drove on the wrong side of the road.

When she reflected on it all, she wanted to go home, and she could not think of any reason why they shouldn't. After all, they didn't really owe anything to the company. Yes, Fred was paid well, but he had always worked harder and brought in more business than most other partners. Jenny felt that she had agreed to this assignment as a favor to Fred and the firm. If anything, they both owed her!

Fred tried to reason with Jenny, but the more he countered, the more determined she became. Then, just the other day, she dropped the bombshell on him: either they could go home together, or he could stay here alone.

THE DECISION

Fred looked out the window once more, wishing that somehow everything could be fixed, or turned back, or something. What had gone wrong? Why was Jenny being so unreasonable? Did he dare call Dave and explain the situation? Dave was very old-fashioned and had once made a derogatory comment about a promising young consultant whose future looked dimmer and dimmer because he "could not control complaints at home."

Looking down again, Fred realized that darkness had fallen. He could see the headlights and taillights of backed-up traffic for blocks in both directions. Though the traffic lights changed, the cars and trucks didn't seem to be moving. Fortunately, under the ground below, one of the world's most advanced, efficient, and clean subway systems moved hundreds of thousands of people from work to their homes for the evening.

NOTE

1. This case was written by Professor J. Stewart Black as a basis for class discussion rather than to illustrate either effective or ineffective handling of an administrative situation. Revised December 12, 2021.

Paula Caligiuri and Henry W. Lane

SELECTING A COUNTRY MANAGER
FOR DELTA BEVERAGES INDIA[1]

Part 1

YOU ARE THE REGIONAL PRESIDENT, Asia, for Delta Beverages, a large US-based firm headquartered in Boston. Delta is one of the world's leaders in the beverage industry (bottled water, carbonated beverages, teas, juice beverages, and sports drinks). After having been with Delta for ten years, you are now responsible for all of the firm's operations in Asia, including the major markets of China, India, Korea, and Japan. Along with the rest of Delta's regional leadership team, you live in the Boston area and travel extensively to the subsidiaries you lead. In the two years since accepting this position, you have logged many frequent-flier miles and, on most days, greatly enjoy the challenges of leading the company's fastest-growing global region.

One of the greatest challenges you have in your role is selecting your direct reports, the Country Managers leading each of the country-level markets within your unit. Delta's Country Managers are hands-on leaders who effectively direct all areas of the subsidiary's operations, including supply chain, logistics, inventory, quality control, government, and customer service. Country Managers need to operate with cultural agility, having a deep understanding of the company's culture, values, and standards of quality, safety, and ethics. At the same time, Country Managers need to, at times, adapt to the client demands and unique challenges inherent in each of their local markets.

For large markets such as India, Delta has traditionally promoted Country Managers from within — leaders who have experience in the Boston-based headquarters and who have experience running smaller and less challenging markets.

DOI: 10.4324/9781003247272-21

Currently, most of your Country Managers are international assignees, with the exception of a few who are running smaller markets.

You understand firsthand what it takes to do this role well. Prior to this role, you had three international assignments, all as Country Manager. Your spouse, two children, and you lived for three years in the UK, two years in Bulgaria, and most recently, two years in China. You recall both the joys and challenges of living and working in each of your host countries. It takes a special person – and a special family – to thrive in this type of work environment.

Today, you need to make one of these critical staffing decisions. Shortly, you are scheduled for a distance communication meeting with the Vice President of Human Resources for International Operations Al Uccello and other members of your leadership team, who are traveling. The meeting is to select someone for the position of Country Manager, India. The job will be not far from New Delhi in the state of Haryana. This position became available a few years ahead of schedule when immediate concerns about government relations and quality control forced you to assign your strongest country leader, Canadian Xiao Zhang, the current Country Manager for India, to China – effective immediately.

The meeting today is important. India is among the largest and most important markets in your unit. You know that selecting the best country manager for India is critical.

EXERCISE 1

Before looking at personnel files, you have decided to review what you know about selecting managers for international assignments. Exhibit 1 shows a list of 15 important characteristics that you think should be considered. You believe this ranking may help you in reviewing candidate files. Working alone, rank these characteristics in importance from high to low. Assign 1 to the most important characteristic and 15 to the least important. Although all are important, you know some may be more important than others in contributing to a successful assignment. After completing your individual ranking, go to Part 2.

EXHIBIT 1 Ranking of Expatriate Selection Criteria

(1 = most important, 15 = least important)

Item	1 Your Individual Rank	2 Your Team's Rank	3 Experts' Rank	4 Your Score (difference between 1 and 3)	5 Team Score (difference between 2 and 3)
Language fluency					
Prior postings					
Technical/business skills					
Availability for preparation training					
Cultural and social interests					
Low sickness record					
Spouse support					
Need for autonomy					
Interpersonal sensitivity					
Few family ties					
Vacations abroad					
Communication skills					
No school-age children					
Extroversion					
Need for achievement					
TOTALS					

Final Team Calculations

1	Average Individual Score (sum of individual scores divided by number in group)	_____	1
2	Team Score (from column 5 above)	_____	2
3	Gain Score (Average Individual Score (item 1) minus Team Score (item 2))	_____	3
4	Best Individual Score (lowest Individual Score in team)	_____	4
5	Ratio (number of individuals in group who scored lower than Team Score (item 2) divided by number of individuals in the group)	_____	5
6	Relative Improvement (Gain Score (item 3) divided by Average Individual Score (item 1))	_____	6

NOTE

1.   This case was written by Paula Caligiuri and Henry W. Lane for the purpose of class discussion. The authors do not intend to demonstrate either effective or ineffective management. Names and other identifying information may have been disguised for the purpose of maintaining confidentiality. Copyright © 2015 Northeastern University, D'Amore-McKim School of Business.

Paula Caligiuri and Henry W. Lane

SELECTING A COUNTRY MANAGER
FOR DELTA BEVERAGES INDIA[1]

Part 2

FIVE CANDIDATES' NOTES FROM THE SUCCESSION PLANNING MEETING

TO PREPARE FOR TODAY'S MEETING, you reviewed the materials from last year's performance review and succession planning meetings. This activity surfaced five possible candidates for the role of Country Manager, India. Your notes on these candidates are as follows:

1. Anika "Ani" Navithar
    Ani has been with Delta for the past 15 years. She joined Delta immediately after completing her MBA at Northeastern University, joining us in the supply chain functional area. She has moved up the ranks quickly to director-level positions in both supply chain and customer service. While based in Boston, Ani has successfully completed several short-term projects internationally, and for the Indian subsidiary specifically. Ani has never been a country manager. She speaks English, Hindi, and Telugu. Part of Ani's leadership development plan is an international assignment. Ani is American.

2. Carlos Delgado
    Between his experience at Delta and his previous employer (Delta's major competitor), Carlos has had three international assignments over the past 18 years. Carlos began his career with Delta at its Boston headquarters and is currently reporting to you as the Country Manager in South Korea. He is highly regarded as a global leader, and as the succession plan indicates, he was on the slate of candidates for your current role. Prior to becoming the

DOI: 10.4324/9781003247272-22

Country Manager in Korea, Carlos was the Argentinean Country Manager for Delta, and was in a supply chain role in Poland with his previous employer. Carlos speaks Spanish and English. He is a Mexican national.

3. **Haziq Tengku**

    Haziq reports directly to you, and is currently the Country Manager for Malaysia, where he has been extremely successful. He is been serving in that role for the past six years and is ready for a promotion, according to the succession plan. With the exception of one three-month orientation at the Boston headquarters when he first joined Delta ten years ago, he has spent his tenure at Delta within the Malaysian subsidiary. Prior to joining Delta, Haziq worked for the Malaysian subsidiary of a US-based fast food chain. Part of Haziq's leadership development plan is to be a country manager for a larger market. He speaks Malay and English, and has a degree in business from University of Malaya. Haziq is a Malaysian national.

4. **Lucas Hansson**

    Lucas was appointed as the Vice President for Delta's Europe, Middle East, and Africa (EMEA) region one year ago. In this current role, he is living and working in Delta's EMEA headquarters location of Basel, Switzerland. Prior to his current role, he was Country Manager in Germany (four years) and has led a variety of functional positions in the International Division from headquarters in Boston, including a two-year global quality initiative. Lucas speaks Swedish, English, French, and German. He is a Swedish national.

5. **Pranav Subramanium**

    Pranav is the Vice President of the Indian subsidiary, reporting to Xiao Zhang, the recently re-assigned Country Manager of India. Pranav joined Delta three years ago after spending five years in a consulting firm in Delhi. The succession plan states that his performance has been exemplary and he is considered in the top rank of the regional talent pool. Pranav has an MBA from the Institute of Advanced Management and Research in Ghaziabad. Part of Pranav's leadership development plan is a short-term assignment in the Boston headquarters. Pranav speaks English, Hindi, and Urdu. He is an Indian national.

YOUR PERSONAL REFLECTIONS

You know all of these candidates personally, some better than others. Here are the mental notes you recall about each of them:

Anika "Ani" Navithar

You know Ani well, and have been extremely impressed with her. She is intelligent and authentic, rising to every leadership role in which she has been placed across multiple functional areas. Last summer at the Delta Company picnic, you enjoyed meeting her family, her husband (who is a university professor in Boston) and their nine-year-old twin girls. Also, when Ani did her short-term project in India, Xiao Zhang said she was very effective. Ani's husband used their short-term experience in India to conduct some research and work with colleagues at Delhi University. You learned at the picnic that he now has a joint appointment at Delhi University.

Carlos Delgado

If you were hit by a bus tomorrow, Carlos would likely be asked to step into your role. He has really proven himself at Delta, with the trajectory of success. He and his family have been willing to relocate to Korea, although the demands they made regarding housing for their family, a cost of living allowance, and education for their teenage children seemed a bit excessive in your opinion. He'd probably enjoy the expatriate community in Delhi, but you wish he was willing to integrate and acculturate more, and at least attempt to learn host national languages.

Haziq Tengku

Haziq has clearly proven himself in Malaysia, and is probably ready for the next step in the Asia region. Six months ago when you were in Malaysia, Haziq was on a short leave of absence to support his wife and care for their two small children while she was going through cancer treatments. Last month, you heard that Haziq's wife is doing well.

Lucas Hansson

Lucas and his family seem to "bloom wherever they are planted," becoming part of the local community in every host country where they have lived. At the last leadership offsite, you and Lucas were speaking about whether he would be interested in accepting the President of EMEA position in the future, becoming your counterpart in EMEA. He noted that he's always looking for the next exciting opportunity – but feels as though he needs more experience running a country in emerging markets. You thought he was being exceptionally humble, but appreciated his self-awareness, probably what makes him such a great international assignee. At one of the social events, Lucas also shared with you that he and his wife had begun to discuss whether they should retire in a few years and move back to Sweden to be with their elderly parents.

Pranav Subramanium

Pranav is a solid performer, but seems as though he needs a few more years as the second-in-command. However, this could be exactly the stretch challenge Pranav needs to launch a global leadership career at Delta.

EXERCISE 2

Still working alone, consider the strengths and weaknesses of each of these four leading candidates for the job to prepare for your meeting with the leadership team. Decide which candidate you think is best suited for the job.

NOTE

1.   This case was written by Paula Caligiuri and Henry W. Lane for the purpose of class discussion. The authors do not intend to demonstrate either effective or ineffective management. Names and other identifying information may have been disguised for the purpose of maintaining confidentiality. Copyright © 2015 Northeastern University, D'Amore-McKim School of Business.

Günter K. Stahl, Mark E. Mendenhall, and Mihaela Dimitrova

ANDREAS WEBER'S REWARD FOR SUCCESS IN AN INTERNATIONAL ASSIGNMENT – A RETURN TO AN UNCERTAIN FUTURE

ANDREAS WEBER'S MIND WOULD NOT stop racing. Normally, an intense run in the evening had the effect of dissipating his worries, but tonight this did not work. The further he jogged along his standard route on the banks of the Hudson River, the more he could not get out of his mind the call he knew he must make tomorrow. "How had it all come to this?" he wondered. This thought triggered his memory back seven years, to the initial event that had set in motion the process that led to his current trouble.

ANDREAS' DECISION TO PURSUE AN INTERNATIONAL CAREER

Andreas remembered the occasion clearly; Marrie Görner, the Managing Director, had walked into his office at the Frankfurt headquarters of his bank, and offered him the chance to participate in a company-wide international leadership development program. Marrie explained that the program involved an international assignment with the intention of fostering the professional development of young, aspiring managers. After their overseas assignments, the trainees would constitute a pool of internationally experienced young managers with the potential for senior management positions at corporate headquarters. Andreas accepted the offer on the spot, with pride. He had worked very hard since joining the bank, and felt that his efforts had finally paid off.

The program started with a one-week seminar at a leading business school in the United States. The CEO had flown in from Frankfurt, demonstrating the

DOI: 10.4324/9781003247272-23

commitment of top management to this program. In his speech to the participants, the CEO stressed that in today's highly competitive global environment, managers and executives must have a global mindset and good grasp of both global imperatives and trends, and the local realities in the markets in which the bank operates. He made it clear that for any aspiring manager or "high potential" in the bank, international experience was a prerequisite for promotion into the ranks of senior management. Andreas felt confident that he had made the right decision in accepting the offer and in pursuing an international career.

Shortly after the program started, an unexpected vacancy opened up in the bank's New York branch, and Andreas was asked if he was interested. He discussed the prospect of a three-year assignment to New York with his wife, Lina. The offer looked very attractive from a career development standpoint. However, Lina was rather reluctant to commit to this move. For her, this meant pausing her career as a tax attorney and becoming a full-time housewife – something she never pictured herself doing. Nevertheless, after some deliberations, they agreed that Andreas should accept the assignment. Two months later, he was transferred to New York.

ASSIGNMENT NEW YORK: THE FIRST YEAR

Andreas remembered the day of his arrival as if it were yesterday. He arrived at JFK Airport early in the afternoon. Since his only contact point about the job assignment was corporate HR in Frankfurt, he assumed that they had made all the necessary arrangements with the New York office for his arrival. However, no one came to the airport to pick him up. He took a taxi and went directly to the New York branch of the bank. When he arrived, he was not sure where he should go. He had not been informed about whom he should contact after his arrival, so he went straight to the office of the head of the corporate finance department where he was supposed to work. When he entered the office and told the office assistant that he was the new manager from Germany, she shook her head, and told him that they were not expecting anybody. Confused, Andreas rushed to the HR department, and soon found that several misunderstandings had occurred. First, it was not the corporate finance department but the credit department that had requested his transfer. Second, contrary to what he was told in Frankfurt, there was only a non-management position vacant. They were looking for a credit analyst, basically the same job that he had done in Germany.

Andreas shook his head in reaction to the memory: "There I stood, in what was supposed to be my new office, with three pieces of luggage on the desk, and wondering whether I should stay or take the next plane home!"

Why he decided to stay in New York, he could never quite figure out. In retrospect, it was probably just a split-second decision to make the best of the situation. The whirl of images of the next two months flashed across his memory: rushed days and nights trying to learn the ropes of a new office with new procedures, looking for a place to live, meeting new people, and exploring new places. Then a clear memory intervened in the collage of memories of those first two months – Lina's arrival. Lina and their three-year-old daughter, Anne-Marie, followed Andreas to New York two months after his arrival. They moved into a small house in the outskirts of New York. Lina knew New York pretty well, as during her studies she had spent an exchange semester at Columbia University. She arrived excited to re-discover her favorite restaurants, art galleries, and museums.

Lina's enthusiasm was unfortunately shortlived. Beyond the frequent attacks of homesickness, she felt isolated and lonely at home with Anne-Marie. All of New York's attractions couldn't distract her from thinking that she had made a big mistake. She missed her job and the daily interactions with her former colleagues. Worst of all, she had a nagging feeling that her career was not simply on pause, but was in fact irrevocably ruined. Money was also an issue. Andreas quickly realized that he should have had negotiated harder for better pay and benefits, rather than accepting the assignment solely because of the potential career development opportunities. Since Lina was unable to work, the family had to rely on Andreas' income, which was barely sufficient for life in New York. Rent for their small house was exorbitant. On top of this, they were not prepared for the high cost of childcare in the United States. The money issues coupled with Lina's general discontent led to frequent arguments and feelings of resentment. Then a few months after their move, Andreas and Lina received a dinner invitation from a young married couple next door. To their surprise, their American neighbors quickly embraced the Webers. Lina joined her new acquaintance in doing volunteer work at a local art museum, which she truly enjoyed. Anne-Marie was now able to spend every second afternoon at a reasonably priced local kindergarten, which gave Lina time to pursue her own interests.

At the end of their first year in the United States, a second daughter, Elena, was born. By then, the Webers had already made several more new friends, both Americans and other expatriates. Things were finally beginning to fall into place for the Webers. When they stepped off the plane at JFK after their first home leave to Germany, it felt more like they were coming home than returning to a temporary assignment.

ANDREAS' FAST-TRACK CAREER AS AN EXPATRIATE

Professionally, things had gone extremely well during this time period. The New York branch of the bank had entered a boom phase that would last for several years. Throughout the boom, the bank's staff increased significantly. After eight months of working in the back office, Andreas was promoted to supervisor of a group of credit analysts. Then, one year after his first promotion, a position opened up at the senior management level. The deputy head of the rapidly expanding corporate finance department – a German expatriate – had unexpectedly left for a job at one of their American competitors, and the bank had to fill her position with a manager who spoke fluent German, was familiar with the finance departments of a number of German and other European companies, and was instantly available. Andreas was asked if he was willing to extend his foreign assignment contract for another three years and accept the position as deputy head of the corporate finance department. After discussing it with Lina, Andreas accepted.

In the fifth year of his assignment, Andreas made another step upward in his career. His boss retired, and Andreas was promoted to head of the corporate finance department. He was now one of five managing directors in the branch. When Andreas signed his new contract, it was agreed that he would stay with the New York branch of the bank for another three years and would then return to the bank's German headquarters.

These were fond memories, memories that somewhat buffered the intensity of Andreas' frustration and anger over his current situation. But as he continued running, the warmth of the past dissipated into the turmoil of the present.

ANDREAS' DILEMMA: STAYING IN NEW YORK OR RETURNING HOME TO AN UNCERTAIN FUTURE

"It all started with that promotion," he muttered to himself. As head of the corporate finance department, Andreas' professional and private lives had unexpectedly changed. He was now responsible for a huge area – his business activities no longer concentrated on North American subsidiaries of foreign-based companies, but included their headquarters in Europe and East Asia. In the first six months of his new job, Andreas had traveled almost 100,000 miles, mainly on business flights to Europe. Frequent virtual meetings were also a common occurrence, where it was expected of him to be flexible and available early in the morning or late at night. All of these responsibilities were exhausting, but he enjoyed the challenge and the opportunity to work with clients from around the world. His extensive traveling and long work hours were initially hard on the family. Lina felt alone, and was concerned about the negative effects of Andreas' absences on their children. Eventually, the Webers adjusted and learned to cherish the times they spent together.

The children's education started to become a source of worry. Their eldest daughter, Anne-Marie, was now nine years old and had spent most of her life outside of Germany. Lina was also concerned about her missing out on a German high school education. Anne-Marie's German language skills had gradually deteriorated over the last two years, and that troubled Lina as well. Their second daughter, Elena, was attending kindergarten, and except for the yearly home leave, she had no contact with other German children. Elena's German was quite poor. In fact, both Anne-Marie and Elena considered themselves Americans.

Lina was once again feeling discontented with her life as a housewife. Continuing her career in the United States remained impossible, and she found volunteer work no longer fulfilling and wanted her own career. To make things worse, Lina's father fell ill and died in that same year, leaving her mother alone. Andreas remembered the long conversations he had had with Lina during this period of time, many of which were from hotel rooms in faraway places. When he was home, they spoke often in the quiet of their living room, and on long walks – Andreas lost count of the multitude of times they had talked as they walked through the same park he was now running through.

"It was an extremely difficult situation," Andreas remembered:

> From a professional standpoint, my assignment to New York was the best thing that could ever happen to me: I worked in the financial center of the world; I loved my job, the freedom of being away from the bureaucracy at corporate headquarters, the opportunities to travel; I became a member of the senior management team at a very young age – impossible if I stayed in Germany. Personally, we were also happy: our children felt at home in New York; we were quickly embraced by our neighbors and the expatriate community; we had many friends … The question we continually wrestled with was: "Does it make sense to give all these up for a return to an uncertain future in Germany?" In principle, the answer would clearly have been: "No." But on a long-term basis, moving back to Germany appeared to be the best solution for our children – that is where all of our extended family are, and they are German citizens. After all, we felt responsible for their future.

After several weeks of consideration and discussion, Lina and Andreas decided to move back to Germany. This was about a year ago. Immediately after the decision was made, Andreas informed his direct superior of his decision and requested a transfer. He also contacted the bank's corporate headquarters and informed the human resource executive in charge of international assignments about his decision. A week later, Andreas received a short email from him, stating that there were currently no positions available in Germany at his level. Part of the problem, Andreas was told, was due to the fact that headquarters staff – including management positions –had been significantly reduced due to organizational restructuring, but since several new branches were due to be opened over the course of the next year, he was told that chances were good that the company would be able to find him a suitable return assignment within the next six months. Since then, Andreas had had several meetings with executives at corporate headquarters, as well as with managers of domestic branches of the bank, but he still had not been offered a reentry position.

Lina gradually became discouraged. She had told her mother that they were coming home immediately after they made their decision to return to Germany, but eight months had passed, and her mother kept asking when they were coming. Andreas' parents were persistent in their queries as well. Finally, last week, Andreas received a call from the corporate HR department, in which he was informed that they had found what they called a "challenging" return assignment. They offered him the position of deputy head of a medium-sized branch of the bank in Dresden – a five-hour drive to the east from Frankfurt. Andreas was told that they would soon send an email explaining the details of the position offer.

THE OFFER

The memory of reading the offer, and the resulting emotions of anger, betrayal, disbelief, and frustration, all came back to him. He stopped running and sat down on a park bench alongside the jogging trail. "Not only will I earn little more than half the salary that I currently make in New York," he thought to himself, "I will not be able to use the skills and experiences that I gained during my international assignment – and I will be out of touch with all the important decisions being made at headquarters as well!"

> With all the frustrations and anger welling up in his chest, Andreas thought, cynically: The bank's promotion policy – if there ever was any rational policy – is to punish those who are really committed to the organization. They assign you to one of those programs for high-fliers and send you abroad, but there is no career planning whatsoever. If there just happens to be a job vacant when you return, you are lucky. If not, they let you wait and wait and wait, until you finally accept the most ridiculous job offer. ... Their slogan that international experience is a key asset and a prerequisite for promotion into the ranks of senior management is rubbish! If you look at the actual promotion and career development practices in this organization, it becomes clear it's only lip service! The better you perform overseas, the more you get stabbed in the back when you return.

He began to wonder if he should accept the offer. Perhaps they should just stay in New York and make their home here. But then, images of Lina, Lina's mother, Anne-Marie, Elena, and his parents, and all of their combined needs enveloped him.

Leaning back on the park bench, he blankly stared down the path that would lead out of the park and into the street, and then home.

PART IV

People Issues in Global Teams, Alliances, Mergers, and Acquisitions

Readings

- Martha L. Maznevski and Celia Chui
  LEADING GLOBAL TEAMS

- Vladimir Pucik, Paul Evans, and Ingmar Björkman
  MANAGING ALLIANCES AND JOINT VENTURES

- Satu Teerikangas, Günter K. Stahl, Ingmar Björkman, and Mark E. Mendenhall
  MANAGING PEOPLE AND CULTURE IN MERGERS AND ACQUISITIONS

Cases

- Yih-teen Lee, B. Sebastian Reiche, and Carlos Sánchez-Runde
  HAIER INDIA: AIMING FOR MARKET LEADERSHIP

- Ingmar Björkman and Günter K. Stahl
  GROWTH THROUGH CROSS-BORDER ACQUISITIONS: CAN LENOVO REPEAT ITS SUCCESS STORY?

- Emma Nordbäck and Maggie Boyraz
  THE RISE AND FALL OF A GLOBAL VIRTUAL TEAM

DOI: 10.4324/9781003247272-24

Martha L. Maznevski and Celia Chui

LEADING GLOBAL TEAMS*

MOST WORK IN ORGANIZATIONS TODAY is done by teams. A team is a defined group of people working together to accomplish a joint task (Hackman, 1990; Kozlowski & Bell, 2013). There are many types of teams, varying by the type of boundary around the group of people and the degree to which they must rely on each other to accomplish the joint task. For example, in a new product development team at Boeing or Airbus, team members represent different functions, such as basic engineering and production, and work together over years in a highly interdependent way to develop and test a new product. In a sales team for Panasonic or Novartis, each salesperson has his or her own territory; team members interact with each other to share ideas and best practices and to work on a limited number of joint accounts. In a global auditing team at Ernst & Young or Deloitte, one auditor from each subsidiary's country develops the accounts for that subsidiary and submits the accounts to a managing partner. The members of this large global audit team interact very little with each other. The managing partner uses a small and representative inner team to bring together all the subsidiary accounts and create a single picture of the global client's operations.

Although teams have always been part of the organizational landscape, they have become increasingly important in the last two decades. Previously, the most important tool for managing people was the hierarchy (Leavitt, 2003; Weber, 1946, 1947): a set of nested levels of authority and responsibility. In a traditional hierarchy, organizations are divided into separate units: each unit has a boss who divides the unit's work into several pieces with a subordinate in charge of each piece; each of those subordinates does the same with his or her part of the organization's work, and so on. The hierarchy is a very simple way

* This is a reproduced version from a chapter published in Mendenhall, M.E., Osland, J.S., Bird, A., Oddou, G.R., Stevens, M.J., Maznevski, M., & Stahl, G.K. (2018), Global Leadership: Research, Practice, and Development. New York: Routledge.

DOI: 10.4324/9781003247272-25

of managing people and work. Everyone's task is clearly defined, and everyone knows with whom to communicate about what.

However, hierarchies are notoriously inflexible, and in today's era of globalization, they fall increasingly short. If the work requirements change—for example, if a supplier changes the specifications on a key component—hierarchies may not clarify who should adapt to the change. If the environment changes—for example, if customer demands shift from one product group to another or a new competitor arrives on the scene—hierarchies may not detect the shift soon enough, and resources are unlikely to be allocated appropriately. And if the task requires high levels of interdependence—for example, if basic development of a new drug should take into account how to manufacture the drug—hierarchies fail as they discourage communication across separate business units or functions. The traditional hierarchy, perfected in the first half of the 20th century, does not manage people to achieve results well in the dynamic and competitive environment of the 21st century.

Hierarchies must be supplemented with more informal modes of organization (for further discussions, see Pfeffer, 1995), especially teams. Teams can be more dynamic and adaptable to change. They can be temporary, formed quickly to achieve a specific task, and then disbanded afterward. Their membership can be fluid, including important skills as they are needed. They can coexist with other forms of organization; members of teams can and usually do hold other organizational roles simultaneously.

Any leader today must be both a good team member and good at leading teams (Biermeier-Hanson, Liu, & Dickson, 2015). Leaders at all levels of the organization are key members of coordination teams, project teams, joint-task teams, and so on. They also find themselves leading such teams at their own level and below. Helping teams perform well, whether as a member or a designated leader, requires a sophisticated understanding of today's teams. And just as leadership itself is more complex in today's global environment than it was previously, teams themselves are also more complex.

In this reading, we begin by reviewing what we know about team effectiveness in general: how teams combine the efforts of individual members to create strong results. The goal here is not to review team research completely, but to provide a representative review highlighting variables relevant to global teams. Then we identify the specific characteristics that differentiate global teams from the more common local variety and apply the research to show how leaders can effectively overcome the barriers to realize opportunities. Next, we briefly look at global teams in the context of connected global organizations. Finally, we discuss the implications for leaders themselves.

EFFECTIVE TEAMS—CONCLUSIONS FROM TEAM RESEARCH

Team research has converged around a clear set of factors that influence team performance, commonly referred to as the Input–Mediator–Output model (Lepine, Piccolo, Jackson, Mathieu, & Saul, 2008). Inputs include individual characteristics of team members, group-level characteristics such as the task type, and organizational elements such as the resources and support for teaming. Mediators are team processes that members engage in, such as communication and conflict resolution, and emergent states or important dynamic conditions within teams, such as trust and cohesion. Outputs are indicators of performance, including quality of decision-making and implementation, development of individual members, and members' engagement with the organization (Hackman, 1990).

INPUTS: SETTING TEAMS UP FOR SUCCESS

Team research has identified three main structural inputs that most affect how teams interact and perform: the configuration of people on the team, the specificity and type of task, and the way the team is organized (Bresman & Zellmer-Bruhn, 2013; Lepine et al., 2008; Stewart, 2006). The research is extensive; here we summarize the most robust findings that build a foundation for leading global teams, as illustrated in Figure 1.

Team Composition

Teams need the right combination of skills and knowledge among members. This includes the right technical and process skills, as well as task-related, functional, and geographical knowledge. It is equally important to have a mix of skills related to managing tasks, such as planning and driving toward milestones, and social skills, such as facilitating participation and resolving conflicts. It is clear that team composition is related to team effectiveness, such as influencing the level of team creativity and innovation implementation (Somech & Drach-Zahavy, 2013) and overall team performance (Woolley, Gerbasi, Chabris, Kosslyn, & Hackman, 2008). In reality, teams frequently have significant skill overlaps and skill gaps. Teams are often composed based on convenience rather than careful assignment, and sometimes the necessary skill combination is simply not available. Team members must assess the adequacy of their capabilities, and gaps should be closed by adding members or developing the skills or knowledge necessary through training or experience.

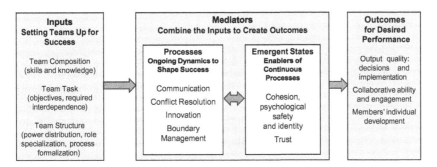

Figure 1 General team effectiveness model, highlighting variables salient for global teams

Defined Tasks and Objectives

It goes *almost* without saying that team members must know clearly what their tasks and objectives are, in order to achieve them (Kleingeld, van Mierlo, & Arends, 2011). Unfortunately, though, many teams do not understand their objectives well or do not agree on them. Sometimes this is due to lack of clear communication from leaders. The leader presents a briefing or mandate that is clear to him- or herself but is difficult or ambiguous to interpret from the point of view of the team. Often, team members have different interpretations of the task and objectives. For example, a marketing professional may think that a successful product launch is defined by high market share, while a finance professional may think it is defined by profitability; these two objectives are potentially conflicting, but many teams neglect to clarify common goals and definitions before working together.

The degree of required (structural) task interdependence is one of the most important contingencies in effective teamwork. In a task with high structural interdependence, team members are obligated to rely on each other extensively. For example, this is necessary for creative marketing communications, product development and launch, systems implementation, and many other global team tasks. When high interdependence is in the task definition, team members tend to develop more collaborative processes and positive states (Pearce & Gregersen, 1991; Van de Ven, Delbecq, & Koenig, 1976; Van Der Vegt, Emans, & Van De Vliert, 2001). More important for leaders, structural interdependence amplifies the effect of other inputs on processes and internal states, such that different inputs are associated with more collaboration, learning, and positive affect when structural interdependence is high (Burke et al., 2006; Gully, Joshi, Incalcaterra, & Beaubien, 2002; Hu & Liden, 2015). Higher interdependence is particularly important in tasks with a need to combine information from different inputs (DeChurch & Mesmer-Magnus, 2010; Guillaume, Brodbeck, & Riketta, 2012), a ubiquitous condition in global teams.

Team leaders in organizations often underestimate the degree of interdependence required to accomplish their team's task and neglect to shape the necessary processes and states (see next section) for outcomes with higher interdependence. It is important at the outset to pay attention to these dimensions.

Team Structure

Like organizations, team structures vary along three dimensions (Zellmer-Bruhn & Gibson, 2006): distribution of power and responsibility, specialization of roles, and formalization of processes. With respect to hierarchy, some teams have formal leaders while others do not. Roles can be more or less specialized, and finally, processes can be more or less formalized. The three variables tend to be correlated, such that teams with a clear leader also tend to have more specialized roles and formal processes. Extensive research suggests that clear structure in teams is generally associated with positive outcomes (Hackman, 1990; Kozlowski & Bell, 2013; Stewart, 2006; Wageman, Hackman, & Lehman,

2005). A clear structure provides a context for psychological safety and effective processes, which supports basic team efficiency as well as more ambitious outcomes, such as learning and innovation (Bresman & Zellmer-Bruhn, 2013; Edmondson, 1999; West, 2012).

Team leaders sometimes avoid implementing a clear structure, believing it goes against the notion of flexibility and fluid collaboration. However, it is much more effective for a team to have a clear structure and adapt it according to the needs of the moment than to have no structure at all.

PROCESSES: ONGOING DYNAMICS TO SHAPE SUCCESS

The two main categories of mediators that shape team success are processes and emergent states (Lepine et al., 2008; Marks, Mathieu, & Zaccaro, 2001; Mathieu, Maynard, Rapp, & Gilson, 2008). Processes are patterns of behaviors that teams enact, such as communication, conflict resolution, problem-solving, and monitoring. Emergent states are the team's shared emotional and cognitive beliefs about the team itself, such as psychological safety and cohesion. Processes and emergent states affect each other in a reciprocal way. For example, effective communication increases team members' beliefs in their ability to complete the task effectively (efficacy), which in turn affects members' willingness to resolve conflict quickly. There are countless processes and states which have been researched. Here we identify the ones which have received the most attention and at the same time are critical to the more complex context of global teams.

Processes: Communication, Conflict Resolution, Innovation, and Boundary Management

These are four fundamental processes that facilitate achieving results. The first two are more basic and fundamental and have been studied for decades, while the importance of the latter two has emerged in the context of more complex teams, including global teams.

Effective communication is the transmission of meaning as it was intended (Maznevski, 1994). Team performance is higher to the extent that each member understands the others' perspectives and the information brought to the team, and to the extent that all members are kept informed of progress in the team in a continuous way (Kozlowski & Bell, 2013; Wageman et al., 2005). Team members can only act in a cooperative way if they know what they are cooperating *about* and what they are contributing *to*. To accomplish this, communication must be an active process, with extensive questioning, checking, and paraphrasing from all parties involved. Many teams find that having a member responsible for facilitating communication is extremely helpful in ensuring effective communication.

Conflict is the expression of differences in opinion or priority due to opposing needs or demands (Tjosvold, 1986). The effect of conflict on a team is complex and research has been unraveling its effects for decades (De Dreu & Weingart, 2003; Jehn, 1995; Jehn & Mannix, 2001; Kostopoulos & Bozionelos, 2011).

Conflict about the relationships in the team or about the team processes is almost always negatively related to the climate within the team and to team performance. Task-related conflict—disagreement and discussion about facts and priorities directly related to the task—is not necessarily negative, and can even enhance task performance (De Church, Mesmer-Magnus, & Doty, 2013; de Wit, Greer, & Jehn, 2012), especially for tasks at more senior levels of the organization and that are more multidimensional. It seems that teams need "the right amount" of conflict. Not enough conflict decreases performance because perspectives are not questioned or improved upon. Many teams assign a formal role of "devil's advocate" to prevent such groupthink. Too much conflict decreases performance because it prevents convergence on a decision and implementation, and teams that experience too much conflict can enhance their performance by assigning someone to facilitate and even mediate such conflict. However, no research has been able to determine exactly how much is "the right amount" of conflict.

Innovation and Creativity. Innovation is the development and implementation of new, valuable solutions. Innovation requires a combination of creativity and deep understanding of the set of challenges the innovation is trying to address (Anderson, Potocnik, & Zhou, 2014; Hülsheger, Anderson, & Salgado, 2009; O'Reilly III, Williams, & Barsade, 1997; West, 2012). Creativity is the consideration of a wide variety of alternatives and criteria for evaluating alternatives, as well as the building of novel and useful ideas that were not originally part of the consideration set. While composition has some impact on innovation, with diverse teams having more ideas, the most important determinants of innovation are the effectiveness of other processes, including communication and conflict resolution, and the emergent states that evolve in the team, such as trust and psychological safety (Barczak, Lassk, & Mulki, 2010; Edmondson, 1999; Gong, Kim, Lee, & Zhu, 2013; Somech & Drach-Zahavy, 2013) (see below).

Many group techniques combine creativity with structured problem-solving to achieve high-quality innovation.

Managing Boundaries and Stakeholders. Most team tasks require extensive interaction between members and various parties outside the team. Effective teams must manage these boundaries well (Ancona & Caldwell, 1992). The three most important aspects of boundary management are resourcing the team, gathering information, and implementing solutions. These activities are characterized by a high need for knowledge management and transfer (Ancona, Bresman, & Caldwell, 2009; Bresman & Zellmer-Bruhn, 2013), and boundaries and stakeholders must be managed carefully. Effective teams map out the external relationships they need and strategically assign members to be responsible for different relationships on behalf of the team. Effective team leaders play a mediating role between the team structure and the way the team manages across its boundaries (Somech & Khalaili, 2014).

EMERGENT STATES: ENABLERS OF CONTINUOUS PROCESSES

Emergent states are beliefs and attitudes that team members hold about the team itself (Marks et al., 2001). They evolve dynamically as the group works together, based on the effect of group experiences. Current research on teams examines a plethora of team states, sorting out which are more important in different situations. Here we summarize the research on two fundamental states which are also especially important to global teams: cohesion and its components of psychological safety and identity, and trust.

Cohesion, Psychological Safety, and Identity

Cohesion, often referred to as social integration, is "the attraction to the group, satisfaction with other members of the group, and social interaction among group members" (O'Reilly, Caldwell, & Barnett, 1989: 22). It is one of the first and most basic states identified in teams, and captures a set of dynamics associated with general group functioning, collaboration, and coordination (Katz & Kahn, 1978; Kozlowski & Bell, 2013; Mudrack, 1989; Mullen & Copper, 1994). Cohesion covers a broad set of dynamics and can even be associated with negative outcomes like groupthink (Janis, 1972), which occurs when team members have such high cohesion they do not question each other or their own assumptions. More recent research, therefore, has sought to identify the specific elements of cohesion most important for team performance. Two are particularly relevant for global team foundations. First, psychological safety is a shared belief that the team is safe for interpersonal risk taking, and is the cohesive sub-state most associated with both caring for each other and satisfaction, on the one hand, and questioning assumptions and challenging for higher performance, on the other (Edmondson, 1999). It is associated with high levels of team learning and innovation, and is developed through effective communication, careful conflict resolution, and boundary management (Bresman & Zellmer-Bruhn, 2013; Edmondson, 1999). Second, social identity is the degree to which team members believe that group membership is an important and positive aspect of their definition of self (Ashforth & Mael, 1989). When individuals identify more strongly with a group, they engage in more participation and cooperation, share information, and coordinate more within the group (Ashforth, Harrison, & Corley, 2008; Ellemers, De Gilder, & Haslam, 2004). Like psychological safety, social identity is enhanced through effective communication, careful conflict resolution, and positive management of the boundaries.

Trust

Interpersonal trust is the extent to which a person is confident in and willing to act on the basis of the words, actions, and decisions of another (McAllister, 1995). It is a positive attitude about other team members, specifically a belief that a team member would make decisions that optimize the team's interests, even in the absence of other team members. When team members trust each other, they allow themselves to be vulnerable; that is, they put themselves at risk of being hurt by the team because of their belief that team members would always try to act to help the team and its members. A long history of research on trust has identified two main forms. Cognitive trust is based on beliefs and expectations about reliability and dependability, while affective trust is based on emotional bonds and emotional reciprocity of care and concern (McAllister, 1995). When people trust each other, they are more likely to take risks for each other (Schoorman, Mayer, & Davis, 2007). Trust among team members tends to increase interpersonal cooperation and teamwork, thereby affecting team performance positively (Balliet & Van Lange, 2013; Jones & George, 1998; Schaubroeck, Lam, & Peng, 2011). Trust develops more easily among people who are more similar to each other, making it difficult to evolve as an emergent state in global teams (Chou, Wang, Wang, Huang, & Cheng, 2008; Hogg, Van Knippenberg, & Rast, 2012). It is important to remember that trust cannot be built without taking risks; team members can only demonstrate to each other that they will act in the team's interests if other team members let them take unsupervised actions.

LEADING THE COMPLEX DYNAMICS OF TEAMS

Team inputs, processes, and emergent states have been reviewed here in a relatively linear fashion. It may imply that a leader first designs the team according to structural inputs, then sets off initiating communication, resolving conflict, innovating, and managing boundaries, and inevitably positive emergent states such as psychological safety, identity, and trust evolve. Of course, the reality is much more complex. "Inputs" constantly change as membership, the task, and the environment change. Moreover, processes and emergent states affect each other in dynamic and sometimes surprising ways, especially as the team and environment change. Newer research captures these processes in more comprehensive ways (Hackman, 2012; Tannenbaum, Mathieu, Salas, & Cohen, 2012; Wageman, Gardner, & Mortensen, 2012). At the same time, these input and mediator factors provide a powerful set of guidelines for team leaders, articulating the main priorities for shaping effective global team performance.

GLOBAL TEAMS: MORE BARRIERS, MORE OPPORTUNITIES

Global teams represent a subset of "teams" in general. While teams are groups of people working together to accomplish tasks, global teams are groups whose members represent different countries and/or whose tasks are multinational in nature. Everything described above with respect to teams applies to global teams, but global teams are more extreme. Global teams face higher barriers to effective performance, and it is much more difficult for global teams to engage effective processes and attain effective emergent states (Jonsen, Maznevski, & Davison, 2012; Pauleen, 2003; Wildman & Griffith, 2015; Zander, Mockaitis,

& Butler, 2012). On the other hand, the characteristics and contexts of global teams provide more potential for high performance and for creating an important impact within organizations, economies, and societies. Global teams that perform well make a big difference (Lane, Maznevski, & DiStefano, 2014).

GLOBAL TEAMS ARE DIVERSE AND DISPERSED

Two characteristics of global teams particularly differentiate them from teams in general, and both of them are inputs to the team model: their composition and their dispersion (Wildman & Griffith, 2015). Both of these characteristics raise barriers and provide opportunities, as summarized in Table 1. The opportunities hold out the promise of global team performance; they are mainly related to inputs and resources available to the group, and contexts in which to implement the group's output. The barriers are unfortunately mainly related to the mediators—both processes and emergent states—for turning inputs into performance. Below, each of these characteristics will be described and their implications for other inputs, processes, emergent states, and outcomes will be discussed.

Diverse Composition

Global teams, on average, have much more diverse composition than teams in general do (Schneider & Barsoux, 2003). This diverse composition has substantial implications: it provides great potential for higher performance by promoting creativity and innovation (Albrecht & Hall, 1991; Payne, 1990) and by bringing in new perspectives and a broader set of external stakeholders; at the same time, it makes smooth team interactions much more difficult. Empirical research has shown that while work team diversity influences communication behaviors that can have negative effects on internal team dynamics, it is also beneficial to team performance (see Jackson & Joshi, 2011, for a review). Diverse teams therefore

Table 1 Diversity and Dispersion: Overcome Barriers to Take Advantage of Opportunities

	Barriers	Opportunities
Diversity	Tendency toward: • Less effective communication • Increased conflict • Lower alignment on task	Potential for: • Increased creativity and innovation • More complete and comprehensive perspectives, stakeholder coverage
Dispersion	Difficult to achieve and maintain basic team conditions, due to: • Limited communication • Invisible relationships • Logistical challenges	Potential for: • More complete and comprehensive perspectives, stakeholder coverage • Focused, objective, balanced communication

tend to perform either better or worse than homogeneous teams, depending on how they are managed (DiStefano & Maznevski, 2000; Earley & Mosakowski, 2000; Staples & Zhao, 2006; Thomas, 1999). Interestingly, the most common reaction to diversity is to suppress it (Richard & Johnson, 2001; Tsui & O'Reilly, 1989), that is, to focus only on similarities. This moves a team from low-performing or value-destroying, to the medium performance of homogeneous teams—an improvement, but still one that misses the potential offered by diversity. In a meta-analysis, Stahl and colleagues found no direct impact of cultural diversity on team performance; however, they found several significant mediators and moderators such that cultural diversity had both a positive and a negative impact on mediators and therefore outputs (Stahl, Maznevski, Voigt, & Jonsen, 2010).

THE PROFOUND EFFECT OF CULTURAL DIVERSITY

Although all types of individual differences affect teams, cultural diversity has a profound impact on many different aspects of teamwork (Thatcher & Patel, 2011). We learn about our culture through years of experiences in families, schools, communities, and other cultural institutions, and people tend not even to be aware that they hold these norms related to their cultural identity. Different cultures even use different metaphors to describe teams; for example, some cultures think of teams as families, while other cultures compare business teams to sports teams.

Quite simply, people from different cultures bring different expectations to the team, and they are often unaware that they do so. Comparative research shows us that although all cultures use teams, cultures differ from each other quite widely in terms of how they tend to work in teams (Zellmer-Bruhn & Gibson, 2006; Zhou & Shi, 2011).

GLOBAL TEAMS ARE ALSO DIVERSE IN OTHER WAYS, RESULTING IN FAULTLINES

Global teams are diverse in terms of nationality, but because they are generally created to address strategic tasks, they are also usually diverse in terms of function, and their members often represent business units with different priorities and needs. This multifaceted diversity means the potential for high performance is even greater than for teams with less diversity, although it is difficult to achieve. Gender, race, function, and other differences that have both surface- and deeper-level implications combine with culture to create complex team dynamics (Stahl et al., 2010). These differences can be exacerbated by what is called faultlines (Lau & Murnighan, 1998): rifts in teams that are created by alignment of different types of differences. For example, a global team may consist of two production engineers, two marketers, and two R&D scientists, from the US, Japan, and Germany. If the engineers are from the US, the marketers from Japan, and the scientists from Germany, then the functional and cultural divisions are aligned and there are likely to be three subgroups within the team who find it very difficult to collaborate.

On the other hand, if each of the functions is represented by people from different countries, the subgroups will be less evident and differences will be easier to bridge (Lau & Murnighan, 2005). The strength of a team's fault-lines affects its performance above and beyond the impact of diversity itself, although empirical research in this area is still emerging (Thatcher & Patel, 2011, 2012).

Diverse composition is an obvious characteristic of global teams, and in fact these teams are usually created to take advantage of at least one aspect of diversity, whether geography, function, or some combination. But global teams are usually even more diverse than intended, and the combinations create nonlinear and challenging effects. The impacts of this input on processes and emergent states are often underestimated or misunderstood by managers.

Dispersed Configuration

In addition to diverse composition, global teams are typically characterized by dispersed distribution: their members are usually based in different locations, often spanning many time zones and climates, and many members travel frequently.

Communication and coordination, therefore, present major challenges for global teams. On the other hand, due to their dispersion and travel, members have access to a wide variety of resources and networks, and therefore can provide a broader variety of inputs to the team and links with its stakeholders.

Dispersed teams, who rely on information and communication technology to conduct much of their work together, are often referred to as "virtual teams." Although research in this field is relatively new (compared with team research in general), it has been extensive. Early research compared virtual teams with face-to-face teams and, in laboratory situations, generally found that face-to-face teams outperform virtual ones. This research identified barriers raised by communications technology and how to overcome them. Later research has accepted that virtual teams are inevitable and valuable. And because companies create virtual teams whenever there is a need to bring together people who are geographically distributed, the tasks are often different from those assigned to face to face teams. Most of the body of research on virtual teams examines their dynamics without comparison to face to face and identifies the key factors contributing to their performance (see Jonsen et al., 2012, for a review).

GLOBAL TEAM INPUTS: CHALLENGES OF ROLE AGREEMENT AND TASK COMPLEXITY

Diversity and dispersion are team inputs, of course. But because both affect so many aspects of social norms and interaction, they also influence other more immediate inputs of teams in significant ways.

Cultural Diversity and Role Agreement

One of the most important differences among cultures is related to how team roles are defined and managed (Maznevski & Zander, 2001). For instance, in more hierarchical cultures, such as Japan and Brazil, it is generally assumed that a team must have a single leader and that the leader must have decision-making authority within the team. If the team is not managed this way, it is believed, then the team will devolve into chaos and inefficiency. In other cultures, such as Scandinavian cultures, it is assumed that team leadership should be more emergent, fluid, and shared, with different people taking the lead at different points in the team's task. It seems that members of all cultures prefer that team leadership is shared among members, but members of cultures that are less hierarchical have a stronger preference for broad sharing (Herbert, Mockaitis, & Zander, 2014). More individualistic cultures, such as America and France, tend to define specific task-related roles clearly so as to identify individual areas of accountability. In these cultures, team members are comfortable differentiating individual performance within the team, rewarding some more than others. More collective cultures, such as Singapore, Malaysia, and Thailand, tend to define roles more fluidly, with people contributing to the team as they can and with higher accountability for the group than for individuals. In these cultures, teams prefer to reward everyone on the team the same. These differences, of course, affect the ease with which team members from different cultures agree on roles within the team. The agreement on roles, in turn, influences significant processes such as communication and conflict resolution, and provides context for assessing emergent states such as cohesion and trust.

Team Dispersion and Task Complexity

Global teams generally work on more complex tasks with less structure and high interdependence requirements (Gluesing & Gibson, 2004). When team members are also dispersed, these task inputs present strong challenges. One critical role of leaders is to provide structure for the task, so team members have a clearer frame in which to engage in processes and build emergent states (Zayani, 2008). The structure of the task affects how work relationships develop, and how frequently team members communicate with each other. This in turn influences trust and shared culture (Earley & Mosakowski, 2000; Hinds, Liu, & Lyon, 2011). Members' very different knowledge contexts can diverge from each other further over time, hindering the task, or can converge in ways that help the task (Baba, Gluesing, Ratner, & Wagner, 2004). Leaders can counteract the dispersion effect by helping team members get to know each other and interact in a way that is consistent with the level of interdependence and structure required by the task (Lampshire, 2009). The negative effect of faultlines created by dispersion can be ameliorated if the team is structured with a strong results orientation (Bezrukova, Thatcher, Jehn, & Spell, 2012), and when leaders pay attention to the diverse contexts in which members are located (Baba et al., 2004). These leadership behaviors improve team processes such as communication and conflict resolution and facilitate the development of emergent states, such as cohesion and trust.

GLOBAL TEAM PROCESSES: BARRIERS TO EFFECTIVE TEAM DYNAMICS

Global teams are complex, and there are many barriers to effective processes and emergent states, as well as many opportunities. Active leadership, therefore, is critical for facilitating the processes and states (Small, 2011).

Communication: Understanding Differences, Restricted Modes

Cultural diversity and dispersion's most obvious impacts are on communication in teams, and indeed, most research on global teams examines this dynamic.

Naturally, people from different cultures speak different languages. Even if there is a common business language—likely English—team members have different levels of fluency, and not everything they are thinking in their native language can be translated into the linear structures and often comparatively imprecise vocabulary of English. Recent research has begun to study the impact of language diversity on communication in global teams. When team members use different languages, subgroups are created and faultlines are reinforced (Kulkarni, 2015). Apart from potential misunderstandings, negative emotions can be provoked by language barriers, including anxiety and resentment (Tenzer & Pudelko, 2015).

Power dynamics can be reflected in language dominance, leading to subgroup imbalances in task input (Hinds, Neeley, & Cramton, 2014). Leaders can reduce the impact of language barriers by diverting attention away from them, decreasing the negative appraisal of people who speak different languages, and counteracting the power imbalances with other sources of power.

Aside from language differences, people from different cultures expect and engage in different norms for communication. In some cultures, such as many Latin cultures, it is acceptable to express one's ideas at any time, even speaking at the same time as others and with openly expressed emotion; in other cultures, such as many East Asian cultures, it is only acceptable to speak when asked a question, and it is never acceptable to speak at the same time as others—silence is preferable.

In many cultures, showing excessive emotion is considered inappropriate. For example, members of collective cultures tend to be more sensitive toward the affective influence of their team members than those in individualistic cultures (Ilies, Wagner, & Morgeson, 2007). With such widely varying norms for communication, it is difficult for culturally diverse teams to communicate effectively, to send and receive meaning as it was intended.

Communication over technology is much less rich than face-to-face communication, even if visual technology such as video conferencing or webcams are used. Subtle nonverbal communication, such as body language and tone of voice, is greatly constrained by technology. Virtual teams therefore find it more difficult to communicate effectively, especially complex and context-sensitive information regarding the task itself, and emotional information regarding team processes (Cash-Baskett, 2011; Cramton & Webber, 2005). And even though most managers conduct a high proportion of their teamwork virtually, most report that they do not like or prefer this mode of communication. It is a "necessary evil."

More specifically, tacit knowledge is extremely difficult to share over technology (Cramton & Webber, 2005; Maznevski & Chudoba, 2000). Tacit knowledge is the type of knowledge that is contextually embedded and cannot be articulated explicitly. Explicit knowledge can be written down in manuals, spreadsheets, patent applications, and so on, and can be transferred relatively easily from one person to another in such forms. Explicit knowledge is copyable and inexpensive; in fact, it can be found free of charge all through the Internet. Tacit knowledge takes explicit knowledge and puts it in context, in use. Tacit knowledge comes from experience and incorporates wisdom and judgment. It is not copyable, and it tends to be expensive. For example, a chemical engineer who just graduated from university has high levels of explicit knowledge: he knows all the latest techniques and applications for combining elements; but he has less knowledge of the complex contexts of different applications. A chemical engineer who has been working on field applications for fifteen years may have less explicit knowledge than the young graduate (that is, she may not know all the latest techniques), but she has more tacit knowledge about how different compounds react to the multitude of variables in different manufacturing contexts. Tacit knowledge is best transferred during face-to-face interactions, which allow for questions, dialogue, and the richness of nonverbal communication. Therefore, if a global team's task requires high levels of tacit knowledge transfer and development, the team will find it challenging without meeting face to face (Sarker, Ajuja, Sarker, & Kirkeby, 2011).

More Conflict, More Difficult to Resolve

Global teams do experience more conflict (Stahl et al., 2010), and both cultural diversity and dispersion influence how global teams detect and address conflict. For example, the different perceptions of power across cultures can influence the type of conflict resolution strategies used (Kaushal & Kwantes, 2006).

Some cultures, such as many Nordic cultures, show respect for each other by expressing conflict only indirectly (it is important not to hurt each others' face or feelings); while others, such as the neighboring Dutch, show respect by expressing disagreement openly (it is important not to waste each others' time on trivial agreement). With such widely varying norms for showing respect in conflict resolution, it is difficult to resolve conflicts constructively. However, when global teams face differences openly and constructively, their different perspectives can be instrumental to resolving conflict (Tjosvold & Yu, 2007).

Creativity and Innovation—Optimism for Diversity and Dispersion

Diverse teams are more creative than teams with low diversity—the former identify more ideas, and more criteria for evaluating the ideas (Stahl et al., 2010). Moreover, collaborative technologies can also lead to increased creativity and innovation in dispersed teams (Cramton & Webber, 2005; Hinds et al., 2011). Achieving innovation in global teams has the same foundation as "normal" teams, although it is more challenging. Global teams who work toward a clear and compelling challenge with involvement and strong information flow achieve strong innovation results (Kerber & Buono, 2004). Teams whose members have more of a global mindset are more innovative and perform better, and transformational leadership in the team is an important predictor of this global mindset and innovation (Gagnon, 2013). Just as for co-located teams, psychological safety is a strong predictor of innovation in global teams (Gibson & Gibbs, 2006). Global innovation teams that manage communication and conflict well in a cycle that creates learning achieve high levels of innovation success (Bouncken & Winkler, 2010).

Boundary Management and Other Processes—the Bright Side of Global Teams

Global teams, by definition, span boundaries already within the team, and face more boundaries outside the team, than "normal" co-located teams. Much of the research on global teams explicitly or implicitly addresses boundary-spanning within the team. However, very little research examines the role of boundary management outside the team, and this is a field where more research is needed (Butler, Zander, Mockaitis, & Sutton, 2012; Zander et al., 2012).

Processes in global teams reinforce each other for higher performance. For example, teams are characterized by learning and adaptability when their leaders facilitate strong communication, boundary-spanning, goal-setting, and task-related skills in the context of managing cultural differences (Furukawa, 2010). Given the complexity of global teams, leaders must deal with paradox and contradiction in team members' expectations and norms, exhibiting a variety of leadership styles simultaneously to facilitate strong processes (Leidner, 2002).

GLOBAL TEAM EMERGENT STATES: DEVELOPING POSITIVE ATTITUDES AND BELIEFS

Positive emergent states are more difficult to build in multicultural teams, and global leadership is critical for enabling good processes to build the states (Stahl et al., 2010). Nevertheless, social integration and trust can be built over time, with predictable positive effects on performance (Kiely, 2001).

Cohesion, Identity, and Psychological Safety Are Threatened by Diversity and Dispersion

Members of multicultural teams tend to be very motivated to work in these teams and enjoy the team experience, yet still find it difficult to develop strong cohesion, identity, or psychological safety. Global teams inevitably feel tensions around which norms to adopt, and this affects their cohesion, identity, and psychological safety. During a crisis, cohesion and psychological safety are especially important for global team motivation and cohesiveness, which in turn leads to motivation to engage with the team (Jenster & Steiler, 2011). Fortunately, culturally intelligent leaders leverage their abilities to develop a synergistic cultural strategy to bring people together for higher-level goals and objectives, which increases team integration and shared identity (Dean, 2007). Global teams that develop a "hybrid culture" seem to develop more cohesion and social integration. A hybrid culture is a shared identity and set of norms that is specific to the team and results from the combination of different norms from team members' "home" cultures (Earley & Mosakowski, 2000; Hinds et al., 2011).

Trust—Starts Fast, Builds Slowly

Global teams experience great challenges overcoming the barriers to trust raised by diversity and dispersion. At the same time, trust is imperative in global teams, because of the need to operate separately in different contexts most of the time (Mach & Baruch, 2015).

Interestingly, dispersed teams often begin with "swift trust," or a willingness to act based on cognitive trust even without experience (Jarvenpaa & Leidner, 1998; Jarvenpaa, Shaw, & Staples, 2004). Reliability and predictability can be developed virtually through task experiences, and global teams should set quick deliverables and communication norms in order to build trust. The deep trust that allows a team member to be vulnerable to others is extremely difficult to build without personal contact.

Multilanguage teams face massive barriers to the development of trust, and the negative emotions and power imbalances associated with language differences (see above) can even prevent the development of trust (Tenzer, Pudelko, & Harzing, 2014). In global teams with high diversity and broad dispersion, consensus-oriented communication and conflict resolution and a collective team orientation can help to overcome diversity and dispersion to build trust (Mach & Baruch, 2015). It is helpful for global teams to experience pieces of the task quickly, to develop reliability, and to create a foundation for trust. For example, the more quickly team members are assigned different aspects of information-gathering and then come together to share initial results, the more "data" team members have about each other to build roles, processes, and eventually trust.

ENABLING POSITIVE OUTCOMES IN GLOBAL TEAMS

When global teams overcome the challenges inherent in their composition and dispersion with strong processes and emergent states, they perform well and achieve outcomes beyond what co-located, less diverse teams could do (DiStefano & Maznevski, 2000). Research shows that multicultural teams who develop a collaborative and cohesive climate outperform homogeneous teams (Stahl et al., 2010).

Realizing the Potential of Diversity through Knowledge and Communication

To turn the input of diversity into high performance, global teams must explicitly address and manage both their similarities and their differences; they must both create social cohesion and acknowledge and respect individual differences (DiStefano & Maznevski, 2000; Lane et al., 2014). Synergy takes enormous energy from the leader, clarifying processes and engaging in discussion around differences (Stumpf & Zeutschel, 2001). Diverse teams that focus only on their differences create great rifts within the team and find it difficult to converge or align. Teams that focus only on their similarities, though, in an effort to maximize social cohesion, also under-perform—they do not take advantage of their differences.

Moreover, their suppressed differences eventually arise in the context of deep and personal conflicts, hurting the team and its performance.

To enable effective processes and high-quality emergent states, it is helpful for team members to map out their similarities and differences, especially with respect to culture, function, or expertise, and business unit perspective. Mapping is creating a picture of the team's diversity, using charts and where possible, data from personality or cultural dimension assessments. If done with an open mindset and motivation, this mapping process itself helps to create cohesion and trust as team members explore their different perspectives and common connections. The team can then identify in which areas it is easily aligned and areas where different members will contribute differently. Teams should develop tight alignment around task-related issues, such as the definition of the task and objectives, while encouraging and respecting diverse perspectives around contributions to the task and ways of getting it done and social needs within the group.

Once the differences are mapped, then team members must bridge these differences using effective communication techniques. Especially important is decentering, or speaking and listening from the others' points of view. For example, an American, through mapping, may understand that her teammates from East Asia prefer to express conflict indirectly. However, she may not be able to bridge that difference by decentering: she may say, "I know you find it difficult to be direct in conflict, but it's okay to do it with me, I won't be offended." If the American were truly decentering, she would find ways to ask questions and check for agreement that allow the East Asians to express conflict indirectly. Referring to a decision about direction, for example, she might ask a teammate "How do you think people in your office would react to this decision?" This question would allow a teammate to express his own disagreement indirectly as a hypothetical third person's opinion and not his own. Equally important in bridging is refraining from blame. Problems and miscommunication in diverse teams are inevitable, and it is a natural reaction to blame others for the problem, or to attribute low motivation or other negative characteristics to them. In effective multicultural teams, team members do not blame each other when such problems arise but engage in creative dialogue to try and understand which types of differences contributed to the misunderstanding. In this way, effective teams turn problems into opportunities for learning about each other.

LEVERAGING DISPERSION BY STRUCTURING THE TASK AND PROCESS

When working over technology, one important implication of the research findings is to maintain discipline and focus around the task and processes. Face-to-face teams can use the immediacy of personal contact to create a sense of urgency and momentum; virtual teams must create it deliberately themselves. Identifying roles, developing a project plan, monitoring progress—all the processes discussed earlier in this chapter—must be accomplished with great deliberation in virtual teams.

Interestingly, teams who develop good discipline and focus find that working over technology can actually facilitate team performance, rather than hinder it. When meeting times are limited, people tend to prepare more effectively and stay focused throughout the meeting. When nonverbal cues are limited, people focus on the spoken or written word and remain much more task focused. Because of this, virtual teams often have lower levels of personal conflict than face-to-face teams. The use of structured communication tools such as conference calls, emails, and web meetings tends to decrease the dominance of extraverts and native language speakers, giving each member more of a chance to participate in a way he or she feels comfortable. This "performance bonus" can only be achieved, though, when the team has built relationships, shared tacit knowledge, and developed discipline and focus (Malhotra, Majchrzak, & Rosen, 2007).

The question is not, then, "should we meet face to face?" but "when should we meet face to face, and what should we do with that time?" Most teams believe they should get together at the team's launch, then whenever there is a crisis, conflict, or a major decision point: "This team is important, and so whenever we really need to see each other, when things aren't going well, we take the effort to jump on a plane and see each other." In fact, high-performing teams do something quite different. They schedule regular meetings and stick to the schedule, for example meeting once every three to four months for two days each time. They create a team heartbeat with a regular rhythm. During their face-to-face meetings, they do not present sales reports or simple updates; instead, they engage in discussions and actions to build shared tacit knowledge and strong relationships. They might visit customers or suppliers together, work on an innovation process, or share cases about best practices or reviews of failures. These activities pump the team's equivalent of oxygen through the team. Research has shown that teams who have a strong heartbeat can manage all other tasks virtually in between their face-to-face meetings and that this is both less expensive and more effective than getting together "whenever we need to" (Maznevski & Chudoba, 2000).

Which technology is most effective? Virtual teams often search for the "one best technology" that will solve all the members' challenges. So far, though, that technology has not yet emerged. Some recent advances such as voice and video over broadband Internet hold promise, as they add richness to normally sparse electronic communication. However, global teams usually face different infrastructures in different countries, company firewalls, people traveling, and other complications that make it difficult for them to rely on these advances.

Effective virtual teams use a range of technology, matching different technologies to different aspects of the team's task. Collaboration technologies facilitate work together and range from straightforward emails to shared documents and virtual meeting applications. Interestingly, high-performing virtual teams that use collaboration technologies well can outperform face-to-face teams, by using the features to leverage diversity and dispersion (Hinds et al., 2011).

For example, such global teams might use email for asynchronous communication, phone for one-to-one discussions, web meetings for joint discussions (some members using the phone and others using the Internet for the voice aspect), and a shared workspace for keeping documents. They might also combine or sequence technologies in specific ways; for example, a good technique for communicating effectively across cultures is to first exchange email background about a topic, then to discuss it on the phone to develop a dialogue with questions and answers in real-time, then to follow up on email to ensure that the main points were shared. In addition, high-performance teams also take team members' personality characteristics into account and match technology with personal preferences well (Jonsen et al., 2012). Recent research shows a relationship between technological communication, personality characteristics, and performance (Jacques, Garger, Brown, & Deale, 2009; Turel & Zhang, 2010). More practically, when choosing technologies, teams should select ones (and provide training if necessary) that all team members can use and that will be supported as needed.

CONNECTED TEAMS CREATE GLOBAL ORGANIZATIONS

Today's multinational organizations typically share some negative characteristics, including impersonality and heavy complexity. Multinationals are large and distributed, and it is often difficult for their members—especially those outside of headquarters—to relate to other parts of the company. Moreover, the use of virtual workers is becoming much more common, such as salespeople with independent territories who only see another member of their own company a couple of times a month or even less. The complexity also makes these organizations heavy and unwieldy, and managers have difficulty getting information where it is needed, when it is needed. Many senior managers today are trying to learn how to motivate people and share information in this difficult situation, to maintain commitment and collaboration so that the opportunities of globalization will not be lost under the burdens. Effective global teams have some important "side effects" related to creating global organizations. "Connected teams" refers to global teams who pay attention to and nurture these higher-order benefits.

First, members of effective global teams tend to feel more committed to the organization as a whole than do people who are not members of such teams. When people have personal and performance-related connections with others in different parts of the organization, those other parts of the organization seem less distant and more real. Team members make the organization more tangible for each other. This may seem trivial, but for a leader trying to enhance and coordinate performance in a multinational organization, this commitment to the company and the individuals within it goes a very long way.

Second, most managers today are members of two or more global teams. As we discussed at the beginning of this chapter, global teams often cross the hierarchy and join people from different parts of the organization. Because of this, the multiple global teams that each manager is part of tend to cross different parts of the company. Each manager (team member), therefore, is a potential conveyor of knowledge across boundaries, and global teams can be conduits for knowledge sharing and organizational learning. This perspective is summarized in Figure 2. As for all other potential benefits of global teams, this knowledge sharing does not happen automatically. In fact, members of global teams tend to focus on the task at hand—which is difficult enough—and not pay attention to passing on knowledge about other aspects of company performance. But as global teams start to master their own task their conversations often turn to "what else is happening at your end?" Effective global leaders and teams encourage this learning, and in fact sophisticated multinational companies see its advantages and facilitate it deliberately.

Most managers are on two or more distributed teams, but tend to see these as separate teams or matrixed teams. This is typically how connected teams are shown, emphasizing the distinct nature of the different teams:

For example, person A is on the "USA and Canada" team, and also on the "Marketing" team.

	USA and Canada	Latin America	Europe	Asia	Middle East and Africa
Marketing	A	F			S
Production	B		J	N	
Logistics	C	G	K		T
R&D	D		L	P	
Finance	E	H	M	Q	U
Call Centers				R	V

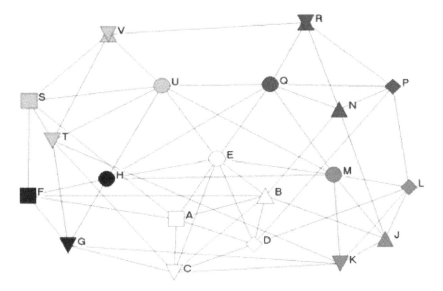

Figure 2 Connected teams

Here are the same teams shown as a network. Shapes the same shade of gray are in the same geographical team, and the same shape are in the same functional team. This network emphasizes the interconnections between team members and highlights the opportunities for learning and distribution of knowledge.

GLOBAL TEAMS: WORTH THE EFFORT

In sum, diverse composition and dispersed configuration raise enormous barriers and opportunities for global teams. Team members are often motivated by this extra challenge, especially at the beginning of a team's life. Working with people in different locations adds variety and new perspectives, and many people find it inspiring to connect with people in other places. By connecting global teams with each other, a large organization can become more human and meaningful, while also learning from this broader configuration. Effective global team leaders can take advantage of momentum to get the team working well together and, using the findings discovered by research about global teams, can turn the challenges into opportunities for high performance.

LEADING GLOBAL TEAMS: ADVICE TO LEADERS

We began this chapter by arguing that effective global leaders must be good both at being global team members and at leading global teams. Throughout this chapter we have identified the characteristics of effective global teams, and global leaders can use the ideas in the chapter as somewhat of a checklist:

- Is the leader paying attention to basic inputs, processes, and emergent states?
- Does the leader have a good understanding of the team's diversity (especially cultural) and dispersion, and the implications of both?
- Is the team overcoming barriers to communication and other processes, to capture the opportunities inherent in its composition and configuration?
- Are team members building cohesion and trust through experiences working together, whether face to face or virtual?
- Are the members leveraging the team as a connected team throughout the organization?

Every global team is different, and therein lies the importance of leadership (Curry, 2015). There are no hard and fast rules about global teams. All global teams should develop trust and respect, and the path to doing that in each team is different. All global teams should be innovative, but the focus of their innovation, the end-user, is different. All global teams must manage external stakeholder relationships, but all have different sets of stakeholders. And so on.

Global and multinational leaders are generally seen to be responsible for defining the goals and direction of the team, organizing and supporting the team in accomplishing their goals, and guiding the implementation of their goals (Zaccaro, Rittman, & Marks, 2002). They must help the team adapt to the environmental constraints including globalization, the different local contexts, and usually a matrix organization (Tworoger, Ruppel, Gong, & Pohlman, 2013). Team leaders who communicate well can mitigate the negative effects of geographical differences, and research suggests that team leaders should communicate more regularly with their globally dispersed teams as well as create team norms that encourage communication among team members.

In global teams, the traditional leadership role tends to be distributed across more people than in traditional teams (Jonsen et al., 2012). In traditional teams, the "leader" tends to be the hierarchical head of the team, the meeting chairperson, the discussion facilitator, the decision-maker, the discipline enforcer, the direction-setter, and often other roles as well. Global teams are too complex and dynamic for one person to take on all of these roles. Experienced leaders of global teams either assign some of these roles to others or facilitate the emergence of multiple leadership roles within the team. This is yet another complexity for leaders of global teams, but as with diversity and distribution, it creates an opportunity for higher performance if well-managed.

This infinite variety of teams and the ambiguity of leadership roles prevent the checklist from being applied like a recipe. It is more like a field guide of which characteristics to pay attention to and which leadership tools might be most effective in different situations. The application is up to the leader, who must match the tools with the situation, including the combination of members, tasks, and external stakeholders. This implies that leaders of global teams must constantly observe and check the condition of the team, monitoring also its context (which includes cultural contextual awareness) and situation.

As emphasized elsewhere in this book, cultural competency is important to global team leadership. Studies have shown a positive relationship between multinational team performance and the degree of cross-cultural competency of their leader (Matveev & Nelson, 2004). For example, individuals who are high on cultural intelligence, global identity, and openness to cultural diversity were found to emerge as global leaders on global student team projects (Lisak & Erez, 2015). One way of increasing cultural awareness is international experience: team leaders who have had international experience are likely to possess a higher level of cultural competence and empathy (Caligiuri & Tarique, 2011). A team leader's cultural intelligence has been shown to influence team members' perceptions of leader performance and team performance (Groves & Feyerherm, 2011). Naturally, leaders who can communicate better with their global followers will be better able to influence the motivation of their team members to exploit, explore, and transfer knowledge within the team.

Importantly, global teams are excellent arenas for developing global leadership skills (Maznevski & DiStefano, 2000). Just as all the global leadership competences and perspectives are important for leading global teams, so they can be developed through experience in global teams. Global leaders encourage meaningful engagement, capture knowledge, and disseminate it while the team is working (Caligiuri, 2015). High-performing global organizations assign emerging global leaders to global teams to support their learning journeys through stretch challenges, peer-level collaborations, and feedback and support (Caligiuri, 2015).

Like global leadership in general, leading global teams is a craft that combines the science of conditions and opportunities in teams—the checklist—with the art of applying the right processes at the right time. Leaders who are open to and careful about learning will develop the skills needed for this craft.

REFERENCES

Albrecht, T.L., & Hall, B.J. 1991. Facilitating talk about new ideas: The role of personal relationships in organizational innovation. *Communications Monographs*, 58(3): 273–288.

Ancona, D., Bresman, H., & Caldwell, D. 2009. The X-factor: Six steps to leading high-performing X-teams. *Organizational Dynamics*, 38(3): 217.

Ancona, D., & Caldwell, D.F. 1992. Bridging the boundary: External activity and performance in organizational teams. *Administrative Science Quarterly*, 37(4): 634–665.

Anderson, N., Potocnik, K., & Zhou, J. 2014. Innovation and creativity in organizations: A state-of-the-science review, prospective commentary, and guiding framework. *Journal of Management*, 40(5): 1297–1333.

Ashforth, B.E., Harrison, S.H., & Corley, K.G. 2008. Identification in organizations: An examination of four fundamental questions. *Journal of Management*, 34(3): 325–374.

Ashforth, B.E., & Mael, F. 1989. Social identity theory and the organization. *The Academy of Management Review*, 14(1): 20.

Baba, M.L., Gluesing, J., Ratner, H., & Wagner, K.H. 2004. The contexts of knowing: Natural history of a globally distributed team. *Journal of Organizational Behavior*, 25(5): 547–587.

Balliet, D., & Van Lange, P.A. 2013. Trust, conflict, and cooperation: A meta-analysis. *Psychological Bulletin*, 139(5): 1090.

Barczak, G., Lassk, F., & Mulki, J. 2010. Antecedents of team creativity: An examination of team emotional intelligence, team trust and collaborative culture. *Creativity and Innovation Management*, 19(4): 332–345.

Bezrukova, K., Thatcher, S.M.B., Jehn, K.A., & Spell, C.S. 2012. The effects of alignments: Examining group faultlines, organizational cultures, and performance. *Journal of Applied Psychology*, 97(1): 77–92.

Biermeier-Hanson, B., Liu, M., & Dickson, M.W. 2015. Alternate views of global leadership: Applying global leadership perspectives to leading global teams. In J.L. Wildman & R. Griffith (Eds.), *Leading global teams: Translating multidisciplinary science to practice*: 195–233. New York: Springer.

Bouncken, R.B., & Winkler, V.A. 2010. National and cultural diversity in transnational innovation teams. *Technology Analysis & Strategic Management*, 22(2): 133.

Bresman, H., & Zellmer-Bruhn, M. 2013. The structural context of team learning: Effects of organizational and team structure on internal and external learning. *Organization Science*, 24(4): 1120–1139.

Burke, C.S., Stagl, K.C., Klein, C., Goodwin, G.F., Salas, E., & Halpin, S.M. 2006. What type of leadership behaviors are functional in teams? A meta-analysis. *Leadership Quarterly*, 17(3): 288–307.

Butler, C.L., Zander, L., Mockaitis, A., & Sutton, C. 2012. The global leader as boundary spanner, bridge maker, and blender. *Industrial and Organizational Psychology*, 5(2): 240–243.

Caligiuri, P. 2015. Developing cross-cultural competences through global teams. In J.L. Wildman & R. Griffith (Eds.), *Leading global teams: Translating multidisciplinary science to practice*: 123–139. New York: Springer.

Caligiuri, P., & Tarique, I. 2011. *Dynamic competencies and performance in global leaders: Role of personality and developmental experiences*. SHRM Foundation Research (Final Report). Alexandria, VA: Society for Human Resource Management.

Cash-Baskett, L.J. 2011. *Global virtual team members' perceptions of leader practices*. Sarasota, FL: A. U. College of Business.

Chou, L.-F., Wang, A.-C., Wang, T.-Y., Huang, M.-P., & Cheng, B.-S. 2008. Shared work values and team member effectiveness: The mediation of trustfulness and trustworthiness. *Human Relations*, 61(12): 1713.

Cramton, C.D., & Webber, S.S. 2005. Relationships among geographic dispersion, team processes, and effectiveness in software development work teams. *Journal of Business Research*, 58(6): 758–765.

Curry, C.D. 2015. Coaching global teams and global leaders. In J.L. Wildman & R. Griffith (Eds.), *Leading global teams: Translating multidisciplinary science to practice*: 141–168. New York: Springer.

De Church, L.A., Mesmer-Magnus, J.R., & Doty, D. 2013. Moving beyond relationship and task conflict: Toward a process-state perspective. *Journal of Applied Psychology*, 98(4): 559–578.

De Dreu, C.K.W., & Weingart, L.R. 2003. Task versus relationship conflict, team performance, and team member satisfaction: A meta-analysis. *Journal of Applied Psychology*, 88(4): 741–749.

de Wit, F.R.C., Greer, L.L., & Jehn, K.A. 2012. The paradox of intragroup conflict: A meta-analysis. *Journal of Applied Psychology*, 97(2): 360–390.

Dean, B.P. 2007. *Cultural intelligence in global leadership: A model for developing culturally and nationally diverse teams*. PhD Dissertation. R. U. School of Global Leadership & Entrepreneurship.

DeChurch, L.A., & Mesmer-Magnus, J.R. 2010. The cognitive underpinnings of effective teamwork: A meta-analysis. *Journal of Applied Psychology*, 95(1): 32–53.

DiStefano, J.J., & Maznevski, M.L. 2000. Creating value with diverse teams in global management. *Organizational Dynamics*, 29(1): 45–63.

Earley, C.P., & Mosakowski, E. 2000. Creating hybrid team cultures: An empirical test of transnational team functioning. *Academy of Management Journal*, 43(1): 26–49.

Edmondson, A. 1999. Psychological safety and learning behavior in work teams. *Administrative Science Quarterly*, 44(2): 350–383.

Ellemers, N., De Gilder, D., & Haslam, S.A. 2004. Motivating individuals and groups at work: A social identity perspective on leadership and group performance. *Academy of Management Review*, 29(3): 459–478.

Furukawa, C. 2010. *Functional multinational team leadership and team effectiveness from a dynamic capability perspective*. PhD Dissertation. B. B. S. College of Social Sciences, University of Birmingham.

Gagnon, J.-P. 2013. *Global team effectiveness: Evaluating the role of transformational leadership and global mindset in geographically dispersed business teams*. PhD Dissertation. University of Pennsylvania.

Gibson, C.B., & Gibbs, J.L. 2006. Unpacking the concept of virtuality: The effects of geographic dispersion, electronic dependence, dynamic structure, and national diversity on team innovation. *Administrative Science Quarterly*, 51(3): 451–495.

Gluesing, J.C., & Gibson, C.B. 2004. Designing and forming global teams. In H.W. Lane, M. Maznevski, M.E. Mendenhall, & J. McNett (Eds.), *The Blackwell handbook of global management: A guide to managing complexity*: 199–226. Hoboken, NJ: John Wiley & Sons.

Gong, Y., Kim, T.-Y., Lee, D.-R., & Zhu, J. 2013. A multilevel model of team goal orientation, information exchange, and creativity. *Academy of Management Journal*, 56(3): 827–851.

Groves, K.S., & Feyerherm, A.E. 2011. Leader cultural intelligence in context: Testing the moderating effects of team cultural diversity on leader and team performance. *Group & Organization Management*. https://doi.org/10.1177/1059601111415664.

Guillaume, Y.R.F., Brodbeck, F.C., & Riketta, M. 2012. Surface- and deep-level dissimilarity effects on social integration and individual effectiveness related outcomes in work groups: A meta-analytic integration. *Journal of Occupational & Organizational Psychology*, 85(1): 80–115.

Gully, S.M., Joshi, A., Incalcaterra, K.A., & Beaubien, J.M. 2002. A meta-analysis of team-efficacy, potency, and performance: Interdependence and level of analysis as moderators of observed relationships. *Journal of Applied Psychology*, 87(5): 819–832.

Hackman, J.R. 1990. *Groups that work (and those that don't)*. San Francisco, CA: Jossey-Bass.

Hackman, J.R. 2012. From causes to conditions in group research. *Journal of Organizational Behavior*, 33(3): 428–444.

Herbert, K., Mockaitis, A.I., & Zander, L. 2014. An opportunity for east and west to share leadership: A multicultural analysis of shared leadership preferences in global teams. *Asian Business & Management*, 13(3): 257–282.

Hinds, P., Liu, L., & Lyon, J. 2011. Putting the global in global work: An intercultural lens on the practice of cross-national collaboration. *The Academy of Management Annals*, 5(1): 135.

Hinds, P.J., Neeley, T.B., & Cramton, C.D. 2014. Language as a lightning rod: Power contests, emotion regulation, and subgroup dynamics in global teams. *Journal of International Business Studies*, 45(5): 536–561.

Hogg, M.A., Van Knippenberg, D., & Rast, I.D.E. 2012. Intergroup leadership in organizations: Leading across group and organizational boundaries. *Academy of Management Review*, 37(2): 232–255.

Hu, J., & Liden, R.C. 2015. Making a difference in the teamwork: Linking team prosocial motivation to team processes and effectiveness. *Academy of Management Journal*, 58(4): 1102–1127.

Hülsheger, U.R., Anderson, N., & Salgado, J.F. 2009. Team-level predictors of innovation at work: A comprehensive meta-analysis spanning three decades of research. *Journal of Applied Psychology*, 94(5): 1128.

Ilies, R., Wagner, D.T., & Morgeson, F.P. 2007. Explaining affective linkages in teams: Individual differences in susceptibility to contagion and individualism–collectivism. *Journal of Applied Psychology*, 92(4): 1140.

Jackson, S.E., & Joshi, A. 2011. Work team diversity. In S. Zedeck (Ed.), *APA handbook of industrial and organizational psychology, volume 1: Building and developing the organization*: 651–686. Washington, DC: American Psychological Association.

Jacques, P.H., Garger, J., Brown, C.A., & Deale, C.S. 2009. Personality and virtual reality team candidates: The roles of personality traits, technology anxiety and trust as predictors of perceptions of virtual reality teams. *Journal of Business and Management*, 15(2): 143.

Janis, I.L. 1972. *Victims of groupthink: A psychological study of foreign-policy decisions and fiascoes.* Boston, MA: Houghton, Mifflin.

Jarvenpaa, S.L., & Leidner, D.E. 1998. Communication and trust in global virtual teams. *Organization Science*, 1999, 10(6): 791–815.

Jarvenpaa, S.L., Shaw, T.R., & Staples, D.S. 2004. Toward contextualized theories of trust: The role of trust in global virtual teams. *Information Systems Research*, 15(3): 250–267.

Jehn, K.A. 1995. A multimethod examination of the benefits and detriments of intragroup conflict. *Administrative Science Quarterly*, 40: 256–282.

Jehn, K.A., & Mannix, E.A. 2001. The dynamic nature of conflict: A longitudinal study of intragroup conflict and group performance. *Academy of Management Journal*, 44(2): 238–251.

Jenster, N.P., & Steiler, D. 2011. Turning up the volume in interpersonal leadership: Motivating and building cohesive global virtual teams during times of economic crisis. *Advances in Global Leadership*, 6: 267–297.

Jones, G.R., & George, J.M. 1998. The experience and evolution of trust: Implications for cooperation and teamwork. *Academy of Management Review*, 23(3): 531–546.

Jonsen, K., Maznevski, M., & Davison, S.C. 2012. Global virtual team dynamics and effectiveness. In G.K. Stahl, I. Bjorkman, & S. Morris (Eds.), *Handbook of research in international human resource management*, 2nd ed.: 363–392. Cheltenham: Edward Elgar Publishing.

Katz, D., & Kahn, R.L. 1978. *The social psychology of organizations.* New York: Wiley.

Kaushal, R., & Kwantes, C.T. 2006. The role of culture and personality in choice of conflict management strategy. *International Journal of Intercultural Relations*, 30(5): 579–603.

Kerber, K.W., & Buono, A.F. 2004. Leadership challenges in global virtual teams: Lessons from the field. *SAM Advanced Management Journal*, 69(4): 4.

Kiely, L.S. 2001. Overcoming time and distance: International virtual executive teams. In M.W. McCall & W. Mobley (Eds.), *Advances in global leadership*, Volume 2: 185–216. Bingley, UK: Emerald Group Publishing.

Kleingeld, A., van Mierlo, H., & Arends, L. 2011. The effect of goal setting on group performance: A meta-analysis. *Journal of Applied Psychology*, 96(6): 1289–1304.

Kostopoulos, K.C., & Bozionelos, N. 2011. Team exploratory and exploitative learning: Psychological safety, task conflict, and team performance. *Group & Organization Management*, 36(3): 385–415.

Kozlowski, S.W.J., & Bell, B.S. 2013. Work groups and teams in organizations: Review update. In N. Schmitt & S. Highhouse (Eds.), *Handbook of psychology: Industrial and organizational psychology*, 2nd ed., Volume 12: 412–469. Hoboken, NJ: Wiley.

Kulkarni, M. 2015. Language-based diversity and faultlines in organizations. *Journal of Organizational Behavior*, 36(1): 128.

Lampshire, C.A. 2009. *Effects of leadership behaviors and communication channels on global intra-team relationships: A qualitative phenomenological study*. Phoenix, AZ: University of Phoenix. ProQuest document ID: 276515675.

Lane, H.W., Maznevski, M.L., & DiStefano, J.J. 2014. *International management behaviour*, 7th ed. New York: Wiley.

Lau, D.C., & Murnighan, J.K. 1998. Demographic diversity and faultlines: The compositional dynamics of organizational groups. *Academy of Management Review*, 23(2): 325–340.

Lau, D.C., & Murnighan, J.K. 2005. Interactions within groups and subgroups: The effects of demographic faultlines. *Academy of Management Journal*, 48(4): 645–659.

Leavitt, H.J. 2003. Why hierarchies thrive. *Harvard Business Review*, 81(3): 96–102, 141.

Leidner, T.R.K.D.E. 2002. Leadership effectiveness in global virtual teams. *Journal of Management Information Systems*, 18(3): 7–40.

Lepine, J.A., Piccolo, R.F., Jackson, C.L., Mathieu, J.E., & Saul, J.R. 2008. A meta-analysis of teamwork processes: Tests of a multidimensional model and relationships with team effectiveness criteria. *Personnel Psychology*, 61(2): 273–307.

Lisak, A., & Erez, M. 2015. Leadership emergence in multicultural teams: The power of global characteristics. *Journal of World Business*, 50(1): 3.

Mach, M., & Baruch, Y. 2015. Team performance in cross cultural project teams. *Cross Cultural Management*, 22(3): 464–486.

Malhotra, A., Majchrzak, A., & Rosen, B. 2007. Leading virtual teams. *The Academy of Management Perspectives*, 21(1): 60–70.

Marks, M.A., Mathieu, J.E., & Zaccaro, S.J. 2001. A temporally based framework and taxonomy of team processes. *Academy of Management Review*, 26(3): 356–376.

Mathieu, J., Maynard, M.T., Rapp, T., & Gilson, L. 2008. Team effectiveness 1997–2007: A review of recent advancements and a glimpse into the future. *Journal of Management*, 34(3): 410–476.

Matveev, A.V., & Nelson, P.E. 2004. Cross cultural communication competence and multicultural team performance perceptions of American and Russian managers. *International Journal of Cross Cultural Management*, 4(2): 253–270.

Maznevski, M. 1994. Understanding our differences: Performance in decision-making groups with diverse members. *Human Relations*, 47: 531–552.

Maznevski, M.L., & Chudoba, K.M. 2000. Bridging space over time: Global virtual team dynamics and effectiveness. *Organization Science*, 11(5): 473–492.

Maznevski, M.L., & DiStefano, J.J. 2000. Global leaders are team players: Developing global leaders through membership on global teams. *Human Resource Management*, 39(2): 195.

Maznevski, M., & Zander, L. 2001. Leading global teams: Overcoming the challenge of the power paradox. In M.E. Mendenhall, T. Kuehlmann, & G.K. Stahl (Eds.), *Developing global leaders*: 157–174. Westport, CT: Quorum Books.

McAllister, D.J. 1995. Affect- and cognition-based trust as foundations for interpersonal cooperation in organizations. *Academy of Management Journal*, 38(1): 24–59.

Mudrack, P.E. 1989. Group cohesiveness and productivity: A closer look. *Human Relations*, 42(9): 771–785.

Mullen, B., & Copper, C. 1994. The relation between group cohesiveness and performance: An integration. *Psychological Bulletin*, 115(2): 210.

O'Reilly, C.A., III, Caldwell, D.F., & Barnett, W.P. 1989. Work group demography, social integration, and turnover. *Administrative Science Quarterly*, 34(1): 21.

O'Reilly III, C.A., Williams, K.Y., & Barsade, S. 1997. Group demography and innovation: Does diversity help? In E. Mannix & M. Neale (Eds.), *Research in the management of groups and teams*, Volume 1: 183–207. Greenwich, CT: JAI Press.

Pauleen, D.J. 2003. Leadership in a global virtual team: An action learning approach. *Leadership & Organization Development Journal*, 24(3): 153.

Payne, R. 1990. *Innovation and creativity at work: Psychological and organizational strategies*. Chichester: Wiley.

Pearce, J.L., & Gregersen, H.B. 1991. Task interdependence and extrarole behavior: A test of the mediating effects of felt responsibility. *Journal of Applied Psychology*, 76(6): 838–844.

Pfeffer, J. 1995. Producing sustainable competitive advantage through the effective management of people. *The Academy of Management Executive*, 9(1): 55–69.

Richard, O.C., & Johnson, N.B. 2001. Understanding the impact of human resource diversity practices on firm performance. *Journal of Managerial Issues*, 13: 177–195.

Sarker, S., Ajuja, M., Sarker, S., & Kirkeby, S. 2011. The role of communication and trust in global virtual teams: A social network perspective. *Journal of Management Information Systems*, 28(1): 273–309.

Schaubroeck, J., Lam, S.S.K., & Peng, A.C. 2011. Cognition-based and affect-based trust as mediators of leader behavior influences on team performance. *Journal of Applied Psychology*, 96(4): 863–871.

Schneider, S.C., & Barsoux, J. 2003. *Managing across cultures*, 2nd ed. Harlow: Financial Times Prentice Hall.

Schoorman, F.D., Mayer, R.C., & Davis, J.H. 2007. An integrative model of organizational trust: Past, present, and future. *Academy of Management Review*, 32(2): 344–354.

Small, L.E. 2011. *An ethnographic study: The impact of leadership styles on the effectiveness of global-multicultural teams*. PhD Dissertation. University of Phoenix.

Somech, A., & Drach-Zahavy, A. 2013. Translating team creativity to innovation implementation the role of team composition and climate for innovation. *Journal of Management*, 39(3): 684–708.

Somech, A., & Khalaili, A. 2014. Team boundary activity: Its mediating role in the relationship between structural conditions and team innovation. *Group & Organization Management*, 39(3): 274.

Stahl, G.K., Maznevski, M.L., Voigt, A., & Jonsen, K. 2010. Unraveling the effects of cultural diversity in teams: A meta-analysis of research on multicultural work groups. *Journal of International Business Studies*, 41(4): 690–709.

Staples, D.S., & Zhao, L. 2006. The effects of cultural diversity in virtual teams versus face-to-face teams. *Group Decision and Negotiation*, 15(4): 389–406.

Stewart, G.L. 2006. A meta-analytic review of relationships between team design features and team performance. *Journal of Management*, 32(1): 29–55.

Stumpf, S., & Zeutschel, U. 2001. Synergy effects in multinational work groups: What we know and what we don't know. In M.E. Mendenhall, T. Kuehlmann, & G.K. Stahl (Eds.), *Developing global leaders*: 175–194. Westport, CT: Quorum Books.

Tannenbaum, S.I., Mathieu, J.E., Salas, E., & Cohen, D. 2012. Teams are changing: Are research and practice evolving fast enough? *Industrial & Organizational Psychology*, 5(1): 2–24.

Tenzer, H., & Pudelko, M. 2015. Leading across language barriers: Managing language-induced emotions in multinational teams. *Leadership Quarterly*, 26(4): 606.

Tenzer, H., Pudelko, M., & Harzing, A.-W. 2014. The impact of language barriers on trust formation in multinational teams. *Journal of International Business Studies*, 45(5): 508–535.

Thatcher, S.M.B., & Patel, P.C. 2011. Demographic faultlines: A meta-analysis of the literature. *Journal of Applied Psychology*, 96(6): 1119.

Thatcher, S.M.B., & Patel, P.C. 2012. Group faultlines: A review, integration, and guide to future research. *Journal of Management*, 38(4): 969–1009.

Thomas, D.C. 1999. Cultural diversity and work group effectiveness. *Journal of Cross-Cultural Psychology*, 30: 242–263.

Tjosvold, D. 1986. The dynamics of interdependence in organizations. *Human Relations,* 39(6): 517–540.

Tjosvold, D., & Yu, Z. 2007. Group risk taking the constructive role of controversy in China. *Group & Organization Management,* 32(6): 653–674.

Tsui, A.S., & O'Reilly, C.A. 1989. Beyond simple demographic effects: The importance of relational demography in superior-subordinate dyads. *Academy of Management Journal,* 32(2): 402–423.

Turel, O., & Zhang, Y. 2010. Does virtual team composition matter? Trait and problem-solving configuration effects on team performance. *Behaviour & Information Technology,* 29(4): 363–375.

Tworoger, L.C., Ruppel, C.P., Gong, B., & Pohlman, R.A. 2013. Leadership constraints: Leading global virtual teams through environmental complexity. *International Journal of e-Collaboration (IJeC),* 9(2): 34–60.

Van de Ven, A.H., Delbecq, A.L., & Koenig, R. 1976. Determinants of coordination modes within organizations. *American Sociological Review,* 41(April): 322–338.

Van Der Vegt, G.S., Emans, B.J.M., & Van De Vliert, E. 2001. Patterns of interdependence in work teams: A two-level investigation of the relations with job and team satisfaction. *Personnel Psychology,* 54(1): 51–69.

Wageman, R., Gardner, H., & Mortensen, M. 2012. The changing ecology of teams: New directions for teams research. *Journal of Organizational Behavior,* 33(3): 301–315.

Wageman, R., Hackman, J.R., & Lehman, E. 2005. Team diagnostic survey. *Journal of Applied Behavioral Science,* 41(4): 373–398.

Weber, M. 1946. Bureaucracy. *From Max Weber: Essays in Sociology,* 196: 232–235.

Weber, M. 1947. *The theory of economic and social organization.* Trans. A.M. Henderson and T. Parsons. New York: Oxford University Press.

West, M. 2012. *Effective teamwork: Practical lessons from organizational research,* 3rd ed. West Sussex: John Wiley.

Wildman, J.L., & Griffith, R. 2015. *Leading global teams: Translating multidisciplinary science to practice.* New York: Springer.

Woolley, A.W., Gerbasi, M.E., Chabris, C.F., Kosslyn, S.M., & Hackman, J.R. 2008. Bringing in the experts how team composition and collaborative planning jointly shape analytic effectiveness. *Small Group Research,* 39(3): 352–371.

Zaccaro, S.J., Rittman, A.L., & Marks, M.A. 2002. Team leadership. *The Leadership Quarterly,* 12(4): 451–483.

Zander, L., Mockaitis, A.I., & Butler, C.L. 2012. Leading global teams. *Journal of World Business,* 47(4): 592–603.

Zayani, F.A. 2008. *The impact of transformational leadership on the success of global virtual teams: An investigation based on the Multifactor Leadership Questionnaire.* PhD Dissertation. C. U. School of Business & Technology.

Zellmer-Bruhn, M., & Gibson, C. 2006. Multinational organization context: Implications for team learning and performance. *Academy of Management Journal,* 49(3): 501–518.

Zhou, W., & Shi, X. 2011. Culture in groups and teams: A review of three decades of research. *International Journal of Cross Cultural Management,* 11(1): 5–34.

Vladimir Pucik, Paul Evans, and Ingmar Björkman

MANAGING ALLIANCES AND JOINT VENTURES

I N THE LATE 1960S, THE US-based chemical company Chemco (name disguised) decided to enter the booming Japanese market. However, Japan's investment policies at the time precluded direct entry. Facing the choice between licensing and a minority joint venture (JV), the company decided to establish a 49:51 percent partnership with a well-known Japanese firm to build a local plant and set up distribution. Chemco would contribute technology in exchange for help in market access. Soon after its launch, the JV, led entirely by local managers, became the leader in its industry segment.

Later, the US parent decided to take advantage of the liberalization of the Japanese economy to obtain a majority position in the JV. In their opinion, the JV was becoming "too independent," and they wanted more influence on its future direction. Besides, drawing upon the support functions of the head office could lower costs. After protracted negotiations, the Japanese partner agreed to sell 2 percent of equity to the Americans to give them control, and the board composition was changed accordingly. The JV management was instructed to streamline the product portfolio and to cut costs by integrating several support functions into the global organization. While the local managers never questioned the need for more efficiency, most of the integration projects never really got off the ground. This was officially justified by referring to pressing local customer needs that took up all available resources.

Frustrated by the difficulties in "integrating Japan," the US management decided that additional equity would give it the necessary influence to push through integration plans. After another round of long negotiations, the US parent gained control of 65 percent of the shares. The company was renamed, putting its US partner's name first. A senior vice president of finance (who did not speak Japanese) was dispatched to join the local management team. In spite of

DOI: 10.4324/9781003247272-26

these changes, the venture continued to be run pretty much as before. While it was profitable, with nearly US$1 billion of sales, margins were well below corporate expectations. As Japanese customers began to migrate to lower-cost sites in other areas of Asia, poor coordination with other affiliates became a serious business problem.

A third generation of US top management decided to address the problem head-on. They retained a consultant to advise them on what to do next. Should they buy even more equity? Send in more expatriates? Or even sell the existing business and start again?

It turned out that the company could not sell the plant in the open market because the surrounding infrastructure belonged to the Japanese parent. In addition, the Japanese partner (located right next door) was the legal employer of the vast majority of employees, including virtually all top managers. Even those recruited well after the JV was established were not employees of the joint venture. Their salaries were determined by their position in the Japanese parent company hierarchy, and they were simply dispatched to the JV at the discretion of the Japanese partner. All the training, starting with new employee induction, was conducted jointly with employees of the Japanese parent—and they all belonged to the same company union.

All of this was seen as a "good deal" when the JV was originally set up in the 1960s—it meant that there was no need to invest heavily in staff or to worry about human resources management (HRM) issues in an unknown market. But ever since the original agreement was signed several decades ago, each step in the evolution of the relationship had focused only on the financial aspects of control. It was only when the consultant was brought in that HRM and organizational issues were analyzed thoroughly for the first time. So the questions had to be rephrased: Would more equity buy more "respect"? Would more expatriates help the integration? What could be done to change the direction of the JV?

OVERVIEW

Alliances are a useful tool for internationalization, but they are also difficult to implement. The example of Chemco illustrates the complexity of alliances, and the dangers of ignoring the management and people dimensions of such a strategy. So first, we will review the many motives for entering an international alliance and the different organizational forms alliances can take, presenting several perspectives on what constitutes alliance success.

An important dimension of alliances is that they are inherently unstable. We will next introduce a framework that helps us to think strategically about alliances and how they may evolve over time. Based on competitive context and knowledge-creation requirements, we will identify four types of alliances, each with a different set of management and HRM challenges. We will illustrate how HR practices and tools can contribute to the long-term success of an alliance strategy.

We will then focus on planning and negotiating alliances, paying particular attention to the human resource factors that must be taken into account. Key management roles in the alliance building process will be presented, along with the implications for how managers for these positions are selected and developed.

Once an agreement has been negotiated, it must be implemented, so we will next review the people and organizational factors involved, highlighting the HRM agenda in international JV management.

The final section of the reading explores the concept of alliance learning. We will first analyze the key obstacles to alliance learning to show the importance of linking HRM to alliance learning objectives. We will then describe the human resource processes that can contribute to successful alliance learning, contrasting examples of successful and unsuccessful learning. To conclude, we will review the evolutionary perspective on alliances and raise the next-generation challenges facing HRM, as alliances become an organic part of the international operations of many multinationals.

THE WHYS AND WHATS OF ALLIANCES

JVs and other forms of cross-border alliance are important and commonly used tools for international growth. Companies engage in alliances for many reasons.[1] Some are created to cut the cost of entry, others to cut the cost of exit. Some are set up with the objective of leveraging opportunities, others with the aim of acquiring knowledge. Some alliances are focused on economies of scale, others on economies of scope. Understanding *why* a company participates in an international alliance is the first step towards deciding the approach to alliance human resource management.

Alliance Business Drivers

International alliances, usually in the form of JVs, began to multiply during the 1960s and 1970s.[2] Their primary objective was to enable firms expanding internationally to secure access to markets where direct presence was not permitted, or where market entry was deemed too costly, too risky, or both. For example, foreign companies targeting the Japanese market, like Chemco, were not allowed to invest independently in Japan until its foreign investment regime was deregulated in the mid-1970s. The only way to enter the booming market early was either to license technology to a local partner or to establish a JV. The early flow of foreign direct investment into China in the 1980s and 1990s followed a similar pattern.

Entering a protected market is only one reason why alliances are formed. Even when a wholly owned subsidiary may be feasible, there are many arguments in favor of market entry through partnership with a local firm. Such a partnership can provide knowledge of local business conditions, a desirable location and infrastructure, access to the distribution system, contacts with government, and a supply of experienced labor and management. The need to enter emerging markets rapidly while minimizing risk is another reason. After the collapse of the Berlin Wall, alliances minimized the risk of entry into uncharted territories in Eastern and Central Europe.[3] As anticipated in the initial agreements, many local partners have since been bought out. Many foreign investors in China and India are following a similar strategy.[4]

Alliances may support internationalization strategies. For example, while global competition often requires "insider" presence in a number of countries, it is difficult for all but the largest firms to achieve such universal market coverage. In car manufacturing, parts suppliers are expected to follow major car companies as they expand around the world, though it may not be viable to set up independent operations everywhere. "Sharing" the customer with a local partner may be a better idea. Many firms are left with only two choices: either to be acquired, or to negotiate alliances with others in a similar position.

Some alliances can remain non-equity contractual agreements for long periods of time. The Airbus consortium was established in 1970 by leading European aerospace firms to compete against the then-dominant US commercial aircraft manufacturers. Risk reduction, economies of scale and scope in research and development (R&D) and production were the primary drivers behind the push for collaboration.[5] But because the vast majority of Airbus employees were on the payrolls of the partner firms, the organization of the consortium presented major challenges, particularly with respect to managing mobility and coordinating cross-border projects. It was only in 2001 that a separate joint stock company was set up.[6]

In high-technology industries today, international alliances are the norm and not the exception. Most high-tech firms are engaged in scores of technological, manufacturing, and marketing alliances. Their objective is to leverage their current know-how quickly over the broadest possible number of markets and to foster the creation of tomorrow's know-how. The early success of IBM and Toshiba in the emerging laptop computer market was partly a result of their long-term collaboration in designing and manufacturing state-of-the-art flat screens. While the two companies never ceased to compete for the final customer, the upstream collaborative efforts allowed them to maximize return on R&D investment, and to gain valuable economies of scale in manufacturing. The challenge for both firms was to ensure that competences created inside the alliance could be quickly transferred to the parents while maintaining learning parity. This was accomplished by a carefully balanced flow of personnel between the alliance and the two partners.

In short, there are many good reasons for companies to engage in international alliances. Some firms are heavily involved with alliances; others find them tangential to their global strategy. However, most companies will engage in some form of international alliance as they expand abroad. Consequently, it is important to understand the strategic and management issues relating to international alliances and the role of human resources management in alliance success. Indeed the question of what is a successful alliance is often not easy to answer, as we can see in Box 1.

BOX 1: Defining alliance success

The Chemco case raises the question of what is a successful alliance. This may seem like an obvious question, but it does not have an obvious answer. Does the mere survival of an international alliance indicate success? Is success measured by the return on the funds originally invested? By current profitability and cash/dividend flow? By market share? By transfer of knowledge or creation of new knowledge? Obviously, the choice depends on the specific objective of the alliance, but objectives typically change as the alliance evolves. From this perspective, the only relevant measure of alliance success is the degree to which an international alliance helps the firm to improve its ability to compete.

Contrary to a popular metaphor, an alliance is *not* like a marriage — longer alliances are not necessarily better. Problematic alliances are a drain on management energy and resources, but they often limp on, since shutting them down would imply "failure."

For an alliance to be sustainable, it must benefit all partners: respect for the partners' needs and mutual value creation is a prerequisite for a successful relationship. But this does not imply that value creation must be equal or that all alliances should be sustainable for an indefinite period. Most are transitory in nature, reflecting a particular competitive situation at a particular point in time. When the situation changes, so does the need for the alliance. A "win–win" strategy is only a tool to create a healthy alliance; it should not be seen as the goal in itself. The definition of a "win" may change as the company strategy evolves, as will the role that the alliance is expected to perform.

From this perspective, Chemco's alliance in Japan, although growing and profitable, was not as successful as it could have been. This does not mean that the original entry decision was wrong. In fact, in terms of return on investment, the deal was the best that the company had ever made. But as the company's internationalization strategy evolved, the alliance in Japan did not follow, largely because of inattention to the management and human resource issues involved.

Ample data show that many alliances fail to meet expectations and that the cause of the failure is, in many cases, poor implementation.[7] It has been estimated that fewer than 50 percent of early JVs in Japan met the foreign partner's business objectives,[8] and observations on more recent experiences with JVs in China suggest a similar pattern.[9] The complexity of managing a business with international partners is a challenge that few firms seem equipped to handle. When alliances break up, HRM issues are often cited as one of the key factors contributing to "irreconcilable differences."[10]

Understanding Alliances

Choosing the right type of alliance for a given strategy is difficult if the strategy is not clear. What is the business objective of the proposed alliance? What is the value added of engaging in a business relationship that will inevitably consume significant resources before yielding results? What form of alliance should a company choose given its objectives? And what are the human resource implications of such a choice?

There are a number of different ways to classify alliances. It is possible to take a functional orientation so as to identify R&D alliances, manufacturing alliances, marketing and distribution alliances, and so forth. Another way to classify alliances is to look at the number of partners involved, from a two-partner agreement to multiple-partner consortia. However, the most common distinction is whether the contractual agreement covering the alliance creates a new jointly owned business unit—usually described as a JV—or whether the collaboration is essentially non-equity based, such as a licensing agreement.

Yoshino and Rangan (1995) present a comprehensive classification of alliances (see Figure 1) based on the fundamental nature of the contractual relationships between the partners.[11] There are many other classifications, some focusing specifically on HR issues.[12]

There is a general agreement that as one moves through the spectrum of alliances from a "simple" marketing agreement with a foreign distributor or original equipment manufacturing (OEM) agreements to stand-alone JVs, the management challenges increase, as does the importance of paying attention to human resource management. Much of the discussion in this reading will therefore focus on the role of HR factors in the most complex of international alliances—JVs between firms based in different countries. However, even among

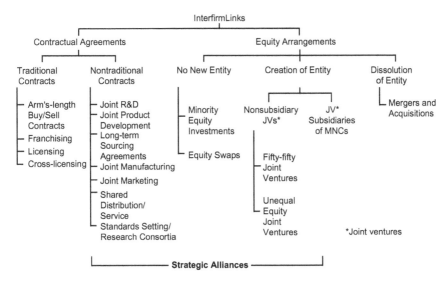

Figure 1 Classification of strategic alliances.

Source: Yoshino and Rangan (1995)

JVs, the differences in strategic logic behind their formation may require differ-ent HRM strategies and HR tools to be applied.

AN ALLIANCE STRATEGY FRAMEWORK

As the Chemco case illustrates, an alliance is typically a dynamic phenomenon. The nature of the alliance may change over time, and shifts in the relative bar-gaining power of the partners and in their expectations about the objectives of the alliance will have corresponding HRM implications.

There are two dimensions of alliances that require careful consideration from an HRM perspective: the strategic intent of the partners, and the expected contribution of the venture to the creation of new organizational capabilities and knowledge. With respect to strategic intent, alliances among firms with competi-tive strategic interests may require different approaches to HRM from those in which interests are complementary. With respect to capability and knowledge-creation, while all alliances involve learning, some are actually formed with the main purpose of capability or knowledge-creation. The learning aspect of alli-ances has major implications for the organizational arrangements, and thus for HR challenges and roles.

Figure 2 shows the four archetypes of alliance strategies based on their strategic and knowledge/capability–creation contexts: complementary, learning, resource, and competitive alliances.

A "complementary" alliance is formed when two (or more) partners with complementary strategic aims join forces to exploit their existing resources or competences—say, by linking different elements of the value chain—and where knowledge creation is not a prime objective. A typical complementary alliance is the traditional JV where one partner contributes technology and the other facilitates entry into a difficult market. Another example may be seen when two partners contribute complementary technologies that may lead to a new product stream. In non-equity alliances, this may take the form of a long-term contract, such as between TI and Nokia in the mobile phone chip manufactur-ing process.

A complementary alliance may evolve into a *learning alliance* if both part-ners share an interest in enhancing their individual capabilities. This can happen through the exchange of existing knowledge between the partners, or through the development of new knowledge where the partners jointly participate in the same value chain activities. An example of a learning alliance is the Fuji Xerox JV in Japan, which will be discussed later in this reading.[13] Originally set up to facilitate Xerox's penetration of the Japanese market, it then shifted its focus to Asia Pacific, and today serves as a critical source of competency development for the Xerox Corporation worldwide. Other alliances may be designed with learning in mind from the outset.[14] Compared to complementary alliances, learning alli-ances require much more interaction, including shared work and interface man-agement, which creates demand for HR systems and processes that can facilitate effective knowledge creation.

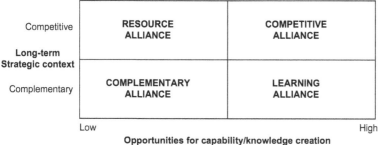

Figure 2 A strategic framework for understanding international alliances.

Notes: Alliances can be evaluated on two dimensions. The first reflects the competitive context of the alliance. The second dimension reflects the need and opportunities for knowledge creation.

Strategic context: competition versus collaboration: The dimension of strategic context positions the alliance with respect to complementarity of interests between the alliance partners. Is the alliance a link with a partner whose long-term strategic interests are in principle complementary (e.g., Airbus), or are they more likely fundamentally competitive?[A]

Capability/knowledge-creation context: low versus high capability/knowledge-creation opportunities. Some alliances rely exclusively on exploiting existing resources and competencies (partners contribute money, patents, production capacity, distribution networks); others are designed explicitly to generate new capabilities or knowledge by combining or extending the resources and capabilities of the partners.[B]

[A] It is important to bear in mind that the strategic interests can change over time, and that what was once a collaborative relationship may turn into a fierce competition or conflict. A common experience of many Western firms with their joint ventures in Japan and two decades later in China are often-cited examples in this regard (Reich and Mankin, 1986; Hamel et al., 1989; McGregor, 2005; Hamilton and Zhang, 2008).

[B] In principle, all alliances have the potential to generate new knowledge—at least partners can learn about each other, and how to work together—the difference is in the intensity of the knowledge-creation process.

Competitive pressures such as resource constraints, political and business risks, or economies of scale may lead competitors to join forces in a "resource alliance." Exploration consortia set up to develop and operate oil and gas fields are increasingly common in the energy industry. One company takes the lead, but the others share the risk by contributing resources, and often staff. For example, BP explored oil deposits off the coast of Vietnam together with Statoil from Norway and the Vietnamese state-owned oil company. Another example would be the sharing of manufacturing facilities in Australia by Nissan and Ford when the Australian government restricted the number of manufacturing sites in the country. Compared to complementary alliances, resource alliances place a greater requirement on HR practices that reduce the frictions that might hamper collaboration.

Finally, there are also learning alliances between partners who are competitors in global markets. One of the best-known examples is NUMMI—a 50:50 JV between General Motors and Toyota.[15] This venture was nominally designed for the joint production of small cars for the North American market, but at the same time it was intended to serve as a "learning laboratory" for the two competitors. GM gained insights into Toyota's manufacturing system, and Toyota learned how to operate a US-based manufacturing facility. Such partnerships can be described as a *competitive* alliance. Another example is Boeing's long-term collaboration with a consortium of Japanese firms that built segments of Boeing airplanes while at the same time pursuing a strategy of becoming aircraft designers themselves.[16] This type of alliance, with its emphasis on knowledge creation in a competitive context, is the most complex to manage and requires the highest level of attention to HRM.

None of these types of alliance is "better" than another. Alliances in all four quadrants can enhance a firm's competitive advantage. However, the management challenges associated with each alliance scenario are fundamentally different, and the HRM strategies, processes, and tools should reflect those differences. Problems occur when the company does not know what kind of alliance it has entered or, as in the case of Chemco, when it does not read and respond appropriately to early signals that the nature of the alliance is changing. For example, in a complementary alliance, it might be possible to rely on the local partner to recruit and train the alliance workforce, since the loyalty factor may not be an issue—at least in the short term. However, such an approach in a competitive alliance could prove costly in the event of any subsequent conflict between the partners.[17]

In a complementary alliance, it may make sense to set up the venture as a standalone entity to promote internal entrepreneurship. In a resource partnership, there are also benefits in creating an entity with clear boundaries so that the competitive strategic context does not inhibit the performance of the alliance—good fences make good neighbors. However, learning alliances should not be constrained by too many fences, as opportunities for knowledge sharing will be greater when the boundaries between the venture and the parent are thin. HR practices in a learning alliance will therefore focus on facilitating the interface between the parent and the venture to increase the speed and quality of information exchange.

In contrast, it is not just fast learning that matters in a competitive alliance, but also speed and effectiveness relative to the partner—maintaining learning parity is the key to sustaining such a relationship.[18] The HR approach has to reflect this, for example by integrating measures of the learning outcomes into the performance management process. At the same time, given the competitive context of the alliance, the flow of knowledge has to be monitored, if not restricted—an approach opposite to what is best for a learning alliance.

In all cases, it is important to remember that alliances do not always fit neatly into conceptual boxes. Some partnerships are complementary in some parts of the value chain but competitive in others, and a nuanced approach to HRM may be needed. The critical issue is that the character of most alliances changes over time. Successful complementary alliances will become learning alliances, and learning alliances may turn into competitive alliances as the strategic intents of partners change over time.[19]

Precisely when a complementary alliance becomes a learning or a competitive alliance is a matter of interpretation. Alliances are typically defined as complementary in the opening public relations statements, but a shift in partnership orientation has to be expected. The anticipation of such shifts needs to be taken into account in formulating the HR strategy so that the appropriate tools can be used proactively to facilitate such a change. In the Chemco case, the alliance started as complementary, combining the technology of the US partner with the market access capability of the Japanese partner. However, the US partner failed to commit the necessary resources at an early stage to ensure the future integration of the JV into its global network (training, exchange of staff, and so forth). There were no incentives for the Japanese staff to pay attention to global strategy. They were rewarded solely on local results, and they saw no future for themselves in Chemco's global organization.

One of the few redeeming factors in the Chemco JV was that the alliance never migrated into the "competitive" domain, simply because the Japanese partner had no wish to enter this particular business segment. Had it chosen to do so, there was not much the US partner could have done to protect its market position because it had little influence over the employees or management in Japan. However, because the partner's position was essentially cooperative, Chemco's top executives and the HR managers did get another opportunity to consider long-term actions to remedy the unsatisfactory situation. We will review later what they did.

ALLIANCE IS A PROCESS, NOT A DEAL

An alliance is not just a deal between two or more partners; it is a complex process that is full of ambiguities and contradictions. Indeed, companies often learn to manage the contradictions of transnational organization through their alliance experiences. Most alliances either die early or evolve, just like any other business venture. Alliance stability is a contradiction in terms.

There is no best way to structure an alliance. Winning and losing alliances cannot be differentiated by specific configurations of organizing patterns, equity ratios, or reporting relationships.[20] In the case of JVs, some argue that 50:50 arrangements work best, since the partners are forced to anticipate each other's interests.[21] Others assert that such arrangements lead to paralysis, for example with respect to staffing and compensation issues, and that it is better when one partner has the power to make a decision when there is deadlock.[22] In fact, both types of venture appear to generate significant but distinct HRM challenges.[23]

It is not the structure of the deal, but the quality of the management process—in planning, negotiating, and implementing an international business partnership—that makes a difference. However, even here there are variations. In HP and Intel, two high-tech firms with extensive histories of successful alliances, the alliance management process is well defined, highly structured, and institutionalized. On the other hand, Corning, which derives most of its income from alliances, favors a more intuitive and informal approach that reflects the company's culture and mode of decision-making. Others use a mix of the two extremes. Whether the approach is formalized or embedded in the company culture, successful alliance players have in common a rigorous and disciplined approach to alliances that includes an appreciation of the HRM contribution.

PLANNING AND NEGOTIATING ALLIANCES

The HR function should be involved early in exploring, planning, and negotiating alliances because a number of key issues relating to control and influence are closely tied to expertise, policies, and practices in human resource management. Unfortunately, HR is often left out at this stage.

Another reason why HR should be involved early is the fact that creating value through superior human resource management can be a source of competitive advantage for the partnership. For example, a partner with proven competence in implementing high-performing work systems, in staffing and recruitment, or in managing innovation through people, has additional negotiating leverage. This competence should contribute to the success of the venture—provided that it can be appropriately adapted to the different cultural and institutional circumstances, and strategic aims.

Outstanding HR strengthens bargaining power in the negotiations. A reputation for good HR systems and practices is part of the corporate "brand equity."[24] Well-managed partners are more in demand than poorly managed ones. A company with poor foundations in its own approach to HRM and without proven know-how in aligning HRM with competitive strategy will find itself disadvantaged when it comes to negotiating and implementing alliances.

HRM Issues in Developing an Alliance Strategy

Successful alliances start with a strategy, not with a partner. This may seem an obvious statement, but it is not always followed in practice. Companies, or more precisely their chief executives, sometimes "fall in love." Notwithstanding the importance of personal relationships at the top, it is dangerous to select the partner before the strategic purpose is clarified.

As discussed in the previous section, it is difficult to identify what kind of relationship and what kind of a partner may be appropriate without fully understanding the long-term objectives. Japanese car component manufacturers entered the United States in the late 1980s because they were following their Japanese customers, for instance Toyota and Honda, into the United States. These customers expected just-in-time support for their newly transplanted assembly plants, but the component manufacturers knew that they did not have the competence themselves to operate in an alien environment. Given the urgency, the alliance route seemed the most feasible entry strategy, though in the long run they intended to establish an independent presence.

Consequently, human resource considerations played a major role in partner selection.[25] The Japanese firms searched for local partners situated in rural environments, perceived as having harmonious labor environments conducive to Japanese manufacturing methods. They also preferred partners who were family-owned but with no clear succession. This would give them the opportunity to acquire full control with a friendly bid once the US partner decided to retire.

While the HR issues in an alliance are always framed by the specific strategic and business context, these considerations are sometimes contradictory, requiring careful analysis. For example, when a firm decides to enter an unfamiliar foreign market, the choice of an experienced local partner may seem to be a smart move that overcomes the existing "market competence" handicap. Yet, with a strong local partner, there may be less urgency to develop internal market know-how, and investments in knowledge-creation may not be a priority. In a complementary alliance, this may not matter. However, if the alliance ever becomes competitive, this may put the foreign partner at a serious disadvantage.

A well-defined alliance management process provides an arena for a full consideration of human resource issues.[26] Early involvement in strategy discussions allows the HR function to understand the business logic of the alliance, highlighting early the issues that may handicap implementation. In addition, important human resource decisions regarding the alliance may need to be taken early on in the implementation process (such as decisions on negotiation training or selection of an alliance manager).

HR's involvement in alliance strategy is often guided by a plan that is fleshed out as implementation proceeds. A sketch of the issues to be considered is shown in Table 1. Given the typical uncertainty surrounding alliance creation, such a plan is only a rough guide. It will become more specific when a partner is selected, paving the way for rigorous implementation when the alliance is launched.

PARTNER SELECTION

There are two main HR issues to consider in selecting a partner: the expected contribution of the partner, and how much the HR systems of the partners will interface within the alliance.

The first issue refers to the degree to which the partner's competences in human resource management are expected to contribute to the alliance. Will the partner be responsible for staffing the alliance? Or, will it be responsible for some of its critical functions? Is the partner expected to provide HR services to the alliance? Does the partner's HR reputation matter? As we will discuss later in this reading, getting the staffing right is the "make or break" issue for many alliances, and the probability of success can be enhanced by making these questions a part of the selection screen.

The second issue addresses the degree to which the organizational and people processes of the partners will be linked in the course of the alliance,

Table 1 The HR alliance strategy plan

HR issues that may influence partner selection:
- Desired competences that a partner should possess.
- Need for venture HR support from the partner.
- Assessment of HR skills and reputation of potential partners.
- Assessment of the organizational culture of potential partners.
- Exit options.

Venture HR issues that need to be resolved in negotiations:
- Desired negotiation outcomes and possible bargaining trade-offs.
- Management philosophy, notably concerning HRM.
- Staffing: sourcing and criteria.
- Compensation and performance management.
- Who will provide what HR service support?

Specific HRM activities that must be implemented early, and resources required:
- Negotiation stage:
  - Negotiation team selection.
  - Negotiation training.
- Start-up stage:
  - Staffing decisions.
  - Alliance management training.

Allocation of responsibility:
- Corporate responsibility.
- Local management team responsibility.
- Partner responsibility.

Measurements to evaluate the quality of HR support:
- Recruitment target.
- Training delivered.
- Skill/knowledge transferred.

which is likely if one of the strategic aims is learning. Will the alliance be clearly separated from the parents? Or will the boundaries be ambiguous? Will there be a lot of mobility between the venture units and the parent companies? Who will evaluate the performance of the venture management? And on what criteria?

When the partner is expected to contribute significantly to HRM, or when the venture is unlikely to be autonomous because of interfaces with the parents, it is vital to include the partner's HR philosophy, policies, practices, and culture as a factor in partner selection (see Box 2). The issue here is not to find a perfect match—a partner who shares the same view on management selection criteria or the role of incentive compensation in the reward package; rather, the purpose is to identify potential differences and then to determine how these differences might influence the execution of the alliance strategy, whether any differences can be reconciled, and whether there are business risks if the gaps cannot be bridged.

BOX 2: Assessing the culture and HR practices of the potential partner

HR policies and practices have a major impact on the culture of the organization, and research has shown that differences in organizational culture may influence alliance success.[27] A cultural audit is therefore an essential part of "due diligence," the audit of a potential partner. A number of factors may impact the cultural compatibility between partners, and these should be included in the audit:

- Communication style (degree of formality).
- Hierarchical boundaries (rigid vs. flexible).
- Control mechanism (tight vs. loose).
- Mode of conflict resolution (explicit vs. implicit).
- Compensation philosophy (market position, degree of salary compression).
- Performance management (open vs. hidden).
- Career stratification (gender, race, age, religion, qualifications).

Various maps exist to understand differences in culture. One simple but useful map has been developed by Goffee and Jones (1998), using two dimensions that are well established in sociological and management theory: *sociability* (friendships, emphasis on relationship, networking) and *solidarity* (collective task and goal orientation).[28] They map out four types of cultures: networked (strong on sociability), mercenary (strong on solidarity), fragmented (low on both), and communal (high on both). Each is reflected in different approaches to management and HRM, and each exists in a positive and negative form (for example, the danger for communal cultures is that they become arrogant and inward-looking, while mercenary cultures can become ruthless).

It is particularly important is to clarify key operating HR policies and the actual practices:

- How do employees enter the company, and what are the selection criteria?
- What are the promotion requirements and timetables?
- Which behaviors are encouraged, and which are scorned?
- What are the performance criteria? And how much do they matter?
- What are the determinants of salary? And how large are the differentials?
- How open is the communication about individual performance?
- How open and transparent is the whole HR system?

This material may not be easily available, but it can be obtained through consultants, a thorough review of press coverage, and local intelligence—and not just leafing through annual reports. Doing the homework eliminates subsequent surprises.

A UK company decided to set up a JV in Malaysia to assemble its product for the local market. Soon after the results for the first year were in, the UK managing director proposed performance bonuses that differentiated by nearly 40 percent between managers at the same level of responsibility. A row erupted at the JV board meeting—the local partner objected because the bonus plan would violate the standards of internal equity among managers and hurt morale. The foreign managing director was puzzled: "You told us that bonuses in your company could be up to 40 percent of the total compensation. That is what I believe our best performers deserve." "Yes," came the answer, "but in our company the bonus percentage is the same for everyone."

Differences in management style and HR practices can, however, sometimes be a powerful argument in favor of an alliance. One of the factors that motivated Toshiba to join forces with General Electric in a Japan-based JV was to get an "insider" view of GE's renowned management system. Toshiba's top management actually encouraged GE to introduce many of its systems and practices into the JV to see how such practices might be adapted in Japan and what learning the Japanese parent might gain from the experience.

SELECTING ALLIANCE MANAGERS

An alliance manager is typically appointed at corporate level, responsible for planning, negotiating, and implementing alliances. Ideally, this role should be kept separate from the role of venture manager,[29] who is responsible for managing a specific project, business unit, or JV within the alliance (see Table 2), though obviously not all firms have the resources to do so.

The alliance manager may monitor several existing alliances, supporting business units in identifying opportunities where a partnership could create value. When such opportunities are identified, the alliance manager will take the lead in developing the negotiating strategy and framing the partnership contract. After negotiations are completed and a new alliance has been formed, they will oversee the evolution of the alliance and the relationship with the partner. This is like managing a portfolio where new ventures get negotiated, added, and monitored.

The alliance manager has a determining impact on the quality of the relationship between the partners and on the ability of a firm to execute its alliance strategy. When selecting alliance managers, it is important to recognize that their role will change from visioning/sponsoring to networking/mediating as the alliance evolves from initial planning through negotiations, start-up, maturity, and on to eventual decline and dissolution.[30]

Typically, the key requirement for the alliance manager's position is a high degree of personal and professional credibility. Mutual trust is the glue that cements alliance relationships, and without credibility, it is difficult to establish trust. When Motorola established a strategically key semiconductor alliance with Toshiba, it appointed as alliance manager a corporate vice president with a stellar business record. This individual played a central role in developing overall corporate strategy in the sector.[31] The focus of the alliance was to share

Table 2 Alliance manager versus venture manager: roles and responsibilities

Alliance Manager Roles and Responsibilities

- **Building trust/setting the tone**—unless there is trust and the right chemistry among managers involved in the alliance, it will not go anywhere.
- **Monitoring partner contributions**—how well a firm meets its obligations to an alliance is the most tangible evidence of its commitment.
- **Managing information flow**—drawing the line between information flow that ensures the vitality of the alliance and unbridled information exchange that could jeopardize competitiveness.
- **Assessing strategic viability/evaluating synergy**—as strategic needs of the firm change over time, what are the implications for the alliance and overall relationship with the partner?
- **Aligning internal relationships**—since an alliance involves many people inside the firm, the alliance manager should mobilize the necessary support across the organization.

Venture Manager Roles and Responsibilities

- **Managing the business**—the venture manager assumes operational responsibility for the success of the venture.
- **Representing venture interest**—the venture manager has to represent without bias the interest of the venture as a business vis-à-vis its parents.
- **Aligning outside resources**—many resources are located outside the venture boundaries in the parent organizations; tapping effectively into those resources is a venture manager's responsibility.
- **Building collaborative culture**—irrespective of the competitive context of the alliance, trust inside the venture is an essential ingredient for success.
- **Developing venture strategy**—successful alliances evolve like any other ongoing business, and this evolution should be guided by solid strategy.

Source: Yoshino and Rangan (1995).

Motorola's microprocessor know-how with Toshiba in exchange for access to Toshiba's memory technology. The alliance manager's personal credibility and reputation were critical in aligning Motorola's internal resources behind the alliance, and in convincing Toshiba that Motorola's management was determined to make the alliance work.

The job of an alliance manager also requires a high degree of flexibility and adaptability in coping with different national and organizational cultures, management styles, and individual behaviors. As discussed earlier, alliances are by nature unstable and uncertain, so it is difficult to operate under precise rules or to expect that an intended strategy will be followed to the letter. Managers who are not comfortable with working under ambiguity will find it difficult to cope. As one experienced alliance manager put it, "High tolerance for frustration is a must."

We have indicated that alliance managers are an example of one of the key lateral coordination roles in a multinational firm—much of what alliance managers are required to do involves mobilizing resources across organizational boundaries. They manage laterally in much the same way as a global account manager or an international project leader, but without large budgets or staff, and without direct authority over resource allocation.[32] Instead, the manager has to rely on influencing networks of people inside and outside the firm. As one senior executive in a Fortune 500 company put it:

> A leader is one who gets people to do what he wants, but who at the same time makes them think that it was all their idea in the first place. An alliance manager also has to work along the same lines. He has no battalions of his own, yet he has to get the job done. He has to get people to buy into his vision of the alliance, make it part of their own job assignment, and actively work to make the alliance a success.[33]

Preparing for Negotiations

Firms need to address HRM issues long before the first encounter between the potential partners. The initial focus is primarily on selecting the negotiating team and facilitating training in handling negotiations.

SELECTING THE NEGOTIATION TEAM

Once the long-term strategy of the alliance is in place, its objectives set, and the potential partners established, it helps if the negotiation team is selected quickly. Different types of venture may require different mixes of entrepreneurial, analytical, and political competences in the team.[34] The context might also influence the choice of the alliance manager, who in most circumstances should be the core member of the team.

There are different opinions as to whether future venture managers should take part in the negotiations. When venture managers are involved in negotiations, they have a vested interested in "getting it right" rather than just "getting the deal," since they will be responsible for implementation. However, when negotiations are protracted (most last longer than anticipated) it is not easy to free up managers who have other responsibilities to participate in negotiations that may fail. An alternative is to assign the responsibility for the venture before the negotiation is completed, but to have another position available in case the negotiations fail.

TRAINING FOR NEGOTIATIONS

Alliance negotiations resemble other business negotiations, though they tend to be more complex due to the strategic and cross-cultural issues involved. For team members who lack experience in alliance negotiations, properly structured negotiation training could be a worthwhile investment.

An essential part of such preparation is to help the negotiators to become familiar with the business and cultural context of the partner's country. Given the stakes involved, a number of studies suggest that companies underestimate the need to prepare carefully.[35] Without preparation, it is all too easy to fall back on cultural stereotypes. It is also important to sort out the individual roles in a team, and to review and practice different negotiation scenarios. HR professionals often have strong process facilitation skills, and they may serve as internal consultants in the alliance negotiations. Especially in more complex negotiations, the presence of an experienced facilitator may be beneficial, observing the flow of interactions, interpreting behaviors, and coaching the key actors.

Negotiation Challenges in Joint Venture Formation

When an alliance takes the form of a joint venture, negotiations regarding control and management of the JV should include HR. There are several negotiation challenges where strategy and HRM interact closely. These include issues of:

- equity control versus operational influence;
- board composition;
- senior management appointments; and
- HR policies for the alliance.

EQUITY CONTROL VERSUS OPERATIONAL INFLUENCE

The issue of control is often difficult to resolve in JV negotiations. Generally, both parties seek to be the majority owner, as this is considered the best way to protect one's long-term interests, particularly in the context of a competitive alliance. However, in the absence of other supporting mechanisms, equity control is no guarantee that the venture will evolve in line with the intended strategy.

Gaining a majority position may provide a tax or financial reporting advantage. However, it is a fallacy to assume that equity control equals management control, as the Chemco case illustrates. A minority equity position, coupled with effective representation on the JV management team and an influence over the flow of know-how, may have more real impact on how the venture operates than a nominal majority exercised from a distance. From an accounting perspective, 51 percent of the shares may entitle the owner to 51 percent of the dividends, but these are often the last piece of the cash pie to be distributed. Internal transfer pricing, purchasing decisions, the cost of services provided by a local partner, payroll determined by compensation levels—all have an impact on cash flow long before any dividends are declared.

Not surprisingly, "the last 2 percent" (going from a 49 percent share to 51 percent) is the most expensive piece of equity. While intangible contributions (the infusion of technical or market know-how, transfer of depreciated assets, brand equity) may substitute for capital in a minority position, a majority position usually requires cash. The important point is that a careful human resource strategy that secures influence can be less costly and more effective than a strategy that focuses on securing equity control.

Acquiring such influence typically starts with the key appointments—the composition of the board and senior management appointments.

BOARD COMPOSITION

Companies often strive for a majority equity position simply to achieve a majority on the board of directors, thus protecting their voting interests in the event of a dispute between partners. In reality, JV boards seldom, if ever, vote. Pushing through a majority vote often constitutes the first step in dissolving an alliance. If the partners have a common interest in maintaining the relationship, then disputes are resolved in private and boards act only to approve such agreements. In addition, the protection of strategic interest can be achieved by other means, such as specific clauses in the agreement or articles of incorporation that stipulate what actions require unanimous or qualified majority consent of the shareholders.

There are side advantages to using the board primarily to oversee rather than to control. Positions on the board can be used for a variety of other purposes. An appointment to the board can be used to recognize the outstanding contribution of an alliance executive. In many countries, "company director" status is considered the pinnacle of a business career, and such opportunities may serve to increase the morale and retention of senior management. Board appointments can be used to expand linkages to outside business circles and the wider community in the local country, broadening learning and business opportunities. A position on the board can also be reserved for an individual who may mediate potential conflicts between the partners.

When setting up the board, there is a natural tendency to appoint alliance champions—people who favored the deal from the outset, who were involved in the negotiations, and who know the partner best. However, it is also useful to appoint at least one "bad cop," who will keep the champions from forgetting that the venture is a business rather than just a relationship—someone a little more skeptical, who sees the potential downfall of various alliance initiatives.[36]

APPOINTING SENIOR MANAGEMENT

In most JVs, senior managers wield far more strategic and operational control and influence than members of the board.[37] Tasks that determine the venture's success—setting business objectives, interfacing with key customers, monitoring the transfer of knowledge, developing the organization's culture—are all operational responsibilities of the senior managers inside the venture. Moreover, it is always preferable to resolve the inevitable conflicts and differences of opinion at the operational level rather than referring disputes to higher levels of alliance governance.

However, there is a paradox here. The shortage of international managers who can implement a market entry strategy in an unfamiliar environment is often a motive for choosing a JV over a wholly owned subsidiary; yet without a pool of suitable candidates, bargaining about positions is a meaningless exercise. Having such a pool ready requires attention to HR from the very early stage of alliance planning, since it takes time to select and groom potential candidates. It may be preferable to recruit in the local market and then provide them with opportunities to learn the organizational ropes before dispatching them to the JV—again, a time-consuming effort. If these HR issues are raised only after the agreement is signed, it may be difficult to find the right candidates in time for the launch. The cost of fixing the problems later grows exponentially with time, since misaligned cultures, attitudes and behaviors are difficult to uproot once embedded.

Note, however, that executive role expectations may vary from one culture to another. In a 50:50 French–Swedish JV located in France, the Swedish company agreed to the appointment of a senior French executive as chairman in exchange for *de facto* control of the operations. But in the French organization, the chairman was not the honorary figure that the Swedes expected. He was seen as the ultimate decision-maker in the venture, while the opinions of the Swedish managers were ignored. Although the venture continued to make strategic sense, the operational frictions generated so much ill will on both sides that it had to be dissolved a few years later.

The leadership and behavioral demands on JV managers are greater than in wholly owned units, and finding suitable managers is not a simple task. Political skills are indispensable because top JV managers need to use influence to balance partner priorities and overcome conflicts. Cross-cultural sensitivity and flexibility are particularly important when partners come from different cultures and where JV staff represent two or more nationalities. Having a cooperative disposition, a high tolerance for ambiguity, and an internal locus of control are additional personal traits that help international alliance managers to perform well.[38]

In particular, the nomination of the venture general manager can generate intense debate. Who should "own" the JV manager? One can argue that the venture manager must have the goodwill of both parents in order to operate effectively.[39] Installing somebody as venture general manager who only represents the interest of one partner may be counterproductive. And special care is needed when the joint entity is essentially independent of the parents' operations, as in the case of many complementary or resource alliances.

However, if the venture activities need to be integrated with those of the parent, then an arms'-length relationship may not be appropriate. There is a fine line between representing the best interests of the venture and those of the parent company. If an insider from one firm seems the logical choice as venture manager—because of his/her knowledge of the business or geographical area—it is important to minimize incentives that show favoritism. It should be clear that the manager's future career depends on the success of the venture. It also helps if alliance managers are seen as its champions—those who believe in the purpose and who work hard to make it succeed—see Box 3.

BOX 3: The role of venture champions

An alliance succeeds because managers and employees believe in the promise of the concept and are willing to invest personal effort to make it happen. Alliances without champions do not survive for long because the ambiguity and uncertainty of the relationship impair participants' capacity to deal with the complex issues embedded in most partnerships.

When Whirlpool Corporation established a manufacturing JV with Tatramat, the Slovak washing machine maker, Tatramat's former top executive, Martin Ciran, became managing director of the JV.[40] The new company later ran into serious financial difficulties that enabled Whirlpool to gain majority control. Yet Ciran retained his position because he was recognized as the key champion of the alliance. His leadership was deemed essential to making the venture a success.

With access to Whirlpool know-how, but under Ciran's leadership, the company was turned around. Today, Whirlpool's Slovak factory—now fully owned—still ranks among its top-performing European subsidiaries.

Identifying alliance champions and recognizing their contribution towards implementing the alliance strategy is a critical driver of its success. Not surprisingly, alliance champions, like alliance skeptics, can be found on both sides of the partnership. Knowing the venture champions on the "other side"—especially those who have sufficient internal credibility to mobilize resources for the benefit of the alliance—is of great value in the negotiations over managerial appointments.

HUMAN RESOURCE POLICIES WITHIN THE ALLIANCE VENTURE

The need to influence alliance strategy is only one of the arguments for addressing HRM issues early in the alliance formation process. When the success of the alliance depends heavily on people issues, such as competence transfer or reaching new standards in quality and productivity, leaving HR until later in order to simplify alliance negotiations may handicap the future chances of success.

It is particularly important to pay early attention to HR policies and practices when there are likely to be many complex interfaces between the venture and the alliance parents.[41] In contrast to licensing or supplier–buyer agreements, up-front agreement on HR philosophy and policies may be vital to success in manufacturing JVs or shared projects in new product development.

Some researchers advocate a detailed contract clarifying HR policies inside the alliance in order to reduce the uncertainty and conflict over matters of staffing, transfers, promotion, and compensation.[42] However, detailed contracts do not guarantee compliance. Venture synergy comes from shared business interests, not from legal formulations. A clear statement regarding HR principles is in most cases sufficient, without limiting contractually what can or cannot be done.

Sometimes companies take the position "when in Rome, do as the Romans" and delegate all responsibility for HR matters to the local partner. This makes sense provided that the "Roman" organization is a paragon of effectiveness, quality, and customer service. If it does not have solid HR foundations in place, then this attempt to show cultural sensitivity will only result in replicating the dysfunctional aspects of local practice. It is said of many foreign JVs in Japan that they represent "museums of Japanese management"—that is, they are repositories of obsolete practices that their Japanese parents ditched a long time ago, but which are still presented to the foreign parent as the "Japanese" way of managing people.

IMPLEMENTING ALLIANCES

Once the contract is signed and the partnership becomes operational, a new set of people-related issues appear. How to manage the evolution of the partnership? How to ensure that the knowledge developed inside the alliance is properly shared among the partners? And how to keep the partnership objectives aligned with those of the parent?

These issues have two major HR implications. The first is managing the interface with the parent, which involves influencing the attitudes and behaviors of staff at home who are in contact with the alliance. The second relates to the management of people inside the venture itself.

Managing the Interfaces with the Parent

An important challenge is to manage the interface between the parent organization and the partnership. The objective is to align the internal processes back home so that they support rather than hinder external collaboration. Often, the organizational units that provide resources to the alliance are not those receiving its outputs. The asymmetry in the perceived costs and benefits of collaboration with the venture may cause internal tensions that undermine willingness to support the partnership. The value of collaboration is sometimes not visible in the hustle and bustle of daily operations, so explicit reinforcements of the message may be required. Ford learned from Motorola's experience, cited earlier, when it entered into broad cooperative agreements in Japan. The question "What have you done to support Ford's alliance strategy?" featured in the performance evaluations for a large part of the organization.

A rapidly growing US securities firm with global ambitions set up an alliance with a European brokerage to offer their European customers "preferential" access to US financial markets. However, even after the alliance was launched to great fanfare, the operational practices at the New York trading desk did not change. The relatively small orders from Europe did not get the same attention as those from large US institutional clients, reducing profit opportunities for the European partner. The new partner received similar second-class treatment from other units of the US firm.

Why was this happening? The rigid "meet-the-numbers" reward system in the United States was incompatible with a strategy that did not yield immediate earnings, like the European partnership. No amount of presentations on the benefits of international expansion could make much difference. In Europe, the initial irritation quickly turned to anger and then to suspicions about the true motives of the American partner. Less than two years later, the alliance was dissolved. As noted by one of the American HR managers involved: "If this alliance was important for our future, then perhaps it should have been partly my job to create an environment where phone calls from our partners would be returned without delay."

TOP MANAGEMENT ROLE

The company's execution of its alliance strategy places particular demands on top management, who must "walk their talk." Box 4 illustrates what happens when top management are not involved.

BOX 4: The anniversary speech

A 50:50 JV between a Japanese and a US firm celebrated its 25th anniversary. Over time, the JV had evolved from a small marketing start-up to a fully integrated firm with an independent R&D and manufacturing capability that enjoyed a very profitable leadership position in the Japanese market. Given its commercial success, the friction between the two partners in the early days regarding the future direction of the business was replaced by a grudging willingness to continue working together. However, on the American side, executives often voiced concerns that the JV operated as if it were a wholly owned affiliate of the Japanese parent, while their influence was being eroded. The loyalty of the workforce was seen as tilted in favor of the local partner.

On the anniversary date, the employees assembled in one of Tokyo's exhibition halls for an afternoon of celebration. The company's glee club warmed up with some speeches and songs. Then, the 96-year-old former chairman of the Japanese parent, who signed the original deal, was helped onto the stage in his wheelchair to deliver a message of thanks to all employees for bringing his dream to life. His speech was short, owing to his failing health, but it was emotional and made a big impact on the audience. His speech was followed by a pre-recorded video message from the current American CEO who, in three years of tenure, had visited the venture once. He said nothing wrong, but the impersonality of the presentation defeated its purpose. Another skirmish in the loyalty battle was lost.

Capturing the loyalty of the alliance workforce is only one of the human resource tasks that require the support of top management. Internal communication is another; top management play an indispensable role in ensuring that the reasons for the partnership are well understood inside the firm, especially when it comes to balancing the competitive and collaborative aspects of the alliance. Top management must also work closely with HR on the selection of alliance managers, on resource allocation for learning activities, and on ensuring that reward systems are well aligned with the partnership strategy.

Human Resource Management Issues in Managing the Alliance

Many of the international HRM issues discussed previously in this book are also relevant to international alliances. Here we will examine those that may have the biggest impact on the success of an alliance strategy:

- staffing of the alliance;
- mobility between the parent(s) and the venture;
- competence and capability development;
- performance management;
- rewards and recognition;
- building influence inside the alliance; and
- aligning the social architecture.

However, just as there are no generic alliance strategies, so too there are few generic blueprints for effective HR policies and practices. Attention to HRM in the alliance depends on the strategic objectives and the position of the alliance in the value chain. The more critical the role of the partnership in creating value, the larger the need to commit HR resources and support.

STAFFING ALLIANCES

Staffing matters! Inappropriate staffing is of one the major causes of alliance failures, and this is typically the most important aspect of HRM in the venture. Perhaps the most important qualification for a potential alliance partner is having sound HR foundations at home. Without that credibility, it may be impossible to establish respect abroad.

Every strategic plan for an alliance should include a review of staffing requirements. Other HR matters, such as training and compensation, have an important impact, but problems in those areas can be addressed—with proper determination—in a relatively short time. Difficulties created by poor staffing, such as correcting the consequences of bad decisions made by people who are not qualified to meet the challenges of managing an alliance, may take years to fix. While the staffing issues will vary from one alliance to another, there are some generic matters to consider:

- What is the number and skill mix of employees required?
- Who is responsible for forecasting manpower demands?
- Who will do the recruiting? Each partner individually? Or will they work jointly?
- Which positions are to be filled by each parent?
- Which positions are to be filled by expatriates?
- In JVs, for whom do the new employees work—for one of the partners, or for the new entity?
- Who decides on new hires? Must there be an agreement among partners?
- How will staffing conflicts be resolved?

In virtually all JVs there will be staff from both partners. Box 5 addresses the tricky question of how to influence the other company's staffing decisions.

BOX 5: "Managing" your partner's staffing

Asymmetry in the quality of the assignees is often an early signal that the venture is heading for trouble, since it raises questions about the managerial competence or sincerity of the deficient partner. If the partner organization is to provide key operational staff, it is important to find ways of ensuring that they possess the required competences and skills. This means developing some way to identify the talented people in the partner organization, and understanding the basis by which the partner differentiates between high potentials, solid performers, and low performers.

Inappropriate staffing decisions are common. The partner's management may not understand the skill level required for jobs in the partnership venture, they may overestimate the capability of their internal candidates, or they may simply not have the necessary basic HR capabilities. It is essential to intervene before any decisions are taken. Forcing a change once an appointment has been made may be difficult.

The right to be consulted on key appointments is a useful stipulation in a partnership agreement. However, exercising this right requires familiarity with the "rules of the game" in the partner's organization, understanding the internal score cards, and knowing how careers evolve there, as well as gaining access to the levers of influence. Much of this is tacit knowledge, acquired through extensive informal interaction and built on trust and personal credibility.

Given the importance of staffing, there is a case for formally addressing these issues in the alliance contract, though, as noted earlier, views are divided since contractual arrangements may be too rigid for evolving staffing needs—mutual agreement on policies may suffice.

ONE-WAY VERSUS TEMPORARY TRANSFER

When partnerships are formed to create a new business, it is important to consider the costs and benefits of two alternative staffing strategies. One approach is to assign personnel to the JV on a temporary transfer from the partner firm. The other is to staff the JV positions on a "permanent" basis. While it is not unusual to combine the two methods, it is important to consider the conflicting priorities and career aspirations of the two groups of employees. Every position filled—usually at higher cost—by a temporary transferee is an opportunity lost for the permanent staff. If the value for money of the transferee is not readily apparent, then resentment and conflict are not far behind.

There is some evidence that it is better to staff JVs with dedicated management teams.[43] If employees are transferred from the parent, then they should expect to remain in the venture without a guaranteed ticket back to the parent, so that their future career opportunities are linked entirely to the growth of the new business. In Japan, a country where few JVs survive, several successful joint ventures have at their helm executives who have spent all or most of their careers in the venture. Fuji Xerox, headed for many years by Yotaro Kobayashi, is probably the most notable example of what strong and stable leadership can do for JV performance.

On the other hand, temporary transfers do have merits. They are useful when a venture is evolving rapidly and the required management skills change, when skill gaps cannot be covered internally, or as a tool for organizational learning. Transferees are more likely to remember that their task is not to preserve the alliance at all costs. Indeed, temporary transfers are generally the only way in which the foreign partner can insert its employees into the venture. However, any assignments should be of a reasonable duration, since new managers will pass through a learning stage before they can contribute fully to the venture. Frequent churn of key venture managers makes it difficult to establish a shared culture.

The foreign partner may experience greater difficulties than the local partner in convincing first-class employees from the parent firm to transfer to the JV.[44] In such cases, the personal involvement of top management can make a difference. When Procter & Gamble first entered the Chinese market in the 1980s, joint venturing with local partners was the only option. In order to encourage its best candidates to accept these challenging assignments, P&G's top management, including the CEO, took a visible role in candidate selection, acting as mentors during the assignment and in repatriation. Such leadership commitment to staffing ensured a ready supply of good managers willing to work in China.

A shortage of qualified candidates, or cost considerations, may persuade foreign partners to limit their representation to a single executive. One person is expected to play the role of corporate ambassador, shadow CEO, chief learning officer, and business developer—quite a challenge! Notably, in competitive alliances, this may not be in the best interest of the business.

In most cases, the best strategy is to recruit and develop local talent. When JVs are an important part of a company's strategy in a particular market, it may be worthwhile establishing a corporate unit that can serve as a holding company for all operations in the country. Local managers can then be hired by the holding company, and trained and dispatched to JVs to represent the interests of the foreign partner, thus lessening the reliance on expensive expatriates with limited local know-how. Many foreign firms investing in JVs in China—for example, ABB and GE—have chosen this route to develop their local management teams.[45]

DEVELOPING CAPABILITIES

The strategic objectives of an alliance often require developing new knowledge, skills, and competences, as in the case of learning and competitive alliances. This in turn requires actions to create a learning environment, including:

- building understanding among people in the parent company who will be involved directly or indirectly in the partnership;
- training employees and managers dispatched to the alliance;
- enhancing collaboration inside the partnership; and
- facilitating integration with the parent firm.

In companies where alliances are critical to the business strategy, alliance training is often used as an integral part of the implementation process. For example, Hewlett-Packard, which is engaged in scores of international partnerships, organizes workshops on a massive scale for managers involved in alliances. The HP alliance management framework, an elaborate knowledge management system focused on alliances, is disseminated using case histories, toolkits, and checklists, as well as comparisons of best practice from other firms.[46]

One of the dilemmas in preparing executives for alliance assignments is that companies may be reluctant to devote resources to alliance management training, or even to select potential venture staff, until the partnership has been agreed. This is a double bind, since there is seldom time for extensive training once an agreement has been reached. Estimates suggest that only a third of firms involved in alliances offer alliance training.[47] One of the authors has directed alliance management seminars for over 25 years. It is not unusual to see participants subscribing to the course at the last minute, departing for a foreign location virtually as soon as the course ends.[48]

One of the focal areas for management development within the alliance venture itself is in helping the members of venture teams to interact and work effectively with each other and with the parents. This process ideally starts when the alliance is launched, helping employees to get to know each other, and learning about each other's company culture and mode of operations. When Corning creates new alliances, venture staff are briefed on the respective organizational cultures and traditions, corporate values, and venture organization in order to minimize confusion and misunderstanding.[49] Other companies organize team-building workshops, ranging from traditional organizational development interventions to outdoor experiential learning.[50] It also pays to follow up the "honeymoon training" with periodic workshops, working jointly through specific business and cultural challenges facing the partnership.

In the Chemco case, the US partner realized that it had to modify the structure of functional training workshops it held to improve coordination in the Asia Pacific. Previously, these had been limited to wholly owned subsidiaries. Although participants complained about the lack of support from the Japanese, no action could be taken since the Japanese, as part of a JV rather than a wholly owned subsidiary, did not attend. In the new format, Japanese JV employees were invited to take part, and the program was redesigned to take language problems into account and to facilitate dialogue. Participants were now able to identify jointly the obstacles to collaboration, suggest actions to remedy the problems, and commit to new joint business initiatives. The bottom line? Profits from joint projects generated by the first three workshops equaled the annual training budget for the whole region.

A good and relatively inexpensive way to foster the alliance integration process is to open up in-house training to the staff in the alliance unit, and when appropriate, to those from the partner. Aside from skill development, this may lead to the creation of personal networks across the alliance boundaries. Real trust cannot be built through contracts, but only through human relationships.

DEFINING PERFORMANCE

During the planning stage, it is generally not difficult for alliance partners to agree that "performance matters." However, for the operating managers dispatched to the actual JV, it can be much more difficult to agree on what constitutes "performance," how to measure it, and what the consequences of high or low performance should be.

Most fundamentally, the partners may have different objectives for the JV and therefore use different criteria to assess performance. A study of Chinese–German JVs revealed that the Chinese parent organization put much higher value on the acquisition of technology and knowledge, while growth and market share were more important for the German parents.[51] However, disagreements about how to appraise performance are often less obvious.

In an oil exploration JV created by British, Norwegian (state-owned), and Vietnamese (government) partners, the parties did not hold the same views about performance management. Yet the split did not cut along East–West cultural lines. British expatriates and locally recruited young Vietnamese managers were in favor of individually focused, achievement-oriented performance criteria with substantial financial benefits for top performers. The Norwegians and the senior representatives of the Vietnamese partner, concerned about equity and harmonious work relations, preferred to give more emphasis to team goals and process implementation, with much less internal differentiation. Although the business principles in the agreement contained a commitment to create a performance-oriented culture, the specifics were never spelled out. The net result was confusion, frustration, conflict, and high turnover—the opposite of what a performance management system is supposed to achieve. It was not that one partner was "right" and the other "wrong," the real issue was the lack of a common perspective.

Many of the dualities involved in performance management can lead to disagreement—short-term versus long-term time horizon, focus on output versus behavior, individual versus group scope, objective versus subjective evaluation, direct versus indirect feedback, and in addition, parent versus venture orientation. This last issue—whether managers are evaluated on the performance of the venture or the parent—can become particularly contentious. But an even bigger problem is to align strategic aims. In Chemco's case, as long as the objective of the local management team was only to grow profitably in Japan, the wider strategic aims of the US firm to grow in the region remained neglected.

Many of the tensions around performance management come from three sources: (1) applying homegrown principles inappropriately in a different context, (2) using different standards for parent company and alliance employees, and (3) attempting to combine incompatible approaches.

In a Japanese-controlled JV in the United States, merit increases were linked to performance evaluations, according to local practice. However, the performance feedback process was decidedly "Japanese," indirect and informal. Japanese bosses spent most time with the laggards, hoping that with some encouragement their performance would improve. On the other hand, they loaded more responsibility on those considered outstanding so as to signal that they were trusted and were on the way to a bright future in the firm. While these signals might have been correctly interpreted in Japan, several of the top American performers quit, complaining that the merit increases did not reflect the additional responsibilities, that the bosses did not care, and that they did not know where they stood. Others complained that the Japanese were not honest, since the encouraging words were not matched by what they saw on their paychecks.

Strategy matters—in a complementary alliance, a hands-off approach to setting the performance objectives may be appropriate, whereas in a competitive alliance, this may be a recipe for disaster. Not surprisingly, resistance to "foreign" ways of managing performance is most pronounced in competitive alliances. This happens because managing performance is one of the keys to having an influence inside the venture. The way that performance is managed indicates to the alliance staff who is in charge and whose interests have to be taken seriously. Without influence over the performance management process, a partner (especially a distant partner) can expect only nominal control over the direction of the venture. Therefore, performance management issues often become a lightning rod in the latent struggle for influence.

The proper measure of influence is not how much the performance management of the alliance resembles that of the parent, but how it furthers the parent company's strategy. First, this means making sure that the parent's strategic objectives are reflected in the performance targets for the alliance. Second, achieving these targets has to be measured. Third, meeting or failing to meet targets should have consequences.

In Chemco's case, the first and second requirements for effective performance management processes were met once the US partner attained formal majority control and regional targets were included in the annual objectives set for the local management team. However, target setting was merely a ritual, since the results had no consequences, positive or negative—and this would remain the case as long as Chemco had no influence over salaries, bonuses, or promotions. This leads us to the reward aspects of performance management.

ALIGNING REWARDS

One of the first actions Chemco took to increase its influence was to negotiate a gradual transfer of all employees in Japan from the payroll of the Japanese parent to JV employee status. The work conditions offered were more favorable, but did not increase the cost as the compensation and benefit system was tailored to the JV workforce. The union and nearly all employees accepted these conditions. As a next step, the management bonus was linked to the achievement of two sets of targets, regional and local, with regional targets being the key objective for senior management. In addition, the variable part of total compensation was increased dramatically, and the company began discussing a stock option scheme. Today, the Japanese partner considers its JV as a "human laboratory" where new HR—novel to the Japanese market—can be tested before being introduced into the parent company.

Of all compensation issues, those relating to variable pay require the most sensitivity and flexibility. Compensation can have a strong impact on strategy implementation because people tend to do what they believe they get rewarded for.[52] But beyond that, people in different countries have very different attitudes to variable pay. This is partly the result of wide differences in accounting standards and tax regimes, for example, regarding stock options.[53] There are also different cultural attitudes to issues like uncertainty avoidance and salary differentials. Again, the primary consideration is to align rewards with the alliance strategy rather than blindly import HR practices because they are successful in the parent firm.[54]

No compensation formula or measurement matrix can overcome a disagreement about strategy. If one partner wants to build market share and the other is interested in cash flow, then developing common performance targets is going to be difficult unless the two partners first agree on priorities. In more complex alliances, building a clear linkage between strategic aims and rewards may not be possible, which is an additional argument for keeping alliances simple and focused.

Another important compensation issue to consider is the tension between external equity with the parent for expatriates and internal equity for venture staff, frequently leading to asymmetry in earnings among different groups of employees within the alliance. For example, expatriate managers often earn many times more than the income of a typical local JV employee (whose pay in turn may be considerably higher than that of a counterpart in a local firm).

The differences in compensation levels may also impact the balance of influence in the alliance since loyalties, not surprisingly, tend to shift towards the higher-paying partner.[55]

These differences, while unavoidable in ventures involving companies from countries with widely different standards of living, may lead to motivational problems and conflict unless the added value of staff who receive superior compensation is visible and appreciated. Disparity in compensation sometimes makes it difficult to persuade the local partner to accept expatriates, even when this could be in the best interest of the venture.[56] Local partners may also try to use the disparity to their own advantage. For example, compensation "equality" between foreign expatriates and local managers was often one of the conditions for JV approval by local authorities in China. In reality, the Chinese managers were paid only a fraction of what was stipulated in the contract, while their state-owned employer retained the rest. Foreign partners in Chinese JVs had to bear the expatriation costs of foreign managers, while the Chinese partner earned a corresponding profit.

Internal equity issues within the parent firm must also be balanced against the supply and demand for high-quality venture managers. Alliances, in comparison with wholly owned subsidiaries, are difficult to manage. They may be seen as risky, since the venture is removed from the politics of getting ahead in the parent company. High-performers, who tend to have options, may elect to stay clear of such assignments unless they are sufficiently compensated. On the other hand, corporate cohesion is better facilitated by a degree of consistency in compensation strategy across all affiliates, irrespective of the organizational form.

This paradox cannot be solved simply by re-calibrating compensation. To achieve the necessary balance, other components of the HR system have to be aligned as well. The deliberate positioning of alliance assignments as a key element of long-term career progression is a powerful tool for ensuring a supply of requisite talent, as we saw in the case of P&G's staffing strategy for entering China. Influencing and shaping careers provides stronger leverage over expatriate staffing than short-term financial incentives.[57]

BUILDING AND MAINTAINING INFLUENCE

One of the best ways to gain allegiance among JV employees is to show commitment to their career development. Shortly after transferring Japanese employees to the JV payroll, Chemco offered some younger staff the possibility of moving to its subsidiaries in South East Asia with the assignment of coordinating sales with Japanese customers in the region. The conditions offered were the same as for any other Chemco expatriate. One benefit for Chemco was improved customer service and sales. The other was a dramatic change in how the Japanese staff perceived regional integration. The earlier view that integration was a power game—us versus them—quickly faded. Expatriate perks such as housing were attractive for the young Japanese since they could not afford this at home. But what made the difference was the feeling that career opportunities were now visibly open to all.

Such career development can promote organizational cohesion, though as with any HRM practice, the execution depends on the alliance's strategic context. In competitive alliances, this needs to be carefully considered. The worst outcome is to accept a transferee for the sake of the relationship, and then to cut him/her off from information and influence because he/she is perceived as untrustworthy. Some transferees will view this as another example of the partner's duplicity and bad intentions.

The form of the alliance also has implications for career development, and again JVs pose most of the challenges.[58] Employees transferred from the parent to a JV can feel left behind, especially if the number of expatriates inside the venture is small. The temporary nature of the assignment only reinforces anxiety about career prospects. Assurances from corporate HR—"Don't worry, we'll take care of you when you come back"—lack credibility in an era of continuous restructuring. The difficulty of managing dual allegiance is one of the arguments in favor of "one-way transfer" staffing strategies. However, this is often not practical from a staffing perceptive, as we will discuss in the next section, or desirable because of a need to foster knowledge exchange between the venture and the parent.

Visible involvement in career development decisions is one of the most effective ways to build influence. Being an "absentee" parent may be a cost-efficient strategy in the short term, but it can be costly in the long term. In a stand-alone JV, when the initial growth levels off, career development prospects may diminish and the best and the brightest may leave unless they see the same opportunity to move to increased responsibilities as they would have in a wholly owned subsidiary. If only one of the parents seems to care, then it is likely that commitment and loyalty will shift accordingly.

DEVELOPING SHARED CULTURE

In contrast to acquisitions, one has to live with conflicting loyalties in alliances. Whether or not this becomes dysfunctional depends on the type of alliance and the ability of the partners to deal with the contradictions in the alliance relationship. One way to cope is to foster a distinct and shared culture inside the alliance that eases tensions between partners, another is to build strong personal relationships. However, as always, this depends on the business strategies underlying the venture. Alliance independence is not a goal in itself—the purpose of an alliance is to create value for the partners. Instructions to general managers, such as "run this like your own business" when the venture does not have decision-making autonomy can only create mistrust and cynicism.

The key outcome of a shared culture is trust.[59] Creating a shared culture inside an alliance does not mean ignoring differences between the partners' strategic priorities. However, even in a competitive alliance, the partnership will not succeed without trust on an operating level. The best way to build trust is to get to know each other. This can be supported by promoting personnel exchanges and by providing visible examples of commitment to common goals.

Another source of cohesion may be a common enemy, as illustrated by the experience of three middle-sized manufacturers of electronic components. American, German, and Japanese, respectively, they established a global alliance aimed at combining R&D resources in a market dominated by two giant competitors. Management teams met regularly around the world to coordinate development activities. However, traditional rivalry, parochial departmental interests, and cultural insensitivity slowed down decision-making, causing the alliance to miss several critical deadlines and to jeopardize relationships with key customers. On the initiative of one of the HR managers, signs bearing the logos of the two competitors were installed on the walls in the conference rooms. The signs could be made to light up by pushing a button hidden under the conference desk, reminding everyone that the competition did not go away while they wasted time in unproductive arguments. After only a few meetings, it became embarrassing for anyone to get flashed for allowing a parochial agenda to get in the way of common interest. The speed, decision-making, and quality of implementation improved dramatically.

SUPPORTING ALLIANCE LEARNING

All alliances include some learning aspects, the least of which is how to work effectively with partners.[60] However, some alliances are created with capability development, knowledge-creation, and learning as the focal objectives.

In both learning and competitive alliances, effective alliance learning is important not only to prevent the erosion of a firm's market position, but also as a building block for future competitive advantage. In the case of Fuji Xerox, the venture was started to facilitate Xerox's entry into the Japanese market. In the late-1980s, other Japanese companies such as Canon and Ricoh aggressively attacked Xerox in its home US market with innovative products, competing on price and quality. Initially, Xerox was not able to respond and lost significant market share. However, recognizing that Fuji Xerox competed successfully against the same players in Japan, the company launched a massive "learning from Japan" campaign, aimed at transferring Fuji Xerox's capabilities back to the US mother firm.[61] Because of this "reverse technology transfer," Xerox was able to stem the market erosion and began to recapture lost share.

The long-term success of Fuji Xerox illustrates the fact that many strong strategic alliances focus on mutual learning. Indeed, selecting partners who are known to be poor learners so as to guard against capability leaks is short-sighted. Weak learning capability is a sign of poor management, and poorly managed firms make poor partners. Trust between the partners allows them to concentrate on managing the business rather than on monitoring and control, and their mutual learning strengthens their position in markets worldwide.

An organization has many tools to manage the process of learning, but in principle, the learning ability of an organization depends on its ability to transfer and integrate tacit knowledge that is difficult to copy, thereby building organizational capabilities. Since the capabilities are typically embedded in people, HRM is critical to organization learning. This is especially true in international alliances where the learning occurs in a complex context of competition and cultural differences. Many of the difficulties in implementing long-term alliance strategies can be traced to the quality of the learning process and the underlying human resource policies and practices. The ability to learn is even more important in competitive alliances, where asymmetry in learning can result in an uneven distribution of benefits.[62]

One objective of human resource management in international alliances is therefore to complement business strategy by providing a climate that encourages organizational learning, and by installing appropriate tools and processes to guide the process of knowledge-creation.[63] We have already discussed many of these, but alliances, particularly competitive alliances, bring particular challenges for HRM.

Obstacles to Alliance Learning

The rapid development of competitive capabilities among leading Japanese firms in the second half of the twentieth century is often attributed to successful alliance learning. Alliances were used as the main vehicle for inward technology transfer and capability improvement. More recently, many other companies in developing countries in Asia and Latin America have pursued the same strategy with success. By contrast, many of the traditional US and European firms have struggled to kick start the learning process and examples of alliance learning like that of Fuji Xerox are relatively rare. So what are the obstacles? Some stem from ill-conceived strategies, others from poor HRM practices, yet others from a combination of both (see Table 3).

DEFENSIVE STRATEGIC INTENT

One obstacle to alliance learning may arise because many alliances are driven by a defensive strategic intent. Firms perceive partnerships primarily as a way of reducing risk and conserving valuable resources.[64] This built-in defensive posture may make managers reluctant to make the necessary investments in learning, especially if one of the alliance objectives is to minimize the cost of developing new competences. Failing to invest in learning will invariably result in the deterioration of a firm's competitive position, leading to an asymmetry in the relationship and eventually to a conflict with the partner. Dissolution of the relationship is then the logical next step. Successful learning alliances are most often driven by a "top-line" orientation where investment in the development of new competences is recovered through the growth of business.

A corollary to defensive intent is the belief that preventing the partner from learning (and thus avoiding asymmetry) may be easier and cheaper than investing in one's own learning. A partner committed to learning will always learn, even if this is made difficult by obstacles put in the way. Meanwhile, the customer feels the obstacles. Secrecy and internal walls lead to sub-optimal solutions,

Table 3 Obstacles to organizational learning in international strategic alliances

HR Activities	HR Practices
Planning	• Strategic intent not communicated. • Short-term and static planning horizon. • Low priority for learning activities. • Lack of involvement by the HR department.
Staffing	• Insufficient lead time for staffing decisions. • Resource-poor staffing strategy. • Low quality of staff assigned to the JV. • Staffing dependence on the partner.
Training and development	• Lack of cross-cultural competence. • Uni-directional training programs. • Career structure not conducive to learning. • Poor culture for transfer of learning.
Appraisal and rewards	• Appraisal focused on short-term goals. • No encouragement to learn. • Limited incentives for transfer of know-how. • Rewards not tied to global strategy.
Organizational design and control	• Responsibility for learning not clear. • Fragmentation of the learning process. • Control over the HR function given away. • No insight into partner's HR strategy.

Source: Adapted from Pucik (1988b).

excessive costs, and delays. In highly competitive markets, companies that hope to build defensive walls around themselves to prevent knowledge "seeping" to the partner often end up losing the customer.

LOW PRIORITY FOR LEARNING ACTIVITIES

Decisions on alliance learning strategy are often based on the assumption that the existing balance of contributions to the venture will not change over time. Consider the case of a partnership where one party provides technology and the other secures market access. The executives of the technology firm may believe that the partner will have to rely on their technological leadership for the foreseeable future, so they see few incentives to invest in learning about the market. However, if the other partner gradually closes the technological gap—after all, technology transfer is often a part of the deal—the basis for the alliance becomes problematic. One partner now has both technology and market access, so why share the benefits?

One problem here is that many firms do not recognize the importance of developing soft or invisible competences. Learning often has to be focused on mastering tacit processes underlying product quality, speed of product development, or linkage to key customers. Firms frequently fail to benefit from alliance learning because they do not recognize the benefits of acquiring the "soft" skills.[65]

Learning through alliances may be faster than learning alone, but it still requires investment. The learning strategy may be compromised by a reluctance to commit the necessary financial resources. In many companies, the traditional focus of the business planning process is return on financial assets, while the accumulation of invisible assets is not evaluated directly since a financial value is hard to assign to these outcomes. Activities that cannot be evaluated in financial terms may be seen as less critical, so learning efforts are given only token support.

INAPPROPRIATE STAFFING

Expatriate staffing is costly, and firms are tempted to reduce alliance costs by limiting the number of expatriate personnel assigned to the foreign venture. As a result, the few expatriates (sometimes only one) are often overwhelmed with routine work, struggling just to get by in an unfamiliar culture. The opportunities for active involvement in new knowledge acquisition—for example, through relationships with local customers or interactions with the partner—are minimal. However keen the expatriate may be to learn, operational matters prevent him/her from doing so.

In Chemco's case, company policy for nearly 20 years was to dispatch only one senior-level executive to Japan, occasionally augmented with an experienced engineer bringing knowledge into Japan. In most cases, the expatriates retired after their assignment in Japan, so there was no organizational transfer of learning. When the company decided to refocus its Japan strategy, the total accumulated experience in the Japanese market among the top management team (Japan was at that time the largest overseas market for Chemco), including business trips longer than one week, was less than six months.[66]

The staffing agenda, however, is not just about how many and where, but also about who. If the managers assigned to oversee or manage an alliance are not credible within their own organization and with the partner, learning will be difficult to achieve. Because these are relatively long-term assignments, they clash with the expectations of fast upward mobility and may not be attractive to high-potential managers. The managers who land in this role may not have the influence to cope with the complex give-and-take of a learning relationship. Long-term career planning is often lacking, as is effective repatriation (as in Chemco's case), which may hinder effective exploitation and dissemination of the acquired know-how.

POOR CLIMATE FOR KNOWLEDGE EXCHANGE

A characteristic of alliance learning is that partner interactions often take place in a context of competitive collaboration.[67] Not surprisingly, competition and learning commonly go hand-in-hand in high-tech industries in which fast learning is an imperative of the business model.

In a competitive alliance, transfer of knowledge to a competitor will often generate legitimate concern among staff over what will happen to job and work groups when their unique knowledge is disseminated to others. Principles of equitable exchange agreed at the venture board meeting do not necessarily translate into perceptions of equity at the operational level. Initial obstacles such as lack of focus and unclear priorities can quickly mushroom into widespread resistance to knowledge exchange. When one partner ignores requests for learning support, it may awaken suspicions of duplicity, inviting retaliation. Very soon, the whole atmosphere of partnership is poisoned.

Internal barriers to the acquisition of learning are often just as serious as unfriendly actions by the partner. The learning from the outside threatens the status quo. The typical attitude is defensive: "It's a good idea, but it will never work here." Contrast this with the attitude guiding GE's approach to alliances: "Stealing with pride" is a message that made it into the company's annual report.

NO ACCOUNTABILITY OR REWARDS FOR LEARNING

Some years ago, one of the authors conducted a survey among foreign JVs in Japan. One of the questions put to the HR managers was, "Who in the parent firm organization is responsible for learning from Japan?" Less than 10 percent identified a person or a function (usually the top representative in Japan), about a third mentioned "nobody," and over half considered the question "not applicable." Since learning is taken more seriously today, the answers might be more positive, but the lack of clear responsibility remains a major obstacle to alliance learning.

Learning targets are unlikely to be taken seriously if there is no accountability for meeting them. In complex organizations, perceptions of the potential value of learning from an alliance may vary according to the business unit, function, and territory, and the commitment to provide the necessary support will vary accordingly. This can lead to asymmetry, where one unit supplies the people while another unit expects the learning. During the dot.com boom, a European high-tech company entered a number of partnerships with companies in Silicon Valley, with the aim of exploring ways of leveraging its technology in the internet world. Several young engineers were dispatched to California to work on specific projects as well as to provide feedback to the technology managers in the mother company. Within a few months, the word came back: "If you want to learn about exploiting the internet, do it yourself. We don't have the time to teach you."

Traditional market-driven reward systems may implicitly encourage the hoarding of critical information rather than the diffusion of learning. People who have valued knowledge can command higher salaries on the market, so diffusing their knowledge to others (for example, by sharing critical alliance contacts) may diminish their market value. Being indispensable is the ultimate in "employability."

HRM Foundations for Effective Alliance Learning

A major role for HR is to help create an organizational context in which alliance learning can flourish (see Table 4). Importantly, alliance learning is not about collecting binders of data in the alliance "war room." Rather, effective alliance learning is focused on absorbing know-how and developing or broadening capabilities.

In the context of learning and competitive alliances, the need to focus on HRM from an early stage is especially critical. Acquisition of new knowledge and competences happens only through people, and if the people strategy is not aligned with the learning objectives, then the chances of this happening are greatly diminished.

SETTING THE LEARNING STRATEGY

One of the first questions to address in developing an alliance learning strategy is the extent to which this issue should be considered in the alliance agreement.

When the alliance is set up as a separate organization, for example as a JV, the partnership agreement or operating principles should provide for at least broad guidelines on key HR policies and practices that influence learning effectiveness. These may involve issues such as freedom to move people across alliance boundaries as necessary, and determination of their learning roles and responsibilities. Clarifying HR issues that influence learning is especially important if the alliance operates abroad, since it is often difficult—and costly—to renegotiate HR policies for the benefit of one of the partners after the venture is launched.

In a learning alliance, the benefits of being clear about learning expectations among partners are self-evident. But what if the learning is to take place in the context of a competitive alliance? Does it make sense to be open about one's learning strategy, or should this remain a closely guarded secret?

The best, but probably hardest, way to deal with the competitive collaboration is to accept and be open about the "race to learn." Hiding the learning agenda increases mistrust and encourages opportunistic behavior. Both parties

---

Table 4 Core principles for alliance learning

---

1. Build learning into the alliance agreement.
2. Communicate the learning intent inside the parent.
3. Assign responsibility for alliance learning.
4. Secure early HR involvement.
5. Maintain HR influence inside the alliance.
6. Staff to learn.
7. Support learning-driven careers, including repatriation.
8. Stimulate learning through training.
9. Reward learning activities.
10. Monitor your partner's learning.

Source: Adapted from Pucik (1988b).

should be explicit about their learning objectives, put forward strategies to accomplish such learning together with their HRM implications, monitor mutual progress, and discuss with each other any important reservations. If the learning objectives cannot be openly discussed, then the merits of the whole alliance may become questionable.[68]

Once the strategy is set, it has to be clearly and consistently communicated across the organization. What is the purpose of the alliance? What are its boundaries? What needs to be learned? What is the partner expected to gain? Sometimes, companies are reluctant to communicate clearly that the alliance is actually competitive in nature because of the fear that such communication may set a bad tone for the relationship. In fact, the lack of communication does not change the reality; competition does not disappear because it is not talked about. The result is confusion and disbelief among the employees. Clear and unequivocal rules of engagement are essential.

While aligning HR processes to the learning strategy is vital, the responsibility for managing learning belongs to the line, not to HR or any other staff function. Who is responsible for learning sends a signal about how important this is. In a product development alliance between an American and Japanese high-tech firm, the HR function put itself forward as the champion of alliance learning, one of the explicit objectives for the alliance.[69] Many of the engineers who were expected to participate dismissed the whole activity as another "HR program." As for the Japanese, the role of the American HR "learning manager" remained a mystery throughout.

There are four basic HR areas where line management and the HR function can leverage alliance learning:

1. Selection and staffing
2. Training and development
3. Career planning
4. Performance management.

STAFFING TO LEARN

The focus on learning starts with appropriate staffing, since the quantity and quality of people involved in the learning effort is fundamental to its credibility and success.[70] There is no such thing as free alliance learning. Strategic intent is no substitute for resource commitment.[71] Obviously, justifying the necessary staffing investments requires fixing clear and measurable learning outcomes. And when some of the desired knowledge resides with partner's employees, as is usually the case, then the partner's commitment to support the alliance with competent staff is also essential.

The most powerful learning often happens in joint alliance teams where employees from both partners work together on solving business issues. Here, it is important to consider the difference between traditional in-company teams and alliance teams. A common company culture and, above all, shared long-term goals facilitate the team process when working in the company. In alliance teams, none of these "glue" factors exist, which introduces additional ambiguity and uncertainty into the learning environment. Selection criteria for alliance learning teams need to take into account the ability of employees to cope with this complexity.

Several years ago, a European consumer products company assigned a group of its fast-track employees to work on a team with its Chinese partner in developing strategies for expansion in China. All assignees had a record of successful postings to wholly owned subsidiaries in the region. However, the added difficulties of working with a partner organization required an adjustment in behavior, communication, and leadership style that several of them could not handle. The project team had to be restructured several times, causing delays and disruptions to the new product launch schedule.

Another critical staffing issue concerns the trade-off between staffing for learning and staffing for effective execution. Consider the case of a joint development project between a US and a European telecommunication company. The main idea behind the collaboration is to pool the complementary technical capabilities of the two firms in order to deliver a novel solution to global customers. A second objective is to learn from each other so that both companies can improve their competitive offerings at home. The execution perspective suggests that each partner should field a team in its areas of special expertise, which will foster speed and efficiency in executing the business plan. However, if the partners only focus on what they are good at, then how will they acquire new skills? In order to learn, additional staff will have to be assigned to join the team, which might hinder progress in getting the job done, not to mention the additional cost that the project would have to bear. Getting this balance right requires a very clear understanding of the strategic objectives behind the alliance.

LEARNING TO LEARN

Different types of training and development activities can stimulate a climate conducive to effective alliance learning. Some training is best conducted internally, with attendance limited to the parent firm so that sensitive issues can be openly discussed. Internal training can help employees to understand the importance of the learning aims of the alliance, as well as how to learn through collaboration, and this type of training should take place early on in the alliance lifecycle. This is especially important if the alliance is or is likely to become competitive in nature.

When a US high-tech manufacturer decided to set up a joint new product development project with a Japanese partner, one of its first actions was to conduct a series of alliance management workshops for all key employees who would be directly or indirectly involved. The strategic logic of the project, its scope and boundaries, the learning objectives and opportunities, as well as ideas on specific learning processes, were presented and discussed in detail. As a result of these discussions, top management decided to redesign the alliance manager role in order to foster clearer accountability for learning and to adjust the resources allocated to specific learning activities.

Since alliance learning is based on relationships with the partner, joint training activities can enhance collaboration by raising both competence and trust. Team-building and joint cross-cultural communication training are especially useful to speed up the getting-acquainted process. These can include intensive discussion on organizational values, structures, decision-making patterns, and the like, so that employees understand the context in which they are expected to work together. Communication problems may otherwise be attributed to "cultural differences"—people learn through such workshops that the real problems are often more tangible matters, such as different interpretations of performance expectations and rewards.

MANAGER CAREER PATHS TO FACILITATE LEARNING

The rotation of employees through alliance positions and back to the parent firm facilitates the transfer of knowledge between the venture and the parent.[72] This requires addressing such issues as the harmonization of salaries/benefits to facilitate moving people back and forth. While these issues do not have to be addressed in the text of the partnership agreement, the transfers need to be planned carefully, especially with respect to future career expectations.[73] If the individual knows that the knowledge acquired in the venture will be put to good use on return, this increases his/her motivation to learn during the assignment.[74]

The need for an explicit strategy to transfer and implement acquired knowledge is well illustrated by the case of NUMMI. Only a handful of selected General Motors managers were assigned to the venture in the early years—apparently in order not to "contaminate" its new culture with old GM practices.[75] After two to three years of working with the Japanese, these managers were converted to the virtues of Toyota's lean manufacturing system, with a good grasp of its workings. They moved back to different GM locations with the mission of implementing the learning from NUMMI within the GM organization. All these efforts ended in failure—not because of inadequate personal learning, but because there was never a critical mass of ex-NUMMI staff to make a difference.

Asymmetry in personnel transfers is usually a good indication of asymmetry in learning. While GM shuffled isolated individuals, Toyota trained more than 100 of its personnel on how to collaborate with NUMMI's American workforce. They were then assigned to Toyota's new wholly owned plant in Kentucky to replicate the NUMMI experience. In contrast, it took over a decade for General Motors to properly leverage its own acquired knowledge. An alumni team from the ventures at NUMMI and CAMI (GM's JV with Suzuki Motors) took charge of a decrepit East German car plant in Eisenach, and within three years they had turned it into the most advanced car manufacturing facility in Europe.[76] The knowledge that specific individuals had gained about Toyota's manufacturing system resulted in action only when there was a coherent organizational strategy for applying that learning.

REINFORCING LEARNING THROUGH PERFORMANCE MANAGEMENT

While successful learning from alliances requires champions of knowledge-cre-ation—people who believe in the value of learning and who support the neces-sary investments—this may not be enough. Thus, alliance learning objectives should be translated into specific measures wherever possible, such as quality or productivity improvement, speed of new product development, or customer expansion.

In Motorola's 12-year alliance with Toshiba to design and manufacture advanced semiconductors (a typical competitive alliance), both companies used explicit learning targets. In Motorola's case, these were translated into individ-ual-level objectives linked to rewards. The explicit measurements allowed both firms to mobilize their internal resources to support learning efforts. Externally, the tangible learning outcomes provided a valuable benchmark for assuring learning symmetry during the life of the alliance. It should be noted that the two executive positions considered most important in this alliance were split between the partners, but rotated every couple of years. One was the role of venture chief executive, the other that of human resource manager.

The climate for learning is best when alliance performance is satisfactory. When the alliance does not meet its expected targets, it may be more difficult to focus attention on the learning agenda, and necessary investments may be cut.[77] But even a failed alliance can be a source of valuable lessons. During its ambitious drive to internationalize in the early 1990s, GE organized a workshop in which executives who had been involved in failed alliances presented their experiences at a company forum. No amount of lectures on alliance strategy can match the impact of a high-level manager explaining how his assumptions about the foreign partner's business culture were wrong, resulting in a loss to GE of US$50 million. Why were these managers willing to share their painful experi-ences? Because sharing experience with others, positive or negative, was part of their performance objectives.

There are also alliances designed solely for the purpose of learning, where the business results are secondary, at least in the short term. However, prob-lems quickly surface if the partners have different priorities in terms of busi-ness results versus learning, especially if this issue was not addressed during the formation of the partnership. In the words of a German manager in a Chinese JV: "We pay the tuition, and they go to school." Conflicting priorities usually translate into ambiguous performance indicators for managers assigned to the venture, generating tension and disagreements among the executive team.

Successful learning alliances exhibit a bias for action. The best way of learn-ing, sometimes the only way, is to do things together. "Don't just talk about learning and collaboration. Do it!" Such was the advice of a Japanese executive in charge of a highly successful learning alliance in the electronics industry. In this alliance, the approach to stimulating mutual learning was straightforward: focused joint development teams were assigned to specific tasks and then held responsible for achieving results, with the co-leaders being directly accountable to their parents. Those who were unwilling to share their know-how were quickly moved aside, those who were not keen to apply what they had learned did not last much longer. The race to learn lasted three years. With the learning mission accomplished, the alliance was dissolved, and the companies renewed their competition, both of them stronger than they would have been if they had operated alone.

THE EVOLVING ROLE OF ALLIANCES

Just as alliances themselves evolve, so the role of alliances as part of corporate strategy is evolving. One increasingly frequent pattern of alliance development is the emergence of alliance networks, whereby firms engage in multiple linkages and relationships, often across the whole spectrum of the value chain from R&D and manufacturing all the way to distribution and after-sales service.[78] Originally limited to the high-tech sector, in which multiple alliances were used as a protective device against obsolescence and other technology risks, today they can be found in a number of sectors, from airlines to fashion to pharmaceuticals. Such networks pose new challenges for HRM.

Managing Network Boundaries

Alliances among carriers in the airline industry are spreading. Such alliances promise the customer a seamless package of air services around the world. Code sharing (where a particular flight is shared by several airlines) is the most visible example. For example, traveling around the world with Star Alliance[79] may involve purchasing a ticket in Asia from Singapore Airlines, flying to Europe via Cape Town with South African Airlines, then on a Lufthansa plane serviced by United to the United States, and completing the final leg of the trip with a Japan-based air carrier. If a service complaint on such a journey were met with the response, "Sorry, but those people were not our employees," then customer loyalty would clearly be compromised. So this raises the question of who the employees work for—their own airline, or also for the Star Alliance?

From the time of reservation until the delivery of luggage at the end of the trip, airlines are a people-intensive business. Some argue that people and the service experience they provide are the only differentiators among carriers.[80] Is it possible to deliver a seamless experience without coordinating or perhaps ultimately integrating HR strategies, ranging from the profile of who will be hired to the kind of training they receive and how they will get paid? How can the airlines share best practices? If at least some amount of coordination of airline HR standards is essential, then what kind of process is needed to make it happen? Who should lead it? And, where is the accountability?

These are new challenges for HRM, particularly since historically, the approach for airlines has been strongly domestic in orientation. A typical airline today is international only because it flies to foreign locations. Most major airlines outside the United States are national flag carriers, with close relationships to their home government and strong national unions. Even if the respective management teams in an alliance agree on what behaviors are expected from the employees, the implementation of HR policies influencing these behaviors may be restricted by historic, institutional, and cultural factors.

In the case of Star Alliance, the Lufthansa Business School took a lead, perhaps because it had played an important role in transforming a bankrupt national carrier with a civil service mentality into one of the most profitable global leaders in the industry in the 1990s. Participation on its project-oriented programs was broadened to include partner members, with the aim of not only facilitating coordination, but also speeding up the internal transfer of learning from one partner to another. Most of the partners bring particular distinctive strengths— Singapore Airlines in customer bonding, United in logistics, Lufthansa itself in maintenance and managing learning. The HRM vision is that the alliance can be used for mutual learning, to convert weaknesses on the part of individual partners into collective strengths.

The HR challenge in airline alliances is an indicator of things to come. As one senior HR executive in a European airline put it: "Anybody who delivers value to my customer is my employee." This is a bold statement, not yet backed up by practice, but with broad implications that go well beyond the airline industry. The density of international alliances is increasing in all sectors as companies engage in a broader variety of relationships across the supply and value chains to the customer. This raises the question of where the boundary of HR's responsibility lies.

Alliances as a Journey towards Transnationalism

The ambiguity of boundaries in an alliance and the need to anticipate future shifts is only one of the tensions in this domain. Alliances are full of tensions between competition and collaboration, between global and local interests, between the venture and its parents, between leveraging and developing competences. Ambiguity and complexity are the norm. Bearing in mind that the principal challenge in the internationalization process is learning to manage tension, dilemma, and duality, mastering alliance dilemmas and contradictions helps firms to learn to manage transnational pressures.

In conclusion, let us therefore summarize some of the paradoxes and dualities that the multinational firm learns to confront through its experience in managing alliances:

- Learning how to manage differentiation. There is no such thing as "an alliance"—each alliance has different aims and strategic objectives, implying different courses of management and HR action. The parallel for the transnational is that it has to differentiate the roles of its units and subsidiaries, managing them in different ways.
- Learning to balance the fundamental tension between short-term performance and the long-term learning or knowledge-creation that come through

collaboration (the exploitation versus exploration duality). As in the Chemco example, being a hands-off parent can be advantageous in the short term, but it can carry a corresponding long-term cost.

- Learning to recognize and deal with trade-offs where a pathology can be created if one extreme is pushed too far. We see many examples in alliances—if either the interests of the venture itself or the interests of the parent are pushed too far, this can make it impossible to achieve the alliance aims. Similarly, the deal itself is critical, though excessive attention to detail can create rigidities (the first Star Alliance document was only one page long).
- Learning that a delicate balance is needed between external equity for expatriates and internal equity for long-term venture staff.
- Learning to take important but "soft" aims such as learning and convert them into "hard" objectives through measurement and accountability.
- Learning "to manage the future in the present"—the strategic aims of tomorrow may be quite different from those of today. Success of the venture must not be confused with the wider strategic aims of the parent.

Individuals involved in alliances face many challenges. They must learn how to manage boundaries, how to deal with ambiguity and conflicting interests, how to mold a culture that balances competing interests, and how to manage the tensions between exploitation (operating results, cash flow, and profit) and exploration (learning). One of the best breeding grounds for transnational managers may be alliance management.

TAKEAWAYS

1. Initially considered only as a means of securing market access, alliances today are an integral part of global strategies in all aspects of the value chain. Using alliances to generate new knowledge is increasingly important.
2. Alliances are mostly transitional entities; therefore, longevity is a poor measure of success. The aim is not to preserve the alliance at all costs, but to contribute to the parent's competitive position.
3. There are four types of alliances: complementary, learning, resource, and competitive. Alliances are dynamic, migrating from one strategic orientation to another. Very few alliances remain complementary for long. Alliances among competitors are increasingly frequent, but they are also the most complex.
4. The approach to HRM is largely driven by the strategic objectives of the partnership. This requires a focus on both managing the interfaces with the parent companies as well as managing people inside the alliance itself.
5. The firm's HRM skills and reputation are assets when exploring and negotiating alliances. Do not enter a complex alliance unless both sides of the

partnership have a good grasp of HRM basics. The greater the expected value from the alliance, the more HR support is required.

6. The failings of an alliance are too easily attributed to cultural differences when the real culprit may be the lack of attention to HRM issues, such as appropriate staffing, performance measures, compensation equity, and career management.

7. Equity control is a costly and relatively ineffective form of alliance control when compared to investing in a carefully designed and implemented HRM strategy.

8. Conflicting loyalties, complex relationships, and boundary management issues, coupled with uncertainty and instability, are characteristic of most alliances. Managers assigned to the alliance need high tolerance for ambiguity.

9. Alliance learning is neither automatic nor free—there must be clear learning targets, sufficient investment in people, and a tight alignment of HRM practices with learning objectives.

10. Alliances are full of tensions between competition and collaboration, between global and local interests, between leveraging and developing competences. Mastering alliances helps firms to learn to manage transnational pressures.

NOTES

1. Contractor and Lorange (1988: 9) identify seven overlapping objectives for the formation of various types of alliances: (1) risk reduction; (2) achievement of economies of scale and/or rationalization; (3) technology exchanges; (4) co-opting or blocking competition; (5) overcoming government-mandated trade or investment barriers; (6) facilitating initial international expansion; and (7) linking the complementary contributions of the partners in a "value chain." See also Kogut (1988).

2. Hergert and Morris (1988); Gomes-Casseres (1988).

3. Cyr and Schneider (1996).

4. Kale and Anand (2006); Luo (2001).

5. Rossant (2000).

6. BAE sold its share in Airbus to EADS in 2006, transforming Airbus into a wholly owned subsidiary.

7. Kanter (1994); Morosini (1998).

8. Pucik (1988a).

9. Luo (2000).

10. Pucik (1988a); Cascio and Serapio (1991).

11. Yoshino and Rangan (1995) describe alliances as linkages based on non-traditional contracts that reflect the long-term and unique nature of the relationship between the partners, such as long-term product development collaboration, not just routine buy–sell agreements. They point out that not all relationships between businesses should be considered alliances—although the word "alliance" has become quite fashionable. They also note that not all equity-based alliances need to be joint ventures; partners may simply decide to invest in each other in order to cement the relationship, or one partner may make a unilateral investment in the other partner. Joint ventures can be further classified based on dominant (majority) or non-dominant

(50:50) partnerships and where they fit in the organizational structure of the firm (integrated or stand-alone).

12. One of these classifications compares different forms of alliances, from licensing arrangements to manufacturing joint ventures, based on the degree of *interaction* between partners and alliance entity employees. This scale is determined by the level and frequency of interaction, and the number of people interacting (Cascio and Serapio, 1991). The intensity of focus on human resource factors and the involvement of the HR function are expected to mirror the intensity of people interaction. Another framework links the HR role with two dimensions of business strategy: the strategic importance of the cooperative venture for the parent organization and the degree of control over own resources by each partner (Lorange, 1996). Alliances fall into four groups: project-based cooperative networks, strings of renegotiated cooperative agreements, ventures with permanently complementary roles, and jointly owned business ventures. Each alliance type requires a different approach to staffing, personnel control, and evaluation. Salk and Simonin (2003) offer a multidimensional map of alliances, encompassing their form, mode, cycle, organization, number of partners, and scope.

13. Fuji Xerox was established in 1962 as a 50:50 partnership of Fuji Photo with Rank Xerox. Rank Xerox was absorbed into Xerox Corporation in 1997. Xerox Corporation transferred its China/Hong Kong Operations to Fuji Xerox in 2000, and Fuji Photo Film Co. raised its stake in the venture to 75 percent in 2001.

14. Inkpen (2005).

15. O'Reilly (1998).

16. Moxon, Roehl, and Truitt (1988).

17. When the Danone and Wahaha alliance in China collapsed, the workforce and managers in the joint ventures overwhelmingly supported the local partner. Danone discovered too late in the game that it had no management capability on the ground to protect its interests (Liu and Liu, 2007).

18. Hamel, Doz, and Prahalad (1989).

19. When business is profitable and provides advantages for both partners in the market as well as contributing to the creation of new knowledge, an alliance may continue even after the original learning objectives of the partners have been fulfilled. NUMMI is a good example.

20. Janger (1980).

21. Beamish (1985).

22. Killing (1982).

23. Zeira and Shenkar (1990).

24. Ulrich (1997).

25. Cole and Deskins (1988); Kenney and Florida (1993).

26. Pucik (1988b); Schuler (2000).

27. Parkhe (1991).

28. Goffee and Jones (1998).

29. Yoshino and Rangan (1995).

30. Spekman *et al.* (1998).

31. Yoshino and Rangan (1995).

32. Yoshino and Rangan (1995).

33. Cited by Yoshino and Rangan (1995: 146).

34. Lorange and Roos (1990).

35. Weiss (1994).

36. Killing (1997).

37. For a review of strategic control and staffing issues in international joint ventures, see Petrovic and Kakabadse (2003).

38. Adobor (2004).

39. Killing (1997).
40. Ferencikova and Pucik (1999).
41. Cascio and Serapio (1991).
42. Shenkar and Zeira (1990).
43. Killing (1982).
44. Tung (1988).
45. Lasserre (2008).
46. In the HP framework, workshop materials are organized in a 400-page proprietary manual, supported by an electronic library devoted to alliances. This serves as a repository for the know-how accumulated by HP over time. Internal knowledge management is important for learning from alliance experience and disseminating that know-how, complemented by internal training if the company has the resources to develop this.
47. Findings from Booz Allen's 1997 survey, as cited in Conference Board (1997).
48. This is one of the management development areas where Web-based distance learning may create opportunities for greater flexibility—providing access to just-in-time relevant information anywhere, including links to the in-company alliance knowledge base.
49. Conference Board (1997).
50. The context of the relationship will determine the most beneficial development applications. However, off-the-shelf cultural training using the traditional "Doing Business with ..." approach is probably of limited value—perhaps even dangerous in building stereotypes.
51. Mohr (2006).
52. Kerr (1995).
53. A common incentive plan (e.g., stock options) could be a logical tool to support synergy among alliance staff. However, among various tax issues that hinder harmonization of compensation across boundaries, incentive plans are probably the area where the differences are the widest. In some countries, such as France, even the initial exercise of stock option rights is a taxable event, which makes awarding options risky and expensive. In addition, even when tax benefits are available, there are differences—for example, which kind of stock option qualifies for tax benefits in the United States and in Germany.
54. Geringer and Frayne (1990).
55. Shenkar and Zeira (1990).
56. Sometimes, expatriate cost alone makes a difference between profit and loss. In a dispute between P&G and its Vietnamese partner, the local company alleged that the high cost of expatriates, brought in to deal with unanticipated product launch difficulties, caused the JV to incur major losses. The local partner was ultimately faced with the choice of accepting the JV bankruptcy or allowing P&G to gain equity control through a recapitalization that the local partner could not match.
57. Lorange (1996).
58. Non-equity alliances are generally temporary, and from a legal perspective, have no "direct" employees. Even those who are assigned to the alliance on a full-time basis are typically paid by and report to their own parent. They expect to return to the parent organization, so that there is no confusion about the focus of their careers. Even if a foreign assignment is involved, a disciplined career development process, which ensures mentoring and a periodic dialogue with the employee, is generally sufficient to avoid a sense of isolation.
59. Child and Faulkner (1998); Parkhe (1993).
60. Barkema et al. (1997); Westney (1988).
61. Gomes-Casseres and McQuade (1992); Kennedy (1989).
62. Hamel (1991).
63. Pucik (1988b).

64. For example, when both partners perceive the partnership as a complementary or resource alliance, the collaboration can be mutually beneficial for a long period of time without much need for new knowledge-creation. However, as discussed earlier in the reading, the focus of the alliance often shifts as the partnership evolves.
65. Doz and Hamel (1998); Tsang (2002).
66. One of Europe's largest banks formed a learning alliance with a major Japanese bank about 20 years ago. The Japanese used this as an opportunity to send hundreds of managers over on two- to six-month learning assignments to Europe, during which time the Europeans only got around to sending two people to learn from the Japanese. By the time the financial services industry started to globalize seriously in the early 1990s and the Europeans awakened to the benefits of the deal, the Japanese had reached their learning objectives and lost interest in maintaining the alliance.
67. Hamel (1991).
68. Open discussion about learning needs may result in explicit limitations on knowledge exchange. A clear definition of what is in and what is out is preferable to fuzzy learning boundaries, which only encourage illicit behavior detrimental to trust between the partners.
69. Pucik and Van Weering (2000).
70. Westney (1988); Schuler (2000); Cyr (1995); Cyr and Schneider (1996).
71. Simonin (1999).
72. Harrigan (1988); Pucik (1988b).
73. Lei, Slocum, and Pitts (1997).
74. Conversely, if there is a perceived imbalance in career opportunities, employees may either be willing to move to the alliance venture but less willing to return to the parent, or not want to move to the venture in the first place (Inkpen, 1997).
75. Inkpen (2005); O'Reilly (1998).
76. Haasen (1996).
77. As argued by Inkpen (1998), unexploited learning opportunities may in turn lead to perceptions that the performance of the alliance is not satisfactory.
78. Doz and Hamel (1998).
79. Star Alliance links the operations of 13 major international airlines, such as United, Lufthansa, and Singapore. The member airlines coordinate schedules, share codes, match frequent flier programs, and coordinate activities to benefit from lower costs in areas such as plane maintenance, ground service, and purchasing.
80. Pfeffer (1998).

REFERENCES

Adobor, H. (2004). Selecting management talent for joint ventures: A suggested framework. *Human Resource Management Review* 14(2): 161–178.

Barkema, H.G., O. Shenkar, F. Vermeulen, and J.H.J. Bell (1997). Working abroad, working with others: How firms learn to operate international joint ventures. *Academy of Management Journal* 40(2): 426–442.

Beamish, P.W. (1985). The characteristics of joint ventures in developed and developing countries. *Journal of World Business* 20(3): 13–19.

Cascio, W.F., and M.G. Serapio, Jr. (1991). Human resources systems in an international alliance: The undoing of a done deal? *Organizational Dynamics* 19(3): 63–74.

Child, J., and D. Faulkner (1998). *Strategies of cooperation: Managing alliances, networks, and joint ventures.* New York: Oxford University Press.

Cole, R.E., and D.R. Deskins, Jr. (1988). Racial factors in site location and employment patterns of Japanese auto firms in America. *California Management Review* 31(1): 9–22.

Conference Board. (1997). HR challenges in mergers and acquisitions. *HR Executive Review* 5(2): 1–18.

Contractor, F.J., and P. Lorange (1988). Why should firms cooperate? The strategy and economics basis for cooperative ventures. In *Cooperative strategies in international business*, eds. F.J. Contractor, and P. Lorange (pp. 3–30). Lexington, MA: Lexington Books.

Cyr, D.J. (1995). *The human resource challenge of international joint ventures*. Westport, CT: Quorum Books.

Cyr, D.J., and S.C. Schneider (1996). Implications for learning: Human resource management in East-West joint ventures. *Organization Studies* 17(2): 207–226.

Doz, Y., and G. Hamel (1998). *Alliance advantage: The art of creating value through partnering*. Boston, MA: Harvard Business School Press.

Ferencikova, S., and V. Pucik (1999). *Whirlpool corporation: Entering Slovakia*. Case study no. IMD-3-0796. Lausanne: IMD.

Geringer, M.J., and C.A. Frayne (1990). Human resource management and international joint venture control: A parent company perspective. *Management International Review* 30 (Special Issue): 103–120.

Goffee, R., and G. Jones (1998). *The character of a corporation: How your company's culture can make or break your business*. New York: Harper Business.

Gomes-Casseres, B. (1988). Joint venture cycles: The evolution of ownership strategies of US MNEs, 1945–75. In *Cooperative strategies in international business*, eds. F.J. Contractor, and P. Lorange (pp. 111–128). Lexington, MA: Lexington Books.

Gomes-Casseres, B., and K. McQuade (1992). *Xerox and Fuji Xerox*. Case study no. 391156. Boston, MA: Harvard Business School.

Haasen, A. (1996). Opel Eisenach GmbH: Creating a high-productivity workplace. *Organizational Dynamics* 24(4): 80–85.

Hamel, G. (1991). Competition for competence and inter-partner learning within international strategic alliances. *Strategic Management Journal* (Summer Special Issue) 12: 83–103.

Hamel, G., Y. Doz, and C.K. Prahalad (1989). Collaborate with your competitors—and win. *Harvard Business Review*, 67(1): 133–139.

Hamilton, S., and J. Zhang (2008). *Danone & Wahaha: A bitter-sweet partnership*. Case study no. IMD-3-1949. IMD, Lausanne.

Harrigan, K. (1988). Strategic alliances and partner asymmetries. *Management International Review (Special Issue)* 28(5): 3–72.

Hergert, M., and D. Morris (1988). Trends in international collaborative agreements. In *Cooperative strategies in international business*, eds. F.J. Contractor, and P. Lorange (pp. 99–109). Lexington, MA: Lexington Books.

Inkpen, A.C., and S.C. Currall (1997). International joint venture trust: An empirical examination. In *Cooperative strategies: North American perspectives*, eds. P.W. Beamish, and J.P. Killing (pp. 308–334). San Francisco, CA: New Lexington Press.

Inkpen, A.C. (1998). Learning and knowledge acquisition through international strategic alliances. *Academy of Management Executive* 12(4): 69–80.

Inkpen, A.C., and E.W.K. Tsang (2005). Social capital, networks, and knowledge transfer. *Academy of Management Review* 30(1): 146–165.

Janger, A.H. (1980). *Organization of international joint ventures*. New York: Conference Board.

Kale, P., and J. Anand (2006). The decline of emerging economy joint ventures: The case of India. *California Management Review* 48(3): 62–76.

Kanter, R.M. (1994). Collaborative advantage: The art of alliances. *Harvard Business Review*, 72 (4): 96–108.

Kennedy, C. (1989). Xerox charts a new strategic direction. *Long Range Planning* 22(1): 10–17.

Kenney, M., and R. Florida (1993). *Beyond mass production: The Japanese system and its transfer to the US*. New York: Oxford University Press.

Kerr, S. (1995). An academic classic: On the folly of rewarding A, while hoping for B. *Academy of Management Executive* 9(1): 7–14.

Killing, J.P. (1982). How to make a global joint venture work. *Harvard Business Review* (May–June): 120–127.

Killing, J.P. (1997). International joint ventures: Managing after the deal is signed. *Perspectives for Managers*, no. 1. Lausanne: IMD.

Kogut, B. (1988). Joint ventures: Theoretical and empirical perspectives. *Strategic Management Journal* 9(4): 319–332.

Lasserre, P. (2008). *Global strategic management*. London: Palgrave Macmillan.

Lei, D., J.W. Slocum, Jr., and R. Pitts (1997). Building cooperative advantage: Managing strategic alliances to promote organizational learning. *Journal of World Business* 32(3): 203–223.

Liu, G., and D. Liu (2007). Danone and Wahaha: China-style divorce (A) and (B). Case study nos. 207-021-1 & 207-022-1. China Europe International Business School (CEIBS), Shanghai.

Lorange, P. (1996). A strategic human resource perspective applied to multinational cooperative ventures. *International Studies of Management and Organization* 26(1): 87–103.

Lorange, P., and J. Roos (1990). Formation of cooperative ventures: Competence mix of the management teams. *Management International Review (Special Issue)* 30: 69–86.

Luo, Y. (2000). *Partnering with Chinese firms: Lessons for international managers*. Aldershot: Ashgate.

Luo, Y. (2001). *Strategy, structure, and performance of MNCs in China*. Westport, CT: Greenwood Publishing Group.

McGregor, J. (2005). *One billion customers: Lessons from the front lines of doing business in China*. London: Nicholas Brealey.

Mohr, A.T. (2006). A multiple constituency approach to IJM performance management. *Journal of World Business* 41(3): 247–260.

Morosini, P. (1998). *Managing cultural differences: Effective strategy and execution across cultures in global corporate alliances*. Oxford and New York: Pergamon.

Moxon, R.W., T.W. Roehl, and J. Truitt (1988). International cooperative ventures in the commercial aircraft industry: Gains, sure, but what's my share? In *Cooperative strategies in international business*, eds. F.J. Contractor, and P. Lorange (pp. 255–277). Lexington, MA: Lexington Books.

O'Reilly, C.A. (1998). New United Motors Manufacturing, Inc. (NUMMI). Case Study. Stanford Graduate School of Business, Stanford.

Parkhe, A. (1991). Interfirm diversity, organizational learning, and longevity in global strategic alliances. *Journal of International Business Studies* 22(4): 579–601.

Parkhe, A. (1993). Partner nationality and the structure-performance relationship in strategic alliances. *Organization Science* 4(2): 301–324.

Petrovic, J., and N.K. Kakabadse (2003). Strategic staffing of international joint ventures: An integrative perspective for future research. *Management Decisions* 41(4): 394–406.

Pfeffer, J. (1998). *The human equation: Building profits by putting people first*. Boston, MA: Harvard Business School Press.

Pucik, V. (1988a). Strategic alliances with the Japanese: Implications for human resource management. In *Cooperative strategies in international business*, eds. F.J. Contractor, and P. Lorange (pp. 487–498). Lexington, MA: Lexington Books.

Pucik, V. (1988b). Strategic alliances, organizational learning, and competitive advantage: The HRM agenda. *Human Resource Management* 27(1): 77–93.

Pucik, V., S. Fiorella, and E. van Weering (2000). American diagnostic systems. Case study no. IMD-3-0870. Lausanne: IMD.

Reich, R.B., and E.D. Mankin (1986). Joint ventures with Japan give away our future. *Harvard Business Review* 64(2): 78–86.

Rossant, J. (2000). Airbus: Birth of a giant. *Business Week*, July 10.

Salk, J.E., and B.L. Simonin (2003). Beyond alliances: Towards a meta-theory of collaborative learning. In *The Blackwell handbook of organizational learning and knowledge management*, eds. M. Easterby-Smith, and M.A. Lyles (pp. 253–277). Malden, MA: Blackwell.

Schuler, R.S. (2000). HR issues in international joint ventures and alliances. In *Human resource management: A critical text*, ed. J. Storey (pp. 314–316). London: International Thomson.

Shenkar, O., and Y. Zeira (1990). International joint ventures: A tough test for HR. *Personnel* 67(1): 26–31.

Simonin, B.L. (1999). Ambiguity and process of knowledge transfer in strategic alliances. *Strategic Management Journal* 20(7): 596–623.

Spekman, R.E., L.I. Sabella, T. MacAvoy, and T.M. Forbes III (1998). Alliance management: A view from the past and a look to the future. *Journal of Management Studies* 35(6): 747–772.

Tsang, E.W.K. (2002). Acquiring knowledge by foreign partners from international joint ventures in a transition economy: Learning-by-doing and learning myopia. *Strategic Management Journal* 23(9): 835–854.

Tung, R.L. (1988). Career issues in international assignments. *Academy of Management Executive* 2(3): 241–244.

Ulrich, D. (1997). *Human resource champions: The next agenda for adding value and delivering results*. Boston, MA: Harvard Business School Press.

Weiss, S.E. (1994). Negotiating with "Romans"—Part 1. *Sloan Management Review* 35(2): 51–61.

Westney, D.E. (1988). Domestic foreign learning curves in managing international cooperative strategies. In *Cooperative strategies in international business*, eds. F.J. Contractor, and P. Lorange (pp. 332–337). Lexington, MA: Lexington Books.

Yoshino, M., and U.S. Rangan (1995). *Strategic alliances: An entrepreneurial approach to globalization*. Cambridge, MA: Harvard Business School Press.

Zeira, Y., and O. Shenkar (1990). Interactive and specific parent characteristics: Implications for management and human resources in international joint ventures. *Management International Review* (Special Issue) 30: 7–22.

Satu Teerikangas, Günter K. Stahl, Ingmar Björkman, and Mark E. Mendenhall

MANAGING PEOPLE AND CULTURE IN MERGERS AND ACQUISITIONS

INTRODUCTION

THIS READING ADDRESSES INTERNATIONAL HUMAN resource management concerns when undertaking mergers and acquisitions (M&As) across borders. M&As are a particular type of an inter-organizational encounter; thus, sharing features with joint ventures, alliances, or outsourcing arrangements (Borys & Jemison, 1989; Parmigiani & Rivera-Santos, 2011). The distinguishing characteristic of M&As is that beyond connecting two organizations, they result in a change in ownership. It is this change of ownership that lies at the heart of many of the human resource-related concerns in M&As: indeed, for the employee, a change of ownership represents not only a change in employer, but also a change in the psychological contract with one's employer.

It has long been argued that the 'human element' explains much of the difficulty of M&A integration (Sarala et al., 2016). Employee-related issues are recognized as causing 30–50% of M&A failures (Cartwright & Cooper, 1993; Davy et al., 1988), while employee resistance affects the potential for synergy realization, i.e. performance, in acquisitions (Larsson & Finkelstein, 1999). A change of ownership is a cause of considerable concern for employees, in turn, causing high levels of uncertainty, stress, and turnover rates following M&As (Bilgili et al., 2017; Martin & Butler, 2015).

In order to support HR scholars and practitioners in appreciating M&As and their critical role therein (Antila, 2006; Schuler et al., 2004), this reading offers an overview of extant research on the sociocultural dimensions of M&As. To this end, the next section offers an extended introduction to the M&A phenomenon.

DOI: 10.4324/9781003247272-27

Employee reactions are reviewed thereafter. The third section focuses on the M&A process and its management, while the fourth section addresses cultural dynamics. The fifth section summarizes the reading's main points by arguing that trust is a critical factor toward M&A success. Finally, the reading concludes with implications for HR practice and future research directions.

WHAT ARE MERGERS AND ACQUISITIONS?

The term 'mergers and acquisitions' is somewhat misleading, given that in terms of transaction numbers, 98% of all M&A transactions are acquisitions (Buckley & Ghauri, 1999). In acquisitions, the 'acquiring' firm purchases the 'target' or 'acquired' firm using cash or stock, whereas in mergers, two or more organizations are combined into one new entity. From a managerial perspective, this means that acquisitions often incur a 'takeover' approach by the acquiring firm, which has the upper hand in the transaction. The post-acquisition era can also be termed a 'merger' even though the transaction has been an acquisition. Thus, the term 'merger' can be used to portray an image of a 'collective, shared' future, thereby alleviating employee concerns (Faulkner et al., 2012).

Taking a historical lens, throughout the 20th century, fuelled by the internationalization of firms, globalization of business, and the liberalization of trade, M&A activity has increased, becoming by the dawn of the 21st century a worldwide phenomenon spanning sectors and industries (Kolev et al., 2012), while driving industry consolidation. Firms engage in M&A activity for various reasons (Bower, 2001). Strategic rationales include product or market expansion, internationalization, access to resources including technology, research and development, and talent, and elimination of excess market capacity. M&As can also represent defensive moves to purchase a competitor or protect against a takeover (Faulkner et al., 2012). In addition to these overt motives, unstated psychological motives exist, including empire-building, managerial hubris and overconfidence, CEO narcissism, the thrill of making deals, and the systemic effect of herd-like behavior (Sudarsanam, 2012). In sum, M&A activity combines strategic and financial dimensions as well as less visible psychological and human dimensions (Faulkner et al., 2012). The corporate liking of M&A activity witnessed via the rising numbers of M&A deals is not matched by the performance results. Though the vending side can gain financially from the transaction, many acquiring firms never gain financially from their M&A activity, and when they do, this positive impact is visible three to 12 years after the transaction (Haleblian et al., 2009; King et al., 2021; Quah & Young, 2005).

The study of M&As had an early focus on the management of M&As (Howell, 1970; Mace & Montgomery, 1962). A financial and strategic focus arose in the 1970s, followed by an interest in the human sides of M&A activity in the 1980s. The 1990s represented an interest in the cross-border cultural dimensions of M&As (Cartwright & Schoenberg, 2006). The early 21st century, in turn, has witnessed identity and power considerations, while studies have been broadened from US and European acquirers to include acquiring firms from emerging markets, including China and India. Presently, M&A scholars are urged to consider the role of M&As in addressing mounting grand challenges and wicked societal and ecological problems (Thanos et al., 2023).

EMPLOYEE REACTIONS TO M&AS

The human side in M&As has been found to have a long-lasting impact on the performance of the acquisition and the acquiring firm. In their meta-analysis of published case studies on M&As, Larsson and Finkelstein (1999) found that employee motivation enables the realization of synergies. Similarly, Birkinshaw et al. (2000) conclude that well-managed human integration has an enabling effect on the progress of integration.

Yet the reality on the ground is bleaker. Studying Australian healthcare mergers, Kavanagh and Ashkanasy (2006) reported that half of the merged workforce experienced significant personal consequences. Reviewing prior work, Martin and Butler (2015) concluded that increased uncertainty experienced by employees during acquisitions results in increased strain and absenteeism, decreased job satisfaction, while increasing turnover intentions. The significance of the human dimension in M&As gains more weight if considered in terms of the long-term nature of these reactions – they persist, and tend even to become emphasized over time (Schweiger & DeNisi, 1991). These negative consequences are experienced increasingly the less powerful the employees and the smaller the acquired partner (Cartwright & Cooper, 1993; Siu et al., 1997). Further, individuals' responses to M&A connect with the individual's appraisal of the effect on one's future career (Pritchett, 1985), thus explaining why mid-career employees can react virulently (Ivancevitch et al., 1987). Following acquisitions, turnover rates increase, particularly for executives (Bucholtz et al., 2003), while differing for CEOs and the top management team (Bilgili et al., 2017). This matters, as executive turnover bears on acquisition performance (Krug et al., 2014). Thus, merged organizations find it difficult to retain key employees (Steigenberger & Mirc, 2020), for example, the technical core of acquired firms, such as research and development engineers (Paruchuri et al., 2006).

Nevertheless, prior research has shed light on the emotional experience as employees adjust to M&As. The emphasis has traditionally been on negative emotions, showing that employees experience feelings of loss and deprivation, leading to heightened stress levels and lowered work commitment (Cartwright & Cooper, 1990). Seminal research around emotions during M&As has argued that employees undergo a merger syndrome (Buono et al., 1985; Buono & Bowditch, 1989), representing the psychological challenges to employees that result from a company undergoing a M&A process. Styhre et al. (2006) point to 'cultural anxieties' that are raised in employees' minds during cross-border M&As. Indeed, post-acquisition cultural change represents an emotionally painful process for organizational members who have to gradually let go of their previous culture whilst developing an allegiance toward the new one. Therefore, M&As can cause acculturative stress (Nahavandi & Malekzadeh, 1988), which bears on acquisition performance (Very et al., 1996). However, the issue of whether domestic or cross-border deals result in higher levels of stress has produced conflicting evidence (Larsson & Risberg, 1998; Very et al., 1996; Weber, 1996). Representing a change of ownership, a merger or acquisition can be experienced emotionally as akin to the loss of a close family member (Schweiger et al., 1987). Similarly, the subsequent integration phase following mergers has been likened to life in a step-family (Allred et al., 2005). Issues of identity also arise, as do power conflicts, particularly in mergers, as the two sides struggle for authority in the new regime (Giessner et al., 2012; Stahl et al., 2013; Tienari & Vaara, 2012). In summary, the greater the cultural discrepancy between the organizations involved and the less attractive the partner, the more likely it is that employees will react negatively to an acquisition.

In parallel, other scholars posit a more nuanced perspective on the emotional journey of employees, arguing that a wide variety of emotions, both negative and positive, are experienced (Hassett et al., 2018, Kiefer, 2002; Sinkovics et al., 2011). Thus, Monin et al. (2013) argue that a feeling of justice matters toward M&A success. In phase-based studies of human reactions during M&A (Ashkanasy & Holmes, 1995; Buono & Bowditch, 1989), employee reactions have been shown to lean toward the negative in the pre-deal phase, and gradually, depending on the quality of integration management and the way in which the acquisition is experienced, turn to the positive in the post-acquisition era. As M&A activity has become increasingly commonplace, employees have been found to develop resilience vis-à-vis the adverse psychological consequences of M&As (Cartwright & Hudson, 2000), for example, by actively engaging in identity work (Langley et al., 2012). In a comparative study of hostile versus friendly mergers, Fairfield-Sonn et al. (2002) found that whilst hostile mergers result in long-term negative employee reactions, friendly mergers result in long-term positive reactions. Moreover, target firm employees react positively to forthcoming transactions if the transaction is viewed as an opportunity (Teerikangas, 2012). Further, certain kinds of post-acquisition changes (e.g., in human resource management practices and organizational culture) (Froese et al., 2007) and expectations of the future (Dackert et al., 2003) bear positively on employee attitudes. In summary, it would seem that M&As are greeted with a mix of positive and negative reactions; yet the media and the early scholarly inquiry have emphasized the negative reactions.

MANAGING M&AS

Paralleling and related to the human factor, the difficulty of post-deal integration and implementation management is considered as another main challenge in making M&As succeed (Graebner et al., 2017; Steigenberger, 2017). The challenge not only concerns change management and strategy implementation, but further, that of combining hitherto separate organizations into one. This combination of organizations introduces cultural clashes, be it at the level of team or organizational or national cultures (Rottig & Reus, 2018; Stahl & Voigt, 2008; Teerikangas & Very, 2006). In this section, we will review research on M&A process management, with an emphasis on post-acquisition integration. The role of the HR function is to support managers in the challenging task of M&A management; the better the HR professionals comprehend M&A process dynamics, the better they are able to support managers throughout its phases.

Overview of the M&A Process

Whilst insights to the managing of M&As can be found in early publications (Howell, 1970; Mace & Montgomery, 1962; Kitching, 1967), the seminal work of Jemison and Sitkin (1986) and Haspeslagh and Jemison (1991) posited a 'process' perspective on M&As. On the basis of a series of in-depth case studies of international acquisitions, Haspeslagh and Jemison (1991) articulated that what distinguishes successful acquisitions is an understanding of the processes through which acquisition decisions are made and through which acquisition integration is managed. The process view (Haspeslagh & Jemison, 1991) portrays acquisitions not as independent, one-off deals, but rather as belonging to a firm's long-term renewal strategy. What is more, whilst concluding a deal is significant, value is realized only if the target is correctly integrated – hence, integration management matters. Their key argument is that instead of viewing (pre-acquisition) decision-making and (post-acquisition) management as separate activities and phases, M&A scholars and practicing managers should treat them as interdependent processes.

This leads to the view of the acquisition process as consisting of two interrelated phases: the phase preceding the deal (the pre-acquisition phase) and the phase following the deal (the post-acquisition phase). The aim of the pre-acquisition evaluation process is to decide whether to engage in an acquisition or not. The acquiring company has a strategic rationale for the purchase, including potential value creation, against which it assesses the attractiveness of the deal. The integration process can be defined as a guided process to implement organizational change affecting mainly the acquired unit (possibly the acquiring organization too, depending on the integration strategy), and ultimately the parties involved, with the aim of aligning the new unit with the sought strategic direction.

Not all M&As are alike, and this bears consequences on the human side of M&A dynamics. The more the transaction incurs integration and post-deal change, the more likely it is that 'people needs' will require significant attention from management. Several typologies of M&A integration strategies have been proposed (Angwin et al., 2022; Buono & Bowditch, 1989; Cartwright & Cooper, 1992; Howell, 1970; Kitching, 1967; Napier, 1989). An oft-cited approach is Haspeslagh and Jemison's (1991) typology, identifying four integration strategies: *absorption*, *symbiosis*, *preservation*, and *holding*, which differ regarding the degrees of target firm strategic interdependence and target firm autonomy. The four-quadrant typology of integration strategies suggests that not all acquisitions are alike in terms of their integration processes, management challenges, and requirements. Using this typology, integration management seems to be the most demanding in 'absorption' or 'symbiotic' acquisitions. One limitation of this typological scheme is that the integration strategies adopted by acquiring firms rarely fit neatly into existing typologies. In practice, acquiring firms tend to adopt integration strategies that combine features of different integration approaches (Haspeslagh & Jemison, 1991).

Best Practices in Integration Management

PLANNING

Planning is a critical factor in ensuring the success of M&A integration. A traditional mistake acquirers have made is being poorly prepared for post-acquisition integration owing to a lack of planning (Howell, 1970). Moreover, the effects of planning on acquisition performance have been confirmed, through the positive impact on the post-acquisition climate and managerial appointments in the target firm (Colombo et al., 2007).

SPEED AND TIMING

The debate regarding whether and how the speed of integration matters toward M&A success is raging (Homburg & Bucerius, 2006). There are diverging views as to whether a quick or slow start is best to accomplish the acquisition (Schweiger & Goulet, 2000; Stahl et al., 2013). Among the practitioner-led proponents of swift post-deal action (Epstein, 2004; De Noble et al., 1988), the immediate post-deal period has been referred to as the 'window of opportunity' (Ranft & Lord, 2002), as the target organization's staff expect change to take place. Angwin (2004) found a correlation between the volume of changes implemented in the first 100 days and perceptions of success three or four years post-acquisition. Positive results on the impact of speed on acquisition performance have also been found by other scholars (Bauer & Matzler, 2014; Colombo et al., 2007).

SOCIALIZATION AND INTERACTIONS

M&As are at heart social encounters – encounters of people who do not yet know one another. Nevertheless, prior research confirms that inter-firm interactions are 'at the heart of integration' (Haspeslagh & Jemison, 1991: 117). To this end, the role of socialization as an informal control mechanism in M&A integration (Calori et al., 1994) and the importance of 'social controls' in fostering acculturation (Larsson & Lubatkin, 2001) have been emphasized. Moreover, prior research calls for recognizing the importance of exchange and interaction in promoting learning, sharing knowledge, and ensuring successful post-deal integration (Larsson & Lubatkin, 2001; Schweiger & Goulet, 2000), particularly in R&D acquisitions, which rely on knowledge transfer (Håkansson, 1995). The degree of inter-firm interaction not only matters toward integration, but further correlates with synergy realization, i.e. acquisition performance (Larsson & Finkelstein, 1999).

COMMUNICATIONS

Communications are another critical factor in securing M&A success (Schweiger & Denisi, 1991). In technology acquisitions, frequent and open communications facilitate post-deal integration (Ranft & Lord, 2002). Moreover, the degree of open communication is positively related to value creation following acquisitions (Ellis et al., 2009). The role of HR is critical with respect to the effectiveness of post-deal communication. However, this role will bear different consequences depending on the size of the acquiring firm. In larger organizations the communications department coordinates external communications, whilst HR typically is in charge of within-firm communications and coaching management teams with respect to the right tone of communicating information. In the Nokia Siemens Networks merger in 2007, HR coordinated a series of town hall meetings for staff in certain countries at the start of the merger, where the merger's strategic aims and typical psychological issues that surface in M&As were presented and discussed. In contrast, in smaller-sized firms that potentially lack a proper HR function per se, communication protocols remain the remit of the founding owner or entrepreneur, with all the risks and opportunities such a personalized approach involves.

ATTITUDES

Attitudes have value-enhancing and value-destructive effects on the progress and outcomes of M&As. For one, prior research emphasizes the importance of the acquiring firm's attitudes in enhancing mutual cooperation in the post-deal phase (Deiser, 1994; Olie, 1994), the need to create an atmosphere supportive of capability transfer (Haspeslagh & Jemison, 1991), the role of 'assertive tolerance' in managing the post-deal integration phase (Napier et al., 1993), and the importance of fairness during post-acquisition integration (Hambrick & Cannella, 1993). The importance of 'respect' in the way acquired firm management and employees are treated was noted by Krug and Nigh (2001) in their study of acquired firm executive departures. Whilst fairness and equality are often emphasized, cases of failed mergers point to the potential ambiguities therein. In a study of the failed Telia and Telenor merger, Meyer and Altenborg (2007) contended that the notion of equality is subject to a myriad of local interpretations. Moreover, in the merger context, the principles of equality in roles and responsibilities might lead to 'structural paralysis' because decisions cannot be taken, and national interests cannot be bridged.

Scholars have also cautioned against the presence of potentially negative attitudes in the aftermath of M&As. To this end, Deiser (1994) alludes to the impact of the acquiring firm's attitude in the post-acquisition process and advises against the acquiring firm blindly imposing its ideas upon the acquired firm.

Further, a 'not-invented-here' syndrome can also hamper integration progress (Buono & Bowditch, 1990). Among potentially destructive attitudes, Haspeslagh and Jemison (1991) identify 'determinism' as a problem, referring to situations, where managers cling to their initial goals for the deal regardless of mounting evidence toward the opposite.

Key Actors in M&A Contexts

TOP MANAGEMENT

While top management are involved in pre-acquisition decision-making and strategic direction-setting, their attention toward the post-acquisition integration phase is also warranted. The role of top management, as institutional leaders, is to set the right atmosphere or tone for integration, so that both sides are interested in sharing ideas and are willing to collaborate in a mutually respectful manner (Haspeslagh & Jemison, 1991). Without such attention, a 'leadership vacuum' might occur, resulting in the failure to make, implement, or effectively communicate decisions throughout the organization.

The manner in which the change process is led has a significant effect on whether post-deal cultural change is accepted, while also bearing on the outcome of a merger or acquisition (Kavanagh & Ashkanasy, 2006). Transformational leadership (i.e. a leadership style involving charisma, inspiration, and transcendental goals) has been found to be the strongest predictors of merger satisfaction (Covin et al., 1997). Yet the competence of managers to effectively deal with a process as complex as a merger or acquisition has been questioned (Teerikangas & Birollo, 2018).

INTEGRATION MANAGER

By developing the firm's M&A capability, acquiring firms with dedicated M&A functions gain in M&A performance (Trichterborn et al., 2016). Moreover, 'enlightened' companies appoint an executive, 'guide,' or 'shepherd' to coordinate post-acquisition phase activities (Ashkenas & Francis, 2000). Studying General Electric's acquisitions, Ashkenas et al. (1998) identified the integration manager's role as: (1) facilitating and managing integration activities, (2) helping the acquired business to understand GE Capital, (3) helping GE Capital to understand the target business, and (4) building a connective tissue between the organizations. The presence and proactivity of integration managers in pre- and post-acquisition phases has been found to have consequences regarding acquisition performance (Teerikangas et al., 2011).

In terms of competences and skills, integration managers need to combine professional expertise with cooperative attitudes, a resilient mindset, as well as emotional, linguistic, and cultural intelligence (Teerikangas & Birollo, 2018). Masking negative emotions can lead to integration failure (Vuori et al., 2018). Amid the highly ambiguous context of M&As, integration managers need to be able to face and deal with uncertainty (Sniazhko, 2022).

ACQUIRED FIRM MANAGERS

The acquired firm managers' attitudes toward a forthcoming acquisition in the pre-deal phase matters, as they can become at best change agents driving the change locally (Teerikangas, 2012). In the post-acquisition phase, evidence advises involving the acquired organization's managers (Angwin et al., 2004) to foster integration, mutual learning, and secure value-creation (Birollo & Teerikangas, 2022). This matters particularly when acquiring in a country in which the acquiring firm has little prior experience (Very & Schweiger, 2001) or when acquiring a technology-based firm (Graebner, 2004). The significance of retaining key target firm talent—e.g., through their early involvement (Krug & Nigh, 2001; Schuler et al., 2004) and mutual relationship-building (Marks & Mirvis, 2001)—has been highlighted.

MANAGING CULTURAL DYNAMICS IN M&AS

As M&As concern the merging of (at least) two hitherto separate organizations into one, cultural change parallels post-acquisition integration management. In parallel, in cross-border M&As, intercultural clashes occur. Yet in the broader setting, the issue of whether and how cultural differences impact merger and acquisition performance continues to be open to debate (Rottig & Reus, 2018; Stahl & Voigt, 2008; Teerikangas & Very, 2006).

The Management of Cultural Change Following M&As

When the aim of the acquiring firm is to integrate the target, some degree of cultural change is to be expected. Prior research provides guidance on the management of cultural change.

To begin with, the direction of cultural change has been found to dictate the ease of change, especially if the change is paralleled with increased levels of openness in the organizational culture (Cartwright & Cooper, 1992, 1993). Where beliefs are widely shared and strongly held in the target firm, cultural change is likely to be challenging (Buono & Bowditch, 1989). Moreover, different cultural change approaches are suggested. To this end, Cartwright and Cooper (1992) identify four approaches to culture change: aggressive, conciliative, corrosive, and indoctrinative. They found that a combinative use of these approaches is fruitful, and argue that culture change should begin with an understanding of both participating cultures followed by an 'unfreezing' of these cultures. Next, a positive and realistic view of the future should be presented to people in both organizations – this ensures the wide-scale involvement of organizational members and creates a realistic timescale for the integration process. Finally, it is necessary to monitor the change process and take corrective action where necessary.

Other authors, in turn, have studied the cultural change process. For example, Buono et al. (1989) unfolded the process of culture change and identified the following factors as meaningful ways of influencing integration in M&As: changing the behavior of organizational members, justifying this change, using cultural communication to facilitate the change, hiring and socializing new recruits to speed up the change, and removing deviants. Similarly, in her study of organizational culture change following M&As, Bijlsma-Frankema (2001) identified factors that promote the progress of cultural integration following M&As. The factors identified include the degree of mutual trust between the parties, which is then strengthened by shared norms, and further enabled by dialogue – even in instances of deviance or conflict resolution. The extent to which cultural change can be achieved has been questioned, though (Buono & Bowditch, 1989), and the importance of attitudes (Deiser, 1994; Morosini, 1998; Napier et al., 1993) when implementing cultural change is arguably critical.

More recent findings posit the mutually reinforcing effects of structural and cultural integration in cross-border acquisitions (Teerikangas & Laamanen, 2014), as cultural integration begins only once structural integration is in progress. All the while, national and organizational cultures impede structural integration if structural integration is not adjusted to the target's cultural regime. Calling for a recognition of the parallel presence of espoused versus practiced cultures in organizations, Teerikangas and Irrmann (2016) present post-acquisition cultural change as a dyadic, bipolar process, whereby targets cohabit the space between espoused and practiced values. Depending on the acquirer's cultural maturity, targets align with either the espoused *or* the practiced culture. Further, whereas previous research parallels cultural change with explicit 'initiatives,' it is argued that cultural change results also from all post-acquisition integration activity, i.e. integration and interactions drive cultural change. This emergent nature of cultural change reflects Brannen and Salk's (2000) work on negotiated cultures in joint ventures, where organizational cultures emerge dynamically.

Cross-cultural Interactions

Studies on acquirer behavior across national boundaries confirm that acquirers from different countries differ in their approach toward due diligence (Angwin, 2000), earn-out (Ewelt-Knauer et al., 2021), and integration management (Child et al., 2001; Larsson & Lubatkin, 2001; Lubatkin et al., 1998). These differences can be reflected back onto the national culture of the involved firms. All the while, some constants across acquirers have been found, just as some acquiring nations would not seem to conform to their cultural stereotype when engaged in acquiring activities (Child et al., 2001). In this respect, based on a study of international firms' acquisitions in Japan, Olcott (2008) points to there not being one approach that characterizes international firms' integration styles in Japan. The Chinese government's 'Go Global' policy in 2000 resulted in a rise in Chinese cross-border acquisitions, paralleled by increasing research on Chinese acquisitions. Thus, their distinctive integration approach suggests a light-touch approach (Liu & Woywode, 2013).

Also, target firms from different countries have been found to prefer different kinds of integration approaches, in line with their home countries' national cultures (Cartwright & Price, 2003; Morosini, 1998). Particular emphasis has been placed on the dimensions of uncertainty avoidance (Morosini, 1998; Schoenberg, 2000), risk orientation (Schoenberg, 2000), and individualism versus collectivism (Morosini, 1998). Despite these preferences, it seems that acquisitions in which the target firm has been involved in the integration through informal activities meet greater success than others (Calori et al., 1994; Child et al., 2001; Larsson & Lubatkin, 2001). This would seem to suggest that the involvement of acquired firms is a critical success factor in M&A activity.

Only few studies have focused on national cultures interacting during acquisitions. Studying the European EADS tri-party merger, Barmeyer and Mayrhofer (2008) found inter-cultural team working to be negatively affected by the involved French, German, and Spanish parties' interpretations of teamwork, cooperation, leadership, and authority. Such differences complicate post-acquisition integration, as members operate with culturally dependent behavioral strategies. Studying the implementation of lean production into a Japanese-owned factory in Sweden, Oudhuis and Olsson (2015) found that cultural clashes relate to national cultures and different approaches to manufacturing. Similarly, Lee et al. (2015) studied how employees experienced cultural differences in Sweden's Volvo's acquisition of South Korean Samsung's business division. Adopting an 11-year interval, the authors find that a classic, positivistic conception of culture predicts culture-related problems, while a social constructivist perspective predicts whether such problems actually materialize. Finally, the trust-building practices of Chinese managers (Sachsenmaier & Guo, 2019; Sun & Zhao, 2020) and the roles of Chinese CEOs in managing individualist cultures when acquiring abroad have received attention (Zhu et al., 2020).

In cross-border contexts, the effectiveness of inter-organizational interfaces is further impacted by language (Feely & Harzing, 2003; Marschan et al., 1997). The lack of a joint native language slows down cooperation, causes misunderstandings, and makes it more difficult and time-consuming to develop a relationship based on trust (Teerikangas & Irrmann, 2013). Moreover, acquired firm managers fear that longer-term, the lack of a joint language has consequences for their potential to climb the parent firm's corporate career ladder (Marschan et al., 1997; Piekkari et al., 2005; Vaara et al., 2005).

BUILDING AND MAINTAINING TRUST IN M&AS

The role of trust has been discussed as a critical success factor in M&A processes. While few attempts have been made to systematically examine trust dynamics in M&As, indirect evidence about the critical role of trust in the M&A process can be drawn from a large body of research that suggests that the development of trust is critical to the successful formation and implementation of inter-organizational relationships (Child, 2001; Inkpen & Currall, 2004; Krishnan et al., 2006). For example, open communication and information exchange, task

coordination, informal agreements, and levels of surveillance are all manifesta-
tions of trust between joint venture partners (Currall & Inkpen, 2002; Krishnan
et al., 2006).

In the context of M&As, case studies (Chua et al., 2005; Olie, 1994) and
interviews with managers and employees affected by M&As (Krug & Nigh, 2001)
suggest that trust is critical to post-merger integration process dynamics and outcomes, as it helps management to overcome resistance, gain commitment from
the employees, and develop a sense of shared identity. It has been observed that
the turbulence following the announcement of a merger or an acquisition creates
a breeding ground for distrust because the situation is unpredictable, easy to mis-
interpret, and people tend to feel vulnerable (Hurley, 2006; Krug & Nigh, 2001;
Marks & Mirvis, 2001). Social networks and mutual understanding established
through years of working together are sometimes destroyed in an instant. With a
new organization, a new top management team, and a new superior, there is little
trust initially, and employees are left wondering what the next wave of changes
will bring. Employees may perceive a merger as a psychological contract violation
or a breach of trust, requiring renegotiation of the broken psychological contract
(Buono & Bowditch, 1989; Cartwright & Cooper, 1996). The period following the
announcement of a merger or takeover is thus one of vulnerability and intense risk
assessment in which employees have to judge whether the acquiring firm's management (and their own management) can be trusted. The following quote from Daniel
Vasella, CEO of Novartis, concerning the merger that created the Swiss pharmaceutical giant highlights both the importance and fragility of trust in M&As:

> Only in a climate of trust are people willing to strive for the slightly impos-
> sible, to make decisions on their own, to take initiative, to feel accountable;
> trust is a prerequisite for working together effectively; trust is also an ally
> to fight bureaucracy. ... We must fill this vacuum as fast as we can, we
> must restore confidence [after the merger]. We must earn it by 'walking
> the talk', with candour, integrity, openness, fairness .... We need to create
> a culture based on trust.
>
> (Chua et al., 2005: 391–392)

Despite the large body of anecdotal evidence supporting the critical role of trust
in M&As, surprisingly little is known about the factors that facilitate or hinder
the development of trust in acquired or merging organizations. Stahl and Sitkin
(2005, 2010) propose that factors related to the firms' relationship history and
interfirm distance, as well as process variables related to the acquirer's integration approach, affect target firm member trust in the acquiring firms' management (see Figure 1).

Relationship History

The extent to which the members of a target firm perceive the acquirer to be
trustworthy is a function of prior *interfirm contact* or, in the absence of a history

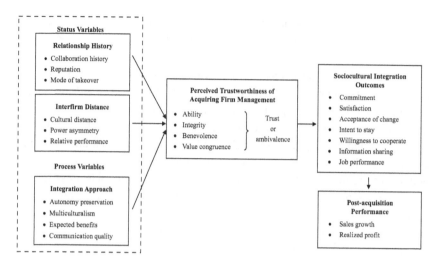

Figure 1 Model of the antecedents and consequences of trust in mergers and acquisitions

of collaboration, the *reputation* of the acquirer. A large body of research on the role of trust in work groups, strategic alliances, and socially embedded partnerships suggests that trust evolves over time through repeated interactions (Inkpen & Currall, 2004; Ring & Van de Ven, 1992; Zaheer et al., 1998). If members of the combining firms had a conflict-rich, inequitable, or otherwise problematic exchange prior to the acquisition (e.g., a failed joint venture), this is likely to limit the potential for trust to emerge. Another important factor in determining target firm members' trust is the *mode of takeover* or tone of the negotiations (whether it is friendly or hostile). It has been argued that hostile takeover tactics can result in sharp interorganizational conflict and difficulties integrating acquired firms (Buono & Bowditch, 1989; Hitt et al., 2001). Hambrick and Cannella (1993) have observed that the atmosphere surrounding a hostile takeover is often characterized by bitterness and acrimony, making smooth social integration after the deal less likely. This is supported by research showing that hostile takeover attempts lead to resistance and increased 'in-group/out-group' bias (Elsass & Veiga, 1994; Krug & Nigh, 2001).

Interfirm Distance

Cultural distance, power asymmetry, and relative performance may affect trustworthiness attributions through perceptions of interfirm distance. Although studies that tested the impact of cultural distance on post-acquisition integration process dynamics and outcomes have yielded inconclusive results (see Cartwright & Schoenberg, 2006; Stahl & Voigt, 2008; Teerikangas & Very, 2006, 2012; Weber & Drori, 2008 for reviews), trust research shows that shared norms and values facilitate the development of trust and the emergence of a shared identity (Lewicki et al., 1998; Sarkar et al., 1997). Conversely, trust can erode and the potential for conflict increase when a person or group is perceived as not sharing key values (Sitkin & Roth, 1993).

Social Identity Theory suggests that in a merger situation, the mere exist-ence of two different cultures is enough to lead to in-group/out-group bias and conflict. Organizational members, while emphasizing their own positive distinc-tiveness, tend to exaggerate the differences between their own and the other's culture (e.g., Hogg & Terry, 2000; Kleppestø, 2005; Vaara, 2003). In cross-border acquisitions, feelings of resentment, hostility, and mistrust may be fur-ther fueled by cultural stereotypes, prejudices, and xenophobia (Vaara, 2003). In addition to cultural distance, *differences in power* between the acquiring and acquired firm are likely to affect trust dynamics. In the case of asymmetrical power relations, target firm members' needs are often overlooked or trivialized by the acquirer (Datta & Grant, 1990; Hambrick & Cannella, 1993; Marks & Mirvis, 2001). Acquiring executives tend to adopt an attitude of superiority and treat the members of the target firm as inferior, thus leading to status degrada-tion and the voluntary departure of key employees (Hambrick & Cannella, 1993; Krug & Nigh, 2001).

Poor Target Firm Performance

Poor target firm performance in the past relative to the acquirer may have a sim-ilar effect, as it is likely to increase an acquirer's tendencies toward arrogance and domination. For instance, Hambrick and Cannella (1993) have observed that even if executives of a poorly performing firm are not fired outright after their acquisition, they may feel inferior or depart voluntarily because they are anticipating the dominating behaviors of their 'conquerors.' Lower-level employ-ees are likely to experience anxiety from fears they might lose their jobs or be unable to meet the acquirer's performance standards. Paradoxically, though, it has been observed that when a smaller or underperforming firm is acquired by a significantly larger or financially healthy buyer, target firm members often welcome the takeover and are energized to become part of something larger or more successful than themselves (e.g., Chaudhuri, 2005; Pucik et al., 2011; Teerikangas, 2012). This is especially true when they see the acquiring company as being a savior or having a more enlightened culture, or when they see other positive outcomes in being associated with the acquirer (better pay, more pres-tige, etc.). Thus, there is not a general effect of power asymmetry and relative performance; rather, the effect on target firm members' trust will depend on the perceived personal risk and benefits resulting from the merger or takeover, as discussed below.

Integration Approach

In addition to the status variables discussed earlier, trust is influenced by a set of process variables relating to the acquirer's post-acquisition integration approach, most notably the removal of autonomy. Autonomy removal can be devastating from the perspective of target firm members, and can lead to feelings of helplessness and open hostility (Hambrick & Cannella, 1993; Marks & Mirvis, 2001) as managers and employees vigorously defend their autonomy – a situation that Datta and Grant (1990) have termed the 'conquering army syndrome.' Research suggests that the degree to which an acquiring firm tends to impose its policies, norms, and expectations on the target firm partly depends on the acquirer's *multiculturalism* (Nahavandi & Malekzadeh, 1988). The term 'multiculturalism' refers to the degree to which an organization values cultural diversity and is willing to tolerate and encourage it (Nahavandi & Malekzadeh, 1988). A multicultural acquirer considers diversity an asset, and is therefore likely to allow an acquired firm to retain its own values and modus operandi. In contrast, a unicultural acquirer emphasizes conformity and adherence to a unique organizational ideology, and is therefore more likely to impose its culture on the target firm. Furthermore, there is evidence that the *expected benefits* of the organizational changes that result from the takeover, particularly the quality of the post-acquisition reward and job security changes, is a critical factor in determining employees' reactions to an acquisition (Cartwright & Cooper, 1996; Van Dick et al., 2006). For instance, Bartels et al. (2006) found that the expected utility of a merger (anticipated benefits such as salary increases or more job security) was the strongest predictor of employees' identification with the post-merger organization. Chaudhuri (2005), in an in-depth case study of one of Cisco's acquisitions, found that strong financial incentives and a vision of the merged entity, including an important role for the acquired employees, helped to promote trust and encouraged acquired employees to stay.

Quality of Communication

Finally, the quality of communication is a key factor in determining the level of trust that target firm members have in the acquirer's management. M&As are associated with high degrees of stress and uncertainty for the individuals affected, especially those from the target firm. Providing acquired employees with credible and relevant information can reduce this uncertainty and mitigate feelings of mistrust and suspicion (Bastien, 1987; Schweiger & DeNisi, 1991), as well as increase employees' identification with the post-merger organization (Ellis et al., 2009). A lack of credible and open communication, on the other hand, has been found to result in intense rumor activity, anxiety over job security, and feelings of suspicion and mistrust (Buono & Bowditch, 1989; Marks & Mirvis, 1998).

Preliminary evidence from several empirical studies (Stahl et al., 2006, 2011, 2012) suggests that the degree to which target firm members trust the acquiring firm management affects a variety of behavioral and attitudinal outcomes, including employee commitment (e.g., Weber et al., 1996), resistance (e.g., Larsson & Finkelstein, 1999), turnover (e.g., Schoenberg, 2004), level of acculturation (e.g., Larsson & Lubatkin, 2001), and cooperation (e.g., Weber et al., 1996), and ultimately, the post-acquisition performance. For example, the results of a case survey (Stahl et al., 2011) suggest that while aspects of the combining firms' relationship history and interfirm distance, such as pre-acquisition performance differences, power asymmetry, and cultural distance, seem to be relatively poor predictors of trust, integration process variables such as the acquirer's tolerance for diversity, the adoption of a hands-off integration approach, the quality of communication, and the quality of the post-acquisition reward and job security changes are major factors influencing target firm member trust. This study further suggested that not only does trust have a powerful effect on target firm members' attitudes and behaviors, it may also contribute to the realization of synergies, as reflected in accounting-based performance improvements. This is consistent with research on post-merger integration that indicates that aspects of the sociocultural integration process, such as the acquirer's ability to build an atmosphere of mutual respect and trust, facilitate the transfer of capabilities, resource sharing, and learning, and conversely, sociocultural and human resources problems can undermine the realization of projected synergies (e.g., Birkinshaw et al., 2000; Larsson & Finkelstein, 1999; Stahl & Voigt, 2008; Stahl et al., 2013).

IMPLICATIONS FOR HR PROCESSES IN M&AS

Having completed our overview of the human and managerial dimensions of M&A activity, we now turn to addressing the direct HR implications of M&A activity. It needs to be recognized that a plethora of acquirer profiles exist. In addition to experienced serial acquirers with M&A program management offices that include professional HR expertise (Laamanen & Keil, 2008), there is a spectrum of acquirers who range from zero to high in terms of their past acquisition experience. This experience tends to parallel the firms' maturity in terms of HR expertise. Whilst the larger-sized multinationals with active acquisition programs tend to boast upper-end HR capability, a large portion of acquisitions are made by small to medium-sized firms with less HR expertise.

Four acquirer scenarios with respect to the degree of the firm's HR expertise and its degree of HR awareness in times of M&A can be identified (see Figure 2). Depending on the acquirer's profile, the human resource challenge in an M&A will be tackled more or less professionally from a human resource standpoint. Whilst the active acquirers aware of human factors in M&A would acknowledge HR as a strategic M&A partner (as in the upper right quadrant of Figure 2), in other cases, a formal HR department may not exist (this is the case in both of the left quadrants of Figure 2). If an HR function exists, but its significance in the M&A process has not been recognized by top management, then the local HR staff will need to sell themselves to management in order to be able to join the negotiating table (this is the case in the lower right-hand quadrant).

Degree of awareness of human
resource issues in M&As

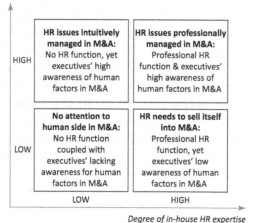

Figure 2 HR's involvement in M&As – four scenarios

HR Roadmap in Times of M&A

The challenge that the HR function faces is not only one of supporting line and top management in dealing with the human dimensions of this change, but further, in enabling simultaneously the change amidst its own organization, i.e. the HR function (Galpin & Herndon, 2000; Antila, 2006) (see Figure 3). Thus, HR bears two roles.

HR professionals need to secure the integration of the HR function in M&A transactions; we term this 'transactional' HR activity. As administrative experts (Antila, 2006), HR professionals are engaged in conducting pre-acquisition HR due diligence (Harding & Rouse, 2007), including compensation and benefits audits, which feed directly into the financial deal valuation schemes driving decision-making about whether to go/not go for the deal. Once a deal has been decided upon, HR needs to secure the functioning of basic HR activities function, regardless of the change in ownership. Rewards, pay, benefits, and pensions become strategic factors that need to be in place before a transaction goes live – who wants to work, let alone commit, if one's pay is not secured? The task of coordinating reward and pay packages in major mergers is a strategic task requiring enormous amounts of work and politics. Finally, HR professionals need to plan and coordinate the integration of HR policies and practices across the merging organizations. Whose sickness absence policy is adhered to? What are the consequences for the party that seemingly loses many of its benefits?

In parallel, HR professionals are ideally called in to support the decision-making, planning, and implementation of the organizational transformation that a merger or acquisition represents. We term this 'transformational' HR activity following a M&A. We use the term 'ideally' as industry experience posits differences between acquirers in this respect. Here, the acquirer types previously identified come into play (see Figure 2).

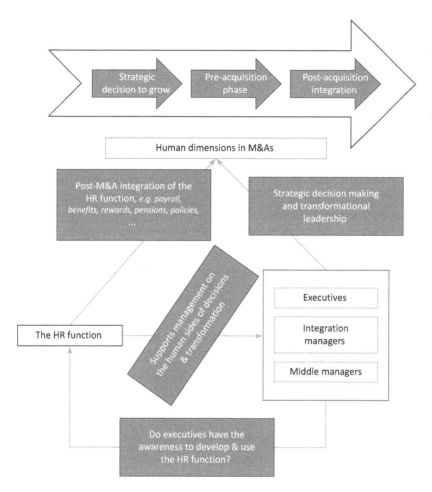

Figure 3 Situating HR's and management's roles in dealing with human dimensions of M&A activity

In order for HR professionals to be able to perform this role, however, they need to step out of an administrative HR role toward a strategic HR role. Using Ullrich's typology of HR roles, in her study of HR roles in M&As, Antila (2006) terms this the strategic partner role. This requires not only courage to act, but beyond this, an appreciation of the M&A process, its strategic, financial and sociocultural implications. This was the purpose of the beginning and middle sections of this chapter: to provide HR professionals with a bird's eye understanding of M&As, the M&A process, and management dynamics therein. It is critical to note that despite frameworks and process maps, the contingency variables shaping M&A activity are numerous (Teerikangas et al., 2012; Angwin et al., 2022): deals differ depending on type of purchase, payment method, countries involved, etc. Thus, whilst an appreciation of M&A process dynamics is critical, it is also important to appreciate how HR approaches might need to be adjusted from one deal and transformation project to the next. In particular, the role of HR will depend on the degree of integration sought in the transaction; when medium to high degrees of integration are sought, the role of HR in transformation support increases. In this role, HR ideally supports executives and middle managers in strategic decision-making and M&A process management both pre- and post-deal. The strategic support roles that HR professionals engage in support of management include:

- Identifying the strategic and sociocultural success factors behind M&As and ensuring that key decision-makers and change agents are aware of them;
- Engagement from the pre-deal phase onward in identifying the strategic rationale for the transaction, target firm search and selection, and M&A process planning and management;
- Gaining early entry into the pre-acquisition phase to provide strategic decision-making support on sociocultural dimensions, including the conduct of management and cultural audits;
- Being involved in the selection of change agents for the transformation phase, i.e. the acquiring firm integration manager(s) and target firm managers in charge of integration;
- Making a change management game plan for the transformation phase;
- Ensuring that a communications plan toward internal and external stakeholders exists;
- Appreciating the challenge that a change of ownership incurs on employees throughout the organizational hierarchy, and providing adequate support;
- Emphasizing the significance of motivating and engaging employees in times of major change, such as acquisitions and mergers;
- Securing the retention of key talent through talent planning exercises;
- Managing the layoff process, if relevant, and liaising with local staff/trade unions;
- Facilitating the cultural clashes and opportunities involved, as well as the sought processes of cultural change;
- Coaching management on the above-mentioned sociocultural dimensions of M&A activity to ensure that in their decision-making and daily behaviors, executives and line managers begin to walk the right talk.

FUTURE RESEARCH DIRECTIONS

Looking forward, the domain of M&A management and its human implications offer exciting and important avenues for future research. Despite the corporate significance of M&As, ample research opportunities in their study remain. In the broader realm, calls have been made to further our appreciation of the dynamics underlying and predicting M&A performance (King et al., 2021; Haleblian et al., 2009). Despite the acknowledged significance of the human factor to M&A success, this raises the question: how does HR enable the creation of value in M&As? Further, which HR-related factors impact M&A performance, and what is the process through which these occur? What is the array of human dimensions that needs to be accounted for, and how do they impact M&A performance? In parallel, calls for greater methodological and philosophical pluralism in the study of M&As have been made (Meglio & Risberg, 2010; Cartwright et al., 2012; Teerikangas & Colman, 2020) in order to secure enhanced appreciations of its dynamics.

A number of specific HR-related research directions can be identified. For one, we noted how extant theorizing has preferred seemingly negative takes on the employee outcries in the portrayal of M&As. This begs the question: under which conditions do employee reactions veer toward the positive? Further, what explains employee engagement and talent retention in M&As (Teerikangas & Välikangas, 2015)? Where are examples of corporations that have successfully maneuvered the human mires following M&As? There would thus appear to be a need to parallel the rise of positive organizational scholarship (Cameron et al., 2003) in the study of M&A processes.

For another, what are the HR and human implications in mega-mergers versus (smaller-scale) acquisitions? Clearly, human and HR dynamics as well as HR roles differ according to transaction type. Yet extant theorizing appears to have paid lip-service to this distinction (Faulkner et al., 2012). There is a need to further refine our appreciation of M&A transactions across contexts. Here, beyond transaction types, country contexts come into play. Whilst emerging market acquirers seem to perform better than acquirers from traditional markets (Gubbi et al., 2010), what are the underlying HR antecedents explaining these results? For example, Indian acquirers are witnessed to have a more 'human' touch than UK or US acquirers (Kale & Singh, 2012).

Third, whilst the culture-performance debate has intrigued scholars, several important questions remain unanswered. In particular, processual research detailing the complex cultural dynamics at play during mergers versus acquisitions is needed (Stahl & Voigt, 2008). Here, recent insights from international business research on the complexity of the modern cultural encounter will be useful.

Fourth, in the realm of M&A integration management, only a handful of papers have addressed individual actors and roles in M&As. Paralleling the increasing interest in strategy as practice (Johnson et al., 2003; Whittington, 2006) and the role of middle managerial agency (Buchanan, 2003; Huy, 2002; Mantere, 2008), HR scholars could further our appreciation of HR roles in mergers versus acquisitions. Under which conditions do acquirers have a mature HR function that is ready to act when an opportunity to purchase emerges? Who has responsibility for the human agenda in M&As? Whilst prior research has seemingly assigned this responsibility to HR, the reality is more complex. What is the process whereby line managers/executives on the one hand and HR professionals on the other come to jointly create a positive HR agenda in M&As? Are there elements of positive emotional contagion in this process (Barsade, 2002; Losada & Heaphy, 2004)? Finally, whilst M&A integration created much buzz in the 1990s in the scholarly literature, less is known about integration within the HR function prior to and following M&A transactions. Looking ahead, there are many opportunities to take these important lines of inquiry forward. Beyond scholarly impact, there is a need for an appreciation of the practiced reality of mergers and acquisitions.

REFERENCES

Allred, B. B., Boal, K. B., & Holstein, W. K. (2005). "Corporations as stepfamilies: A new metaphor for explaining the fate of merged and acquired companies." *Academy of Management Executive*, 19(3): 23–37.

Angwin, D. (2000). "Mergers and acquisitions across European borders: National perspectives on pre-acquisition due diligence and the use of professional advisers." *Journal of World Business*, 36(1): 32–57.

Angwin, D. (2004). "Speed in M&A integration: The first 100 days." *European Management Journal*, 22(4): 418–430.

Angwin, D., Urs, U., Apadu, N., Thanos, I. C., Vourloumis, S., & Kastanakis, M. (2022). "Does M&A strategy matter? A contingency perspective." *European Management Journal*, 40(6): 847–856.

Antila, E. (2006). "The role of HR managers in international mergers and acquisitions: A multiple case study." *International Journal of Human Resource Management*, 17(6): 999–1020.

Ashkanasy, N. M., & Holmes, S. (1995). "Perceptions of organizational ideology following merger: A longitudinal study of merging accounting firms." *Accounting, Organizations and Society*, 20(1): 19–34.

Ashkenas, R. N., DeMonaco, L. J., & Francis, S. C. (1998). "Making the deal real: How GE Capital integrates acquisitions." *Harvard Business Review*, 76(1): 165–178.

Ashkenas, R. N., & Francis, S. C. (2000). "Integration managers: Special leaders for special times." *Harvard Business Review*, 78(6): 108–116.

Barmeyer, C., & Mayerhofer, U. (2008). "The contribution of intercultural management to the success of international mergers and acquisitions: An analysis of the EADS group." *International Business Review*, 17(1): 28–38.

Barsade, S. G. (2002). "The ripple effect: Emotional contagion and its influence on group behavior." *Administrative Science Quarterly*, 47(4): 644–675.

Bartels, J., Douwes, R., De Jong, M., & Pruyn, A. (2006). "Organizational identification during a merger: Determinants of employees expected identification with the new organization." *British Journal of Management*, 17(S1): 49–67.

Bastien, D. T. (1987). "Common patterns of behaviour and communication in corporate mergers and acquisitions." *Human Resource Management*, 26(1): 17–33.

Bauer, F., & Matzler, K. (2014). "Antecedents of M&A success: The role of strategic complementary, cultural fit, and degree and speed of integration." *Strategical Management Journal*, 35: 269–291.

Bijlsma-Frankema, K. (2001). "On managing cultural integration and cultural change processes in mergers and acquisitions." *Journal of European Industrial Training*, 25(2/3/4): 192–207.

Bilgili, T. V., Calderon, C. J., Allen, D. G., & Kedia, B. L. (2017). "Gone with the wind: A meta-analytic review of executive turnover, its antecedents, and post-acquisition performance." *Journal of Management*, 43(6): 1966–1997.

Birkinshaw, J., Bresman, H., & Håkansson, L. (2000). "Managing the post-acquisition integration process: How the human integration and task integration processes interact to foster value creation." *Journal of Management Studies*, 37(3): 395–425.

Birollo, G., & Teerikangas, S. (2022). Acquired middle managers' strategy roles and value creation in cross-border acquisitions. *European Management Journal*, 40(6): 895–905.

Brannen, M. Y., & Salk, J. E. (2000). "Partnering across borders: Negotiating organizational culture in a German-Japanese joint venture." *Human Relations*, 53(4): 451–487.

Borys, B., & Jemison, D. B. (1989). "Hybrid arrangements as strategic alliances: Theoretical issues in organizational combinations." *Academy of Management Review*, 14(2): 234–249.

Bower, J. L. (2001). "Not all M&As are alike – And that matters. *Harvard Business Review*, 79(3): 93–101.

Buchanan, D. (2003). "Demand, instabilities, manipulations, careers: The lived experience of driving change." *Human Relations*, 56(6): 663–684.

Bucholtz, A. K., Ribbens, B. A., & Houle, I. T. (2003). "The role of human capital in post-acquisition CEO departure." *Academy of Management Journal*, 46: 506–514.

Buckley, P. J., & Ghauri, P. N. (1999). *The Internationalisation of the Firm: A Reader.* London: Thomson Learning.

Buono, A. F., Bowditch, J. L., & Lewis, J. W. (1985). "When cultures collide: The anatomy of a merger." *Human Relations*, 38(5): 477–500.

Buono, A. F., & Bowditch, J. L. (1989). *The Human Side of Mergers and Acquisitions: Managing Collisions between People, Cultures and Organizations.* London: Jossey-Bass.

Buono, A. F., & Bowditch, J. L. (1990). "Ethical considerations in merger and acquisition management: A human resource perspective." *SAM Advanced Management Journal*, 55(4): 18–33.

Calori, R., Lubatkin, M., & Very, P. (1994). "Control mechanisms in cross-border acquisitions: An international comparison." *Organization Studies*, 15(3): 361–379.

Cameron, K. S., Dutton, J. E., & Quinn, R. E. (2003). *Positive Organizational Scholarship.* San Francisco, CA: Berrett-Koehler.

Cartwright, S., & Cooper, C. L. (1990). "The impact of mergers and acquisitions on people at work: Existing research and issues." *British Journal of Management*, 1(2): 65–76.

Cartwright, S., & Cooper, C. L. (1992). *Managing Mergers, Acquisitions and Strategic Alliances: Integrating People and Cultures.* Oxford: Butterworth-Heinemann.

Cartwright, S., & Cooper, C. L. (1993). "The role of culture compatibility in successful organizational marriage." *Academy of Management Executive*, 7(2): 57–70.

Cartwright, S., & Cooper, C. L. (1996). *Managing Mergers, Acquisitions, and Strategic Alliances: Integrating People and Cultures.* New York: Routledge.

Cartwright, S., & Hudson, S. L. (2000). "Coping with mergers and acquisitions." In R. Burke & C. L. Cooper (Eds.), *The Organization in Crisis: Downsizing, Restructuring and Renewal* (pp. 269–283). London: Blackwell.

Cartwright, S., & Price, F. (2003). "Managerial preferences in international merger and acquisition partners revisited: How much are they influenced?" *Advances in Mergers and Acquisitions*, 2: 81–95.

Cartwright, S., & Schoenberg, R. (2006). "Thirty years of mergers and acquisitions research: Recent advances and future opportunities." *British Journal of Management*, 17(1): 1–5.

Cartwright, S., Teerikangas, S., Rouzies, A., & Wilson-Evered, E. (2012). "Methods in M&A: A look at the past, and the future, to forge a path forward." *Scandinavian Journal of Management*, 28(2): 95–106.

Chaudhuri, S. (2005). "Managing human resources to capture capabilities: Case studies in high-technology acquisitions." In G. K. Stahl & M. E. Mendenhall (Eds.), *Mergers and Acquisitions: Managing Culture and Human Resources* (pp. 277–301). Stanford, CA: Stanford Business Press.

Child, J., Faulkner, D., & Pitkethly, R. (2001). *The Management of International Acquisitions.* Oxford: Oxford University Press.

Chua, C. H., Engeli, H. P., & Stahl, G. (2005). "Creating a new identity and high-performance culture at Novartis: The role of leadership and human resource management." In G.

K. Stahl & M. Mendenhall (Eds.), *Mergers and Acquisitions: Managing Culture and Human Resource* (pp. 379–400). Stanford, CA: Stanford Business Press.

Colombo, G., Conca, V., Buongiorno, M., & Ghan, L. (2007). "Integrating cross-border acquisitions: A process-oriented approach." *Long Range Planning*, 40(2): 202–222.

Covin, T. J., Kolenko, T. A., Sightler, K. W., & Tudor, R. K. (1997). "Leadership style and post-merger satisfaction." *Journal of Management Development*, 16: 22–33.

Currall, S. C., & Inkpen, A. C. (2002). "A multilevel approach to trust in joint ventures." *Journal of International Business Studies*, 33(3): 479–495.

Dackert, I., Jackson, P., Brenner, S.-O., & Johansson, C. R. (2003). "Eliciting and analysing employees' expectations of a merger." *Human Relations*, 56(6): 705–725.

Datta, D. K., & Grant, J. H. (1990). "Relationships between type of acquisition, the autonomy given to the acquired firm, and acquisition success: An empirical analysis." *Journal of Management*, 16(1): 29–44.

Davy, J. A., Kinicki, A., Kilroy, J., & Scheck, C. (1988). "After the merger: Dealing with people's uncertainty." *Training and Development Journal*, 42(11): 56–62.

Deiser, R. (1994). "Post-acquisition management: A process of strategic and organisational learning." In G. Von Krogh, A. Siknatra, & H. Singh (Eds.), *The Management of Corporate Acquisitions* (pp. 359–390). London: Macmillan Press.

De Noble, A. F., Gustafson, L. T., & Hergert, M. (1988). "Planning for post-merger integration: Eight lessons for merger success." *Long Range Planning*, 21(4): 82–85.

Ellis, K. M., Reus, T. H., & Lamont, B. T. (2009). "The effects of procedural and informational justice in the integration of related firms." *Strategic Management Journal*, 30: 137–161.

Elsass, P. M., & Veiga, J. F. (1994). "Acculturation in acquired organizations: A force-field perspective." *Human Relations*, 47(4): 431–453.

Epstein, M. J. (2004). "The drivers of success in post-merger integration." *Organizational Dynamics*, 33(2): 174–189.

Ewelt-Knauer, C., Gefken, J., Knauer, T., & Wiedemann, D. (2021). "Acquirers' cultural background and the use of earnouts." *Journal of Accounting, Auditing and Finance*, 36(1): 30–55.

Fairfield-Sonn, J. W., Ogilvie, J. R., & DelVecchio, G. A. (2002). "Mergers, acquisitions and long-term employee attitudes." *Journal of Business & Economic Studies*, 8: 1–16.

Faulkner, D., Teerikangas, S., & Joseph, R. (2012). *The Handbook of Mergers and Acquisitions*. Oxford: Oxford University Press.

Feely, A. J., & Harzing, A.-W. (2003). "Language management in multinational companies." *Cross-Cultural Management: An International Journal*, 10(2): 37–52.

Froese, F. J., Pak, Y. S., & Chong, L. C. (2007). "Managing the human side of cross-border acquisitions in South Korea." *Journal of World Business*, 43(1): 97–108.

Galpin, T. J., & Herndon, M. (2000). *The Complete Guide to Mergers and Acquisitions: Process Tools to Support M&A Integration at Every Level*. San Francisco, CA: Jossey-Bass.

Giessner, S. R., Ullrich, J., & van Dick, R. (2012). "A social identity analysis of mergers and acquisitions." In D. Faulkner, S. Teerikangas, & R. Joseph (Eds.), *Handbook of Mergers & Acquisitions* (pp. 474–494). Oxford: Oxford University Press.

Graebner, M. E. (2004). "Momentum and serendipidity: How acquired firm leaders create value in the integration of technology firms." *Strategic Management Journal*, 25(89): 751–777.

Graebner, M. E., Heimeriks, K., Huy, Q. N., & Vaara, E. (2017). "The process of post-merger integration: A review and agenda for future research." *Academy of Management Annals*, 11(1): 1–32.

Gubbi, S. R., Aulakh, P. S., Ray, S., Sarkar, M. B., & Chittoor, R. (2010). "Do international acquisitions by emerging-economy firms create shareholder value? The case of Indian firms." *Journal of International Business Studies*, 41(3): 397–418.

Haleblian, J., Devers, C. E., McNamara, G., Carpenter, M. A., & Davison, R. B. (2009). "Taking stock of what we know about mergers and acquisitions: A review and research agenda." *Journal of Management*, 35(3): 469–502.

Hambrick, D. C., & Cannella, A. A. (1993). "Relative standing: A framework for understanding departures of acquired executives." *Academy of Management Journal*, 36(4): 733–762.

Harding, D., & Rouse, T. (2007). "Human due diligence." *Harvard Business Review*, 85(4): 124–131.

Haspeslagh, P. C., & Jemison, D. B. (1991). *Managing Acquisitions: Creating Value through Corporate Renewal*. New York: The Free Press.

Hassett, M. E., Reynolds, N. S., & Sandberg, B. (2018). "The emotions of top managers and key persons in cross-border M&As: Evidence from a longitudinal case study." *International Business Review*, 27(4): 737–754.

Hitt, M. A., Harrison, J. S., & Duane Ireland, R. (2001). *Mergers and acquisitions: A guide to creating value for stakeholders*. New York: Oxford University Press.

Hogg, M. A., & Terry, D. J. (2000). "Social identity and self-categorization processes in organizational contexts." *Academy of Management Review*, 25(1): 121–140.

Homburg, C., & Bucerius, M. (2006). "Is speed of integration really a success factor of mergers and acquisitions? An analysis of the role of internal and external relatedness." *Strategic Management Journal*, 27(4): 347–367.

Howell, R. A. (1970). "Plan to integrate your acquisitions." *Harvard Business Review*, 48(6): 66–76.

Huy, Q. N. (2002). "Emotional balancing of organizational continuity and radical change: The contribution of middle managers." *Administrative Science Quarterly*, 47(1): 31–69.

Håkansson, L. (1995). "Learning through acquisitions, management and integration of foreign R&D laboratories." *International Studies of Management and Organization*, 25(1–2): 121–157.

Hurley, R. F. (2006). "The decision to trust." *Harvard Business Review*, 84(9): 55–62.

Inkpen, A. C., & Currall, S. C. (2004). "The coevolution of trust, control, and learning in joint ventures." *Organization Science*, 15(5): 586–599.

Ivancevich, J. M., Schweiger, D. M., & Power, F. R. (1987). "Strategies for managing human resources during mergers and acquisitions." *Human Resource Planning*, 10: 19–35.

Jemison, D. B., & Sitkin, S. B. (1986). "Corporate acquisitions: A process perspective." *Academy of Management Review*, 11(1): 145–163.

Johnson, G., Melin, J., & Whittington, R. (2003). "Guest editors' introduction: Micro strategy and strategizing: Towards an activity-based view." *Journal of Management Studies*, 40(1): 3–22.

Kale, P., & Singh, H. (2012). "Characteristics of emerging market mergers and acquisitions." In D. Faulkner, S. Teerikangas, & R. Joseph (Eds.), *Handbook of Mergers & Acquisitions* (pp. 545–565). Oxford: Oxford University Press.

Kavanagh, M. H., & Ashkanasy, N. M. (2006). "The impact of leadership and change management strategy on organizational culture and individual acceptance of change during a merger." *British Journal of Management*, 17(S1): S81–S103.

Kiefer, T. (2002). "Understanding the emotional experience of organizational change: Evidence from a merger." *Advances in Developing Human Resources*, 4(1): 39–61.

King, D., Wang, G., Samimi, M., & Cortes, F. (2021). "A meta-analytic integration of acquisition performance prediction." *Journal of Management Studies*, 58(5): 1198–1236.

Kitching, J. (1967). "Why do mergers miscarry?" *Harvard Business Review*, 45(6): 84–100.

Kleppestø, S. (2005). "The construction of social identities in mergers and acquisitions." In G. K. Stahl & M. Mendenhall (Eds.), *Mergers and Acquisitions: Managing Culture and Human Resources* (pp. 130–151). Stanford, CA: Stanford Business Press.

Kolev, K., Haleblian, J., & McNamara, G. (2012). "A review of the merger and acquisition wave literature: History, antecedents, consequences and future directions." In D. Faulkner, S. Teerikangas, & R. Joseph (Eds.), *Handbook of Mergers and Acquisitions*: 19–39. Oxford: Oxford University Press.

Krishnan, R., Martin, X., & Noorderhaven, N. G. (2006). "When does trust matter to alliance performance?" *Academy of Management Journal*, 49(5): 894–917.

Krug, J. A., & Nigh, D. (2001). "Executive perceptions in foreign and domestic acquisitions: An analysis of foreign ownership and its effect on executive fate." *Journal of World Business*, 36(1): 85–98.

Krug, J. A., Wright, P., & Kroll, M. J. (2014). "Top management turnover following mergers and acquisitions: Solid research to date but still much to be learned." *Academy of Management Perspectives*, 28(2): 147–163.

Laamanen, T., & Keil, T. (2008). "Performance of serial acquirers: Toward an acquisition program perspective." *Strategic Management Journal*, 29(6): 663–672.

Langley, A., Golden-Biddle, K., Reay, T., Denis, J.-L., Hebert, Y., Lamothe, L., & Gervais, J. (2012). "Identity struggles in merging organizations: Renegotiating the sameness–difference dialectic." *Journal of Applied Behavioral Science*, 48(2): 135–167.

Larsson, R., & Risberg, A. (1998). "Cultural awareness and national versus corporate barriers to acculturation." In M. Gertsen, A.-M. Söderberg, & J. E. Torp (Eds.), *Cultural Dimensions of International Mergers and Acquisitions* (pp. 39–56). Berlin: De Gruyter.

Larsson, R., & Finkelstein, S. (1999). "Integrating strategic, organizational, and human resource perspectives on mergers and acquisitions: A case survey of synergy realization." *Organization Science*, 10(1): 1–26.

Larsson, R., & Lubatkin, M. (2001). "Achieving acculturation in mergers and acquisitions: An international case study." *Human Relations*, 54(12): 1573–1607.

Lee, S. J., Kim, J., & Park, B. I. (2015). "Culture clashes in cross-border mergers and acquisitions: A case study of Sweden's Volvo and South Korea's Samsung." *International Business Review*, 24(4): 580–593.

Lewicki, R. J., McAllister, D. J., & Bies, R. J. (1998). "Trust and distrust: New relationships and realities." *Academy of Management Review*, 23(3): 438–458.

Liu, Y., & Woywode, M. (2013). "Light-touch integration of Chinese cross-border M&A: The influences of culture and absorptive capacity." *Thunderbird International Business Review*, 55(4): 469–483.

Losada, M., & Heaphy, E. (2004). "The role of positivity and connectivity in the performance of business teams." *American Behavioral Scientist*, 47(6): 740–765.

Lubatkin, M., Calori, R., Very, P., & Veiga, J. (1998). "Managing mergers across borders: A two-nation exploration of a nationally bound administrative heritage." *Organization Science*, 9(6): 670–684.

Mace, M. L., & Montgomery, G. (1962). *Management Problems of Corporate Acquisitions*. Cambridge, MA: Harvard University Press.

Mantere, S. (2008). "Role expectations and middle manager strategic agency." *Journal of Management Studies*, 45(2): 294–316.

Marks, M. L., & Mirvis, P. (1998). *Joining Forces*. San Francisco, CA: Jossey-Bass.

Marks, M. L., & Mirvis, P. (2001). "Making mergers and acquisitions work: Strategic and psychological preparation." *Academy of Management Executive*, 15(2): 80–94.

Marschan, R., Welch, D., & Welch, L. (1997). "Language: The forgotten factor in multinational management." *European Management Journal*, 15(5): 591–598.

Martin, J. A., & Butler, F. C. (2015). "The moderating effects of executive political skill on employee uncertainty post-acquisition." *Journal of Managerial Issues*, 27: 28–42.

Meglio, O., & Risberg, A. (2010). "Mergers and acquisitions – Time for a methodological rejuvenation of the field?" *Scandinavian Journal of Management*, 26(1): 87–95.

Meyer, C. B., & Altenborg, E. (2007). "The disintegrating effects of equality: A study of a failed international merger." *British Journal of Management*, 18(3): 257–271.

Monin, P., Noorderhaven, N., Vaara, E., & Kroon, D. (2013). "Giving sense to and making sense of justice in post-merger integration." *Academy of Management Journal*, 56: 256–284.

Morosini, P. (1998). *Managing Cultural Differences: Effective Strategy and Execution across Cultures in Global Corporate Alliances.* Oxford: Pergamon.

Nahavandi, A., & Malekzhadeh, A. R. (1988). "Acculturation in mergers and acquisitions." *Academy of Management Review*, 13(1): 79–90.

Napier, N. K. (1989). "Mergers and acquisitions, human resource issues and outcomes: A review and suggested typology." *Journal of Management Studies*, 26(3): 271–289.

Napier, N. K., Schweiger, D. M., & Kosglow, J. J. (1993). "Managing organizational diversity: Observations from cross-border acquisitions." *Human Resource Management*, 32(4): 505–523.

Olcott, G. (2008). "The politics of institutionalization: The impact of foreign ownership and control on Japanese organizations." *International Journal of Human Resource Management*, 19(9): 1569–1587.

Olie, R. (1994). "Shades of culture and institutions in international mergers." *Organization Studies*, 15(3): 381–405.

Oudhuis, M., & Olsson, A. (2015). "Cultural clashes and reactions when implementing lean production in a Japanese-owned Swedish company." *Economic and Industrial Democracy*, 36(2): 259–282.

Parmigiani, A., & Rivera-Santos, M. (2011). "Clearing a path through the forest: A meta-review of interorganizational relationships." *Journal of Management*, 37(4): 1108–1136.

Paruchuri, S., Nerkar, A., & Hambrick, D. C. (2006). "Acquisition integration and productivity losses in the technical core: Disruption of inventors in acquired companies." *Organization Science*, 17(5): 545–562.

Piekkari, R., Vaara, E., Tienari, J., & Säntti, R. (2005). "Integration or disintegration? Human resource implications of a common corporate language decision in a cross-border merger." *International Journal of Human Resource Management*, 16(3): 330–344.

Pritchett, P. (1985). *After the Merger: Managing the Shockwaves.* Homewood, IL: Dow Jones and Irwin.

Pucik, V., Evans, P., Björkman, I., & Stahl, G. K. (2011). "Human resource management in cross-border mergers and acquisitions." In A.-W. Harzing & A. Pinnington (Eds.), *International Human Resource Management* (3rd ed., pp. 119–152). London: Sage.

Quah, P., & Young, S. (2005). "Post-acquisition management: A phases approach for cross-border M&A." *European Management Journal*, 23(1): 65–75.

Ranft, A. L., & Lord, M. D. (2002). "Acquiring new technologies and capabilities: A grounded model of acquisition implementation." *Organization Science*, 13(4): 420–441.

Ring, P. S., & Van de Ven, A. H. (1992). "Structuring cooperative relationships between organizations." *Strategic Management Journal*, 13(7): 483–498.

Rottig, D., & Reus, T. (2018). "Research on culture and international acquisition performance: A critical evaluation and new directions." *International Studies of Management and Organization*, 48(1): 3–42.

Sarala, R. M., Junni, P., Cooper, C. L., & Tarba, S. Y. (2016). "A sociocultural perspective on knowledge transfer in mergers and acquisitions." *Journal of Management*, 42(5): 1230–1249.

Sachsenmaier, S., & Guo, Y. (2019). "Building trust in cross-cultural integration: A study of Chinese mergers and acquisitions in Germany." *International Journal of Cross Cultural Management*, 19(2): 194–217.

Sarkar, M., Cavusgil, T., & Evirgen, C. (1997). "A commitment-trust mediated framework of international collaborative venture performance." In P. W. Beamish & J. P. Killing (Eds.), *Cooperative Strategies: North American Perspectives* (pp. 255–285). San Francisco, CA: New Lexington Press.

Schoenberg, R. (2000). "The influence of cultural compatibility within cross-border acquisitions." *Advances in Mergers and Acquisitions*, 1: 43–60.

Schoenberg, R. (2004). "Dimensions of management style compatibility and cross-border acquisition outcome." *Advances in Mergers and Acquisitions*, 3: 149–175.

Schuler, R. S., Jackson, S. E., & Luo, Y. (2004). *Managing Human Resources in Cross-Border Alliances.* London: Routledge.

Schweiger, D. M., & Denisi, A. S. (1991). "Communication with employees following a merger: A longitudinal field experiment." *Academy of Management Journal*, 34(1): 110–135.

Schweiger, D. M., & Goulet, P. K. (2000). "Integrating mergers and acquisitions: An international research review." In C. Cooper & A. Gregory (eds.), *Advances in Mergers and Acquisitions* (Vol. 1, pp. 61–91). Amsterdam: JAI Press.

Schweiger, D. M., Ivancevich, J. M., & Power, F. R. (1987). "Executive actions for managing human resources before and after acquisition." *Academy of Management Executive*, 1(2): 127–138.

Sinkovics, R. R., Zagelmeyer, S., & Kusstatscher, V. (2011). "Between merger and syndrome: The intermediary role of emotions in four cross-border M&As." *International Business Review*, 20(1): 27–47.

Sitkin, S. B., & Roth, N. L. (1993). "Explaining the limited effectiveness of legalistic 'remedies' for trust/distrust." *Organization Science*, 4(3): 367–392.

Siu, O., Cooper, C. L., & Donald, I. (1997). "Occupational stress, job satisfaction and mental health amongst employees of an acquired TV company in Hong Kong." *Stress Medicine*, 13(2): 99–107.

Sniazhko, S. (2022). "Integration team members' approaches to uncertainty management in M&A." *European Management Journal.* https://doi.org/10.1016/j.emj.2022.10.002.

Stahl, G. K., Chua, C. H., & Pablo, A. (2006). "Antecedents of target firm members' trust in the acquiring firm's management: A decision-making simulation." In *Advances in Mergers and Acquisitions* (Vol. 5, pp. 69–89). Amsterdam: JAI Press.

Stahl, G. K., Larsson, R., Kremershof, I., & Sitkin, S. (2011). "Trust dynamics in acquisitions: A case survey." *Human Resource Management*, 50(5): 575–603.

Stahl, G. K., & Voigt, A. (2008). "Do cultural differences matter in mergers and acquisitions? A tentative model and examination." *Organization Science*, 19(1): 160–176.

Stahl, G. K., & Sitkin, S. (2005). "Trust in mergers and acquisitions." In G. K. Stahl & M. E. Mendenhall (Eds.), *Mergers and Acquisitions: Managing Culture and Human Resources* (pp. 82–102). Stanford, CA: Stanford University Press.

Stahl, G. K., & Sitkin, S. (2010). "Trust dynamics in acquisitions: The role of relationship history, interfirm distance, and acquirer's integration approach." In *Advances in Mergers and Acquisitions* (Vol. 9, pp. 51–82). Amsterdam: JAI Press.

Stahl, G. K., Chua, C. H., & Pablo, A. (2012). "Does national context affect target firm employees' trust in acquisitions? A policy-capturing study." *Management International Review*, 52: 395–423.

Stahl, G., Angwin, D., Very, P., Gomes, E., Weber, Y., Tarba, S., Noorderhaven, N., Benyamini, H., Bouckenooghe, D., Chreim, S., Durand, M., Hassett, M. E., Kokk, G., Mendenhall, M. E., Mirc, N., Miska, C., Park, K. M., Reynolds, N., Rouzies, A., Sarala, R. M., Seloti, S. L., Søndergaard, M., & Yildiz, H. (2013). "Sociocultural integration in mergers and acquisitions: Unresolved paradoxes and directions for future research." *Thunderbird International Business Review*, 55(4): 333–356.

Steigenberger, N. (2017). "The challenge of integration: A review of the M&A integration literature." *International Journal of Management Reviews*, 19(4): 408–431.

Steigenberger, N., & Mirc, N. (2020). "Should I stay or should I go? Multi-focus identification and employee retention in post-acquisition integration." *Human Relations*, 73(7): 981–1009.

Styhr, A., Börjesson, S., & Wickenberg, J. (2006). "Managed by the other: Cultural anxieties in two anglo-Americanized Swedish firms." *International Journal of Human Resource Management*, 17(7): 1293–1306.

Sudarsanam, S. (2012). "Value creation and value appropriation in M&A deals." In D. Faulkner, S. Teerikangas, & R. Joseph (Eds.), *Handbook of Mergers & Acquisitions* (pp. 195–253). Oxford: Oxford University Press.

Sun, Z., & Zhao, L. (2019). "Chinese reverse M&As in the Netherlands: Chinese managers' trust building practices." *Chinese Management Studies*, 25(3): 69–91.

Teerikangas, S. (2012). "Dynamics of acquired firm pre-acquisition employee reactions." *Journal of Management*, 38(2): 599–639.

Teerikangas, S., & Birollo, G. (2018). "Leading M&As in a middle managerial role: A balancing act." In J. Raitis, R. Harikkala-Laihinen, M. Hassett, & N. Nummela (Eds.), *Socio-Cultural Integration in Mergers and Acquisitions: The Nordic Approach* (pp. 65–94). London: Palgrave Pivot Series.

Teerikangas, S., & Colman, H. (2020). "Theorizing in the qualitative study of mergers and acquisitions." *Scandinavian Journal of Management*, 36(1): 1–16.

Teerikangas, S., & Irrmann, O. (2013). "Unbundling the linguistic dynamics in cross-border acquisitions." Paper presented at the *Annual Meeting of the Academy of Management*, Orlando, August 2013.

Teerikangas, S., & Irrmann, O. (2016). "Cultural change following international acquisitions: Cohabiting the tension between espoused and practiced cultures." *Management International Review*, 56(2): 195–226.

Teerikangas, S., Joseph, R., & Faulkner, D. (2012). "Mergers & acquisitions: A synthesis." In D. Faulkner, S. Teerikangas, & R. Joseph (Eds.), *Handbook of Mergers & Acquisitions* (pp. 661–685). Oxford: Oxford University Press.

Teerikangas, S., & Laamanen, T. (2014). "Structure first! Temporal dynamics of structural & cultural integration in cross-border acquisitions." *Advances in Mergers and Acquisitions* (Vol. 13, pp. 109–152). Amsterdam: Emerald.

Teerikangas, S., & Välikangas, L. (2015). "Engaged employees in mergers & acquisitions: Illusion or opportunity?" In A. Risberg, D. King, & O. Meglio (Eds.), *Routledge Companion to Mergers and Acquisitions* (pp. 130–149). London: Routledge.

Teerikangas, S., & Very, P. (2006). "The culture-performance relationship in M&A: From yes/no to How." *British Journal of Management*, 17(S1): 31–48.

Teerikangas, S., & Very, P. (2012). "Culture in mergers and acquisitions: A critical synthesis and steps forward." In D. Faulkner, S. Teerikangas, & R. Joseph (Eds.), *Handbook of Mergers & Acquisitions* (pp. 392–430). Oxford: Oxford University Press.

Teerikangas, S., Very, P., & Pisano, V. (2011). "Integration manager's value-capturing roles and acquisition performance." *Human Resource Management*, 50(5): 651–683.

Thanos, I., Angwin, D., Bauer, F., & Teerikangas, S. (2023). "Editorial: Boundary spanning and boundary breaking research in M&A: Taking stock and moving forward to reinvent the field. Introduction to the special issue on Reshaping M&A scholarship – Broadening the boundaries of M&A research." *European Management Journal*, 41(2): 181–190.

Tienari, J., & Vaara, E. (2012). "Power and politics in mergers and acquisitions." In D. Faulkner, S. Teerikangas, & R. Joseph (Eds.), *Handbook of Mergers & Acquisitions* (pp. 495–516). Oxford: Oxford University Press.

Trichterborn, A., Knyphausen-Aufseß, D. Z., & Schweizer, L. (2016). "How to improve acquisition performance: The role of a dedicated M&A function, M&A learning process, and M&A capability." *Strategic Management Journal*, 37(4): 763–773.

Vaara, E. (2003). "Post-acquisition integration as sensemaking: Glimpses of ambiguity, confusion, hypocrisy, and politicization." *Journal of Management Studies*, 40(4): 859–894.

Vaara, E., Tienari, J., Piekkari, R., & Säntti, R. (2005). "Language and the circuits of power in a merging multinational corporation." *Journal of Management Studies*, 42(3): 595–623.

Van Dick, R., Ullrich, J., & Tissington, P. A. (2006). "Working under a black cloud: How to sustain organizational identification after a merger." *British Journal of Management*, 17: 69–79.

Very, P., Lubatkin, M., & Calori, R. (1996). "A cross-national assessment of acculturative stress in recent European mergers." *International Studies of Management and Organization*, 26(1): 59–86.

Very, P., & Schweiger, D. (2001). "The acquisition process as a learning process: Evidence from a study of critical problems and solutions in domestic and cross-border deals." *Journal of World Business*, 36(1): 11–31.

Vuori, N., Vuori, T. O., & Huy, Q. N. (2018). "Emotional practices: How masking negative emotions impacts the post-acquisition integration process." *Strategic Management Journal*, 39(3): 859–893.

Weber, Y. (1996). "Corporate cultural fit and performance in mergers and acquisitions." *Human Relations*, 49(9): 1181–1202.

Weber, Y., & Drori, I. (2008). "The linkages between cultural differences, psychological states, and performance in international mergers and acquisitions." *Advances in Mergers and Acquisitions*, 7: 119–142.

Weber, Y., Shenkar, O., & Raveh, A. (1996). "National and corporate cultural fit in mergers & acquisitions: An exploratory study." *Management Science*, 42(8): 1215–1227.

Whittington, R. (2006). "Completing the practice turn in strategy research." *Organization Studies*, 27(5): 613–634.

Zaheer, A., McEvily, B., & Perrone, V. (1998). "Does trust matter? Exploring the effects of interorganizational and interpersonal trust on performance." *Organization Science*, 9(2): 141–159.

Zhu, H., Zhu, Q., & Ding, Z. (2020). "The roles of Chinese CEOs in managing individualistic cultures in cross-border mergers and acquisitions." *Journal of Management Studies*, 57(3): 664–697.

Yih-teen Lee, B. Sebastian Reiche, and Carlos Sánchez-Runde

HAIER INDIA

Aiming for Market Leadership*

CHANGING PEOPLE IS NOT EASY. The biggest and hardest work in the overseas market is changing people. Otherwise, people change you.

Song Yujun, managing director of Haier India

INTRODUCTION

Sitting face to face in their office in the outskirts of Delhi, Song Yujun and Eric Braganza—managing director and president of Haier India, respectively—were contemplating their strategic objectives to drive Haier India to become one of the top brands in the Indian white goods market in the years to come. Forming a stable leadership team at the helm of Haier India since 2011, Yujun and Braganza consistently achieved double-digit growth and had started closing the gap between Haier and the top brands in the market (LG and Samsung). Yet the distance between the company and its key competitors in terms of both market share and brand influence was still huge. Furthermore, the unique management model created by the visionary CEO Zhang Ruimin had not yet been fully implemented in India.

"I know what CEO Zhang wants," Yujun said to Braganza. However, they needed to figure out together how to make it happen. For example, how could they continue to consolidate the team and attract more talent to meet the demands for growth? What could be done to further implement the Rendanheyi[1] principle and the concept of microenterprises (MEs) advanced by Haier's headquarters? How could they further improve the mutual understanding and collaboration

* Originally published by IESE Publishing.

DOI: 10.4324/9781003247272-28

between all the departments so that Haier India could effectively obtain strategic guidance and support from the HQ in China while maintaining its agility and flexibility in order to stay ahead in the fast-changing Indian market?

HAIER INDIA

Haier India was established in 2004 as a wholly owned subsidiary of Haier Group, a leading brand in a wide range of white appliances, originating from Qingdao, China. In the earlier years of Haier's operation in India, the local community generally expected it to fail and close down, as many other foreign brands in India had done previously. However, in 2009, Haier India entered a phase of growth as it transitioned towards Haier's management philosophy. Under the leadership of Yujun (who joined Haier India in 2011) and Braganza (who joined in 2009), Haier India became a serious competitor for India's leading brands, such as LG, Samsung, and Whirlpool. More specifically, over the previous five years Haier India had experienced annual growth of around 20%; it had also targeted doubling its 2017 revenues to become one of the top three white-goods brands with a market share of 12–15% by 2021. This would place Haier among the top three players in India. In addition, Haier India had recently expanded its factory located in Pune.

This growth had been fueled by a series of factors that reflected the spirit of Haier's Rendanheyi system. First, Haier India generated a series of innovations to satisfy local user needs. For example, 80% of the Indian population were vegetarian and would cook fresh meals on a daily basis. This required comparatively large and accessible refrigerator space to store vegetables and relatively less freezer space. The correspondingly introduced fridges which placed freezers at the bottom demonstrated the initiative of local teams to design and decide on the right model for local users. Second, Haier India actively built up brand awareness and credibility through a relentless pursuit of product quality and clear strategic positioning and planning. For example, Haier India intentionally refrained from discounting its products for competition and established Haier as a higher-quality brand. Third, Haier developed a qualified and motivated workforce that believed in future growth—Haier India was now perceived as the best work environment in the Indian appliances industry, which had resulted in unsolicited talent attraction (i.e., good candidates applying for jobs) and lower than average attrition.

Yujun joined Haier Group in 1998 and, with his expertise in operation management, had participated in and contributed to the establishment and systematic operation of multiple Haier factories all over the world. In 2007, Yujun was commissioned to run Haier Pakistan and turn it around. Back then, Haier Pakistan ran an annual loss of several million US dollars. When he succeeded in bringing Haier Pakistan back into the black, Yujun was sent to run Haier India in 2011, while maintaining his responsibilities of overseeing and coordinating the Pakistan operation. Braganza joined Haier India in 2009, when it was still an extremely small company in the Indian market. Yujun's operational expertise and Braganza's commercial background complemented each other well and helped form a strong partnership in leading Haier India.

HAIER'S INNOVATIVE MANAGEMENT SYSTEM

Since its creation in 1984 in Qingdao, China, under the visionary leadership of Zhang, Haier experienced five stages of expansion, each representing different strategies:

- brand building (1984–1991),
- diversification (1991–1998),
- internationalization (1998–2005),
- global brand (2005–2012), and
- networking (2012–present).

Although each stage was marked by a unique strategic focus and management systems that matched the needs of the time, three themes consistently cut through Haier's management philosophy:

- maximizing employees' individual initiative and accountability,
- satisfying customer needs through close proximity, and
- leveraging an innovative technological and management system.

The most recent developments of Haier's system included the Rendanheyi model, salary-paid-by-user, and microenterprises within Haier (see Exhibit 1 for the historical development of Haier's system and the Rendanheyi model).

As the basic operating units at Haier, microenterprises were independent operational entities with the power to make decisions, to recruit and deploy personnel, and to distribute profit. Haier maintained an investor–investee relationship—instead of a superior–subordinate relationship—with microenterprises and provided them with entrepreneurial resources through Haier's ecosystem.

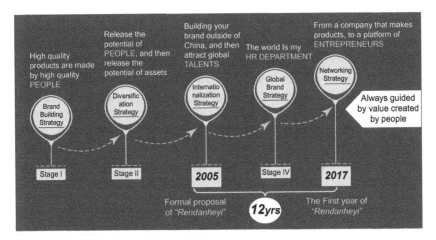

Exhibit 1 Developmental stages of Haier's model and Rendanheyi.

Source: Information provided by the company.

Microenterprises might thus survive, die, or grow depending on their competitiveness in the market. Rendanheyi, or the Win–Win Mode of Individual-Goal Combination, was the foundational philosophy at Haier. Here, "individual" referred to employees and "goal" appeared to refer to customer orders in general, but further implied the needs and value of resources of both internal and external users. Thus, the Individual-Goal Combination focused on the integration of employees' capabilities with the value they created for users and their resources. With this concept, Haier redefined the organization into a network between users and employees. The win–win principle was reflected in the incentive system that was based on microenterprises managing their own profits and losses in collaboration with other (internal and external) units to generate profit. In other words, employees' salaries were calculated based on the customer value they could create.

THE IMPLEMENTATION OF THE HAIER MODEL IN INDIA

> What I keep telling my staff is what was valid yesterday is not valid today, and what is valid today is not necessarily going to be valid tomorrow.
>
> Eric Braganza, president of Haier India

Under the leadership of Song Yujun and Eric Braganza, Haier India continued to experiment and innovate in order to respond to the needs of different developmental stages. In particular, the focus was placed on the efficient and effective operation and management of the organization, as well as on maintaining and mobilizing employees' initiative. Yujun and Braganza started transforming Haier India by introducing a tight target-budget system and an intensive evaluation process to keep the operation transparent. Based on their individual business targets, individuals were given a specific budget to fulfill their key performance indicators (KPIs), which were associated with individual incentives. Unlike other companies in India, which conducted annual evaluations, workers at Haier India received monthly evaluations, sometimes with daily feedback. Moreover, in line with Haier's culture at HQ, cross-functional collaboration and integration were encouraged at Haier India. All these measures were intended to provide employees with a strong sense of ownership. Haier India also emphasized promoting people internally, thus giving people the opportunity to grow with the company. Given the ongoing growth and concrete results over the previous years, people were gaining enough confidence in the model and in their team to further embrace the new system and mindset. The sales director once told a new hire, "This is your individual area, and it is controlled by you as an individual. There are only very few parts that are controlled by our organization."

In other words, people were the masters of their destiny.

In contrast to the traditional way of thinking about planning, Haier created a non-linear and self-evolving, commitment-oriented planning system that included five key elements:

- a target-to-lead system, which defined network value and user value to be achieved at a specific space and time (i.e., the node);
- breakthroughs at nodes of timing and space;
- differentiated models and paths for various types of actors in the system (e.g., sector owner, industry owner, microenterprise owner, and member);
- an open talent system, which allowed goal-based gathering and dispersing of people and teams, resulting in dynamically optimized teams; and
- target-team mechanism alignment.

Haier India fully adopted such a preset budgeting process. Targets tended to increase by about 20–30% from one year to the next, while the market was growing by around 15% per year. This illustrated Haier India's ambitions to out-grow the market. In many ways, this process was a cultural buffer that effectively reduced potential misunderstandings and ensured continuity in case employees left the organization. Managers and employees at Haier India saw many benefits to the annual budgeting process, as it:

- fostered ownership and accountability;
- created transparency for how higher-level organizational targets were linked to individual goals;
- created predictability and made preset goals (predict the "win" or profit beforehand); and
- drove each individual to create a careful action plan in advance.

Haier India had also made substantial progress in adopting the Rendanheyi model. All heads of department (HoDs) understood that their objective was to: (1) be profitable and (2) drive their unit to be a separate, independent company with its own profit and loss (P&L). In the case of platform services, such as logis-tics, after-sales, or human resources (HR), this might also entail serving other external clients or looking for external resources. For example, Haier India put great effort into making the operation more user-centric and measuring the final "sales out" to end users in order to be able to adequately calculate and distrib-ute the value generated across the different business and service units operating within Haier India. Similarly, the factory in Pune measured relevant KPIs and linked them to each individual plant worker (usually, each worker had about ten different KPIs). Haier's factory footprints were used for group review meetings three times a day (in the morning, to define the targets for the day; a midday review; and an evening meeting to close the day: see Exhibit 2). Motivating slo-gans consistent with the spirit of the Rendanheyi model were present on the shop floor of the factory.

However, as of 2019, Haier had not completed the implementation and adop-tion of Rendanheyi in India and was still looking for ways to improve. For exam-ple, according to Yujun, the company was still exploring the question of how to share profits effectively and in a fair manner, consistent with each unit's and individual's value-generation. In line with Rendanheyi and the concept of being

Exhibit 2 Stage imported from Haier HQ in the Pune factory.
Source: Information provided by the company.

one's own CEO, such profit sharing should be introduced by the heads of department and self-driven microenterprises themselves rather than by Yujun, but this
had not yet occurred. Similarly, the concept of the microenterprise was often
not yet fully understood, and therefore required a lot of teaching, coaching, and
handholding on the part of the managers—both for new employees and external
partners (e.g., service centers, dealers, etc.). This also required providing more
tangible benefits to the external partners of a microenterprise. As Braganza
recounted, "Our external after-sales engineers are expected to provide service
to a customer at temperatures that can reach up to 50°C. So we need to think of
ways to reward this sort of behavior."

Under the KPI budget system, Haier India started transforming its existing
compensation system, shifting from the unitary system of "fixed salary" to "variable compensation," as a move to motivate employees to attain their variable
compensation by meeting their KPI targets. For example, several Indian managers mentioned the need to increase the fixed salaries of Haier India employees to
be able to attract better talent, given that LG tended to pay about a 50% higher
fixed salary than Haier. This difference could be partly explained by Haier's
competitors not paying any variable compensation (i.e., 100% of salary was
fixed), while Haier India's current distribution was 40% fixed and 60% variable.
However, employees were only eligible for variable pay if they achieved at least
80% of their target in what was a relative and publicly transparent evaluation
system. While salary was not the only motivating factor, the sentiment among
Indian managers and employees suggested that more could be done in terms of
helping to adapt their mindset towards more ownership and reaching their salary
potential through introducing innovative ideas, process improvements, etc. At
the same time, factory workers faced a bonus ceiling at about 120% of achievement levels, which would limit the scale of variable compensation. According to
the sales director, the challenge was changing people's mindset.

To help with this process, Haier India had simplified the model to some
extent and used the term "ownership" to capture the spirit of Haier, while avoiding expressions that might create confusion in the local culture (e.g., "everyone

is their own CEO"). Indian managers generally understood and appreciated the much deeper sense of ownership at Haier India compared with other companies. It was also challenging for Indian workers to fully understand the concept of the microenterprise. "Creating a win–win" was another term used locally to help workers understand the system. Some Indian managers mentioned the challenges of explaining the Haier system to potential new hires, especially about practices such as being evaluated on a monthly (or sometimes daily) basis.

To facilitate the effective and localized implementation of the Rendanheyi model and strategy, Haier India adopted the "1+1" model (one local employee and one Chinese member) in key management and operation units. All members in the unit shared leadership and the responsibility for setting unit targets. As of 2019, quality and technical units had also adopted a similar model. In 2019, there were 30 such posts in Haier India.

These Chinese members were expected to fulfill several roles, including:

- ensuring strategy alignment with HQ and knowledge transfer to/from HQ;
- creating infrastructure platforms for management and operation;
- training for future positions (management development);
- enhancing local performance through improving communication with HQ;
- ensuring subsidiary operations were in accordance with HQ's globalization strategy; and
- ensuring a homogeneous corporate culture throughout the global organization.

The group of Chinese expatriates lived together in a company dormitory, together with a cook hired to prepare three meals a day for them. The Indian cook learned to prepare a wide range of Chinese dishes over time.

This mode of functioning had several key benefits that facilitated Haier India's progress and growth. First, the presence of Chinese liaison personnel ensured the consistent implementation of the HQ strategy in the local context and helped Indian colleagues obtain HQ resources and support through their knowledge of and contacts at HQ. As Braganza commented, "The Chinese members serve a critical role in coordinating with the HQ in Qingdao. Our Indian colleagues simply don't have the knowledge or contact network in China to do so."

Second, it also enabled more structured international talent development for Haier, at least for its Chinese talent, as they rotated to different country markets. Third, this mode of functioning offered a balancing mechanism between Indian managers who faced short-term considerations and immediate pressures on the one hand, and the Chinese heads who were in charge of ensuring HQ strategy implementation and long-term functioning on the other. Fourth, the structure was instrumental for a two-directional model of knowledge transfer and interaction, in which the Indian counterpart would share local market knowledge while the Chinese counterpart could translate HQ strategy, policies, practices, and the Rendanheyi model. In general, the liaison structure generated good synergies.

For such a mode of functioning to work, agreement on common targets and mutual trust and respect were all necessary. In many ways, this trust and respect could only develop if both Indian and Chinese counterparts brought complementary, similarly valuable knowledge to the table, which required experienced candidates on both sides. Both partners also needed to be humble and open-minded, and understand when they should listen and accept the other's lead and opinion in order to ensure that timely agreement and consensus could be reached.

While this mode of functioning brought with it several benefits, it also entailed a number of challenges. First, there was a risk of decision-making delays when the Chinese counterpart happened to be absent at that specific moment, or when the Chinese counterpart was not sufficiently knowledgeable about the local environment and objective local conditions.

For its part, the Chinese team also faced disadvantages, as they had to deal with a highly complex local context and the local English accent in India required additional communication efforts. Moreover, given their expat assignment, the Chinese team could generally only nurture their familial relationships in a limited way on a daily basis, due to the distance. This added stress to the already culturally challenging local life.

MICROENTERPRISES IN HAIER INDIA

As of 2017, Haier India adopted a multi-tier approach to their exploration in a localized implementation of the Rendanheyi model. The first step was the formation of parallel linked microenterprises and their collaboration through a value-adjusted mechanism (VAM) agreement. According to the Rendanheyi model, Haier implemented the system of pursuing ambitious goals defined by markets and users outside, rather than taking the previous year's performance as a starting point. Such goals were internally called "leading targets." In May 2017, guided by strategic leading targets, and based on user interaction, Haier India began its company-wide top-down transformation towards the microenterprise structure. As of 2019, six industry MEs and four platform MEs had emerged. The six industry MEs were fridge, freezer, air conditioning, washing machine, TV, and electric water heater enterprises; the four platform MEs were market, aftersales, logistics, and manufacturing enterprises.

Each ME adhered to the following principles: being able to predict a win beforehand, being self-funded, being responsible for their own profits and losses, and having independent accounting and a rolling budget. The MEs were required to duly perform their strategic tasks and market planning and to be responsible for maintaining the whole-process competitiveness of their respective ME/platform. The strategic targets of the MEs were formulated with the assistance of the platform. Mature and stand-alone MEs could bid for goals, establish their implementation system (self-managed), and continue to optimize their goals (self-driven). Industrial MEs signed a VAM agreement with platform MEs, which set out the competitiveness goals for market leadership and the resources needed. All MEs used independent accounting systems. Industry MEs identified resources through leading targets. Platform MEs provided services according to the goals and resources set out in the VAM. Eventually, the goal for a win–win situation in which industrial MEs could make gains and platform MEs could achieve leading targets was established.

After MEs emerged with independent accounting and goal-driven win–win had been carried out through VAM among MEs, Haier India introduced the value-added sharing mechanism which upholds the principle: the higher the value added, the higher the share. MEs were motivated to set higher targets in order to attain higher value, which served to encourage MEs/members to always seek out higher goals and improve their operational efficiency. MEs/members could cash in their share of the value created after goals were achieved. This profoundly changed the mindset of all the entrepreneurs—and particularly of the Indian employees—who started to set higher expectations for themselves by seeing the challenging goals as a base line; they also started to take the initiative to connect with relevant nodes (MEs) in the process. From an unwillingness to accept challenging goals in the beginning to actively undertaking these same goals, Haier India took a qualitative leap not just in its corporate management model, but also in people's way of thinking.

By the end of 2017, the refrigerator ME had already set its strategic target to sell one million units in 2018. However, during the last target setting meeting, Braganza proposed that based on the company's future strategic development outlook and market assessment, the challenging target could be set at 1.3 million units, and expected to establish added-value sharing after reaching the challenging target, in order to encourage the refrigerator ME and the platform MEs to connect and collaborate in new ways in order to reach the challenging goal. In the end, the refrigerator ME sold 1.33 million units in 2018, thus not only surpassing its challenging goal, but also achieving profitability. The additional portion of profits would first be allocated to strategic projects for the following year: for example, it could become part of the strategic reserve to ensure sustainable development for the following year or years. Subsequently used for value-added sharing with the refrigerator ME and platform MEs, it helped achieve the goal. Getting their share instilled the MEs and their members with confidence for achieving future goals.

Led by Yujun, Haier India never ceased to explore ways to innovate the mechanism and to motivate its employees. The company remained committed to its goals, and was open to trying out new ideas for mobilizing employees' initiative. In 2019, Haier India first tried the "real-time incentive" mechanism with the aftersales platform ME to motivate frontline employees to become self-driven and self-developing. The aftersales ME developed a "work dashboard" for its frontline engineers and changed their income source from "management-determined" to "self-determined"/"user-determined." On the day of launch, every engineer could see their monthly incentive in real time, motivating them to focus more on customer satisfaction, productivity, and revenue. Since its launch in September 2019, it spread rapidly, covering 1,500 network engineers as of 2020. The performance-based income of all engineers saw a gradual increase on a daily basis, with more and more engineers working even harder for higher gains.

DIFFERENCES AND SIMILARITIES IN THE SALAD CULTURE

Although both situated in Asia, the differences between Chinese and Indian cultures were tremendous, given their rich traditions and diversity.

Workers at Haier India perceived some noteworthy differences between the Chinese and Indian staff. For example, a shared observation from the Chinese side was that the Chinese were fast and efficient in execution, whereas the Indian colleagues sometimes slowed things down and required additional follow-up. One Chinese manager joked, "It happens time and again that Indian colleagues may commit to a task but not actually achieve it. When they say, 'I will do that,' one cannot be fully sure whether they will really do it or not."

Such situations frustrated the Chinese employees, but both sides were learning more about each other with time. By contrast, the Indian colleagues considered alertness, agility, quick thinking, and fast decision-making as their particular strengths. Thus far, the perceived differences, however, had not created big obstacles in the collaboration between the two cultures.

In addition, Haier India faced a number of specific challenges due to the complexities of the diverse Indian market. For example, the provision of after-sales services was quite difficult in India in the early stage because the market was both vast and fragmented. Similarly, while Haier India had started to experiment with e-commerce, its proportional clout was still very small, as e-commerce in India was still in its early stages. The infrastructure in India (e.g., Internet coverage) sometimes also dictated how far Haier India could implement the Haier system, which required more timely sharing of user data and feedback. Moreover, Haier India was in the process of a retail transformation, moving from "sell in" (i.e., selling products to dealers) to "sell out" (i.e., selling products to end users). Such a move represented an effort to get closer to the market to better understand and serve its needs.

In the process of its global expansion (including recent acquisitions of foreign brands, such as Sanyo in Japan, Fisher & Paykel Appliances in New Zealand, and GE Appliances in the United States), Haier developed a "salad culture" approach towards cultural integration. Specifically, instead of viewing cultural integration as one culture changing the other, the salad culture approach emphasized the identification and pursuit of commonalities among different cultures. For example, the spirit of Rendanheyi was in line with the common human needs for self-realization. Different cultures could be seen as different ingredients (vegetables, fruits, etc.) in the salad—each with its unique flavor and color. However, they could all coexist perfectly in harmony in the form of a salad, integrated by the salad dressing—the Rendanheyi spirit[2] (see Exhibit 3). Yujun was convinced that Haier's management system and the spirit of Rendanheyi could be implemented in India, as he strongly believed in the salad culture model proposed by Zhang and had seen some initial results. However, he felt that he could not relax or turn a blind eye to the cultural differences that were present in everyday work and company operations. Some of these differences were minor and inconsequential.

Exhibit 3 Haier's salad culture integration model.

Source: Zhang Ruimin, chairman and CEO of the Haier Group, "Creating a Business Model for the IoT Era—Rendanheyi," September 2017.

Yet, left unaddressed, some of them could accumulate and eventually trigger bigger tensions in the future.

THE ROAD AHEAD

Yujun emphasized the importance of starting with the fundamental platform and operation processes (such as the creation of a backup system for key positions, the creation of a talent pool in each department, and a rotation and relocation policy), which laid a solid foundation for a more far-reaching implementation of the Haier model and Rendanheyi in India. Over several years, Yujun and Braganza had started to enjoy the fruits of their labor. Generally, the Indian and Chinese coworkers maintained good relationships in working together towards common goals. As one Indian manager exclaimed, "My Chinese counterpart and I should be happy. We should be healthy. We should all prosper together." Another Indian manager commented, "We should work hard together and enjoy our time together." The company was growing fast, and people seemed happy and confident about the future.

At the same time, Haier India had still faced a challenging battle in terms of capturing talent. It needed to continue to recruit and retain people with the right values and beliefs, and "keep building the fire inside them," in the words of Braganza. Furthermore, the Chinese members were paying a heavy toll, traveling back and forth between China and India, to serve as key bridging and liaison figures between HQ and the Indian operation. Was this system sustainable in the long run, especially when the market was moving so quickly and required the Chinese employees' physical presence and timely decisions? Were there ways to further implement the Rendanheyi model in India so that Haier India could connect itself more closely with the global platform of the Haier Group? Yujun and Braganza paused their conversation, taking a sip from the teacups in their hands, and pondered in silence the future of Haier India, of which they were the owners.

NOTES

1. *Rendanheyi*, 人单合一 in Chinese. Literally, it could be translated as "Individual-Goal Combination." Here "individual" refers to employees and "goal" refers to customer orders in general, but further implies the needs and value of resources of both internal and external users. Thus, the Individual-Goal Combination focuses on the integration of employees' capabilities with the value they create for users and user resources. It was the founding philosophy of all management systems in Haier.
2. *Haier Culture Special Report*, No. 53, October 21, 2016.

Ingmar Björkman and Günter K. Stahl

GROWTH THROUGH CROSS-BORDER ACQUISITIONS: CAN LENOVO REPEAT ITS SUCCESS STORY?

FOUNDED IN 1984 IN A dusty, two-bedroom Beijing guardhouse by Liu Chuanzhi and a team of engineers from the Chinese Academy of Sciences, Lenovo soon began to manufacture and sell computers. It carried out a successful Initial Public Offering on the Hong Kong Stock Exchange in 1994, and by 1996 the company had become the market leader in China and had also began selling its own laptops.

In 2005, Lenovo acquired IBM's personal computer division for US$1.25 billion. Through the deal, Lenovo would be transformed from a firm exclusively focusing on the Chinese market to being a major global player. Lenovo was now the third largest PC manufacturer and had sales, support, and delivery operations across the globe. Lenovo also obtained the right to use the IBM brand for five years. The headquarters of the company was to be in the US. Lenovo's CEO, Yang Yuanqing, agreed to step down to make way for an IBM executive, Steve Ward, while Yang became the Chairman of the Board.

In April 2005, shortly after the merger, Lenovo's founder, Liu Chuanzhi, explained the appointment of Steve Ward as CEO of the leading Chinese brand – and soon-to-be global technology leader:

> All of us agreed when we were choosing our CEO that we would choose the best one possible, no matter what nationality he or she might be …. We want to establish a global company, so it is very natural to find a global CEO for our company.
>
> (cited in Stahl & Lengyel, 2012, p. 1)

DOI: 10.4324/9781003247272-29

Of the 13 members of the new management team, six were from IBM, giving the company almost parity at top management level. Consistent with the goal of creating a new company that was neither Chinese nor American, but would combine the best of both worlds – a "marriage of equals, based on trust, respect, and compromise," in the words of Yang (cited in Stahl & Lengyel, 2012, p. 1) – a decision was made to pursue a gradual integration approach to ensure a smooth transition. There was true excitement on both the Lenovo and IBM sides from the outset. However, although the positive attitude spanned several levels in the organization, the challenges across different time zones were obvious from the start.

Simple geographical distance was a major barrier: The flight from Beijing to New York took 13 hours and crossed 12 time zones. Without any direct flights from Beijing to Raleigh, North Carolina, where the new headquarters was located, that trip took an additional few hours. Any meeting or information exchange face to face had to be planned weeks in advance to make the trip worthwhile. The thousands of miles separating the company's main locations made information exchange and transfer of best practices very difficult. The regular business hours of New York and Beijing overlap only for three to four hours each day; if the company needed to include European colleagues, having a joint meeting became nearly impossible – or required employees to join meetings at very odd hours.

Language barriers and differences in communication styles also proved challenging. Especially tricky were conference calls, which offered no visuals to help participants interpret the meanings and nuances of others' verbal comments and where "IBM leaders would do most of the talking and the Lenovo leaders would do most of the listening" (Stahl & Köster, 2013). A business transformation team was assigned with the task of exploring the cultural differences between Lenovo and IBM, and efforts were made to ensure that the cultural differences between the two parties were openly highlighted and the employees on both sides received cultural and communication training.

After less than one year, Steve Ward was replaced with William Amelio, a senior executive at Dell. English was introduced as the official work language, and the frequency of meetings between the Chinese and US senior managers was increased. This led to a number of senior Chinese leaders leaving the company, but gradually the remaining managers learned more about each other's cultures. Additional cultural integration activities were initiated in 2006, and a number of managers were sent from the US to China and from China to the US to learn about their respective cultures and practices. Gradually, the two parties became more integrated, Lenovo strengthened its position in the global PC business, and profitability also improved as the global economy continued to grow rapidly in 2005–2007.

However, in the second half of 2008, the global financial crisis broke out and Lenovo's performance deteriorated rapidly. As one PC analyst commented: "[Lenovo] spent all this time integrating their operations .... The competition was out there grabbing opportunities in the market, but they still had internal challenges distracting them" (Balfour, 2009). In 2009, "Lenovo's Godfather" Liu gave a speech to more than 10,000 employees in which he said that the biggest problem with the integration process was that it had led to inefficiency. While US culture emphasized talking, Lenovo's brilliance had been based on doing and this had to be brought back. Approximately 10 percent of the workforce were laid off, including several US managers. CEO Amelio also left in February 2009, being replaced with Yang, while Liu returned as the Chairman of the Board. The number of members of the Executive Committee fell to eight. Even with these cuts, Liu and Yang worked at retaining a fair balance between Chinese and Western executives, reflecting their drive to turn Lenovo into a truly global firm. The work paid off, with Lenovo in 2013 surpassing HP to become the largest PC manufacturer in the world.

As demands for PCs slowed, Lenovo recognized the need to grow outside of its core PC business. As part of its new "PC+" strategy, Lenovo was seeking to enter the market for mobile phones and acquire a major player. In 2014, Lenovo announced that it would take over Motorola Mobility – yet another American icon – from Google for US$2.9 billion. Although Motorola clearly showed signs of losing its historical position (it had been a leading global brand in the late 1990s) – and Lenovo was up against strong competitors like Apple, Samsung, and Xiaomi – Yang saw Motorola as a key platform to expand into the lucrative smartphone sector in developed markets. Just a few weeks earlier, Lenovo had acquired IBM's x86 Server business for $2.3 billion. A marginal business in IBM, it was deemed a core business and future growth engine in Lenovo (Ran et al., 2016).

The acquisition of IBM's x86 Server business put Lenovo ahead of Dell in the Chinese market, giving it 24 percent market share and propelling the company from sixth to third place in the global server market. With the Motorola acquisition, Lenovo became one of the world's largest mobile phone makers. As Lenovo was celebrating the tenth anniversary of the acquisition of IBM's PC business, the company looked back with some pride on what it had accomplished during the past decade. Lenovo had grown from a $3 billion company whose interests were mostly in China to a $46 billion global technology leader. Lenovo's share of the global PC market had risen from 2 percent to 21 percent. The company had gone from selling only PCs to being the world's third biggest tablet maker, and had become a Global Fortune 500 company. During this decade, Lenovo had made eight cross-border acquisitions, making a growth-through-acquisitions strategy Lenovo's mode of becoming a global player (Nylander, 2016).

However, the questions now facing Yang and the management team were similar to those they had confronted ten years earlier when they acquired IBM's PC division: How to integrate Motorola Mobility and IBM's x86 Server business into its existing operations in such a way that the projected synergies would be realized? And how to deal with the myriad of cultural and people challenges that can undermine the success of cross-border acquisitions? Should Lenovo take the same approach to cultural and people integration as the one used over the previous decade? The integration of IBM's PC division proved to be a bumpy ride, but ultimately, was successful. However, each acquisition is unique, and each integration process different. Should Lenovo's management team try a new way to minimize cultural frictions and other people-related problems?

CASE STUDY QUESTIONS

1. Evaluate what you view as the most important success factors in Lenovo's integration of IBM's PC business. How would you characterize Lenovo's approach to cultural integration?
2. What are the most important organizational, cultural, and people issues that the management needs to address to make sure the integration of Motorola Mobile and IBM's x86 Server business is successful?
3. What recommendations would you make to the management team regarding how to approach the post-merger integration? Which of the learnings from the integration of IBM's PC business are likely to apply to the new acquisitions, and in which areas might a new approach be needed?

REFERENCES

Balfour, F. (2009). Lenovo CEO is out; Chinese execs return. *Businessweek,* February 5. https://www.bloomberg.com/news/articles/2009-02-05/lenovo-ceo-is-out-chinese-execs-return#xj4y7vzkg, accessed November 20, 2022.

Nylander, J. (2016, March 20). How Lenovo became the largest PC maker in the world. *Forbes.* https://www.forbes.com/sites/jnylander/2016/03/20/how-lenovo-became-the-largest-pc-maker-in-the-world/?sh=271dd4f5388b, accessed November 20, 2022.

Ran, A., Liu, X., Dong, J., Liu, Y., & Cui, M. (2016). Lenovo: Is the cultural integration template reusable? Ivey publishing. Case W16631-PDF-ENG.

Stahl, G.K., & Koester, K. (2013). *Lenovo-IBM: Bridging cultures, languages, and time zones: Integration challenges.* WU Case Series, 5. WU Vienna University of Economics and Business, Vienna.

Stahl, G.K., & Lengyel, A. (2012). *Lenovo-IBM: Bridging cultures, languages, and time zones: Becoming a global leader.* WU Case Series, 5. WU Vienna University of Economics and Business, Vienna.

Emma Nordbäck and Maggie Boyraz

THE RISE AND FALL OF A
GLOBAL VIRTUAL TEAM

MONIKA LEFT HER OFFICE WITH tears in her eyes. She had just read the resignation letter from one of her closest colleagues, Dimitar, with whom she had shared laughter and tears over the past year. They were among the first to join a brand-new subsidiary of a multinational corporation, GlobeTech in Bulgaria, and they had looked forward to building up this new site together with the rest of the new hires in Bulgaria, as well as together with their team members and leader in Finland. However, their journey at GlobeTech was far from a walk in the park. Dimitar's resignation hit Monika hard as they had become partners in crime. They had fought so many battles in an attempt to improve the ways of working and the quality of their product. It was now exactly ten months since Monika and Dimitar had started working at GlobeTech, and Monika read Dimitar's email again, pondering whether there was a future for her within GlobeTech or not.

AN EXCERPT FROM THE FIVE-PAGE RESIGNATION LETTER BY DIMITAR

From: Dimitar Davidor
To: nikolay.haruzov@globetech.com [country manager and administrative super-
    visor in Bulgaria]
Cc: monika.mladeno@globetech.com [closest colleague]
Subject: Feedback regarding my resignation
Dear Nikolay (CC: Monika),
In this email I'm going to explain the reasons I decided to leave GlobeTech.

I chose to work at GlobeTech because I was excited about the opportunity to be involved in building up a new office in Sofia which would be part of a multinational

DOI: 10.4324/9781003247272-30

company, and to build up a new product. Prior to joining GlobeTech, I had been working in three other global IT companies for eight years in total, and I knew that my knowledge, skills, and abilities would bring value to GlobeTech. I looked forward to working in a globally distributed team with colleagues both in Bulgaria and in Finland. To some degree, my expectations were met, and our team in Bulgaria has become tight over the past year. I call my colleagues over here friends now. But over the past year, the drawbacks have exceeded the advantages, and I got to a point where I was only wasting my time and the company's money.

I expected to work at GlobeTech on a high-quality product, with high-quality code and rigorous Quality Assurance. I was wrong about that. Although we work on a new project, the code is a total mess with thousands of duplicated lines of code, numerous compilation warnings, inconsistent naming of objects, not to mention poor architecture. The worst thing is that we are not allowed to make any improvements to the code. Our ideas are shut down every single time.

I also expected to work with professional people. For instance, a good Software Architect must be able to do research, be a good programmer, have excellent teamwork abilities, know and understand the methodology and practices of the development teams, know and enforce the product's life cycle, and among many other qualities and skills, he/she must be an excellent communicator. Now, when it comes to our project's main architect, Kari, my expectations definitely haven't been met, either.

Kari is mediocre at coding, isn't willing to learn new technologies and coding languages (including any other Java language than Java 8. The developed world uses Java 15 now), and he complains when people use any modern techniques. What kind of software architect isn't willing to adapt to the most widely used standard technology in the industry? And another thing is that the code review process goes through him only, and he is very reluctant to accept any changes. He is never willing to delegate any work, even though he seems stressed all the time. In effect, this makes him the absolute bottleneck in our project and a poor leader. Then there are the soft skills and professionalism of the Finns in our project (particularly the management). The Finns are really bad at dealing with criticism. They never accept accountability for any of the problems in the project. Just a few days ago, we Bulgarians were blamed for poor decisions made by the Finnish management. For me personally, this was too much to handle. All I have ever done is to raise problems and to offer solutions so that we can improve our way of working and the quality of the product. Honestly, no one in Bulgaria is interested in who made a mistake, we just want the problems fixed.

After all this ranting, it's quite obvious that I feel that my potential was unused at GlobeTech. But even worse, I ended up lowering my standards and ambitions just to keep peace in the project. Bottom line, you don't hire experts with vast work experience just to shoot down all their ideas, and tell them how they're young, and how they need to grow old in order to understand how things work, etc. You don't tell people they are equals and then make decisions behind their backs. You don't ask team members to follow processes that you don't follow yourself.

Towards the end of my time at GlobeTech, I felt that my work was ruining my self-esteem. I had no hope in sight, and I felt worthless. My team was blamed for poor performance which was beyond our control. At this point I felt that the whole Bulgarian site was mistreated by the management, and I could no longer stay and watch. I want to work in a workplace where my colleagues and I are thriving.

Overall, I enjoyed working with my colleagues in Bulgaria, as well as with most people in Finland, but it was not enough for me to stay. I wish you all the best!

Sincerely,
Dimitar

MONIKA MLADENO

Monika was a young software developer in her mid-20s, born and raised in Sofia, the capital of Bulgaria. She was ambitious, hard-working, and empathetic, with a purpose in life to develop more sustainable software on planet earth. Monika received a Bachelor of Science in Computer Science, and a Master's from one of the most prestigious universities in Bulgaria. She received A's both in the computer programming major courses (with a focus on both backend and frontend development), and in her minor in user interface design, making her a desirable candidate for any software development position on the global market. Even before she earned her degree, she received a job offer as a trainee at a global outsourcing company AlphaIT. At AlphaIT, however, she had little say in any decisions, and was simply expected to quietly accept her assigned tasks. Being an ambitious woman, knowing her own worth, and being confident in her own expertise, she wanted a career rather than a job where she was micromanaged. She wanted to make an impact and to feel valued. To pass time one day at the office, she began browsing job offerings on LinkedIn to see if something interesting would pop up. Soon enough, Monika was over the moon to find a job advertisement with a global multinational corporation, GlobeTech, looking for a full stack (generalist) software developer, and importantly, as an inhouse employee. The inhouse position promised a rather different outlook than her previous outsourcing experience. The job post listed information such as:

Excerpt from Job Ad

Software Developer
GlobeTech is a world leading multinational corporation within Energy, Process & Utility, looking to expand its operations by building up a new subsidiary in Bulgaria. GlobeTech employs around 400 employees, with

operations in Finland (where it is headquartered), England, and Indonesia, but is now looking to build up a new unit in Bulgaria with the aim to house 100 employees within five years. The Bulgarian subsidiary will include a variety of high-priority business functions, including units within IT, sales, marketing, and support.

Do you want to be a key member of the GlobeTech team? Then come and work with us. Here's your unique chance to be involved in building up a new workplace where people and products can thrive. Through this job ad, we are looking for a software developer, and if you answer yes to the following questions, you might be just the one:

- Are you the whole package gluing together the frontend with the backend?
- Do you value high-quality IT, without losing sight of customer-centricity?
- Do you want to have an impact and make your mark in a sustainable IT world?
- Do you have a curious mindset and want to develop your skills?
- Are you a global thinker?
- Are you ready to take accountability and to bring your expertise to the table?

"Could this be real?" Monika asked herself. Not thinking twice, she found herself writing the job application. Monika, who had grown tired of the authoritarian leadership style at AlphaIT and the feeling of being a square peg in a round hole, was delighted to find a job that offered a different outlook.

THE FINNISH PERSPECTIVE ON THE EXPANSION TO BULGARIA

Sven Virtani, GlobeTech's Director of Software Solutions, based at the head-quarters in Finland, had helped draft the job ad Monika was reading. He had initiated the expansion of the company to Bulgaria together with the top management team, who were all convinced that the expansion would be another success story for the growing company. Why Bulgaria? Due to its excellent education system and salaries paid in Bulgarian levs (making worker salaries three times less in value than if paid in euros), Bulgaria, and particularly the capital city, Sofia, had recently begun to attract attention from companies looking to internationalize their business and operations. The advantage of having a subsidiary in Bulgaria would be that Helsinki (the HQ) and Sofia were in the same time zone. Sven, who had experience from leading globally distributed teams spread across Asia, Europe, and the US, felt confident about the unified time zone of Finland and Bulgaria: "It will eliminate all challenges of communication."

At lunch one day, Kari Pyynno, a senior software architect at HQ, had questioned Sven about his ambitions to create an integrated team in which Bulgarian and Finnish team members had equal responsibility: "Soon they might take our jobs. I mean, is all development going to be moved to Bulgaria?" Kari was not the only one suspicious about the Bulgarian subsidiary, and there was a lot of gossip at HQ within the IT department. Mostly it was the developers who felt threatened and suspicious about the quality of the work performed by the Bulgarians – fearing that they would have to do double the work to account for the poor quality of Bulgarian workers. Nevertheless, the subsidiary was established in Sofia, and Bulgarian workers were recruited.

ONBOARDING IN FINLAND

Among the first employees recruited by GlobeTech in Sofia were four software developers and one designer. The intent was to not only make them the first set of employees in the IT department of the Bulgarian subsidiary, but also to immerse them in the organizational culture of the parent company and to implement this culture in Bulgaria. Finally, the aim was to make the newcomers part of a global virtual team. A small three-person team in Finland was going to welcome these five members as part of their team, and transition from being a local team to a global one. Before even meeting up in Bulgaria, all Bulgarian members traveled to Finland to go through onboarding training at the company headquarters. The onboarding training and site visit were set to last one month, and included a set of training sessions for the new hires. Monika looked forward to the trip to Espoo, where HQ was located, as she had never been to Northern Europe before, and she very much looked forward to getting to know her new colleagues. On the first day in the Finnish office, Monika went to grab coffee at the office coffee machine, where she was approached by one of the Finnish employees who welcomed her to Finland and asked her about the purpose of the trip. She answered:

> Thank you, it feels nice to be here. I think the purpose of us [Bulgarian new hires] being here in Espoo is that we have to take in as much information as possible about how you all work here and soak in the organizational culture. I hope that after this trip we'll be prepared to go back to Bulgaria to work independently. And then there are the social aspects, of course, we have to get to know the people working here at the headquarters so that we'll be able to collaborate as a global team when we continue our collaboration over distance as we go back.

As a response, the employee responded "Well, good luck with socializing with Finns, haha," grabbed his coffee cup, went back to his desk to put his headphones back on, and continued working. Monika didn't reflect on the comment at the time, but three weeks later, when she looked back at the site visit, she realized that it had not turned out the way she had imagined. She began to question the purpose of the visit. Firstly, about her hopes of getting to know the people she was going to work with in Finland, she started to realize that the comment about Finns not socializing might have had some truth to it. Monika, who was used to Bulgarian employees being very keen on socializing both at work as well as after work, left Finland feeling that no one was interested in getting to know her and her Bulgarian colleagues. She already felt like an outsider. When the workday was over, Finnish employees commonly packed up and left the office. Not a single time was there any joint informal get-together after work with the Finns and Bulgarians. And around the kitchen lounge people would speak Finnish to each other, disregarding the Bulgarian visitors. On top of this, Monika's calendar had been filled with one formal onboarding training after another, with requirements to read and pass exams in between, as well as formal meetings where she would remain a silent listener. "How on earth am I going to get to know the people at GlobeTech, or they me?" she asked herself. Making the outlook even worse, the Bulgarians were the only ones participating in training sessions. After one particular training, which was about cross-cultural collaboration, Monika asked herself: "Are we really the only ones who need to be taught about how to collaborate in a global work environment?" On top of this, she felt that the training materials were outdated. Having already been trained in scrum and other agile work methodologies at university, she felt that leadership practices, especially in the IT industry in Bulgaria, were far more egalitarian than indicated by the normative cultural values presented in the training sessions.

In the training sessions at HQ, it was evident that there was a wish from management for the Bulgarian subsidiary to mimic the parent company's values and culture. Backstage, in the top management team, there was, however, talk about transferring only "best practices" to Bulgaria, and not the bad habits that also existed at HQ. In any case, it was the Bulgarians who needed to be trained and who needed to fit in with current practices. Among the company values, accountability and inclusion were listed. She was particularly keen on the company value of "accountability," which she elaborated upon to her colleague Dimitar:

> From a technical point of view [chuckles], it means actually having responsibility over some piece of code. Doesn't matter if it's a small thing or a bigger thing. It matters for a person in general, I think it matters to have accountability over something because then you are a lot more involved in making that thing better. If you are not responsible, then it's very easy to say it's not my problem, I did my job and I don't care to do anything more than that. I think this is one of the key things in software development in general.

Monika and the other newcomers left Finland with mixed feelings — on the one hand, excited about the responsibility they were going to have and to be involved in building up an entire new site for the company, but on the other hand, afraid of not satisfying the expectations of management (as there had been little discussion about the roadmap ahead). There had, for instance, been no talk about the performance expectations of the Bulgarians for the upcoming months. Monika was, however, confident that she would be a quick learner ready to deliver high-quality software as soon as within the first month. Finally, it seemed like she would be able to have a position in which she would be able to make an impact and feel valued.

BEGINNING WORK AS A GLOBAL VIRTUAL TEAM

The newly established global virtual team included the five Bulgarian hires, who had been recruited into software developer roles and one designer role, as well as three Finnish members, including the team leader Matti, software architect Kari, and a tester named Anna. At the Bulgarian site, a country manager, Nikolay, had also been recruited, who would oversee the operations in Bulgaria and be the administrative supervisor of the Bulgarian workers. The Bulgarians didn't really see a need for direct supervision by the country manager in their daily work, but appreciated that they had someone who would have their back at the Bulgarian site, given that their team leader and the executive leadership team were all located in Finland. The project they were going to work on was a new product which was going to be launched in the market in one year. Since it was a new product, it had little legacy code (i.e., old existing code base), which enabled the programming work to be more open for modern solutions. Monika was excited about being able to apply her recently acquired programming skills, and already had multiple ideas on how to improve the software and its prospects on the market four weeks into her working time at GlobeTech.

First Global Meeting

When the Bulgarians entered their new office for the first time, a month after being hired, they felt like superstars as they started their very first real work tasks at height-adjustable standing desks and chairs with brand new computers in their hands. They quickly divided the desks in their open office so that everyone would have a desk they could decorate and call their own. Soon after, they had a meeting with the global virtual team where they decided that they would have short daily status meetings every morning at 10 a.m., in addition to a longer weekly meeting where the focus would be on planning upcoming tasks as well as evaluating past performance. In the first global meeting, they discussed priorities and the upcoming tasks for the next month. Everyone left the meeting motivated and excited about the work that lay ahead. There were no bigger responsibilities assigned to the Bulgarians, but they knew that they needed some time to get into their tasks and get to know the work practices and the product. It was, after all, a new industry for several of the software developers, and they knew that the domain knowledge mostly resided within Finland.

First Demo Meeting

A month later, the Bulgarians were sitting in a meeting room at 10 a.m., about to participate in their first demo meeting. Another team from Finland was going to present their progress on their product, and it was a habit that everyone from the IT department participated in the demo sessions to grow awareness of each other's work and to help improve it.

Minutes passed and the time approached 10:10 a.m. "Where is everyone?" the Bulgarians wondered. They knew that they had the correct time as there was a formal meeting invitation in their calendar, and both Finland and Bulgaria shared the same time zone. "Do meetings follow academic quarters in Finnish companies? Perhaps the meeting will start at 10:15?" Around 10:20, they knew that something was off. A minute later, the connection was suddenly opened from Finland's side, and a Finnish employee commented: "I am so, so sorry, we forgot to open the connection." Monika politely responded: "That's okay, I guess we all have to get used to the fact that we are global now." The Bulgarians followed the final ten minutes of the demo, but didn't get a chance to comment or ask questions as they were afraid of asking something that they should have known if they had participated in the demo meeting from the start. The atmosphere in the meeting room in Bulgaria was heated after the call, with strong words being used. Monika, trying to be the reasonable one, calmed her colleagues down by reassuring them that the Finns were going to adapt, they just needed to move outside their local bubble. The Bulgarians went back to work, but with growing irritation and suspicion.

This was, in fact, not the only incident where they felt excluded. They had witnessed other meetings in which the Finns led the discussions and Bulgarians felt left out. They had witnessed decisions being made behind their backs. Such decisions commonly were revealed in the daily status meetings, where everyone reported their progress on their current tasks – with the tasks completed by Kari commonly being completely different from the tasks previously agreed upon together. Overall, his leadership style revealed that he was an autocratic leader who did not take the opinions of the Bulgarian team members or the collective global team into consideration. Monika was puzzled since Finland was supposed to be highly egalitarian, according to the lessons learned about national culture during the new hire orientation (see Exhibit 1 for a comparison of Finland and Bulgaria on some key cross-cultural differences).

The Planning and Review Meeting

Two months after launching the team, the Bulgarians collectively made a decision to bring up the issues that were bothering them in the next planning and review meeting. In planning and review meetings, the last two weeks of a team's work was usually reviewed, and there was an opportunity for the team members to express the things that had gone well in the past two weeks and things that needed improvement, as well as to plan which tasks were to be performed in the

Geert Hofstede

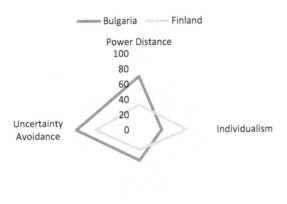

Exhibit 1 Comparison of Finland and Bulgaria on key cross-cultural dimensions, according to Geert Hofstede.

Source: Own elaboration based on Geert Hofstede, https://www.hofstede-insights.com/country-comparison/bulgaria/.

following two weeks. The following is an excerpt from a dialogue between the team leader Matti (based in Finland) and the administrative supervisor Nikolay (in Bulgaria) during the meeting:

Matti: In today's meeting, we need to discuss what tasks have been completed in the past two weeks and what tasks from the queue have not been done. We will also take turns in discussing what could be improved in terms of process.

Nikolay: I would like to start by saying that we here in Bulgaria have realized that our way of working is fundamentally different from the way that some other people from Espoo are used to working. We think some people are very conservative, they are very protective of the code. We are writing code. Some are, like, "Let's not change the code not to introduce issues," you know? You can't protect the code too much because it doesn't evolve. It has to evolve to improve, and you don't let us.

Matti: Wait, what do you mean?

Nikolay: Yes, it became clear that our hands are tied and we cannot contribute much to improve the code, and would like to be provided with more freedom to do so. We would like to participate more in decision making. Some of us here in Bulgaria like clear rules and written procedures, but others, like Monika here, would prefer more freedom.

Matti: This can't be right, we have been very happy with what you've been producing in Bulgaria, and we are very pleased with how you value collaboration.

Nikolay: Well it depends on how you define collaboration. See, I think this is where we diverge across locations. When we say "collaborate," we work and make decisions as a team. My workers feel undervalued and would like to contribute more. The tasks you've given us are menial, and we have much more knowledge and would want to use our time more effectively. Currently, much time is also wasted because of the messiness of the code.

Matti: Thank you for bringing this up. Well, since this is news to me, let me talk to Kari after the meeting and get back to you.

Reflections after the Planning Meeting

After the meeting, Monika and her colleagues Ivan and Dimitar opened up about their feelings:

Ivan: Well, things are not working by the book in Finland. I feel that the process that they follow and the values they show with their actions are not what we learned at the new hire orientation.

Monika: I agree. I guess we can't say it's a bad thing yet, though. We are still observing and trying to make sense of it all, to understand what the positives and the downsides are.

Dimitar: Yeah, but there is this other thing bugging me as well. We were supposed to be able to influence and take ownership. I don't really see that happening in any near future. How could we, if we are not included?

Ivan: Exactly. I don't like being left in the dark. I have a feeling that it may be on purpose, that they're withholding something from us. I don't think Kari is going to admit to Matti that his code is anything else than perfect. And why the heck couldn't this discussion have taken place with all of us online? I may be overreacting, but yeah, the communication from the Finns is not transparent, if you can even say that they are communicating. I feel that Anna [a tester based in Finland] is the only one who gets us and would want to see us more included. But she avoids conflicts.

Dimitar: I suppose they [Finns] don't want to lose power. I get the impression that they expect me to work really slowly, just to do the tasks that are assigned to me, but nothing more. It's quite different from all the beautiful and ambitious company values conveyed in the training we had in Finland. In reality, we are basically left with no responsibility since we cannot make any decisions as a team on our own.

Monika: I agree, but let's try to remain positive and continue to learn so that we can base our opinions on more knowledge, okay? I am pretty sure we'll get more responsibility soon.

Dimitar: Whatever. [Dimitar threw up his hands and abruptly left the room.]

Meanwhile, in Finland, the architect Kari raised his concerns to their team leader Matti:

Kari: The Bulgarian team keeps complaining about lack of voice and inclusion. This is driving me nuts. How are we supposed to lead them if they are not following our lead?

Matti: Yeah, right. But I do get a sense that they feel that there is not enough collaboration, particularly from our side. Kari, help me understand this. I am not that involved in your day-to-day tasks, so it's hard for me to see where the issues are. And what was the messiness of the code and poor quality assurance that they kept bringing up in the meeting?

Kari: The Bulgarian team is too strict with the way they follow the development process. They don't see the bigger picture. They concentrate too narrowly on the issues in our processes and code, forgetting that we have a paying customer to deliver to. Besides, they are really good at complaining over there. It's driving me crazy having to explain to them all the time how things work over here. There is nothing wrong with the code, there are just differences in preferences, and they just want to reach group consensus on everything.

Matti: Okay, well, keep up the good work and I'll be in touch with you later in the week with new business requirements.

As months passed, incidents showing that the Finns were not willing to yield power to the Bulgarians continued. While the Bulgarians grew tired of this lack of inclusion, the Finns grew frustrated with the work style of the Bulgarians, who would often not get to the office before 10 a.m. For instance, Kari was expecting a prompt response to an instant message he sent to Dimitar first thing on Monday morning at 8 a.m., but he received a response at 10:13 a.m. Rather than getting to know Dimitar's (and the other Bulgarians') working habits, Kari began complaining to his team leader Matti about the Bulgarians' laziness and lack of responsiveness. These frustrations were never openly discussed, even though it was known that Bulgarians spent much longer hours in the Sofia office working late, but also socializing and going out to lunch collectively.

The Last Straw

The last straw for both Dimitar and Monika was when at the end of the year the team had their annual evaluations. This was also when Dimitar sent his resignation letter, leaving Monika broken and devastated. On top of all the hurdles of the past year, the feedback she and her team got in the yearly evaluation meeting where the team met with the management left her puzzled. In the feedback session, the Bulgarian team got to hear about their poor performance from the top management team in Finland – who listed numerous failed sales attempts and negative feedback from customers. This feedback was a total surprise to the Bulgarian team members, who until now had not seen any data from user research, nor had they been involved in a single discussion where user requirements were specified. Despite numerous attempts to find out about the results from user studies, they never saw any of this data. Instead, the Finnish management always provided reasons such as "We want you to focus on what you do best, programming," or "We want to protect your time." Therefore, the Bulgarian team members had implemented exactly the features they were told to implement. At this stage, being blamed for poor performance in terms of failed sales and poor customer satisfaction, the Bulgarians had had enough. The Bulgarian members pondered how on earth they could be blamed for actions they had no control over. "How could we have ensured that we implemented code which met user requirements and needs, when we never had any say in which features were prioritized and implemented?" Instead of holding themselves accountable for poor strategic planning, poor design choices, and communication breakdowns, the Finnish top management team blamed the Bulgarian workers for their own flaws. Monika talked about this experience with her administrative supervisor Nikolay after the meeting:

Monika: As you know, our project only released one copy for the year, and we had a target of nine or ten. And stakeholders asked why, of course, and management said because the developers weren't working fast enough, when it was actually because the customers wanted features that hadn't been implemented because the management didn't prioritize those features. When we asked about them, and we asked what the customers want, and why we aren't implementing this and this, they just said no, this is what we want, you just shut up and do it. They didn't say it like that, but that was the message. And then, when it turned out that the features weren't prioritized correctly and the requirements were not correctly specified to the Bulgarian team members, Sven said, "yeah, you have to work more, and you have to do a better job."

Nikolay: I know. I am as puzzled as you are. I see how hard you are all working every day at the office. I don't like this blaming culture either, and quite frankly, the Finns should really look at themselves in the mirror. They haven't even received training on how to collaborate on a global team. We did.

Monika: Exactly!

Nikolay: I'm sorry that I could not have your back more. I hope you understand that I tried to defend you, without burning totally the bridge to headquarters?

Monika knew that Nikolay only meant well, but she also had come to understand that he had little power to influence anything beyond things like approval of her summer vacation time. She had come to understand that no one really had her back.

To Stay or Not to Stay?

A few days later, Sven (GlobeTech's Director of Software Solutions) met with Monika online and encouraged her to stay with the company and to become the process-focused leader of the global virtual team. If she accepted this offer, she would be promoted (and receive a higher salary) and would be responsible for implementing a team intervention to "fix the team in Bulgaria." After the meeting with Sven, Monika was wondering what to do. Would this additional responsibility be a suicide mission, or a chance for her to flip the coin and improve things for the global teams at GlobeTech?

ANALYSIS

Power Distance

This dimension deals with the fact that all individuals in societies are not equal – it expresses the attitude of the culture towards these inequalities among us.

Finland scores low on this dimension (a score of 33), which means that the following characterizes the Finnish style: being independent, hierarchy is for convenience only, employees have equal rights, management facilitates and empowers. Power is decentralized, and managers count on the experience of their team members. Employees expect to be consulted. Control is disliked, and attitudes towards managers are informal and on a first name basis. Communication is direct and participative.

Bulgaria scores high on this dimension (a score of 70), which means that people accept a hierarchical order in which everybody has a place. Hierarchy in an organization is seen as reflecting inherent inequalities, decisions are centralized, and subordinates expect to be told what to do. Consequently, an autocratic leadership style is likely to be accepted.

Masculinity

A high score (Masculine) on this dimension indicates that the society will be driven by competition, achievement, and success, with success being defined by the winner or an expert – a value system that starts in school and continues throughout organizational life.

Finland scores 26 on this dimension, and is thus considered a Feminine society. In Feminine countries, the focus is on "working in order to live," managers strive for consensus, people value equality, solidarity, and quality in their working lives. Conflicts are resolved by compromise and negotiation.

Bulgaria scores 40 on this dimension, and is thus considered a relatively Feminine society, but it is more masculine in comparison with Finland, therefore competition, achievement and success may be relatively more valued.

Uncertainty Avoidance

The dimension of Uncertainty Avoidance has to do with the way a society deals with the fact that the future can never be known: should we try to control the future, or just let it happen?

Finland scores 59 on this dimension, and thus has a high preference for avoiding uncertainty. Countries exhibiting high Uncertainty Avoidance maintain rigid codes of belief and behavior and are intolerant of unorthodox behavior and ideas. In these cultures, there is an emotional need for rules (even if the rules never seem to work).

Bulgaria scores 85 on this dimension, and thus has a very high preference for avoiding uncertainty. Bulgarian workers will feel an even higher need for clear roles, rules, and policies than Finnish workers.

Individualism

This dimension has to do with whether people's self-image is defined in terms of "I" or "We." In Individualist societies, people are supposed to look after themselves and their direct family only. In Collectivist societies, people belong to "in groups" that take care of them in exchange for loyalty.

Finland, with a score of 63, is an Individualist society. This means there is a high preference for a loosely knit social framework in which individual achievement and success are valued. In Individualist societies, leadership should focus on management of individuals.

Bulgaria, with a score of 30, is considered a Collectivistic society. This is manifested in a close, long-term commitment to the member "group." This group could be an immediate family, extended family, or extended relationships. Leadership must involve managing groups and group member expectations.

BIBLIOGRAPHY

Hofstede, G. (2001). *Culture's consequences: Comparing values, behaviors, institutions, and organizations across nations* (2nd ed.). Thousand Oaks, CA: SAGE Publications.
Hofstede, G., Hofstede, G. J., & Minkov, M. (2005). *Cultures and organizations: Software of the mind* (Vol. 2). New York: McGraw-Hill.
Hofstede Insights. (2022). Retrieved from https://www.hofstede-insights.com/country-comparison/bulgaria/.

PART V

Responsible Leadership in a Global and Cross-cultural Context

DOI: 10.4324/9781003247272-31

Philip H. Mirvis

DEVELOPING GLOBALLY RESPONSIBLE LEADERS[*]

INTRODUCTION

THIRTY YEARS AGO, BUSINESS EXECUTIVES were not expected to concern themselves with community welfare, the natural environment, the heightened aspirations of employees, and human rights in global supply chains, among numerous other issues. These matters were delegated to staff functions and specialists—or ignored. No more.

Today, executives face socially conscious investors, customers, employees, and a public that expect businesses to take a larger and more responsible role in society. Accordingly, they need to understand and calibrate social and environmental issues that affect their firms and devise strategies that respond to challenges as varied as climate change, a COVID-19 pandemic, the rich–poor gap, and increased workforce diversity. They must also be prepared to deal with activist groups, the threat of protest, calls for greater transparency, and the dramatic increase in exposure provided by the internet and social media.

Amid all these changes, business leaders still have to do what they have always had to do: produce growth, deliver results, develop relationships with people, and innovate to meet marketplace needs and beat competitors. What does it take for leaders to be successful in the business world today? It requires new forms of *individual* and *collective learning*.

LEADING RESPONSIBLY

In nearly every survey and study, leadership stands out as the number one factor driving responsible behavior in companies (Conference Board, 2016; PWC,

* This is a reproduced version from a chapter published in Mendenhall, M.E., Žilinskaitė, M., Stahl, G.K., & Clapp-Smith, R. (2020). *Responsible Global Leadership: Dilemmas, Paradoxes, and Opportunities*. New York: Routledge.

DOI: 10.4324/9781003247272-32

2016). This starts with the CEO, of course, but includes managers at every level and leaders of work councils. In popular imagination, the high-powered, profit-driven, take-charge model of leadership is the prototype for big business, particularly in the US, but in favor by degrees around the world (Khurana, 2002). Yet the benefits of that model are increasingly suspect.

In a study of over 500 CEOs operating across 17 countries, for instance, researchers compared CEOs who gave primacy to economic factors (profits, cost control, and market share) in their decision-making versus those who stressed stakeholder values (customers, employee relations, environmental concerns, and communities). They found that economic leaders were seen as authoritarian by their direct reports, whereas CEOs with a stakeholder orientation were viewed as more visionary. Stakeholder CEOs were also more likely to lead firms that performed better financially, and their followers were more apt to show extra effort and make sacrifices for the sake of the firm (Waldman, Seigel, & Javidan, 2006).

GLOBAL OPERATING ENVIRONMENT

Calls for responsible leadership are relevant for leaders in business, government, and civil society, and in organizations small and large. But the message takes on added significance in multinational corporations (MNCs), which have achieved historic scale and influence in the 21st century. As one indicator, a scan of the world's 100 largest economic "entities" includes 69 corporations along with 31 countries! With their reach, ability to innovate and problem-solve, knowledge of brand management and customers, and vast resources, MNCs are power players that reach across national boundaries and shape the global operating environment.

The benefits of globalization to business—open markets, global labor supply, lower communication and transportation costs, and decreased regulations—have offered the world rising standards of living, given consumers lower prices and a greater variety of goods and services, and provided access to technology to ease their life and work burdens. However, these benefits have not come without well-documented costs (WBCSD, 2006; Waddock & McIntosh, 2011; Korten, 2015).

In recent decades, for instance, the gap between the average per capita GDP in the 20 richest and poorest countries has doubled, and today, half of the world's population lives on less than US$5.50 per day. More than 2 billion people lack adequate sanitation facilities, and more than 1 billion lack access to clean water. On the environmental side, besides global warming, one in four mammal species is in serious decline, fish stocks are eroding, the world's wetlands and forest cover are shrinking markedly, and desertification puts some 135 million people worldwide at risk of being driven from their lands.

Business leaders operate in a complex ecosystem of diverse expectations where critical social and environmental issues can affect the entire increasingly interconnected planet. Amid all of this, boundaries between government, business, and civil society are shifting dramatically across the globe, with heightened expectations that MNCs should "step up" and contribute their talents and treasure to the sustainability of society (Googins, Mirvis, & Rochlin, 2007). Responsible leadership is required not only for business to meet its obligations in this new social contract, but also to retain its license to operate and to grow (Schwab, 2015).

Thus, leading companies today are greening their operations, applying "shared value" principles to global supply chains and business lines, and striving for more robust social impact through their corporate social responsibility (CSR) programs and employee volunteering. These activities require executives to stretch beyond their current frames of reference to assimilate what is happening in the world and to reach out in creative ways to communities and customers who have unmet needs.

Meanwhile, a new frontier calls for responsible leadership in complex webs of converging interests, multilateral partnerships, and multinational social movements concerned with collective prosperity, well-being, and the future of the planet (Maak & Pless, 2008). Competing companies are cooperating to tackle water shortages, extend microcredit, set green standards, and even promote peace in troubled lands. Governments, businesses, and nongovernmental organizations (NGOs) are, in different configurations, joining forces to reduce corruption, encourage healthier eating habits, and address climate change. These forums provide a vehicle for leaders to act collectively—and on the global stage.

RESPONSIBLE LEADERSHIP: SCOPE AND COMPETENCIES

A variety of scholars, thought leaders, and consortia of academics and practitioners have sought to define responsible leadership in contemporary organizations (GRLI, 2006; Maak & Pless, 2006; Stahl, 2016; Miska & Mendenhall, 2018). Many connect it to CSR and sustainability by stressing that responsible leaders create long-term economic value and protect the planet and its peoples. The Globally Responsible Leadership Initiative (GRLI, 2008), involving representatives of business schools, learning institutions, and companies, declares responsible leadership to be "the art of motivating, communicating, empowering, and convincing people to engage with a new vision of sustainable development and the necessary change that this implies" (p. 4).

To frame this in the global operating environment, responsible leadership encompasses the following (Voegtlin, Patzer, & Scherer, 2012):

1. The work of the individual leader.
2. Leadership exercised throughout a corporation.
3. Responsible business practiced in the larger ecosystem of investors, consumers, competitors, regulators, and other interests.

This multilevel paradigm threads responsibility from individual to organization-wide to collective multiparty leadership—or, in a more colloquial expression, "from Me to We to all of Us" (Mirvis, Googins, DeJongh, Quinn, & van Velsor, 2010).

The foregoing has stimulated considerable theorizing and research on what is different about the doings of responsible leaders. Waldman and Galvin (2008), for example, emphasize that responsible leaders operate via moral principles, values, and respect; engage a full range of stakeholders; think globally while acting locally; and enable their enterprise to do good while doing well commercially. Maak and Pless (2016) stress the *relational* aspects of responsible leadership, and advise leaders to build, cultivate, and sustain "trustful relationships" among diverse stakeholders and create an "inclusive integrity culture." And Maak, Pless, and Voegtlin (2016), in turn, find that responsible leaders must reconcile corporate interests with the claims of other parties and operate under accords of co-responsibility and co-accountability.

Given the kinds of challenges that executives face in the globalized world of work, four "meta-competencies" have been identified for responsible leadership (Mirvis, Thompson, & Marquis, 2010):

1. Self-leadership: The need for heightened self-awareness and emotional intelligence already informs the developmental agenda of executives in leading companies. But in addition to these intra-personal skills, global leaders also need cognitive complexity and emotional resilience to adapt to new and unfamiliar situations and to deal with dilemmas encountered in meeting the interests of multiple stakeholders.
2. Leading others: As top-down, hierarchical management systems reinforced by centralized control are being replaced by more bottom-up, globally distributed management systems, leaders need to expand their interpersonal, group, and social integration skills. Learning how to operate in and exert authority in fluid, loosely structured, often leaderless task groupings is a crucial part of the leader's global work. So is applying cultural intelligence—the capacity to get "inside" how different people think and feel and to understand how societal cultures are built on different foundations of philosophy, faith, and history.
3. Leading an organization: Within the firm, traditional divisions by hierarchy and function are giving way to multilevel and cross-functional forms of collaboration that span countries and cultures. This calls for leaders who can think strategically, adopt multiple perspectives, and promote continuous, adaptive change. Leading with vision and leading with purpose are requisites, but in a global context, doing so by listening, eliciting, and catalyzing may be more effective than by speaking, persuading, and directing.
4. Leading in society: Meanwhile, across firms, collaboration encompasses the extended enterprise—from supply chain to customers—and includes multi-sector partnerships and multi-business alliances. Gaining experience in and a comfort level with navigating across so many boundaries is integral to the development of responsible executives. Learning how to best form, align, and leverage multiparty structures is also becoming a requisite for leaders in global companies today.

Learning to Lead

Not surprisingly, there is a considerable gap between these requisite competencies and current methods for training business leaders. There is, for example, rising angst about the relevance of management research and teaching, particularly in the US, but also about the spread of the "American" model to business schools around the world (Pfeffer & Fong, 2004; Bennis & O'Toole, 2005; Khurana, 2010). Among the central concerns are that leading business schools have defined themselves as theory- and research-based institutions where academic theorizing about business and its leadership has become more distant from practice, research rigor has been emphasized over its relevance, and university-based academics themselves spend little time interacting with and learning from practitioners and companies.

This rap on management scholarship extends as well into the business school classroom. In many instances, the typical American MBA class focuses on "analytics" rather than discovery and diagnosis, considers situations from a functional rather than integrative management perspective, and gives scant attention to the development of interpersonal and leadership skills. As Leavitt (1989) aptly put it, MBA education has been "distorting those subjected to it into critters with lopsided brains, icy hearts, and shrunken souls."

Accordingly, rather than send their current and future leaders to university executive and MBA programs, many firms now provide in-house leadership development. A first step was to emulate the academic model and construct corporate universities. And although this offered a practical and organizationally relevant curriculum for general and functional leaders in a firm, it did not typically engage them in the complex issues facing business or provide them any hands-on practice in addressing them. A next step was to introduce project-based learning into the corporate curriculum (Tichy, Brimm, Charan, & Takeuchi, 1992) such that participants could tackle real-time business problems to both develop themselves as leaders and deliver business results for the firm. Senior business leaders often serve as faculty, role models, and mentors for participants in programs.

But to operate responsibility today, firms must experiment with new business models, develop new ways of making and marketing goods and services, connect more deeply to society, and forge and manage cross-sector partnerships. This calls for a shift in mindset and requires new ways of leading and operating the business. Leaders are needed who can address complex socio-commercial problems with fresh perspectives and compassion, generate on-the-ground insight, and navigate sociopolitical dynamics in effecting change. Conventional project-based learning programs in companies seldom address these topics experientially, nor do they confront participants with stakeholders whose interests and needs don't necessarily align with the strategies and offerings of the firm. Thus, the latest step in leadership development in leading companies has been to expose current and future leaders to real-world business problems in situ, where issues of responsible leadership and sustainable development are front and center.

FOUR "REAL-WORLD" LEARNING PLATFORMS TO DEVELOP RESPONSIBLE LEADERS

The author has, for the past two decades, worked with leadership educators and MNCs to design and assess learning platforms to develop responsible leaders

(Mirvis, 2009; Mirvis, Hurley, & MacArthur, 2014; Mirvis & Googins, 2018). Four distinct models are notable (see Figure 1):

1. Real-world sustainability projects engage participants in innovation teams focused on delivering business results while addressing relevant (environmental, social, and governance, or ESG) challenges.
2. Learning journeys take executives to see firsthand the contours of economies, societies, and natural environments around the world to raise consciousness about and motivate action toward sustainable development.
3. Pro bono service learning has employees team up in global service assignments where they cocreate innovations with an NGO, social enterprise, small business, or government agency to address social problems in situ.
4. Partnering with social entrepreneurs has company leaders function like social venture capitalists and run workshops and labs for social entrepreneurs and enterprises, and provide mentoring, business guidance, and technical assistance. Sometimes, these engagements develop into partnerships between firms and social enterprises.

Table 1 summarizes these leadership development platforms and their rationales and relevance for employee and company learning.

Learning via Sustainability Projects

Can the corporate classroom be transformed into a laboratory for learning about how to lead for sustainable development? Project-based learning is a requisite, but it must also immerse participants in the sociopolitical context of corporate affairs and confront them with myriad corporate stakeholders. Charoen Pokphand Group, a Thai conglomerate, uses its CP Leadership Institute (CPLI) to foster this kind of experiential learning to promote sustainable development.

CPLI runs several multi-month programs where new, mid-, and upper-level leaders work in teams to produce solutions and innovations relevant to CP's various business units. These project-based learning programs have CP managers,

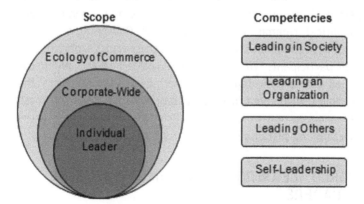

Figure 1 Responsible leadership

Table 1 Four "real-world" learning platforms to develop responsible leaders

	Real-world Sustainability Projects	Learning Journeys	Pro Bono Problem-solving	Partnering with Social Entrepreneurs
Description	Global leadership program engages leaders in real-time sustainability projects.	Leaders see at first hand economies and societies, customers and communities.	Leaders provide service to communities, NGOs, government agencies, and SMEs.	Leaders provide mentoring and innovation support for social entrepreneurs and enterprises.
Rationales	Projects expose leaders to relevant socioeconomic and environmental challenges to factor into business. Coursework on responsible leadership—leading self, others, responsible business.	Collective exposure to global environment. Relevant socioeconomic and environmental issues in market development. Continuous reflection on personal and organizational implications.	Intensive exposure to operating in emerging markets. Manage socioeconomic and environmental issues with client organization. Extensive personal reflection.	Intensive exposure to startup and scaling of social ventures. Co-creation of new ideas with social entrepreneurs. Potential evolution into a sustainable partnership.
Exemplar	Charoen Pokphand: Leaders engage in six-month sustainability projects (many outside home region) to develop global mindset and confront real-time ESG issues and dilemmas.	Unilever Journeys: Executives explore region to understand peoples/societies and come together as leadership community.	IBM Corporate Service Corps: Pro bono teams work with "clients" in emerging markets. Innovative solutions to problems. Strong focus on employees' development in global context.	SAP Social Innovation Labs: For social entrepreneurs to develop and scale innovations. Expert mentoring and tools from employees. Also, leaders host "bootcamp" for social entrepreneurs around the world.
Employee Learning	Multilevel learning means self-leading and co-leading with others; how to deliver socially beneficial results beyond border.	Participants open eyes to regional ESG issues. Raising consciousness about self and responsible global development.	Participants learn to co-create with stakeholders and gain global knowledge and hands-on skills in emerging markets. Cultural intelligence and expand vision on role of business in society.	Employees learn to cocreate and develop entrepreneurship skills. Also, cultural intelligence. Partnership skills develop with sustained relationships.
Company Learning	Projects expose ESG issues, and learnings spread via executive reviews and knowledge management platform.	Journeys expose ESG issues, and learnings translate into new business practices/processes.	High Mutual Knowledge Exchange: Companies learn about society; client community learns modern methods/technology.	High Mutual Knowledge Exchange: Companies learn about social innovation; enterprise learns modern methods/technology.

from different businesses and geographies, directly engage market demands and opportunities, and develop new business processes and products. In so doing, they must address questions of sustainability and strive to minimize harms and maximize benefits to society and the planet. What are the key design features?

SOCIALLY CONSCIOUS LEADERSHIP

To build leadership capability, CPLI incorporates experiential and reflective exercises into its learning programs, and features constant dialogue among participants with the group's senior leaders. Leadership development inputs focus on the following:

- Self-leadership, including 360-degree feedback from bosses, peers, and employees, and coaching from team members and CPLI specialists, enables future leaders to "look into the mirror" and explore strengths and weaknesses, attitudes, and values. The idea here is that self-reflection and personal development are essential to becoming a more socially conscious leader.
- Co-leading has leaders develop not only their smarts (IQ), but also their emotional intelligence (EQ) via interactive learning, collective attention to team dynamics, and candid team discussions of what is going well and what needs improving. Sessions featuring tai chi, yoga, and meditation also tune spiritual development.
- Leading in service to society has teams raise funds for and undertake community service for those in need. This can take them to children's schools, homes for the aged, healthcare centers, and the like, where they connect with and help out the neediest in society. This raises their consciousness about CP's role in society and their own understandings of social needs.

DESIGN THINKING FOR SUSTAINABILITY

Project teams are trained in *design thinking* and *customer-centric innovation*. Teams may access "big data" to identify different consumer segments and community concerns, and meet face to face with consumers to understand their lifestyles and aspirations. They also engage other stakeholders—government officials, civil society leaders, academics, and so on—to see the big picture and determine what actions are needed to enlist their support for new ideas.

Then they translate these inputs into insights, develop product prototypes and run pilot tests, and share their findings with the group's chairperson and vice-chairperson, CEOs, and other executives who challenge their thinking and refine their approach.

FACTORING IN ESG: MINIMIZE HARMS, MAXIMIZE BENEFITS

Projects teams are challenged to increase revenue or reduce costs in their projects. How does sustainability factor in? Teams look carefully at the potential environmental, social, and governance impact of their projects. What are the issues we face? Are there any risks to the company, or people, or the planet? Are there opportunities to create benefits? These analyses inform action plans.

Attention is also given to ESG issues in developing prototypes and providing "proof of concept" for teams' new ideas. CPLI's Business Leader Program has hosted several projects where current and future CP leaders have developed new products, processes, and programs aiming toward sustainable development in every CP business:

- Non-GMO soybeans introduced into India.
- Reduced energy and waste in fertilizer distribution systems in Southeast Asia.
- Nutritious ready-to-eat meals designed for the aged in Thailand.
- Environmentally friendly diapers made from plants in China.
- New channels to bring traditional Thai crafts and foods to market.
- Healthy foods and snacks for convenience stores in Thailand and China.
- Pesticide-free vegetables in Southeast Asia.
- Traceability for seeds and agriculture products.
- Biodegradable packaging in several product lines.
- Reduced costs/improved service for telecom customers—university students, and farmers.
- Fortified eggs (omega 3, 6, 9; vitamin E; antioxidants).

LEARNING FROM REAL-WORLD PROJECTS

How do CP trainees learn about responsible leadership via their real-world sustainability projects? In their coursework, CP leaders are exposed to a variety of tools, exercises, and experiences geared to enhancing their intellectual, emotional, and spiritual development. The projects broaden perspectives about the world around CP and also facilitate personal development. An encounter with a complex socio-commercial business problem, for example, can stretch interpersonal consciousness when executives have to personally interact with and explain themselves to people uninformed about or even critical of their business and its purposes. It can also impinge on their personal beliefs and conscience and give them a better sense of and feel for working with diverse stakeholders. Multi-stakeholder consciousness is, according to Schein (1966), integral to the moral development of executives.

In addition, CP learners have many in-depth discussions with CP's top managers about the company's "three-benefit" philosophy of meeting the needs of people, the company, and countries where CP does business. They also have experiences that challenge them to reconcile the three benefits with attendant costs. For instance, a team proposing new "safe produce" standards was taken to task on social media for threatening the livelihoods of Bangkok's street food vendors, whose fare wouldn't pass the safety criteria. In another instance, a proposal to provide microcredit to rural students ran afoul of government regulations on lending arrangements. Such real-world experiences bring to life the complexity of leading responsibly.

Leadership Journeys

Business leaders are being urged to apply their business acumen to fast-paced changes in the world around them, and, in particular, to come to grips with the social, moral, and environmental impact of their organizations. This means, among other things, that they operate as "global citizens" and develop a point of view about the role of business in society (Waddock, 2002). On these counts, exposure to a broader array of social and environmental stimuli and situations can stretch and deepen a leader's world view. Mintzberg and Gosling (2002) refer to this as "educating managers beyond borders."

The author had an opportunity to educate managers beyond borders with Unilever Asia. A starting point was to connect senior leaders of 17 national companies in the Asia Pacific region—which had previously operated independently—and to include the next layers of country marketers, supply chain managers, and corporate staff in setting strategy and reviewing performance for the whole of the regional business. In turn, a cross-national forum was created to expose the next generation of leaders to the ideas of Western thinkers like Maslow, Fromm, and Frankl and to have them share the tenets of Buddhism and Eastern philosophy. These young leaders also engaged in community service learning projects. Behind this was a desire to build the capacity of the entire Asian leadership body to think, feel, and work together—that is, to operate as a community of leaders (Mirvis & Gunning, 2006).

SEEING THE WORLD WITH FRESH EYES

Responsible leadership development came in when the Asian leaders created deeper bonds among themselves and with communities throughout Asia via a series of annual learning journeys. They traveled to locales of historical and cultural relevance; hiked through mountains and deserts; met with school children, Indigenous peoples, everyday consumers, and the poor; learned from leaders in business, government, and community organizations; and talked deeply with one another about their personal and business lives.

At their initial meeting in Sarawak (once part of Borneo), Unilever's Asian leaders gathered to experience firsthand the terrible costs incurred in the clear-cutting of tropical rainforests. They first learned about the state of the natural environment in Asia from a talk by a director of a global natural resources group. Then, to get closer to the scene and symbolically lend a hand, the executives cleaned a nearby beach of industrial flotsam and tourist trash. A trip upriver in hollowed-out wooden canoes took them to the village of the Penan. There they met villagers and hunters, in their tribal dress and loincloths; talked through translators to the chief, spiritual healer, and tribespeople; and took a long walk with them through their clear-cut forests.

Periodic group reflections along the way opened up hearts and led to an earnest discussion of the benefits and costs of economic growth in Asia. This in turn led to calls to incorporate sustainability into strategic plans. One leader commented:

> The beauty of the nature and the majesty of the place helped deepen our insights about our roles as leaders and individuals on this earth. To be in the jungles of Borneo helped us feel and see the potential in this region, almost feel and touch the vision. We were able to move from discovering self to building a mental picture about the future with a clear direction of where you want to go and where you want to be. And it is extremely powerful when you see around you a lot of people sharing the same picture.

Subsequent journeys took these leaders to China and India to look at the migration from farms to cities and the social side of sustainability, to post-tsunami Sri Lanka to help care for the distressed and rebuild the commercial supply chain, and to the northern mountains of Vietnam, where they participated in an extended service-learning program with the Hmong peoples, teaching them about sanitation, hand washing, and tooth brushing. These journeys raised the consciousness of leaders about the perilous state of agriculture in their region, at the center of the business model, including water shortages, the loss of family farms, and the toxic side effects of certain types of fertilization.

MAKING BUSINESS MORE SUSTAINABLE

This deep engagement with society affected many of Unilever's Asian leaders personally. Said one:

> The communities we visited reminded me of an "itch" that has been bugging me for the longest time, that is, to give my time and effort to a cause which is beyond myself (and even beyond my family). I have been blessed so much in this life that the least I can do is to help my fellow men. I need to act now.

Motivated by this knowledge, Unilever journeyers applied it to environmental cleanup and social improvement projects in their own nations and to sustainable certification schemes for their products. Many also took their own teams on consciousness-raising journeys. In addition, the Asian journeys were a source of inspiration for community-based business initiatives and a testing ground for new-product and market development ideas under the company's base-of-the-pyramid business strategy and socially relevant brands. "Connecting with poverty reminds us that our company, as a member in Asia, has strong social responsibilities," said one participant, who continued: "We need to build our business success while taking on social responsibilities to help to protect the environment, to relieve poverty. ... At the same time, these actions will help our business grow."

LEARNING FROM LEADERSHIP JOURNEYS

Unilever's learning journeys were intentionally designed as consciousness-raising journeys (Mirvis, 2008). The participants learned important lessons about consciousness in China when they practiced with a tai chi master. When one asked, "How does a master do tai chi?", he told them that masters must be aware of themselves, their opponent, and the situation around them, and then forget it all when fighting. This opened up deep conversations among the leaders about how to integrate consciousness of the self, other, and the world around when taking action. The fact that the teacher, nearly 80 and revered around in the world, did not yet consider himself a true master, provoked a new appreciation of the importance of discipline, persistence, and especially humility on a leader's journey.

Pro Bono Problem-solving

Studies document the desires of the millennial generation (born 1978–1998) to work for a company that "cares about how it impacts and contributes to society" (Deloitte, 2016). Many want to contribute to society actively and directly through their work and volunteerism. At the behest of CEO Sam Palmisano, young IBMer Kevin Thompson came up with a bold idea to attract and motivate his millennial peers: a "peace corps" operated by the company. Since 2008, IBM's Corporate Service Corps (CSC) has sent 3,000 employees in over 275 teams to nearly 40 countries for one-month service assignments where they co-create innovations with an NGO client, social enterprise, or government agency.

INNOVATING FOR SOCIETY

Major corporations have sponsored employee volunteerism for decades. With the advent of global pro bono programs, they are expanding their scope and turning their focus to social innovation. In these efforts, innovation is about problem-solving for society and pooling corporate thinking and community wisdom to do things in a new way. Pro bono employees bring a business mindset, management tools, and technology to their assignments, whereas local clients bring their facility in bricolage—applying or recombining existing "resources at hand" to address social issues seldom encountered in corporate jobs (Mair, Wolf, & Seelos, 2016). The task is to co-create solutions to the problems at hand—something that actually works.

What do corporate service teams do on the ground? A Dow Corning team of ten employees went to Bangalore, India, to develop more energy-efficient cooking stoves for street vendors and introduce renewable energy products for rural housing with partners including international development NGO PYXERA Global and the Indian Institute of Science. Innovations included using stabilized mud blocks as a low-carbon emission alternative in building affordable homes. When confronting technical challenges, the Dow Corning team emailed, blogged, and tweeted ideas with scientists and engineers back home, bringing the expertise of not just ten but hundreds of fellow employees to their Bangalore partners.

PRO BONO AS SOCIAL BUSINESS

Gib Bulloch, founder of Accenture Development Partnership (ADP), recalls how reading an article in the London Underground about a volunteer agency seeking business "skills" (not cash) to enhance community development caused a "switch to go off in my head." He devised a program whereby Accenture would volunteer its high-performers free of profit and corporate overhead; these employees would voluntarily give up a substantial percentage of their salary; and non-profits would pay Accenture for consulting and technology services at significantly reduced rates. ADP went through a pilot phase, a development phase with a few social sector partners, to its institutionalization in the business. To date, ADP has undertaken over 600 projects in 55 countries where its professionals, at 50% salary reduction, work in partnership for up to six months with NGOs to bring business solutions to humanitarian problems.

As an example, ADP worked with NetHope, a consortium of over 40 NGOs, to launch the first global IT help desk for international NGOs. Staffed jointly by NetHope and ADP employees, the help desk was a pioneering example of business–NGO collaboration in the development sector. In 2013, the partners conducted a study of technology use in developing markets. They found, for instance, that although mobile technology featured in many development success stories, simpler, text-based applications were more practical for rural workers who don't own smartphones. Commenting on the learnings from this joint research and development (R&D) effort, NetHope's Lauren Woodman and Accenture's Jessica Long wrote:

> It's no longer good enough to arrive in developing countries and proclaim to have all the answers. We need to refine our solutions by researching local markets, learning lessons from trial and error and welcoming feedback and possibilities from those on the ground.

LEARNING FROM PRO BONO SERVICE

Global pro bono service provides a training ground in which executive volunteers are schooled on how to get things done in an emerging market with limited resources; how to work in complex, multi-stakeholder environments; and how to operate in an unfamiliar culture. Amanda MacArthur (2014), who leads the pro bono practice at PYXERA Global, an NGO that matches corporate employees with service clients in social enterprises, small businesses, and government agencies, makes the business case on the basis of their impact on employees:

Walking through open-air markets to learn about consumer purchasing preferences, speaking with patients with non-communicable diseases at community clinics, examining agricultural supply chains, and discussing infrastructure and funding challenges with government officials contribute to a deep understanding of the needs of a particular market. Perhaps the most important aspect of an executive program is the opportunity to actively engage with a local community, especially stakeholders at the bottom of the pyramid, to understand their needs and aspirations, if only for a moment. Beyond market insights, experiencing the realities of everyday people—not just the local business elite—encourages participants to stretch their listening and observational skills.

(MacArthur and Ginsberg, 2014)

There is a growing literature documenting the impact of pro bono programs (e.g., Caligiuri, Mencin, & Jiang, 2013; Caligiuri, Mencin, Jayne, & Traylor, 2019; Pless, Maak, & Stahl, 2011). PYXERA's surveys of over 2,000 executive volunteers from large companies found that over 90% of global pro bono participants believed they had a better understanding of business's role in society, and 92% felt more culturally aware as a result of their experience. IBM's internal assessment went further, by asking participant's managers to rate the impact of the program on their people. Some 85% of managers of CSC participants agreed that the experience increased their employees' "knowledge/understanding of IBM's role in the developing world," and 72% agreed that the experience increased their employees' leadership skills.

Partnering with Social Entrepreneurs and Enterprises

Firms have historically worked with established NGOs and charities to deliver on their social responsibility agendas. Why would a company have its employees support budding social entrepreneurs and their enterprises? For one, it is a new way to connect deeply to society where employees help catalyze innovative social action and, as a social enterprise accelerates, help to build its capacities and heighten its impact. This adds vitality to the social sector and exposes a firm to new ideas and practices promulgated by creative startup NGOs, social businesses, and hybrids. Second, as employees interact with and mentor social actors, they gain insights into social issues and innovations, sharpen their own coaching and project management skills, and develop new relationships that expand the social capital of their companies (Muthuri, Matten, & Moon, 2009).

SOCIAL LABS AND ACCELERATORS

Software maker SAP taps its employees and R&D resources to support social innovators around the world. SAP began its work in this space in 2013, when its employees partnered with Barclays to host Startup@RISE Africa, where South African tech entrepreneurs participated in training focused on how to develop prototypes by using the SAP HANA Cloud technology. Over several years, teams of SAP employees were sent on assignments to consult with innovation hubs, incubators, academic centers, and the like to reach to many more social entrepreneurs and their enterprises. SAP employees have, to date, assisted over 350 NGOs and social businesses, including blueMoon, Ethiopia's first youth agribusiness incubator that selects, mentors, and accelerates impact entrepreneurs, and the University of Johannesburg's Centre for Social Entrepreneurship and Social Economy, which helps to redesign and build funding models for the incubator web site.

Closer to HQ, SAP employees staff Social Impact Labs in Berlin, Hamburg, and other German cities for social entrepreneurs that are set to scale. When leading workshops on design thinking, sharing their business acumen, and deploying SAP technology, employee volunteers connect with innovators at the grassroots of society and also offer them access to a network of impact investors geared to SAP's nonprofit entrepreneur partners.

SOCIAL R&D

Connecting with social innovators is a form of social R&D. On this count, Kanter (1998) foresaw the social sector as a "beta site" for business innovation. Barclays hosts a 13-week innovation accelerator for fin-tech startups, in partnership with Techstars. Employees sorted through applications from more than 300 companies from 50 countries to fill the 11 places in the first program. The prototypes developed included an alternative to payday loans, a credit scoring system for startups, and peer-to-peer funding for real estate.

Singapore, like other nations in Asia, has comparatively few civil society organizations and social enterprises compared to the West. To address this gap, Leona Tan, head of the Development Bank of Singapore (DBS) Foundation, adapted the bank's platforms for assisting commercial startups to the social sector. The first stage of support is geared to startup enterprises. DBS employees serve as advisors to social startups, and the foundation offers them pilot/prototype grants. In the second stage, for enterprises that are two to five years old, there are employee-run incubators, innovation tool kits and case studies, and a full ecosystem of DBS mentors who can provide counsel on every aspect of growing an organization. The third stage of support is for scaling the enterprise. At this phase, social enterprises have access to a full suite of DBS banking services, which, according to Leona, are provided "almost free." Beyond the social benefits, Singaporean startups are exposed to banking culture, and DBS staff gain from the cultural exchange on how startups innovate and grow.

LEARNING FROM PARTNERING

Working with social entrepreneurs introduces employees to young, passionate, and creative innovators operating beyond the corporate boundary. This opens eyes to social issues and conditions, can reawaken minds and ideals, and often yields emotionally resonant learning. Said one SAP staffer about to launch a social innovation lab for female entrepreneurs, "I want to help these women get new hope for a better future. And I want to use this time to get to know who I am and what my potential is."

In addition, many of these endeavors have evolved into full partnerships between companies and social enterprises. This gives future leaders an opportunity to fully engage in a cross-sector partnership and learn the ins and outs of, for example, building trust, managing conflicts, and aligning different interests in service of creating something useful for society (Kania & Kramer, 2011; Worley & Mirvis, 2013).

RESPONSIBLE LEADERSHIP: COLLECTIVE LEARNING

In launching their leadership development and engagement platforms, many of the companies studied here also sought to create firm-relevant knowledge about social issues and opportunities (Mirvis, Herrera, Googins, & Albareda, 2016). For instance, CP's top executives and the relevant business sponsor sustainability projects of the teams regularly coach team members and review results, and in the end, implement project solutions. Thus, they are actively engaged in learning more about responsible leadership in its practical applications. They also participate collectively in a review of the projects of six or more teams, where, guided by the group's vice-chairperson, lessons about business and sustainable development are harvested. Finally, these executives participate in a review of all of the CP leaders who participated in the program, rating them not only on their business performance, but also on how they exemplified and practiced CP's three-benefits principles.

As for learning from journeys, Unilever Asia's journeys were stepping stones to an organization-wide review of the company's CSR profile and objectives (Mirvis, 2011). Hundreds of executives were engaged in fact-finding about current realities and future trends, and thousands of stakeholders were engaged in open discussions. New knowledge has catalytic potential: it can simultaneously disconfirm old understandings and point to new directions. And new relationships can also be catalytic: they can disrupt existing structural configurations and establish new ones. Suddenly, marketers were talking to business leaders, HR was talking to the supply chain, and everyone was talking about sustainability and CSR. The collective learning exercises culminated in 2010, when Unilever unveiled its Sustainable Living Plan, whereby it intends to improve the health of 1 billion people, to buy 100% of its agricultural raw materials from sustainable sources, and to reduce the environmental impact of everything it sells by half, all while doubling its revenues.

On the pro bono side, companies seem to be more or less proactive in promoting collective learning in this space. IBM, for instance, gives its pro bono participants three months of online prework about the country and cultures they will encounter, along with background on the social issues to be faced. In the aftermath, participants prepare written summaries of lessons learned and have face-to-face debriefings with their managers on personal learnings and any implications for the business. Furthermore, many of IBM's Corporate Service Corps graduates participated, along with 15,000 other individuals, in its global electronic "service jam" on October 10–12, 2010. The jam was designed to raise consciousness about global service broadly, and build a global knowledge base and community of practice around it.

As for engaging social entrepreneurs, testimonials abound as to the learnings about responsible business. For example, an SAP manager who works with entrepreneurs in Kenya said:

> I am in my ninth year of working at SAP and have had a tremendous amount of support and coaching from leaders and mentors. I have increased confidence and learning that came with being placed in another country, drawing from my own knowledge and learning at the same time. The ability to make an impact on people's lives ensures it's an experience I will never forget and I will continue to stay connected to CSR at SAP and ensure many employees are given ample opportunities to gain the same experience.

Besides participants' learnings, corporate leaders and managers who serve as their sponsors and mentors are exposed to ideas and issues pertinent to running a responsible global business.

Telefónica's Innovation and Research group also learned some things from working with external social entrepreneurs:

> We have learnt that lean innovation can help us to break the commercialization glass ceiling that innovations usually face, thus reducing risk and minimizing resource consumption. But we have also validated that it is an extraordinary motivational tool because it gives employees more autonomy, mastery and, last but not least, a purpose.
>
> (Apruzzese & Olano Mata, 2014)

LEARNING TO LEAD RESPONSIBLY

There is still today a considerable gap between stakeholders' expectations of responsible business and corporate performance in these regards. The four learning platforms explored in this reading provide one means of partially bridging that gap by promoting individual and collective learning about what it takes to lead responsibly. But adopting any one of them requires thoughtful consideration.

DEPTH AND DURATION OF LEARNING

All four learning platforms feature what is called 3D learning: they stimulate learning at cognitive, emotional, and behavioral levels. Real-world sustainability projects, especially like those at CP that start in the corporate classroom, are strongest in introducing leaders to new concepts, frameworks, and applications regarding responsible leadership and providing structured mechanisms for reflection and knowledge exchange. To an extent, this was also built into Unilever's learning journeys. On the emotional side, by comparison, pro bono problem-solving and partnering with entrepreneurs have leaders engage more intensely with social problems and work with key actors to address them. These platforms also invite leaders to "practice" new behaviors in collaborative problem-solving and innovation.

Although each of these platforms promotes deep learning, each is limited in its duration. Typically, learning journeys are a one-off, and the other initiatives engage participants for a period of three to six months. A risk with these short-term learning experiences is that the enrichment gained fades fast upon return to a work "cubicle." What is key, then, is the transfer of learning to responsible leadership in everyday practice—and its continuous development. Companies like Danone and Interface provide a model by regularly engaging employees in sustainability projects throughout the enterprise and hosting forums where they can share their experiences and best practices on both the operational and the sustainability aspects of projects, learn from successful models, and analyze what went wrong in unsuccessful ones (Vilanova & Dettoni, 2011).

STRATEGIC FIT AND THE "BUSINESS CASE"

Another key question for a company is which model for developing responsible leaders (if any of them) best fits with its strategy and yields the greatest cost–benefit return. On this point, Vogel (2006) notes that the "market for virtue" varies across firms and industries as well as employment markets. Arguably, the absence of market demand and perceived rewards accounts for the fact that some companies pay scant attention to developing their leaders in these regards. Where conditions are right, however, some trade-offs have to be considered.

For instance, pro bono problem-solving and partnering with entrepreneurs are primarily individual (or small-group) learning platforms. Although the experiences can be deep and can translate into action within an organization, the lessons learned don't necessarily transfer to collective learning and action. Learning journeys and real-world sustainability projects, by comparison, allow for broader engagement: they can be large-group or even organization-wide experiences. Yet learning journeys are often keyed to raising consciousness, and projects hosted by a corporate university are necessarily limited in time and scope. Much of the sustained impact of any of these learning platforms depends on the extent to which they are fully aligned with the strategy and employee engagement culture of an organization versus a "bolt-on" or peripheral consideration (Grayson & Hodges, 2004). Companies are well advised to connect them to broader, strategic, and systematic efforts to become more responsible (Mirvis, 2012).

REALISTIC EXPECTATIONS

Finally, can these learning platforms "drive" responsible leadership in a company? Consideration must be given to what "stage" a company is in with regard to CSR and sustainability. One formulation sees companies progressing from an elementary to an engaged, innovative, integrated, and, in some instances, transformative approach to CSR (Mirvis & Gunning, 2006). The benefits of these learning platforms are apt to be more appealing to and ultimately significant in firms that are further along in embracing a larger role in society.

That said, there is evidence that involvement in socially responsible activities can promote prosocial motivation and behavior among employees (Grant, 2012), affect firm practices and outlooks (Garavan & McGuire, 2010), and even affect the socially responsible identity of a firm (Haski-Leventhal, Roza, & Meijs, 2017). On these counts, pro bono problem-solving and partnering with entrepreneurs are particularly strong in enabling employees to "give" service to society and generate considerable publicity inside and outside a firm. Perhaps this, in and of itself, can generate momentum toward promoting more-responsible leadership in a company.

On this count, realism is called for—leadership development is but one force in a field of powerful ones that shape corporate commitments to and progress toward responsible leadership. In my experience, when participants find that their new and motivating thoughts, feelings, and behaviors concerning responsible leadership are not congruent with the values and practices of their boss or firm, they are more apt to leave rather than engage in a "bottom-up" transformation strategy. Certainly, consciousness-raising learning programs helped to launch Unilever's drive toward sustainability. But it took strong and purposeful CEO leadership, regular engagement with stakeholders, and a compelling business case to bring it to the fore. Learning journeys are today integrated into a suite of programs at Unilever that includes socially relevant project-based learning, partnerships with entrepreneurs, and other means of fostering responsible leadership development (Polman & Bhattacharya, 2016).

REFERENCES

Apruzzese, S. J., & Olano Mata, M. L. (2014). *Lean elephants: Addressing the innovation challenge in big companies.* Madrid: Telefónica I+D.

Bennis, W. G., & O'Toole, J. (2005). How business schools lost their way. *Harvard Business Review, 83*(5), 96–104.

Caligiuri, P., Mencin, A., Jayne, B., & Traylor, A. (2019). Developing cross-cultural competencies through international corporate volunteerism. *Journal of World Business, 54*(1), 23–24.

Caligiuri, P., Mencin, A., & Jiang, K. (2013). Win—win—win: The influence of company sponsored volunteerism programs on employees, NGOs, and business units. *Personnel Psychology, 66*(4), 825–860.

Conference Board. (2016). *The seven pillars of sustainability leadership.* Retrieved from http://pages.conference-board.org/rs/225-WBZ-025/images/TCB-1604-Sustainable -Leadership-CEO.pdf.

Deloitte. (2016). *The 2016 Deloitte millennial survey: Winning over the next generation of leaders.* Retrieved from https://www2.deloitte.com/content/dam/Deloitte/global/ Documents/About-Deloitte/gx-millenial-survey-2016-exec-summary.pdf.

Garavan, T. N., & McGuire, D. (2010). Human resource development and society: Human resource development's role in embedding corporate social responsibility, sustainability, and ethics in organizations. *Advances in Developing Human Resources, 12*(5), 487–507.

Googins, B., Mirvis, P. H., & Rochlin, S. (2007). *Beyond "good company": Next generation corporate citizenship.* New York: Palgrave Macmillan.

Grant, A. M. (2012). Giving time, time after time: Work design and sustained employee participation in corporate volunteering. *Academy of Management Review, 37*(4), 589–615.

Grayson, D., & Hodges, A. (2004). Corporate social opportunity! 7 steps to make corporate social responsibility. *Work for Your Business.* Sheffield: Greenleaf.

GRLI The Globally Responsible Leadership Initiative. (2006). *Globally responsible leadership: A call for engagement.* Brussels: The Global Compact and European Foundation for Management Development.

GRLI The Globally Responsible Leadership Initiative. (2008). *Globally responsible leadership: A call for action.* Brussels: The United Nations Global Compact and European Foundation for Management Development.

Haski-Leventhal, D., Roza, L., & Meijs, L. C. (2017). Congruence in corporate social responsibility: Connecting the identity and behavior of employers and employees. *Journal of Business Ethics, 143*(1), 35–51.

Kania, J., & Kramer, M. (2011, Winter). Collective impact. *Stanford Innovation Review,* 36–41.

Kanter, R. M. (1998). From spare change to real change: The social sector as beta site for business innovation. *Harvard Business Review, 77*(3), 122–132.

Khurana, R. (2002). *Searching for a corporate savior.* Englewood Cliffs, NJ: Princeton University Press.

Khurana, R. (2010). *From higher aims to hired hands: The social transformation of American business schools and the unfulfilled promise of management as a profession.* Princeton, NJ: Princeton University Press.

Korten, D. C. (2015). *When corporations rule the world* (2nd ed.). San Francisco, CA: Berrett-Koehler.

Leavitt, H. J. (1989). Educating our MBAs: On teaching what we haven't taught. *California Management Review, 31*(3), 38–50.

Maak, T., & Pless, N. M. (Eds.). (2006). *Responsible leadership.* London: Routledge.

Maak, T., & Pless, N. M. (2008). Responsible leadership in a globalized world: A cosmopolitan perspective. In A. G. Scherer & G. Palazzo (Eds.), *Handbook of research on global corporate citizenship* (pp. 430–443). Cheltenham: Edward Elgar.

Maak, T., & Pless, N. M. (2016). Responsible leadership in a stakeholder society—A relational perspective. *Journal of Business Ethics, 66*(1), 99–115.

Maak, T., Pless, N. M., & Voegtlin, C. (2016). Business statesman or shareholder advocate? CEO responsible leadership styles and the micro-foundations of political CSR. *Journal of Management Studies, 53*(3), 463–493.

MacArthur, A. (2014). *The state of Global Pro Bono.* The Conference Board. Retrieved from www.conference-board.org/retrievefile.cfm?filename=TCB-GT-V1N8-State _of_Global_Pro_ Bono1.pdf&type=subsite.

MacArthur, A., & Ginsberg, H. (2014). *Three ways companies build better leaders with Global Pro Bono.* Retrieved from https://www.pyxeraglobal.org/three-ways -companies-build-better- leaders-with-global-pro-bono-2/.

Mair, J., Wolf, M., & Seelos, C. (2016). Scaffolding: A process of transforming patterns of inequality in small-scale societies. *Academy of Management Journal, 59*(6), 2021–2044.

Mintzberg, H., & Gosling, J. (2002). Educating managers beyond borders. *Academy of Management Learning & Education, 1*(1), 64–76.

Mirvis, P. H. (2008). Executive development through consciousness raising experiences. *Academy of Management Learning & Education, 7*(2), 173–188.

Mirvis, P. H. (2009). Educating for sustainability: The power of learning journeys to raise consciousness. In C. Wankel & J. Stoner (Eds.), *Management education for global sustainability* (pp. 159–174). Charlotte, NC: IAP.

Mirvis, P. H. (2011). Unilever's drive for sustainability and CSR—Changing the game. In S. Mohrman & R. Shani (Eds.), *Organizing for sustainability* (pp. 41–72). New York: Emerald.

Mirvis, P. H. (2012). Employee engagement and CSR: Transactional, relational, and developmental approaches. *California Management Review, 54*(4), 93–117.

Mirvis, P. H., & Googins, B. (2018). Catalyzing social entrepreneurship in Africa: Roles for western universities, NGOs, and corporations. *Africa Journal of Management, 4*(1), 57–83.

Mirvis, P. H., Googins, B., DeJongh, D., Quinn, L., & van Velsor, E. (2010). *Responsible leadership emerging: Individual, organizational and collective frontiers.* University of Pretoria: Centre for Responsible Leadership.

Mirvis, P. H., & Gunning, L. (2006). Creating a community of leaders. *Organizational Dynamics, 35*(1), 69–82.

Mirvis, P. H., Herrera, M. E. B., Googins, B., & Albareda, L. (2016). Corporate social innovation: How firms learn to innovate for the greater good. *Journal of Business Research, 69*(11), 5014–5021.

Mirvis, P. H., Hurley, S. T., & MacArthur, A. (2014). Transforming executives into corporate diplomats: The power of global pro bono service. *Organizational Dynamics, 43*(3), 235–245.

Mirvis, P. H., Thompson, K., & Marquis, C. (2010). Preparing next generation business leaders. In R. Burke & M. Rothstein (Eds.), *Self-management and leadership development* (pp. 464–486). Cheltenham: Edgar Elgar.

Miska, C., & Mendenhall, M. E. (2018). Responsible leadership: A mapping of extant research and future directions. *Journal of Business Ethics, 148*(1), 117–134.

Muthuri, J. N., Matten, D., & Moon, J. (2009). Employee volunteering and social capital: Contributions to corporate social responsibility. *British Journal of Management, 20*(1), 75–89.

Pfeffer, J., & Fong, C. T. (2004). The business school 'business': Some lessons from the US experience. *Journal of Management Studies, 41*(8), 1501–1520.

Pless, N., Maak, T., & Stahl, G. K. (2011). Developing responsible global leaders through international service learning programs: The Ulysses experience. *Academy of Management Learning & Education, 10*(2), 237–260.

Polman, P., & Bhattacharya, C. B. (2016). Engaging employees to create a sustainable business. *Stanford Social Innovation Review, 14*, 34–39.

PwC. (2016). *Redefining business success in a changing world.* CEO Survey. Retrieved from www.pwc.com/gx/en/ceo-survey/2016/landing-page/pwc-19th-annual-global-ceo -survey.pdf.

Schein, E. H. (1966). The problem of moral education for the business manager. *IMR; Industrial Management Review, 8*(1), 3.

Schwab, K. (2015). Business in a changing world: Stewarding the future. *Foreign Affairs.* Retrieved from www.foreignaffairs.com/articles/global-commons/2015-01-06/ business- changing-world.

Stahl, G. K., Miska, C., Puffer, S. M., & McCarthy, D. J. (2016). Responsible global leadership in emerging markets. *Advances in Global Leadership, 9*, 79–106.

Tichy, N. M., Brimm, M. I., Charan, R., & Takeuchi, H. (1992). Leadership development as a lever for global transformation. In V. Pucik, N. M. Tichy, & C. K. Barnett (Eds.), *Globalizing management* (pp. 47–60). New York: Wiley.

Vilanova, M., & Dettoni, P. (2011). *Sustainable innovation strategies: Exploring the cases of Danone and interface.* Barcelona: ESADE, Institute for Social Innovation.

Voegtlin, C., Patzer, M., & Scherer, A. G. (2012). Responsible leadership in global business: A new approach to leadership and its multi-level outcomes. *Journal of Business Ethics, 105*(1), 1–16.

Vogel, D. (2006). *The market for virtue: The potential and limits of corporate social responsibility.* Washington, DC: Brookings Institution Press.

Waddock, S. (2002). *Leading corporate citizens: Visions, values, and value added.* New York: McGraw-Hill.

Waddock, S., & McIntosh, M. (2011). *SEE change: Making the transition to a sustainable enterprise economy.* Sheffield: Greenleaf.

Waldman, D., & Galvin, B. M. (2008). Alternative perspectives on responsible leadership. *Organizational Dynamics, 37*(4), 327–341.

Waldman, D., Seigel, D., & Javidan, M. (2006). Components of CEO transformational leadership and corporate social responsibility. *Journal of Management Studies, 43*(8), 1703–1725.

WBCSD World Business Council for Sustainable Development. (2006). *From challenge to opportunity: The role of business in tomorrow's society.* Retrieved from wbcsd.org.

Worley, C., & Mirvis, P. H. (Eds.). (2013). *Organizing for sustainability: Building networks & partnerships* (Vol. 3). New York: Emerald.

Günter K. Stahl, Christof Miska, Laura J. Noval, and Mary Sully de Luque

THE CHALLENGE OF RESPONSIBLE GLOBAL LEADERSHIP

THE AFTERMATH OF THE COVID-19 pandemic has created a social and economic ripple effect experienced through communities, countries, and regions around the world (Sneader & Singhal, 2020). These social and economic ripples are colliding to create a shift in, and raise demands for, responsible leadership (Hope Haile & Jacobs, 2022). With societal grand challenges escalating (George et al., 2016), responsible leaders are expected to deal with multifarious issues such as the climate crisis, increasing inequality, and military conflicts (e.g., in Ukraine and large parts of Africa).

Calls for more responsible corporate governance and leadership are not novel, but they have intensified (e.g., Pucik, Björkman, Evans, & Stahl, 2023; Todnem By, 2021). In the wake of major economic crises and highly publicized corporate scandals (Robison, 2021), ethical breaches have become front-page news. Occurrences of reprehensible and unethical business behaviors are on display, from misuse of company funds at Merrill Lynch and Elf in France, to questionable accounting practices at Enron and Arthur Andersen, to corrupt leader behavior at Odebrecht in Brazil and Samsung in Korea, to improper payments for government officials by Xerox managers in India, and bribes by Siemens to government officials in Asia, Africa, Europe, the Middle East, and the Americas. Some ethics scandals involve encroachments of human rights, exhibited through Nike's use of child labor in Pakistan and Shell's handling of human rights violations in Nigeria. Other company ethics malfeasance has resulted in environmental degradation, such as the scandal surrounding Volkswagen's emissions-cheating program and BP's massive oil spill in the Gulf of Mexico. Perhaps the most captivating, inappropriate trading and other illegal activities have been reported in

DOI: 10.4324/9781003247272-33

the financial services sector at Credit Suisse, Deutsche Bank, Citigroup, Goldman Sachs, and Wirecard – the list is seemingly endless.

These highly visible instances of managerial misconduct might suggest that public faith in business worldwide would be eroded through the realization that business leaders engage in irresponsible behavior more frequently than previously assumed (Pearce & Stahl, 2015). Yet recent research does not support this assumption. According to the 2021 Edelman Trust Barometer, 61% of the general public believe that business leaders can be trusted to tell the truth and make ethical decisions when confronted with a difficult issue. Among the four collective institutions of NGOs, the media, government, and business, respondents reported "My Employer" as the most trusted, at 77% globally. The Edelman Trust Barometer has been gathering data on trust, around the world for more than a decade. In 2022, the data indicated that government is not seen as a leader on most societal grand challenges, such as climate change, economic inequality, or workforce reskilling (Edelman, 2022). However, multinational corporations are uniquely situated to become a significant steadying influence to manage such pressing global challenges and facilitate change. Thus, business can be both a source of problems and a force for good (Pucik et al., 2023).

The calls for more responsible leadership are not only a reaction to business scandals and concern for improved ethical managerial conduct and attention to societal problems, but also a result of increased stakeholder activism and scrutiny (see, e.g., Aguilera et al., 2007; Knowles & Hunsaker, 2022; Voegtlin, Patzer, & Scherer, 2012). In light of the growing economic, social, and environmental challenges around the world, there are increasing demands among and across stakeholder groups, from governments and local communities to NGOs and consumers. These groups are pressuring corporations and their leaders to engage in self-regulation, to take part as active citizens in society, and to promote "the creation of economic and societal progress in a globally responsible and sustainable way" (EFMD, 2005, p. 3). At the supranational level, since its official launch on July 26, 2000, the UN Global Compact has grown to more than 20,000 participants, including over 15,000 businesses and 3,800 non-business participants in more than 170 countries around the world (UN Global Compact, 2022). Together, these participants have produced over 95,000 public reports, with 81% of companies attributing progress on sustainability efforts to their participating in the UN Global Compact. Equally, the UN Sustainable Development Goals (SDGs), which reflect $12 trillion in business opportunities, have garnered wide-ranging attention from companies to meet global goals by 2030 (Hoek, 2018). The 17 goals and 169 sub-targets encompass numerous domains such as clean energy, gender equality, justice and strong institutions, and sustainable growth. Playing an integral role is the societal expectation that for-profit companies proactively contribute to sustainable development by focusing on strategic SDGs (Wettstein, Santangelo, Giuliani, & Stahl, 2019).

Responsible leadership thus includes decisions and actions taken by corporations and their leaders to both avoid harmful consequences and enhance societal welfare for stakeholders and society at large (Crilly, Schneider, & Zollo, 2008; Stahl & Sully de Luque, 2014). These dual goals correspond with two major themes in the corporate social responsibility (CSR), sustainability, and business ethics literature: namely, concerns about businesses' detrimental impacts on society (avoiding "negatives") and the objective of contributing to society (creating "positives"). In this reading, we will illustrate the increasing trend of companies operating in cross-border contexts intensifying the demands on managers in these two key aspects of social responsibility.

Executives are regularly confronted with VUCA – volatile, uncertain, complex, and ambiguous – environments (Miska, Economou, & Stahl, 2020). Navigating a VUCA world requires embracing a wider-ranging view of diversity, comprehending a broader range of stakeholders when making decisions, as well as engaging in advanced boundary-spanning activities within and across national borders. This leads executives to face challenging and competing tensions both on and off the job. The past few years of the pandemic and ongoing geopolitical tensions featured heightened ambiguity surrounding decisions and related outcomes, and more thorny ethical dilemmas related to globalization (e.g., Hope Hailey & Jacobs, 2022; Lane et al., 2009). When analyzing these issues, four major areas in which global executives confront significant challenges have been identified (Stahl, Pless, Maak, & Miska, 2017). These include:

1. Diversity and inclusion: The need to deal with the legitimate rights, claims, and expectations of a diverse group of stakeholders, both within and outside the organization, and create inclusive and equitable work environments.
2. Ethics: The need to strengthen principle-driven and ethically acceptable behavior.
3. Sustainability: The need to preserve, protect, and restore the resources of the environment while improving human well-being and social equity.
4. Human rights: The need to skilfully identify, competently understand, and proficiently address human rights issues in the countries where the organization operates.

While responding to these challenges, executives make decisions that consider the needs of a diverse set of stakeholders, with sometimes conflicting values, perspectives, and interests. The increasing complexity of doing business across global supply chains has greatly exacerbated this dilemma, not only for leaders from multinational companies (MNCs) in developed economies, but also for those from emerging economies (see Stahl, Miska, Puffer, & McCarthy, 2016). As a result of these complexities, executives often find it difficult to determine when different is different and when different is wrong (Donaldson, 1996). Examples of recent corruption scandals illustrate that MNCs from developed economies continue to participate in bribery, especially when operating in countries where law enforcement is weak and ineffective (Zyglidopoulos, Dieleman, & Hirsch, 2020).

Global managers may engage in unethical or unlawful behavior believing it is acceptable in the host country, or that it will not be discovered due to inadequate control systems and lax enforcement practices (Donaldson & Dunfee, 1999; Pontes & Anselmo, 2022; Puffer & McCarthy, 2008). Such environments, combined with only a partial understanding of the local context, may tempt executives to adopt an attitude of cultural relativism toward CSR, sustainability, human rights, and ethics. Thus, they "follow the lead of those who know the ropes". At the other end of the spectrum, managers may be induced by factors such as company policies, codes of conduct, training programs, and incentive systems to act everywhere in the world the same way as "things are done at headquarters", which can lead to neglecting local stakeholders' needs. Global companies and their managers thus face a perennial dilemma: how to balance the need for consistency in CSR approaches and ethical standards with the need to be sensitive to local stakeholder demands (Scholz, de los Reyes, & Smith, 2019).

Next, we will explore the foundations of responsible global leadership at multiple levels, from the micro (i.e., ethical decision-making processes and managerial behavior), to the meso (i.e., characteristics of the team and organizational context within which global executives operate), to the macro (i.e., aspects of the broader institutional and cultural environments that may affect executive decision-making and responsible behavior). The multi-level framework guiding our discussion is depicted in Figure 1. Our analysis begins with a broad overview of the growing body of research on ethical decision making and its implications for managerial behavior. Then we identify the individual and situational antecedents of managerial ethical choices and outline the processes that hinder and promote managerial ethical decision making in a global context. We give particular focus to the mechanisms of moral disengagement, the role of intuition and emotions, and the influence of a key situational factor: moral intensity.

MANAGERIAL ETHICAL DECISION-MAKING AND BEHAVIOR

Research that falls under the term "behavioral business ethics" or "managerial ethical decision making" (see Kish-Gephart, Treviño, Chen, & Tilton, 2019; O'Fallon & Butterfield, 2005; Tenbrunsel & Smith-Crowe, 2008 for reviews) examines the antecedents of managerial unethical behavior – such as cheating, lying, stealing, and discriminatory practices – as well as the antecedents of managerial behavior that exceed moral minimums, such as engaging in philanthropy, contributing to environmental causes, supporting community development, and whistle-blowing (Crilly et al., 2008; Treviño, Weaver, & Reynolds, 2006). To date, the majority of the work in this field has focused on the unethical behavior; however, research on what motivates managers to go beyond moral minimums and behave prosocially is gaining attention (Crilly, Ni, & Jiang, 2016; Mayer, 2010; Stål, Marttila, & Macassa, 2022). For organizations, it is important to understand the dual sides of moral behavior, from what motivates managers to avoid unethical or harmful behavior ("avoid harm") to what motivates managers to proactively contribute to society ("do good").

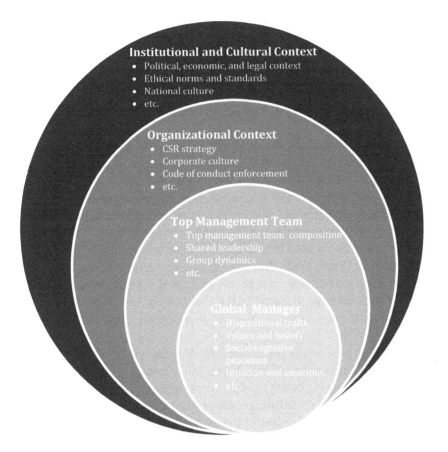

Figure 1 Multiple levels and factors influencing responsible global leadership.

To better comprehend why managers avoid harm or do good, we will review four different aspects of individuals' ethical decision making and behavior. These are comprised of individual dispositions (including personality, philosophies, and identity), moral disengagement and motivated reasoning processes, the role of intuition and emotions, and characteristics inherent to the ethical issue (i.e., moral intensity; Jones, 1991).

Individual Differences: Traits, Moral Development, Moral Philosophies, and Moral Identity

Examining all dispositional traits and individual variables that have been associated with unethical behavior at the workplace is beyond the scope of this review. Instead, we will focus on those garnering extensive empirical support, based on reviews and meta-analyses of the literature (Kish-Gephart, Harrison, & Treviño, 2010; Treviño et al., 2006). Among dispositional traits, a well-studied example is Machiavellianism, which characterizes individuals who use interpersonal relationships opportunistically and deceive others for personal gain (Christie

& Geis, 1970). Similarly, narcissism and locus of control are personality traits linked to unethical workplace behavior that describe individuals with an excessive self-focus and driven by self-interest at the expense of others (Kish-Gephart et al., 2010). Recent studies have examined the role of dispositional and situational influences on employees' unethical pro-organizational behavior (Chhabra & Srivastava, 2022; Veetikazhi, Kamalanabhan, Malhotra, Arora, & Mueller, 2022).

Another important antecedent of managerial ethical behavior (less stable than personality traits) is related to the manager's level of cognitive moral development (CMD; Kohlberg, 1984). According to the CMD approach, people have different levels of sophistication with which they assess moral dilemmas, and according to which they decide whether a certain course of action is morally right or wrong. Managers who are at the higher levels of cognitive moral development consider societal good in their decisions and are less likely to engage in unethical behavior (Blasi, 1980; Trevino et al., 2006; Kish-Gephart et al., 2010). Importantly, scholars find that most people operate at the "conventional" (middle) level of CMD, largely influenced by the environment, including social norms and organizational characteristics, in which they operate (Kish-Gephart et al., 2010).

In addition to personality traits and level of cognitive moral development, managerial ethical decision making is highly influenced by moral philosophies, which refers to managers' "stated beliefs or personal preferences for particular normative frameworks" (Kish-Gephart et al., 2010, p. 3). For example, a relativistic moral philosophy refers to the inherent belief that moral principles are situationally determined rather than universal, whereas an idealistic moral philosophy refers to the inherent belief that moral principles are universal (Kish-Gephart et al., 2010). Global managers who endorse a relativistic moral philosophy are more likely to adopt a "when in Rome do as the Romans do" approach, embracing ethical norms that operate in the local context. Such an approach can be dangerous when working in countries with ethical standards that differ from international ones, such as where the employment of under-aged children is allowed, where security standards are very low, or where bribery is common practice (Donaldson, 1996). On the other hand, global managers who endorse an idealistic moral philosophy need to be wary of engaging in what is often referred to as ethical imperialism – that is, imposing international ethical standards onto local contexts when it is not warranted (Donaldson, 1996).

Finally, managerial ethical decision making is also influenced by the importance that managers attribute to their moral identity (Aquino & Reed, 2002). According to the moral identity approach, individuals are motivated to behave morally because of what they believe about "who they are" (Blasi, 2004). The importance that people attribute to their moral identity has been linked to a number of positive ethical behaviors in organizations and other social contexts (e.g., Reed & Aquino, 2003; Reynolds & Ceranic, 2007). Interestingly, this self-importance of moral identity has been found to expand individuals' circle of moral regard by making them consider the welfare of those considered as "out-group" members (i.e., those who are different to the decision maker; Reed & Aquino, 2003). Given that the ethical decisions reached by global managers are likely to have an impact on out-group members, such as employees or customers of different nationality or ethnic background, the importance that global managers attribute to their moral identity should facilitate ethical decision making in international contexts.

Social-cognitive Processes: Moral Disengagement and Motivated Reasoning

The traditional approach to address ethical decision making in organizations is based on the notion that there are certain managers who are "bad apples" and who can be clearly identified and avoided in organizations. More recent approaches in the field of behavioral business ethics, however, are based on the notion that the ethicality of individuals is malleable rather than stable (Monin & Jordan, 2009; Moore & Gino, 2013), and that many failures of ethical behavior result from individuals' unconscious and automatic biases rather than from their stable dispositions (Bazerman & Tenbrunsel, 2011). Such an approach echoes Hannah Arendt's exploration of the "banality of evil" (1963), in which she argues that much of what we call evil does not arise from the deliberate intention to do harm, but from the failure to think about what we are doing (cited in Werhane et al., 2014, p. 2). The social-cognitive approach to ethical decision making argues that feelings of discomfort (e.g., guilt, shame, or dissonance) arise when individuals consider behaving contrary to their own moral standards, prompting individuals to behave ethically (Bandura et al., 1996). However, people are capable of engaging in several cognitive mechanisms that reframe an unethical or harmful act so as to make it appear right, which in turn enables them to engage in such behavior without feelings of guilt or dissonance (Bandura et al., 1996).

This process is referred to as "moral disengagement", and has been found to be an important predictor of unethical behavior in organizations (Moore, 2008; Moore et al., 2012; Newman, Le, North-Samardzic, & Cohen, 2020). Next, we will review some mechanisms of moral disengagement, grouped into three types of cognitive restructuring, and provide examples of how these mechanisms can affect global managers. Table 1 provides an overview of all moral disengagement mechanisms.

- The first group of mechanisms consists of *reframing the harmful act by employing moral justification* (e.g., justifying the means with the ends), advantageous comparison (e.g., thinking that "others do worse things"), or disregarding/minimizing the consequences (e.g., thinking that "it is not a big deal"). Global managers may, for example, seek to reframe a harmful and/or unethical act by arguing that such behavior is in line with local standards,

Table 1 Examples of moral disengagement

Mechanism	Example
Moral justification	"We answered to a more important cause." "My arm was twisted, I couldn't have done anything else."
Advantageous comparison	"Others do worse things."
Euphemistic language	"Being a team player"; "rightsizing"; "creative accounting"
Displacement of responsibility	"My boss told me to do it."
Diffusion of responsibility	"Everyone else in my group was doing it."
Distortion of consequences	"Nobody was really harmed. "It could have been worse."
Dehumanization	"They do not deserve better."
Attribution of blame	"They brought it upon themselves."

and that inculcating other cultures with his or her home values would be ethically wrong, even if the act in question clearly results in harm to others (e.g., bribery, poor security measures, etc.). Likewise, global managers may be able to use advantageous comparison if they work in countries with poor reinforcement of ethical norms and where worst atrocities or violations of human rights occur compared to the ones perpetrated by the manager and his or her organization.

- The second group of mechanisms of moral disengagement consists of *reframing the role of the decision maker* in the ethical decision, for example by displacing responsibility (e.g., "my boss told me to do it") or diffusing responsibility (e.g., "it was a group decision"). As we will see in the next section, managers often take decisions in groups (top management teams and shared leadership), which can facilitate diffusion of responsibility. In addition, global managers may displace responsibility to the government(s) or to a weak institutional context for questionable ethical practices, as discussed in more detail later in this reading. If the manager is able to displace or diffuse responsibility, he or she may feel relieved from his or her responsibility to address or improve the situation, under the excuse that "someone else" has made the decision.

- The third group of mechanisms of moral disengagement consists of *reframing the role of the victims* of the harmful behavior by either blaming (e.g., "they deserved it") or dehumanizing the victim (e.g., perceiving the victim as less than human and thus as unworthy of consideration). Scholars argue that dehumanization and blame processes are evident in "accounts of Wall Street traders who viewed clients not as unique individuals but as suckers asking to be conned" (Ashforth & Anand, 2003, p. 20). Perceiving the victims of harmful behavior as belonging to the "out-group" can facilitate dehumanization processes (Bandura, 2002; Moore & Gino, 2013). This suggests that global managers may find it easier to dehumanize or blame those affected by their decisions when the latter are psychologically and culturally different from themselves, as is likely to be the case in a global environment.

In addition to moral disengagement, scholars have found several instances of motivated reasoning in ethical situations – that is, reasoning that allows people to reach the conclusions they want to reach (Kunda, 1990; Ditto et al., 2009). For example, a study by Paharia et al. (2013) illustrated that individuals are likely to justify the use of sweatshop labor if they want to acquire the products elaborated with that type of labor, while such justification does not take place if those products are not desirable. Other scholars have also shown that people engage in motivated moral reasoning by selecting the moral principles and ideologies that best fit their desired conclusions (Ditto et al., 2009). In an international context, this suggests that global managers could make selective use of moral philosophies (e.g., relativistic vs. idealistic) that best justify harmful local practices, if they have sufficient motivation for engaging in such behavior (e.g., monetary incentives, career advancement, etc.). To sum up, the research on motivated moral reasoning and moral disengagement demonstrates that even when managers have ethical predispositions and want to act in line with those predispositions, they may still act unethically, and re-interpret their unethical behavior in several ways so as to make it appear morally acceptable.

The Social-intuitionist Approach: The Role of Intuition and Emotions

Parallel to the findings on the limitations and biases of moral reasoning in facilitating ethical decision making, researchers have discovered that ethical judgment and behavior are often the result of automatic and intuitive affective processes rather than of deliberate and analytical reasoning (Haidt, 2001; Greene & Haidt, 2002; Sonenshein, 2007). This line of research was inspired by Damasio's seminal study which discovered that patients with damage to the brain areas responsible for the processing of emotions (but with intact analytical brain functioning) were incapable of reaching moral decisions (Damasio, 1994). Further neuroscientific evidence has provided evidence that when individuals contemplate moral dilemmas, the brain areas responsible for the processing of emotions are more likely to be activated than the brain areas responsible for analytical and deliberate reasoning (Greene et al., 2001). Partly based on these discoveries, the social-intuitionist model of ethical decision making proposes that moral decisions result from "a sudden appearance in consciousness of a moral judgment, including an affective valence (good-bad)" (Haidt, 2001, p. 818), and that deliberate reasoning serves as a post hoc rationalization of those initial intuitive/affective reactions to the moral dilemma. Empirical evidence in the social sciences has found that such affective-laden intuitions, often in the form of moral emotions such as empathy and guilt, are essential in promoting ethical and prosocial behaviors, and inhibiting harmful and unethical behaviors (Eisenberg, 2000; Zhong, 2011).

The prevalence of intuition and emotions in determining ethical decision making presents some additional challenges for global managers. For instance, moral emotions are more likely to be aroused in moral dilemmas when the people affected by the decision maker are in his or her proximity (Greene et al., 2001). Given that global managers often reach decisions with ethical implications for others who are not only physically (in other countries) but also psychologically (out-group members) distant from themselves, they may be less likely to experience the moral emotions that would facilitate ethical behavior. Indeed, neuroscientific research has demonstrated that moral emotions that facilitate helping, such as empathic concern, are more often activated in the presence of in-group members (Mathur et al., 2010), and that individuals experience less emotional distress when they contemplate harming out-group members (Cikara et al., 2010). Moreover, scholars have also identified interventions that help individuals consist of "out-group" members in their circle of moral regard (Reed & Aquino, 2003), including intergroup contact (Pettigrew & Tropp, 2006), emphasis on shared identity (Gaertner & Dovidio, 2000), re-categorization of out-group individuals into a superordinate, common group (Dovidio et al., 2009), and identication with all humanity (McFarland, Webb & Brown, 2012)

Characteristics of the Ethical Issue: Moral Intensity

In his seminal paper in the field of behavioral business ethics, Thomas M. Jones (1991) argues that managerial ethical choices are determined by the immediate characteristics inherent to the ethical issue, which the author terms the "moral intensity" of the issue. Although not an individual characteristic per se, the moral intensity of the issue has been consistently found to determine individual ethical choices (Kish-Gephart et al., 2010; Valentine & Godkin, 2019). In the following, we will review how different features of the ethical issue may relate to moral disengagement and emotional processes. The moral intensity of the ethical issue is defined by six main characteristics, which are illustrated in Table 2.

Two aspects related to the moral intensity of the ethical issue are particularly likely to pose challenges for global managers: proximity and social consensus. As previously mentioned, global managers are likely to experience low proximity (either physical, cultural, or psychological) to those who are affected by their behavior (both harmful and prosocial). Such low proximity inherent to the ethical issue may in turn facilitate dehumanization and blame processes toward others affected by the ethical behavior, as reviewed in the section on moral disengagement. At the same time, low proximity may decrease feelings of concern and empathy for those others, as we reviewed in the section on intuition and emotions.

In addition to low proximity, social consensus about the rightness or wrongness of an ethical act is likely to be low for managers who operate in global environments. For instance, employment of under-aged children, bribery, poor security standards, and other business practices may have high social consensus in certain local societies, whereas the social consensus about these same

Table 2 Components of the moral intensity of the ethical issue

Mechanism	Definition/Example
Magnitude of consequences (MC)	Sum of the harms and/or benefits of the action e.g.: An act that causes the death of a human being has greater MC than an act that causes a person to suffer a minor injury
Probability of effect (PE)	Likelihood that the action will take place and that it will result in the predicted outcome e.g.: selling a gun to a known armed robber has more PE than selling a gun to a law-abiding citizen
Social consensus (SC)	To what extent the issue is approved by society e.g.: the wrongness of bribing an official in Texas has greater SC than the wrongness of bribing an official in Mexico
Proximity (PR)	Feeling of closeness to the objects/individuals affected e.g.: layoffs in a manager's work unit have greater PR than layoffs in a remote plant
Temporal immediacy (TI)	Time period before the onset of consequences e.g.: reducing the retirement benefits of old employees has greater TI than reducing the retirement benefits of young employees
Concentration of effect (CE)	Number of people affected by an act of given magnitude e.g.: Cheating an individual or small group of individuals out of a given sum has a more concentrated effect than cheating an institutional entity

Source: Adapted from Jones (1991).

practices in an international context may be low. In face of such ambiguous social consensus, the manager has no clear indication of what the "right" course of action to follow is, and may thus be more likely to find justifications for engaging in harmful behavior (or for refusing prosocial behavior). Indeed, several managers who have engaged in unethical behavior have claimed that if something is not labeled as illegal, it must be "OK" (Gellerman, 1986, p. 88, cited in Ashforth & Anand, 2003), and that practices are justified as long as they are standard industrial practice (Elsbach, 1994; Ashforth & Anand, 2003). As already mentioned, such beliefs are problematic in a global environment, in which standard practices and illegality are different and conflicting between and within local and global contexts (Donaldson, 1996).

ROLE OF THE TOP MANAGEMENT TEAM AND SHARED LEADERSHIP

After having reviewed the micro-level explanations as to why individual managers may behave in an ethical or unethical manner, we will now consider important aspects at the meso level of our framework and explore the immediate organizational context of those managers who operate at the top of companies. In the following, we will discuss the idiosyncratic characteristics of the top management team (TMT), mainly team diversity and the role of shared leadership. We will also address the ways in which these characteristics may promote or impede TMT ethical decision making and, consequently, corporate social performance.

The decisions and actions of a company's top executives are key to its social performance and long-term viability. Indeed, it is the leaders who are making the responsible decisions, not the businesses (Waldman, 2011). Beyond the day-to-day routine administration planning, organizing, coordinating, and controlling tasks (Finkelstein, Hambrick, & Cannella, 2009), top managers are in charge of setting a company's strategic direction (Cohen & Bailey, 1997), designing CSR and sustainability strategies (Waldman, Siegel, & Javidan, 2006), and promoting the integration of CSR principles and ethical norms within the company's structure, policies, and corporate culture (Desai & Rittenburg, 1997; Quinn & Dalton, 2009; Sun & Govind, 2022). Yet executive managers are often not the only decision makers in a corporate setting. They are part of a team, the TMT, in which the decision making power and control are distributed and shared among a range of senior executives such as the chief operations officer or the chief financial officer (Aggarwal & Samwick, 2003).

When investigating the influence of the TMT on corporate social performance, a range of team- or group-related factors need to be considered. These include: group composition design variables (e.g., demographics, diversity, size, and tenure), organizational context variables (e.g., corporate culture, reward system, supervision, training, and resources), group processes (e.g., communication and conflict among internal group members or external parties), and group psychological traits (e.g., group norms, cohesiveness, team mental models, and group affects) (Cohen & Bailey, 1997). As a group composition design variable, diversity has gained particular attention (Van Knippenberg & Schippers, 2007). Global managers are confronted not only with differing institutional and international contexts, and more diverse sets of stakeholders (Arthaud-Day, 2005), but also with more heterogeneous TMTs.

Diversity in a group context is known to pose both opportunities and challenges (Horwitz & Horwitz, 2007; Milliken & Martins, 1996), which can be explained by means of several mechanisms. Diversity can lead to social categorization, which may provoke stereotyping, polarization, and anxiety among group members (Williams & O'Reilly, 1998). In groups, individuals often classify themselves and others into social categories on the basis of visible attributes such as sex, age, or status (Tajfel, 1982; Tajfel & Turner, 1986). Through such classification processes, individuals create a favorable self-identity and perceive others as less trustworthy, honest, and collegial. In diverse groups in particular, this can lead to dissatisfaction, incoherence, conflicts, and as a result, poor performance outcomes. Similarly, influences on performance can arise from the degree to which group members perceive themselves to be similar to or different from others within the group (Pfeffer, 1983). Similarity based on characteristics stemming from attitudes or demographic variables enhances interpersonal liking, yet may make diverse groups, including their communication, cohesion, and integration, less effective (Williams & O'Reilly, 1998). In a TMT context, this means that teams whose members share certain characteristics — for example, who are in the same age group or have the same nationality, values, or hobbies — may yield better results than heterogeneous teams, since lower levels of diversity would seem to promise harmonious social interactions and unity. However, cases such as Enron illustrate vividly how too much unity in the boardroom can bring about disastrous outcomes (Skapinker, 2003). With very few exceptions, Enron's board mainly consisted of white male Americans, who uniformly described internal board relations as harmonious (US Government, 2002).

Although there were a multitude of factors that had contributed to Enron's collapse (McLean & Elkind, 2003), psychological phenomena such as "groupthink" may explain why the company's board members did not call a halt to the scandalous corporate malpractices in the first place. Next to the persuasion of doing something truly innovative, the tendency to favor consensus and harmony over disagreement and conflict has likely provoked the unreasonable decisions that resulted in one of the largest corporate bankruptcies in US history. Irving Janis (1972), in his now classic study of the processes that lead to disastrous policy decisions such as The Bay of Pigs or Watergate, describes how individuals in groups are more likely to thoughtlessly conform to collective judgments without voicing their reservations for fear of being seen as disloyal or being ostracized. Groupthink predominantly occurs in groups that are highly cohesive and homogeneous, and it has been argued that the presence of diversity can reduce the probability of its occurrence (Cox & Blake, 1991; Stahl et al., 2010). From this perspective, diversity may be regarded as a potential measure to facilitate healthy dissent and critical evaluation among TMT members, thereby promoting responsible leadership.

In addition to reducing peer pressure, diversity is further recognized to contribute to higher sensitivity toward social issues (Hafsi & Turgut, 2013), to enhance a team's ability to handle differing environmental conditions, and to better respond to stakeholder needs around the world (Wong, Ormiston, & Tetlock, 2011). Moreover, diverse TMTs are considered to be more creative and innovative in solving CSR issues, as they have access to larger and more diverse informational networks (Ancona & Caldwell, 1992). In this context, not only diversity in general, but also distinct types of diversity may be of importance when composing TMTs. Researchers find that educational diversity, which is similar to national diversity, allows for a broader array of relevant information (Dahlin, Weingart, & Hinds, 2005). While age diversity has been found to positively influence philanthropic decisions (Post, Rahman, & Rubow, 2011), gender diversity has been linked to positive CSR outcomes (Hafsi & Turgut, 2013). The above findings illustrate that there are several different ways of boosting diversity in a TMT.

Apart from the diversity aspect, the concept of shared leadership is the second crucial factor that may influence ethical decision-making in TMTs and corporate social performance. Shared leadership reflects the idea that "leadership is not merely the influential act of an individual or individuals but rather is embedded in a complex interplay of numerous interacting forces" (Uhl-Bien, Marion & McKelvey, 2007, p. 302). In other words, process toward productive outcomes is shaped not by a single manager or TMT member, but rather by multiple social actors in the organization (Carson, Tesluk, & Marrone, 2007; Pearce, Wassenaar, & Manz, 2014; Zhu, Liao, Yam, & Johnson, 2018). Shared leadership contributes to the idea that every member of the organization is an important part of a "checks and balances system" that ensures responsible managerial behavior and eventually prevents corruptive tendencies (Pearce & Manz, 2011). The lack of shared leadership has been identified as a major cause of irresponsible decisions and behaviors (Christensen, Mackey, & Whetten, 2014; Pearce et al., 2014). Hence, raising awareness and implementing the notion of shared leadership in the minds and business cultures of global managers and their organizations may not only create a common sense of responsibility, but also be an important measure to evoke critical thinking and to avoid corporate fraud in the future.

THE ORGANIZATIONAL CONTEXT

Continuing with the meso level of analysis, further influences on responsible managerial behavior lie within the organizational context. This is supported by a large body of research in social psychology: classic experiments such as Asch's (1951) conformity studies, Milgram's (1974) work on obedience to authority, and Zimbardo's (1972) prison experiment have demonstrated that the social context in which individuals are embedded can influence their revealed good and bad characteristics. The previously discussed research on ethical decision making also points to the importance of the organizational context (e.g., Craft, 2013; Lehnert, Park, & Singh, 2015; Treviño et al., 2014) and its ethical infrastructure – such as the ethical climate in the organization, the existence and enforcement of a code of conduct, as well as reward and sanctioning mechanisms – in influencing ethical and unethical choices.

Another important feature of the organizational context is the approach to CSR a company adopts. As discussed earlier, companies operating across different countries and societies are confronted with the dual needs of globally integrating and standardizing their various CSR activities for consistency reasons and at the same time adapting these activities locally in order to meet the demands of local stakeholders. Building on Bartlett and Ghoshal's (1998) global–local framework, a growing number of scholars (e.g., Arthaud-Day, 2005; Filatotchev & Stahl, 2015; Miska, Witt, & Stahl, 2016) have studied organizational approaches to CSR by focusing on three prototypical strategies: globally standardized, locally adapted, and transnational CSR approaches. Figure 2 provides an overview of the three prototypical CSR approaches.

The *globally standardized CSR approach* implies global CSR consistency and standardization regardless of the country in which a company operates. It relies on universal principles comparable to "hypernorms" (Donaldson & Dunfee,

Potential pros:
- ❑ Global CSR consistency
- ❑ Clearly defined rules of conduct for global managers
- ❑ Worldwide transfer of CSR best practices
- ❑ Leverage of MNC's global resources and capabilities
- ❑ Worldwide endorsement of MNC's responsibility culture

Potential cons:
- ❑ Neglect of local stakeholders' needs and interests
- ❑ "Ethical imperialism"
- ❑ Blind application of CSR rules and policies

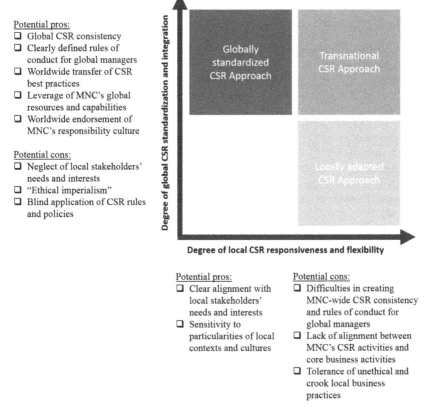

Potential pros:
- ❑ Clear alignment with local stakeholders' needs and interests
- ❑ Sensitivity to particularities of local contexts and cultures

Potential cons:
- ❑ Difficulties in creating MNC-wide CSR consistency and rules of conduct for global managers
- ❑ Lack of alignment between MNC's CSR activities and core business activities
- ❑ Tolerance of unethical and crook local business practices

Figure 2 Three prototypical CSR approaches.

Source: Adapted from Stahl et al. (2017).

1994; Scholz, de los Reyes, & Smith, 2019), embodied in corporate codes of conduct that are assumed to apply across societies. While such a strategy ensures clear global rules and consistency, employee awareness of ethical dilemmas, and the importance of responsible conduct worldwide, it may lead to ethical imperialism and arrogance. The mirror opposite of this strategy – the *locally adapted CSR approach* – aims at counterbalancing such risks, as it emphasizes the need for sensitivity and responsiveness to local conditions when business is conducted in multiple countries. However, this approach poses the risk of decreasing the credibility of company-wide and universally accepted codes of conduct. The third approach – the *transnational CSR approach* – can be seen as a hybrid strategy which aims to balance global and local demands. It involves providing a global template to guide managerial decision making and behavior regarding CSR, sustainability, and business ethics, while offering the flexibility required in specific situations and by particular local stakeholders.

Filatotchev and Stahl (2015), based on extensive case study research, conclude that the transnational CSR approach is the most effective in helping MNCs to coordinate their worldwide CSR activities. Israel-based Teva Pharmaceuticals, the world's largest generic drug company, provides an example of a company that

Table 3 Competencies required to support different CSR approaches

Globally Standardized CSR Approach	Locally Adapted CSR Approach	Transnational CSR Approach
• Strong commitment to head office • Understanding of global stakeholders' needs • Big-picture thinking • "Helicopter" view • Understanding of universal ethical standards • Integrity and behavioral consistency	• Strong commitment to local stakeholders • Non-judgmental and open to different views • Local knowledge and experience • Intercultural sensitivity and perspective-taking skills • Adaptability and behavioral flexibility	Competencies required for Globally Standardized and Locally Adapted CSR Approaches plus: • Dual citizenship • Global mindset • Ability to balance paradoxes and contradictions • Tolerance of uncertainty • Multicultural identity • Long-term orientation • Moral imagination

Source: Stahl et al. (2017).

has adopted a transnational CSR approach. At Teva, a global code of conduct applies to all managers and employees in the company's countries of operation. However, there are four specific areas in which subsidiaries have a high degree of flexibility when enacting the code: protection of the natural environment, workplace safety, access to global healthcare, and support of regions affected by natural disasters through medical help (Filatotchev & Stahl, 2015).

These three CSR approaches have far-reaching implications for responsible global leaders' decision making, as they define the space for maneuver in terms of leaders' ability (and opportunity) to engage in "do good" and "avoid harm" behaviors. Each approach requires specific skills and competencies to support it, both at the individual and organizational levels. The various key competencies required on the part of responsible global leaders to successfully implement the three approaches are summarized in Table 3. Based on this analysis, the transnational CSR approach is the most demanding, as it requires that responsible global leaders balance various, often contradictory expectations, demands, and interests on the part of both global and local stakeholders. To successfully perform this balancing act, leaders need to possess the capacity to integrate multiple cultural and strategic realities, as well as the ability to recognize, understand, and identify with both global and local perspectives, and to reconcile potential conflicts between them (Javidan & Bowen, 2013; Miska, Stahl, & Mendenhall, 2013).

THE INSTITUTIONAL AND CULTURAL CONTEXT

At the macro level of analysis, the institutional and cultural environments within which global companies operate pose major constraints on the implementation of the previously discussed CSR approaches and on the enactment of responsible leadership (see, e.g., Aguilera et al., 2007; Schneider, Barsoux, & Stahl, 2014; Waldman, Sully de Luque, Washburn, & House, 2006). In 2012, when IKEA still relied on printed catalogues as a key marketing instrument, the multinational furniture company of Swedish origin systematically removed women from the Saudi Arabian version of its catalogue. This step was followed by considerable criticism from global media as well as by Swedish politicians, seriously damaging IKEA's reputation as a socially responsible company and an employer of choice for women and minorities. It appears that in Saudi Arabia, IKEA was leaning toward Saudi sensibilities, rather than promoting its own values such as "daring to be different" and promoting human rights universally through a global CSR approach (Miska & Pleskova, 2016). In the end, IKEA took full responsibility and apologized – in accordance with what the public in the Western world and respective institutional influences required.

Institutional factors include cultural norms and values, and they can constrain responsible managerial behavior in the global context, as they embody societies' and nations' formal and informal rules (North, 1990). Hall and Soskice's (2001) "varieties of capitalism" is an approach intended to systematically capture the variations in institutional rules across countries. Traditionally, these variations can be classified into two types of political economies: liberal market economics (LMEs) prevalent in Anglo-Saxon countries and characterized by companies coordinating their activities by means of competitive market arrangements and formal contracting; and coordinated market economies (CMEs), prevalent in Continental Europe, where companies depend on non-market relationships, resulting in the need for relational networks rather than competitive activities. Largely consistent with this dichotomous distinction, Witt and Stahl (2016) found evidence for executives' responsibility orientations to differ across two Western (Germany, United States) and three Asian (Hong Kong, Japan, South Korea) economies, albeit there was variance between the two broad LME and CME categories. For instance, for US executives (LME) shareholder primacy was important, whereas business leaders in Japan (CME) considered many more stakeholders to be important, including employees and society as a whole.

Beyond the dichotomous LME–CME distinction, more recent research (e.g., Fainshmidt et al., 2018; Witt et al., 2018) indicates a broad variety of alternative institutional systems. This specifically mirrors the nature of many emerging and advancing economies, where institutional environments tend to be less clearly explicable as they are frequently characterized by arbitrary law enforcement, bureaucratic irregularities, and corruption practices (Dobers & Halme, 2009). For instance, Fainshmidt et al. (2018) suggested additional institutional categories such as state-led (e.g., Argentina, China, India), family-led (e.g., Brazil, Mexico, Nigeria), and centralized tribe (e.g., Iran, Saudi Arabia, UAE). As with LMEs and CMEs, it is likely that within these types of institutional systems, executives' responsibility orientations follow patterns mirroring the characteristics of these environments.

Institutional environments not only shape CSR requirements and expectations on the part of various stakeholders, they also influence global managers' values, attitudes, and assumptions (Miska & Mendenhall, 2018). As organizations and their members operate in different cultural and institutional environments, they experience various societal values related to CSR (Waldman et al., 2006; Witt & Stahl, 2016) and encounter assorted constraints on behaviors that are considered acceptable in a society (Jackson, Gelfand, De et al., 2019; Martin, Resick, Keating, & Dickson, 2009). Thus, in the context of CSR, the role of culture needs to be examined with other institutional influences, which may reveal numerous interdependencies that are often underappreciated (Caprar & Neville, 2012).

Societal cultural values frequently examined in CSR research are largely based on the Hofstede Values Framework (Hofstede, 2001) and the GLOBE Project (House et al., 2004). Although there are other cultural value models (Inglehart & Baker, 2000; Schwartz, 1999), we will focus on those extensively assessed across CSR research. Drawing from the Hofstede model (2001), studies using two cultural value dimensions, individualism (IDV) and power distance index (PDI), demonstrate both similar and disparate findings. Societies ranking higher on Hofstede's IDV have independence from the broader group and show greater affinity toward the self, whereas lower-IDV societies give precedence to the group over the individual. Societies ranking higher on PDI accept that power or privilege is duly stratified as a result of tradition or experience, whereas lower-PDI societies believe that power is more equally distributed and interaction minimizes differences between its members (Carl et al., 2004).

Researchers found societies characterized as lower-IDV were significantly related to higher corporate social performance (Ho et al., 2012). PDI showed a negative association with studies assessing corporate social performance (Cai et al., 2016) and charitable behavior (Winterich & Zhang, 2014). Other studies (Gallego-Álvareza & Ortas, 2017; Gallego-Álvarez & Pucheta-Martínez, 2020; Peng et al., 2014) indicate that individualistic societies exhibit stronger associations with CSR-related activities, while societies having a greater power differential have less concern for these activities. However, through an institutional perspective (e.g., Hartmann & Uhlenbruck, 2015; Scholtens & Dam, 2007) and in other studies, relationships between IDV or PDI and CSR-related outcomes are rather mixed (Ho et al., 2012; Park et al., 2007; Ringov & Zollo, 2007). While assessing culture and corporate non-financial performance globally, some studies showed that higher PDI had a significant negative effect on corporate social and environmental performance (Husted, 2005), with IDV having no significant effect (Ringov & Zollo, 2007). In other studies where the PDI dimension was significant, the hypothesis was not supported because higher PDI revealed an opposite relationship than anticipated, showing a positive relationship with corporate social performance (Ho et al., 2012).

Along these lines, the GLOBE culture dimensions of institutional collectivism (ISC), and power distance (PD) are frequently used to examine CSR. Hofstede's dimension of collectivism (IDV), however, is different than the GLOBE institutional collectivism (ISC) (Gelfand et al., 2004). Whereas the Hofstede IDV cultural dimension is defined as in-group or family collectivism, the GLOBE ISC dimension exemplifies societies where people identify with the larger collective, as well as where institutional practices reward and encourage collective rather than individual action (Javidan, Dorfman, Sully de Luque, & House, 2006). Research has found that GLOBE institutional collectivism (ISC) is positively related to sustainability initiatives, CSR decision-making, and responsible leadership (Parboteeah et al., 2012; Waldman et al., 2006; Witt & Stahl, 2016).

The GLOBE dimension of power distance (PD) is to some extent similar to the Hofstede power distance (PDI) construct. The PD dimension describes how power is accepted in societies, with higher PD typifying societies that are more accepting and lower PD representing those less accepting of the power differential. PD has been negatively related to ethics, CSR, corporate social and environmental performance, and sustainability initiatives (Alas, 2006; Parboteeah et al., 2012; Ringov & Zollo, 2007). In one study, Waldman and colleagues (2006) assessed the impact that societial institutional collectivism (ISC) and PD cultural values have on managers' CSR decision-making values involving stakeholders and overall community/state welfare. These researchers find that societies with higher ISC cultural values have a positive impact on managers' CSR values, while societies with higher PD culture values showed they had less concern for, and interest in, stakeholders such as employees, customers, and the environment.

Investigating culture and its effects on "doing good" is presented in studies on topics such as firms' CSR commitment (Peng et al., 2014) or corporate social performance (Ho et al., 2012; Ringov & Zollo, 2007). In one study, Thanetsunthorn (2015) examined several culture dimensions and CSR. For community CSR performance, which aligns closest with "doing good" specifically, negative effects were consistently identified for Hofstede's PDI and IDV. In another study, Winterich and Zhang (2014) examined why some societies are more inclined to donate both money and time, and others are less inclined to do so. They discovered that societies depicted as higher on PDI create a diminished sense of responsibility to support others, resulting in less charitable behavior.

When looking at comparative research with a focus on "avoiding harm", we have identified two broad thematic areas that align with CSR/CS: environmental concerns as well as corruption and bribery. To gain deeper appreciation for governance issues from a cross-national perspective, researchers have examined the relationship between national culture dimensions and the nature of corruption (e.g., Boateng et al., 2021; Jain & Jain, 2018; Pillay & Dorasamy, 2010; Scholl & Schermuly, 2020). Through these studies, both national differences and social institutions were shown as important when considering cross-national differences. Investigating the association between national cultural dimensions and corruption, using the Corruption Perception Index (CPI), Seleim and Bontis (2009) showed the impact of GLOBE institutional collectivism (ISC) practices on the level of corruption in a society. In another study employing the Hofstede

cultural dimension, Achim (2016) showed that lower IDV societies (more collectivistic societies) display greater degrees of corruption; whereas higher PDI societies exhibit elevated levels of corruption. Overall, power imbalances, as well as
individualism versus collectivism, appear to be cultural features most frequently
linked to corruption and bribery.

When it comes to navigating cultural differences relevant for responsible
managerial behavior in the global context, culture can be a particular asset in
understanding the idiosyncrasies of specific institutional environments in which
global managers operate. Culture can also pose a constraint on managers' ability
to engage in responsible behavior, especially if they are unaware of the informal
rules of specific contexts, lack cultural understanding, or have a "cultural imperialism" attitude. In this sense, Fitzsimmons, Miska, and Stahl (2011) pointed to
the potential of multicultural managers who have acquired experience in multiple
cultural settings. Due to their insights into different cultural contexts and their
attendant perspective-taking abilities, multicultural managers might be better at
reconciling conflicting cultural values and norms. Consequently, global managers
who possess experience in various cultural settings are likely to deal more effi-
ciently with institutional and cultural variations in the global context.

Institutional and cultural differences can result in tough choices for global
managers. Based on their own cultural values and ethical norms, they frequently need to decide when different is different and when different is ethically
wrong. For example, the 2013 collapse of the Savar building in Bangladesh
caused more than 1,000 deaths, making it one of the most lethal garment
factory accidents at that time. At first, the factory owners and government
officials were considered the main culprits, since they had failed to enforce
proper safety standards, although soon after the disaster, international brands
and retailers like Walmart, Mango, Primark, and Matalan (Mail Online, 2013;
The Economist, 2013) were criticized, as they had garments produced in the
factory. In most of the international brands' and retailers' countries of origin, labor safety standards are considerably higher. However, these companies
relied on the less stringent institutional environment in Bangladesh – leading
to fatal consequences.

These findings indicate that responsible leaders must have a comprehensive
understanding of culture and how it matters in the design, implementation, and
adoption of CSR practices, as well as managers' CSR-related choices. Answering
these questions will necessitate that responsible leaders focus on both procedures and context by exploring mediating processes linking culture with CSR, as
well as clarifying the conditions through which culture matters most in influencing CSR practices and outcomes.

CONCLUSION: THE CHALLENGE OF
RESPONSIBLE GLOBAL LEADERSHIP

As societies rise from the ashes of the global pandemic, there is increasing
pressure on organizations and their managers to act in a globally responsible,

sustainable, and ethically sound manner. Compounding these challenges, the world landscape is changing and discussions abound regarding the "deglobaliza-tion" of business. Bremmer (2022) argues that the era of "hyperglobalization" ended with the 2008 global financial crisis, but this does not portend the end of global trade. However, with the disruption of global supply chains, it may mean rethinking the global process through which business is done. In this read-ing, we have provided an overview of existing and emerging research relevant to responsible global leadership – including work on ethical decision making, shared leadership, and corporate social responsibility – highlighting the multiple influ-ences on responsible managerial behavior and the conditions under which global executives may engage in responsible or irresponsible conduct. Global execu-tives need to address the diverse, and often conflicting, demands of multiple cross-boundary stakeholders. The complexities of leading responsibly in a global environment span multiple layers, comprising characteristics of the individual manager, aspects of the organizational context, including top management team decision making and corporate CSR strategies, as well as the broader institu-tional and cultural environments in which global corporations are embedded. In navigating these complexities, executives need to be aware of their own perspec-tives, orientations, and biases in situations of ethical decision making. Global managers need to possess a specific skillset and mindset to implement corporate CSR strategies. In particular, they must be able to balance global integration and local responsiveness with respect to CSR, sustainability, and ethics. While responsible leadership in a cross-border and culturally diverse context is highly demanding, it offers vast opportunities for global executives to make a differ-ence for their companies and society.

REFERENCES

Achim, M. (2016). Cultural dimension of corruption: A cross-country survey. *International Advancement of Economic Research*, 22(3), 333–345.

Aggarwal, R. K., & Samwick, A. A. (2003). Why do managers diversify their firms? Agency reconsidered. *The Journal of Finance*, 58(1), 71–118.

Aguilera, R., Rupp, D. E., Williams, C. A., & Ganapathi, J. (2007). Putting the s back in corporate social responsibility: A multilevel theory of social change in organizations. *Academy of Management Review*, 3(3), 836–863.

Alas, R. (2006). Ethics in countries with different cultural dimensions. *Journal of Business Ethics*, 69(3), 237–247. https://doi.org/10.1007/s10551-006-9088-3.

Ancona, D. G., & Caldwell, D. F. (1992). Bridging the boundary: External activity and performance in organizational teams. *Administrative Science Quarterly*, 37(4), 634–665.

Aquino, K., & Reed, A. (2002). The self-importance of moral identity. *Journal of Personality and Social Psychology*, 83(6), 1423–1440.

Arendt, H. (1963). *Eichmann in Jerusalem*. New York: Penguin.

Arthaud-Day, M. L. (2005). Transnational corporate social responsibility: A tri-dimensional approach to international CSR Research. *Business Ethics Quarterly*, 15(1), 1–22.

Asch, S. E. (1951). Effects of group pressure on the modification and distortion of judgments. In H. Guetzkow (Ed.), *Groups, leadership and men* (pp. 177–190). Pittsburgh: Carnegie.

Ashforth, B. E., & Anand, V. (2003). The normalization of corruption in organizations. In R. M. Kramer & B. M. Staw (Eds.), *Research in organizational behavior* (Vol. 25, pp. 1–52). Amsterdam: Elsevier.

Bandura, A. (2002). Selective moral disengagement in the exercise of moral agency. *Journal of Moral Education*, 31(2), 101–119.

Bandura, A., Barbaranelli, C., Caprara, G. V., & Pastorelli, C. (1996). Mechanisms of moral disengagement in the exercise of moral agency. *Journal of Personality and Social Psychology*, 71(2), 364–374.

Bazerman, M. H., & Tenbrunsel, A. E. (2011). Good people often let bad things happen – Ethical breakdowns. *Harvard Business Review*, 89(4), 58–65.

Bartlett, C. A., & Ghoshal, S. (1998). *Managing Across Borders: The Transnational Solution* (2nd ed.). Boston: Harvard Business School Press.

Blasi, A. (1980). Bridging moral cognition and moral action: A critical review of the literature. *Psychological Bulletin*, 88(1), 1–45.

Blasi, A. (2004). Moral functioning: Moral understanding and personality. In D. K. Lapsley & D. Narvaez (Eds.), *Moral development, self and identity* (pp. 335–348). Mahwah, NJ: Lawrence Erlbaum.

Boateng, A., Wang, Y., Ntim, C., & Glaister, K. (2021). National culture, corporate governance and corruption: A cross-country analysis. *International Journal of Financial Economics*, 26(3), 3852–3874..

Bremmer, I. (2022, October 25). Globalization isn't dead: The world is more fragmented, but interdependence still rules. *Foreign Affairs,* https://www.foreignaffairs.com/world/globalization-isnt-dead

Cai, Y., Pan, C., & Statman, M. (2016). Why do countries matter so much in corporate social performance? *Journal of Corporate Finance*, 41, 591–609.

Caprar, D. V., & Neville, B. A. (2012). "Norming" and "conforming": Integrating cultural and institutional explanations for sustainability adoption in business. *Journal of Business Ethics*, 110(2), 231–245.

Carl, D., Gupta, V., & Javidan, M. (2004). Power distance. In R. J. House, P. J. Hanges, M. Javidan, P. W. Dorfman, & V. Gupta (Eds.), *Culture, leadership, and organizations: The globe study of 62 societies* (pp. 513–563). Thousand Oaks, CA: Sage.

Carson, J. B., Tesluk, P. E., & Marrone, J. A. (2007). Shared leadership in teams: An investigation of antecedent conditions and performance. *Academy of Management Journal*, 50(5), 1217–1234.

Chhabra, B., & Srivastava, S. (2022). Paved with good intentions: Role of situational and dispositional influences on employees' unethical pro-organizational behavior. *International Journal of Organizational Analysis*. https://doi.org/10.1108/IJOA-03-2022-3191.

Christensen, L. J., Mackey, A., & Whetten, D. (2014). Taking responsibility for corporate social responsibility: The role of leaders in creating, implementing, sustaining, or avoiding socially responsible firm behaviors. *Academy of Management Perspectives*, 28(2), 164–178.

Christie, R., & Geis, F. (1970). *Studies in Machiavellianism*. New York: Academic Press.

Cikara, M., Farnsworth, R. A., Harris, L. T., & Fiske, S. T. (2010). On the wrong side of the trolley track: Neural correlates of relative social valuation. *Social Cognitive and Affective Neuroscience*, 5(4), 404–413.

Craft, J. L. (2013). A review of the empirical ethical decision-making literature: 2004–2011. *Journal of Business Ethics*, 117(2), 221–259.

Crilly, D., Ni, N., & Jiang, Y. (2016). Do-no-harm versus do-good social responsibility: Attributional thinking and the liability of foreignness. *Strategic Management Journal*, 37(7), 1316–1329.

Crilly, D., Schneider, S. C., & Zollo, M. (2008). Psychological antecedents to socially responsible behavior. *European Management Review*, 5(3), 175–190.

Cohen, S. G., & Bailey, D. E. (1997). What makes teams work: Group effectiveness research from the shop floor to the executive suite. *Journal of Management, 23*(3), 239–290.

Cox, T. H., & Blake, S. (1991). Managing cultural diversity: Implications for organizational competitiveness. *The Executive, 5,* 45–56.

Dahlin, K. B., Weingart, L. R., & Hinds, P. J. (2005). Team diversity and information use. *Academy of Management Journal, 48*(6), 1107–1123.

Damasio, A. R. (1994). *Descartes' error: Emotion, reason, and the human brain.* New York: Free Press.

Desai, A. B., & Rittenburg, T. (1997). Global ethics: An integrative framework for MNEs. *Journal of Business Ethics, 16*(8), 791–800.

Ditto, P. H., Pizarro, D. A., & Tannenbaum, D. (2009). Motivated moral reasoning. In B. H. Ross, D. M. Bartels, C. W. Bauman, L. J. Skitka, & D. L. Medin (Eds.), *Moral judgment and decision making* (pp. 307–338). San Diego, CA: Academic Press.

Dobers, P., & Halme, M. (2009). Corporate social responsibility and developing countries. *Corporate Social Responsibility and Environmental Management, 16*(5), 237–249.

Donaldson, T. (1996). Values in tension: Ethics away from home. *Harvard Business Review, 74*(5), 48–62.

Donaldson, T., & Dunfee, T. W. (1994). Toward a unified conception of business ethics: Integrative social contracts theory. *The Academy of Management Review, 19*(2), 252–284.

Donaldson, T., & Dunfee, T. W. (1999). When ethics travel: The promise and peril of global business ethics. *California Management Review, 41*(4), 45–63

Dovidio, J. F., Gaertner, S. L., Schnabel, N., Saguy, T., & Johnson, J. (2009). Recategorization and prosocial behavior: Common in-group identity and a dual identity. In S. Stürmer & M. Snyder (Eds.), *The psychology of prosocial behavior: Group processes, intergroup relations, and helping.* Oxford: Wiley-Blackwell.

Edelmann. (2022). Edelman Trust Barometer: Global report. https://www.edelman.com/trust/2022-trust-barometer.

Eisenberg, N. (2000). Emotion, regulation, and moral development. *Annual Review of Psychology, 51,* 665–697.

Elsbach, K. D. (1994). Managing organizational legitimacy in the California cattle industry: The construction and effectiveness of verbal accounts. *Administrative Science Quarterly, 39*(1), 57–88.

EFMD. (2005). Globally responsible leadership – A call for engagement. Retrieved from http://www.oasishumanrelations.org.uk/content/uploads/2015/01/grli-call-forengagement.pdf.

Fainshmidt, S., Judge, W. Q., Aguilera, R. V., & Smith, A. (2018). Varieties of institutional systems: A contextual taxonomy of understudied countries. *Journal of World Business, 53*(3), 307–322.

Filatotchev, I., & Stahl, G. K. (2015). Towards transnational CSR: Corporate social responsibility approaches and governance solutions for multinational corporations. *Organizational Dynamics, 44*(2), 121–129.

Finkelstein, S., Hambrick, D. C., & Cannella, A. A. (2009). *Strategic leadership: Theory and research on executives, top management teams, and boards.* New York: Oxford University Press.

Fitzsimmons, S. R., Miska, C., & Stahl, G. K. (2011). Multicultural employees: Global business' untapped resource. *Organizational Dynamics.* 40, 199–206.

Gaertner, S. L., & Dovidio, J. F. (2000). *Reducing intergroup bias: The common ingroup identity model.* Philadelphia, PA: The Psychology Press.

Gallego-Álvarez, P., & Ortas, P. (2017). Corporate environmental sustainability reporting in the context of national cultures: A quantile regression approach. *International Business Review, 26*(2), 337–353.

Gallego-Álvarez, M., & Pucheta-Martínez, I. (2020). Corporate social responsibility reporting and corporate governance mechanisms: An international outlook from emerging countries. *Business Strategy and Development*, 3(1), 77–97.

Gelfand, M. J., Bhawuk, D. P., Nishii, L. H., & Bechtold, D. J. (2004). Individualism and collectivism. In R. J. House, P. J. Hanges, M. Javidan, P. W. Dorfman, & V. Gupta (Eds.), *Culture, leadership, and organizations: The globe study of 62 societies* (pp. 437–512). Thousand Oaks, CA: Sage.

Gellerman, S. W. (1986). Why "good" managers make bad ethical choices. *Harvard Business Review*, 86(4), 85–90.

George, G., Howard-Grenville, J., Joshi, A., & Tihanyi, L. (2016). Understanding and tackling societal grand challenges through management research. *Academy of Management Journal*, 59(6), 1880–1895.

Greene, J., & Haidt, J. (2002). How (and where) does moral judgment work? *Trends in Cognitive Sciences*, 6(12), 517–523.

Greene, J. D., Sommerville, R. B., Nystrom, L. E., Darley, J. M., & Cohen, J. D. (2001). An fMRI investigation of emotional engagement in moral judgment. *Science*, 293(5537), 2105–2018.

Hafsi, T., & Turgut, G. (2013). Boardroom diversity and its effect on social performance: Conceptualization and empirical evidence. *Journal of Business Ethics*, 1–17. https://doi.org/10.1007/s10551-012-1272-z.

Haidt, J. (2001). The emotional dog and its rational tail: A social intuitionist approach to moral judgment. *Psychological Review*, 108(4), 814–834.

Hall, P. A., & Soskice, D. (2001). An introduction to varieties of capitalism. In P. A. Hall & D. W. Soskice (Eds.), *Varieties of capitalism: The institutional foundations of comparative advantage* (pp. 1–70). Oxford: Oxford University Press.

Hartmann, J., & Uhlenbruck, K. (2015). National institutional antecedents to corporate environmental performance. *Journal of World Business*, 50(4), 729–741.

Hoek, M. (2018). *The trillion dollar shift*. London: Routledge.

Hofstede, G. (2001). Culture's recent consequences: Using dimension scores in theory and research. *International Journal of Cross Cultural Management*, 1(1), 11–17.

House, R. J., Hanges, P. M., Javidan, M., Dorfman, P., & Gupta, V. (2004). *Culture, leadership, and organizations: The globe study of 62 societies*. Thousand Oaks, CA: Sage.

Ho, F. N., Wang, H. M. D., & Vitell, S. J. (2012). A global analysis of corporate social performance: The effects of cultural and geographic environments. *Journal of Business Ethics*, 107(4), 423–433.

Hope Hailey, V., & Jacobs, K. (2022). *Responsible business through crisis: Has COVID-19 changed leadership forever?* London: Chartered Institute of Personnel and Development.

Horwitz, S. K., & Horwitz, I. B. (2007). The effects of team diversity on team outcomes: A meta-analytic review of team demography. *Journal of Management*, 33(6), 987–1015.

Husted, B. W. (2005). Culture and ecology: A cross-national study of the determinants of environmental sustainability. *Management International Review*, 45(3), 349–371.

Inglehart, R., & Baker, W. (2000). Modernization, cultural change, and the persistence of traditional values. *American Sociological Review*, 65(1), 19–51.

Jackson, J. C., Gelfand, M., De, S., & Fox, A. (2019). The loosening of American culture over 200 years is associated with a creativity–order trade-off. *Nature Human Behaviour*, 3, 759.

Jain, S., & Jain, S. (2018). Power distance belief and preference for transparency. *Journal of Business Research*, 89, 135–142.

Janis, I. L. (1972). *Victims of groupthink: A psychological study of foreign-policy decisions and Fiascoes*. Boston, MA: Houghton Mifflin.

Javidan, M., & Bowen, D. (2013). The "global mindset" of managers. *Organizational Dynamics*, 42(2), 145–155.

Javidan, M., Dorfman, P. W., Sully De Luque, M. S., & House, R. J. (2006). In the eye of the beholder: Cross cultural lessons in leadership from project globe. *Academy of Management Perspectives*, 20(1), 67–90.

Jones, T. M. (1991). Ethical decision making by individuals in organizations: An issue-contingent model. *Academy of Management Review*, 16(2), 366–395.

Kish-Gephart, J. J., Harrison, D. A., & Treviño, L. K. (2010). Bad apples, bad cases, and bad barrels: Meta-analytic evidence about sources of unethical decisions at work. *Journal of Applied Psychology*, 95(1), 1–31.

Kish-Gephart, J. J., Treviño, L. K., Chen, A., & Tilton, J. (2019). Behavioral business ethics: The journey from foundations to future. In D.M. Wasieleski and J. Weber (Eds.), *Business and society 360, Business ethics:* Volume 3, (pp. 3–34). Bingley: Emerald Publishing Limited.

Knowles, J., & Hunsaker, T. (2022). The new math of Multistakeholderism. *MIT Sloan Management Review*, 64(1), 1–4.

Kohlberg, L. (1984). *The psychology of moral development: essays on moral development.* San Francisco, CA: Harper & Row.

Kunda, Z. (1990). The case for motivated reasoning. *Psychological Bulleting*, 108(3), 480–498.

Lane, H. L., Maznevski, M. L., Mendenhall, M. E., & McNett, J. (Eds.). (2009). *The Blackwell handbook of global management – A guide to managing complexity.* Malden, MA: Blackwell Publishing Ltd.

Lehnert, K., Park, Y. H., & Singh, N. (2015). Research note and review of the empirical ethical decision-making literature: Boundary conditions and extensions. *Journal of Business Ethics*, 129(1), 195–219.

Mail Online. (2013). Miracle survivor of Bangladesh factory collapse changed into clothes of her dead colleague before being rescued: 19-year-old who lived off water from dripping pipe for 17 days emerged from ruins in a mauve wrap and pink scarf. *Mail Online*. Retrieved June 11, 2013, from http://www.dailymail.co.uk/news/article -2322391/Bangladesh-survivor-Reshma-Akhter-changed-dead-colleagues-clothes -trapped-rubble.html.

Martin, G. S., Resick, C. J., Keating, M. A., & Dickson, M. W. (2009). Ethical leadership across cultures: A comparative analysis of German and US perspectives. *Business Ethics: A European Review*, 18(2), 127–144.

Mathur, V. A., Harada, T., Lipke, T., & Chiao, J. Y. (2010). Neural basis of extraordinary empathy and altruistic motivation. *Neuroimage*, 51(4), 1468–1475.

Mayer, D. M. (2010). From proscriptions to prescriptions: A call for including prosocial behavior in behavioral ethics. In M. Schminke (Ed.), *Managerial ethics: Managing the psychology of morality* (pp. 257–271). New York: Taylor and Francis Group.

McFarland, S., Webb, M., & Brown, D. (2012). All humanity is my ingroup: A measure and studies of identification with all humanity. *Journal of Personality and Social Psychology*, 103(5), 830–853.

McLean, B., & Elkind, P. (2003). *The smartest guys in the room: The amazing rise and scandalous fall of Enron.* New York: Portfolio.

Milgram, S. (1974). *Obedience to authority: An experimental view.* New York: Harper & Row.

Milliken, F. J., & Martins, L. L. (1996). Searching for common threads: Understanding the multiple effects of diversity in organizational groups. *The Academy of Management Review*, 21(2), 402–433.

Miska, C., Economou, V., & Stahl, G. K. (2020). Responsible leadership in a VUCA world. In M.E. Mendenhall, M. Žilinskaitė, G.K. Stahl, & R. Clapp-Smith (Eds.), *Responsible global leadership: Dilemmas, paradoxes, and opportunities* (pp. 11–28). New York: Routledge.

Miska, C., & Mendenhall, M. E. (2018). Responsible leadership: A mapping of extant research and future directions. *Journal of Business Ethics*, 148(1), 117–134.

Miska, C., & Pleskova, M. (2016). IKEA's ethical controversies in Saudi Arabia. In C. Barmeyer & P. Franklin (Eds.), *Case studies in intercultural management: Achieving synergy from diversity.* (pp. 120–133). London: Palgrave Macmillan.

Miska, C., Stahl, G. K., & Mendenhall, M. E. (2013). Intercultural competencies as antecedents of responsible global leadership. *European Journal of International Management*, 7(5), 550–569.

Miska, C., Witt, M. A., & Stahl, G. K. (2016). Drivers of global CSR integration and local CSR responsiveness: Evidence from Chinese MNEs. *Business Ethics Quarterly*, 26(3): 317–345.

Monin, B., & Jordan, A. H. (2009). The dynamic moral self: A social psychological perspective. In D. Narvaez & D.K. Lapsley (Eds.), *Personality, identity, and character: Explorations in moral psychology*, (pp. 341–354). Cambridge University Press.

Moore, C. (2008). Moral disengagement in processes of organizational corruption. *Journal of Business Ethics*, 80(1), 129–139.

Moore, C., Detert, J. R., Treviño, L. K., Baker, V. L., & Mayer, D. M. (2012). Why employees do bad things: Moral disengagement and unethical organizational behavior. *Personnel Psychology*, 65(1), 1–48.

Moore, C., & Gino, F. (2013). Ethically adrift: How others pull our moral compass from True North, and how we can fix it. *Research in Organizational Behavior*, 33, 53–77.

Newman, A., Le, H., North-Samardzic, A., & Cohen, M. (2020). Moral disengagement at work: A review and research agenda. *Journal of Business Ethics*, 167(3), 535–570.

North, D. C. (1990). *Institutions, institutional change and economic performance.* Cambridge: Cambridge University Press.

O'Fallon, M. J., & Butterfield, K. D. (2005). A review of the empirical ethical decision-making literature: 1996–2003. *Journal of Business Ethics*, 59(4), 375–413.

Paharia, N., Vohs, K. D., & Deshpandé, R. (2013). Sweatshop labor is wrong unless the shoes are cute: Cognition can both help and hurt motivated reasoning. *Organizational Behavior and Human Decision Processes*, 121(1), 81–88.

Parboteeah, K. P., Addae, H. M., & Cullen, J. B. (2012). Propensity to support sustainability initiatives: A cross-national model. *Journal of Business Ethics*, 105(3), 403–413.

Park, H., Russell, C., & Lee, J. (2007). National culture and environmental sustainability: A cross-national analysis. *Journal of Economics and Finance*, 31(1), 104–121.

Pearce, C., Wassenaar, C., & Manz, C. (2014). Is shared leadership the key to responsible leadership? *Academy of Management Perspectives*, 28(3), 275–288.

Pearce, C. L., & Manz, C. C. (2011). Leadership centrality and corporate social ir-responsibility (CSIR): The potential ameliorating effects of self and shared leadership on CSIR. *Journal of Business Ethics*, 102(4), 563–579.

Pearce, C. L., & Stahl, G. K. (2015). Introduction to the special issue: The leadership imperative for sustainability and corporate social responsibility. *Organizational Dynamics.* 44(2), 83–86.

Peng, Y. S., Dashdeleg, A. U., & Chih, H. L. (2014). National culture and firm's CSR engagement: A cross-nation study. *Journal of Marketing & Management*, 5(1), 38–49.

Pettigrew, T. F., & Tropp, L. R. (2006). A meta-analytic test of intergroup contact theory. *Journal of Personality and Social Psychology*, 90(5), 751–783.

Pfeffer, J. (1983). Organizational demography. In B. Staw & L. Cummings (Eds.), *Research in organizational behavior* (Vol. 5, pp. 299–357). Greenwich, CT: JAI Press.

Pillay, S., & Dorasamy, N. (2010). Linking cultural dimensions with the nature of corruption: An institutional theory perspective. *International Journal of Cross Cultural Management*, 10(3), 363–378.

Pontes, J., & Anselmo, M. (2022). *Operation car wash: Brazil's institutionalized crime and the inside story of the biggest corruption scandal in history.* London: Bloomsbury Academic.

Post, C., Rahman, N., & Rubow, E. (2011). Green governance: Boards of directors' composition and environmental corporate social responsibility. *Business and Society,* 50(1), 189–223.

Pucik, V., Björkman, I., Paul Evans, P., & Stahl, G. K. (2023). *The global challenge: Managing people across borders* (4th ed.). Cheltenham, UK: Edward Elgar Publishing.

Puffer, S. M., & McCarthy, D. J. (2008). Ethical turnarounds and transformational leadership: A global imperative for corporate social responsibility. *Thunderbird International Business Review,* 50(5), 303–314.

Quinn, L., & Dalton, M. (2009). Leading for sustainability: Implementing the tasks of leadership. *Corporate Governance: The International Journal of Business in Society,* 9(1), 21–38.

Reed, A. I., & Aquino, K. (2003). Moral identity and the expanding circle of moral regard towards out-groups. *Journal of Personality and Social Psychology,* 84(6), 1270–1286.

Reynolds, S. J., & Ceranic, T. L. (2007). The effects of moral judgment and moral identity on moral behavior: An empirical examination of the moral individual. *Journal of Applied Psychology,* 92(6), 1610–1624.

Ringov, D., & Zollo, M. (2007). The impact of national culture on corporate social performance. *Corporate Governance: The International Journal of Business in Society,* 7(4), 476–485.

Robison, P. (2021). *Flying blind: The 737 MAX tragedy and the fall of Boeing.* New York: Doubleday.

Schneider, S., Barsoux, J.-L., & Stahl, G. K. (2014). *Managing across cultures.* London: Prentice Hall.

Scholl, W., & Schermuly, C. (2020). The impact of culture on corruption, gross domestic product, and human development. *Journal of Business Ethics,* 162(1), 171–189.

Scholtens, B., & Dam, L. (2007). Cultural values and international differences in business ethics. *Journal of Business Ethics,* 75(3), 273–284.

Scholz, M., de los Reyes, G., & Smith, N. C. (2019). The enduring potential of justified hypernorms. *Business Ethics Quarterly,* 29(3), 317–342.

Schwartz, S. H. (1999). A theory of cultural values and some implications for work. *Applied Psychology: An International Review,* 48(1), 23–48.

Seleim, A., & Bontis, N. (2009). The relationship between culture and corruption: A cross-national study. *Journal of Intellectual Capital,* 10(1), 165–184.

Skapinker, M. (2003, January 25). Too much unity in the boardroom. *The Financial Times,* 26.

Sneader, K., & Singhal, S. (2020). *Beyond coronavirus: The path to the next normal.* McKinsey & Company, p. 5.

Sonenshein, S. (2007). The role of construction, intuition, and justification in responding to ethical issues at work: The sensemaking-intuition model. *Academy of Management Review,* 32(4), 1022–1040.

Stahl, G. K., & Sully de Luque, M. S. (2014). Antecedents of responsible leader behavior: A research synthesis, conceptual framework, and agenda for future research. *Academy of Management Perspectives,* 28(3), 235–254.

Stahl, G. K., Maznevski, M. L., Voigt, A., & Jonsen, K. (2010). Unraveling the effects of cultural diversity in teams: A meta-analysis of research on multicultural work groups. *Journal of International Business Studies,* 41(4), 690–709.

Stahl, G. K., Miska, C., Puffer, S. M., & McCarthy, D. J. (2016). Responsible global leadership in emerging markets. In J. S. Osland, M. Li, & M. E. Mendenhall (Eds.),

Advances in global leadership, (Vol. 9, pp. 79–106). Bingley: Emerald Group Publishing Limited.

Stahl, G. K., Pless, N. M., Maak, T., & Miska, C. (2017). Responsible global leadership. In M. E. Mendenhall, J. Osland, A. Bird, G. R. Oddou, M. J. Stevens, M. L. Maznevski, & G. K. Stahl (Eds.), *Global leadership: Research, practice, and development* (3rd ed., pp. 363–388). New York: Routledge.

Stål, F., Marttila, A., & Macassa, G. (2022). Business executives' perceptions of responsible leadership and corporate social responsibility for stakeholders' health and wellbeing. *International Journal of Applied Research on Public Health Management*, 7(1), 1–14.

Sun, W., & Govind, R. (2022). A new understanding of marketing and "doing good": Marketing's power in the TMT and corporate social responsibility. *Journal of Business Ethics*, 176(1), 89–109.

Tajfel, H. (1982). Social psychology of intergroup relations. *Annual Review of Psychology*, 33(1), 1–39.

Tajfel, H., & Turner, J. (1986). The social identity of intergroup behavior. In S. Worchel & W. Austin (Eds.), *Psychology and intergroup relations* (pp. 7–24). Chicago, IL: Nelson-Hall.

Tenbrunsel, A. E., & Smith-Crowe, K. (2008). Ethical decision making: Where we've been and where we're going. *Academy of Management Annals*, 2(1), 545–607.

Thanetsunthorn, N. (2015). The impact of national culture on corporate social responsibility: Evidence from cross-regional comparison. *Asian Journal of Business Ethics*, 4(1), 35–56.

The Economist. (2013). Battle of the brands. *The Economist*. Retrieved May 19, 2013, from http://www.economist.com/blogs/schumpeter/2013/05/factory-safety.

Todnem By, R. T. (2021). Leadership: In pursuit of purpose. *Journal of Change Management*, 21(1), 30–44. https://doi.org/10.1080/14697017.2021.1861698.

Treviño, L. K., den Nieuwenboer, N. A., & Kish-Gephart, J. J. (2014). (Un)ethical behavior in organizations. *Annual Review of Psychology*, 65, 635–660.

Treviño, L. K., Weaver, G. K., & Reynolds, S. J. (2006). Behavioral ethics in organizations: A review. *Journal of Management*, 32(6), 951–990.

Uhl-Bien, M., Marion, R., & McKelvey, B. (2007). Complexity leadership theory: Shifting leadership from the industrial age to the knowledge era. *The Leadership Quarterly*, 18(4), 298–318.

United Nations Global Compact. (2022). *United Nations Global Compact*. https://www.unglobalcompact.org/.

U.S. Government. (2002). *The role of the board of directors in Enron's collapse*. Washington, DC: U.S. Government Printing Office.

Valentine, S., & Godkin, L. (2019). Moral intensity, ethical decision making, and whistleblowing intention. *Journal of Business Research*, 98, 277–288.

Van Knippenberg, D., & Schippers, M. C. (2007). Work group diversity. *Annual Review of Psychology*, 58, 515–541.

Veetikazhi, R., Kamalanabhan, T. J., Malhotra, P., Arora, R., & Mueller, A. (2022). Unethical employee behaviour: A review and typology. *The International Journal of Human Resource Management*, 33(10), 1976–2018.

Voegtlin, C., Patzer, M., & Scherer, A. G. (2012). Responsible leadership in global business: A new approach to leadership and its multi-level outcomes. *Journal of Business Ethics*, 105(1), 1–16.

Waldman, D. A. (2011). Moving forward with the concept of responsible leadership: Three caveats to guide theory and research. *Journal of Business Ethics*, 98(1), 75–83.

Waldman, D. A., Sully de Luque, M. S., Washburn, N., House, R. J., Adetoun, B., Barrasa, A., Bobina, M., Bodur, M., Chen, Y., Debbarma, S., Dorfman, P., Dzuvichu, R. R., Evcimen, I., Fu, P., Grachev, M., Gonzalez Duarte, R., Gupta, V., Den Hartog, D. N., de Hoogh, A. H. B., Howell, J., Jone, K., Kabasakal, H., Konrad, E., Koopman, P. L., Lang, R., Lin, C., Liu, J., Martinez, B., Munley, A. E., Papalexandris, N., Peng, T. K., Prieto, L., Quigley, N., Rajasekar, J., Rodríguez, F. G., Steyrer, J., Tanure, B., Thierry, H., Thomas, V. M., van den Berg, P. T., & Wilderom, C. P. M. (2006). Cultural and leadership predictors of corporate social responsibility values of top management: A globe study of 15 countries. *Journal of International Business Studies*, 37(6), 823–837.

Waldman, D. A., Siegel, D. S., & Javidan, M. (2006). Components of CEO transformational leadership and corporate social responsibility. *Journal of Management Studies*, 43(8), 1703–1725.

Werhane, P. H., Hartman, L. P., Archer, C., Englehardt, E. E., & Pritchard, M. S. (2014). *Obstacles to ethical decision-making mental models, Milgram and the problem of obedience*. Cambridge: Cambridge University Press.

Wettstein, F., Santangelo, G. D., Giuliani, E., & Stahl, G. K. (2019). International business and human rights: A research agenda. *Journal of World Business*, 53(1), 54–65.

Williams, K. Y., & O'Reilly, C. A. (1998). Demography and diversity in organizations: A review of 40 years of research. *Research in Organizational Behavior*, 20, 77–140.

Winterich, K. P., & Zhang, Y. (2014). Accepting inequality deters responsibility: How power distance decreases charitable behavior. *Journal of Consumer Research*, 41(2), 274–293.

Witt, M. A., Kabbach de Castro, L. R., Amaeshi, K., Mahroum, S., Bohle, D., & Saez, L. (2018). Mapping the business systems of 61 major economies: A taxonomy and implications for varieties of capitalism and business systems research. *Socio-Economic Review*, 16(1), 5–38.

Witt, M. A., & Stahl, G. K. (2016). Foundations of responsible leadership: Asian versus Western executive responsibility orientations toward key stakeholders. *Journal of Business Ethics*, 136(3), 623–638.

Wong, E. M., Ormiston, M. E., & Tetlock, P. E. (2011). The effects of top management team integrative complexity and decentralized decision making on corporate social performance. *Academy of Management Journal*, 54(6), 1207–1228. https://doi.org/10.5465/amj.2008.0762.

Zimbardo, P. G. (1972). *Stanford prison experiment: A simulation study of the psychology of imprisonment*. Philip G. Zimbardo, Incorporated.

Zhong, C. B. (2011). The ethical dangers of deliberative decision making. *Administrative Science Quarterly*, 56(1), 1–25. http://doi.org/10.2189/asqu.2011.56.1.001.

Zhu, J., Liao, Z., Yam, K. C., & Johnson, R. (2018). Shared leadership: A state-of-the-art review and future research agenda. *Journal of Organizational Behavior*, 39(7), 834–852.

Zyglidopoulos, S., Dieleman, M., & Hirsch, P. (2020). Playing the game: Unpacking the rationale for organizational corruption in MNCs. *Journal of Management Inquiry*, 29(3), 338–349.

Mike Rosenberg

BUSINESS AND SUSTAINABILITY

ALTHOUGH THE EARLY 2020S HAVE been marked by the global COVID-19 pandemic, shortages of key commodities such as microchips, and Russia's invasion of Ukraine, one positive aspect has been the growing interest in environmental and social sustainability among the international business community.

Of course, many companies have a long history of environmental stewardship and concern for people and the communities in which they operate. The Henkel Corporation, for example, has been doing full life cycle assessments of the environmental impact of its products since the 1950s.

What is different is that over the last 10–15 years the number of companies which are making clear and well-publicized progress on goals related to both environmental and social sustainability has been growing, and companies with some history in this area are making increasingly bold and public targets.

Today, thousands of companies and other organizations publish formal sustainability reports or integrate sustainability into their annual reports. In fact, a combination of factors has led to what one might call a tipping point on this topic which has brought businesses of all kinds around the world to the conviction that they must go even further and integrate sustainability into their strategy and human resource practices.

This increased focus on sustainability is part of the larger question of the role of business in society. The need for a company to balance the financial interests of its shareholders with other stakeholders and the connection between that and human resource management has been well established since the 1980s.[1]

This reading will explore the link between sustainability, business strategy and international human resources management (HRM). It adds to a growing body of literature which looks at the links between HRM and the broader issues of corporate social responsibility (CSR).[2] The reading starts by going into some detail on the origin of the United Nations' 17 Sustainable Development Goals (SDGs). It then discusses why we may have reached a tipping point on this issue,

DOI: 10.4324/9781003247272-34

then circles back to the central role currently played by the SDGs. The reading closes with a discussion of what strategic sustainability means in the corporate context and the specific role that the human resources (HR) area needs to play in this regard.

THE SUSTAINABLE DEVELOPMENT GOALS

The SDGs are the result of a process that was led by the UN's Secretary-General Ban Ki-moon to launch a new set of targets to replace the Millennium Development Goals (MDGs) which had helped the world to focus its attention between 2000 and 2015.

The MDGs began in the 1990s in a series of conferences during which UN member states were discussing the most urgent priorities of human development for the 21st century. These conferences included the United Nations Conference on Environment and Development in 1992, the International Conference on Population and Development in 1994 and the Fourth World Conference on Women in 1995.

Together with the *Brahimi Report* (2000),[3] these conferences led to the *Millennium Declaration* which was signed by 189 heads of state in September, 2000.

In 2001, Kofi Annan, the Secretary-General at that time, signed a report titled *A Road Map towards the Implementation of the United Nations Millennium Declaration* which defined the implementation of the eight Millennium Development Goals (see Exhibit 1), which had 18 targets and 48 indicators. These targets were defined as global aspirational achievements to be adopted by national governments and to be measured by using quantifiable indicators.

About two years before signing the *Millennium Declaration*, Annan challenged world business leaders to implement the triple bottom line, an idea put

Exhibit 1 The eight Millennium Development Goals.

Source: United Nations Development Program (https://www.un.org/sustainabledevelopment/blog/2015/05/jeffrey-sachs-interview/mdgs/).

forward by John Elkington,[4] who argued that companies should report not only on their financial performance, but also their environmental and social achievements.

These ideas were developed, and finally included ten principles, which were called the UN Global Compact. Since it was launched in July 2000, more than 16,000 organizations from 160 countries have signed the Global Compact.

Embracing the MDGs and signing the Global Compact was a break from Milton Friedman's negative view of corporate philanthropy, or what came to be called corporate social responsibility.

In a famous article,[5] Friedman argued that corporate philanthropy was a form of theft. In his view, a corporation existed to provide jobs for its staff, products and services for its customers, and a return for its shareholders. Money spent on anything that did not directly contribute to its core activities would have to be diverted from paying higher wages, lowering the cost of those products and services or generating profits. Friedman felt that it would be better to put the money into the pocket of these different stakeholders and then let them contribute to society.

Speaking at Chatham House in 2008, Cynthia Carroll, the former CEO of Anglo American, disagreed with this view and argued that:

> Companies are major economic actors who can play a significant role in areas like poverty alleviation, climate change, trade liberalization, supporting good governance, technology transfer and capacity-building. Indeed, without the involvement of the private sector it is difficult to see progress on many of these fronts.[6]

Over time, more and more corporate leaders came to understand that environmental and social responsibility were good for business, for a number of reasons.

In the first place, developing economies offered tremendous opportunities for growth, but could only do that if they developed economically and socially.

Second, those companies that were perceived as being helpful in this process would increase the value of what came to be called their social license to operate, or in other words, the reputation they have with civil society in the countries they operate in.

Third, many business leaders came to believe that bringing hundreds of millions of people out of poverty would increase political and economic stability, thus decreasing risk.

Overall, the UN felt that the MDGs were an unparalleled success. One report said that "even though the progress rate had been insufficient and uneven, the results were remarkable. One major achievement, for example, was that by the end of 2013 extreme poverty were reduced by half."[7]

However, some of the goals did not achieve the stipulated objectives. Child mortality for under-fives, for example, had not been cut by two-thirds, the maternal mortality rate was not reduced by three-quarters, and the population without access to basic sanitation was not halved.

Some non-governmental organizations claimed that the MDGs were too simplistic. In their view, some countries prioritized those actions that would make their numbers better at the expense of concentrating on the poorest of the poor or taking a longer-term perspective.

They also felt that important topics such as world peace, security and human rights, environmental sustainability, inequality or decent work were missing from the list.

In addition, some questioned the process that had been followed to develop the eight goals in the first place, and others challenged the data quality. By 2015, for example, some 40 countries around the world lacked the ability to accurately report on poverty and hunger.

A final critique of the MDGs, which also applied to their successors, the SDGs, was that the goals and targets did not reflect the interconnectedness of different issues. Child mortality, for example, is found to fall as a result of rising levels of prosperity and the fact that women tend to have fewer but healthier babies as they move up the economic ladder.

The global financial crisis of 2009 also had a negative impact on the MDGs and the world's ability to meet the 2015 targets. Many developing countries were hit by the crisis, and wealthy countries struggled to fulfill their promises with respect to foreign aid and assistance.

Moving past the MDGs, the SDGs increased the scope of the UN's ambition and made sustainable development the main driver of economic growth, social justice and environmental conservation for future generations.

The SDGs were also developed in line with the expected transformation the world would undergo in the coming years. It was expected that by 2050, the emerging economies in developing countries such as China, India, Brazil and South Africa would bring about an increase of the size of the middle class, a shift in the balance of political and economic power and a need to accelerate the transition to a low-carbon economy.

The costs of achievement of the new goals in the following 15 years was estimated at $3.3–4.5 trillion annually, and it was thought at that time that the private sector would provide about half the necessary funds.

The SDGs were first officially debated in the United Nations Conference on Sustainable Development in Rio de Janeiro in 2012. Two years later, in July 2014, the Open Working Group on SDGs of the United Nations presented its findings. Its proposal defined 17 goals, which are detailed in Exhibit 2.

In December 2014, UN Secretary-General Ban Ki-moon presented *The Road to Dignity by 2030: Ending Poverty, Transforming All Lives and Protecting the Planet.* The report summarized the impact of the MDGs and called for a new set of goals which would run to 2030. A panel of 27 people drawn from civil society and the private and public sectors was put together to develop the *Post-2015 Development Agenda*, which eventually became the Sustainable Development Goals.

In addition, the United Nations invited other stakeholders – such as local communities, volunteer groups and foundations, migrants and families, as well as older persons or people with disabilities – to participate in this process.

Exhibit 2 The 17 Sustainable Development Goals.

Source: United Nations Sustainable Development Goals (https://www.un.org/sustainabledevelopment/). Note: The content of this publication has not been approved by the United Nations and does not reflect the views of the United Nations or its officials or Member States.

In summary, the 17 SDGs and the 169 targets were the result of a long and complex political process in which the international development community was largely represented.

Interestingly, what happened is that organizations around the world adopted the SDGs as a kind of language to communicate what they had been and would be doing in terms of corporate social responsibility and sustainability.

One critic of the SDGs is Bjorn Lomborg, author of *The Skeptical Environmentalist* and the head of the Copenhagen Consensus Center. Lomborg's view is that the SDGs are fundamentally a political compromise. Most of the goals would not withstand a simple cost–benefit analysis, and there is no discussion of priorities or deep analysis of cause and effect.

Nevertheless, up to the onset of the global pandemic in March 2020, the world was making significant progress on the SDGs. A detailed snapshot of where the world is with respect to the 2030 goals can be found in the United Nations' 2020 report and also on a number of websites and platforms.[8]

The economic fallout from COVID-19 and Russia's invasion of Ukraine in March 2022 has had a negative impact on people all over the world, making it difficult to imagine how the world will achieve the targets on hunger, poverty and access to health care and water.

Even more difficult will be some of the more socially oriented goals such as gender equality, as there are still a large number of countries around the world which do not support these goals, citing cultural considerations.

While the situation is complex at the level of public policy, at the corporate level there is an increasing interest in pushing forward on both environmental and social sustainability.

Many companies now routinely use the 17 SDGs as a way of explaining what they are doing to their employees, shareholders and civil society as a whole.

MATERIALITY

In the world of sustainability reporting, the Global Reporting Initiative (GRI) is the most widely recognized and adopted set of standards. Since 2002, the GRI has published guidelines designed to help make reports more complete and comparable. One of the ideas that GRI insists on is for companies to explicitly identify which of the many issues connected to sustainability are the most relevant for them.

The concept that is used is called *materiality*, and is often applied to the SDGs and their sub-targets. This is done by plotting different ideas against two axes. One looks at which of the topics are most important to the company itself, and the other is about what is important to society.

The idea is to focus on those issues which are important for both.

If you look at the sustainability reports from a number of different companies, you will see each firm's discussion of materiality and typically find three to five large initiatives or focus areas. In the best cases, these are areas in which it makes some intuitive sense or obeys some compelling business logic. In others, there seems to be little to no connection with the initiatives and the company's business model.

In the reports, you will also find a list of which of the 17 SDGs (and 169 targets) the company is particularly interested in and what it is doing to make progress on them.

Some companies may not be doing new things, but simply classifying activities using the SDGs as a way of explaining what they are doing. The Coca-Cola company, for example, highlights its focus on water management in its sustainability reports, but has in fact been working on the issue for 20 years.

In the early 2000s, Coke was criticized for overtaxing the water table in Pachimede, a village in India, and then embarked on a program to become water-neutral by 2020, which it achieved in 2015.

Coke operates in 200 countries around the world, and has the data to show that in all of those places which suffer from water stress, meaning that fresh water is in short supply, it invests in helping the region develop new water sources to compensate for the water used in its bottling plants.[9]

In a rigorous effort to evaluate the efforts large companies were making because of the SDGs in 2019, Harvard's Mark Kramer and his colleagues found that companies had simply "relabeled" their CSR initiatives, and that efforts were largely cosmetic.[10]

In their view, companies should focus on fewer goals which could actually help their business. An additional point, which is discussed later in this reading, is that it is important to break down long-term bold objectives such as reaching net zero into meaningful near-term targets and allocate the resources needed to reach them.

THE TIPPING POINT

Although interest in sustainability has steadily increased, a step change in interest and commitment occurred in the years following the Paris Climate Accord in December 2015.

One very visible sign of these activities is the announcement by many CEOs of bold targets for 2025, 2030, 2035 or 2040. Targets include becoming carbon-neutral, implementing aspects of the circular economy or achieving specific goals concerning equity, diversity and inclusion.

Another very visible sign is the Business Roundtable's decision in August 2019 to depart from the shareholder primacy principle and explicitly embrace a broader stakeholder orientation, including making sustainability and social responsibility an explicit part of the purpose of the firm.[11]

There are a number of reasons why companies are stepping up their commitments at this time.

One is that recent weather around the world is increasingly making it evident to politicians, business people, consumers and civil society as a whole that climate change is real and that action is required.

Although this reading is not the place for a detailed discussion of the physics of climate change, it is important to acknowledge that the phenomenon has begun and is already affecting weather patterns around the world. Heat waves, forest fires, droughts, floods and stronger storms are all plain to see, and their increases are well documented.

The essential physics concerning the greenhouse effect have been well established since the 1950s. Higher levels of carbon dioxide and other greenhouse gasses interfere with the planet's ability to cool itself.

According to the International Panel on Climate Change (IPCC), an organization founded in 1988 by the United Nations Environment Programme and the World Meteorological Organization, our industrial society had, by 2022, already warmed the earth about 1.1°C (1.8°F).

In its most recent report, the IPCC is unequivocal in its conclusion that the weather we are experiencing is a direct result of man-made climate change, and that it will get worse in the best-case scenario.[12]

Wildfires, for example, are more frequent and widespread when the forests are drier and high temperatures combine with strong winds. Large fires are also more likely because of civilization encroaching on the world's forests. Residents tend to put out smaller bush fires, thus leaving the bushes and small trees in place. These are then available as fuel in a large conflagration, which can become unstoppable.

Slightly higher temperatures also give storms more energy. They then do more damage because we have built houses, hotels and other infrastructure on the world's coastlines and have often drained some of the wetlands which protected our coasts.

Climate change is also affecting weather patterns, causing flooding in some parts of the world and drought in others, such as California and the Cape in South Africa.

The point of this very brief synopsis is that many of these issues are already affecting people's lives.

A second reason for increasing attention and urgency is that young people around the world are getting increasingly anxious about the changes they see, and some of them are turning to political agitation and activism.

One of the best-known of these eco-warriors is Greta Thunberg, an autistic Swedish teenager who went on a school strike to try to encourage her parents and their entire generation to take things seriously and start to change.

There are tens of millions of "Gretas" all over the world, and they are demanding that their parents clean up their act at home, at work and in terms of the politicians they elect.

The impact these young people have on business is enormous. In the first place, many senior managers and CEOs have children who are pushing them to do more.

A very public example of this was the decision of Kleiner Perkins' John Doerr to set up Silicon Valley's first major clean tech fund and then to donate $1.1 billion to Stanford University to establish the university's first new school in 70 years, the Stanford Doerr School of Sustainability. In his TED Talk from 2007,[13] Doerr said that his interest began when his 15-year-old daughter asked him what he was doing to help the environment.

Young adults are an important segment of the population, and they are increasingly less likely to buy products and services from companies they perceive to be part of the problem.

In addition to being consumers, young people are also joining the workforce. In a recent study by Deloitte, environmental and societal impact turned out to be key points in retaining talented Generation Zs and Millennials.[14] Scholars have also clearly established the link between motivation in the workplace and a company's efforts on corporate social responsibility.[15]

A third major push towards environmental and social sustainability has come from the financial sector. Although many companies have been gradually adopting the idea of a triple bottom line and publishing some type of sustainability report, one got the sense that much of the activity during the first 15 years of the new millennium was just for show or to "tick the box".

What changed is that the world of finance – i.e., investors, banks, and insurance companies – all began talking about ESG, which is really the intersection of three separate streams of activity.

The E is for environment. Carbon emissions, for example, are reported on three levels. Scope 1 emissions are what a company produces as a result of its own operations. Scope 2 emissions are the result of the company using energy provided by a third party. Scope 3 emissions are the hardest to measure and to reduce. Scope 3 are the emissions from a company's supply chain and also the use of its products and services by its customers or end consumers.

A company's environmental impact, of course, goes beyond the emissions of CO_2 and other greenhouse gasses, and includes air and water pollution, the circularity of its products as well as other impacts. Circularity is the idea that rather than make, use and dispose of the things we use, it makes more sense to re-use them in ways that mimic nature.

Recycling can be considered part of this idea, although there are a number of issues with the way recyclable material is collected, treated and eventually re-created into usable products. Much of the material collected for recycling, for example, never actually gets recycled, and the process often uses large amounts of energy in any case.

The S is for social, and typically has to do with health and safety as well as the increasingly important aspects of diversity, equity and inclusion. These ideas mean different things in different parts of the world, but all have to do with treating people with dignity and respect.

The G is for governance. This stream really got underway after the Enron scandal of 2001. Enron, an energy company, had overstated its growth and profits by using unconventional and even illegal accounting procedures. Neither its board of directors nor the auditors they hired to check the books stopped the process until the bubble burst, wiping out billions of dollars of its investors' money.[16]

The result of the scandal was a wave of legislation such as Sarbones-Oaxley in the US and similar laws around the world making the board of directors criminally liable for the way a company managed its accounts. It also stimulated a movement around the world to improve the way a company is managed or governed at the highest level.

By combining these three ideas into ESG, the financial community has established a language it can use to communicate with companies. Perhaps the most public example of this has been when the CEO of BlackRock, the world's largest asset management firm, added a paragraph to his annual letter to CEOs in 2016. Mr. Fink has been writing these annual letters for years, and uses them as a way of telling the CEOs what his company considers to be important in evaluating investment opportunities.

In his 2016 letter, which was mainly about taking a medium- and long-term view on creating value, Fink added a paragraph discussing the Paris Accord and ESG:

> Generating sustainable returns over time requires a sharper focus not only on governance, but also on environmental and social factors facing companies today. These issues offer both risks and opportunities, but for too long, companies have not considered them core to their business – even when the world's political leaders are increasingly focused on them, as demonstrated by the Paris Climate Accord. Over the long-term, environmental, social

and governance (ESG) issues – ranging from climate change to diversity to board effectiveness – have real and quantifiable financial impacts.

The message to the world's CEOs was that if you do not take these issues seriously, BlackRock will not invest in your company.

By 2022, there are a large number of agencies which rate the ESG performance of publicly listed companies, and most major funds have followed BlackRock in demanding such performance.

Banks are also being placed under scrutiny and are being asked to publicly state what industries they are supporting and which they are not. Several global banks, for example, have stopped funding the construction of coal-fired power plants. In Europe, the European Union has published a taxonomy which it requires banks to use to classify their lending and assets.[17]

The insurance industry is also using ESG and climate risk when looking at its own investments and in providing coverage to corporate customers.[18]

What the evidence shows is that companies with higher ESG scores have a higher share price and a lower cost of capital and insurance than companies with lower scores.[19]

In many ways, finance is the language of business, and when it talks, people listen.

Yet another reason that may explain the increased interest in sustainability has to do with the wave of corporate scandals that have come to light, in addition to the Enron case discussed earlier, and have been seen in many different parts of the world and the economy. These scandals and the financial collapse of 2009 have all worked to undermine faith in business as a force for good in the world.

To compensate, many firms have since placed more emphasis on the role they play in the world at the center of their communications efforts, often going far beyond what has been referred to as corporate social responsibility.

Going even further, a number of scholars, such as Harvard's Rebecca Henderson, have, in parallel, established that companies which can articulate a clear sense of purpose outperform others which only seem to work to maximize shareholder value.[20] For many firms, their commitment to sustainability has become central to that definition of purpose.

IMPLICATIONS FOR HUMAN RESOURCE MANAGEMENT

To understand the link between sustainability and HRM, it is important to first distinguish between strategic issues and operational issues.

The distinction is that operational issues are either mandated by regulations or show a clear business case in terms of costs and benefits. Strategic issues are more complex, in that the costs and benefits are not as clear.

For example, making a company's hiring practices compliant with local diversity regulation is an operational issue. There is a legal requirement, and non-compliance runs the risk of lawsuits, fines, etc. Taking the example further, however, the benefits of diversity go well beyond compliance, and could include improving the climate in the workplace, making better decisions and improving a company's image among civil society. These could be thought of as strategic goals.

In addition to issues such as diversity, equity and inclusion, Rosenberg (2015) explores a number of strategic issues associated with environmental sustainability.[21] What is critical is that there is full alignment between a company's market and non-market strategy and the human resource management policies and processes it develops.

One strategic issue, for example, is to make sure that the company limits its exposure to catastrophic risks such as an explosion in a petrochemical facility or the collapse of a tailing dam at a mining site. While firms do have insurance for these kinds of disasters, the environmental and social impact can be overwhelming.

Besides injuring or even killing employees, large disasters can affect larger populations. In perhaps the worst such case in history, a plant operated by a joint venture of Union Carbide, an American chemical company, released a cloud of toxic gas in 1984 in Bhopal, India, killing approximately 20,000 people who lived close to the plant. The company first exited the insecticide business, and was eventually sold off to other firms.

While catastrophic risks usually require deep technical and operational knowledge to understand and mitigate, the human resources function has a fundamental role in making sure that senior management has a clear view of what may happen and is prepared. Many firms have a crisis management protocol in place which includes operations people as well as corporate communications and, of course, human resources.

The COVID-19 crisis in many ways highlighted the importance of this role, and in some cases required the function to develop new crisis management capabilities.[22]

Short of disaster, companies are increasingly being called to account by activists and other interest groups in terms of their social and environmental performance.

The idea is that people may not want to support a company they feel is a bad corporate citizen. Coca-Cola's commitment to protecting water resources around the world, for example, was driven by its concern that Coke's brand could be sullied if it was associated with causing people in rural India to lack basic supplies of water for drinking, irrigation and sanitation.

Coca-Cola is about happiness, and the product is associated with positive feelings and actions. Reacting to consumers' concerns about waste and plastic, for example, Coke has announced a new target to become waste-neutral by 2030.

While tracking how a company is perceived is primarily the job of corporate affairs, it is also deeply linked to internal communications, and in many cases this function reports to HR.

As mentioned earlier, the financial industry is increasingly looking at the ESG performance of many firms and using that performance as a way to make investment decisions as well as to price access to capital and evaluate risk.

In this context, a company's performance on social issues has moved from the sphere of human resources management to the boardroom. These issues include health and safety as well as diversity, equity and inclusion.

While these issues are discussed at length in other readings (see, e.g., Reading 2.1), the critical idea is that the HR function not only needs to make progress on these issues, but to fully understand how the different ratings agencies, activists and others evaluate the company and how it compares to others.

More than anything, HR needs to understand how much progress the company needs to make and how fast in order to be where it needs to be in terms of these issues.

An added complexity is that companies are increasingly doing business all over the world where regulations and social standards are very different. Is diversity, for example, about nationality, race, gender, sexual orientation or all of the above?

The question which needs to be addressed at the highest levels of the company is whether it should have exactly the same policy everywhere in the world. This question has an important aspect in terms of sustainability at the technical and operational level, but also in the social sphere.

The issue is complex, as it can affect the competitiveness of the company on the one hand, but also its social license to operate on the other. If, for example, a company were to insist on minority rights in one part of the world, it might offend people in another. However, if it does not insist on those rights, it may open itself up for attack by groups promoting such diversity.

A fifth strategic issue is the interests a company's customers have in its performance on environmental and social sustainability. The good news is that this interest is rapidly increasing, both at the business-to-business as well as the business-to-consumer levels. In most industries and segments, business customers appear to be more demanding than consumers, and simply will not do business with companies which do not meet some minimum level of performance.

In the automotive industry, for example, the large car manufacturers have made commitments to their customers to become carbon-neutral, and are therefore requiring such commitments from their first-tier suppliers. The firms, in turn, are scrambling to find green aluminum and green steel in order to meet these commitments.

Consumers are more difficult to read, as it seems that many people in the developed world would like products and services that are more sustainable, but few will pay more money for such services, and even fewer will do the necessary research to compare claims and try to determine what is really more sustainable when given a dizzying array of options.

The challenge for HR is that if a company does choose to make sustainability an integral part of its product offering, then it may have to ensure that its own employees, and in particular its senior managers, are actually walking the talk.

This may mean implementing sustainability in all aspects of the business, and even in personal choices with regard to vehicles and travel policies.

A sixth issue which was mentioned earlier is about matching the company's environmental and social performance to the expectations of its current and future employees.

Google, Apple, Meta and other so-called tech giants have all become carbon-neutral, for example, and take enormous pains to ensure that they are perceived to be socially progressive.

One reason to do this is to make these companies attractive to Millennials and people in Generation Z who care deeply about these issues and want to feel they are making a difference. As young adults enter the workforce, they are looking for companies that share some of their values.

A stark example of how important this is was seen at Google in 2018. Google staffers around the world came out in protest when it was found that the company had quietly paid off a manager accused of sexually harassing his female co-workers.[23]

One of the primary tasks of human resources is attracting and retaining the people a company needs. The challenge for human resources in this context is to develop the employee branding proposition that the company needs to have, but also to connect it with the practical aspects of assuring that senior management fully understands the scope and difficulty of developing a real and meaningful sustainability strategy.

WHAT TO DO?

This reading has discussed the roots of sustainability in a business context, reviewed the origin of the 17 Sustainable Development Goals and touched on a number of strategic issues facing many companies from the perspective of human resources.

While it might seem self-evident that the human resources function needs to play a leading role in helping companies achieve their ambitions in the area of sustainability, the evidence shows that this has not always been the case in the broader area of CSR.[24]

What is missing, in some cases, is a clear and overarching approach to sustainability that has been adopted by the organization at the highest level. Once that approach is clear, then human resources can proceed to identify lines of action, programs, specific targets and key performance indicators (KPIs).

In some cases, for example, a company is controlled by an individual or a family who chooses to direct the firm to do more on environmental and/or social sustainability than the law or pure business logic would call for. Famous examples of this strategy include Patagonia and Interface, a carpet tile company based in Atlanta, Georgia. Both firms are, for example, not only carbon-neutral, but actually have a negative carbon footprint and adhere to the highest levels of social standards.

In this case, the objective of human resources will be to ensure that all aspects of its people management strategy, from hiring to promotion and retention and even the development of the company culture itself, are imbued with the principles senior management have adopted. The selection of the members of the senior management team and ensuring their cultural fit with the owner or founder may be one of the most critical functions in organizations which are purpose-driven and for which that purpose is related to environmental and/or social sustainability.

Other companies may have decided that they have no choice but to develop a leading sustainability position at some point in the future. Such decisions are usually based on senior management's judgment about where the strategic issues discussed earlier are going. This is often the logic behind bold commitments for 2030 or 2040 made by CEOs. What is key in these cases is to first break such commitments down and develop a clear roadmap that will achieve these goals over time.

The role of human resources in these cases is to manage the cultural and behavioral change that is required to support such a journey. Such a transformation cannot happen without real leadership from the top, but it is equally critical that managers across the company, and eventually all collaborators, receive the training they need and that people management processes are gradually aligned with the overall objective.

A specific issue may be that a number of capabilities need to be developed, perhaps including hiring new people with the requisite skills. What might make sense is to lay out a series of phases which will take the company and its culture from where it is today to the future in logical and doable steps.

There are, of course, other paths which might be chosen by the CEO and the board of a specific company. At a minimum, a company must be fully compliant with the law in every location in which it operates. The thing to be aware of, however, is that the law is changing in many places, and what was acceptable at one time may not be at another. The challenge is to be sure to change policy and procedures fast enough to stay fully compliant.

Another strategic choice some firms take is to adopt a wait-and-see approach to sustainability and to hold off on taking bold steps for the time being.

From a human resources viewpoint, the key issue here is to get hold of the data on where the company is at this point in time and also be ready to discuss what it would take to make improvements. Changing the gender balance of senior managers in some industries, for example, can be very difficult, and should only be done with a full understanding of what would have to happen and how long it would take.

The last approach is to take a leading stance on specific environmental and social issues, and many companies are doing just that. As mentioned earlier, this typically involves choosing which issues to focus on and making an explicit link to some, but not all, of the Sustainable Development Goals and their sub-targets.

For companies following this path, the final question is how much to talk about what they are doing, both internally to employees and externally to shareholders, customers, communities and to civil society.

Some companies choose to make sustainability a critical aspect of their communications policy and to bake it into everything they say and do. A terrific example of this over the last ten years has been Unilever, the European consumer products giant. Under the Leadership of Paul Polman (co-author of *Net Positive*), the company fully embraced sustainability and turned it into a real competitive advantage.

The danger of this approach is that the marketing and communications people may go too far and overstate what the company is actually doing. Such proactive communications can attract the attention of, and potential attacks from, activist groups such as Greenpeace and others.

"Greenwashing" is the term applied to firms which make bold claims on some aspects of sustainability in order to cover up other aspects in which they are not performing to the same standard, or worse, are doing significant damage to the environment or specific groups of people.

Volkswagen, in another example, had publicly signed the Global Compact and was advertising its "Blue Motion" sustainable approach to mobility at the same time it installed software in thousands of vehicles to turn off the car's pollution control device in normal driving conditions. Volkswagen not only broke the law, but lied about it for years before the scandal was uncovered, eventually resulting in billions of dollars of fines and damages and prison for two of its executives.

Nestlé is a direct competitor to Unilever, but has taken a different approach to sustainability. At an operational level, Nestlé does many of the same things that Unilever is doing, but has not, by and large, made the same communications effort to consumers and civil society. Part of the logic behind this approach is that Nestlé has experience with highly critical campaigns that have been directed against it in the past and has made a strategic choice to have very advanced policies and procedures in place, but to keep a relatively low profile.

In either case, human resources has a fundamental role to play in supporting the company's desire to have a leading position. This entails both crafting that approach as well as delivering real progress on the large array of issues and KPIs which are consistent with it. In many ways, this effort will be easier in those companies which communicate more rather than less – especially in terms of employer branding, recruitment, etc.

CONCLUSION

In his latest book on human resources, Dave Ulrich[25] argues that human resources management essentially has nine areas in which it needs to add value. These are then divided into core drivers (strategic positioner, paradox navigator, credible activist), enablers of the organization (culture and change champion, human capital curator, total rewards steward) and enablers for the firm to deliver (compliance manager, analytics designer and interpreter, technology and media integrator).

At the core, the human resources function has a critical role to play in helping the CEO and the rest of the management team develop the strategy itself. In the context of sustainability, that means fully exploring the benefits which can be achieved in terms of employer branding, retention and other issues for taking a stronger position on sustainability. It also requires human resources to work out how difficult the transition, to the degree it is needed, will be in terms of modifying people's beliefs, rewards system and behaviors.

The issue is that a balance must be struck between managing the company for success in today's world while listening to the needs of younger employees and customers and preparing it for tomorrow.

To do that, of course, the organization's culture needs to reflect its sustainability agenda, and this may also require changing the mix of people and skills as well as realigning reward systems.

Finally, the compliance side of sustainability is becoming increasingly challenging, and the role of human resources in collecting and analyzing the data to prove increased diversity, equity and inclusion as well as health and safety is critical. For this to be done effectively, human resources also needs to fully integrate new digital tools and even social media in the process of cultural renewal.

As the climate crisis becomes more acute, businesses around the world will adopt a more sustainable approach to how they operate and what they stand for. This will, of course, be different in different sectors and different parts of the world. In any case, human resources is essential for making such a sustainability journey successful.

NOTES

1. Beer, M., Boselie, P. & Brewster, C. (2015). Back to the future: Implications for the field of HRM of the multistakeholder perspective proposed 30 years ago. *Human Resource Management*, 54(3): 427–438.
2. Voegtlin, C. & Greenwood, M. (2016). Corporate social responsibility and human resource management: A systematic review and conceptual analysis, *Human Resource Management Review*, 26(3): 181–197.
3. Brahimi, L. (2000). The report of the Panel on UN Peace Operations ("Brahimi report"). https://peacekeeping.un.org/sites/default/files/a_55_305_e_brahimi_report .pdf, accessed October 15, 2022.
4. Elkington, J. (1994). Towards the sustainable corporation: Win–win–win business strategies for sustainable development. *California Management Review*, 36: 90–100.
5. Friedman, M. (1973). The social responsibility of business is to increase its profits. *New York Times*, September 13.
6. Speech by Cynthia Carroll, Chief Executive, Anglo American plc, Chatham House, June 18, 2008.
7. www.givingwhatwecan.org/sites/givingwhatwecan.org/files/reports/CCC%20MDG %20Report.pdf, March 2015.
8. See *The SDG Tracker* which is offered by a commercial website called *Our World in Data* (https://sdg-tracker.org/).

9.   https://www.coca-colacompany.com/au/news/we-are-water-neutral--how-coca
     -cola-matches-every-drop-it-uses-.
10. Kramer, M.R., Agarwal, R. & Srinivas, A. (2019). Business as usual will not save
     the planet. *Harvard Business Review*, June 12, https://hbr.org/2019/06/business-as
     -usual-will-not-save-the-planet.
11. See   https://s3.amazonaws.com/brt.org/May-2022BRTStatementonthePurposeofa
     CorporationwithSignatures.pdf.
12. *Climate Change 2022: Impacts, Adaptation and Vulnerability*, Geneva, Switzerland:
     IPCC, February 2022.
13. https://www.ted.com/talks/john_doerr_salvation_and_profit_in_greentech?lan-
     guage=en.
14. https://www2.deloitte.com/content/dam/Deloitte/at/Documents/human-capital/at
     -gen-z-millennial-survey-2022.pdf.
15. Mirvis, P. (2012). Employee engagement and CSR: Transactional, relational, and
     developmental approaches. *California Management Review*, 54(4): 93–117.
16. McLean, B. & Elkind, P. (2013). *The Smartest Guys in the Room: The Amazing Rise
     and Scandalous Fall of Enron*, New York: Portfolio, 10th ed.
17. https://ec.europa.eu/info/business-economy-euro/banking-and-finance/sustainable
     -finance/eu-taxonomy-sustainable-activities_en.
18. Cleary, P., Harding, W., McDaniels, J., Svoronos, J.-P. & Yong, J. (2019). *Turning
     Up the Heat: Climate Risk Assessment in the Insurance Sector*, FSI Insights on
     Policy Implementation, 20, Basel, Switzerland: Bank for International Settlements,
     Financial Stability Institute.
19. Kölbel, J. & Busch, T. (2017). The link between ESG, alpha, and the cost of capital:
     Implications for investors and CFOs. *corporate finance biz*, 3/4: 82–85.
20. Henderson, R. (2020). *Reimagining Capitalism in a World on Fire*, New York:
     PublicAffairs.
21. Rosenberg, M. (2015). *Strategy and Sustainability*, London: Palgrave Macmillan.
22. Kumar, A. & Chaudhuri P. (2021). New role of human resource development in
     Covid-19 crisis, *KIIT Journal of Management*, 17(1): 283–291.
23. https://www.nytimes.com/2018/10/26/technology/sexual-harassment-google.html.
24. Stahl, G.K., Brewster, C.J., Collings, D.G. & Hajro, A. (2020). Enhancing the role
     of human resource management in corporate sustainability and social responsibil-
     ity: A multi-stakeholder, multidimensional approach to HRM. *Human Resource
     Management Review*, 30(3): 100708.
25. Ulrich D., Kryscynski, D., Brockbank, W. & Ulrich, M. (2017). *Victory Through
     Organization: Why the War for Talent Is Failing Your Company and What You Can
     Do About It*, New York: McGraw Hill.

B. Sebastian Reiche and Yuan Liao

NESTLÉ'S ALLIANCE FOR YOUTH (A)*

IT WAS LATE SEPTEMBER 2017, and Frederique Naulette, Human Resources (HR) and project manager of Nestlé needs YOUth (NNY) for Zone Europe, felt invigorated by the recent announcement from Nestlé's CEO Mark Schneider at events around the UN General Assembly week in New York. As the CEO explained, the company would commit to helping 10 million young people around the world have access to economic opportunities, thereby lifting Nestlé's Alliance for YOUth (A4Y) to a global level. Nestlé further backed up its commitment by being one of the first companies to join the Global Initiative on Decent Jobs for Youth led by the International Labour Organization. As Naulette pondered the implications of this expanded ambition, she started to reflect on the initiative's beginnings and the various challenges in implementing it at a European level. She remembered some of the issues they had discussed as they embarked on the initiative. How would Nestlé adapt the initiative to each European country? How would they overcome country-specific hurdles to implementation?

COMPANY BACKGROUND

Nestlé is the largest food and beverage company in the world in terms of revenues, reaching 89.8 billion Swiss francs in 2017. Nestlé owns 442 factories in 86 countries, has operations in 197 countries and employs 323,000 workers (approximately half in factories and the other half in administration and sales).

The company is divided into Zone Europe, Middle East and North Africa (26.1 billion Swiss francs in 2017); Zone Americas (40.7 billion Swiss francs in 2017); Zone Asia, Oceania and Africa (23 billion Swiss francs in 2017); Nestlé Waters (7.4 billion Swiss francs in 2017); and Nestlé Nutrition (9.6 billion Swiss francs in 2017).

* Originally published by IESE Publishing.

DOI: 10.4324/9781003247272-35

The company's product range is divided into seven groups: Powdered and Liquid Beverages (20.4 billion Swiss francs in 2017), Milk Products and Ice Cream (13.4 billion Swiss francs), Prepared Dishes and Cooking Aids (12.0 billion Swiss francs), Nutrition and Health Science (15.3 billion Swiss francs), PetCare (12.5 billion Swiss francs), Confectionery (8.8 billion Swiss francs) and Water (7.5 billion Swiss francs).

A selection of Nestlé's key brands includes Maggi, KitKat, Milo, Nesquik, Nestea, Pure Life, Perrier, S. Pellegrino, Nescafé, Nespresso, Friskies, Buitoni, Lean Cuisine, Dolce Gusto, Stouffer's, Nestlé Ice Creams, Dreyer's and Carnation.

THE BIRTH OF A NEW INITIATIVE

As a result of the economic crisis that began in 2008, Europe experienced a huge increase in unemployment. Youth were especially hard hit, and in some countries youth unemployment stood at double, or more than double, the overall unemployment rates. According to Eurostat, youth unemployment across Europe was 24% in 2014 and 22% in 2015.[1] However, there was a huge variation between countries. Spain had the highest unemployment rate for young people, with 48% in 2015 (53% in 2014), followed by Italy with 40% (43% in 2014), Portugal with 32% (35% in 2014), France with 25% (24% in 2014) and Poland with 21% (24% in 2014). It was during this period of stubbornly high youth unemployment rates that Nestlé started its Nestlé needs YOUth (NNY) initiative.

To Nestlé, young people suffered from high unemployment because they lacked the appropriate qualifications and/or training for the job. For example, in 2011, 23% of young Portuguese withdrew from school, which made it more difficult to be integrated into the labor market.[2] This also contributed to Portugal's higher emigration rates in the European Union (EU). In Poland, where only 34% of people under 25 were actively employed in the labor market, many Polish factories still faced a dramatic shortage of qualified vocational school graduates. As Laurent Freixe, CEO for Zone Europe at that time, explained:

> Although we are starting to see job opportunities increasing, unemployment is still rising in some countries. This reflects problems in the job matching process. There are mismatches between the skills or educational qualifications young people have and what certain jobs require.

Nestlé had a long tradition of recruiting young people directly from schools or universities. The company would invest in them, build their capabilities and develop their professional careers, embracing diversity of cultures, traditions and opinions. This practice had helped the company close the gap between young hires' capabilities and the requirements of the job. With the worsening economic context, Nestlé felt it could do even more to help address youth unemployment by focusing on creating first professional experiences. This ambition was not at all far-fetched. The private sector was by far the biggest employer in Europe, and businesses that wanted to continue investing and growing in Europe needed to count on young people at work and give them hope for the future of Europe. In addition, Nestlé often encountered difficulties in finding properly trained young people across Europe due to the unattractiveness of jobs in the food and drinks industry. The food sector also faced huge challenges, such as a transformation towards a more sustainable food system to feed 8 billion people by 2030, consumer demand for more nutritious and healthy products, and the digital revolution. Nestlé needed to attract, train and retain the best young talent to successfully handle these challenges. To tackle Europe's youth unemployment crisis, Nestlé set up a European steering committee, composed of human resources (HR) and business leaders, to develop a long-term commitment for Europe, asking all European country units to develop their own actions in line with Nestlé's European plan. The project formed part of the Creating Shared Value axis of the company, which comprised 41 commitments related to its long-term impact on society.

In November 2013, Nestlé launched the NNY initiative, whose main objective was to improve the employability of young people. Freixe, CEO for Zone Europe at the time, led the initiative that involved business leaders of all countries and their HR teams (mainly those responsible for recruiting and contact with education organizations and schools). The initiative aimed to hire 10,000 young people aged below 30 and to offer 10,000 apprenticeship and traineeship positions across Nestlé sites and functions in Europe by 2016. The NNY initiative also created Readiness for Work programs, delivered at schools, colleges and Nestlé sites across Europe, including interventions such as interview training, CV cleaning, job market tips, etc. to help facilitate young people's transition from school to employment.

Nestlé pioneered the introduction of dual learning schemes in countries without such a tradition (e.g., Spain and Italy), or where this practice had disappeared (Poland, Hungary and Slovakia). Nestlé also developed internal strategies to decrease the generation gap by supporting the transmission of collective skills. First, it increased the number of tutors among the aging population in order to support new apprentices in factories. Second, Nestlé introduced reverse mentoring programs to allow young people to coach aging workers on digital skills.

In 2014, the second stage of the NNY initiative, the Alliance for Youth (A4Y) was launched in collaboration with like-minded business partners across Europe to provide more opportunities to young people. A4Y aimed to develop individual and joint initiatives to give work experience, internships and training opportunities to 100,000 young people. The founding partners of A4Y included companies like Adecco, AXA, Cargill, DS Smith, Ernst & Young, Facebook, Google, Nielsen, Salesforce, Twitter and almost 200 local partners.

During its first year, A4Y aimed to provide 50,000 training and job opportunities and readiness for work activities. Nestlé also engaged in a number of programs to further smooth the transition from education to employment, such as launching the digital platform All4YOUth, hosted by Facebook, which offered education, jobs and services in an interactive way. Other activities included signing the European Youth Forum initiative on Skills for the Future to launch quality internship and apprenticeship programs, and organizing a workshop and panel debate in Brussels with A4Y apprentices and trainees, parliamentary assistants and youth organizations to discuss achievements and future actions. Nestlé also became a founding member of the European Pact for Youth, created by CSR Europe and the European Commission with the objective to work together with businesses, youth organizations, education providers and other stakeholders to reduce skills gaps and increase youth employability by introducing dual learning schemes.

In 2017, Nestlé joined forces with Junior Achievement Europe to activate youth employment through a new avenue – entrepreneurship, which complemented its work on apprenticeships. Under the lead of Ernst & Young (EY), many A4Y members (including AXA, EY, Firmenich, Nestlé, Nielsen, Salesforce and White & Case) committed to contribute to the Company Program, providing entrepreneurship education dedicated to training, coaching and mentoring students. The aspiration of this unique pan-European collaboration was to support more than 1,000 secondary school and vocational students in obtaining the Entrepreneurial Skills Pass™. Successfully launched in Spain and the UK, the initiative was looking to bring on board more companies and to potentially expand its support in Bulgaria, France and Romania for future school entrance.

At the same time, Nestlé was also conscious of possible challenges in rolling out its initiative. For one, it faced an arduous connection with the education sector, which made it difficult to set up new apprenticeship schemes in the various countries. In addition, the education system in some countries lacked necessary preconditions for implementing the initiatives. For instance, there was no tradition of dual training programs in Spain, nor was there a dual career system in Poland. In other cases, such as France, budget constraints restricted the development of apprenticeship programs.

As Naulette drifted further into her thoughts, she remembered the distinct conditions in four specific European countries: Spain, Germany, Italy and the Czech Republic.

SPAIN

The population in Spain was 46.77 million in 2014. Migration trends observed a significant change in 2014. Although the country registered 102,309 more emigrants than immigrants, the number was 59.3% lower relative to the previous year. The change was due to a 9.4% increase in immigration and a 23.1% decrease of emigration compared with the previous year.[3] On the other hand, the attitude of the Spanish population towards immigrants was positive. The opportunities for people born outside Spain were only slightly inferior to those born in Spain in terms of education and employment, showing good integration of immigrants in the country.

Spain suffered the highest level of unemployment in the EU. In 2014, its unemployment rate was 24.5%, the youth unemployment rate was 53.2% and the youth unemployment ratio was 19.0% – double the EU averages of 10.2%, 22.2% and

9.2%, respectively.[4] Spain also had the highest share of early school leavers in the EU. The rate was 21.9% in 2014, again double the EU average of 11.2%.[5]

Dual vocational training was a new concept in Spain. In November 2012, the government published a Royal Decree establishing the foundations of the dual principle in vocational education and training (VET) in Spain. Companies and VET providers joined forces to combine theory and training embedded in a real-life work environment. The dual system was characterized by close cooperation between publicly funded vocational schools, providing theoretical and general education, and companies extending such theoretical education to practical training. The dual vocational training program aimed to increase youth employment by increasing the number of people who could obtain post-secondary education degrees through vocational education, decreasing early school leaving, facilitating labor market entry as a result of greater contact with companies, and so on. Its implementation depended on each region.[6]

GERMANY

The population of Germany rose to 81.2 million at the end of 2014. This increase was mainly due to high immigration – a total of 1,465,000 people immigrated to Germany, while 914,000 people departed the country. A main source of immigrants was asylum seekers. In 2014, 202,834 asylum seekers filed a first-time or follow-up application for asylum. This number increased twofold to 476,649 in 2015, and further increased to 745,545 in 2017.[7]

Germany suffered the least unemployment threat among the EU countries. Its unemployment rate was 5.0%, the youth unemployment rate was 7.7% and the youth unemployment ratio was 3.9% in 2014 – much lower than the EU average. The unemployment rate also showed a decreasing trend since the economic crisis in 2008.[8]

The German dual training system, called the vocational education and training system, had been firmly established in the German education system for a long time. The cooperation between vocational schools and companies has been regulated by law since the Vocational Training Act was introduced in 1969. Trainees in the dual system usually spend part of each week at a vocational school and the rest at a company, or they may spend longer periods at each place before alternating. Dual training typically lasts two to three-and-a-half years. The German dual training system has proved vital for business competitiveness. Companies participating in the scheme consider vocational training the best way to save on recruitment costs and to avoid the risk of hiring the wrong candidates. The domestic success has attracted international attention, and Germany has cooperated with other European countries in supporting apprenticeship initiatives.[9]

ITALY

Demographics in Italy have been changing, with three significant trends. First, the country is facing a decreasing population. While it was 60.79 million in 2014, it is forecast to be only 56 million in 2050. The number of newborn babies has been decreasing since 2008. Second, Italy's population is aging. In 2014, 22.0% of the Italian population were older than 65 years, whereas the European average was 17.6%. The number is forecast to increase to 34.9% in 2055, compared with a European average of 28.4%. The Oldness Index, the ratio of people aged 65+ years to those aged 0–14 years, was 1.57 in 2014. Third, the country was receiving more and more immigrants. Between 2006 and 2016, 900,000 immigrants arrived, and the share of immigrants in the population was 8.2% in 2014, increasing by 3% compared to 1995.

Italy has the EU's fourth highest level of youth unemployment, behind Spain, Greece and Croatia. In 2014, 42.7% of youth were unemployed. Further, almost one in three (27.4%) of young Italians aged 15–34 were not in employment, education or training, compared to the EU average of 16.6%.[10]

The practice of irregular contracts was widespread – creating job insecurity in the country. About 15% of Italian employees aged 25–39 had this kind of contract, compared with less than 5% in the UK, for example. There was also a significant gap between the educational system and the real-life working environment, further contributing to youth employment.

CZECH REPUBLIC

The Czech Republic had a population of 10.52 million and a youth population of 1.06 million in 2014. The unemployment rate stood at 6.1%, the youth unemployment rate was 15.9% and the youth unemployment ratio was 5.1% – all lower than the EU averages in 2014.[11]

In the Czech Republic, VET schemes had a long tradition in the 20th century. Most of them, however, were abandoned in the 1990s as a result of the transformation of the entire society and economy after the regime change. The need for VET programs soon arose again. In 2008, the Ministry of Education, Youth and Sports adopted a National Action Plan to support vocational education and training. In 2013, the government adopted new measures that defined the main steps related to the organization, administration and legislation planned in the next few years to enhance participation in VET and its quality.[12]

VET programs at the upper secondary level are provided by different types of secondary schools, and vocational education accounts for almost three-quarters of secondary education in terms of student numbers. However, people still perceived a lack of opportunities for young people. In a yearly survey in 2014, about 75% of respondents answered "rather not" or "definitely not" to the question, "Do young people have enough opportunities to gain experience while studying?"

Given the many differences across countries, Naulette and her team had been well aware of the need to leave specific implementation to each local country operation. The initiative had only provided an overarching objective, which left each country with a lot of autonomy to decide how to carry it out. With the expanded scope of the initiative on the horizon, she realized that she needed to better understand how the specific implementation had actually occurred in each country.

B. Sebastian Reiche and Yuan Liao

NESTLÉ'S ALLIANCE FOR YOUTH (B)

Frederique Naulette knew that the Nestlé CEO's recent public announcement at the United Nations to globalize the Alliance for Youth (A4Y) initiative provided a strong commitment to follow through with their ambition. She confidently looked back at the success they had achieved so far. The initial success of both the A4Y and the Nestlé needs YOUth initiatives exceeded the original objectives. Between 2014 and 2016, the NNY initiative hired 20,000 young people across Europe, provided 12,000 apprenticeship and traineeship positions, and conducted 5,000 Readiness for Work workshops. In one year, A4Y hired 34,000 young people, provided 18,000 quality apprenticeships and traineeships, and ran 5,400 Readiness for Work workshops on the Facebook platform. In the period 2014–2016, A4Y, together with its partners, provided 115,000 jobs, apprenticeships and traineeships.

In addition, the initiatives had a huge social impact. Nestlé won the 2016 European HR Excellence Award for NNY in the Corporate Social Responsibility category. The initiative was also included in the best practices for responsible entrepreneurship for the Reinhard Mohn Prize in 2016. Further, the two initiatives obtained strong support from key stakeholders, such as European Union Employment Commissioner Marianne Thyssen and national authorities in all European markets, and received massive media coverage.

Nestlé management, both at the European and national levels, were satisfied with the achievements of both initiatives. According to their view, the success was due to a strong empowerment by the CEO of Europe and alignment across all teams, especially Human Resources departments, but also Production, Communication & Marketing and Supply Chain at the European level and in each country. Further, a close working relationship with the EU authorities helped

DOI: 10.4324/9781003247272-36

to push the dual learning schemes through concrete actions, and the company also partnered with food industry associations and government institutions at European and national levels to gain wider public visibility and support. Nestlé also collaborated with non-governmental organizations (NGOs), suppliers, clients and media.

However, Naulette also knew that to scale the initiative effectively to the global level and reach the ambitious goal of helping 10 million young people around the world have access to economic opportunities, Nestlé would have to better share and leverage the experiences from each country, especially since the implementation of the initiative was largely a local affair.

She decided to meet with representatives from four different Nestlé country organizations to understand how NNY had been implemented and what could be learned for the expansion to other countries. Her first stop was Spain, where the initiative had originated.

SPAIN

The NNY initiative started in 2013, shortly after the Spanish government had introduced a new legal framework for training programs that facilitated the development of dual training programs, combining both studies and in-company practical experience. As such, it was Nestlé that pioneered the development of these programs in different Spanish regions. This involved collaboration with the German operation, where dual training programs had a much longer history. This collaboration also enabled an apprenticeship exchange between the two Nestlé country units.

According to Maria Castelló, the initiative's project leader in Spain, the reaction to NNY was generally positive:

> The educational system welcomed us with open arms. They were, in fact, looking for companies that would set up dual training programs, and so we could help with this. Suppliers who joined our initiative realized the benefits of hiring new workers after extended traineeships that allowed them to make better selection decisions. Ultimately, the initiative has become a social movement that even involved NGOs, such as Once and the Red Cross, to address people at risk of social exclusion.

However, to make the initiative work, especially A4Y, Castelló had to work with a multitude of stakeholders, whose interests did not always fully coincide. For example, the Spanish regions differed in their educational quality standards, which made it more difficult to roll out and scale the initiative. Nestlé had to go to each region to work closely with local politicians and to share best practices among regions. In the beginning, some students were not sure whether such practical experience would provide value to their future career, since the dual training program was new to Spain. In more rural areas, where factories were often located away from the main urban centers, the participating organizations faced the added difficulties of attracting enough students that were prepared to commute between their home and schools on the one hand and the factory on the other. As the initiative mainly targeted public schools in poorer socioeconomic areas, Castelló realized that compared with local students, second-generation Spanish students whose parents had immigrated to Spain were initially more inclined to try out a dual training program, which often involved the same number of subjects as traditional vocational programs, in addition to the apprenticeship.

At a time when staffing increasingly focused on the attraction of key talent, many companies initially did not see the value of youth trainees. Cost-cutting pressures after the financial crisis similarly put potential partners off. What was more, given the high unemployment rate in Spain, some Nestlé employees internally perceived the initiative as substituting full-time employment with apprenticeships. As Castelló explained:

> We had to be very careful to distinguish between traineeships and normal employment. Our main purpose was the training of the youth and so we established clear rules to clarify this distinction. For example, trainees could spend a maximum of six months in the company, and hiring managers published vacancies for trainees targeted at specific schools rather than the wider job market.

Still, the benefits of such extended training paid off, and as many as 33% of trainees were subsequently hired and given full-time employment, mainly in the factories. The initiative had several other benefits for the Spanish organization. While Nestlé maintained a positive reputation in Spain, Castelló highlighted that the initiative played an important role in showcasing Nestlé's continued social concern and impact in the media. As she further elaborated:

> Partnering with suppliers on the initiative also made us realize that we share the same values – beyond specific business objectives – which helped us deepen the relationships with our long-term suppliers. Internally, the initiative helped engage our employees. In fact, the initiative involved a specific program to teach our own employees' children to look for work. And by integrating the trainees I believe we have also become a more inclusive workplace.

Naulette left the conversation with Castelló with a better understanding of the local realities in Spain. However, she wondered how much of her learning was relevant to other settings. Given the collaboration between Nestlé Spain and Germany, Naulette decided to visit the latter operation next.

GERMANY

In Germany, NNY also covered different pillars. For example, as part of the Readiness for Work program, which trained young people for the job application process, Nestlé Germany ran 109 events in 2017 alone. The context conditions in Germany differed markedly from those in Spain, though. Germany had a relatively low unemployment rate and youth unemployment was not a substantial issue, so the German initiative focused relatively more on disadvantaged youth, including refugees. For example, of the 700 traineeships organized, 51 were provided to refugees.

Internally, employees at Nestlé Germany were very supportive of NNY. The favorable labor market meant that employees did not perceive the same potential threat from incoming trainees that was initially the case in Spain. Further, Nestlé Germany already had in place a program through which employees would get three days off work to help refugees, the young or an NGO, so the initiative was seen as consistent with previous measures.

At the same time, Nestlé Germany faced unique challenges of its own. As Boris Stojevic, project lead for NNY in Germany, explained:

> Germany, just like Austria and Switzerland, has a long tradition of dual apprenticeship systems, so this concept was neither new to us nor the educational system more broadly. However, the system in Germany is a two- to three-year program, compared with much shorter programs in other countries. International candidates do not understand our program, so you really need to find the right candidate who will stay for these two to three years. For companies, this makes it a more substantive decision and also a higher investment.

Naulette was aware of these differences, and she had begun to lobby at the European level for standardization of the apprenticeship model, which would not only help NNY, but, importantly, also facilitate exchange of trainees between countries. Germany had already experienced an inflow of trainees, either through the European-wide Erasmus Plus program that provided financial support for apprentices from other countries to come to Germany or in near-border regions where specific apprentice exchange programs existed. However, these exchange trainees were mostly young, did not speak German and often experienced homesickness, which required social programs to help integrate them.

Nestlé Germany also faced challenges for its A4Y pillar of the initiative. Nestlé tried to engage the same multinational companies that were present across Europe as partners in each respective country, in addition to some local partners. However, finding partners in Germany turned out to be difficult, and the number of partners in A4Y was lower in Germany compared to other countries. As Stojevic highlighted:

> We have a few local partners, such as Barmer, Lekkerland and Joblinge. But many companies already have their own trainee programs in Germany or they don't have a budget for multi-year apprenticeships, so we needed to clearly explain the benefits for all involved.

For those joining the initiative, a key motivator was to engage in social work at a time when social issues, like the refugee crisis, were high on the agenda. Helping the disadvantaged find employment was a noble cause. Partners also gained public attention and visibility through their contributions.

Having learnt from the German experience, Naulette decided to travel to Italy next.

ITALY

Italy faced a similar labor market situation to Spain. Given the high unemployment in general and youth unemployment in particular, NNY was well received both internally and externally. As David Gaal, Head of Recruitment, Learning and Development and project lead in Italy, explained:

> The initiative was welcomed by a lot of people. For example, many of our older employees have kids who experience employment difficulties. So this is also a social project for which it was relatively easy to find sponsors and get our employees to contribute; for example, in specific programs or events. In fact, of our 4,500 employees in Italy, annually around 100 employees participate with great enthusiasm and commitment.

Furthermore, Nestlé Italy tried to orientate the initiative as closely as possible to its business priorities. For example, on malnutrition – together with colleagues from the Nestlé Health Science business – Nestlé Italy built a campus that involved students coming from universities specializing in nutrition and biology, where there are not many opportunities in the market.

After the first few years, the initiative exceeded its initial objectives in terms of number of young people hired (over 1,300), apprenticeship and traineeship positions offered (over 1,050) and Readiness for Work programs organized (over 300). Encouraged by the initial success, Nestlé Italy further expanded the scope and engaged its partners in the initiative. Among its partners were European-level companies like Accenture, Facebook and Nielsen, with their own programs on traineeships and Readiness for Work events. Then there were local companies that only participated in Italy and contributed mainly with local knowledge and through their participation in local initiative-related events.

For partners in Italy, the initiative also served as an important recruitment tool. Gaal stated:

> In Italy, where work experience schemes yet need to be fully utilized, companies realized that you could actually select better candidates if you get to know them over the course of a traineeship, apprenticeship or internship. But beyond that I think the initiative also helped our employer branding. I think our Swiss company culture sculpted in many ways the manner in which we communicate with our future employees: modest and through

actions rather than through marketing campaigns. The initiative certainly helped positively influence future candidates and other stakeholders. Still, the most important thing for us was the positive energy behind the initiative that created such a strong impact in the local community.

Challenges in Italy mainly stemmed from how to involve public partners. For local government institutions, the dual apprenticeship models are still being explored and tested in many ways. The education system still needs to catch up with the world of business. As Gaal explained:

> One of the objectives is still to engage teachers in the local program, together with the students, but we found it difficult to motivate them for activities outside their roles.

Another challenge came from how the initiative might be perceived by other stakeholders. For example, in 2017, high school students across the country protested against a mandatory government program that required students in their last three years of secondary education to participate in work experience schemes, because of discontentment that the program had not been implemented properly. As a result, Gaal was conscious of the importance of collaborating closely with external stakeholders in order to explain the objectives of the various initiatives. In addition, Nestlé Italy focused on offering high-quality activities and experiences to young apprentices or trainees in order to improve their future employability. In 2017, Nestlé Italy hired 43% of the interns after their initial planned six-month experience on regular or temporary contracts, demonstrating Nestlé's commitment and achievements in this initiative.

CZECH REPUBLIC

The NNY initiative in the Czech Republic started with the aim of increasing youth employment, and faced similar challenges to those in other countries. As Andrea Brožová, Corporate Communication Manager in the Czech Republic, explained:

> The initiative received some internal resistance in the beginning. Since vocational education and training programs were interrupted for years, many people were unfamiliar with the idea and thought they would be babysitting the young trainees. It took my team a few months to persuade our colleagues and change their mindset.

Gradually, the initiative received support from both internal and external partners. A4Y was launched in the Czech Republic in September 2014, and was supported by the Minister of Education and Vice-chairwoman of the Committee for Culture and Education of the European Parliament. The initiative overachieved its 2014–2016 targets, with direct hiring reaching 360%, hiring of trainees and apprentices 125%, and Readiness for Work events and workshops 140%.

However, youth unemployment was not a major threat in the Czech Republic. Its youth unemployment rate decreased to 12.6% in 2015 and 10.5% in 2016, well below the EU average of 20.3% and 18.7% in the respective years. For this reason, the focus of the initiative gradually shifted from solving the unemployment problem to better connecting theory with practice and creating a talent pool. To bring theoretical education closer to business practices, Nestlé cooperated with universities to develop curriculums for courses such as marketing and sales. Nestlé also actively engaged public authorities, presented issues at local parliaments, and sought help from politicians and lawmakers to build the link between theory and practice.

New challenges in this phase came from attracting young people and engaging business partners. Since similar vocational training programs already existed in other companies, Nestlé needed to distinguish its initiative from others in order to attract young talent. It emphasized several benefits from becoming a trainee at Nestlé, such as receiving hands-on experience in a multinational company, doing real work with real responsibilities and the possibility of making a difference in the local market. In addition to the traditional apprenticeship model already in place in factories, Nestlé Czech, in cooperation with four A4Y members, organized two-day workshops that focused on innovation. In order to reach the young generation growing up in the digital age, Brožová and her team established extensive communication channels on social media, such as Facebook, Twitter, LinkedIn and Snapchat, instead of using newsletters.

Engaging business partners was another main challenge. As Brožová explained:

> We should have been more careful in inviting alliance members. We have 60 members signed up for the Alliance for Youth, but many of them are not active. We have been working mainly with their HR departments in the past, now my goal is to engage their CEOs to better align our objectives.

Naulette was aware that establishing the initiative at the European level gave it a huge boost and created many multipliers. More than 200 companies participated either directly or indirectly in one of the initiative's projects across Europe. However, she also knew that making it a global initiative would change the fabric considerably. As Nestlé had to bring in additional partners who would help roll out the initiative globally and create even greater impact, Nestlé would naturally lose some ownership. As Gaal put it in the conversation with her:

> This is about Nestlé orchestrating the whole initiative, but evidently other partners will also take more credit for it. So there is some internal debate around how much ownership we should maintain, how much we can leverage the initiative ourselves, or whether this is strictly about the "right thing to do."

As she pondered what she had taken from the four visits, she was both inspired by the expanded scope of the initiative and anxious about how best to get it off the ground.

NOTES

1. http://ec.europa.eu/eurostat/statistics-explained/index.php/Unemployment _statistics.
2. http://ec.europa.eu/eurostat/statistics-explained/index.php/Early_leavers_from _education_and_training#Source.
3. www.ine.es/en/prensa/np917_en.pdf.
4. http://ec.europa.eu/eurostat/statistics-explained/index.php/Unemployment_statis-tics#Longer-term_unemployment_trends.
5. https://ec.europa.eu/info/sites/info/files/file_import/european-semester_thematic -factsheet_early-school-leavers_en.pdf.
6. www.empleo.gob.es/es/garantiajuvenil/home.html.
7. https://www.destatis.de/EN/FactsFigures/SocietyState/Population/Population .html.
8. http://ec.europa.eu/eurostat/statistics-explained/index.php/Unemployment _statistics.
9. https://www.bmbf.de/en/the-german-vocational-training-system-2129.html.
10. http://appsso.eurostat.ec.europa.eu/nui/show.do?dataset=edat_lfse_20&lang=en.
11. https://ec.europa.eu/info/sites/info/files/file_import/european-semester_thematic -factsheet_early-school-leavers_en.pdf.
12. https://unevoc.unesco.org/wtdb/worldtvetdatabase_cze_en.pdf.

Atri Sengupta and Nicola M. Pless

JUGGLING THE INTERESTS OF
DIFFERENT STAKEHOLDERS?
The Roles of Responsible Leadership
and Human Resource Management[1]

KRISHNA, A TRIBAL VILLAGER FROM Kashipur Block, Odisha,[2] furiously said, "They should never be allowed to step onto our own land." He continued with tears in his eyes, "Police killed my brother. Do you think we should be punished for protecting our own land?"

The reference point was Utkal Alumina International Limited (UAIL), an ambitious greenfield alumina refinery, co-generation power plant, and bauxite mine, which began its journey in 1992–93 in the most remote and hilly terrain of Odisha, where epidemics, starvation, and atrocities were rampant. It was a joint initiative of three conglomerates – Indal, Tata Industries Limited (TIL), and Norsk Hydro Aluminum (NHA) of Norway – intended to set up a 100% export-oriented 1 million ton per annum (MTPA) alumina refinery. The capacity of the alumina refinery was planned to be 1.5 MTPA, expandable to 3 MTPA, while bauxite mining was to be 4.5 MTPA, expandable to 8.5 MTPA. The capacity of the co-generation power plant was to be 3 × 30 MW.

Despite having a progressive plan and the necessary approval from the state government, this greenfield project faced stiff resistance from a range of stakeholders, especially from the local tribal people, who would be most affected by the project. The project was shut down for more than a decade due to a mass protest by indigenous people supported by non-governmental organizations (NGOs) and environmental activists. The UAIL leaders were struggling to find ways to commission the project. They wondered if the project would need to be shut down permanently amid the resistance.

DOI: 10.4324/9781003247272-37

BACKGROUND

The Project

UAIL, which was initiated as a joint venture of Indal, TIL, and NHA, changed status soon after an incident in which police fired into a violent protest, which resulted in the deaths of three tribals. TIL and NHA sold their stakes to Indal and Alcan in 2000. Subsequently, Indal was acquired by Hindalco, a flagship metal company of Aditya Birla Group (ABG)—an Indian conglomerate. UAIL became a wholly owned subsidiary of Hindalco[3] when Alcan sold its stake in UAIL to Hindalco. UAIL was a part of Hindalco's ambitious expansion plan to become a premium global metal producer. The company initiated multiple greenfield projects in India under its expansion plan, and UAIL was one of them.

As per the then law of Odisha, land acquisitions for the UAIL plant, long-distant conveyor, railway siding, raw water intake, and waste disposal areas began in 1993 under the direct supervision of the state government. The company was not directly involved in the land acquisition. A total of around 3,000 acres of land spread across 24 villages in Kashipur Block of Odisha was selected for the purpose. Due to the mass protests and resistance, Hindalco changed its site plan and proposed a new site, which was 21 km away from the bauxite mine. Nonetheless, the resistance was not resolved. This massive delay in the project created bottlenecks for all its stakeholders—employees, vendors, management, local administration, and the community as a whole—including a massive financial burden. UAIL welcomed a new leader in December 2008 amid these chaotic conditions. The leader was given the responsibility for commissioning the project successfully at the earliest possible time. This would be a difficult task!

The Socio-economic Status of the Region and the Protest

Dominated by the tribal inhabitants (indigenous people), Kashipur Block in Rayagara District was characterized by low socio-economic status, in which per capita income for each family was far below the poverty line. Malnutrition, death from perennial diseases, a high illiteracy rate, and poor education and medical facilities were dominant in the area. The population earned their livelihood mainly from crop production with little support from the administration. Sometimes farmers received seeds free of cost, but irrigation, guidance on cultivation of new and improved varieties of seeds, and other forms of support were not available. Some of the families were dependent on non-agricultural activities to earn their livelihood as they did not have their own land. Although the region suffered from poor socio-economic and health status, it was rich in minerals and other natural resources. The quality of the region's bauxite attracted many aluminum companies to set up their plants there.

Despite the poor socio-economic and health status of the local population, the land acquisition for the project in the region faced stiff resistance, criticism, and opposition from anti-industrialization groups sponsored by organizations from different regions of the country, environmentalists, and political parties. These groups held the view that industrialization in the area would adversely affect the lives of indigenous people, and they demanded the land be given back to the indigenous people. The mass protests were often directed by those groups. The agitations accelerated as time went on. When one such protest in 2000 became violent, the police fired openly to control the fierce mob, resulting in the deaths of three tribals. The incident received immediate attention from the media and the international community, which intensified the conflict further. As a result, the project remained stuck until 2008.

THE PERSPECTIVES OF THE TRIBAL VILLAGERS[4]

Savitri, a tribal villager, was looking very sad. She said:

> Getting sufficient food twice a day for all the members of my family is difficult. Several days a month it happens that we offer food to our children only with nothing available for the adults. The small area of land we had for cultivation could not generate enough earnings for our survival. However, we were happy with that small piece of land. Now we do not know how to earn our livelihood. The money we received for my land long ago will be finished soon. What will we do next?

She said, crying:

> Each family in the village has experienced the death of a child very often. I lost my one son last year. He was only two years old. He had cholera. When he was taken to the health center in the next village, it was closed. We couldn't give any medicine to my son. He died. Nobody is there to think about us.

Although a health center was available in the next village, it remained closed several days a month due to the unavailability of doctors or nurses. Even medicine was rarely available there. For emergencies, villagers had to travel 50 km or more to be treated. Even the education system in the locality was pitiable. The few affluent families used to send their children to the nearby school, 7 km away. However, because of a lack of teachers, the quality of education at the school was very poor.

The villagers' primary source of income was crop production. Only a few families had poultry. Sabita, another tribal villager, said:

> We collect wood for cooking and herbal medicines from the nearby forest, which is not very dense. Agency Babu [an NGO] are our only source of free medicines and seeds, though it is not enough. They also teach us basic calculations and literacy. They are good to us.

Choton, Sabita's husband, added:

> We survive only by the mercy of God. One day some well-dressed babu
> [UAIL company officials] came and talked to our village head, who told
> us afterward that they wanted to set up a company on our land. We could
> not understand the purpose of the company, and we were scared about our
> future livelihood. We were not ready to sell our land.

He continued:

> Then somebody told us that the land where we farmed originally belonged
> to the government, which was the ultimate owner of the land. However,
> the government was ready to compensate us with a lump sum of money in
> exchange for reacquiring the land. The proposed amount seemed exorbi-
> tantly high to us, so we finally handed over our land to them.

Another villager, Murmu, offered:

> Then came agency officials who told us that these arrangements would in
> fact make us poorer. We were told to protest and get our land back. They
> would support us in this. We were utterly confused. But soon we realized
> that we had no work when the land was taken from us. Because we were
> sons of the soil, losing our land became an identity crisis for us. We wanted
> to return the money and get our land back.

Lagan nodded his head in support of Murmu and said:

> This is why we began protesting and stopped the company's construc-
> tion work. They called the police. Nobody was interested in listening
> to us. We also couldn't understand what they said. Our conversations
> soon turned into a confrontation leading to the police shooting, which
> caused the deaths of three of our villagers. We felt hatred for both the
> company and the police. We understood the company and its officials
> were not acting for our benefit. We decided not to allow those people
> to enter our land.

Kalu, an elderly person, added sadly:

> My son died in the police shooting. He was an important earning member of
> my family. He left his widow and two small daughters behind him. They are
> my responsibilities now. I have worked hard to earn our livelihoods so far.
> Now I am ill. Soon my physical health won't permit me to do hard work. I
> don't know what will happen to them after me.

"Can the company offer us jobs? We are mostly illiterate or semi-literate. What
type of jobs can we do there even?" Piku asked worriedly.

An agitated community with mounting socio-economic and health-related issues posed great challenges for the new leader.

THE PERSPECTIVES OF THE UAIL EMPLOYEES

Anjan, a Hindalco manager, said:

> We, a team of fifteen senior and junior officers, were initially transferred to the UAIL project from other units of Hindalco. Because the project site was remotely located, our families stayed in the city, where our children could attend their schools. When we visited the site, we found a partially completed boundary wall, some civil construction here and there, and evidence of blasting at the small hills in the designated area. The local farmers were busy preparing the land for planting. We were given accommodation in Rayagada district, and from there we commuted 70 km to the project site.

He added:

> It was beautiful hilly terrain, with dark green forest all along. Though we appreciated the natural beauty, we were scared about the hostile environment and the absence of law and order in the region. The local administration was avoiding the location of the upcoming project. The entire region seemed backward, with the local population appearing poor, malnourished, ill, and half-clothed.

Mahendra, another employee of UAIL, said:

> Almost every day, there was intense rain. At first, we were visiting the designated construction site only twice or thrice per week to measure the progress of civil construction by the contractors, which we had to report to the corporate office.

He added:

> Eventually, we started visiting the site more regularly. However, it proved very difficult to carry out routine activities smoothly. Every now and again, the villagers entered the plant premises in unsafe and disruptive ways. Hence, we had to stop work until they left the premises. Moreover, there were always two to three festivals occurring in one or more of the nearby villages, and we were forced to provide donations for those celebrations. Reluctance to provide donations led to further disruptions and work stoppages.

Anjan stated further:

> On a few occasions, we were under severe pressure to stop work due to local protests. We were helpless, as the villagers had difficulty

understanding either our language or the importance of maintaining progress on the project. Many of our officers were threatened, and some of us were beaten by the villagers, who demanded that work cease. On four to five occasions, while returning from the plant site to district headquarters in the evening, we encountered road blockages from them putting large trees on the road. Fearful for our safety, we began taking longer, less direct routes to commute to the plant. It was quite impossible for us to continue work there. Many of us considered approaching the management for another transfer. We even contemplated resigning if a transfer proved impossible.

He added: "Contractors were also threatened and prevented from working. In this situation, how to take the project forward was a big challenge for us." Prafull, another manager, said, "We are yet to have a proper HR policy in place that will motivate our employees."

When the new leader, after joining the project, considered shifting all the employees directly associated with the project along with him and his family to the project site as residents, this created further turmoil amongst the employees.

THE PERSPECTIVES OF THE CONSTRUCTION CONTRACTORS

Hari, the project supervisor of a contractor, said:

We secured the bid to construct the township at the UAIL project. The proposed land, bordering a perennial stream, was rolling and boulder-strewn, which rendered it difficult to even walk. However, UAIL management assured us they would provide the major raw material, like steel and cement, along with the heavy machinery required to prepare the site for construction. The company accepted our proposal. Necessary drawings and estimates were submitted accordingly.

He continued:

We moved our resources to the site. Then we erected temporary offices in portable cabins, as well as similar arrangements for the engineers in my team. Because the major part of our work would be unskilled and labor intensive, we visited nearby villages and hired rural laborers for construction work on a daily wage basis. We started with small construction activities. Our first task was to build the engineer hostel and cafeteria. However, the situation soon became a nightmare for us. Many villagers, rather than working as directed, started physically abusing our engineers for money. We were understandably worried, as were the UAIL officers. The progress of construction was slow and halting.

He added:

> Finally, we decided to invest a large sum of money to establish peace at the site. In the meantime, we experienced widespread theft of our equipment, steel, and cement. UAIL management was against using hard power, in the form of security agencies like CISF, to resolve the situation. Moving ahead with a soft approach, despite the ongoing complications, we filed complaints at the local police station. Unfortunately, the police response was also very weak. As a result, we had to manage as best as we could on our own, with support from UAIL management.

He said further:

> The site engineers and supervisors, however, were not inclined to work at the UAIL site. A few of the villagers engaged by us for construction work had a habit of becoming inebriated with locally made alcohol, after which they would demand more money and threaten our staff. Our short-term solution was to provide them with some money, simply to maintain progress on construction and peace at the site. It was a horrible time for us and our staff. Accordingly, we had to offer extra compensation to attract and retain the services of engineers and supervisors. Furthermore, the delay in the project cost us more. We were therefore unable to manage the construction expenses with the agreed-upon contract amount, so we requested that UAIL management amend our contract with revised rates.

THE PERSPECTIVES OF HINDALCO MANAGEMENT

Being a leader in integrated aluminum production in India, Hindalco's management framework was crafted on the principle of "excellence by design," which encompassed the five core values of ABG:

- *Integrity*: Honesty in every action—ethical, transparent, truthful, upright, principled, respectful
- *Commitment*: Founded on integrity, doing what it takes to deliver as promised—accountability, discipline, responsibility, results orientation, self-confidence, reliability
- *Passion*: Missionary zeal arising out of an emotional engagement with work—intensity, innovation, transformational, fire in the belly, inspirational, deep sense of purpose
- *Seamlessness*: Thinking and working together across functional silos, hierarchy levels, businesses, and geographies—inclusion, teamwork, integration, involvement, openness, global, learning from the best, empowering
- *Speed*: Responding to stakeholders with a sense of urgency—response time, agile, accelerated, timelines, nimble, prompt, proactive, decisive.

With an ambition of becoming a premium global metal leader, the management decided on an ambitious expansion of its aluminum metal business with four major greenfield projects: one alumina refinery, two smelters, and one flat-rolled product division. The alumina refinery (UAIL), which was planned in Kashipur Block of the Kalahandi-Bolangir-Koraput region of Odisha, was supposed to be the major feeder to the other two greenfield smelters. However, the turmoil faced by UAIL derailed this plan.

Massive delays and other nuisances created in and around the project site resulted in the project costs mounting heavily (to around US$1.5 billion), with minimal hope of commissioning the project within the next few years. Despite this critical situation, Kumar Mangalam Birla, the Chairman of ABG, remained highly passionate about the project. Birla was insistent that, in spite of the critical situation, the new leader of UAIL must act with the highest values and with the utmost morality.

THE PERSPECTIVE OF THE NEW LEADER

"My earlier experiences in leading different companies bestowed me with a high sense of self-efficacy and determination, which fueled me to take up the challenges," Suryakant Mishra, the new leader, said. He added:

> After joining as CEO and Managing Director of UAIL, I started investigating the details of the project. I found that the root causes of the crisis were multifold, but mostly people related. On one side, local tribal people (sons of the soil) along with NGOs active in the area opposed the project, while on the other side, the state government and local administration were in favor of the project. For the government, the project would surely add value to their industrialization agenda.

He continued:

> Soon I found myself amidst the multiple conflicting stakeholders with different vested interests. The local community was resisting and was adamant there would be no project in the demarcated land. Those tribals were supported by NGOs and environmental activists. Government and local administrators who were in favor of the project lost interest as it became a permanent law and order problem for them. The media was always searching for the controversy in the project to increase television ratings. The construction contractors, for their part, began with a quoted price that was already 30% higher than typical bidding for similar projects elsewhere. Due to all of the local resistance, the contractors couldn't complete the construction on time and within budget. Hence, they were also requesting an increase in budget to meet their additional expenses. The overall project cost was mounting for Hindalco management despite having done a lot of investment in the project.

He added:

> Even the company employees had become demoralized. I found officers were operating in the project by commuting 70 km to reach the project site. Constant resistance, occasionally life-threatening, from the tribal villagers led many employees to lose faith in the project. Above all, poor facilities and the prolonged separation from their families had led some to quit the organization. Getting efficient employees was therefore a challenge, as no one was eager to go to that remote location. Officers were accustomed to visiting the site once or twice a week only, so no supervisor remained available on site to shepherd the project on a daily basis. This situation ultimately sent the signal to the tribal villagers and NGOs, in turn, that no company would ever actually occupy the land, which they interpreted as meaning the land still belonged to them. They demanded extra monetary compensation for giving us possession of the project site. In fact, the villagers developed a habit of issuing an additional monetary demand at every opportunity. In reality, however, these demands arose not from the villagers themselves but from the mediators, who wanted to get benefits out of the situation and proved difficult to remove from the system of communications.

"With the complications proliferating as time passed by, I have realized that restoring the confidence of all stakeholders would be a tough challenge and critical for commissioning the project," he opined finally.

NOTES

1. This case is based on Pless et al. (2021) and Sengupta and Sonawane (2020). Names of individuals have been disguised to maintain confidentiality. Data were collected following the ethics protocol of the Indian Institute of Management Sambalpur and based on permission by the company. This case is intended to be used as the basis for class discussion rather than to illustrate either effective or ineffective handling of a management situation.
2. A state in India.
3. www.hindalco.com.
4. Villagers spoke in local languages that were translated into English for this case.

REFERENCES

Pless, N. M., Sengupta, A., Wheeler, M. A., & Maak, T. 2022. Responsible Leadership and the reflective CEO: Resolving stakeholder conflict by imagining what could be done. *Journal of Business Ethics, 180,* pp. 313–337. https://doi.org/10.1007/s10551-021-04865-6.

Sengupta, A., & Sonawane, B. 2020. Collective resistance to collective collaboration: A leader's introspection. *Emerald Emerging Markets Case Studies*, 10(1). https://doi.org/10.1108/EEMCS-09-2019-0229.

Barbara Coudenhove-Kalergi and Christian Seelos[2]

EVN IN BULGARIA[1]

Engaging the Roma Community

A S AN ENERGY AND ENVIRONMENTAL services provider, we fulfil the daily needs of our customers. Through our reliable and high quality services, we make a sustainable contribution to their quality of life.

(EVN corporate policy statement)

I want to live like a normal human being and not like in the dark age.

(Mehmet Denev, a Stolipinovo resident who won a court case against EVN on the grounds of ethnical discrimination of the prevailing electricity regime)

Stefan Szyszkowitz, Managing Director of EVN Bulgaria, a subsidary of the Austrian energy provider EVN, was nervous. He was walking to the office building of EVN, close to the historic center of Plovdiv, Bulgaria's second largest city, when a horse cart was passing by. Horse carts are still the typical vehicles of the Roma minority in Bulgaria and a quite common sight in Plovdiv, which is home to Europe's biggest Roma ghetto, Stolipinovo. This afternoon, Szyszkowitz would meet some of the most influential Roma leaders in this settlement. He wanted to discuss EVN's plans on how to improve the supply of electricity to the inhabitants of Stolipinovo after long years of a tight electricity regime that only supplied electricity during the night—leaving an estimated 70,000 people without the possibility to cook, heat or switch the lights on during the day.

It was early July in 2007, and the air was stuffy, Szyszkowitz didn't like the idea of going to Stolipinovo. He knew the quarter only from the outside, but he had heard the stories from his technicians about angry mobs, broken sewage systems, inadequate water supply, and garbage that piled up on the streets because the municipal

DOI: 10.4324/9781003247272-38

waste collections had stopped servicing Stolipinovo. However, Szyszkowitz knew that EVN had arrived at a turning point, a crucial moment for the success or failure of his plans on how to deal with this complex and emotional situation.[1]

EVN had inherited this problem from the old Energy Distribution Company of Plovdiv as part of the acquisition of two distribution companies in Southeastern Bulgaria in 2004. But now, Stolipinovo was EVN's problem. It was not the only challenge that EVN faced in Bulgaria. Already after a few years of operating, the company was cornered on all sides with every step being watched very closely.[3] EVN could not afford to lose any more credibility. Municipal elections were scheduled later that year, which usually meant that rival political parties would readily exploit any opportunity to frame a foreign company as a scapegoat for all kinds of local problems.

Stefan Szyszkowitz knew this meeting had to be successful, but wondered whether he could reason with the Roma. This was a discriminated population group that has been displaced, segregated and oppressed for centuries. They were the poorest of the poor in Bulgaria. Would they be willing and able to pay if EVN decided to improve the much-needed electricity supply? If left unresolved, would EVN be judged as an accomplice to a growing humanitarian disaster in one of the youngest member states of the European Union? And how would this affect EVN's business strategy in the country and the region?

BULGARIA'S ELECTRICITY SUPPLY CHALLENGES

In many countries of the former Eastern bloc, the energy industry played an important role in the national ideology. Electricity was seen as a symbol of the social compact between state and citizen as well as a practical necessity for industrialization, and thus progress. Electricity presented the good life.[4] This attitude was also true for Bulgaria. During the communist regime and the Russian influence, Bulgarian engineers were trained in the Soviet Union, and the utilities were state-owned and promoted as the nation's pride in public. "Each year in June the day of the electrical engineer was celebrated. The Bulgarians took great pride in their electro-technical competence and were very self-confident," observed Stefan Szyszkowitz. In addition, Bulgaria has traditionally been a significant net exporter of power to neighboring countries. However, due to rapid industrialization, irrational energy use, energy waste and the fragile transmission network, the electricity supply was highly unreliable. This was causing a growing sense of disillusionment with the communist party as early as the mid-1980s. In most large towns, an electricity regime of three hours on and three hours off for at least six days a week was introduced, but even these supplies could not be guaranteed, and the power was frequently suspended without warning. As R.J. Crampton wrote, "The dark nights played a prominent role in the demoralization of society and in the draining away of faith in a system which after forty years of socialism was not able to guarantee a normal daily life."[5] The socialist economy responded to the emerging shortages in the only typical way for that system—by building new capacity. The construction and commissioning of four additional nuclear reactors in Kozloduy also strengthened Bulgaria's role as a net exporter of energy.[6] Kozloduy later became one of the critical issues in Bulgaria's negotiations when the EU made the shutdown of the nuclear power plant a precondition for the country's EU membership. The government agreed reluctantly to the closure of the two oldest reactors by 2002, and reactors three and four by 2006.

Power Sector Reform[7]

Due to the deterioration of the relationship with Russia, power sector reform became indispensable. It would pave the way to effective privatization of the state-owned utilities. Part of the appeal of privatization was the money to be earned by the state as well as attracting desperately needed investment in the infrastructure of the networks, mainly to reduce commercial and technical losses and to bring effective management to the companies. This meant breaking up the state monopoly represented by the national electricity utility NEC, which owned almost all nuclear, hydro and pumped hydro power plants in Bulgaria and con-trolled 87.9% of total capacity.

In April 2000, the seven state-owned power distributors and the independent power generation companies, including Kozloduy and the thermal power plants of Maritsa East, were thus separated from NEC and registered as legal enter-prises. In autumn of the same year, a State Commission on Energy Regulation was set up, responsible for electricity prices of the energy carriers, licensing and permits for energy facilities. NEC was transformed into the national power transmission company, acting as a so-called single buyer—i.e., purchasing elec-tricity from independent producers and selling it to the utilities that, in their function as distributors, would sell the power to end-users.

Even though the power sector reform was deemed a success in general, sev-eral issues were insufficiently tackled.

1. *Economic issues*

A transparent and independent pricing policy as one of the most important objectives of the reform was lacking. In fact, the State Commission on Energy Regulation remained largely financially dependent on the state budget. Moreover, the reform started with the freezing of electricity prices for end consumers, not allowing the market mechanism to form competitive and cost-covering prices. In addition, NEC continued to export energy to neighboring countries like Greece or Turkey at cheaper rates than its domestic customers, thus undermining the market mechanism.

At the same time the independent power distributors could not procure the necessary collection rates of electricity bills. Generally, 30–35% of electricity was lost in the frail transmission network or due to theft. A large portion of the outstanding payments belonged to the municipalities financed by the state budget, which in turn relied in part on the revenue of the NEC operations.

2. *Environmental issues*

Environmental issues posed a substantial challenge to the reform efforts—mostly in relation to the projected high costs of dealing with environmental destruction during the transition period. The communist five-year plans had not been geared towards making production cleaner or repairing damage already caused. Sofia and the surrounding areas remain today one of the most polluted regions in the country. According to a World Bank study published in 2000, the Bulgarian energy industry was the biggest source of air pollution, and the total investment costs of meeting EU requirements for the rehabilitation of the thermal power plants up to the year 2010 were estimated at US$1.6 billion at a minimum. As so often, there are intrinsic trade-offs between Bulgaria's objective to ensure the lowest-cost energy supply to the country while remaining a dominant energy supplier in the region, minimizing its dependence on energy imports and complying with national and international environmental commitments.

3. *Social issues*

The social impact of the power sector reform was never subject to any specific studies and seemed not to be considered in relation to the reforms. However, the social challenges are critical. Bulgarian end users are not only faced with relatively high costs of energy, but at the same time burdened by low household incomes. Low-income households accounted for 38% of the total in 2000. They spent 14% of their income on energy. International benchmarks such as the UK energy poverty threshold of 10% would categorize a large share of the Bulgarian population as energy-poor.[8] In the same year, 20% of the households relied on social assistance to cover energy costs.

4. *Non-payment and electric power theft*[9]

According to the World Bank, the electricity market in Bulgaria has among the highest hidden costs of EU member states. These hidden costs include poor bill collection rates, excessive technical losses and losses due to theft. The amount of unpaid bills is a result of both household and business indebtedness. In 2005, the EDCs lost 20–23% of distributed electric power due to technical losses or thefts.

Theft of electricity in Bulgaria is generally carried out by companies and by households in an approximate proportion of 1:5. In 2003, about 50 million euros of losses from electricity thefts were recorded, with average losses accounting for 6–7% of distributed energy.[10] Reportedly, small energy-intensive companies or production facilities, restaurants and hotels are among the most frequent violators. Anton Gramatikov, director of the metering department, observed:

> After the privatization the technical losses were discussed in one of the working groups set up for the integration process. The Austrians could not grasp that the majority of the technical losses was due to energy theft.

They couldn't believe that this was even possible. For them it was a completely new problem and they had no ready solution."

A particular problem faced by the EDCs in Bulgaria was the en masse non-payment of electricity bills in neighborhoods populated by the Roma ethnic minority such as Stolipinovo in Bulgaria's second largest city, Plovdiv (see Chart 1).

ROMA, "THE PEOPLE"[11]

The Roma are considered the European Union's largest and most vulnerable ethnic minority group. Although precise figures are unavailable, it is estimated that about 10 million Roma live in Europe as a whole—a population size higher than that of a number of European Union member states. However, Roma-related issues remained overwhelmingly absent from the political agendas in most of the EU member states until the beginning of the 21st century, when the rights and living conditions of Roma were incorporated into the EU accession process of the new member states of Eastern Europe, such as Bulgaria.

As an endogamous culture with a tendency to self-segregation, the Roma have generally resisted assimilation into other communities in whichever countries they have moved to, the positive aspect being that they have managed to successfully preserve their distinctive and unique culture. The price of this cultural persistence, however, has been isolation from the surrounding population, and this has made them vulnerable to being stereotyped. Discrimination against and stereotyping of Roma is still widespread and permeates many aspects of life, including education, employment and housing.[12] The poverty of many Roma

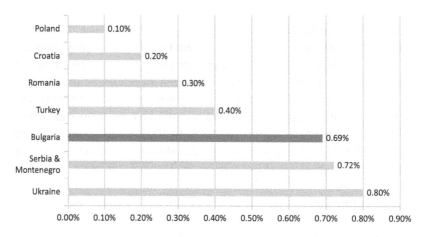

Unaccounted losses from inefficient operations and thefts as % of GDP (2003)

Poland 0.10%
Croatia 0.20%
Romania 0.30%
Turkey 0.40%
Bulgaria 0.69%
Serbia & Montenegro 0.72%
Ukraine 0.80%

Chart 1 Hidden costs in the energy sector.

Source: Ebinger, J., *Measuring Financial Performance and Infrastructure: An Application to Europe and Central Asia,* World Bank, 2006.

communities, which is even more obvious in ghettos, contributes to general resentment, as Roma are perceived as parasites living off state welfare payments, thieves, etc. In summary, the persistent disadvantages in education, which limit future opportunities and access to the labor market, the poor health service and the inadequate housing and marginalization of settlements characterize the situation of the Roma population in Europe.

Roma in general are not a homogeneous group. The diversity among Roma populations is tremendous, and ranges from the various dialects of the Romany language to the proportions living in cities, integrated neighborhoods or segregated rural settlements. Also, Roma are not a united community, but rather are divided into many subdivisions—depending, for example, on their exact descent or language and religious affiliation. This diversity creates significant challenges regarding research and the collection of quantitative and qualitative data on the Roma population. Information and reliable and precise data on true Roma living conditions and poverty are often scarce and fragmented, making it extremely hard to develop policies for this community.

The Roma of Bulgaria—the Socio-economic Context[13]

It is estimated that about 800,000 Roma live in Bulgaria—the official census of 2001 reported only 370,000, or 4.68% of the total population. The difference is attributed to a large number of Roma self-identifying as Bulgarians or Turks. The Bulgarian Roma were primarily nomadic or semi-sedentary until 1958, when the communist regime launched a campaign of forced assimilation, restricting their traditional customs and forced them to settle down. The communist government also banned the public use of the Romany language.[14] The so-called "process of revival" in the mid-1980s, in which Turks and the Muslim Roma were forced to adopt Bulgarian names, was followed by a period when the official position more or less denied the very existence of Roma in Bulgaria. During the socialist-era policies of resettlement, assimilation programs or employment provision, Roma communities became heavily reliant on state social support. Despite extensive involvement in the shadow economy, Roma households are still heavily dependent on welfare payments today (see Table 1 and Chart 2).

In Bulgaria, the long and painful transition from a planned state economy to a free market has hit the Roma the hardest. When subsidies for state-owned enterprises were slashed, it was often Roma who were the first to be dismissed. Many have never recovered from the economic restructuring. The community's geographical isolation increased, resulting in negative effects on the Roma's ability to find jobs. Many Roma neighborhoods turned into ghettos, which were abandoned by most state institutions, making access to administrative, medical and other services very difficult. A large number of young Roma dropped out of school, causing functional illiteracy that again hampered labor market integration and led to more poverty.[15]

In 1992, the term Bulgarian Ethnic Model emerged, and soon became part of the political rhetoric. This coincided with the signing of the association

Table 1 Source of income that provides the most money for a Roma household (%)

Source of income	Bulgaria	Czechia	Hungary	Romania
Regular wage job	25.9	40.3	14.8	10.6
Occasional job	2.5	2.8	3	0.5
Salary/payment for work at a civil organization	1.1	0.4	0.2	0
Self-employment/own business	2.1	2.8	0.4	1.1
Pension	26	15.5	23.6	13.3
Unemployment benefits	15.2	23.2	22.4	9.1
Scholarship	0.3	0.6	0.3	0.4
Child support (including paid maternity leave)	15.3	10.6	27.2	25.4
Other	11.6	3.8	8	38.7

Source: UNDP survey, 2004.

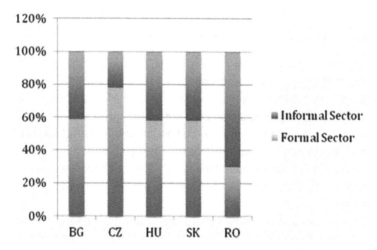

Chart 2 Formal and informal sector employment.
Source: UNDP (2002).

agreement of Bulgaria with the EU, which insisted on including an article safe-guarding the human rights of ethnic minorities.[16] Even if it is true that many positive steps have been taken to protect the Roma's ethnic and cultural iden-tity—also under the watchful eye of the EU—Roma have largely remained at the very bottom of Bulgarian society.

No Voice—No Power

The Roma population is poorly represented in the Bulgarian political system. The Roma community has never managed to unify behind one Roma party to attend and participate at the National Assembly, despite potentially having more than enough votes to do so.[17] This damages the situation of Roma on a national and local level even further, as they have almost no political power to voice their concerns. Also, the non-Roma parties have generally ignored Roma issues, even though Roma-dominated organizations have supported the election of municipal councilors in many municipal elections. Every post-communist election has also seen the open buying of Roma votes by competing non-Roma politicians offering cash handouts, food, jobs, and promises of other post-election services and benefits to Roma voters—for example, the cancellation of their electricity bills.

The Roma Housing Situation[18]

Roma never were landowners, and therefore possessed limited economic resources. They continued to be poor during the era of central planning, and had no property to reclaim when post-communist restitution began. As a result, Roma migration to urban and suburban areas intensified, leading to the expansion of ghettos, with all the corresponding social consequences.[19]

A relatively high percentage of the Roma population live in inadequate housing conditions such as sub-standard housing or shantytowns. Bulgaria particularly stands out in comparison with other Central and Eastern European countries with a large Roma population. According to the Bulgarian National Statistical Institute, almost half of the Roma population in Bulgaria still lacked running water in their homes in 2001 and were forced to use water from street pipes or wells. Most Roma neighborhoods have damaged sewage systems or none at all, and this increases the risk of infectious diseases and epidemics such as hepatitis. Overpopulation in Roma neighborhoods and homes is the norm. Often, more than three generations live under the same roof. As most municipal authorities have abandoned Roma neighborhoods, there is no control over illegal construction and use of sidewalks and streets for building on.[20] The majority of the buildings in Roma ghettos are constructed illegally, making it very difficult for the utility services to reach customers. Some housing projects aimed specifically at Roma actually maintain the isolation and segregation of these communities.[21]

In 2007, 64% of the Bulgarian Roma population lived in neighborhoods with poor health conditions, and 34% in areas separate from surrounding cities, or in the cities themselves[22] where they concentrated in ghettoized neighborhoods such as Fakulteta in Sofia, Nadejda in Sliven, Komluka and Meden Rudnik in Burgas, and Stolipinovo and Sheker Mahala in Plovdiv.

Energy Supply and Bad Debts in Roma Neighborhoods[23]

Many people in Bulgaria fail to pay their electric bills, and many of them are Roma. Bad debts in terms of electricity or water bills have existed for years in Roma neighborhoods. The accumulating debts have posed a growing economic problem for the utilities that serve Roma settlements all around the country. The roots of the problem are multi-dimensional. Since the fall of the communist regime, there had been almost no new investment in the communal infrastructure. Technical connection to electricity or heating networks was particularly difficult, if not impossible, in the settlements mainly inhabited by Roma or Turks. This structural situation, combined with the existing bad socio-economic situation, led many Roma to steal electricity by illegally tapping into the grid. This again led to frequent blackouts because of the instability of the grid, and subsequently to an unreliable supply. At the same time, as bills have remained unpaid, the utilities have had no capital to invest in the upgrading or renovation of the electricity infrastructure, which has led to a further downgrading in service quality.

There are two quick answers one hears when asking why the Roma in Bulgaria do not pay their electricity bills: first, they are too poor, and second, they are manipulated by political forces. However, it is not that simple. Failure to pay is not only due to factors like affordability, the general income situation, or a household's budgeting and management skills. The reasons also lie in the dynamics within the community and a widespread feeling of being treated unfairly by general society and its institutions.

Bad Debts—a Sociological Phenomenon[24]

> The Roma people in Stolipinovo feel very powerful because they are large in numbers. They live in a city within a city. When they are isolated like this, they only follow their own rules. Even the police hasn't dared to go into this ghetto. But if they live in smaller settlements or if they live in mixed districts with non-Roma families, then they abide the rules of society.
>
> (Anton Gramatikov, director of the metering department of EVN Bulgaria)

Some Roma simply refuse to pay, for example, when they know that many of their neighbors are refusing to pay, or because their electricity lines have been tapped by neighbors who run up their bills. Some Roma do not pay because they believe they are being unfairly overcharged by the electrical utility company or by its corrupt employees.

The endemic non-payment reveals a complex process of social, economic and psychological factors leading to the refusal to pay. A research study by the Open Society Institute revealed how a vicious circle has developed: deprivation and prejudice lead to the segregation of the already marginalized Roma minority. As a result, they lose effectively most of their links and bridges to other segments within society. At the same time, they are deprived of effective access to institutions and authorities. All that holds the community together are its close internal links. When the payment of utility bills appears against such a background and in the context of poverty, the absence of immediate punishment for non-payment can lead to a process that normalizes non-payment as accepted behavior and even a group norm.[25]

Ineffective Responses and Growing Tensions

> The Roma were blamed for stealing the electricity. The truth is, the stealing happened everywhere, the Bulgarians did it, too! But the electricity company decided to install the meters on poles 15 meters high in special

boxes, which are secured and locked. The consumers were actually pre-vented from tracking their consumption; they did not know how much energy they were using. In the end it's a matter of trust. If you don't trust, you don't pay.

(Daniela Michalova, a lawyer working for the Open Society Institute)

The electrical utilities responded in a variety of ineffective ways to the Roma's failure to pay their bills. In districts where the companies were technically able to cut off electricity to individual customers, Roma had illegally reconnected their houses, bypassing electricity meters. Therefore, the electricity meters, some of which are more than 30 years old and very easy to manipulate, were installed on exterior boards that were fixed on poles at about 15 meters above the ground. Anton Gramatikov remembered:

The Roma destroyed the boards and the meters, and illegally connected themselves to the electricity lines. They are very creative. The high poles were no real obstacles for them, but it made them angry. They attacked the electricians, for whom it became dangerous to go into Stolipinovo or other Roma ghettos.

However, the installation of the electric meters on high poles became common practice in Roma neighborhoods in all Bulgarian cities, and the meters turned into a much-contested symbol of discrimination and distrust among the Roma.

For self-protection, the electricity distributors eventually started to col-lectively cut off the electricity supply in whole districts or blocks without dis-tinguishing between residents who paid their bills and those who failed to pay. This led to more unrest, as regularly paying households were also "punished", among them ethnic Bulgarian families. "We pay our bills regularly but we get no electricity because of the Roma. They have brought us back to the 18th cen-tury," said furious Diana Ilieva after the power cuts in 2002 that affected about 300 households of non-Roma families living in Stolipinovo.[26]

STOLIPINOVO—A SPECIAL CONFLICT AREA

During 2002 the Roma ghettos in Bulgaria began to resemble enclaves of the third world in a country that dreams of joining the first world.[27]

The majority of Roma living in the southeastern territory of Bulgaria, the operat-ing area of EVN, are concentrated in the towns of Plovdiv and Sliven. According to the official census, around 27,000 Roma live in the Plovdiv region, which has a total population of over 700,000. However, the real numbers of Roma in Plovdiv are estimated as much higher, and considered to be close to 80,000. This figure represents 11% of the population of the Plovdiv region and around 20% of the population of the town of Plovdiv. Plovdiv is home to four districts that are mainly inhabited by Roma: Stolipinovo, Sheker Mahala, Hadji Hassan Mahala and Arman Mahala—the biggest being Stolipinovo. The number of its inhabitants is estimated to be around 35,000 during summer, with almost double the figure in winter due to migration patterns. "Even though Stolipinovo is a desperate place to live, many people move there during the winter months," explained a Bulgarian consultant for EVN. "Some Roma even use it as a resource and make a business out of it. They 'collect' and charge other Roma for using the water and the electricity."

Stolipinovo is considered the most problematic Roma district in Plovdiv, partly because of its sheer size, but also because of the particularly depressed socio-economic situation of its residents. It is estimated that the unemployment rate in Stolipinovo is up to 90%, according to information from the Employment Agency Plovdiv, and 97% of those 90% do not qualify for welfare subsidies.

Moreover, the housing shortage in Stolipinovo is acute. People live either in run-down blocks built in the communist era or houses, many of which are illegally built with no connection to water, sewage, electricity or gas for heating. Illegal construction presents a potential danger for inhabitants because of bad construction materials, and of streets obstructing emergency services and exits as well as the provision of utilities. Garbage is not collected in Stolipinovo by the city, resulting—together with an inappropriate and patchy sewage system—in bad water quality and the danger of infection and epidemics.[28]

The Political Game

In Stolipinovo, yet another dimension has added to the complexity of the situation. During Bulgaria's transition from the communist regime to democracy and consequent democratic elections, the votes of the Roma and Turkish minorities became valuable, particularly on a municipal level. Because of their weak socio-economic situation, the Roma are easy to manipulate. Many observers claim that parties of all political camps have paid for Gypsy votes with cash and food supplies, or by bribing Roma with festivals and conferences. Various political forces have lured in the Roma population with promises to improve their living conditions.

In Stolipinovo, the major bait was the cancellation of accumulating debts for electricity bills. This created and fostered a sense of immunity from punishment among the irregular payers. In addition, the exertion of political pressure of the political decision makers on the EDCs to play along was well established, originating in the culture of dominant political influence in the former state-owned enterprises.

The Genesis of the Electricity Regime

On February 21, 2002, the long-lasting conflict between the state-owned electricity supplier in Plovdiv and the Roma in Stolipinovo finally erupted into violence. When the utility disconnected the whole neighborhood after unpaid bills dating back several years reached the multi-million leva (the Bulgarian currency) mark, riots broke out. Outraged Roma erected roadblocks with garbage cans and started to throw stones at cars passing by.[29] The regional coordinator of the Internal Macedonian Revolutionary Organization commented on the events in Stolipinovo:

> What happened is a sad epilogue of a policy of manipulation, demagogy and compromise that had been conducted over the past four, five years. The debts of the Roma residents were not collected so that the ruling political force in Plovdiv could win the votes of the people living in the Roma residential areas. The problem of paying the money was being settled by a telephone call by the former district governor and of ex-mayor.[30]

The disturbances went beyond any previous incidents in terms of numbers of demonstrators and readiness for violence. "The Bulgarians will regard the Taliban in Afghanistan as angels if they leave us in darkness," threatened an angry Roma resident in connection with the cut-off electric power supply of the residential areas of Stolipinovo and Sheker Mahala. This eruption of violence and the fear of repeats forced the public authorities to seek a way out of the dilemma.

Local authorities, executives of EDC Plovdiv and representatives of the protesting Roma reached an agreement by which the power supply debtors in the Roma suburbs were to pay 10% of the amount due for January accounting for 299,000 leva (US$134,000). According to EDC Plovdiv's executive director, the company was prepared to restore the power supply if the agreement was honored and the sum agreed was paid.[31] The agreement seemed of little value. Only a few weeks later, five power supply posts were destroyed in the residential areas of Hadzhi Hassan, Arman Mahala and Stolipinovo.

Finally, as a last sanction, the neighborhood was put on a restricted regime — the electricity supply was cut off from 8 a.m. until 7 p.m. — in order to protect the EDC from more excessive losses. Stolipinovo was soon regarded as a lost cause.

Stolipinovo — Looking for a Way Out

> We have inherited a disaster.
>
>   (Stefan Szyszkowitz)

"We became aware of the importance of Stolipinovo when the media began to hunt us and we didn't know how to react properly to their accusations. Facts just didn't count anymore," said Stefan Szyszkowitz as he recalled the events. Suddenly, Stolipinovo emerged as the most important question about the economic future of the company, its image and its long-term strategy in Bulgaria, inseparably linked to the question of social responsibility.

After bad press regarding the court decision on the discrimination issue was reported in one of the leading Austrian newspapers in December 2006 — triggering even more bad press in Austria — Rudolf Gruber, EVN's chairman of the supervisory board, urged the taking of action and assured it would have the full backing of the board.

Risky Customers

The issue of "risky customers", as the non-paying customers mainly living in Roma ghettos were called, was not new to the Bulgarians who worked for EVN's predecessor. To learn about the dimension of the risky customers on EVN's territory, the customer service center organization KEZ carried out an analysis of the neighborhoods' risk potential. The analysis included questions about topics such as safety, the height at which the meters were installed, and an assessment by KEZ regarding the level of tension and the risk of escalation.

KEZ reported that in 147 neighborhoods with 99,000 customers, 50,500 could be classified as risky customers—corresponding to 51%.

In 85 neighborhoods, the quota of risky customers was over 50%, and in 76 neighborhoods, the meters were installed higher than 2 meters off the ground.

A total of 41 neighborhoods were classified as having a "very high" risk of social tension and escalation regarding maintenance of the electric installations, and 70 neighborhoods were classified as having a "high" risk (see Chart 3).

The data for Stolipinovo were the most disturbing:

- Of the 5,500 electronic meters installed in an area of 1.7 square meters, 3,400 were sabotaged or destroyed; 2,000 houses were not connected to the grid at all.
- The electricity infrastructure, consisting of 17 transformer substations and 112 km of electricity lines, was found to be in a bad and neglected state.
- The transformer substations were easy targets for continuous vandalism. Maintenance was impossible without police protection.
- The accumulated bad debts amounted to 6 million euros, with a collection rate of only 3%.
- EVN estimated that it had to invest around 34,000 Euro in the maintenance of the electricity supply and around 17,000 Euro in the security measures.
- Yearly energy consumption was estimated to be 50 GWh. Technical losses in Stolipinovo amounted to 41%.

A Technical Approach

Even though the Bulgarians were well aware of the high-risk customer problem, a solution had never been prioritized or promoted, either due to political pressure or lack of leadership, or both. Nevertheless, in 2003, one of the predecessor companies of EVN, EDC Stara Zagora, installed electronic meters with distant meter reading and built-in relays to turn on or cut off the electricity to reduce the presence of employees and prevent social conflicts and attacks in Roma neighborhoods. The new meters were installed at eye level to make maintenance more convenient. In order to prevent tampering or vandalism, a security firm was

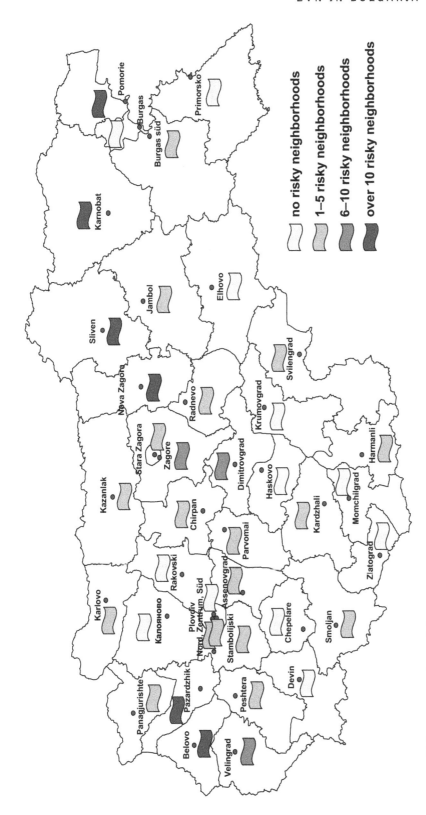

Chart 3 Risky customers/potentials.

Source: EVN Bulgaria.

recruited. It turned out that this concept unintentionally also led to a higher collection rate.

This important lesson provided a strong argument for the technical concept
EVN developed to replace the old meters and repair the grid as well as transmission substations. In May 2006, a proposal on how EVN could proceed in the
seven most risky Roma neighborhoods was submitted to the management board
(see Chart 4).

To build a sustainable economic model, five targets were set for the investment to pay off. The new technical solution should lead to:

- an increase of collectability of the electricity bills up to 100%,
- a reduction of energy consumption of 30–50%,
- a reduction of technical losses to 10%,
- a payback rate of the old debts of about 15%, and
- the acquisition of new customers by preventing illegal tapping.

Moreover, in its proposal the technical working group listed the following "non-
economic" reasons to justify the investments:[32]

- Legal requirements: We don't have the right to cut off customers who are
  paying their bills regularly.
- We have to create conditions for the equal treatment of customers. Special
  rules or exemptions for non-paying customers will lead to the assumption
  that some customer groups are privileged. This will undermine the payment
  practices of paying customers.
- The current situation of differing customer treatment leads to political spec-
  ulation and social tensions.
- The current situation has a negative impact on the image of our company.

Getting in Contact with the Roma—a Viral Approach

It is a legend that all Roma have tribal leaders. In Stolipinovo they are
totally unstructured. The only thing that holds them together is their belief
that they cannot leave Stolipinovo.

(Stefan Abadjiev, EVN consultant)

At the same time, Stefan Szyszkowitz still had no idea with whom to negotiate
in the Roma community in Stolipinovo. "Their claim to leadership is built on
mutual dependencies, economic power and rivalry. The biggest risk for EVN was
to step into an unknown situation and get involved in any of the ongoing political, religious or internal fights," he said. Several attempts to find influential but
trusted personalities failed, as political groups tried to influence any discussions
in their interest.

No	Data / Indicators	Units	Plovdiv - WV Stolipinovo	Plovdiv - WV Shekera	Stara Zagora – WV Makedomski	Stara Zagora - WV Zora	Burgas- WV Pobeda	Sliven WV Komluka	Yambol- WV D.Sjuleimezova	Total
						ERP				
1	Number of customers	Number	5 330	810	950	850	790	1 010	990	10 730
	BEFORE ACTION									
2	Delivered Energy per Transformer Station per Year	KWh	54 300 000	8 840 000	8 100 000	7 300 000	10 350 000	10 200 000	4 300 000	103 390 000
		Leva	3 118 449	507 681	465 183	419 239	594 401	585 786	246 949	5 937 688
3	Sales Quantity per Year	KWh	34 600 00	6 800 000	5 500 000	5 500 000	3 800 000	4 850 000	1 600 000	62 650 000
		Leva	3 820 532	750 856	673 750	673 750	465 500	594 125	196 000	7 174 513
4	Collection Rate per Year	Leva	38 205	7 509	640 063	579 425	148 960	404 005	7 840	1 826 006
		% of Sales	1,00%	1,00%	95,00%	86,00%	32,00%	68,00%	4,00%	25,45%
5	Balance of Receivables per March 1, 2006	Leva	9 707 000	2 067 000	17 000	10 700	143 000	145 000	1 890 000	13 979 700
6	Grid Losses per Year	KWh	19 700 000	2 040 000	2 600 000	1 800 000	6 550 000	5 350 000	2 700 000	40 740 000
		% of energy to be distributed	36,28%	23,08%	32,10%	24,66%	63,29%	52,45%	62,79%	39,40%
	OUTCOMES AFTER IMPLEMENTATION OF MEASURES									
7	Delivered Energy per Transformer Station per Year	KWh	38 010 000	6 188 000	6 885 000	5 840 000	7 245 000	7 140 000	3 010 000	74 318 000
		Leva	2 182 914	355 377	395 406	335 391	416 080	410 050	172 864	4 268 083
8	Sales Quantity per Year	KWh	34 209 000	5 569 200	6 196 500	5 256 000	6 520 500	6 426 000	2 709 000	66 886 200
		Leva	3 777 358	614 951	759 071	643 860	798 761	787 185	331 853	7 713 039
9	Collection Rate per Year incl, Old Debts	Leva	3 966 226	676 446	759 071	643 860	878 637	865 904	381 630	8 171 774
		% of Sales	105,00%	110,00%	100,00%	100,00%	110,00%	110,00%	115,00%	105,95%
10	Grid Losses per Year	KWh	3 801 000	618 800	688 500	584 000	724 500	714 000	301 000	7 431 800
		% of distributed energy	10,00%	10,00%	10,00%	10,00%	10,00%	10,00%	10,00%	10,00%
	OUTCOMES AFTER IMPLEMENTATION OF PROJECT									
11	Economic Effectiveness of Electricity Sales	KWh	0	0	696 500	0	2 720 500	1 576 000	1 109 000	6 102 000
	Economic Effectiveness of Electricity Distribution	KWh	16 290 000	2 652 000	1 215 000	1 460 000	3 105 000	3 060 000	1 290 000	29 072 000
		Leva	935 535	152 304	146 685	83 848	478 718	349 758	196 540	2 343 388

Chart 4 Risky neighborhoods—opportunity overview.

Source: EVN Bulgaria.

According to an insider, there were three influential groups within Stolipinovo:

- *The "bandits"*: families or groups who had become relatively rich by trafficking drugs, alcohol or humans. Some of them were busy in the scrap metal business, stealing cables and metal parts for resale.
- *The "rich families"*: families who drew their power from setting up NGOs and benefited from the huge sums from European or US institutions that were flowing into projects labeled "support for Roma". Critical voices said that the funds were mainly used to build power networks and benefit family members rather than the needy persons.
- *The religious communities*: mainly the Protestant and the Muslim faiths had influence in Stolipinovo.

None of them was an acceptable partner for EVN, especially as one of the most influential powers—the Muslim community—was closely related to the political party MRF, which was already infamous for manipulation during election campaigns.

Finally, with the help of Daniela Michalova, a lawyer working with the Open Society Institute and the Helsinki Committee for Human Rights who was experienced in working with Roma, they were able to identify a handful of Roma leaders who assured in a credible way that their agenda was the improvement of the living conditions in Stolipinovo and who were prepared to lobby for this issue in community meetings. Daniela Michalova spoke Romany and managed to convince them to be at least prepared to meet with EVN representatives and discuss their proposition regarding the technical approach. "It took us a couple of months to find partners who were willing to talk but in the end, it is essential to have the Roma leaders on your side," explained Michalova. "In Stolipinovo we have identified nine leaders for 35,000 people. Also, the leaders only talk to other leaders." Therefore, the meetings had to be arranged as senior-level events.

INVESTING IN A "LOST CAUSE"?

Stefan Szyszkowitz took a deep breath. It was time to go. He checked again the dos and don'ts that Daniela Michalova had written down for the meeting. Show respect, don't refuse anything that is offered, don't put a drinking glass on the floor, don't whisper. He would meet her at the periphery to Stolipinovo, where the car could not pass because the illegal building activities left only narrow streets. It was not advisable to leave a company car in Stolipinovo without protection anyway. When he rode through the busy streets of Plovdiv, it was hard to believe that a neighborhood like Stolipinovo even existed. However, now he had to deal with it. Many questions arose:

- *How should he proceed, given that the local authorities were not prepared jointly to tackle the problems in Stolipinovo? Should EVN try to go ahead* and push the technical solution right away? Or should it continue the electricity regime for the time being and try to get support from other stakeholders? There were indications that the public were starting to understand the complex situation better and acknowledged the need for a period of grace for EVN to deal with the problem.

- *Was the technical approach developed by his technicians enough to tackle the complex problem of Stolipinovo?* Evidence showed that the new digital meters facilitated the targeting of defaulters and made mass cut-offs unnecessary. The big hope was that the collection rates would go up as a result, but by how much and for how long?

- *Could he afford to put a huge investment into the grid renovation of a neighborhood that was seen as "lost cause"?* Or should he focus on the modernization of the infrastructure elsewhere in its service area? Would EVN ever be able to earn back these investments? The investment would only pay off if the Roma were (1) willing and (2) could afford to pay their bills. Could he even trust them if an agreement was reached?

- *How could EVN ensure a sustainable solution in Stolipinovo?* Was it even EVN's role to deal with a long-standing local problem like this? What was EVN's responsibility in this conflict?

- *How would EVN's shareholders react?*

NOTES

1. This case can be used together with the case *EVN in Bulgaria: Making it work. These two cases* can be used as standalone cases or together with the following case which is available from IESE Business School Publications (http://www.iesep.com/en/): *EVN in Bulgaria: "Eastern Fantasy" Meets Eastern Reality* (SM-1565-E).
2. This case was prepared by Barbara Coudenhove-Kalergi and Christian Seelos as the basis for class discussion rather than to illustrate either effective or ineffective handling of an administrative situation. No part of this publication may be reproduced without permission by Christian Seelos who can be reached at: cseelos@stanford.edu. Last edited: August 20, 2012
3. EVN in Bulgaria: "Eastern Fantasy" Meets Eastern Reality, 2011, IESE Business School Case SM-1565E.
4. The World Bank, 2006, Reforming Power Markets in Developing Countries.
5. Crampton R.J., 2007, The Oxford History of Modern Europe: Bulgaria, p374.
6. Business Insights, The Eastern European Electricity Market Outlook, 2009.
7. Main sources: Doukov, 2001, Bulgaria Power Sector Reform; Austrian Energy Agency: https://enercee.net.
8. See www.poverty.org.uk.
9. See The Energy Sector in Bulgaria, Major Governance Issues 2010.
10. Novinite.com, January 8, 2004, BGN 100 M Annual Losses of Power Theft in Bulgaria.
11. Main sources: The National Deliberative Poll: Policies towards the Roma in Bulgaria, 2007; The Situation of Roma in an Enlarged European Union, European Commission 2004; Crampton R.J., 2007, The Oxford History of Modern Europe: Bulgaria; Petrova D., 2004, The Roma: Between a Myth and the Future.
12. Ringold D., Orenstein M., Wilkens E., 2005, Roma in an Expanding Europe: Breaking the Poverty Cycle, World Bank, p13.

13. Main sources: EURoma Report: Roma and the Structural Funds, 2010; Ringold D., Orenstein M., Wilkens E., 2005, Roma in an Expanding Europe: Breaking the Poverty Cycle, World Bank; Revenga A., Ringold D., Tracy W.M., 2002, Poverty and Ethnicity: A Cross-Country Study of Roma Poverty in Central Europe, World Bank.

14. Crampton R.J., 2007, The Oxford History of Modern Europe: Bulgaria, p440.

15. EDIS S.A., 2007, European Survey on Health and the Roma Community, p97.

16. Crampton R.J., 2007, The Oxford History of Modern Europe: Bulgaria, p438.

17. Hajdinjak M., 2008, Political Participation of Minorities in Bulgaria, p17.

18. Main sources: European Union Agency for Fundamental Rights FRA, 2009, Housing Conditions of Roma and Travellers in the European Union; EDIS S.A., 2007, European Survey on Health and the Roma Community.

19. UNDP, 2002, Roma in Central and Eastern Europe, Avoiding the Dependency Trap, p15.

20. EDIS S.A., 2007, European Survey on Health and the Roma Community, p98.

21. FRA, 2009, Housing Discrimination against Roma in Selected EU Member States—an Analysis of EUMIDIS Data, p19.

22. EDIS S.A., 2007, European Survey on Health and the Roma Community, p25.

23. Sources: if not stated otherwise, Report PR Agency ICONA.

24. See Pallai K., 2009, Who Decides? Development, Planning Services and Vulnerable Groups, OSI.

25. Ibid., p8.

26. Associated Press, February 21, 2002, Power cuts spark Roma riot, Sofia Echo.

27. Bulgarian Helsinki Committee, 2002, Human Rights in Bulgaria in 2002: Annual Report, p24.

28. Nahabedian M., 2002, The Roma in Plovdiv, European Center for Democracy and Solidarity.

29. Associated Press, Power cuts spark Roma riot.

30. Research PR Agency ICONA.

31. Associated Press, Power cuts spark Roma riot.

32. EVN Bulgaria, May 2, 2006, Implementation Strategy of the Technical Concept in the Risky Quarters.

Index